Ledger Narratives

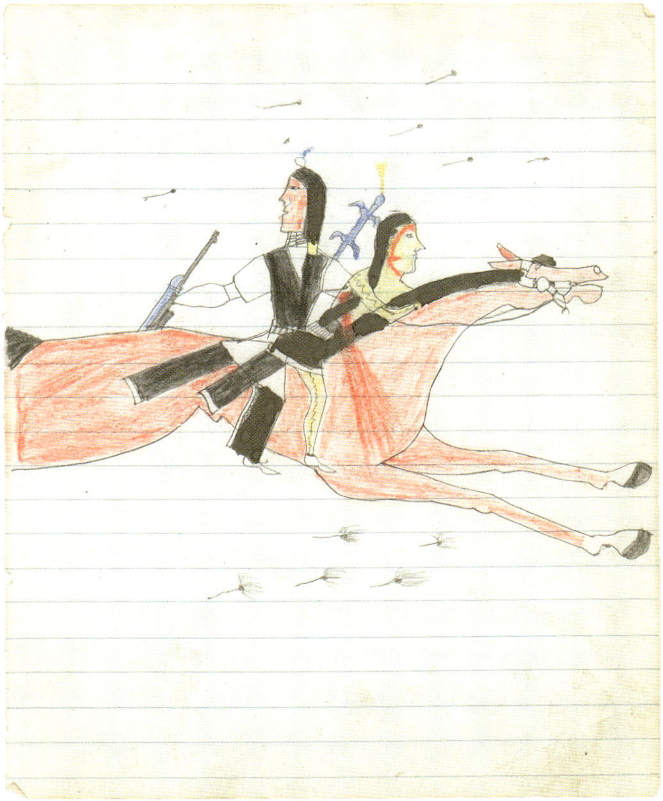

New Directions in Native American Studies

Colin G. Calloway *and*
K. Tsianina Lomawaima, *General Editors*

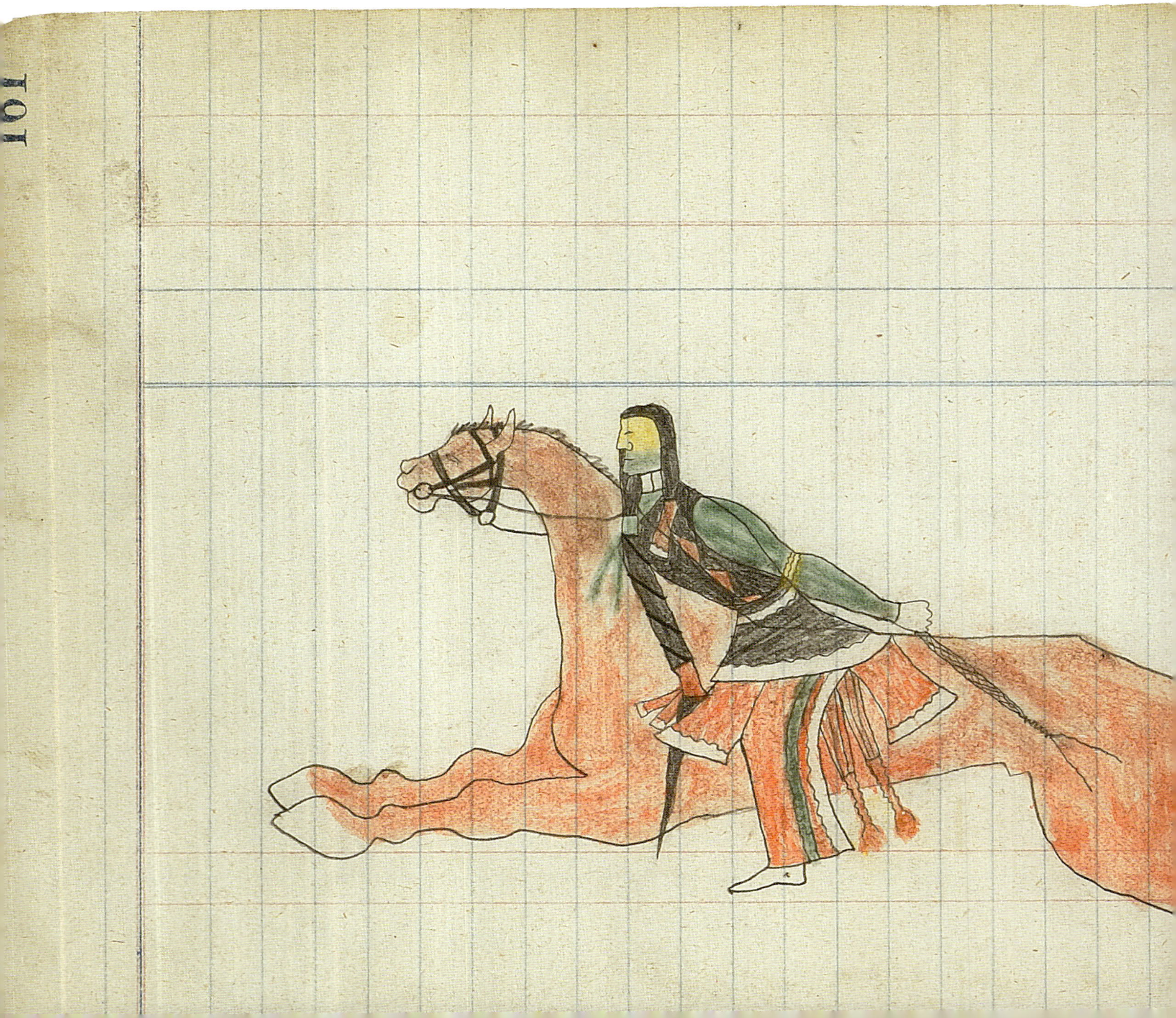
101

LEDGER NARRATIVES

The Plains Indian Drawings of the Lansburgh Collection at Dartmouth College

Edited by COLIN G. CALLOWAY

UNIVERSITY OF OKLAHOMA PRESS : NORMAN

Published in Cooperation with the
HOOD MUSEUM OF ART, DARTMOUTH COLLEGE,
HANOVER, NEW HAMPSHIRE

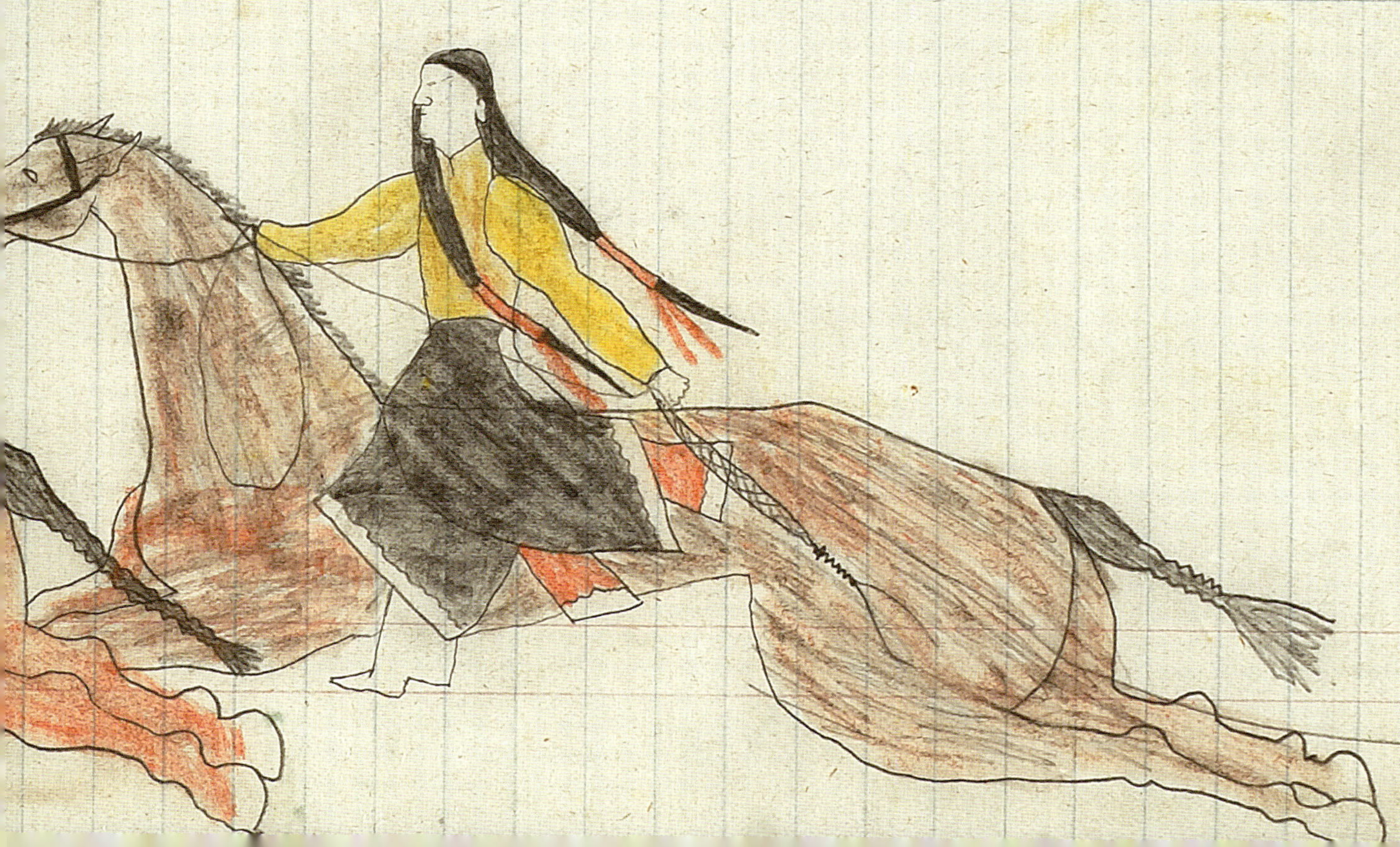

The following illustrations, appearing uncaptioned on the pages noted, are reproduced courtesy of the Hood Museum of Art, Dartmouth College, Hanover, New Hampshire:

Page i: Unknown artist, Tsistsistas (Cheyenne), active late nineteenth century, *Untitled [Tsistsistas (Cheyenne) warrior rescuing a wounded comrade]*, from the "Robert Allen Guthrie Notebook," c. 1874–75 (2007.65.89) (plate 38, p. 82).

Pages ii–iii: Unknown artist, Southern Tsistsistas (Cheyenne), active late nineteenth century, *Untitled [Tsistsistas (Cheyenne) warriors on horseback]*, page 161 from the "Arrow's Elk Society Ledger," c. 1874–75 (2008.70.3) (detail, plate 30, p. 74). Purchased through the Mrs. Harvey P. Hood W'18 Fund.

Page 1: White Swan, Apsáalooke (Crow), 1851–1904, *Untitled [White Swan riding through gunfire]*, c. 1890 (2007.65.93) (detail, plate 136, p. 182).

Page 43: Unknown artist, Tsistsistas (Cheyenne), active late nineteenth century, *Untitled [A procession of Tsistsistas (Cheyenne) warriors]*, page 190 from the "Old White Woman Ledger," c. 1880–90 (2007.65.74) (detail, plate 112, p. 158).

LIBRARY OF CONGRESS CATALOGING-IN-PUBLICATION DATA

Ledger narratives : the Plains Indian drawings of the Lansburgh collection at Dartmouth College / edited by Colin G. Calloway. — First [edition].

pages cm — (New directions in Native American studies ; v. 8)

This book is the product of the exhibition "Native American Ledger Drawings from the Hood Museum of Art: The Mark Lansburgh Collection," held Oct. 2–Dec. 19, 2010, Hood Museum of Art, and the 2010 Leslie Humanities Institute, "Multiple Narratives in Plains Indian Ledger Art," Dartmouth College, Hanover, New Hampshire.

Includes bibliographical references and index.

ISBN 978-0-8061-4297-5 (hardcover : alk. paper) — ISBN 978-0-8061-4298-2 (pbk. : alk. paper)

1. Indian ledger drawings—Great Plains—Catalogs. 2. Lansburgh, Mark—Art collections—Catalogs. 3. Drawing—New Hampshire—Hanover—Catalogs. 4. Hood Museum of Art—Catalogs. 5. Indians of North America—Great Plains. I. Calloway, Colin G. (Colin Gordon), 1953–

E78.G73L43 2012

741.089'97078—dc23

2012007470

Ledger Narratives: The Plains Indian Drawings of the Lansburgh Collection at Dartmouth College is Volume 8 in the New Directions in Native American Studies series.

The paper in this book meets the guidelines for permanence and durability of the Committee on Production Guidelines for Book Longevity of the Council on Library Resources, Inc. ∞

2 3 4 5 6 7 8 9 10

Contents

Acknowledgments

The acquisition, exhibition, and publication of the Mark Lansburgh collection would not have been possible without the dedication and collaboration of many people. An avid collector himself, Mark Lansburgh always acknowledges the assistance of Malcolm Grimmer, formerly of the Morning Star Gallery in Santa Fe, in building this remarkable collection. He also wishes to express his appreciation to Ania Kamienska for her kindness and assistance. Mark's loyalty and generosity to his alma mater opened the way for the college to obtain the collection through purchase and partial gift. Brian Kennedy, director of the Hood Museum of Art from 2005 through 2010, and Barbara Thompson, former curator of the Native American collections at the Hood and now a curator at the Cantor Center for the Visual Arts at Stanford University, both worked tirelessly with Mark preparing the groundwork. Former Dartmouth president James Wright, former provost Barry Scherr, and the late Dartmouth College librarian Edward Connery Lathem made sure that the possibility became reality. Katherine Hart, interim director of the Hood in 2010–11 and Barbara C. and Harvey P. Hood Curator of Academic Programming, sustained the momentum and ensured that the exhibition proceeded smoothly during a time of transition at the museum. In this she was ably aided by Karen Miller, Assistant Curator for Special Projects; independent scholar Sherry Brydon, who researched and provided object documentation; data manager Deborah T. Haynes, who did a tremendous amount of work cataloguing and standardizing the cataloguing of the drawings in the collection, and whose attention to detail and consistency was invaluable at the copyediting and proof stages; Kathleen O'Malley, Associate Registrar; and Nils Nadeau, Communications and Publications Manager, all of whom, as always, were generous and unstinting in their support and assistance of the Native American Studies program during the project. Joe D. Horse Capture, Associate Curator at the Minneapolis Institute of the Arts, served as guest curator of the exhibition and as a willing and frequent consultant during the symposium.

Barbara Thompson coauthored the proposal that secured funding from the Leslie Humanities Center at Dartmouth for the "Multiple Narratives in Plains Indian Ledger Art" institute and symposium. Adrian Randolph, Leon B. Williams Professor of Art History and former Director of the Leslie Humanities Center, gave the project enthusiastic and consistent support, and center administrator Isabel Weatherdon managed the arrangements for the institute with her customary grace, good humor, and competence.

Joyce M. Szabo, Regents Professor of Art History at the University of New Mexico, came to Dartmouth as William H. Morton Distinguished Fellow for the fall 2010 institute. In that capacity she served as director of the institute's weekly seminars and afterwards continued to work closely with the staff of the Hood Museum of Art in fine-tuning the descriptions and information relating to the drawings. In all of her contributions (and despite a series of misadventures involving cars, dogs, and ankle bones), Joyce was generous with her time and her knowledge and wore her expertise lightly. In the course of the three-month seminar, many students and visitors dropped in for one, two, or several sessions. Regular participants and short-term fellows, besides those contributing essays to this volume, included Elaine Brown, then the Charles Eastman Dissertation Fellow at Dartmouth College; Mary Coffey, Associate Professor of Art History, Dartmouth College (and her newborn baby, Irena); Mike Cowdrey, independent scholar; Chris Dueker, then a doctoral candidate in Native American art at Columbia University; Bruce N. Duthu, Samson Occom Professor and Chair of Native American Studies,

Dartmouth College; Deborah T. Haynes; Joe D. Horse Capture; Ben Madley, then a Mellon Postdoctoral Fellow at Dartmouth; Karen Miller; Chris Parsons, then a PhD candidate at the University of Toronto; Dale Turner, Associate Professor of Government and Native American Studies, Dartmouth College; and Lola Van Wagenen of Clio Visualizing History, an organization dedicated to developing innovative American history projects designed to engage students, inform educators and researchers, and appeal to a wide public audience.

This book is a joint publication between the Hood Museum of Art and the University of Oklahoma Press, where Alessandra Tamulevich demonstrated immediate interest in the publication and guided it through its early stages. Jo Ann Reece handled the copyediting with attention to detail and a thoughtful awareness of the overall project. Managing editor Steven Baker shepherded the publication along with care and consideration. Designer Julie Rushing was patient and responsive to our concerns and wishes. The work of Deborah T. Haynes and Kathleen O'Malley at the Hood Museum of Art was invaluable in compiling the images. Janet C. Berlo, Professor of Art History and Visual and Cultural Studies, University of Rochester, was unable to attend the exhibition and symposium as planned, but her insightful comments on the manuscript made a valuable contribution to the final product. From planning to publication, *Ledger Narratives* has been a truly collaborative effort.

Colin G. Calloway
Hanover, New Hampshire, 2011

LEDGER NARRATIVES

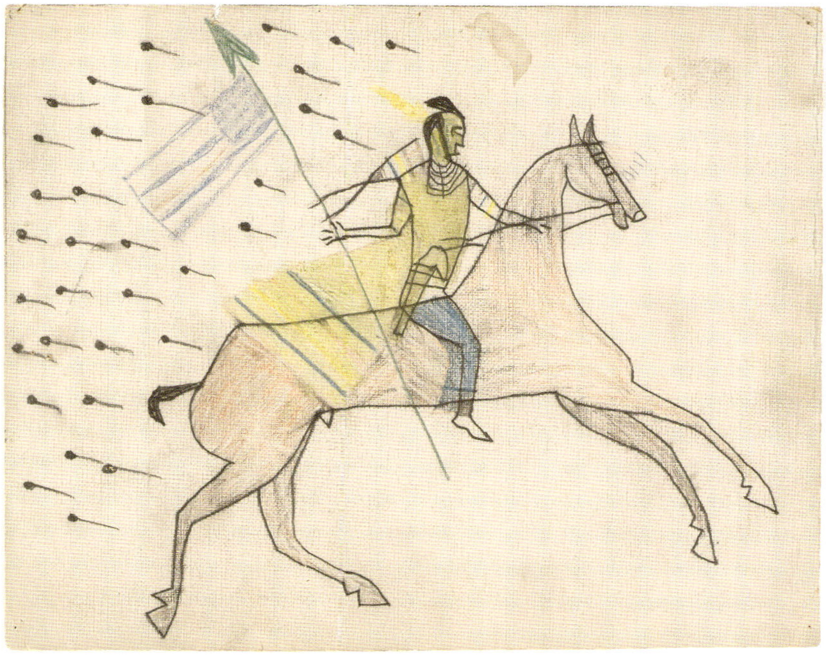

Introduction

COLIN G. CALLOWAY

In 2007 Dartmouth College acquired a remarkable collection of Native American ledger art. Over more than a quarter-century, Mark Lansburgh, Dartmouth class of '49, brought together a body of nineteenth-century Plains Indian drawings that was widely considered to have been one of the largest and most diverse collections in private hands. Now housed at Dartmouth's Hood Museum of Art, the Lansburgh collection not only includes many rare works but also embodies a wealth of information about lifeways, events, and cultural changes among the Plains peoples in the nineteenth century. In the fall of 2010, with generous funding from the Leslie Center for the Humanities and in conjunction with the Hood Museum of Art, which staged a major exhibition of the collection, Dartmouth hosted a symposium in which faculty and visiting scholars explored the interdisciplinary merits of the collection and considered ways of using ledger art in developing new approaches to Native American history and cultural studies. This book is the product of that symposium and that exhibit, serving as both a catalogue of the collection and an introduction to a major resource for understanding Native American history and cultural transitions during the second half of the nineteenth century.

Historically, figurative arts among the Plains Indians of North America chronicled the heroic achievements of warriors and chiefs. Predominantly a male art form, visual representations of war, hunting, and ceremony were painted onto rock, buffalo robes, and tipi covers to publicly memorialize the great accomplishments of warrior-artists and their cohorts. From the mid-nineteenth century, increased contact with Euro-Americans, much of it driven by the migrations of settlers and the construction of railroads across the Great Plains toward the Pacific Coast, led to multiple encounters and a series of conflicts that ultimately transformed life on the Great Plains. Smallpox, cholera, and other alien diseases decimated Native populations. Treaties lopped off huge chunks of Native American homelands. Native American participation in the fur trade and commercial hunting by Americans, aided and abetted by a United States campaign of systematic slaughter, virtually exterminated the buffalo herds that had constituted the foundation of Plains Indian economy and culture. Military campaigns targeted Indian villages in their effort to "pacify" the plains. The survivors were confined to reservations where they were subjected to government programs of civilization that replaced hunting with farming, outlawed their dances and rituals, and took their children away to boarding schools to be stripped of their Native language and culture and remade into "productive" American citizens.

As a result of their greater exposure to American settlers and soldiers, Plains warrior artists appropriated new perspectives, themes, materials, and artistic styles to capture and document their personal experiences. In particular, they developed their figurative graphic arts, usually executed on animal hides, into a unique genre that now used the new media of pencils and crayons and bound ledger or account books, the most readily available source of paper. Their drawings became known as "ledger art," and the term has come to be applied to the genre in general even if, as in the Lansburgh collection, many drawings were done on plain paper rather than lined accounting pages.

Many of the drawings in the Lansburgh collection document the tumultuous decades of the late nineteenth century and depict struggles for cultural survival as well as adaptations to imposed change. These autobiographic and storytelling ledger drawings contain multiple narratives. They served to prompt memories of heroic exploits in battle and horse raids, and often contained details that would have had particular meaning for the Native artist and audience. They became an important form of communication about different tribal cultures and between Natives and non-Natives. They chronicled both past and contemporary experiences, but especially addressed the cultural transitions that resulted from relocation to reservation life, forced abandonment of traditional lifestyles, imprisonment, and policies of assimilation that attempted to strip Plains peoples of their Native identities.

Battle scenes record fights not only against soldiers but also against Indian enemies, sometimes warriors who were allies of the United States. The Great Plains by the early nineteenth century was a cauldron of competition and conflict as different peoples moved onto the rich grasslands, adopted the horse and buffalo culture that brought unprecedented power and prosperity, and battled with rivals for hunting territory, for access to guns and horses, and for survival. The expansion of the Lakota, or western Sioux, onto the northern and central plains brought them and their Cheyenne and Arapaho allies into conflict with Pawnees, Arikaras, and Crows; Comanches and Kiowas who moved south and established hegemony on the plains of Oklahoma and Texas clashed with Apaches, Osages, and Caddos. Intertribal competition for space and resources intensified as Euro-Americans intruded onto tribal territories and decimated the buffalo herds. The Crows' rich hunting territories in the Bighorn basin came under virtual siege as neighboring tribes saw their own herds diminish. "Look at our country, and look at our enemies," Crow chiefs declared in 1870, "they are all around it; the Sioux, Blackfeet, Cheyennes, Arapahos, and Flatheads, all want our country, and kill us when they can."[1]

American expansion and wars against the Sioux offered some Indian peoples an opportunity to secure powerful allies in their own struggles. It made sense for the Crows to align themselves with the Lakotas' new enemies, the Americans. Crows and Shoshonis fought with General George Crook against Crazy Horse at the Battle of the Rosebud in June 1876, and a week later Crow and Arikara scouts guided George Armstrong Custer to the Little Bighorn.[2] The Crow artist White Swan was severely wounded during the retreat of Major Reno's command in that battle.

The Pawnees, too, sided with the United States, and they figure in drawings in the Lansburgh collection. Hit hard by repeated epidemics of diseases—smallpox in 1780–81, 1825, 1831, 1837–38, and 1852; cholera in 1849; measles and diphtheria in 1864—the Pawnees turned to the new power on the plains as an ally in a war of resistance against the Sioux that was rapidly becoming a war of survival. Pawnees formed a battalion of scouts that served alongside U.S. troops during the height of the Plains Indian wars between 1864 and 1877, guarded construction crews on the Union Pacific Railroad as they made their way across the plains, and served under Major Frank North in scouting expeditions and skirmishes with the Sioux and Cheyennes. They donned blue U.S. military uniforms (usually out-of-date).[3] Not surprisingly, Pawnee enemies feature in several of the Cheyenne drawings, where they are identifiable not only by their distinctive roach hairstyle and cuffed moccasins but also by the blue coloration of their bodies.

Although only about 10 percent of the drawings in the Lansburgh collection came from Fort Marion, the incarceration of Southern Plains prisoners there from 1875 to 1878 looms large in any history of Plains Indian ledger art. The men who developed their drawing at Fort Marion had been selected as prisoners because of actual or alleged involvement in the events of the Red River War of 1874–75, often called the Buffalo War.

By the terms of the Treaty of Medicine Lodge in October 1867, the Kiowas, Comanches, Plains Apaches, Southern Cheyennes, and Southern Arapahos were supposed to move to a reservation and make the transition from a way of life based on buffalo hunting to one based on farming. But delays in delivering the promised annuities produced hunger on the reservations and pushed men back to hunting at the very time that white hunters were slaughtering the herds. Black Kettle's Southern Cheyenne band strayed outside the reservation to find food. Black Kettle remained peaceful toward whites in the region, but the Dog Soldiers, the elite military society of the Cheyennes, did not. The United States launched a series of winter campaigns to punish the Indians who were "off the reservation" and raiding. In November 1868, George Custer's Seventh Cavalry attacked Black Kettle's village on the Washita River, killing many people, including the chief and his wife, and slaughtering nearly one thousand horses. The following summer, Pawnee scouts were the first to reach the Cheyenne village at the Battle of Summit Springs, where the Dog Soldier chief Tall Bull was killed. Meanwhile, with their families going hungry on the reservation, young Kiowas and Comanches returned to long-established patterns of raiding for livestock, and raids into Mexico escalated.[4] Continuing clashes exploded into full-scale conflict in the Red River War. Once again, Pawnee scouts served against the Kiowas, Comanches, and Southern Cheyennes.

After the war, seventy-one men and one woman were designated war criminals and shipped to imprisonment in Fort Marion, a disused Spanish colonial fortress that had been built, in part by Indian labor, at St. Augustine, Florida. There were twenty-seven Kiowa prisoners, thirty-three Cheyennes, nine Comanches, two Arapahos, and one Caddo.[5] The government hoped that removing this troublesome element would help facilitate the tribes' transition to reservation life. Their jailor was Lieutenant Richard Henry Pratt, who had served as an officer in the Tenth Cavalry (the regiment was composed of black enlisted men—known as Buffalo Soldiers—but the officers were white) and with Indian scouts during the Red River War. Pratt's autobiography, written late in life, reveals much about his plans and attitudes, but also provides information and insights into the life of the warrior-artists in his charge.[6] Pratt seized this opportunity to show how "savages" could be transformed by education and civilization. He cut their hair, put them in army uniforms, and imposed a military-style daily regimen. The prisoners did military drills, attended church, and went to school, where some learned to read, write, and speak English. In addition, Pratt encouraged his prisoners to create drawings to be sold to tourists in St. Augustine and used their artwork, along with evidence of their "progress" and Christianity, as part of his public relations campaign to generate support and funding for his Indian education program. Many of the adult prisoners turned to producing art as a means of earning money to send home to their families on the reservation. The marketability of these drawings also encouraged reservation-bound artists to create art for sale to non-Native consumers and influenced the content of the drawings—battle scenes (particularly against whites) gave way to buffalo hunts and courtship scenes.

Over the course of three years, from 1875 to 1878, the prisoners became so accomplished in their work and conducted themselves so well in the white world that they were trusted to work outside the prison walls and even to travel up the Eastern Seaboard. Some of the younger men decided to continue their education in the East and were accepted at Hampton Institute, a school opened in 1868 for African Americans. But Pratt's educational experiment with the Plains prisoners had mixed success: Kiowa artist Paul Caryl Zotom and Cheyenne artist Making Medicine, who took the name David Pendleton Oakerhater, were both ordained as deacons in the Episcopal Church, but most of the former prisoners returned to live the kind of life on the reservations that Pratt had hoped they would help eradicate.[7] Pratt became convinced that he was targeting the wrong population. He lobbied Congress for funding to establish a school that would apply the same strategies of cultural transformation to Indian *children*, and within a year of the prisoners' release he opened the Indian Industrial School in Carlisle, Pennsylvania. A few of the Fort Marion artists followed Pratt to Carlisle and, for a short time, may have passed their artistic traditions along to a younger generation of students before white art teachers arrived. The boarding school system, which began operation in 1879 and lasted well into the twentieth century, grew out of an "experiment" that subjected many of the most famous ledger artists to both incarceration and education (see chapter 6).

By the turn of the century, as Western-oriented fine arts curricula became a part of the boarding school experience, the production of ledger art waned. By the early twentieth century this art form had all but disappeared. Few of the Fort Marion artists, most notably Howling Wolf, continued the genre after they returned home from St. Augustine. But their work influenced younger artists who changed the map of modern Indian art after receiving Western fine art training. Some of these artists adopted mainstream international fine arts practices, setting the stage for subsequent generations of Native American artists to work in diverse media to document and comment on current events and issues, politics, and cultural change. In recent years, several Native artists have revived, invoked, and been inspired by the ledger art tradition, incorporating it into their own work and adding another dimension to its history (see chapters 4 and 5).

The Lansburgh collection reveals the great depth, complexity, and diversity of Plains Indian ledger drawing while also setting up a backdrop for understanding subsequent developments of both visual and text-based Native narratives. The collection includes drawings by, or at least attributed to, some of the most celebrated warrior artists of the time, including Howling Wolf (Ho-na-nist-to, Southern Cheyenne), Chief Killer (Noh-hu-nah-wih, Southern Cheyenne), Ohettoint (Kiowa), Arrow (Southern Cheyenne), Wooden Leg (Kum-mok-quiv-vi-ok-ta, Northern Cheyenne), Short Bull (Brulé Lakota), Old White Woman (Southern Cheyenne), Dull Knife (Northern Cheyenne), and White Swan (Crow), among others. Also in this collection are works by as yet unnamed artists from ledgers known by the names of their collectors, the "Frederick Douglas Ledger," "Peter W. Edwards Ledger," "Carl S. Dentzel Ledger," and "Vincent Price Ledger" (the late movie star was an avid collector of ledger art).

Dating from the mid-1860s to the end of the 1890s, these drawings illustrate as much about the different characteristics of the Plains cultures within which the artists lived as they do about the individual artists' lives. They offer Native alternatives to the artistic, romanticized, and often ahistorical representations of Plains cultures in the works of well-known Western artists such as Karl Bodmer, George Catlin, Charles M. Russell, and Frederic Remington. Focusing on individual lifestyles, responses, and perspectives, they provide important visual contexts and documentation of Native clothing, practices, and material culture of the time. They also provide alternative views and interpretations of Native and non-Native interactions specifically as seen through the eyes of people who directly witnessed or took part in the depicted events. With scenes depicting martial confrontations, hunting, courting, dance and religious ceremony, landscape, incarceration, travel by foot, horse, train, and boat, and more, the collection offers a wide selection of themes through which scholars can reevaluate historical interpretations of life on the plains at that time. Filled with detailed and dramatic scenes of milestone moments in the lives of Plains warriors, the drawings illustrate their struggles to retain land, resources, and cultural freedom. The participation of the artists in key battles includes a representation of the Battle of Summit Springs, White Swan's involvement in the Battle of the Little Bighorn, and the experience of Dull Knife (also known as Morning Star) during the capture of his Northern Cheyenne village in 1876. Drawings by Howling Wolf, Chief Killer, and Ohettoint record their daily observations of life as captives at Fort Marion. A sequence of drawings by Old White Woman provides a rare glimpse into the negotiation of privacy and intimacy between two individuals as it depicts the process of courtship between a man and a woman, beginning with their introduction by a female mediator and ending with the couple's sexual encounter.

The Lansburgh collection provides both the source material and the focus to bring together many new approaches in Native American studies and to significantly advance how scholars and students think about and interrogate these unique cultural productions. The research potential of the collection lies in the importance of the drawings not only as an artistic genre but also as historical and sociological documents that illuminate the complex encounters and relationships between Natives and non-Natives and the renegotiation of Native identity in the second half of the nineteenth century. The collection holds opportunities for exploring issues of gender, identity, social status, sovereignty, tribal and intertribal politics, exchange and economy, confinement and space in a changing world.

How can the examination of Plains ledger art reinform our understanding of the relationships between traditional Plains oral narratives and text-based non-Native as well as Native histories? How did these drawings demonstrate cultural resilience and subtle resistance within a state of cultural oppression? What are the mechanisms through which Plains ledger artists established new ways of visually negotiating identities? This book features a sampling of essays from the Dartmouth "Multiple Narratives in Plains Indian Ledger Art" symposium by scholars who tackle some of these questions, focusing primarily but not exclusively on the Lansburgh collection. One of the leading authorities on ledger art, well-known for her work on the Southern Cheyenne artist Howling Wolf and the Fort Marion art in the Silberman Collection, Joyce M. Szabo, begins with an overview of the Lansburgh collection, how it came to Dartmouth, and what it contains. Anthropologist Michael Jordan situates the drawings within the cultural and historical contexts in which they were produced, and explores the role ledger art played in constructing, maintaining, and reflecting status, honor, and wealth among Southern Plains men. Whereas Jordan examines how ledger art sustained relations within communities, Jenny Tone-Pah-Hote, a Kiowa historian who specializes in the study of Kiowa expressive culture, considers what the drawings reveal about relations *between* communities, in a volatile world where alliances and enmities could have life-and-death significance and where shifting patterns of trading and raiding brought people of different cultures into collaboration and conflict.

As the "Multiple Narratives" symposium encouraged contributions by scholars from multiple disciplines, some of the essays are written by authors who claim no specific expertise in ledger art but who approach the subject from new perspectives, ask different questions, and suggest some alternative ways to assess its significance. A Native scholar from New England whose work focuses on the literature of the Southeast, Melanie Benson Taylor warns against looking at ledger art to find what we *want* to be there, too easily assuming that the artists were engaged in subtle and not-so-subtle acts of resistance against the cultural and capitalist dominance of their oppressors when in fact there is evidence to suggest ambivalence and compliance. Mary Peterson Zundo, an art historian, focuses on the drawings of Cheyenne artist and Fort Marion prisoner Chief Killer to draw attention to differing treatments and conceptions of landscape and space. Where Zundo considers issues of space, Vera B. Palmer reflects on issues of confinement. Like Melanie Benson Taylor, Palmer makes no pretention to expertise in ledger art: her engagement with the Lansburgh collection stems from working with Native American inmates in maximum-security prisons in upstate New York. Accordingly, her essay requires more than the normal use of the authorial "I." Palmer revisits the historical roles of prison and school for Native people and identifies parallels in the experiences and artistic expressions of modern-day and Fort Marion prisoners. Although she frames her essay around two sets of art and artists, she is primarily concerned with the ethical issues raised by such prison art, and interested in its therapeutic possibilities as much as its specific content. Finally, Joyce Szabo explores the challenges and opportunities in reading ledger art, and suggests ways in which piecing together fragments of information can help reconstruct the often spare images on the pages into fuller stories and reveal additional meanings in the drawings.

This book, then, contributes to the rich and growing literature on ledger art, as well as showcasing the Lansburgh collection. Some of the authors look at these drawings in new ways and some from disciplines outside of the usual historical and art historical paradigms. Allowing each essay to stand on its own as well as be a part of the collection required a degree of editorial tolerance for repetition of examples, images, and even observation. The essays do not claim or attempt to address all or even most of the issues raised in the Lansburgh collection, and the authors of the essays do not necessarily agree with each others' interpretations. But individually and collectively the essays convey the richness of the collection for scholars of Plains Indian life and history and the possibilities for incorporating these Native perspectives into revisions of Native American history and cultural understanding.

NOTES

1. Calloway, "The Only Way Open to Us," 24–34; quote at 33.
2. Calloway, "Army Allies or Tribal Survival?" 62–81.
3. Van de Logt, *War Party in Blue*; Dunlay, *Wolves for the Blue Soldiers*, ch. 9.
4. Rand, *Kiowa Humanity*, chs. 3–4.
5. Lookingbill, *War Dance at Fort Marion*, 205.
6. Pratt, *Battlefield and Classroom*, chs. 10–13.
7. Viola, *Warrior Artists*, 15–17.

CHAPTER I

Battles, Courting, and Changing Lives

THE MARK LANSBURGH COLLECTION

JOYCE M. SZABO

OVER THE PAST SEVERAL YEARS the Hood Museum of Art at Dartmouth has increased its holdings of Native American art in major ways, the most significant of which is the acquisition of the Mark Lansburgh collection of Plains Indian ledger art. Comprised of 144 drawings, the Lansburgh works are invaluable for their diversity of subject matter, dates of creation, and cultural authorship. Mark Lansburgh, Dartmouth class of 1949, spent twenty-five years collecting Plains drawings; a collection such as his would be impossible to amass in today's market. Dartmouth is extremely fortunate to have acquired these important drawings.

Plains drawings are not the only gifts that Mark Lansburgh has bestowed on Dartmouth. He has given the Hood Museum of Art six important additional works over the years. These include a late Celtic bronze ewer, dating from approximately 300 BCE; two late-twelfth-century Islamic bronze mortars; an iron and bronze European lock from the late sixteenth to early seventeenth century; a seventeenth-century graphite portrait on vellum by the Dutch artist Bartholomeus van der Helst (c. 1613–1670); and a contemporary ledger-style drawing on paper by the Siksika artist Terrance Guardipee (b. 1968). In addition, the Lansburgh family presented a stunning third-century Roman cast-bronze ram with copper inlay to the museum in 2000.

Rauner Special Collections Library houses eighty-nine other items that Mark Lansburgh has presented to Dartmouth over the years. These reflect not only the focus of his undergraduate major in English, but also his growing attraction to both history and medieval art. Lansburgh works in the Rauner library include numerous medieval manuscript leaves; several fifteenth-century incunabula books printed just after the invention of movable type; a 1521 letter from Pope Clement VII; a 1627 papal bull from Urban VIII; British legal documents; and Guillaume Durand's *Rationale Divinorum Offiorum* of 1484. Many additional broadsides and personal letters are among the gifts, including a 1952 letter from Robert Frost, with whom Mark developed a friendship. In 1956 he began operating his own hand press, having learned from Professor Ray Nash of Dartmouth how to set type and print. An author and poet, as well as a calligrapher, Mark has given Dartmouth various works that he printed. Lansburgh's *Leaves by the Wayside*, printed when he was a student, reflects his all-encompassing approach to creativity. He wrote the verse, created woodcut illustrations, printed the pages on a hand press, and bound the volumes.

Mark Lansburgh grew up in Washington, D.C., and entered Dartmouth directly following his service as an airplane navigator in the Second World War. In fact he came to his initial meeting in the admissions office still dressed in his Army Air Force uniform. The outlook was not promising. Admissions was overcome with applicants returning from the war, but said they would check the scores from Mark's Army Air Force tests. The next day he was greeted with a warm handshake and welcomed to Dartmouth. He received his AB degree in English, but art was always an important part of his life. During the early years following his graduation, a love of medieval art absorbed Mark as he traveled much of the world photographing, collecting, and lecturing about the various arts of the Middle Ages. He received grants from the American Council of Learned Societies and the Ford Foundation to help finance these photographic projects. His photographs of illuminated manuscripts, housed in libraries in the United Kingdom and throughout Europe, are now in the collections of the National Gallery of Art in Washington, D.C., and in the Getty Museum Research Library in California.

But it was ledger art, a comparatively new kind of art both chronologically and more recently discovered by

Mark Lansburgh, that began to fascinate him, ultimately leading to the gift of his collection of late nineteenth and early twentieth-century Native American works on paper. This additional gift lifted the Hood Museum of Art at Dartmouth to its new position as a major repository of this singular art form.

Mark Lansburgh began collecting Plains drawings in 1986 when he was captivated by a series created by a late nineteenth-century Lakota artist that was for sale at Morning Star Gallery in Santa Fe, New Mexico.[1] Their sure draftsmanship, delicacy of color, and overall artistic quality attracted him in much the same way as medieval art. He has written about the "ineffable spirit" of Plains drawings, noting that many have a tension that "makes us part of the action" depicted;[2] such comments reflect his strong personal connection to ledger art. Mark started visiting galleries whenever he learned new ledger drawings had become available and purchased many more over the years. While he selected works by warrior-artists from various Plains cultures, it was apparent from the beginning that he had a sophisticated collector's eye.[3] Malcolm Grimmer, then of Morning Star Gallery, has observed that Mark is one of the most consummate collectors he has ever known and that once hooked he became totally absorbed in his new passion. During the initial years of collecting Plains drawings, Mark was drawn to images of village life and dances, particularly drawings with many figures and a great deal of color; over time, he also began to collect simpler compositions.[4]

Mark Lansburgh's approach to collecting was certainly impacted by his many years of working with medieval art, especially illuminated manuscripts. He also taught and lectured about art at various universities including Colorado College, where he was a lecturer in art from 1965 to 1972. When Lansburgh was at Colorado College, he was only the second person in the then one-hundred-year history of that school to receive an award from the American Council of Learned Societies; he had been nominated for the award by Princeton's Institute for Advanced Study. He also lectured at the University of California–Santa Barbara, the University of California–Los Angeles, Stanford University, New York University, and, of course, Dartmouth College. This background in the arts is the foundation for his unique appreciation of ledger art.

Unlike many collectors of Plains drawings, Mark Lansburgh was not drawn to possess other genres of Native American art, beyond a few examples of Southwestern ceramics. Even the ceramics are not those that typically attract collectors. His are Apache ceramics, large utilitarian vessels beautiful for their simple, undecorated sculptural form, not for any elaborate painted decoration. Rather, it was Plains drawings that enthralled him and continue to do so.

Ledger drawings became more prevalent as more non-Native people came onto the plains from the mid-nineteenth century forward and previously immense herds of buffalo were depleted. Such drawings began as the same type of visual records of valiant achievements in battle that men had traditionally painted on hide robes and shirts. Hide paintings were very public records that associated the wearer with his accomplishments, assuring all who saw him of his status. Books of drawings were not the same widely visible historic documents, but they were opened at gatherings where men recounted their actions, especially those of individual warrior societies within Plains cultures. Many Plains cultures had several men's associations or warrior societies, one of which most men joined; often a man became a member of the society to which his father or an uncle belonged. Warrior societies served various functions including bolstering members in war, celebrating victories after battle, and holding ceremonies. Ledger books may have been shared by members of the same warrior societies or war parties. Drawings were a visual record of actions, but oral storytelling and sometimes partial reenactments were vital opportunities for those involved to add details and context surrounding the incidents portrayed. Ledger drawings depicting battle encounters were, then, historic records that allowed commemoration and celebration of specific events. In some cultures at least, a warrior could render his own brave actions or ask another, perhaps more artistically skilled man, to do so. Other subjects beyond battles began to appear, apparently slowly at first and then more rapidly with the strict enforcement of the reservation system following the end of the Plains wars, approximately mid-1875 on the southern plains and a year and a half later in the north. By the reservation years, non-Native people on the plains, particularly military men, began to purchase ledger drawings in increasing numbers.

The initial use of accountants' ledgers and other types of books as surfaces upon which to record battle prowess and other related subjects coincides with an increase in the number of non-Native people on the plains, because they were the ultimate source of the books that were incorporated into Plains lifestyles. How and why this occurred was the result of complex intersections of cultures, but one example is indicated by a brief account offered by Fanny Kelly, a young woman who was held captive by a group of Lakota Sioux for five months in 1864. One of the younger warriors brought her clothes taken from the wagon train

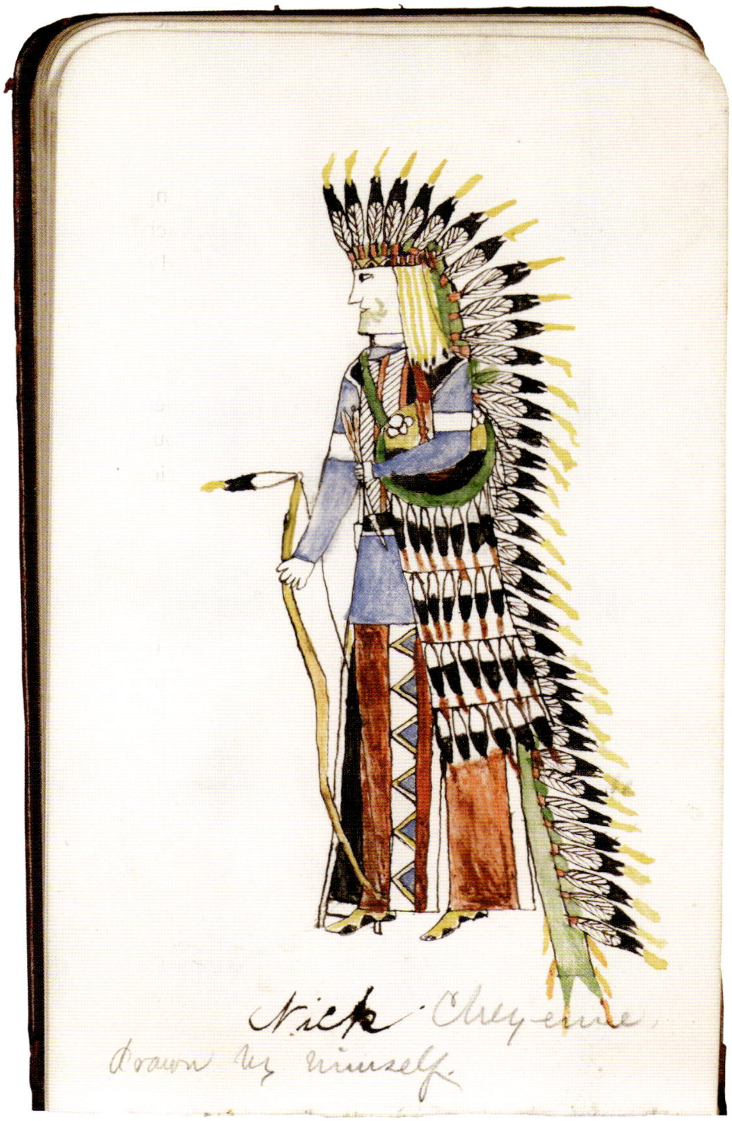

FIGURE 1.1
Nick (1855–1879), Southern Cheyenne. "Nick, Cheyenne, Drawn by Himself," mid-1875–mid-1878. Yale Collection of Western Americana, Beinecke Rare Book and Manuscript Library, 1073237

on which she had been traveling west; he looked "kindly as he laid these articles before me . . . He also brought me some books and letters."[5] That the warrior placed books and letters before her suggests he was aware of the value these articles held for non-Native people like Kelly. While Native people had been incorporating newly available materials into their lives from the time of initial contact with non-Natives, as well as trading widely with each other for materials only available from great distance, the use of books may well have carried additional messages. Recognizing the importance of books, as Kelly's account implies they did, warriors could and did absorb them and other sources of paper into their own cultures and use them to document images of their battle successes, often victories over the same non-Native intruders.

The smaller size of pieces of paper, in comparison to large buffalo hides and clothing, required adjustments, but warriors expanded what could be represented on single sheets in many ways, such as rendering partial figures to stand for whole ones and guns firing from the edges of pages to suggest larger forces. Two facing pages in a book were also occasionally used to relay a larger view of one specific scene, and consecutive pages seem, at times, to refer to serial events. The Lansburgh collection offers clear potential for comparative examination of these approaches to chronicling information deemed important to the people who drew the images. Sometimes individual warrior-artists appear to have created all of the images in a specific ledger book, but, in many others, multiple warriors drew within a single volume. Individual and perhaps even cultural variations in the ways information is relayed on various pages are clear.

The discussion within this essay, and most others concerning ledger drawings, focuses on men as the exclusive artists of these drawings. Men were the primary warriors in Plains societies, but there were women warriors as well; the possibility remains that women who exhibited bravery in battle might have drawn images of their accomplishments meriting recognition, although no evidence supporting this has come to light. There are drawings that depict heroic actions of women in battle, including two attributed to Yellow Nose, a Ute captive raised by the Northern Cheyennes.[6]

The collection includes works created both before the enforcement of the reservation system and during the reservation era. An additional group of drawings came from the unique three-year period between mid-1875 and mid-1878 when seventy-two Southern Plains warriors and chiefs were imprisoned at Fort Marion in Saint Augustine, Florida. Fifteen drawings from the Fort Marion confinement created by two different prisoners, the Kiowa Ohettoint (1852–1934) and the Southern Cheyenne Chief Killer (1849–1922), are in the collection (see plates 46–60). Fort Marion art is almost exclusively drawn by Southern Cheyenne and Kiowa men with a few known examples by the two Arapaho inmates. Drawings made in Saint Augustine are very different from art created on the plains. Images rarely overtly refer to battle but focus more on genre scenes of the lives from which the prisoners were exiled and on many of their new experiences in Saint Augustine.[7]

Inmate-artists made drawings at Fort Marion for multiple reasons, not the least of which was as a means of communication. Communication was part of the attraction for tourist-purchasers of the drawings; making the images open-ended to allow understanding of them must have been, at least in part, a goal. The drawings were also a potentially important source of communication between the inmates themselves. Prisoners from five different cultures were confined in Florida and understanding each other through spoken word was not always possible, although sign language would have helped. Visual documents relayed important and multilayered information about one's culture to a person from another in a very direct manner. Perhaps this is why so many images of specific warrior societies appear in Fort Marion drawing books and why, in part, when the men depicted themselves in single-figure self-portraits they did so with signs of their status as warriors on the plains rather than as prisoners in Florida where, with limited exception, the men were forced to dress alike. Individual men presented themselves as they would have been on the plains (see figure 1.1), wearing the regalia and indications of their rightful position; these images and the way the men wished to be seen, both at Fort Marion and in their representations of life on the plains, remain strongly connected. Such depictions may also have been a way to defy the rigid conformity the men were forced to endure, a way to reassert their identities in the midst of stifling sameness. The drawings allowed the men to make their achievements as warriors clear without generally depicting the specific battles that led to their elevated positions. These were perhaps more acceptable to Richard Henry Pratt and other non-Native viewers of the drawings, while battle representations may have been less so. Aspects of Pratt's assimilation program are also clear from the Fort Marion record. For example, various artists created drawings of the classroom where some of the prisoners were learning to read and write and of church services they attended.

The Lansburgh collection, then, comprises pre-reservation, reservation, and Fort Marion drawings—all three of the primary periods of ledger art appear. These drawings provide a wide view of the changing cultural history of Plains people as well as individual stylistic variation. The majority of extant ledger drawings, whether in the Lansburgh collection or elsewhere, are by Lakota, Cheyenne, and Arapaho warrior-artists. Kiowa drawings are known from Fort Marion and from the reservation era, but Kiowa battle-oriented art before Fort Marion is particularly elusive. Thus far no concretely dated pre-reservation Kiowa drawings have been identified. Drawings by Crow warriors are rare, and the fact that the Lansburgh collection contains drawings by a Crow artist adds to the importance of the collection.

Some drawings, both those created on the plains and by prisoners at Fort Marion, bear captions that were added at unknown times and by people who may or may not have known what the artist intended to represent; some even record names purported to identify the artists. Captions or titles for drawings and descriptions or identities associated with those works often take precedence over the visual information provided by the work itself and lead viewers to accept what the words say, rather than what the visual language says. Critical examination of captions and descriptions associated with Plains drawings is vital, and that scrutiny is equally important in studies of the works in the Lansburgh collection.

Many of the Cheyenne Lansburgh drawings that were created on the plains came from a single ledger book that was sold through a gallery in Santa Fe that, fortunately, published a full facsimile of the book with detailed

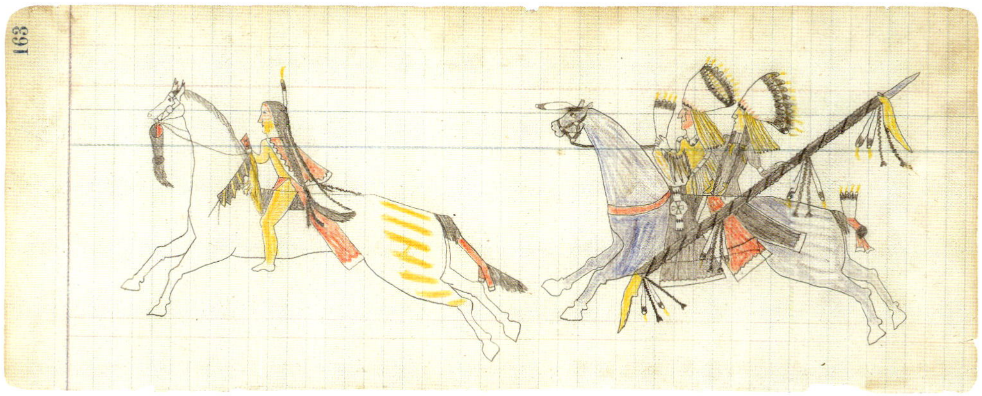

FIGURE 1.2
Unknown artist, Southern Tsistsistas (Cheyenne), active late nineteenth century, ***Untitled [Tsistsistas (Cheyenne) Elk Society warriors],*** c. 1874–75, Hood Museum of Art (plate 32)

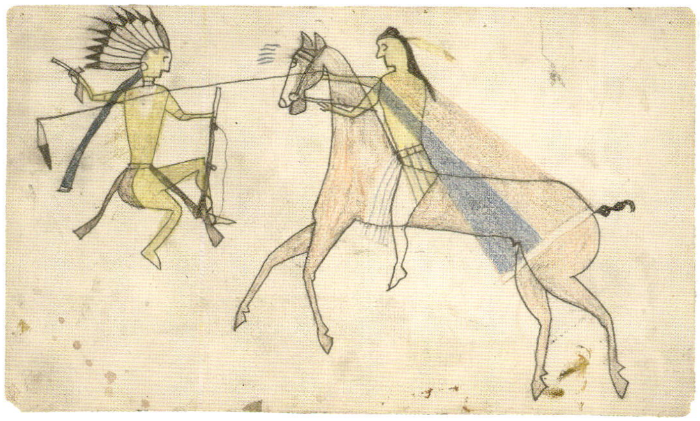

FIGURE 1.3
White Swan, Apsáalooke (Crow), 1851–1904, ***Untitled [White Swan counting coup on a warrior, possibly Lakota],*** c. 1890, Hood Museum of Art (plate 138)

commentary by Mike Cowdrey.[8] (See figure 1.2 and plates 17–33.) Such resources, preserving the context of the drawings, are vital to a greater understanding of what the warrior or, in this case, warriors valued sufficiently to represent in two-dimensional form. Ledger books have been given titles based on the predominance of a single figure that appears in the drawings, sometimes because of a known artist whose work appears in a book, and sometimes by an historic or a contemporary collector's name. The book that Cowdrey studied intently was titled "Arrow's Elk Society Ledger" for the frequency in which a figure appears that seems to have a name sign of an arrow; name signs are small images that most often appear above the head of a figure and are sometimes connected to that man by a line. Name signs are not artists' signatures; rather, they identify protagonists rendered in various drawings. Since some men drew their own battle exploits, while in other instances different men rendered them, the identity of the artist and the warrior depicted are not necessarily the same. The arrow-glyph figure carries and wears objects that associate him with the Cheyenne Elk Warrior Society. These drawings, whether by someone actually named Arrow or only depicting someone named Arrow, provide detailed information about a man and a specific Cheyenne warrior society. The individual pages from the book that are in the Lansburgh collection include various battle and hunting scenes, social events such as courting, and ceremonial activities. This diversity of subjects illustrating Plains cultures in transition and the detailed way in which the artist or artists rendered them place the drawings from the Arrow Ledger among the most important in the Lansburgh collection.

Some of the other artists with works in the collection are known to us today by name; for others there is not even a suggestion of the creator's identity. There are works here by the Southern Cheyenne warrior-artist Howling Wolf (1849–1927) (see figure 1.6 and plates 34–36); he created these during the late pre-reservation period prior to his imprisonment in Florida and they are currently his earliest known drawings. Howling Wolf created additional works that probably date before the enforcement of the reservation system, many more when he was imprisoned at Fort

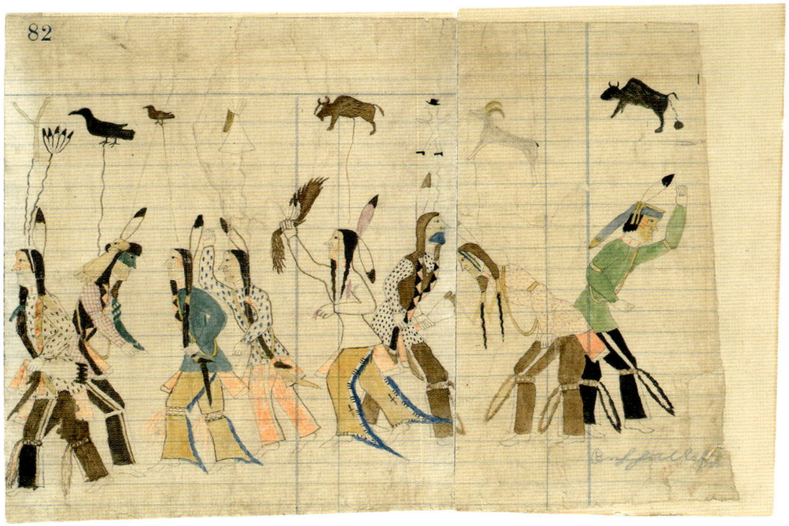

FIGURE 1.4
Wooden Leg (Kum-mok-quiv-vi-ok-ta), Northern Tsistsistas (Cheyenne), 1858–1940, ***Untitled [Joined ledger pages: social dancers, including part of page 82]***, c. 1882, Hood Museum of Art (plate 123).

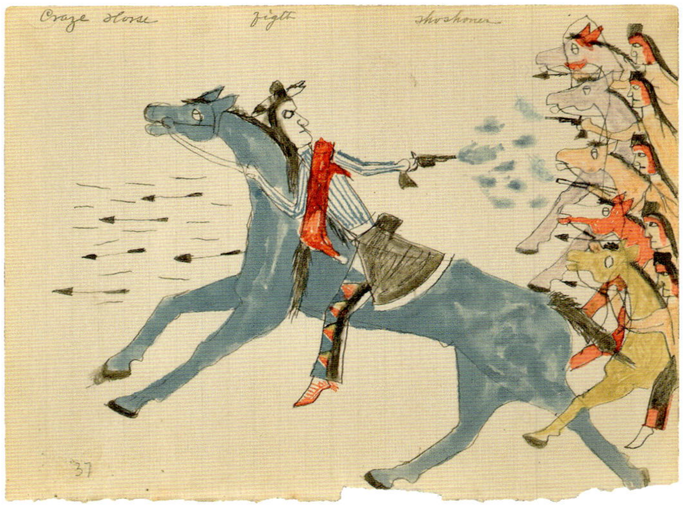

FIGURE 1.5
Short Bull (Tatanka Ptecela), Lakota (Sioux), c. 1845–1915, ***Untitled [Crazy Horse fighting the Apsáalooke (Crow)]***, c. 1885–90, Hood Museum of Art (plate 132).

Marion, and one known book of twelve drawings created after his return to the Cheyenne and Arapaho Reservation following his release from exile.[9] White Swan (1851–1904), one of the Crow scouts with George Armstrong Custer at Greasy Grass, or the Battle of Little Bighorn, is also represented in the Lansburgh collection (see figure 1.3 and plates 134–38); his works, rather than being on paper, are on a textured woven cloth that has been cut into small pieces similar to the size of ledger drawings in books. White Swan's drawings may originally have been one large work that was subsequently subdivided into multiple compositions. Well known both as a scout and as an artist, White Swan made other works both on paper and cloth, the latter larger in scale. Northern Cheyenne ledger artist Richard Wooden Leg (1858–1940) has two drawings in the collection (see figure 1.4 and plates 122–23). He, too, is a recognized artist who created many drawings throughout his life, and, like various other Cheyenne warrior-artists, he rendered very precise, detailed images.[10] Ten drawings attributed to Short Bull (c. 1845–1915) are powerful representations of battle with both Native and non-Native enemies, especially Pawnee and Crow (see figure 1.5 and plates 124–33). Short Bull was a Lakota warrior, Ghost Dance advocate, and artist who created various works on both paper and canvas, some dated as late as 1912.[11] If the captions that appear on the drawings are correct, Short Bull rendered not only himself in battle but also the famous warrior Crazy Horse.

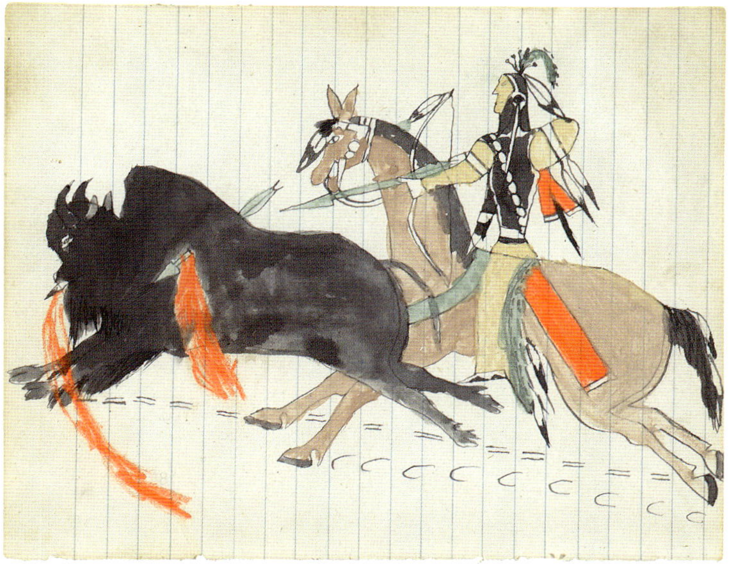

FIGURE 1.6
Howling Wolf (Ho-na-nist-to), Southern Tsistsistas (Cheyenne), 1849–1927, ***Untitled [Warrior on a buffalo hunt],*** c. 1874–75, Hood Museum of Art (plate 36)

Howling Wolf's drawings were part of a small book that included the work of four or five additional artists, one or two of whom are represented in the Lansburgh collection (see plates 34–42). This small book is sometimes referred to as the "Robert Allen Guthrie Notebook." Together with the three drawings by Howling Wolf, these additional six drawings illustrate the manner in which men shared drawing books. Five of the images depict battle encounters but, of the remainder, two are courting scenes, one is a buffalo hunt, and the last is an image of a warrior, identified by caption as Howling Wolf, standing behind his horse. Although this is a book that, by its inscription and the style of Howling Wolf's drawings, predates the enforcement of the reservation system, the subject matter has broadened to include renditions well beyond those illustrating battle prowess.

Drawings such as those by Howling Wolf, White Swan, and Wooden Leg offer the possibility of study and comparison to known works by these men contained in other collections. Howling Wolf's drawings can, for example, be viewed as the predecessors of those found in a book containing over fifty drawings now in the collection of the Allen Memorial Art Museum of Oberlin College.[12] Ohettoint and Chief Killer, the Fort Marion artists represented here, also have drawings in various other collections that can be examined in relation to those at the Hood Museum.[13]

Many drawings cannot be attributed with any precision to individuals currently known by name. They also illustrate that captions appearing on drawings need to be closely interrogated, their accuracy always in question. The Kiowa drawings that Mark Lansburgh collected came from two different volumes. One book, known as the "Julian Scott Ledger" for the man who probably obtained it in 1890 when he was in Indian Territory, was reproduced with a commentary by Ronald McCoy.[14] The single drawing in the Lansburgh collection from the Scott Ledger depicts seven men engaged in an Osage Dance (see plate 100). Two men are drummers while the remainder are dancing, moving in different directions. While the caption on the drawing indicates that men from three different cultures are represented, McCoy underscores that the dress, hairstyles, and face paint make an Osage identity for all of the participants more likely.

The other drawings with a Kiowa association have been identified as potentially Mexican-Kiowa in origin based largely on the subjects depicted (see plates 92–99). Kiowas had repeated contact with Mexican people. They traded with them, and they raided into Mexico. Mexican youth were, on occasion, captured and adopted into the Kiowa culture.[15] Most of the ten Kiowa drawings in the collection detail Kiowa encounters with Mexican soldiers. Fringed, vibrantly patterned Mexican textiles appear in two drawings. One of these drawings bears a questionable caption, with the protagonist identified as Cheyenne but dressed, instead, in Kiowa-style clothing.[16]

Various works in the collection were probably made by Arapaho men. But these attributions are more complex given the frequency with which both Southern Arapaho and Cheyenne men went to war together; the two cultures were strong allies during the years of the Plains wars and afterward they were assigned to a joint reservation in

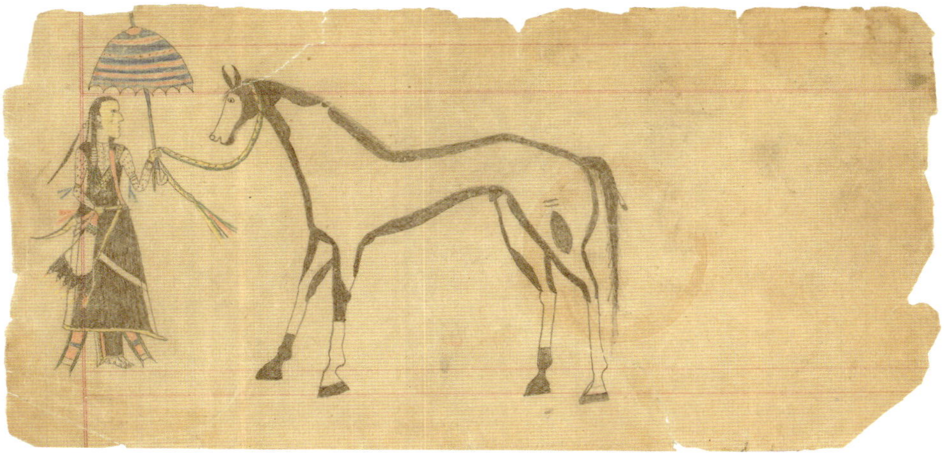

FIGURE 1.7
Unknown artist, Tsistsistas (Cheyenne) and/or Inunaina (Arapaho), active late nineteenth century, ***Untitled [A man holding a parasol leads a horse],*** late nineteenth century, Hood Museum of Art (plate 87)

Indian Territory. If men in war parties shared drawing books, then warriors from both Arapaho and Cheyenne societies could have rendered images in the same volume. What may be the earliest concretely datable drawings in the collection came from a ledger book probably collected during the late 1860s by Peter Edwards when he was on the plains (see plates 6–8); he died in 1872.[17] Most of those drawings have been reproduced in the book titled the "Peter W. Edwards Ledger," again based on the collector's identity. These works have been attributed to Arapaho men, but some of the drawings may be by Cheyenne warriors.

Thirty-one of the drawings in the Lansburgh collection are from a ledger book previously owned by the actor and art collector Vincent Price (see figure 1.7 and plates 61–91). Given the details of clothing and warrior society regalia depicted, some of these works were either created by both Arapaho and Cheyenne warriors or else members of one culture drew very specific representations of people from the other. Work by at least four different artists is apparent and the drawings are stylistically diverse, but the vast majority are battle scenes as warriors encounter both non-Native and a variety of Native enemies. Artists successfully rendered the action of battle and the important details that designate both protagonists and their enemies. One artist, in particular, was exceedingly adept at rendering fine-line details of humans and animals, clothing and regalia. He turned figures in space, presenting frontal views of faces and portions of bodies for both humans and animals (see plate 71). Within the wealth of battle scenes, a few additional subjects appear including a well-dressed man with a parasol, perhaps on his way to visit a woman, and two agency policemen on horseback.[18]

An intriguing book now known as the "Frank Henderson Ledger" was created as a gift and sent in December 1882 to an elderly woman in Carlisle, Pennsylvania, by a young Arapaho boy, Frank Henderson (1862–1885) (see figure 1.8 and plates 116–19). He had met Martha Underwood, a teacher, when he was a student at Carlisle Indian School. After his return to Indian Territory, Henderson recorded inside the book: "I have to say to you this Monday afternoon I try hard to make you Indian picture. I wish you could write soon. Ah you pleased with it. I am your friend Henderson."[19] While he appears to take credit for all of the images within the book, multiple artists contributed drawings to it. Some of those artists may have been Cheyenne while others were Arapaho, for the two cultures were then sharing a reservation in present-day Oklahoma. One of the artists in the Henderson book is the same artist who was such an adept draftsman in the "Vincent Price Ledger"; the manner of rendering animals, humans, and details of clothing and paraphernalia makes the identity clear. (Compare plates 71 and 119.) The same artist created a single, fully landscaped drawing in the collection from an unknown ledger. (See plate 121.) Drawings by this extremely precise visual narrator found in three different ledger books suggest some of the range of his experimentation; even if his actual identity remains unknown, his stature as a Plains artist is clear.

Three drawings from a book known as the "Carl S. Dentzel Ledger" are in the Lansburgh collection (see plates 43–45). Again, these may have been drawn by either Arapaho or Cheyenne warriors, or both, because they depict what appear to be insignia of specific warrior societies from each culture. One drawing depicts a warrior on horseback counting coup on, or touching, a fallen soldier using a lance with what might be a Cheyenne Bowstring warrior society round-shaped rattle attached to it. Another illustrates a warrior who uses an Arapaho warrior society

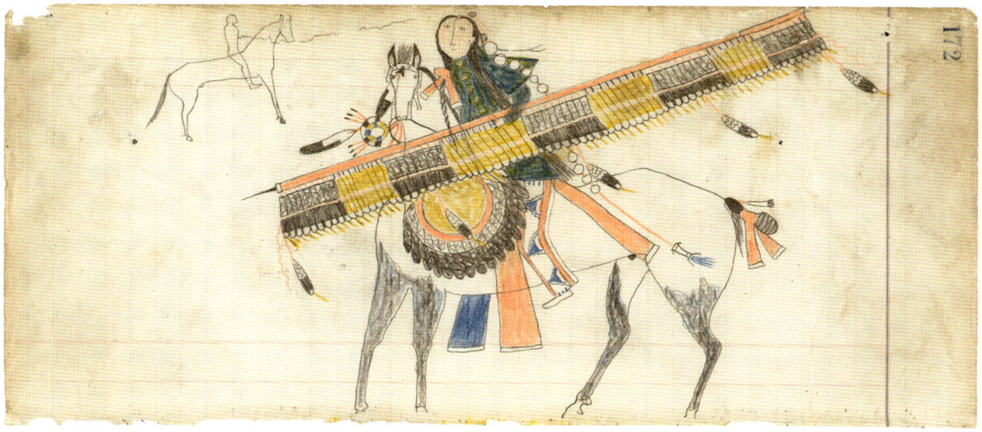

FIGURE 1.8
Unknown artist, Southern Inunaina (Arapaho) and/or Southern Tsistsistas (Cheyenne), active late nineteenth century, ***Untitled [A Crazy Dog Society warrior],*** June 1881–December 1882, Hood Museum of Art (plate 119)

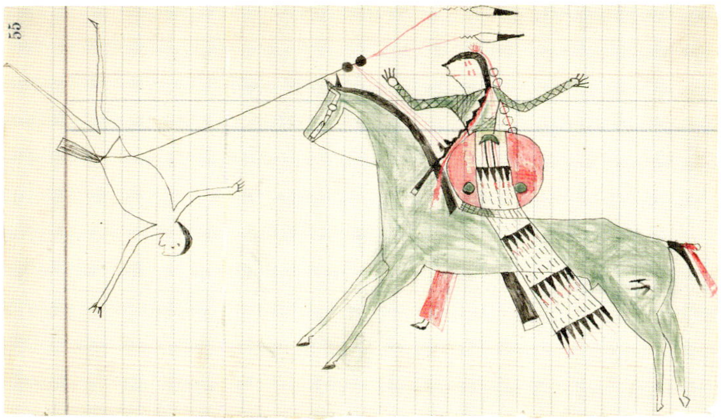

FIGURE 1.9
Unknown artist, Tsistsistas (Cheyenne), active mid- to late nineteenth century, ***Untitled [A Tsistsistas (Cheyenne) warrior counts coup on an enemy],*** 1860s, Hood Museum of Art (plate 2)

clubboard, a specific sign of membership in the Tomahawk Society, to count coup on a fallen enemy (see plate 44).

Mark Lansburgh's growing attraction to less complex images is reflected in the five drawings that came from a book known as the "Frederic H. Douglas Ledger," after a previous owner who was a curator at the Denver Art Museum (see figure 1.9 and plates 1–5). In these the artists used an economy of line and, in several cases, less color than most of the other works in the collection to render the vital details of figures on horseback with their shields and warrior society regalia. The battle action is, however, effectively relayed. Two of the warriors engage in battle with enemies, one apparently a Native man while the other is non-Native.

Eight Cheyenne drawings, two of which are only pencil sketches, came from an unknown book, but the artists who rendered these images have works in other known volumes and collections (see figure 1.10 and plates 9–16).[20] Several of the pages represent the heroic battle actions of a man whose name sign appears to be a lance. In two of the drawings, he is represented as what is commonly referred to as a "naked fighter," one who has stripped to his loincloth or a blanket for battle. Such men were recognized as extremely brave and powerful. His yellow body paint with a black moon on his chest and buffalo tracks on his face and legs marks him as a warrior with special spiritual protection.[21]

Many drawings in the Lansburgh collection suggest, on first examination, that they were probably made during the reservation era. The diversity of subject matter, a large number of courting scenes, and some ceremonial representations argue for a later date than their creation during the active years of the Plains wars. Among the drawings of genre scenes or courting are the fifteen images from what is known as the "Old White Woman Ledger," based on an interpretation of a name sign that appears repeatedly on the drawings (see figure 1.11 and plates 101–15). Moments of intimacy are suggested in most of the drawings, while several others depict ceremonies and one presents a man with many of his possessions arrayed around him. There are a few drawings in which a man, or men, with shields or warrior society regalia

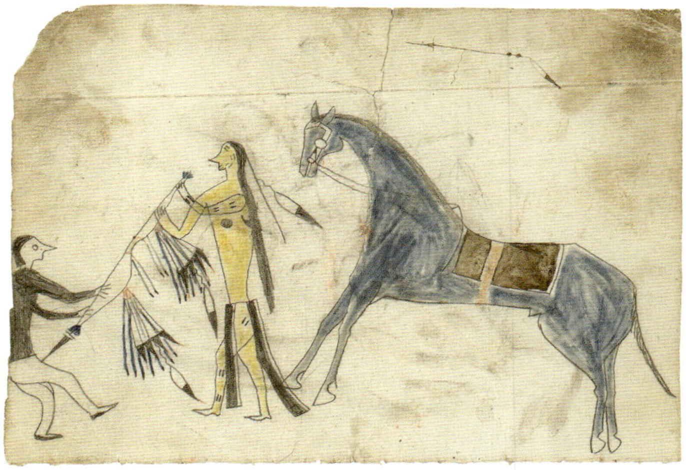

FIGURE 1.10
Unknown artist, possibly Tsistsistas (Cheyenne), active mid- to late nineteenth century, ***Untitled [A Tsistsistas (Cheyenne) counting coup on a non-Native enemy],*** late 1860s–early 1870s, Hood Museum of Art (plate 9)

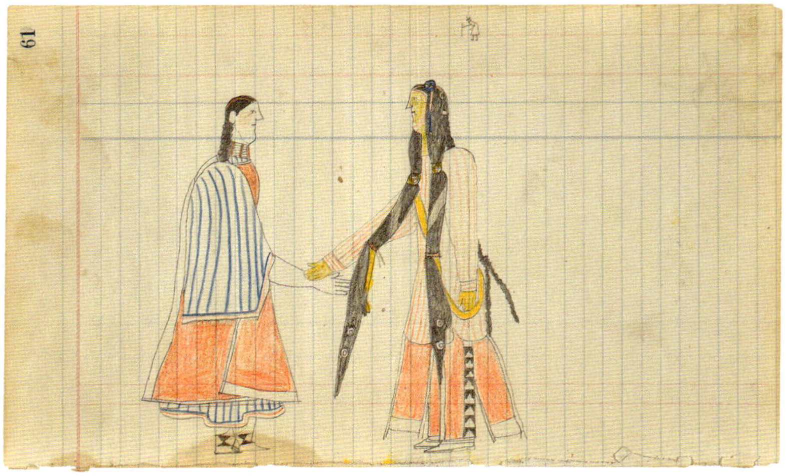

FIGURE 1.11
Unknown artist, Tsistsistas (Cheyenne), active late nineteenth century, ***Untitled [A Tsistsistas (Cheyenne) courting couple meet],*** c. 1880–90, Hood Museum of Art (plate 105)

appear, but there are no clear battle images among the Lansburgh drawings from this book. Four drawings in the collection that are by far the smallest in size are associated with a Northern Cheyenne man, Robert Ridge Walker (c. 1867–c. 1965), who served as a scout with the army in 1890 (see plates 139–42). These images suggest varied activities associated with reservation life and new occupations for Plains men; a 1901 date is associated with other drawings from the same book.[22] But without correlating dates and information concerning artists or contemporaneous collectors, subject matter alone is no guarantee that the drawings were made during the reservation era—just as representations of war are not confined to drawings from the pre-reservation era. Battle images did continue to be made, particularly by men who had earned the right to illustrate their successes.

Mark Lansburgh's collection of drawings that are now in the Hood Museum are distinct, vivid representations of aspects of Plains history, whether they were drawn on the plains or in a Florida prison. Ledger drawings taken from their original context are only portions of complete books; they are parts of wholes. But even individual works provide multiple narratives, and one of those concerns the subsequent lives of the drawings—how they have been perceived by various generations and diverse audiences. No two individuals today, and undoubtedly none in the past, see any of these drawings in the same way.

Extant or known drawings, both those now at the Hood Museum as well as those held in other collections, are a microcosm of what the whole of ledger art might have been. As a significant part of this larger history, the Lansburgh drawings become an image gallery, a museum unto themselves. The drawings that comprise that gallery are open to perpetual reconfiguration as different drawings are placed on view, categories altered, and one image placed next to another in new ways that change how we see those images and how we potentially reconstruct some of their numerous meanings. Such observations offer rich avenues of study and potential ways to reconstruct an image of the past from these separate pages. With its rich, new collection of Plains drawings, made possible by Mark Lansburgh's generosity, the Hood Museum of Art at Dartmouth has seemingly limitless opportunities for continuing interpretations and understandings, as these powerful drawings allow their multiple narratives to emerge.

NOTES

1. I am indebted to Mark Lansburgh for his overwhelming generosity in sharing his enthusiasm, memories, and knowledge concerning ledger art over the more than twenty years I have known him. Malcolm Grimmer, formerly the owner of Morning Star Gallery, has also been extremely helpful during the years that I have studied ledger art, most recently by examining his records to determine specific dates referenced in this essay and in offering his observations on Mark Lansburgh as a collector.

2. Mark Lansburgh, "Foreword," in McCoy, *Kiowa Memories*, iv.

3. Conversation and e-mail correspondence with Malcolm Grimmer, February 10, 2011.

4. Conversation and e-mail correspondence with Malcolm Grimmer, February 10, 2011.

5. Kelly, *My Captivity among the Sioux Indians*, 41.

6. These are now at the Smithsonian Institution's National Anthropological Archives as INV 08704700 and INV 08708400.

7. Thirty-three Cheyennes, twenty-seven Kiowas, nine Comanches, two Arapahos, and one Caddo were selected for exile in Florida.

8. Cowdrey, *Arrow's Elk Society Ledger*.

9. Howling Wolf's work has been discussed and reproduced in various places. The drawings at the Allen Memorial Art Museum of Oberlin College all appear in Szabo, "Howling Wolf: An Autobiography of a Plains Warrior-Artist," 4–87. The twelve drawings he made after his return to the Cheyenne and Arapaho Reservation in mid-1878 are in Petersen, *Howling Wolf*. Szabo, *Howling Wolf and the History of Ledger Art*, offers a comparative discussion of the artist's works before the reservation, at Fort Marion, and after his return to Indian Territory.

10. A drawing from West Point that is very similar to those by Richard Wooden Leg in the Lansburgh collection was reproduced as figure 17 in Szabo, *Howling Wolf and the History of Ledger Art*.

11. Wildhage, "Material on Short Bull," 35–42.

12. Szabo, "Howling Wolf: An Autobiography of a Plains Warrior-Artist," 4–87.

13. See, for example, Szabo, "Chief Killer and a New Reality," 50–57; Vincent, Brydon, and Coe, eds., *Arts of the North American Indians*, 126; and Petersen, *Plains Indian Art from Fort Marion* , 165, 235.

14. Scott (1846–1901), born in Vermont, was a painter who specialized in American history paintings, especially of the Civil War. His painting *Battle of Cedar Creek* is still in Montpelier, Vermont, in the Governor's Reception Room. Scott was employed with the Census Bureau on President Benjamin Harrison's project to provide an accurate count of Indians in the nation. Working in the Southwest and Southern Plains, Scott created sixty oil paintings during his tenure as an agent with the bureau. McCoy, "Kiowa Memories: The Julian Scott Ledger," in *Kiowa Memories*, 1–2.

15. See the discussion of captives from Mexico and what would become the state of New Mexico in Methvin, *Andele, or The Mexican-Kiowa Captive*, especially the "Introduction" by James F. Brooks. See also Mooney, *Calendar History of the Kiowa Indians*.

16. The drawing in question is plate 99a, b.

17. Petersen, "Peter W. Edwards," in *The Edwards Ledger Drawings*, xi.

18. Two incomplete sketches also appear.

19. Peterson, *American Pictographic Images*.

20. Afton, Halaas, and Masich, *Cheyenne Dog Soldiers*, reproduces a book of drawings taken from the battlefield at Summit Springs in present-day Colorado in 1869. This book is now in the collection of the Colorado Historical Society. Various warrior-artists worked in the ledger, but one is the same man who drew the images with the lance name-glyph in the Lansburgh collection. Other works by the same artist are also contained in the collections of the Museum of Mankind, London. See Taylor, "The 'Tall Bear' Drawings," 1–12, especially figures 10–12. Afton, Halaas, and Masich, *Cheyenne Dog Soldiers*, also includes one of the drawings from London on page 10.

21. Page 15 of the Dog Soldier ledger contains a representation drawn by the same artist and includes not only the lance name-sign but also a depiction of the warrior with the same body paint. Afton, Halaas, and Masich, *Cheyenne Dog Soldiers*, 20–22.

22. Morning Star Gallery, *Native American Ledger Drawing Book*; Vincent, Brydon, and Coe, eds., *Arts of the North American Indians*, 165.

CHAPTER 2

Striving for Recognition

LEDGER DRAWINGS AND THE CONSTRUCTION AND MAINTENANCE OF SOCIAL STATUS DURING THE RESERVATION PERIOD

MICHAEL PAUL JORDAN

PLAINS PICTOGRAPHIC DRAWINGS HAVE BEEN widely recognized as valuable historical documents capable of providing insights into nineteenth-century Plains Indian life.[1] Yet ledger drawings did not merely reflect the societies in which they were produced; they also played an active role in constituting these societies by shaping the social relations between individuals. This essay addresses the ways in which men's social status was both constructed and expressed through the production of ledger drawings during the late nineteenth century. The present study confines itself to an analysis of drawings from the southern plains, focusing on the work of Southern Arapaho, Southern Cheyenne, and Kiowa artists in the Mark Lansburgh collection. A comparison of works produced before and following the cessation of warfare on the southern plains indicates that the production of ledger drawings continued to be fueled by the pursuit of male status into the reservation period.

Theoretically, this study builds on British anthropologist Alfred Gell's work on the agency of art. Gell maintains that individuals seek to influence others through the production of material objects, arguing that objects are imbued with the intentions and agency of their originators. He refers to this process as objectification, noting that "objectification in artefact form is how social agency manifests and realizes itself, via the proliferation of fragments of 'primary' intentional agents in their 'secondary' artefactual forms." Gell focuses on the "origin-stories" of objects and the motivations underlying their creation.[2] This essay combines an analysis of drawings in the Lansburgh collection with a reconstruction of the cultural and historical contexts in which they were created. This approach reveals that the pursuit of male status contributed directly to the production of ledger drawings and highlights the role these drawings played in shaping social relations within Southern Plains communities.

SUBJECT MATTER AND DATING

The lack of precise information regarding when many of the drawings in the Lansburgh collection were executed makes it difficult to determine whether specific works were created before or after the Red River War in 1875, which effectively marked the end of warfare on the southern plains. Scholars can arrive at a terminal date for a set of drawings' production if they can determine when the ledger book was initially collected. Fortunately this information exists for several of the ledgers in the Lansburgh collection. For example, since Peter W. Edwards died in 1872, one can be sure that the Arapaho drawings he collected were produced no later.[3] In the case of the Henderson Ledger, a dedication inscribed on the first page is dated December 12, 1882.[4] While the inscription establishes that the drawings were produced before this date, it does not indicate how long before. The same is true of the "Old White Woman Ledger," which contains an inscription dated April 3, 1887. The Dentzel Ledger was reportedly collected at Fort Reno, Indian Territory, in 1878. Unfortunately, there is no reliable way of determining how much time may have elapsed between when a set of drawings was made and when it was collected, and one cannot assume that the drawings were created the same year they were acquired.

While the subject matter of the drawings might provide a clue as to when they were created, it is often impossible to date a ledger book based solely on its content. Despite the conventional wisdom that images of courting, hunting, ritual, and daily life appeared following the end of warfare, these new subject matters actually found their way into ledger books before the cessation of hostilities.[5] Furthermore, the notion that these subjects quickly supplanted images of warfare during the reservation period is also false. As anthropologist Candace S. Greene notes, "scenes of war continued to be the single most prominent topic in ledger art throughout reservation times."[6] We cannot simply assume that a ledger book containing courting or hunting scenes dates to the reservation period, or that a set of drawings containing combat scenes dates to 1875, or before. However, the relative proportions of the different subject matter depicted in a ledger book provide a better indication of when the drawings were made and ledgers containing a higher percentage of hunting, courting, or ceremonial scenes compared to scenes of warfare, and ledgers lacking any combat scenes, can be assigned to the reservation period with some certainty.

But, how could drawings that circulated outside the subject's community have impacted his social status within the community? Here, it is worth considering anthropologists Arjun Appadurai and Igor Kopytoff's work on the cultural biographies and social lives of objects. Appadurai and Kopytoff recognized that a commodity is not a specific type of thing, but rather a phase in the life of an object.[7] Ledger books that were sold to military officers, agency employees, traders, or ethnologists did not necessarily begin their "lives" as commodities, just as books that were presented as tokens of friendship were not necessarily created with that specific end in mind. These drawings may have initially been created for an indigenous audience, and may have remained within the artists' community for years before circulating outside it. Indeed, the inclusion of name glyphs in many of the drawings suggests that this was the case. While community members would have had no difficulty deriving an individual's identity from his name glyph, the glyph would have been relatively meaningless to an individual from outside the community. Name glyphs appear in drawings from the Edwards Ledger, "Vincent Price Ledger," Dentzel Ledger, Henderson Ledger, the "Old White Woman Ledger," and one of the unidentified sketchbooks in the collection, suggesting that each of these books was at least initially produced for an Arapaho or Cheyenne audience. Furthermore, many of these ledgers contain the work of multiple artists, indicating that they were produced in a communal context.[8] At the very least, the artists who collaborated on a book would have viewed one another's drawings, and it is likely that they would have circulated the book among their peers.

Some drawings are biographical rather than autobiographical. According to Greene, "Not all men depicted their own exploits. There appears to have been a measure of specialization in which particularly gifted artists were called upon to represent their friends as well as themselves."[9] The subjects of these scenes commissioned the drawings, narrating their war exploits for the artist, who then depicted them on paper. Among the Kiowas, war deeds were treated as a form of intellectual property. A warrior owned his martial exploits, as well as the right to depict them, and a man could not depict another's deeds unless he first obtained his permission.[10] Similar protocols likely existed among the Southern Arapahos and Southern Cheyennes. One can therefore be confident that the drawings were produced with the subjects' assent.

WARFARE AND STATUS

Scholars have long recognized the link in historic Plains Indian societies between a man's achievements in warfare and his social standing.[11] Discussing the connection between war deeds and social status among the nineteenth-century Kiowa, anthropologist Bernard Mishkin stated unequivocally that, "At the root of rank differentiation was war."[12] Indeed, it was a man's accomplishments in war more than any other factor that determined his standing in Kiowa society. For example, many respected and relatively wealthy religious specialists were never recognized as members of the uppermost echelon of Kiowa society, because they lacked the requisite war honors.[13] Furthermore, when Kiowa men quarreled regarding their relative status, they inevitably made recourse to their war records, attempting to demonstrate the superiority of their courage and martial prowess.[14]

Martial achievement and social status were closely linked among the Southern Cheyennes as well. An exceptional war record was a necessary qualification for men hoping to assume an office in one of the warrior societies.[15] The members of the societies routinely selected men who had demonstrated their bravery and distinguished themselves in warfare as their leaders.[16] In 1878, Howling Wolf, reflecting back on his career as a warrior, told Agent Lawrie Tatum, "I did not think it wrong to raid and fight, which I now believe to be wrong; for I was an Indian, and I thought and acted as an Indian. I wanted to be a leader."[17] Howling Wolf draws a clear connection between a man's war exploits and his rise to prominence, noting that his own martial exploits were fueled by his personal ambition.

Writing of the nineteenth-century Arapaho, anthropologist Alfred Kroeber observed that "honor and fame are primarily to be obtained through war."[18] This was most evident in the ranking of members of the age-graded men's societies or lodges. While there was no internal differentiation among the members of the first two societies, the Kit Foxes and Stars, when an age set entered the Tomahawk or Clubboard Lodge, four members were singled out and honored with leadership positions.[19] The Clubboard Lodge

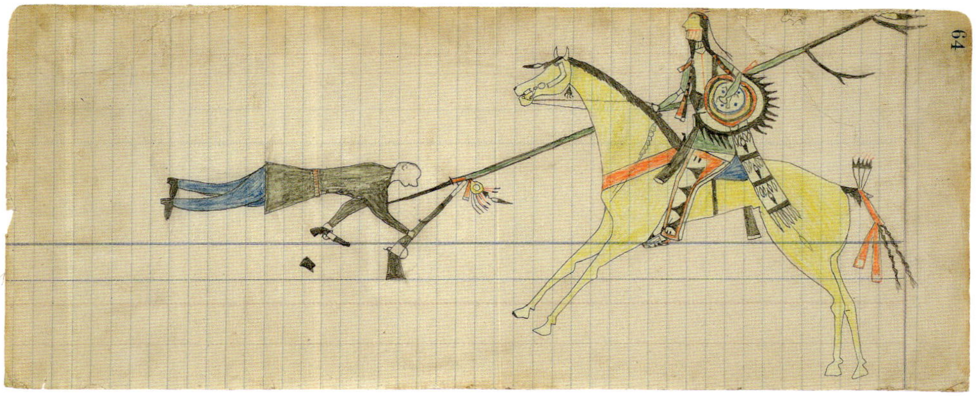

FIGURE 2.1
Unknown artist, Southern Tsistsistas (Cheyenne) and/or Southern Inunaina (Arapaho), active late nineteenth century, ***Untitled [A Tsistsistas (Cheyenne) warrior counts coup on a soldier]***, c. 1875–78, Hood Museum of Art (plate 45).

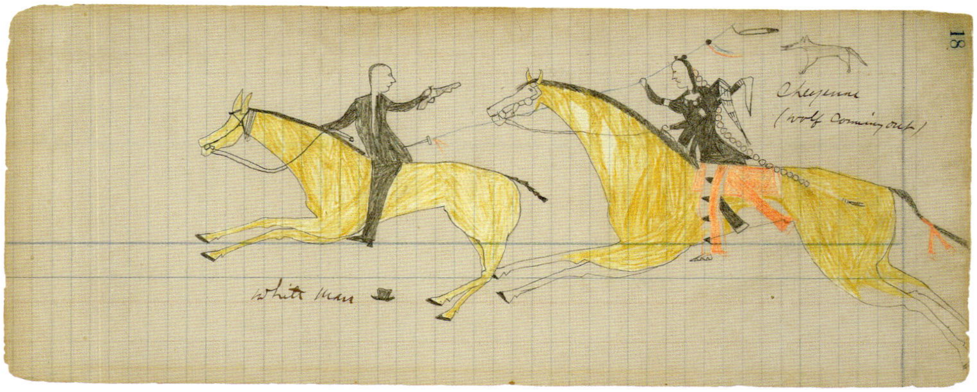

FIGURE 2.2
Unknown artist, Southern Tsistsistas (Cheyenne) and/or Southern Inunaina (Arapaho), active late nineteenth century, ***Untitled [A Tsistsistas (Cheyenne) or Inunaina (Arapaho) warrior counts coup on a non-Native enemy]***, c. 1875–78, Hood Museum of Art (plate 43).

marked "a shift to specialized roles and from unranked equality to formally ranked membership within the age set."[20] These ranks were "distinctions of respect and tribal confidence" awarded "chiefly for bravery."[21]

Arapaho, Cheyenne, and Kiowa men recognized a number of deeds, the performance of which they considered worthy of recognition. One of the most prestigious acts was counting coup, which entailed making physical contact with the enemy or striking him with an object held in the hand, such as a quirt or a bow. Coup could be counted on men, women, or children. In addition, multiple warriors could count coup on the same individual. The Cheyennes recognized the first three men to strike an enemy, while the Kiowas and Arapahos recognized the first four. The first man to touch the enemy garnered the most honor, the last the least.[22] Some of the most prestigious acts entailed the warrior risking his life for his comrades.[23] These included charging the enemy to cover a party's retreat, rallying a routed party, and rescuing a companion who had been wounded, unhorsed, or cut off by the enemy.[24] A few deeds, while not as prestigious as counting coup, were nevertheless recognized as noteworthy, including scalping an enemy, or capturing his horse, weapon, or shield.[25] Riding down a pedestrian enemy was also considered an exploit worthy of recognition.[26] This fact may account for the numerous ledger drawings depicting mounted warriors riding over prostrated foes. Men also received acclaim for leading successful expeditions against the enemy.[27]

In Southern Plains cultures, the recitation of war deeds was an integral component of the ritual associated with warrior society meetings. Among the Cheyennes, the narration of martial exploits marked the opening and closing of most warrior society functions.[28] In addition, an account of a "coup-counting bout" or contest, engaged in by the Elk and Bowstring societies, in which emissaries passed between the two sodalities, reciting their exploits and proffering gifts in an effort to outdo one another, may describe a more widespread practice.[29] Similar competitions occurred within the context of some of the Arapaho men's lodges, with half the membership of the lodge pitted against the other half.[30]

Many of the preparations for the Cheyenne Sun Dance could be undertaken only by men who had performed certain deeds in war. These men typically prefaced the performance of their ritual functions with the recitation of a coup or other war exploit. For example, only a man who had served as a scout, and in the process had counted coup inside an enemy's lodge, could ceremonially "scout" for the tree that would furnish the center pole for the Sun

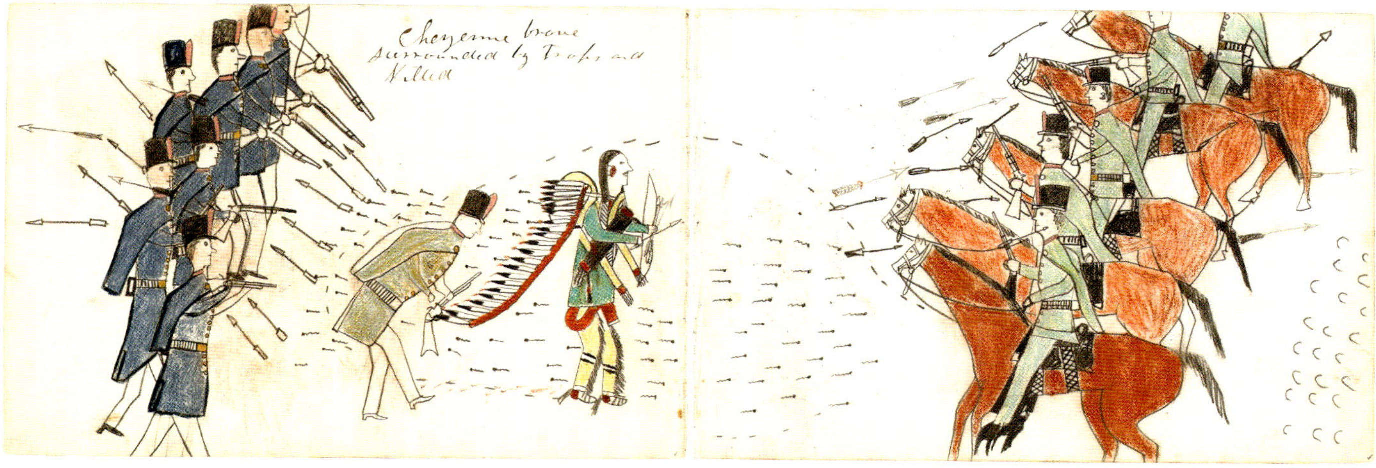

FIGURE 2.3

Unknown artist, Kiowa and/or Mexican, active late nineteenth century, ***Untitled [Kiowa warrior in battle with Mexican soldiers]***, late nineteenth century, Hood Museum of Art (plates 99a, 99b).

Dance Lodge. The individual would ride out on a horse painted for war. After selecting the tree, he would recount his exploit, and then strike the tree, counting coup on it. A man who had stabbed an enemy with a knife or struck one with a hatchet or an axe was asked to strike the first blow in cutting down the tree, but before doing so, he was expected to narrate this encounter with the enemy.[31]

The contexts in which men recited their war deeds did not disappear immediately following the cessation of hostilities. Kiowa and Southern Cheyenne warrior societies continued to meet into the 1880s, and the Southern Cheyennes continued to perform the Sun Dance.[32] The end of warfare and the advent of reservation life may have actually increased the standing of men who had distinguished themselves in war. These individuals would have been part of an ever shrinking cadre of men with the qualifications to perform the preparations for the Sun Dance, as well as other ritual functions. For example, in 1901 there were only two Southern Cheyenne men living who possessed the requisite deeds entitling them to select the center pole for the Sun Dance lodge.[33]

According to anthropologist Marion Smith, "A coup was honored, not because of any result which accrued from the act itself, but because of the danger which had been successfully overcome, and the emphasis naturally fell upon the conditions under which the act was accomplished."[34] Consequently, ledger drawings frequently record details concerning the protagonist's encounter with the enemy, including the armaments the parties carried and the odds that he confronted.

Careful attention to the weaponry wielded by the protagonist and his foe was important, because such details reflected on the warrior's courage.[35] Commenting on the Cheyennes, ethnologist George Grinnell noted that, "It was regarded as evidence of bravery for a man to go into battle carrying no weapon that would do any harm at a distance. It was more creditable to carry a lance than a bow and arrows; more creditable to carry a hatchet or war club than a lance; and the bravest thing of all was to go into a fight with nothing more than a whip, or a long twig—sometimes called a coup stick."[36] Arapaho, Cheyenne, and Kiowa warrior-artists frequently contrasted their own preference for weapons suited for hand-to-hand combat with their enemy's preference for weapons that were lethal at far greater range, such as firearms or bows and arrows. In this manner, Southern Plains warriors contrasted their own willingness to close with the enemy with their opponents' desire to hold their foe at bay, a contrast that underscored their superior courage. For example, three drawings from the "Carl S. Dentzel Ledger" (see figures 2.1 and 2.2) depict Cheyenne and Arapaho warriors armed with lances, striking opponents armed with firearms. The Lansburgh collection also contains two similar drawings from "Arrow's Elk Society Ledger." Implicit in all of these drawings is the idea that the protagonist has willingly exposed himself to great danger by charging through the enemy's fire in order to strike him.

Drawings depicting a protagonist defying overwhelming odds were intended to emphasize the warrior's courage and superior fighting abilities. Three ledger books in the Lansburgh collection contain drawings addressing this theme: the unidentified sketchbook with Kiowa drawings, "Arrow's Elk Society Ledger," and the "Vincent Price Ledger." One of the Kiowa drawings (figure 2.3) depicts a

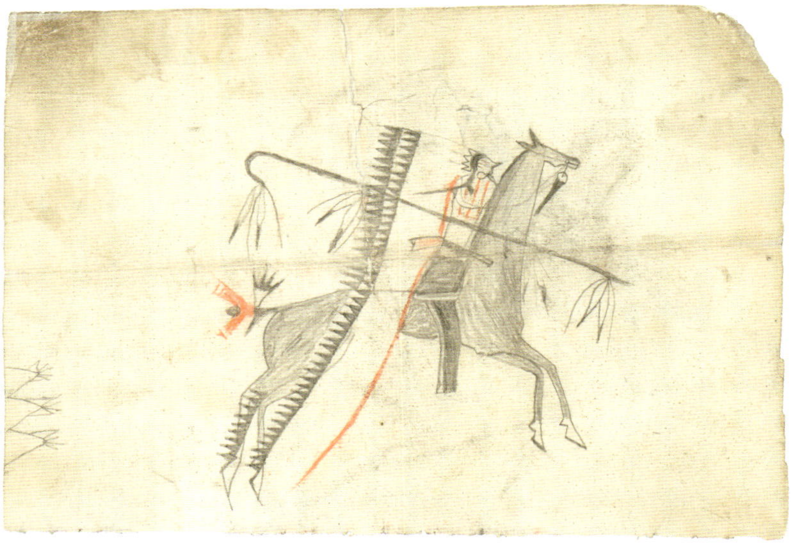

FIGURE 2.4
Unknown artist, possibly Tsistsistas (Cheyenne), active mid- to late nineteenth century, ***Untitled [A Tsistsistas (Cheyenne) Crooked Lance Society warrior]***, late 1860s–early 1870s, Hood Museum of Art (plate 10).

warrior surrounded by Mexican cavalry and infantry.[37] He faces both overwhelming odds and firepower; however, the inscription indicating that the warrior was killed in this encounter is undoubtedly incorrect. Southern Plains warriors rarely depicted the deaths of their comrades. The drawing is part of a larger corpus of Kiowa pictographic art that honors the deeds of men who escaped after being surrounded by the enemy. Warriors who fought their way out after being encircled or who fought so bravely that they convinced the enemy to abandon their attack were afforded special recognition in nineteenth-century Kiowa society. Each time the Tipi with Battle Pictures—a Kiowa tipi painted with pictographic images of warfare—was renewed, one of these men was asked to include his experience on the cover. The established convention dictated that the warrior depict himself inside a circle, variously identified as representing either the hastily constructed breastworks behind which he had fought or the enemy force that had surrounded him.[38] The drawing of the Kiowa warrior surrounded by Mexican soldiers recalls the scenes on the Tipi with Battle Pictures, and celebrates a Kiowa warrior's triumph over a much larger force.

Men who occupied leadership positions in the various warrior societies sometimes depicted themselves with symbols of their office, such as a distinctive lance or club. Because these positions were reserved for men who had distinguished themselves in combat, the drawings served to reference not only the man's elevated standing within his warrior society, but also his war record, bringing to mind the deeds that enabled him to ascend to his position. A drawing in one of the unidentified sketchbooks (figure 2.4) depicts an officer of the Cheyenne Elk Society. The mounted warrior bears a crooked lance wrapped with otter hide. This was the insignia carried by two of the Elk Society's officers.[39] Indeed, Crooked Lances was a popular alternative name for the society among the Southern Cheyennes.[40]

The connection between the warrior's position and his martial accomplishments was made even more explicit when he was pictured wielding his emblem of office in battle. Such drawings provided proof that the warrior was faithfully discharging the duties attendant to his position. As Kroeber notes regarding the ranked positions within the Arapaho men's lodges, "the bestowal of these honors was not only a recognition of past deeds, but an obligation involving future risk."[41] A Southern Arapaho drawing (figure 2.5) from the Dentzel Ledger depicts a second degree officer of the Tomahawk or Clubboard Lodge counting coup on a prostrate Pawnee with the club or "sword" that served as the insignia of his office.[42] In an engagement, duty demanded that the ranking members of the Tomahawk Lodge charge ahead of their comrades and count coup on the enemy using their clubs before returning to lead the general charge.[43] Men's society leaders were expected to exemplify the ideals of courage and fearlessness, and ledger drawings provided a way for warriors to demonstrate that they were living up to these ideals.

A Southern Cheyenne ledger, the "Robert Allen Guthrie Notebook," contains two similar drawings created around 1874 to 1875. The first is a self portrait by Howling Wolf (see plate 34), in which he depicts himself wearing an eagle bonnet and carrying a lance that emblemizes his status as an officer in the Bowstring Society. In the second drawing, by an unidentified artist, a mounted warrior

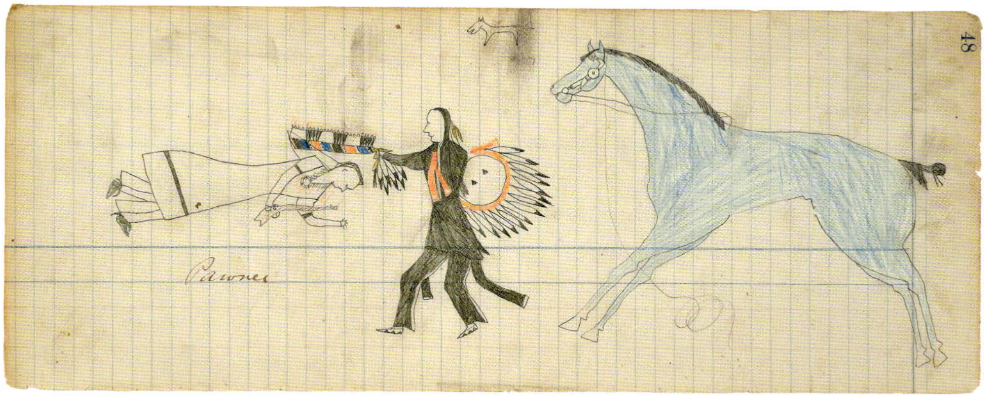

FIGURE 2.5
Unknown artist, Southern Tsistsistas (Cheyenne) and/or Southern Inunaina (Arapaho), active late nineteenth century, ***Untitled [Inunaina (Arapaho) warrior counts coup on an enemy, possibly a Chaticks Si Chaticks (Pawnee) warrior]***, c. 1875–78. The Arapaho warrior is an officer in the Tomahawk Society. Hood Museum of Art (plate 44).

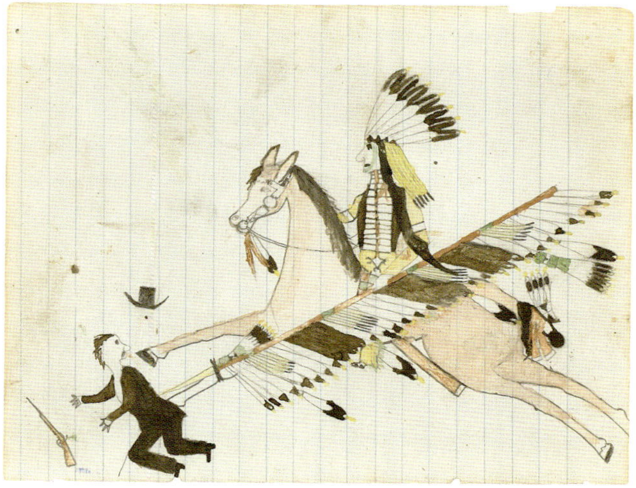

FIGURE 2.6
Unknown artist, Tsistsistas (Cheyenne), active late nineteenth century, ***Untitled [A Tsistsistas (Cheyenne) Bowstring Society warrior counts coup on a non-Native enemy]***, c. 1874–75, Hood Museum of Art (plate 37).

uses his Bowstring Society lance to strike a fleeing Anglo civilian (figure 2.6).

WEALTH AND STATUS

Martial achievement, despite its importance, was not the only factor that contributed to social status. Wealth also added to a man's standing. In reporting his rise to prominence, one Kiowa attributed his advancement in part to his ability to accumulate property and dress himself well. This same individual explained that a man whose wife had been unfaithful might turn the situation to his own advantage, noting that, as the aggrieved party, the husband could lay claim to his wife's lover's property, and thereby increase his wealth and status.[44] Summarizing information from his interviews, Mishkin observed that one of the markers of the highest ranking Kiowa men was possession of the "finest horses, clothes, arrow quivers, [and] saddles."[45]

Among the changes in Plains pictographic art that accompanied the adoption of ledger books and other bound compendia as mediums of expression was the adoption of new subject matters. According to Greene, "One new type of picture that emerged was of an individual man, shown standing or on horseback but not engaged in any particular activity. These pictures focused on appearance rather than on action, with men displaying their personal finery rather than their personal prowess in war."[46] Since an individual's social status was determined in part by wealth, depictions of material goods in drawings served to mark that status.

Drawings in the Lansburgh collection provide ample proof that this genre was well established before the end of warfare on the southern plains. The existence of books containing both combat scenes and portraits illustrating details of individuals' dress and accoutrements indicates that Southern Plains artists considered both subject matters worthy of representation. For example, of the five drawings from the "Frederic H. Douglas Ledger" in the Lansburgh collection, two focus on combat, while three depict solitary warriors. Although mounted and outfitted

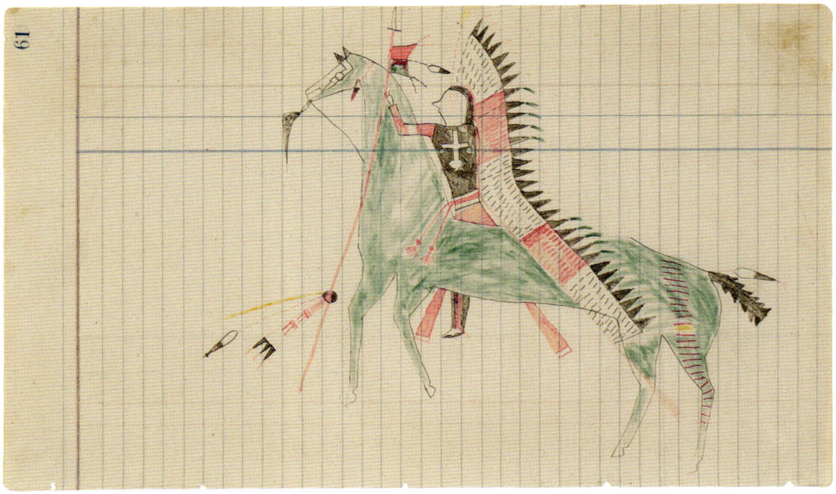

FIGURE 2.7
Unknown artist, Tsistsistas (Cheyenne), active mid- to late nineteenth century, ***Untitled [A Tsistsistas (Cheyenne) Bowstring Society warrior]***, 1860s. Note the silverwork and bonnet. Hood Museum of Art (plate 4).

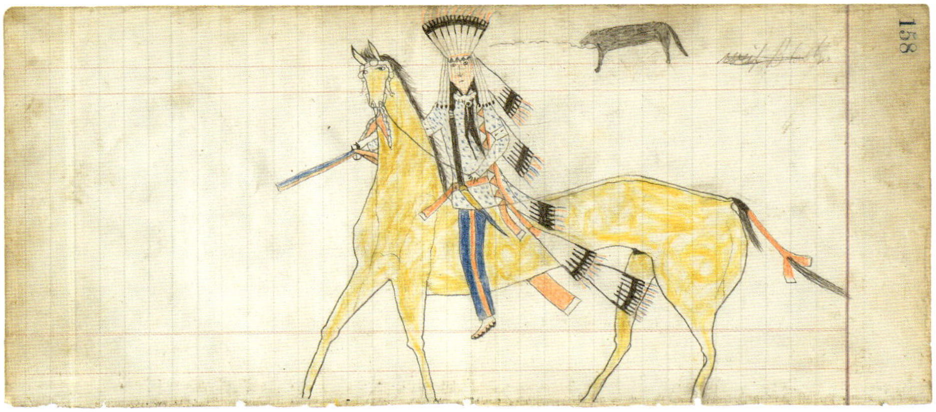

FIGURE 2.8
Unknown artist, Southern Inunaina (Arapaho) and/or Southern Tsistsistas (Cheyenne), active late nineteenth century, ***Untitled [An Inunaina (Arapaho) warrior]***, June 1881–December 1882. The artist depicted the man's clothing and accoutrements in great detail. Hood Museum of Art (plate 118).

for war, the latter figures are not shown engaged in the act of counting coup or killing an enemy, suggesting that it was their personal appearance and trappings that the artist and the subjects themselves wished to display. Although the figures lack facial features, the artist rendered their clothing and accoutrements in great detail. He paid special attention to their silverwork, including armbands, a pectoral ornament, a cross, a set of hair plates, and the decorations on their horses' bridles (see figure 2.7). In addition, two of the figures wear eagle feather bonnets, one with an extremely long trailer.

During the reservation period, individuals' anxiety regarding their economic circumstances likely intensified. Military actions in 1874 and 1875 resulted in the destruction of significant personal property, as the army targeted Cheyenne and Kiowa villages for destruction. The military seized large numbers of horses, capturing some in battle, and confiscating others when the bands surrendered at military posts. What remained of the tribes' herds soon became the target of Euro-American horse thieves.[47]

In letters written following his return from Fort Marion to the reservation in 1878, Howling Wolf repeatedly laments being reduced to a state of poverty, and speculates regarding how he might improve his lot. In a letter to Lieutenant Zalinski, whom he had met during his exile in the east, he writes, "I am very poor, as the Northern Cheyennes stole every one of my horses when they left this place last September. When I get some more ponies I shall feel better."[48] In a letter to Richard Henry Pratt, he contrasts his earlier life on the plains and at Fort Marion with his current condition, concluding that "At the fort you gave us cloths but we have bin here one year and they are about all gon . . . When I hunted the Buffalo I was not poor; when I was with you I did not want for eney thing[,] but here I am Poor."[49] A dearth of employment opportunities only added to the poverty and distress of young men adjusting to reservation life.[50]

Drawings produced in the 1880s evidence this concern with wealth and status. The Lansburgh collection contains four Arapaho drawings from the "Frank Henderson

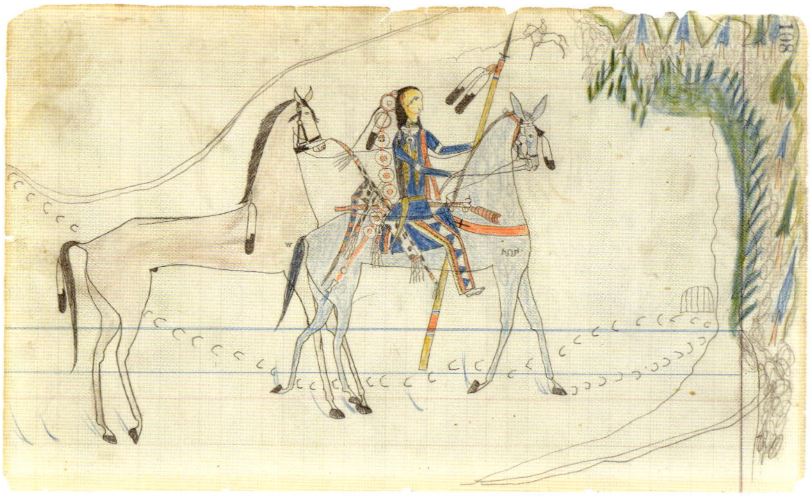

FIGURE 2.9
Unknown artist, Southern Inunaina (Arapaho) and/or Southern Tsistsistas (Cheyenne), active late nineteenth century, ***Untitled [An Inunaina (Arapaho) warrior traveling],*** early 1880s. An elaborately dressed warrior: note his beaded leggings, silverwork, and armaments. Hood Museum of Art (plate 121).

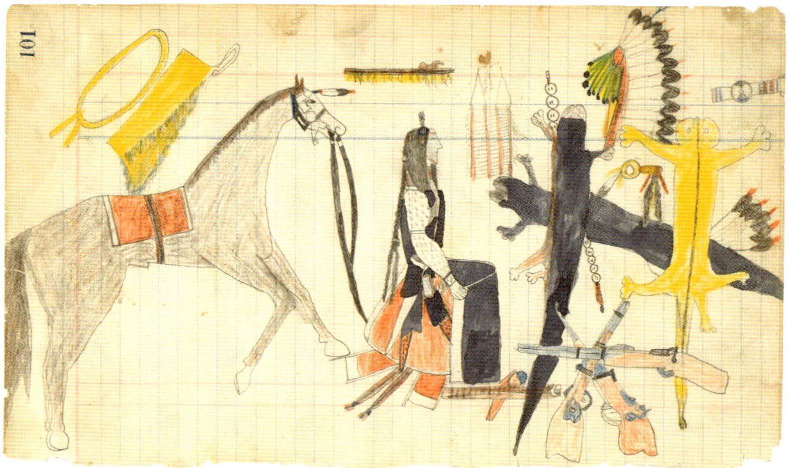

FIGURE 2.10
Unknown artist, Tsistsistas (Cheyenne), active late nineteenth century, ***Untitled [A Tsistsistas (Cheyenne) Bowstring Society warrior with his possessions],*** c. 1880–90, Hood Museum of Art (plate 107).

Ledger," three of which are portraits similar to those in the "Frederic H. Douglas Ledger." The figures are depicted mounted and arrayed for war; all of the men carry weapons, and their horses' tails are tied up or bound for war. The drawings are more detailed than those in the Douglas Ledger, and the warriors' dress is carefully rendered. Two of the men wear beaded leggings and the third wears beaded moccasins (figure 2.8). Each man's horse is equipped with a silver mounted bridle. The men themselves wear an array of silverwork, including armbands, hair plates, and a pectoral ornament. Two of the men wear bonnets. A man's everyday dress during this period consisted of a "calico shirt, undecorated trade cloth leggings, un-beaded moccasins and … [a] wool breechcloth."[51] In contrast, beaded leggings, war shirts, and bonnets were prestige goods.[52] Judged by these standards, the Arapaho warriors in the Henderson Ledger are dressed to impress.

One of the figures depicted in the Henderson Ledger appears in a drawing from another book (figure 2.9), where he is identified by the same name glyph. While the two-page drawing clearly records a journey the warrior undertook, the detailed rendering of the man's clothing and weapons suggests that it was also intended to call attention to his material possessions. Dressed in his finest, he wears beaded leggings and moccasins, a set of hair plates, armbands, and a pectoral ornament. He carries an array of weapons. In addition to his lance, he is shown with a percussion lock muzzle-loading rifle and a bow in an elaborately decorated cowhide bow case.

A drawing in the "Old White Woman Ledger" contains perhaps the most explicit expression of an individual's wealth. The Cheyenne artist's self-portrait represents a marked departure from the drawings heretofore considered. Unwilling to settle for depicting only those items of clothing and articles which he could wear or carry at any one time, the artist portrays himself literally surrounded by his possessions (figure 2.10). He provides an inventory of his material goods. In addition to his horse, with its silver-decorated bridle, the artist includes buckskin leggings, a breastplate, a beaded blanket strip, an eagle feather fan and

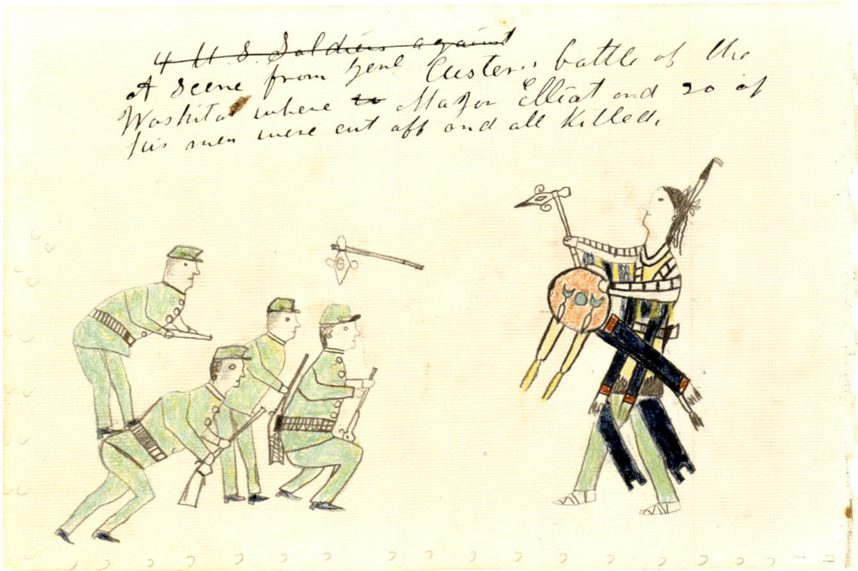

FIGURE 2.11
Unknown artist, Kiowa and/or Mexican, active late nineteenth century, ***Untitled [A Kiowa warrior counts coup on the cavalry]***, late nineteenth century. The warrior carries a shield bearing a design that originated in 1862 in a vision experienced by a man named Akopti (Timber Mountain). Hood Museum of Art (plate 97).

bonnet, a bandolier, and a set of hairplates. He references his society membership, including among his belongings a type of rattle used by members of the Bowstring society.[53] Located in the bottom right of the drawing are the man's armaments: three carbines and a pistol with its associated gun belt and holster. He also includes what appear to be two otter hides and a mountain lion hide. The hides of both animals were prized by the Cheyenne for making bow cases and quivers.[54]

While material possessions served as markers of wealth, it is important to recognize that forms of intangible or intellectual property, including shield designs, were also highly valued by members of the nineteenth-century Cheyenne, Arapaho, and Kiowa communities.[55] Shield designs may be referred to as visionary art, because the designs originated in visions or dreams in which men encountered supernatural powers that offered them aid and assistance.[56] Often associated with the medicine was a set of rules that would henceforth govern the visionary's behavior.[57] The shield design was part of a complex package that included detailed instructions regarding "the system of tabu and other regulations, the rules for painting and decoration of the shield, the owner and his horse, with the accompanying war cries, songs, and other ceremonials."[58]

The instructions frequently authorized the visionary to share the medicine with others, allowing him to produce additional copies of the shield.[59] In addition, warriors nearing the end of their careers might bequeath their medicine and shields to younger men. This resulted in a situation among the Kiowa in which "Most of the shields in use derived from the vision encounters of relatively few individuals, replicated and dispersed through the community."[60] The majority of warriors obtained access to medicine and shield designs through fellow tribal members rather than direct revelatory encounters with the supernatural.

The transfer of intellectual property between individuals was customarily accompanied by a corresponding transfer of wealth. Young men from the wealthiest Kiowa families preferred to purchase their medicine.[61] It seems likely that they sought the power of proven warriors, whose successful careers demonstrated the efficacy of their medicine. Kiowa transactions that accompanied the transfer of medicine were conspicuously devoid of any bargaining or haggling.[62] A Cheyenne man could secure a shield of any design, provided he had the ability to pay for it.[63] For example, a man who made a copy of his shield for another might receive a horse in exchange.[64] Thus, representing a man with a painted shield may have served as a way of reminding the viewer that the individual possessed the means to transact in such intellectual property. The inclusion of painted shields and other material manifestations of intellectual property referenced the link between wealth and social status.

SPIRITUAL POWER AND STATUS

Depictions of men with their shields also served to emphasize these individuals' access to powerful spiritual forces. In combat, a warrior's medicine furnished him both a protective mantle and the power to vanquish his

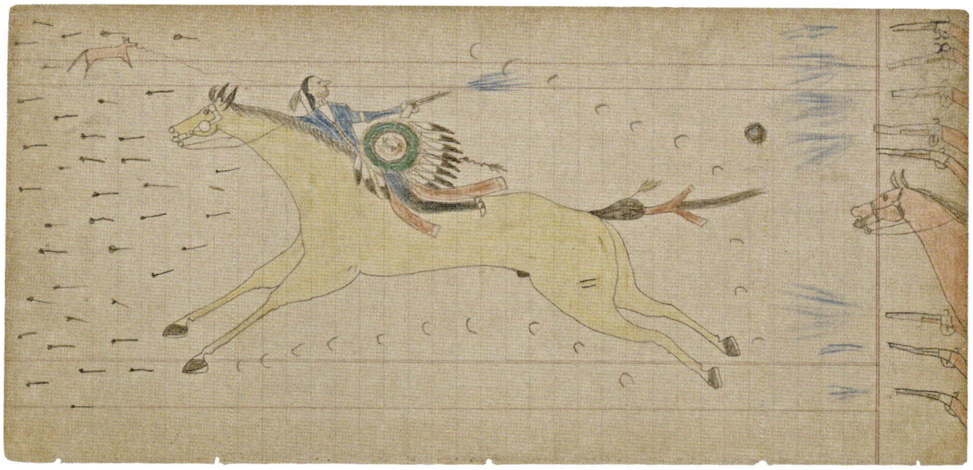

FIGURE 2.12
Unknown artist, Tsistsistas (Cheyenne) and/or Inunaina (Arapaho), active late nineteenth century, ***Untitled [An Inunaina (Arapaho) warrior fires back at U.S. soldiers]***, late nineteenth century. An Arapaho or Cheyenne warrior demonstrates his bravery by charging a cavalry skirmish line. A second set of horse tracks mark the course of his previous charge. Hood Museum of Art (plate 73).

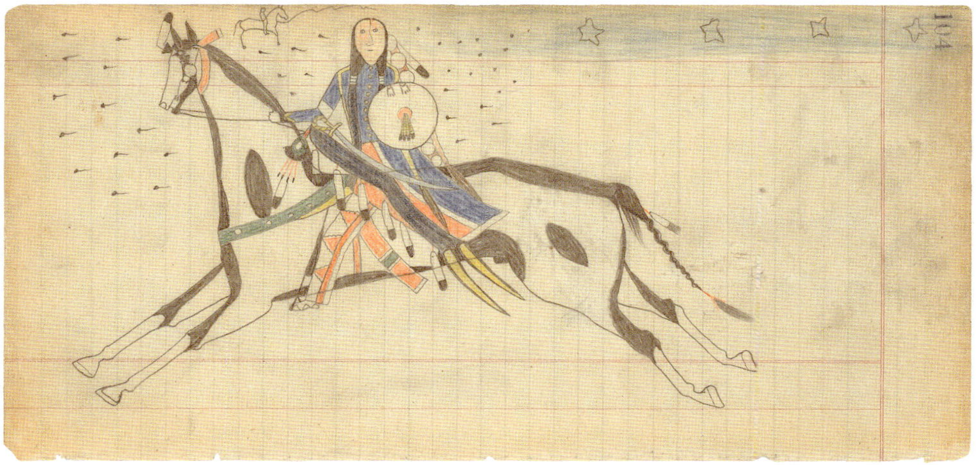

FIGURE 2.13
Unknown artist, Tsistsistas (Cheyenne) and/or Inunaina (Arapaho), active late nineteenth century, ***Untitled [An Inunaina (Arapaho) warrior in the midst of gunfire]***, late nineteenth century. The warrior, relying on his medicine, rides unscathed through the shower of bullets. Hood Museum of Art (plate 71).

enemies.[65] Each warrior's courage and ability were seen as linked to the individual's "relationship to the supernatural."[66] Consequently, drawings of men overpowering their enemy or emerging unscathed from showers of bullets or arrows may be read as "religious testimonies" that index the efficacy of the protagonist's personal medicine, which is often referenced in the drawing through the depiction of his shield.

A Kiowa drawing of a warrior counting coup on four dismounted soldiers (figure 2.11) is a prime example of this genre. The warrior carries a shield bearing a design that originated in the vision of a man named Akopti (Timber Mountain) in 1862. These shields were associated with the Taime, the Kiowa Sun Dance medicine, and were displayed outside the Medicine Lodge during the Sun Dance.[67] The drawing testifies to the power of the shield's medicine. Although each of the soldiers is armed with a carbine, none of them makes an effort to fire at the warrior. They seem awestruck and appear to almost cower before him, as if his shield has rendered them defenseless.

Several drawings in the "Vincent Price Ledger" portray men relying on the protection afforded by their shields' medicine. In one (figure 2.12), a warrior charges a line of soldiers and then veers away, firing a parting shot with his pistol. The soldiers are represented in pictorial shorthand by a line of carbines and the heads of their officers' mounts. The muzzle blasts of the troopers' carbines and the resulting cloud of bullets indicate the grave danger inherent in such a reckless act. Yet this is not the first time this day that the warrior has exposed himself to the enemy's fire; a second series of hoof prints extending across the front of the soldiers' formation marks the path of a previous charge.

Another drawing (figure 2.13) depicts a nighttime raid in which an Arapaho warrior rides through a hail of bullets. The man's name glyph identifies him as the same man depicted in two of the portraits discussed earlier. In this drawing, the warrior is depicted with what appears to be a different shield than the one he is shown with in the Henderson ledger. Perhaps the two designs represent

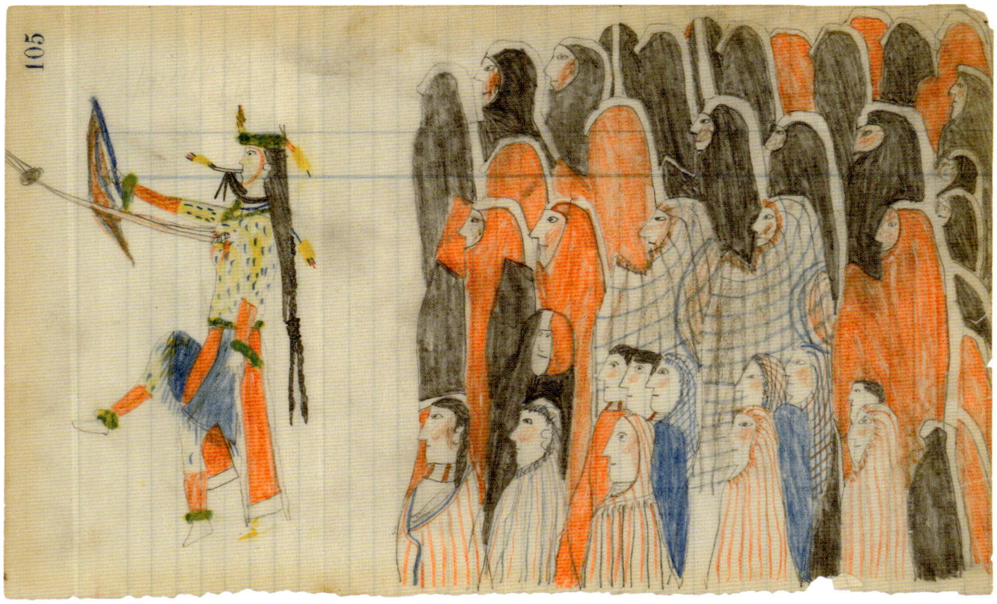

FIGURE 2.14
Unknown artist, Tsistsistas (Cheyenne), active late nineteenth century, ***Untitled [Undertaking the sacred Tsistsistas (Cheyenne) sun dance],*** c. 1880–90. A Cheyenne Sun Dancer fulfills his vow. Hood Museum of Art (plate 108).

the outer and inner covers of the same shield. It is also possible that the warrior acquired a new shield at some point in his career.

In these two drawings, as in all of the drawings of warriors with shields from the "Vincent Price Ledger," the artist has oriented the shield so that its painted surface or cover is visible to the viewer. This is the case even when, as in the last drawing (figure 2.13), the warrior would almost surely have been wearing the shield in a different manner than the one shown. A warrior riding away from the enemy would have slung his shield over his back, exposing its powerful and protective imagery to the source of danger.[68] Given the tendency in Plains pictographic art to depict mounted figures from the waist up in a frontal or three quarter view, rendering a fleeing warrior's shield as it was likely worn would mean that the only the edge of the reverse or back side of the shield would be visible. Artists seem to have eschewed this view, preferring to depict shields in a manner that would render their painted designs and attachments visible. The representation of distinctive aspects of men's clothing and accoutrements, including shields, often functioned as a means of identifying these individuals.[69] However, the protagonists in the "Vincent Price Ledger" are identified through the use of name glyphs, indicating that the detailed depictions of the shields served some other purpose. The evidence strongly suggests that the shields were included as acknowledgements of the potent spiritual powers that interceded on these warriors' behalf, each shield serving as a reminder of its owner's communion with spiritual forces.

While drawings of men emerging unscathed from showers of bullets may be read as "religious testimonies" that index the efficacy of the protagonists' personal medicine, scenes portraying individuals' participation in corporate rituals served a similar purpose, emphasizing their access to spiritual power. The "Old White Woman Ledger" contains an example of such imagery: a striking drawing of a Cheyenne Sun Dancer (figure 2.14). The drawing differs significantly from the detailed illustrations of the Medicine Lodge or Sun Dance ceremony produced by other Cheyenne artists, both at Fort Marion and later. These drawings typically present a panoramic view of the ceremony that encompasses not only the Medicine Lodge, but also the surrounding camp (figure 2.15). In the drawing from the "Old White Woman Ledger," the focus of attention is a single participant rather than the ceremony as a whole.

All eyes are on the man who is undergoing one of the piercing rites. While a man might drag buffalo skulls suspended from skewers inserted in the skin of his back, the subject of this drawing has decided to "swing to the pole."[70] Those who vowed to be pierced in this manner had "the skin pinched up on the right side and the left side of the breast, a knife run through the skin, and then a wooden skewer passed through each incision, which skewers were tied to the end of a rope fastened to the center-pole of the Medicine Lodge."[71] The drawing contains a wealth of detail. Blood can be seen where the wooden skewers pass through the incisions in the man's breast. Buckskin thongs connect the skewers to the end of the rawhide rope. The subject dances tethered to the center pole. As he dances, he pulls backward, attempting to break free by tearing the skin that holds the skewers in place.[72]

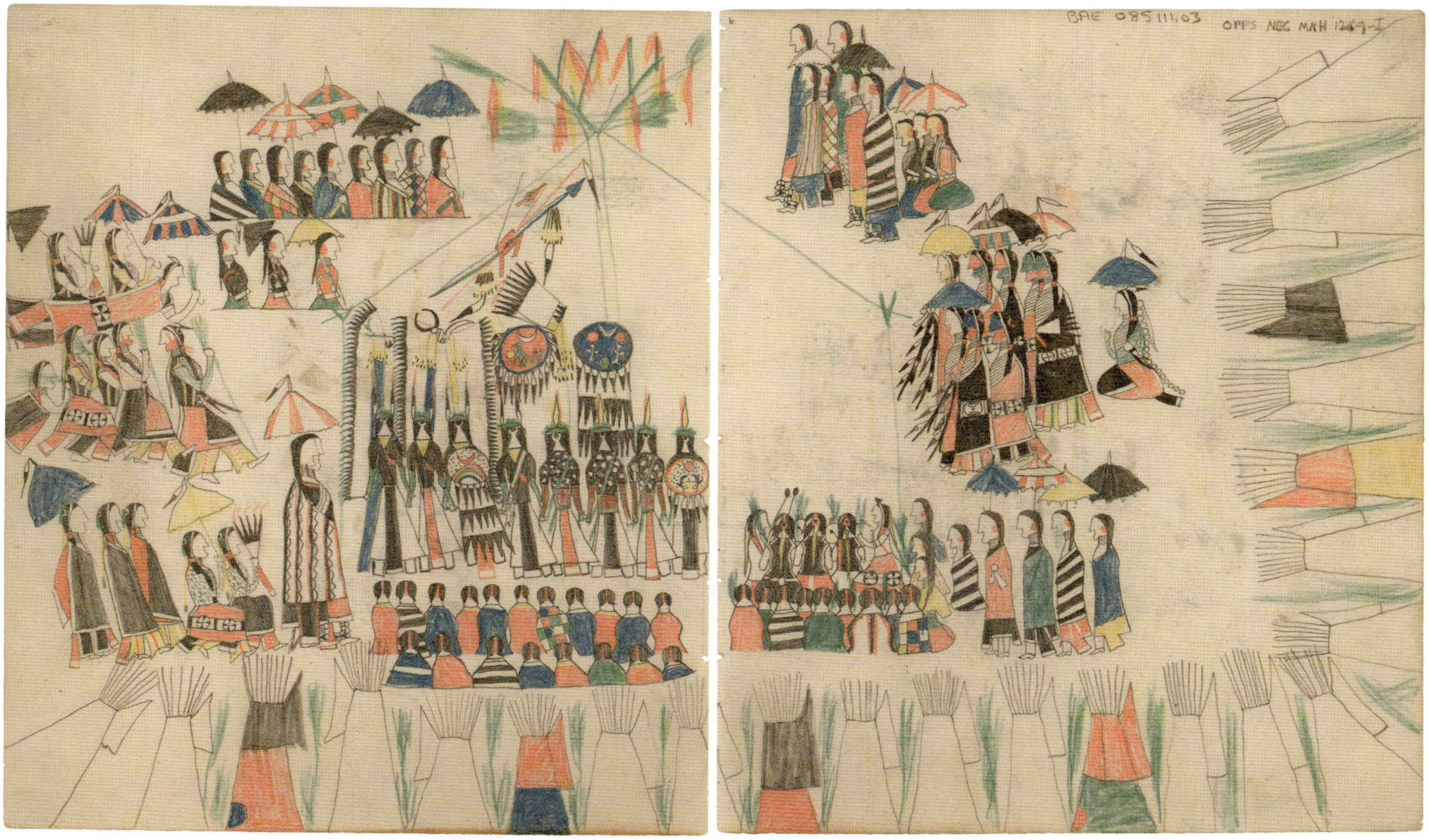

FIGURE 2.15
Unknown Artist, Cheyenne, ***A Cheyenne Sun Dance encampment,*** c. 1875–78. Manuscript 154064C. National Anthropological Archives, Smithsonian Institution, 08511103.

Piercing was not required of those participating in the Medicine Lodge ceremony. It was the result of a personal vow, an act of self sacrifice offered in exchange for supernatural assistance. A man might vow to pierce to secure a loved one's recovery from illness or to obtain medicine to aid him in a particular endeavor. Although the vow might be fulfilled during the Sun Dance, it did not have to be.[73] Indeed, Grinnell's consultants indicated that in the past, it had been much less common for a man to fulfill his vow during the Sun Dance than at some other time. A man who had vowed to be pierced "was altogether likely to make his sacrifice quietly, among the hills at a distance from the camp, seeking no notoriety, but rather striving, so far as possible, to keep the matter quiet."[74] The subject's decision to perform this rite during the Sun Dance was unusual for his time. His suffering and sacrifice occurs not in relative seclusion, but before a crowd of witnesses.

The drawing captures the totality of the subject's sacrifice. Men were pierced in the context of the Sun Dance without fully participating in the ceremony; however, the subject's body paint, kilt, eagle bone whistle, and willow headband, wristlets, and anklets mark him as a Sun Dancer.[75] As a dancer, he makes additional sacrifices, abstaining from food or water during the final days and nights of the ceremony and dancing in the heat and sun.[76]

Just as an image of a warrior with his shield references the man's ability to invoke spiritual forces, this drawing testifies to the subject's encounter with the sacred. Like the crowd assembled outside the Sun Dance lodge, the drawing serves as a witness to the subject's sacrifice. Having fulfilled his vow to "swing to the pole," he is now in a position to instruct others who might make the same vow.[77] Likewise, his experience in the Medicine Lodge set him on a path to one day guide others through the ceremony.[78] This is little different from the way in which a successful warrior might share his medicine and shield design with a younger man.

CONCLUSION

Situating the drawings in the Lansburgh collection in the cultural and historical contexts in which they were created provides insight into the motivations that lay behind their production. Southern Arapaho, Southern Cheyenne, and Kiowa men created and commissioned drawings depicting their martial accomplishments, wealth, and access to spiritual power in order to increase their social standing within their respective communities, a practice that continued well into the reservation period. And drawings imbued with the agency and intentionality of the artists that created them, and depicting the subjects that sanctioned their production, played an active role in constituting social relations in nineteenth century Southern Plains communities.

NOTES

1. Afton, Halaas, and Masich, *Cheyenne Dog Soldiers*; Keyser, "Painted Bison Robes"; McCoy, Kiowa Memories; Moore, "Cheyenne Political History."

2. Gell, *Art and Agency*, 18, 21, 67.

3. Petersen, *Edwards Ledger Drawings*, xi.

4. Petersen, *American Pictographic Images*, viii, xvii.

5. Greene, "From Bison Robes to Ledgers," 24–25.

6. Ibid., 25.

7. Appadurai, "Introduction: Commodities and the Politics of Value," in *The Social Life of Things*, 13, 17, 25–29; Kopytoff, "The Cultural Biography of Things," in Appadurai, ed., *The Social Life of Things*, 64–67, 73.

8. Greene, "Artists in Blue," 53.

9. Ibid., 53.

10. Greene and Drescher, "Tipi with Battle Pictures," 423.

11. Parsons, "Plains Indian Portable Art," 258; Smith, "War Complex," 425, 433–34.

12. Mishkin, *Rank and Warfare*, 37.

13. Ibid., 36; Richardson, *Law and Status among the Kiowa Indians*, 14–15.

14. Mishkin, *Rank and Warfare*, 37.

15. Dorsey, *The Cheyenne Indians*, 15–16, 21.

16. Berthrong, *Southern Cheyennes*, 69.

17. Petersen, *Howling Wolf*, 24.

18. Kroeber, *The Arapaho*, 157.

19. Anderson, *Four Hills of Life*, 146.

20. Ibid., 146.

21. Kroeber, *The Arapaho*, 156.

22. Grinnell, "Coup and Scalp," 296, 298, 302; Mishkin, *Rank and Warfare*, 39.

23. Foster, "Introduction" to Mishkin, *Rank and Warfare*, viii, ix.

24. Berthrong, *Southern Cheyennes*, 69; Mishkin, *Rank and Warfare*, 39.

25. Berthrong, *Southern Cheyennes*, 43, 69; Grinnell, "Coup and Scalp," 303; Mishkin, *Rank and Warfare*, 37.

26. Berthrong, *Southern Cheyennes*, 43.

27. Ibid., 69; Mishkin, *Rank and Warfare*, 39.

28. Petersen, "Cheyenne Soldier Societies," 164, 167–69.

29. Llewellyn and Hoebel, *The Cheyenne Way*, 187.

30. Anderson, *Four Hills of Life*, 148.

31. Dorsey, *Cheyenne Indians*, 82, 84, 110; Greene, "Women, Bison, and Coup," 106; Grinnell, *Cheyenne Indians*, vol. 2: 228–33.

32. Meadows, *Kiowa, Apache, and Comanche Military Societies*, 103; Petersen, "Cheyenne Soldier Societies," 149, 157, 160. It is unclear precisely when the Southern Arapaho men's lodges ceased to meet, although it occurred sometime before 1898. Kroeber, *The Arapaho*, 158.

33. Dorsey, *Cheyenne Indians*, 81.

34. Smith, "War Complex," 427.

35. Berthrong, *Southern Cheyennes*, 43.

36. Grinnell, "Coup and Scalp," 297.

37. This drawing bears a striking similarity to the sole surviving example of pre-reservation Kiowa warrior art; a painted bison robe collected by Dr. Edward Palmer in 1864. The Palmer robe depicts a Kiowa warrior wearing a buffalo horn bonnet and firing a bow, surrounded by non-Indian figures armed with firearms. Greene, "Southern Plains Graphic Art," 4.

38. Greene and Drescher, "Tipi with Battle Pictures," 423; Ewers, *Murals in the Round*, 16; Petersen, *Plains Indian Art from Fort Marion*, 168; "Shield Societies," n.d., Box 9, Folder 18, Alice Marriott Collection, Western History Collection, University of Oklahoma. In 1936, Alice Marriott collected the following account by Saíoma, describing her husband's participation in the renewal of the Tipi with Battle Pictures, "They were attacked by white people, but they escaped and were only wounded. . . . It was such a brave deed that whenever anybody painted a tipi they would come and get him. Up at the top at the back he would paint a circle for the people who surrounded them, and the figures of the two men in the center." Ibid.

39. The regular membership of the society carried straight lances wrapped with otter hide. While the use of the crooked lance was not confined to the officers of the Elk Society, the distinctive manner in which the lance in the drawing is "decorated" confirms its association with the society and its leadership. Petersen, "Cheyenne Soldier Societies," 159, 169. Describing the lances carried by members of the Elk Society, Mike Cowdrey notes that, "At four points along the shaft were affixed as pendants a pair of golden eagle tail feathers, usually tipped with yellow-dyed horse hair; and a pair of narrow strips of otter fur, each tipped with a dewclaw that almost certainly was from the society's tutelary animal." Cowdrey, *Arrow's Elk Society Ledger*, 20. The pendant eagle feathers and otter hide strips are clearly visible in the drawing, identifying the lance as an emblem of the Elk Society and its owner as one of the society's officers.

40. Petersen, "Cheyenne Soldier Societies," 158–59, 169.

41. Kroeber, *The Arapaho*, 157.

42. Anderson, *Four Hills of Life*, 147; Kroeber, *The Arapaho*, 185–86. The sword consisted of a flat piece of wood approximately three feet long, painted with a series of six to eight contrasting colored rectangles. Attached along the bottom side of the sword was a strip of hide, identically painted, from which were suspended white and black feathers. Ibid., 185–86.

43. Mooney, *Ghost Dance and the Sioux Outbreak*, 349.

44. LaBarre, "Typescript of Students' Notes," in Papers of Weston LaBarre.

45. Ibid.

46. Greene, "Bison Robes to Ledgers," 25.

47. Berthrong, *Cheyenne and Arapaho Ordeal*, 3, 13, 17, 19, 129–30; Mooney, *Calendar History of the Kiowa Indians*, 339–40; Nye and Soule, *Plains Indian Raiders*, 174–76.

48. Petersen, *Howling Wolf*, 25.

49. Ibid., 25.

50. Berthrong, *Cheyenne and Arapaho Ordeal*, 81.

51. Cowdrey, *Arrow's Elk Society Ledger*, 34.

52. Coleman, "Riders of the Storm," 54.

53. Petersen, "Cheyenne Soldier Societies," 147.

54. Grinnell, *Cheyenne Indians*, vol. 1: 184.

55. Ewers, Murals in the Round, 7–8, 50; Greene, "The Tepee with Battle Pictures," 423–24; Grinnell, *Cheyenne Indians*, vol. 1: 233–35; "War Societies," January 29, 1936, box 9, folder 24, Alice Marriott Collection, Western History Collection, University of Oklahoma; "Shield Societies," n.d., Alice Marriott Collection.

56. Harris, *Between Two Cultures*, 9–10.

57. Greene, *Silver Horn*, 188; Grinnell, *Cheyenne Indians*, vol. 1: 189, 195; Harris, *Between Two Cultures*, 9–10; Mishkin, *Rank and Warfare*, 49.

58. Mooney, "The Cheyenne Indians," 417.

59. Coleman, "Riders of the Storm," 54; Greene, *Silver Horn*, 189; Grinnell, *Cheyenne Indians*, vol. 1: 192–93, 195; Mishkin, *Rank and Warfare*, 49.

60. Greene, *Silver Horn*, 189.

61. Mishkin, *Rank and Warfare*, 49.

62. "Assimilation," n.d., box 8, folder 15, Alice Marriott Collection, Western History Collection, University of Oklahoma.

63. Cowdrey, *Arrow's Elk Society Ledger*, 64.

64. Grinnell, *Cheyenne Indians*, vol. 1: 193; Nagy, "Typology of Cheyenne Shield Designs," 33.

65. Cowdrey, *Arrow's Elk Society Ledger*, 43, 64; Greene, *Silver Horn*, 189; Grinnell, *Cheyenne Indians*, vol. 1: 187–88.

66. Smith, "War Complex," 429.

67. Mooney, "Unpublished Manuscript 2531,"; Greene, *Silver Horn*, plate 36, plate 38, 188; Merrill, et al., *Guide to the Kiowa Collections at the Smithsonian*, 33, 34; McCoy, "Miniature Shields," 69.

68. Cowdrey, *Arrow's Elk Society Ledger*, 43.

69. McCoy, "Searching for Clues in Kiowa Ledger Drawings," 58–59; Szabo, "Shields and Lodges, Warriors and Chiefs," 3.

70. Grinnell, "Cheyenne Medicine Lodge," 249.

71. Grinnell, *Cheyenne Indians*, vol. 2: 211.

72. Dorsey, *Cheyenne Indians*, 175–76; Grinnell, "Young Dog's Dance," 307; Grinnell, "Cheyenne Medicine Lodge," 253; Grinnell, *Cheyenne Indians*, vol. 2: 211.

73. Dorsey, *Cheyenne Indians*, 175–77; Grinnell, "Cheyenne Medicine Lodge," 246–47, 250.

74. Grinnell, "Cheyenne Medicine Lodge," 249–50.

75. Dorsey, *Cheyenne Indians*, vol. 2: 149, 152, 175; Grinnell, *Cheyenne Indians*, 252, 265.

76. Dorsey, *Cheyenne Indians*, 60; Grinnell, *Cheyenne Indians*, vol. 2: 251.

77. Grinnell, "Cheyenne Medicine Lodge," 249.

78. Moore, *The Cheyenne*, 221.

CHAPTER 3

Illustrating Encounter

TRADE, TRAVEL, AND WARFARE IN SOUTHERN PLAINS LEDGER DRAWING, 1875–1880

JENNY TONE-PAH-HOTE

IN 1880, JULIAN SCOTT, AN ARTIST, purchased a book of drawings at Fort Sill in what would become Oklahoma.[1] Multiple Kiowa men had contributed to this book; one of them, now known simply as Julian Scott Ledger Artist A, drew "Osage War Dance," now part of the Lansburgh collection (figure 3.1). The drawings in the Julian Scott book depict scenes of celebration and of social life among neighboring peoples, interspersed with scenes of warfare—a prominent theme of nineteenth-century Plains drawing. Although "Osage War Dance" does not feature intercultural encounter as a subject, the drawing itself was a product of multiple encounters. Julian Scott Ledger Artist A, identified as a Kiowa, drew and described the Osage men through their dress and dance.[2]

In this drawing the artist highlights the military and political force of a people whom the Kiowas had known both as neutral neighbors and as enemies, and he emphasizes this theme by paying special attention to dress and the objects that the figures in the image carry. By 1880, Kiowas had been at peace with the Osages for forty years, but as anthropologist James Mooney noted, "relations with the Osage were somewhat strained in consequence of their serving as scouts against the allied southern plains tribes."[3] The man on the far left and others carry pipe tomahawks as they dance. Native men valued these items for their utility and "as a symbol of Indian prestige and power in diplomacy and warfare"; this was particularly true for chiefs and headmen who traveled to Washington, D.C., for political purposes.[4] The historic relationship between Kiowa and Osage people may have colored and influenced the artist's decision to create a work that focused on military power.

"Osage War Dance" and other pictorial images in the Lansburgh collection illuminate the central role of intertribal and intercultural connections for Native peoples. This drawing and others show that external ties shaped how artists presented moments of intercultural encounter. In this chapter, I discuss various levels of encounter to demonstrate its relevance in pictorial arts from the southern plains. For example, Chief Killer, a Cheyenne Fort Marion artist, focused on trade and visiting with other peoples in two of his drawings. Another Fort Marion artist, either Etahdleuh or Koba, demonstrated the significance of engagement more subtly through the dress of his subjects in a courting image. The work of an unknown Kiowa artist captures the opportunity and peril of military expeditions and alludes to the significance of warfare for Kiowa men socially and economically.

In part, this essay examines and discusses drawings by Fort Marion prisoners who were sent to Saint Augustine, Florida in the aftermath of the Red River War. Individual warrior-artists in this intertribal group made drawings for sale. Scholars now view Fort Marion drawings as composed for multiple audiences, including other Native peoples and Euro-Americans who bought drawings as tourist items.[5] The prisoners drew images of plains social life and of their activities in Saint Augustine.[6] Fort Marion artists primarily depicted hunting, courting, and other scenes of their homes in the southern plains.[7] Richard Henry Pratt also encouraged them to depict their lives at the fort and in Saint Augustine. Etahdleuh Doanmoe, Zotom, and others illustrated their journey from Fort Sill and their daily experiences of military regimentation, western education, and various kinds of labor.[8]

The context for works by the Unknown Kiowa and the Julian Scott ledger artists was distinct from that of Fort Marion. The audience for drawings from the Kiowa, Comanche, and Apache (KCA) reservation during the 1870s and 1880s was different in two important ways. Individuals who bought Native items lived in close proximity to or on the KCA reservation. They served

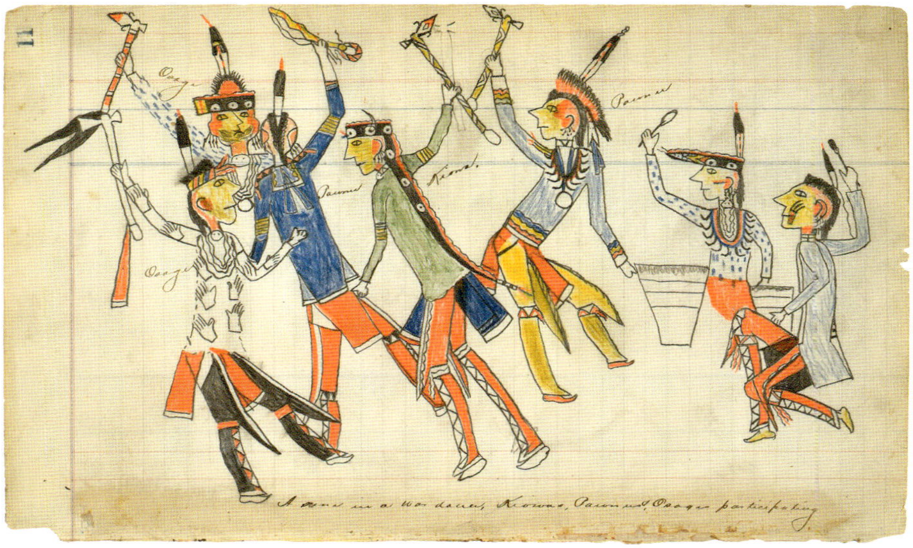

FIGURE 3.1
Unknown artist, Kiowa, active late nineteenth century, ***Untitled [Osage war dance]***, 1880, Hood Museum of Art (plate 100).

in the army at Fort Sill, or worked on the reservation in some capacity.[9] The military component of this audience may have taken an interest in men's pictorial art because of their own connections with plains warfare during the nineteenth century.[10]

PLAINS DRAWINGS: ILLUSTRATING ENCOUNTER

Images featuring trade and encounter developed from scenes of warfare in representational drawing on hide and paper. Hide painting and works on paper illustrated warfare between Native and non-Native actors. Cheyenne men produced a number of drawings before the reservation era, along with their Lakota and Arapaho contemporaries.[13] During the 1860s, ledgers and books became more accessible and encouraged the production of drawings on paper.[12] Men explored the defining subject of military encounter and rendered subjects connected to their social roles.[11] Pictorial artists also began to depict events other than warfare, including images centering on religion, hunting, and courting, which were also connected to men's roles and achievements.[14] To fully elaborate on an episode in battle, Plains men often drew identifying details of their opponents' hair and dress. Similar visual elements were also a feature of Kiowa calendars. Calendar keepers drew pictographs of widely known events of each year.[15] These drawings often included encounters with Native and non-Native others. Each of these pictorial forms helped elaborate intertribal interactions, and this intercultural theme also emerges from some of the reservation era drawings and Fort Marion works.

Kiowa calendars also illustrated the theme of intertribal encounters, which ranged from warfare to intertribal visiting during the Medicine Lodge. Calendars presented two events per year. The summer image represented the Sun Dance and another image illustrated a second well-known event of that year. For example, in 1844, the Dakotas had traveled south for the Medicine Lodge in the summer, and their visit was symbolized on the calendar by a figure of a man near the lodge wearing a necklace. Mooney explained that Kiowas referred to Dakotas as "Necklace people" because they were the first to don these items.[16] The summer of 1851 was marked by a dance for Kiowa men who killed Pawnee warriors and took their horses from an encampment, and the pictograph from that year featured a Pawnee man complete with a shaved head standing near a representation of where the Medicine Lodge took place.[17]

UNKNOWN KIOWA ARTIST: EPISODES OF MILITARY ENCOUNTER

Works by the Unknown Kiowa are distinctive in the Lansburgh collection because they focus on battle scenes with Mexican forces (see "An Unidentified Sketchbook," plates 92–99). They foreground the dangers and opportunities that expeditions created. Drawings by the Unknown Kiowa also express Kiowa social imperatives in warfare with Mexicans. Throughout the 1850s and 1860s Kiowas and other tribes raided Mexico to acquire war honors and horses, which played a central economic role in Kiowa

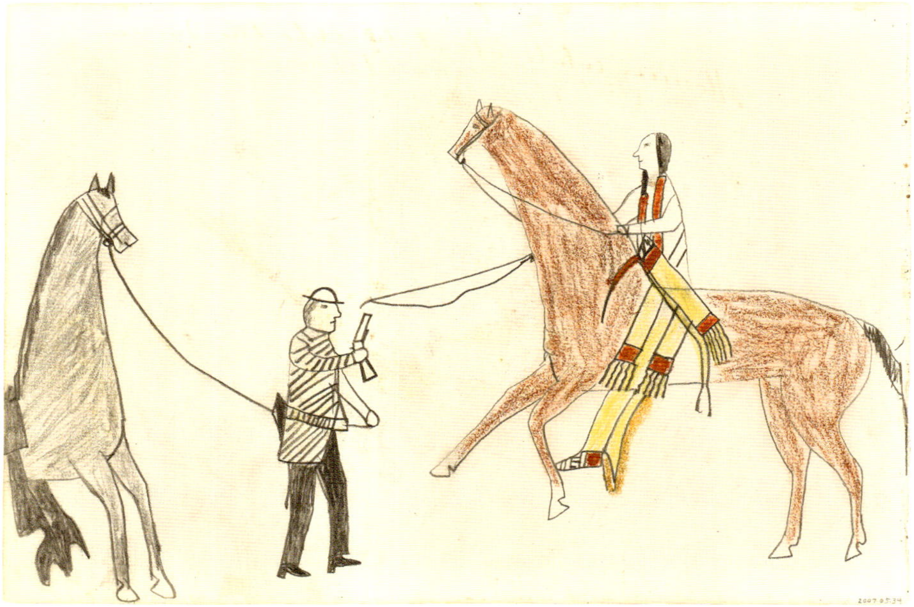

FIGURE 3.2
Unknown artist, Kiowa and/or Mexican, active late nineteenth century, ***Untitled [A Kiowa warrior counts coup on a non-Native man]***, late nineteenth century, Hood Museum of Art (plate 92).

society. The images from the Unidentified Sketchbook provide a glimpse of a broader social and economic connection between Natives and Mexicans that formed a basis for trade and exchange in the southern plains.

Kiowa men engaged in warfare in Mexico to build and secure their reputations. Gaining military honors and accumulating horses for redistribution were central to men's social roles and their status.[18] In the words of one scholar, in the 1830s and 1840s both Comanches and Kiowas "were fighting to win honor, avenge fallen comrades, and grow rich."[19] Often young men served as primary actors in warfare to prove themselves and to demonstrate their talents and capacities as warriors and leaders.[20] Older men traveled as well, and there were many expeditions that journeyed far into the interior. By studying Mexican archival materials, historian Brian DeLay found that Kiowas and Comanches participated in "at least forty-four major raiding campaigns south into Mexican territory, each one involving one hundred men or more." He explained, on "at least four occasions Mexican officials reported expeditions of eight hundred to a thousand men," and he estimated, "these largest endeavors involved upward of half of the region's total fighting force."[21] DeLay points to a critical mass of raids during the 1830s and 1840s, but the Kiowas continued to send expeditions later as well.

The Unknown Kiowa Artist generated a number of images of Kiowas counting coup that reflected broader patterns of warfare. For example, in "A Kiowa warrior counts coup on a non-Native man" he illustrates this time-honored theme of warrior art (figure 3.2). The Kiowa warrior rides directly toward the armed Mexican scout, who stands near his horse outfitted with a saddle and tapaderos. The Kiowa man counts coup from the moving horse. The other man appears to have removed his gun from the holster, preparing to fire at the oncoming warrior. Here the artist also demonstrates the danger inherent in close combat.

In addition to battle honors warfare also served an economic purpose, giving Kiowa men and others in the southern plains more access to horses. The winter entry for a Kiowa calendar notes that in the winter of 1858, Kiowa men went to Chihuahua to seek horses and returned with more animals.[22] George Bent, a Cheyenne, recalled that Kiowas and Comanches rode into Mexico, as well as Texas and New Mexico, to acquire horses every year. Bent remembered seeing the horses "grazing along the river for fifty miles."[23] By obtaining more horses, Kiowa men could access other trade goods more easily.[24] In the 1840s, Cheyenne men also traveled into Mexico to obtain horses and goods through warfare.[25] When Howling Wolf, another Fort Marion artist, arrived home to Indian Territory, he described his poverty there, noting that he wanted to go to Mexico and saying, "I could capture a herd and bring them back here then I would not be poor."[26] He associated horses with material resources and showed that the Cheyenne people also viewed Mexico as a prime place to acquire horses.

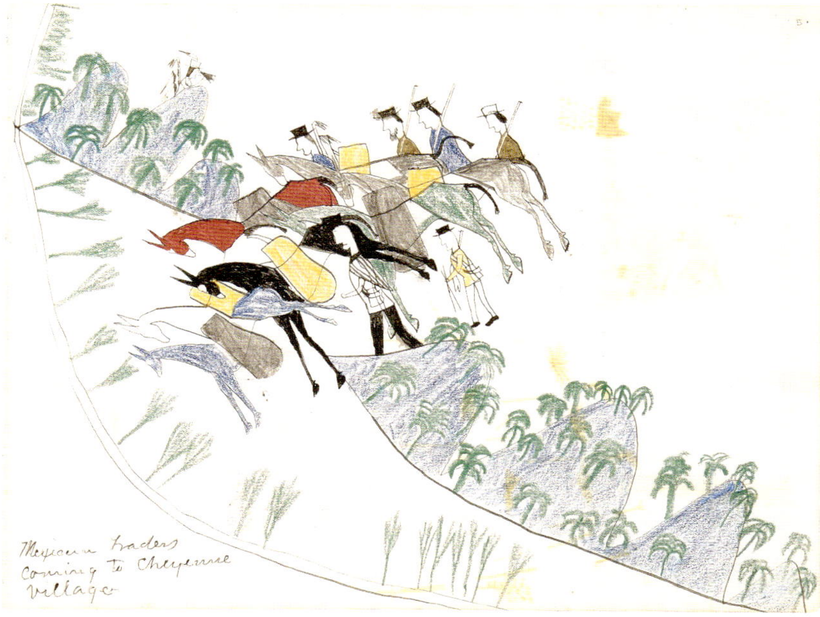

FIGURE 3.3
Chief Killer (Noh-hu-nah-wih), Southern Tsistsistas (Cheyenne), 1849–1922, ***Untitled ["Mexican traders Coming To Cheyenne village"]***, mid-1875–mid-1878, Hood Museum of Art (plate 54).

CHIEF KILLER: VISITING AND TRADE

Chief Killer, a Cheyenne prisoner at Fort Marion, demonstrated the importance of trade and visiting in pictorial arts by rendering detailed images of particular subjects as well as their dress and adornment.[27] Chief Killer's works explore the varied and significant roles of hunting, trade, and intertribal visiting among the Cheyennes in the late nineteenth century, and they also emphasize how intertribal relationships played a role in his depictions of these themes. Chief Killer's drawing of a Cheyenne visit to the Lakotas demonstrates the ongoing ties between the Cheyenne and Sioux peoples that continued throughout the nineteenth century. Another work highlighted ongoing trade in the 1860s and 1870s between Comancheros, or Mexican traders, and Native peoples.

At the turn of the nineteenth century, the Cheyennes often served as middlemen for trade between Northern and Southern Plains tribes. They gained horses through expeditions among the Comanches and Kiowas and by trading in the Western Comanche trade center, and the Cheyennes then exchanged these animals in trade to the villages of the Mandan, Hidatsa, and Arikara people.[28] As waves of diseases like small pox diminished these villages, the Cheyennes began to move south to gain greater access to horses and bison.[29] Throughout the 1830s, the Cheyennes took horses from the Kiowas and Comanches. Cheyenne bands also moved further south to gain access to Euro-American goods and markets.[30]

Changes in intertribal relationships molded the region and its representation at the hands of Southern Plains men. Warfare among the Kiowas, Comanches, Southern Cheyennes, Southern Arapahos, and Kiowa Apaches ended in 1840. Peace resulted in a lasting alliance that shifted the power dynamics of Southern Plains tribes and altered each party's access to military power, horses, and other resources. After 1840, men from these tribes fought in joint military expeditions and traded in the center that the Western Comanches formed and controlled within the region. Here, horses were the main commodities and circulated with some foodstuffs, guns, and other items of European manufacture.[31] Trade slipped from American Indian to Euro-American control as William Bent, an American trader built Bent's Fort on a location that had long been used for trade by many Native peoples who made their home within the region.[32]

Other traders also worked throughout the southern plains, and Comancheros were itinerant traders in the eighteenth and nineteenth centuries until the Red River Wars of the 1870s. Though not officially licensed to trade with the Indians, the Comancheros traded among Plains villages, circulating a range of goods from captives to horses, as well as guns, cooking vessels, manufactured tools, and other objects.[33] For instance, they exchanged horses from Kiowa and Comanche camps to various locations in New Mexico. The Comancheros were so deeply enmeshed in the regional economy that they operated in Cheyenne villages as far north as Fort Laramie.[34]

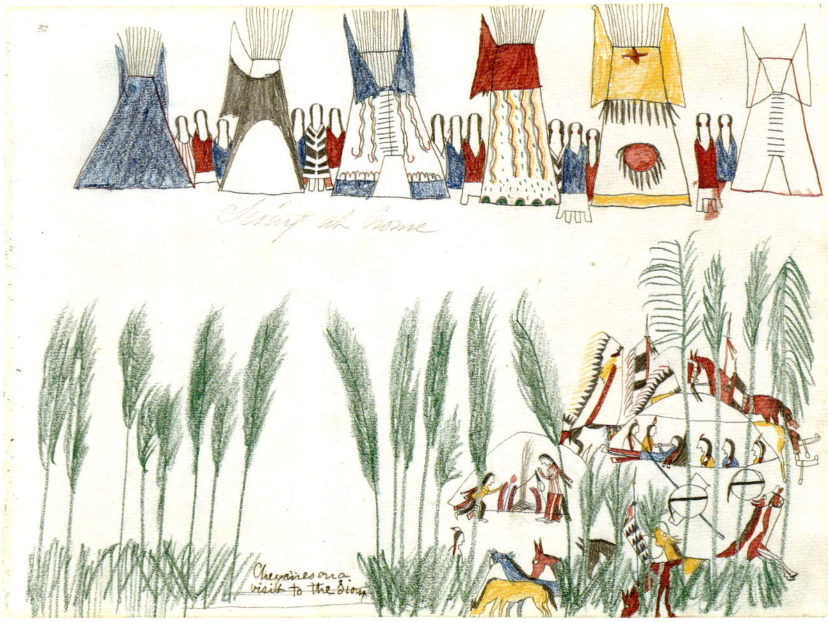

FIGURE 3.4
Chief Killer (Noh-hu-nah-wih), Southern Tsistsistas (Cheyenne), 1849–1922, ***Untitled ["Cheyennes on a visit to the Sioux"],*** mid-1875–mid-1878, Hood Museum of Art (plate 60).

Cheyenne people enjoyed trading with the Comancheros and the goods that they brought. George Bird Grinnell, who wrote about Cheyenne social life, noted that when the Comancheros arrived in the village "almost the whole tribe had gone out to where the Mexicans were to get a taste of the food they brought to trade."[35] Kiowas also recorded their presence, marking the winter of 1872 as the "Winter that the Pueblos came," and noting the arrival of not just the Pueblos, but also the Mexicans who exchanged, "*biscocho*, or Pueblo bread, and eagle feathers for horses and buffalo robes." Like the Mexicans in Chief Killer's drawing (figure 3.3), the Pueblo man represented in the calendar also traveled with a pack mule.[36]

The Cheyennes participated in a network of exchange which incorporated a diverse group of people, and Chief Killer's drawing illustrates one portion of this network. In the drawing "Mexican Traders coming to Cheyenne village," each of the traders wears a hat. Indian artists in the early nineteenth century often depicted Euro-Americans with hats because of their association with trade.[37] Plains people also used a sign for hats when referring to or describing Euro-Americans in sign language.[38] Chief Killer may have represented these men with hats because of their role as traders in the southern plains. The traders traveled armed with guns as well as bows and arrows; that one of these Comancheros also carried a bow and arrow indicates the mutual exchange between peoples. Presumably, the fringed quiver was also an item acquired from Native peoples or it was fashioned in the style of a plains quiver; in either case it illustrates a sense of reciprocity and the influence of Native peoples on the material life of these men.[39]

Encounter is the central theme of the drawing, and the man on the ridge watches them with binoculars from a concealed location some distance from where the traders travel. Chief Killer uses hills that span the page to indicate the distance between the individual who watches from afar and the Mexican traders. He presents these traders as a comparatively large, well-defended trading party who travel in the direction of a river that he has drawn across the page. The Comancheros urge the donkeys with their large packs forward; perhaps in anticipation of trade in the village they are approaching.

Chief Killer's drawing provides a snapshot of not just the traders, but of changing social and economic relations. It portrays the continuation of Comanchero trade in spite of rising militarization of the plains as a region. As William Bent and his partners became successful traders, they also minimized the Comanchero trade.[40] In 1859 the War Department purchased the new version of Bent's Fort, and it eventually became Fort Wise.[41] The transition from trading center to a military fort signaled the heightened military presence of Euro-Americans in the region but, as the drawing illustrates, the Comanchero trade continued until U.S. army officials officially ended this system of trade in 1872.[42]

Chief Killer also highlighted other regional connections by illustrating intertribal visiting. We might interpret "Cheyennes on a Visit to the Sioux" as depicting an event

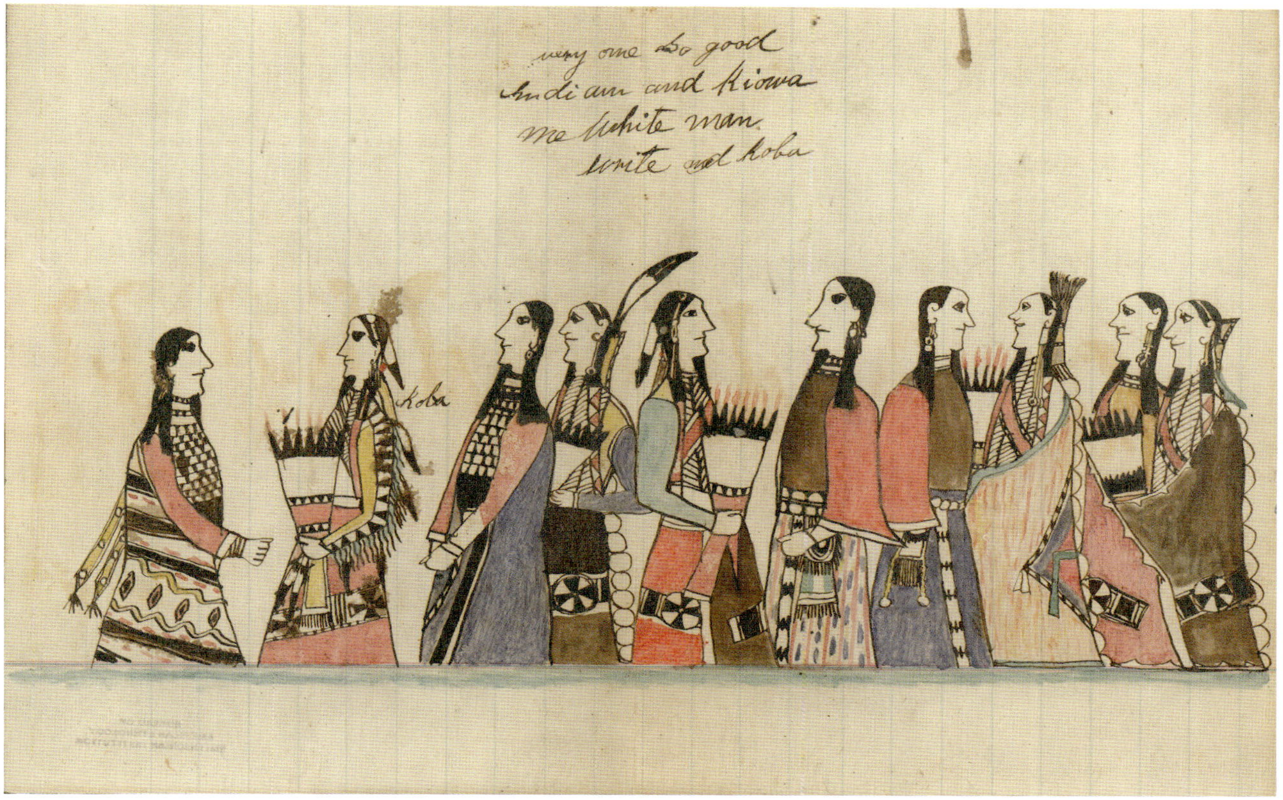

FIGURE 3.5
Koba or Etahdleuh, *"Kiowa drawing, possibly by Koba or Etahdleuh, of courting scene with five couples,"* 1875–78, National Anthropological Archives, NAA Inv 08547624.

that had occurred on a regular basis (figure 3.4). By the early nineteenth century, the Cheyennes facilitated Lakota expansion into the plains by engaging in warfare against the Pawnees and by pressing the Kiowas further into the southern plains.[43] Military endeavors and kinship ties allowed for convergence as well, and by the 1860s, the Cheyennes had split into northern and southern divisions, with the Northern Cheyennes maintaining Lakota allies. A third group emerged as a Cheyenne band composed of intermarried Cheyenne and Lakota families.[44] Long-standing relationships cemented through kinship ties, political, and military alliances would have required visiting among Cheyenne and Lakota peoples. For instance, Southern Cheyenne individuals paid a visit to their northern relatives during 1865. They camped part of the spring near the Lakotas and both of their warrior societies hosted events.[45]

Chief Killer's work of art alludes to the connections between warfare and courting in this drawing of a leisurely visit among long-term allies with linked histories.[46] In the drawing, Cheyenne men are partially concealed away from the village. They smoke, cook, and tend their horses, and the men travel with their shields, society lances, and war bonnets, items frequently depicted in drawings of military encounter. However, in this drawing the accoutrements may indicate that they wanted to make an entrance into the village. In contrast, the line of outlined figures stands alongside the group of painted tipis in a very orderly fashion. They appear to await the arrival of the Cheyenne men. A few of these figures appear to be women, which may also indicate that this is a courting image. The caption below reads "Sioux at Home." Chief Killer has presented a drawing that combines courting with visiting. Broad conventions of ledger drawing and men's roles shaped how Chief Killer depicted this moment of intertribal encounter.

COURTING SCENE: ILLUSTRATING TRADE THOUGH DRESS

Koba or Etahdlueh Doanmoe emphasizes the significance of trade goods in the dress and adornment of Kiowa men and women in a drawing that includes courting couples (figure 3.5). Each of the individuals wears goods that were the product of diverse groups of people interconnected though webs of trade. The artist illustrates the way that Kiowas and others incorporated items like textiles as adornment and displayed them to communicate their social standing. Both men and women's clothing emphasized and documented the variety of trade objects that flowed though the southern plains.

The artist reflects how important self-presentation was in courting scenarios like the one featuring the five couples. The couple on the left illustrates finery that was composed of goods acquired through intertribal and Euro-American trade, and these goods expressed their social standing. The woman at the far left and the man labeled as Koba stand out in this drawing because of their interaction with each other. The artist has constructed them as the center figures in the image, not just because they speak together. He emphasizes their importance and equivalence though their adornment and comportment. The figure on the far left wears a black dress with red sleeves decorated with shells or elk teeth. This dress features the "saved list," or the white trim of the fabric, that many Native women favored in broad cloth.[47] Though it is unclear from the image whether the dresses are adorned with shell or elk teeth, the dresses also communicate social standing. Elk teeth were highly valued because they were difficult to obtain. Women tapped into broad webs of exchange for elk teeth, various kinds of shells, and other items of adornment.[48] The figure labeled as Koba wears equally fine regalia for the occasion. He is dressed in a fringed yellow buckskin shirt with beadwork along the arm. He wears a beaded red wearing blanket over his shirt.

The other well-dressed men and women in the picture are also involved in courting, or the observation of it. The second couple from the left may be chaperones of sorts. The woman who is third from the left, perhaps a relative, wears very similar clothing to the woman on the far left and observes with her hands clasped in front of her. Her counterpart also appears to watch the couple on the left. The man and woman on the right may be observing the courting couples as well.

The textiles that appear in this drawing and others illustrate the desirability of these goods and their use in clothing. Kiowa and Comanche individuals actively sought out textiles. In Cuesta, New Mexico, in 1831, Comanche and Kiowa warriors gave several horses for ammunition and blankets.[49] As trading relationships with Mexico deteriorated into raiding, which continued into the 1870s, Comanche and Kiowa warriors continued to obtain woven textiles.[50] Mexican and Navajo women made textiles that circulated throughout the Southwest and beyond. Kiowa people wore Saltillo serapes so frequently that one anthropologist has suggested these blankets influenced their beadwork patterns.[51] Ledger artists, like Koba, Etahdleuh, and others captured the decorative use of textiles in their drawings.[52]

Each of the men in the image also wears German silver metalwork, which was associated with exchange and was regarded as "a highly valued prestige item."[53] Kiowa calendars recorded the use of metalworking techniques and silver trade items during the nineteenth century, and they illustrate that German silver was valued as an item of adornment. The Kiowas referred to the winter of 1832–33 as the "Winter that they captured the money," when Kiowa warriors took a sum of silver coins from an American group. They flattened and shaped them into disks that they wore in their scalp locks.[54] The figure labeled Koba wears such an ornament in his own scalp lock. Anthropologist James Mooney recorded that the Sun Dance of 1866 was known as the "Flat metal (i.e., German silver) Sun Dance," because Charles A. Whittacre, a trader, came and traded "a large quantity of German silver," which Kiowas received "in sheets which they cut and hammer into the desired shapes." The image for that year was the Sun Dance lodge with an accompanying set of hairplates.[55] Three of the men in the image also wear sets of hairplates.

The men and women wearing German silver also reflect its prominence in Southern Plains dress styles. Travelers and missionaries described the prominence of metalwork in both men's and women's dress during the nineteenth century. When Catlin traveled the plains during the 1830s he painted a portrait of Tohausen, the principal chief of the Kiowa, and wrote "his long hair, which was up in several large clubs, and ornamented with a great many silver broaches, extended quite down to his knees."[56] Randolph Marcy, an army officer who mapped and explored the Red River, remarked upon Comanche men in his journal, noted their long hair, and recalled that they "ornament it upon state occasions with silver and beads."[57] When Thomas Battey, a Quaker missionary arrived on the KCA reservation during the 1870s, he also described the metalwork that men and women wore. He explained, "they wear a profusion of rings on their fingers and in their ears, from the latter of which hang small brass chains, terminated by small pieces of tin, or German silver, cut in fanciful forms."[58] Men and women in this picture wear a number of earrings in their ears in various styles.

As a whole, the image conveys the integration and desirability of goods acquired in intertribal and Euro-American trade. The courting scene, which does not deal with encounter per se, demonstrates that the products of encounter were central to individual Kiowa people who deployed these goods in various ways. They illuminated the wealth and prestige of the wearer who had access to various markets that were the source of beads, sheet metal, shells, and other items.

The artist of the courting scene and others represented in the Lansburgh collection demonstrate the significance of intercultural encounter not just in pictorial drawings, but also in the social lives of men and women who lived on and traveled the plains and beyond. The drawings featured in this essay elaborate on subjects ranging from warfare to the influence of cultural encounters and intertribal relationships on adornment. The conventions of pictorial arts and historical circumstance shaped these drawings, which were also the product of encounter on various levels. The Unknown Kiowa Artist illustrated scenes of individual acts of valor in battles, with descriptive images of Mexican opponents, whom Southern Plains Indians had long fought. Julian Scott Ledger Artist A and Chief Killer showed that historical relationships, and the topical conventions of drawing, influenced how men depicted commerce and intertribal relations. Finally, the artist of the courting scene demonstrates how trade goods, and relationships that provided access to indigenous and Euro-American markets shaped expressions of one's person and place in Kiowa society.

NOTES

1. McCoy, *Kiowa Memories,* 1–2. McCoy argues that "three warrior-artists contributed to the Julian Scott Ledger" (p. 5). However, Janet Catherine Berlo asserts that "at least three artists' hands are evident in this book." She distinguishes two of them as Julian Scott Ledger Artist A and Julian Scott Ledger Artist B. Berlo, *Plains Indian Drawings,* 150, 154.

2. McCoy, *Kiowa Memories,* 1–2; Meadows, *Kiowa Military Societies,* 261. Meadows explained that the Osage did not acquire the I'nlonschka, sometimes referred to as the war dance, until 1884.

3. Mooney, *Calendar History,* 170. For a discussion of warfare with the Osage and the Cut Throat Gap Massacre see Mooney, 257–60.

4. Shannon, "Queequeg's Tomahawk," 620.

5. Szabo, *Art from Fort Marion,* 44.

6. Ibid., 41–42

7. Ibid., 41.

8. Earenfight, ed., *A Kiowa's Odyssey*; Szabo, *Art from Fort Marion.*

9. Greene, "Changing Times, Changing Views," 19.

10. Bol, "Defining Lakota Tourist Art," 224.

11. Greene, "From Bison Robes to Ledgers," 26.

12. Ibid., 22.

13. Szabo, *Howling Wolf,* 45.

14. Greene, "Changing Times, Changing Views," 19; Greene, "Structure and Meaning," 32.

15. Greene, *One Hundred Summers,* 2

16. Mooney, *Calendar History,* 281.

17. Ibid., 291.

18. Mishkin, *Rank and Warfare,* 21–22.

19. DeLay, *War of a Thousand Deserts,* 138.

20. Rand, "Primary Sources," 145.

21. DeLay. *War of A Thousand Deserts,* 117.

22. Mooney, *Calendar History,* 306.

23. Hyde, *Life of George Bent,* 37.

24. Mishkin, *Rank and Warfare,* 22.

25. Jablow, *Cheyenne in Plains Indian Trade Relations,* 76–77.

26. Howling Wolf to Richard Henry Pratt, June 5, 1877, Richard Henry Pratt Papers. Yale Collection of Western Americana, Beinecke Rare Book and Manuscript Library.

27. Szabo. "Chief Killer and a New Reality," 52. Szabo argues here that Chief Killer's illustration of details about the dress and actors were a significant focus in drawings from the Anne S. K. Brown Military collection. I think this is also the case with his drawings in the Lansburgh collection.

28. Jablow, *Cheyenne in Plains Indian Trade,* 79; Hämäläinen, "Western Comanche Trade Center," 506.

29. West, *Contested Plains,* 79.

30. Moore, "Cheyenne Political History," 345; West, *Contested Plains,* 83.

31. Hämäläinen, "Western Comanche Trade Center," 508.

32. Ibid., 512–13.

33. Hagan, *United States–Comanche Relations,* 13. Charles Kenner has emphasized that Comanchero traders exchanged mostly subsistence goods and foodstuffs and not ready-made goods. Kenner, *Comanchero Frontier,* 85

34. Mooney, *Calendar History,* 165; Berthrong, *Southern Cheyennes,* 92.

35. Grinnell, *Cheyenne Indians,* vol. 1:24.

36. Mooney, *Calendar History,* 336.

37. Ewers, "Images of White Man," 413, 416.

38. Clark, *Indian Sign Language,* 402–403.

39. Kenner, *Comanchero Frontier,* 213.

40. Hämäläinen, "Western Comanche Trade Center," 513.

41. Hyde, *Life of George Bent*, 108.

42. Brooks, *Captives and Cousins*, 343–44.

43. Moore, *The Cheyenne*, 91.

44. Ibid., 97.

45. Hyde, *Life of George Bent*, 200–201.

46. Greene, "From Bison Robes to Ledgers," 26.

47. Emil Her Many Horses, "Portraits of Native Women and Their Dresses," in *Identity By Design*, 27.

48. Ibid., 24; Ewers, "Climate, Acculturation, and Costume," in *Plains Indian History and Culture*, 146; Hail, *Hau Kóla!*, 92 and 94.

49. DeLay, *War of A Thousand Deserts*, 58.

50. Ibid., 92.

51. Hail, *Gifts of Pride and Love*, 29.

52. Janet Catherine Berlo, "Creativity and Cosmopolitanism: Women's Enduring Traditions," in Her Many Horses, ed., *Identity By Design*, 120.

53. Swan, *Peyote Religious Art*, 63.

54. Mooney, *Calendar History*, 254; Douglas and Marriot, "Metal Jewelry of the Peyote Cult," 77

55. Mooney, *Calendar History*, 318–19; Greene, *One Hundred Summers*, 93.

56. Catlin, *Letters and Notes*, vol. 2:74.

57. Marcy and McClellan, *Adventure on the Red River*, 161.

58. Battey, *Life and Adventures of a Quaker Among the Indians*, 325.

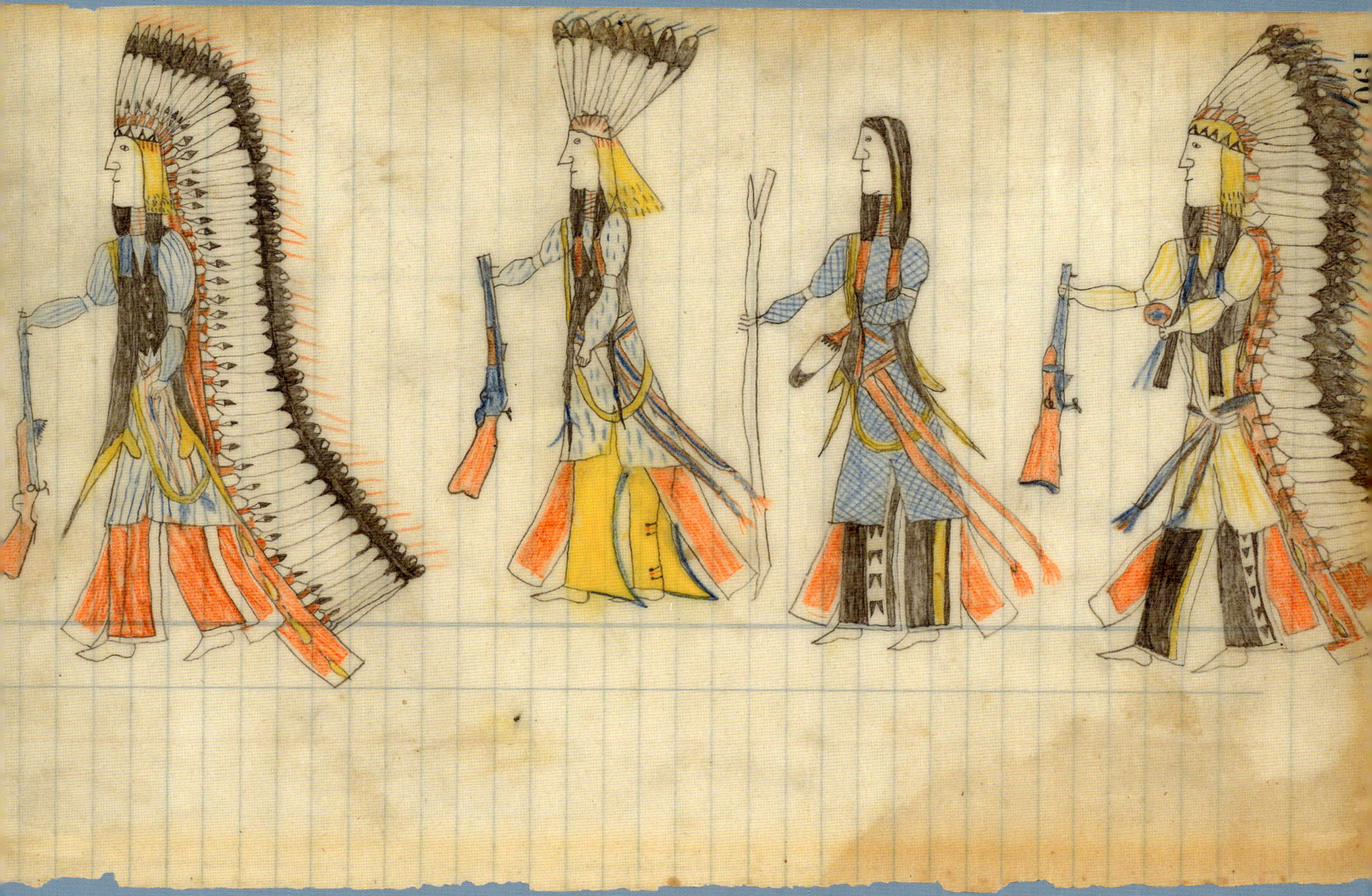

The Mark Lansburgh Collection

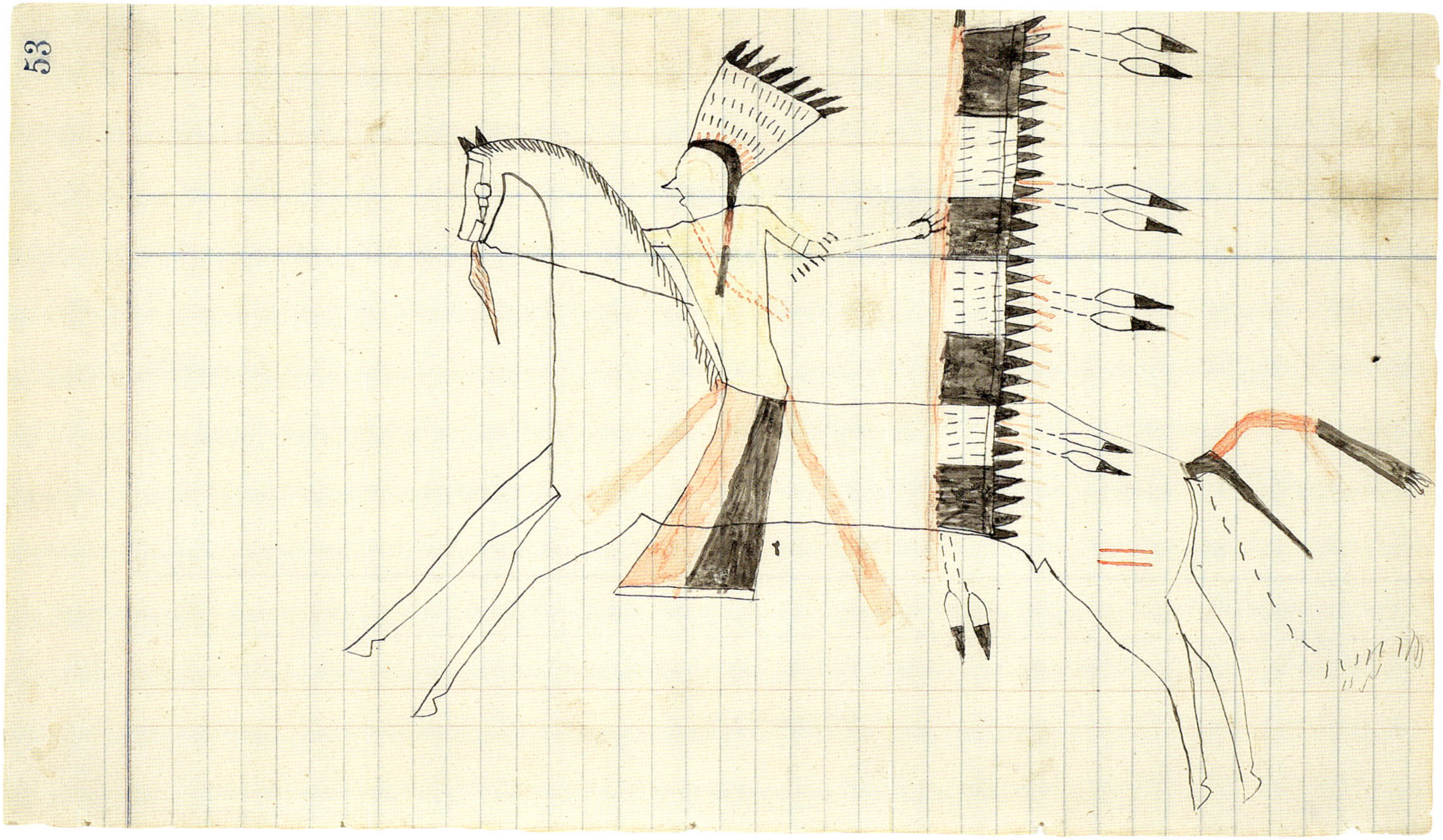

PLATE 1

Unknown artist, Tsistsistas (Cheyenne), active mid- to late nineteenth century, ***Untitled [A Tsistsistas (Cheyenne) Bowstring Society warrior],*** page 53 from the "Frederic H. Douglas Ledger," 1860s, ink and watercolor on laid ledger paper, reverse: page 54 (no drawing), sheet: 7 3/8 × 12 1/4 in. (18.6 × 31.2 cm); 2007.65.1.

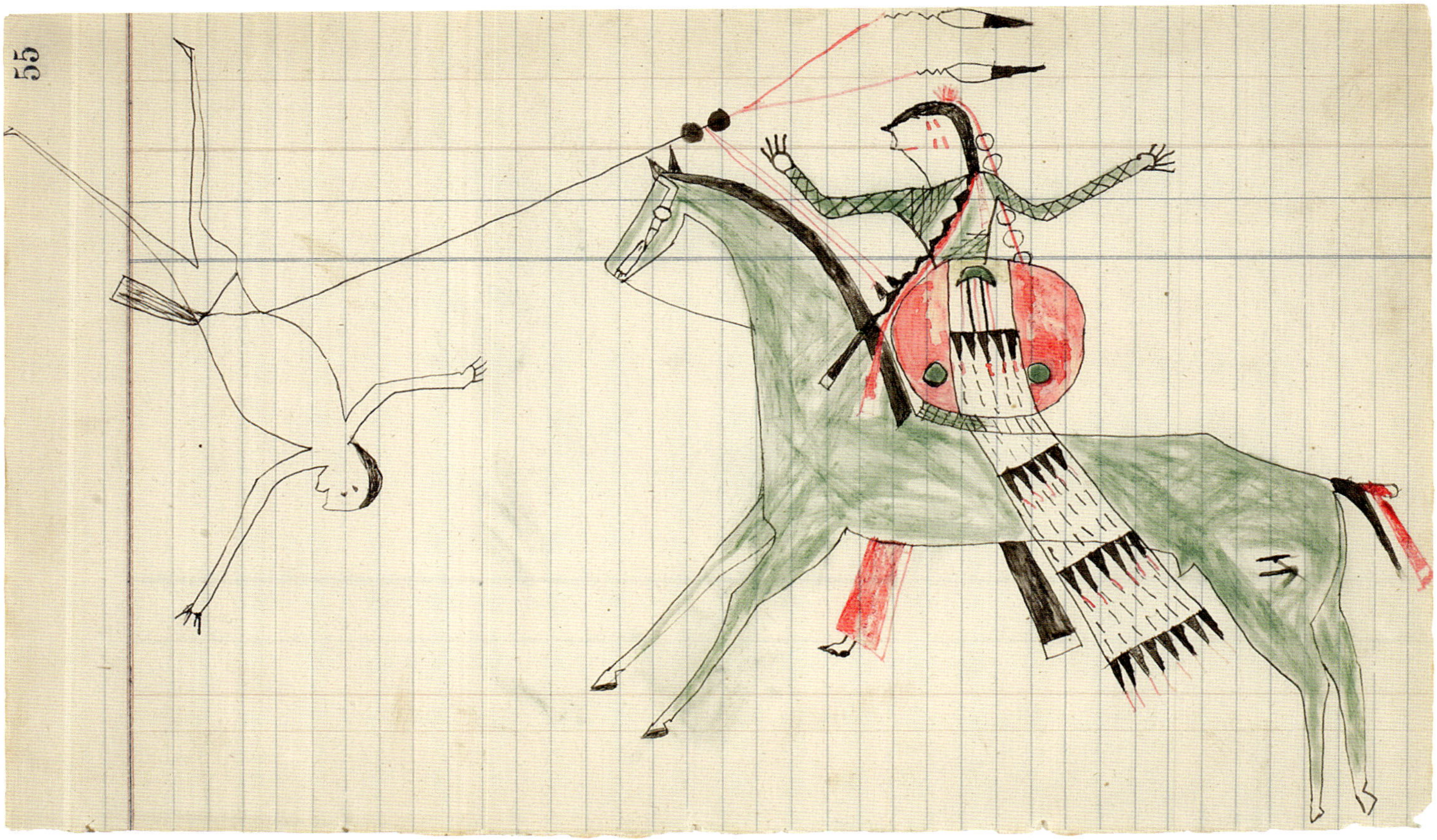

PLATE 2

Unknown artist, Tsistsistas (Cheyenne), active mid- to late nineteenth century, ***Untitled [A Tsistsistas (Cheyenne) warrior counts coup on an enemy],*** page 55 from the "Frederic H. Douglas Ledger," 1860s, ink, colored pencil, and watercolor on laid ledger paper, reverse: page 56 (no drawing), sheet: 7 3/8 × 12 1/4 in. (18.7 × 31.2 cm). Purchased through the Robert J. Strasenburgh II 1942 Fund and the Julia L. Whittier Fund; 2007.26.1.

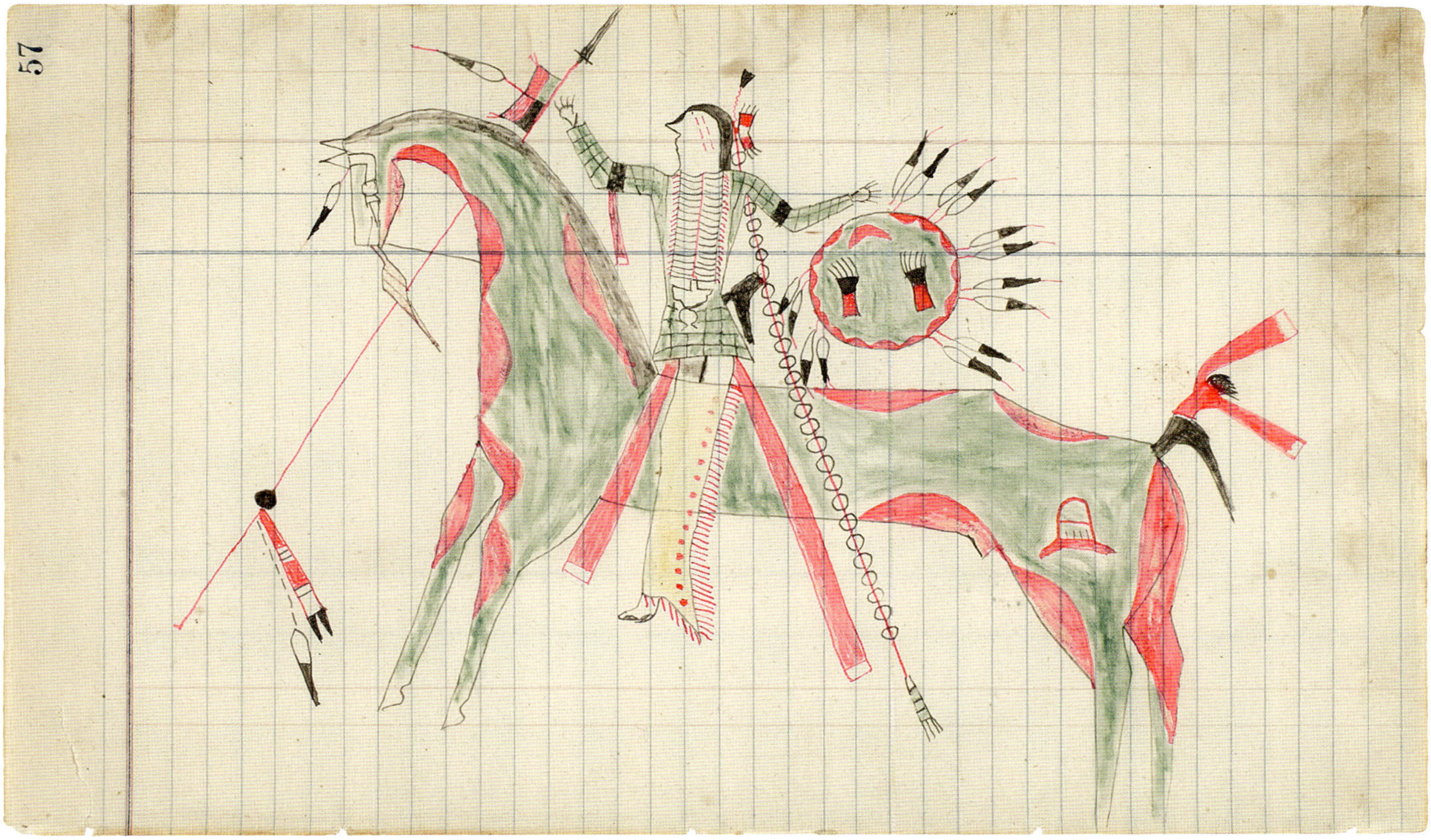

PLATE 3

Unknown artist, Tsistsistas (Cheyenne), active mid- to late nineteenth century, ***Untitled [A Tsistsistas (Cheyenne) Bowstring Society warrior],*** page 57 from the "Frederic H. Douglas Ledger," 1860s, ink, graphite, colored pencil, and watercolor on laid ledger paper, reverse: page 58 (no drawing), sheet: 7 ⅜ × 12 ¼ in. (18.7 × 31.2 cm). Purchased through the Robert J. Strasenburgh II 1942 Fund and the Julia L. Whittier Fund; 2007.26.2.

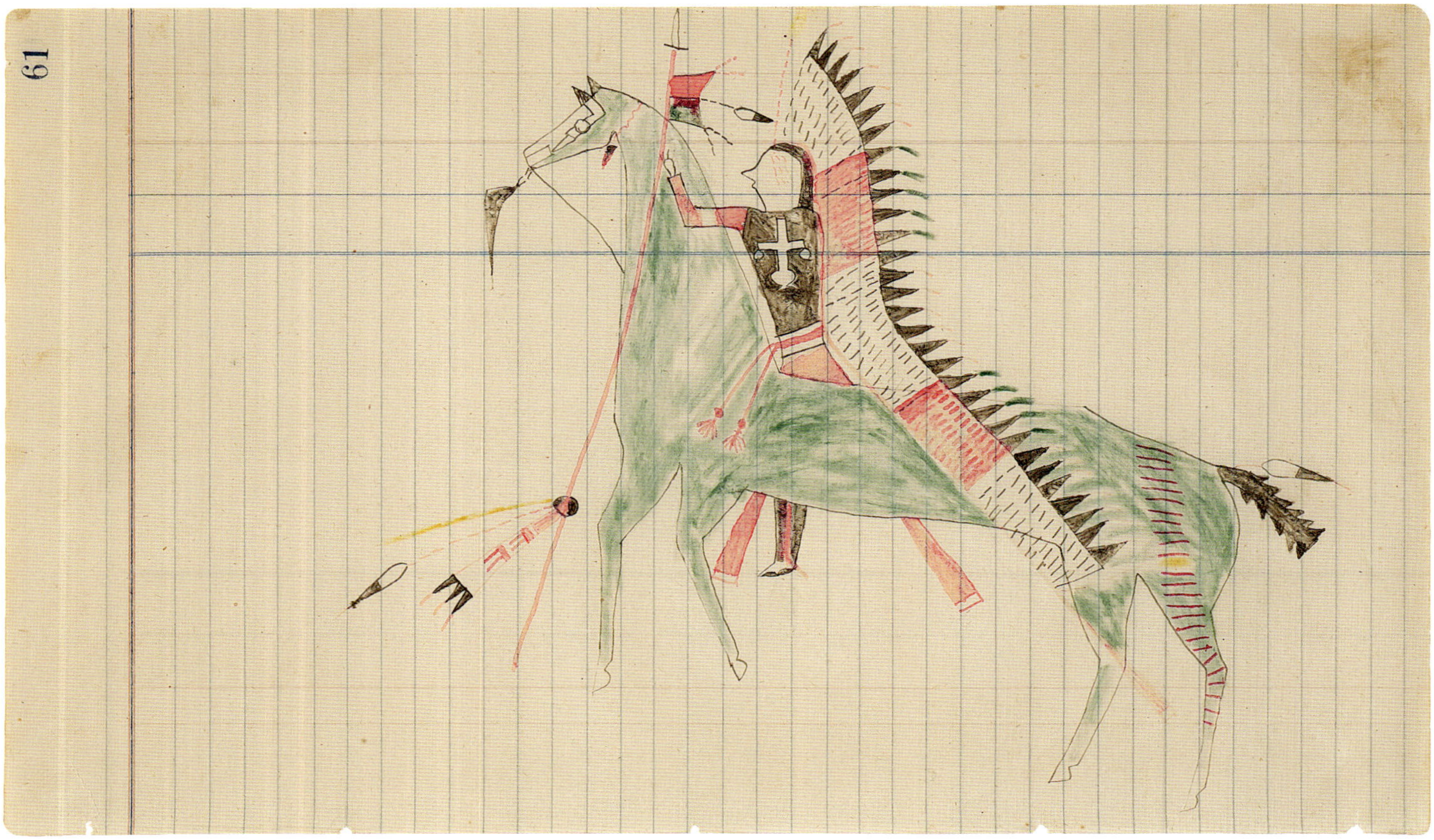

PLATE 4

Unknown artist, Tsistsistas (Cheyenne), active mid- to late nineteenth century, ***Untitled [A Tsistsistas (Cheyenne) Bowstring Society warrior],*** page 61 from the "Frederic H. Douglas Ledger," 1860s, graphite, colored pencil, and watercolor on laid ledger paper, reverse: page 62 (no drawing), sheet: 7 3/8 × 12 3/8 in. (18.7 × 31.2 cm); 2007.65.3.

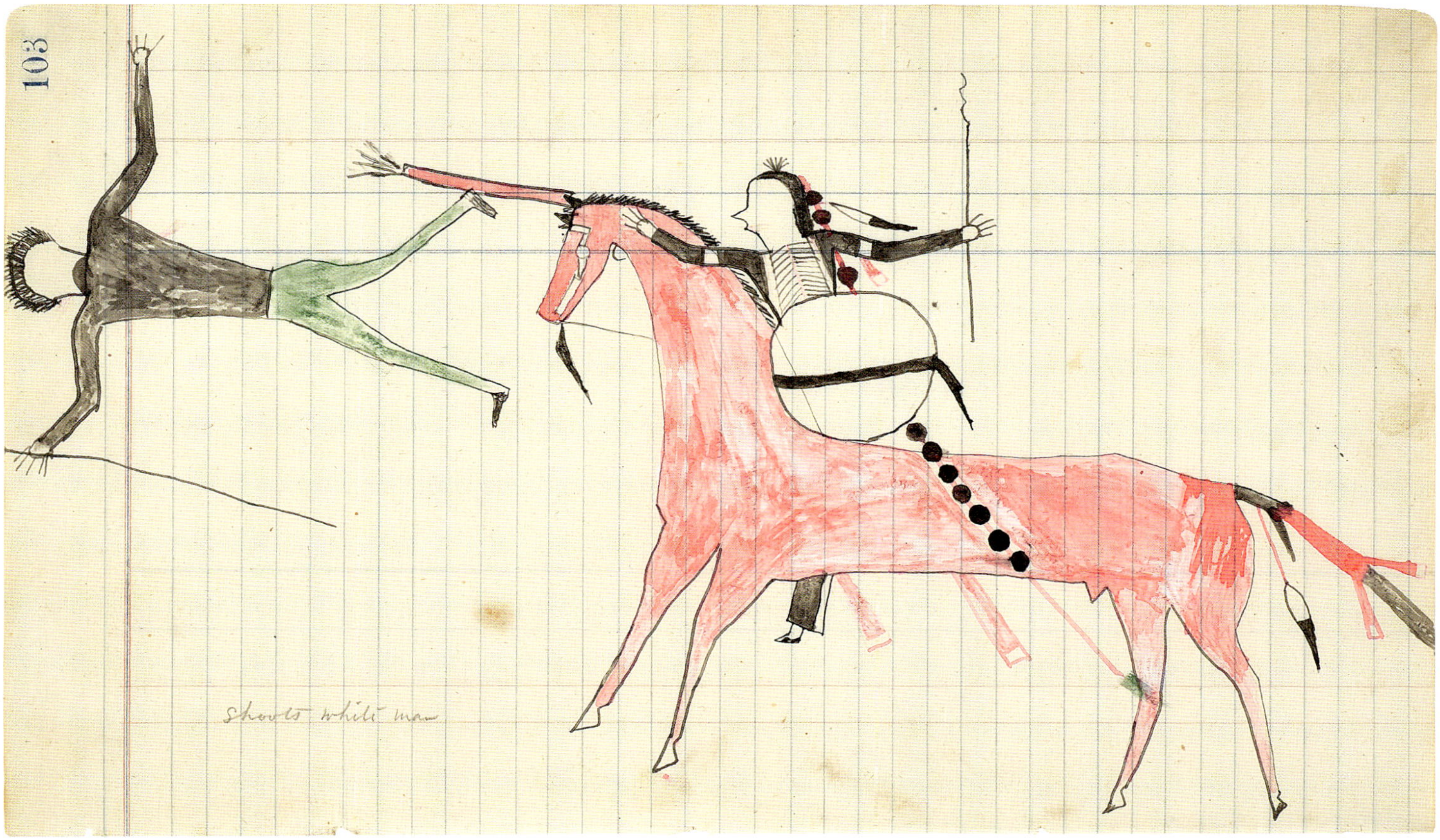

PLATE 5

Unknown artist, Tsistsistas (Cheyenne), active mid- to late nineteenth century, ***Untitled [A Tsistsistas (Cheyenne) warrior shoots a non-Native man],*** page 103 from the "Frederic H. Douglas Ledger," 1860s, ink, watercolor, colored pencil, and graphite on laid ledger paper, reverse: page 104 (no drawing), sheet: 7 3/8 × 12 1/4 in. (18.7 × 31.2 cm); 2007.65.2.

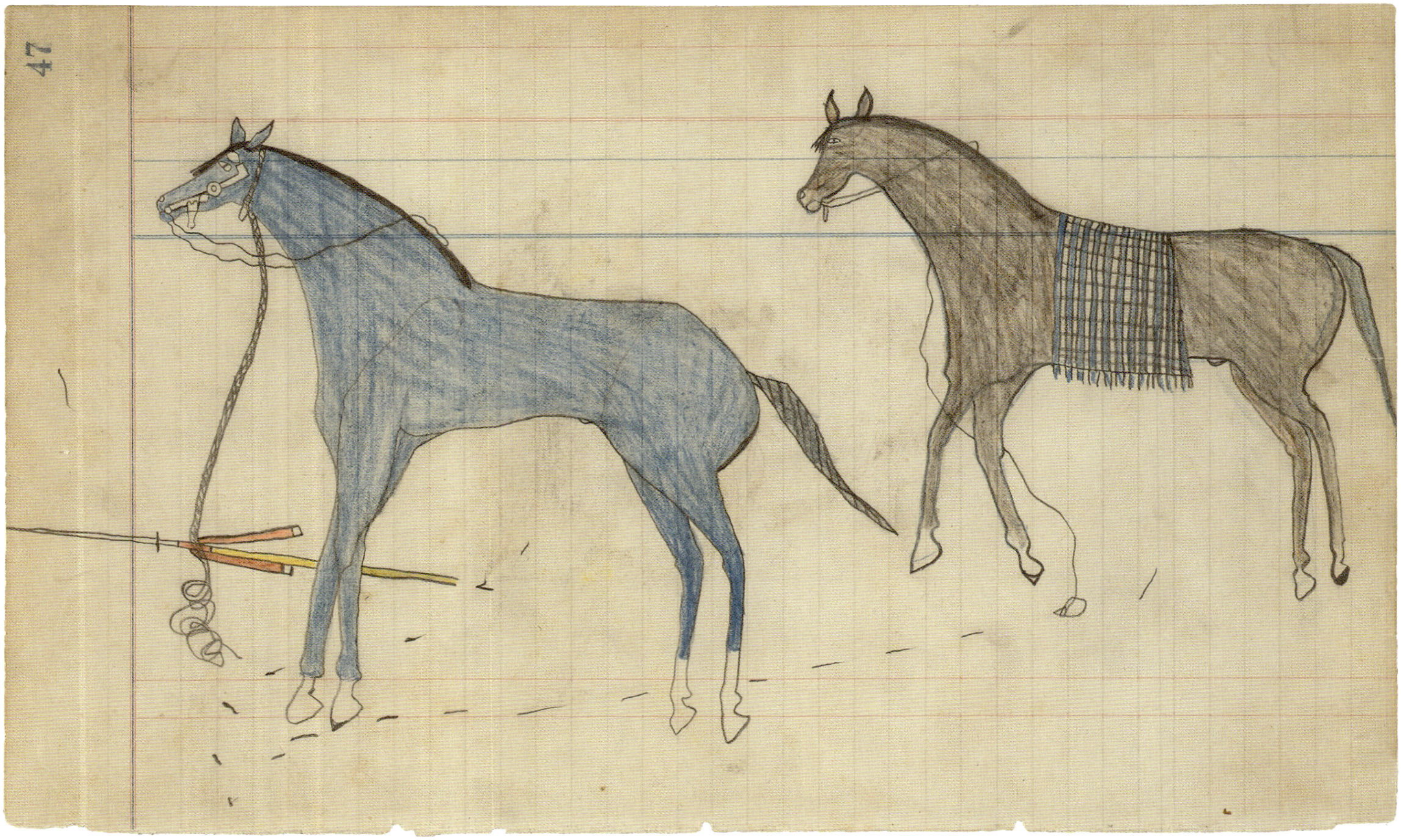

PLATE 6

Unknown artist, Southern Inunaina (Arapaho) and/or Southern Tsistsistas (Cheyenne), active mid- to late nineteenth century, ***Untitled [A horse and mule]***, page 47 from the "Peter W. Edwards Ledger," 1860s, graphite and colored pencil on laid ledger paper, reverse: page 48 (2007.65.5), sheet: 7 5⁄8 × 12 7⁄8 in. (19.4 × 31.5 cm); 2007.65.4.

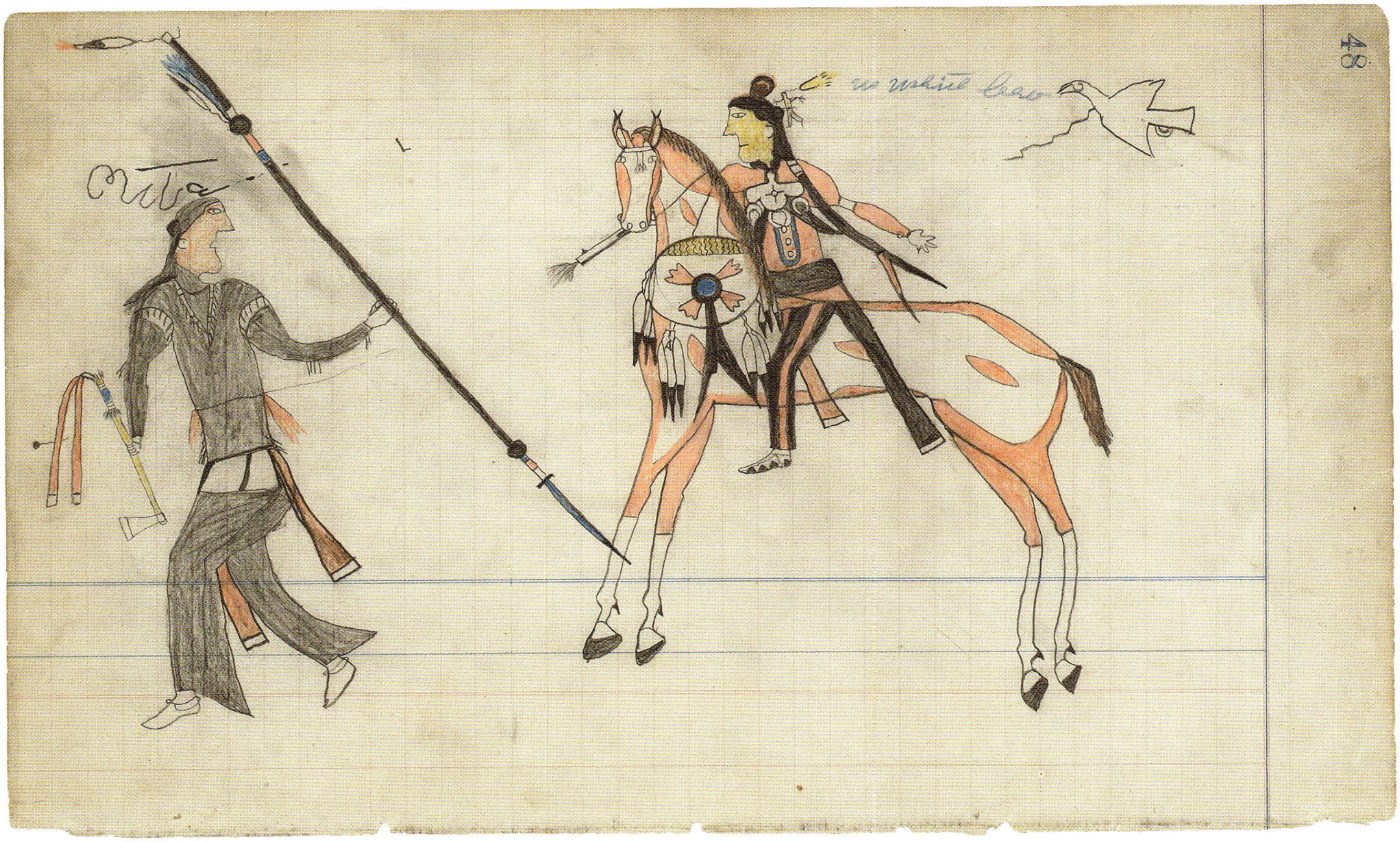

PLATE 7

Unknown artist, Southern Inunaina (Arapaho) and/or Southern Tsistsistas (Cheyenne), active mid- to late nineteenth century, ***Untitled [A warrior fires upon a fleeing enemy],*** page 48 from the "Peter W. Edwards Ledger," 1860s, graphite and colored pencil on laid ledger paper, reverse: page 47 (2007.65.4), sheet: 7 5/8 × 12 7/8 in. (19.4 × 31.5 cm); 2007.65.5.

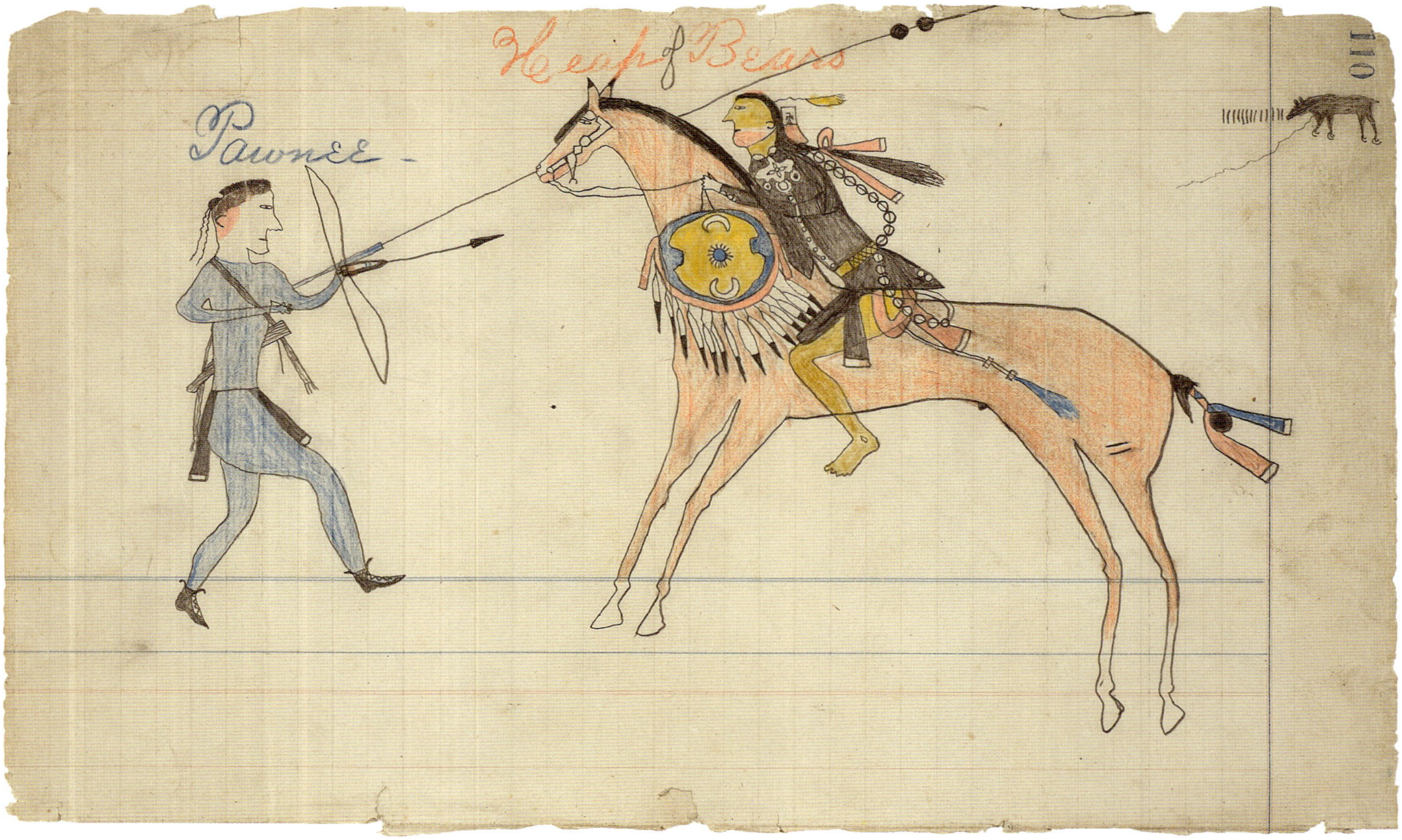

PLATE 8

Unknown artist, Southern Inunaina (Arapaho) and/or Southern Tsistsistas (Cheyenne), active mid- to late nineteenth century, ***Untitled [A warrior counts coup on a Chaticks Si Chaticks (Pawnee) warrior]***, page 110 from the "Peter W. Edwards Ledger," 1860s, graphite and colored pencil on laid ledger paper, reverse: page 109 (no drawing), sheet: 7 ¾ × 12 ⅜ in. (19.5 × 31.4 cm); 2007.65.6.

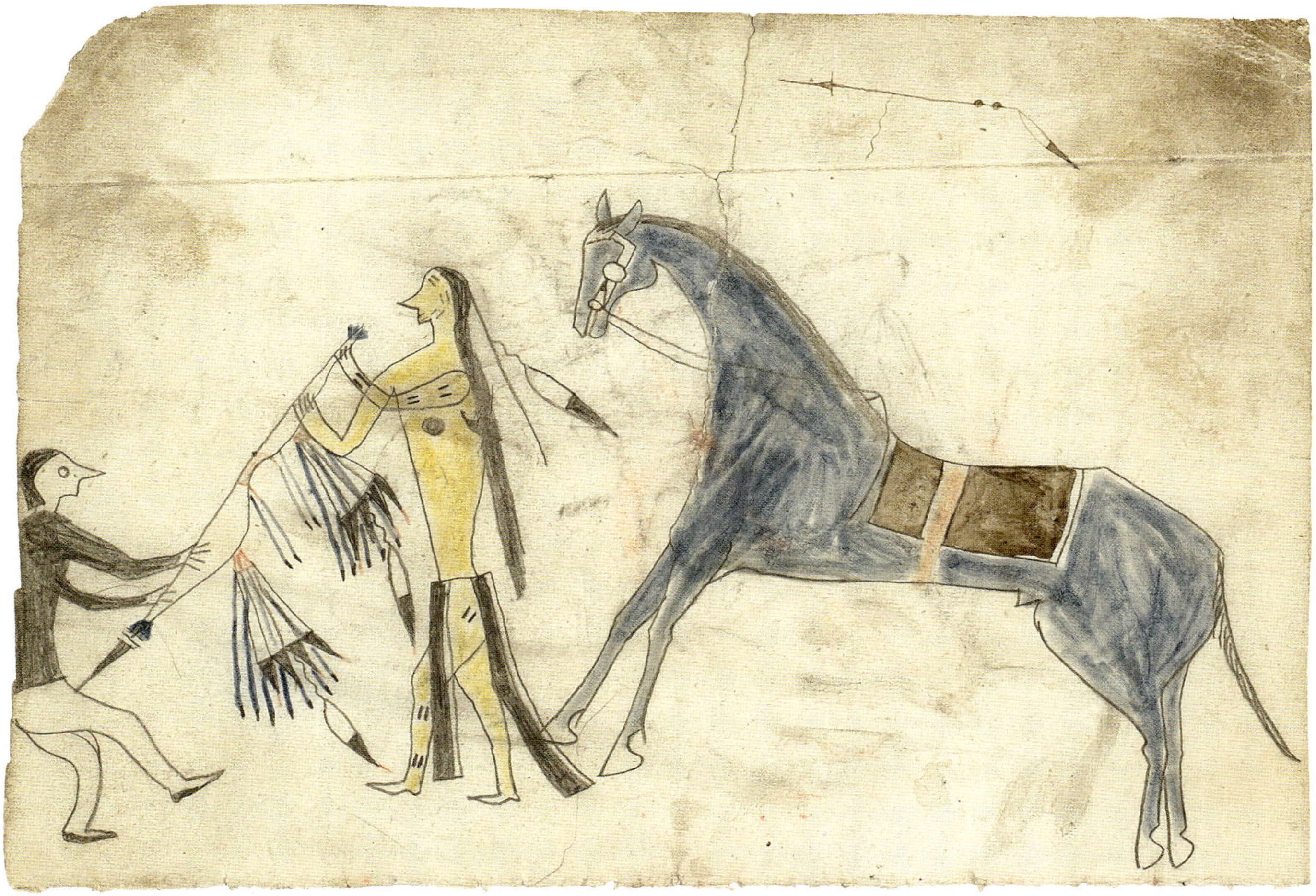

PLATE 9

Unknown artist, possibly Tsistsistas (Cheyenne), active mid- to late nineteenth century, ***Untitled [A Tsistsistas (Cheyenne) counting coup on a non-Native enemy],*** from an unidentified sketchbook, late 1860s–early 1870s, graphite, colored pencil, and watercolor on wove paper, reverse: (2007.65.86), sheet: 6 × 8 5⁄8 in. (15.2 × 21.9 cm); 2007.65.85.

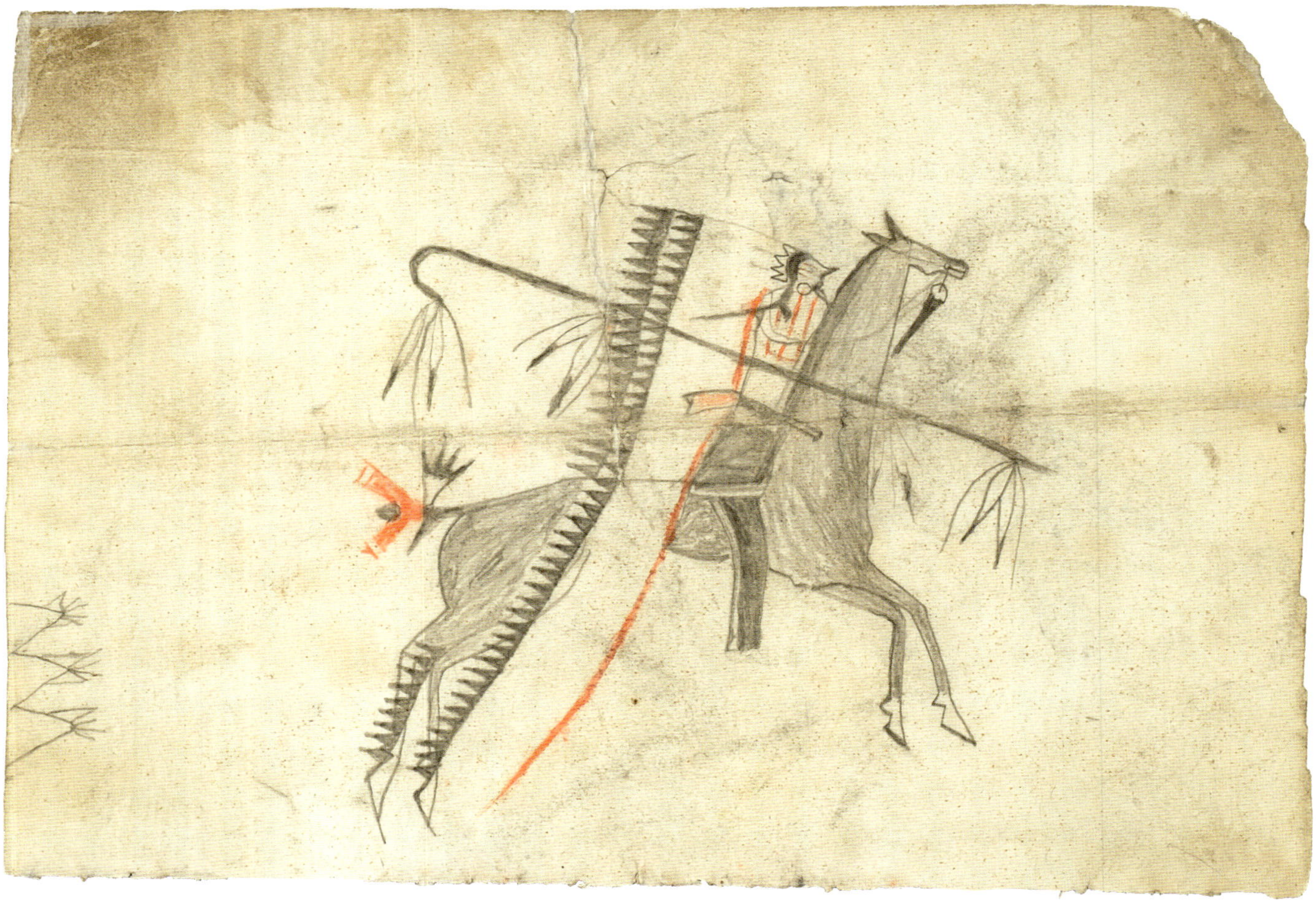

PLATE 10

Unknown artist, possibly Tsistsistas (Cheyenne), active mid- to late nineteenth century, ***Untitled [A Tsistsistas (Cheyenne) Crooked Lance Society warrior],*** from an unidentified sketchbook, late 1860s–early 1870s, graphite and colored pencil on wove paper, reverse: (2007.65.85), sheet: 6 × 8 5⁄8 in. (15.2 × 21.9 cm); 2007.65.86.

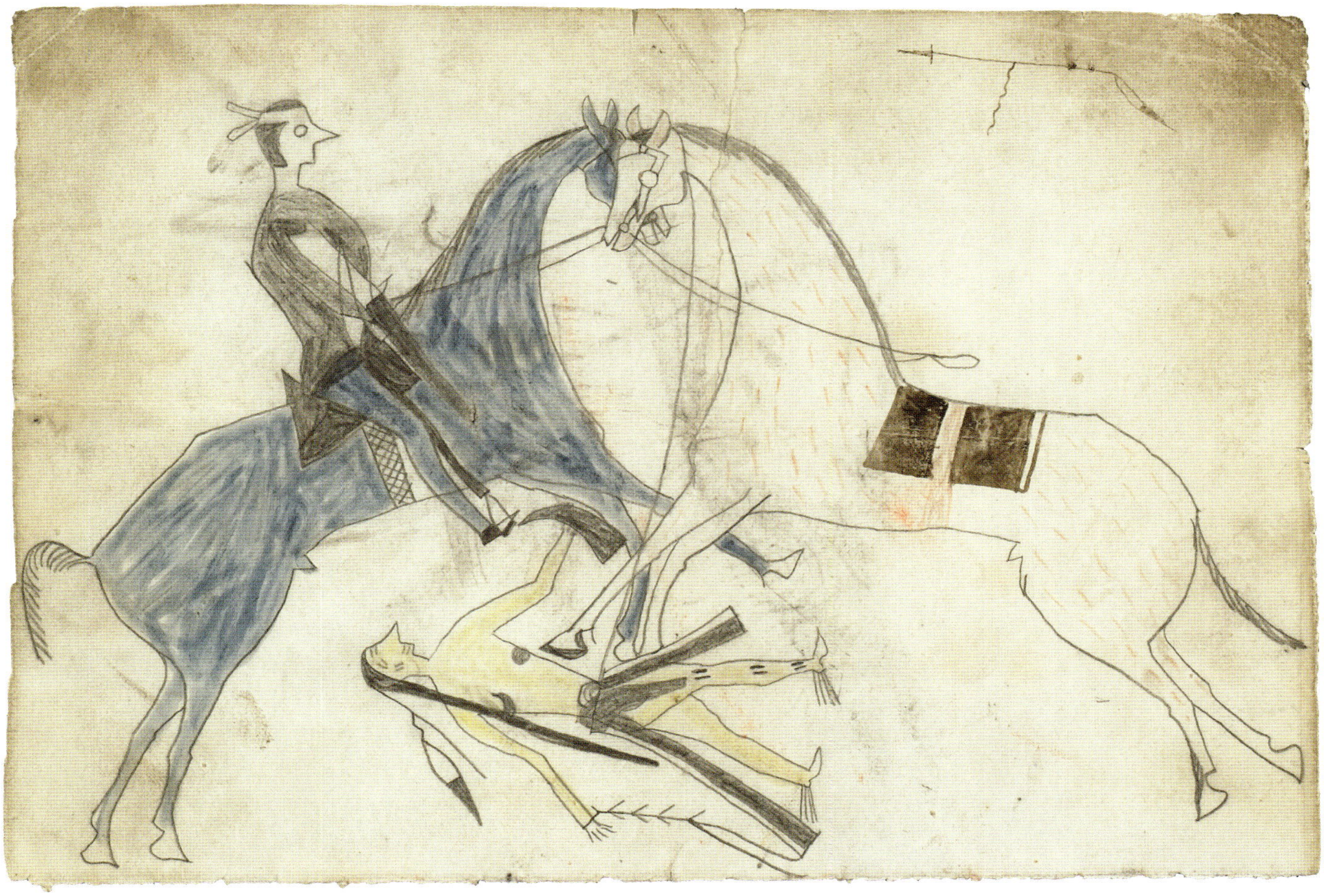

PLATE 11

Unknown artist, possibly Tsistsistas (Cheyenne), active mid- to late nineteenth century, ***Untitled [Counting coup],*** from an unidentified sketchbook, late 1860s–early 1870s, graphite, colored pencil, and watercolor on wove paper; reverse: (2007.65.84); sheet: 6 × 8 ¾ in. (15.3 × 22.2 cm); 2007.65.83.

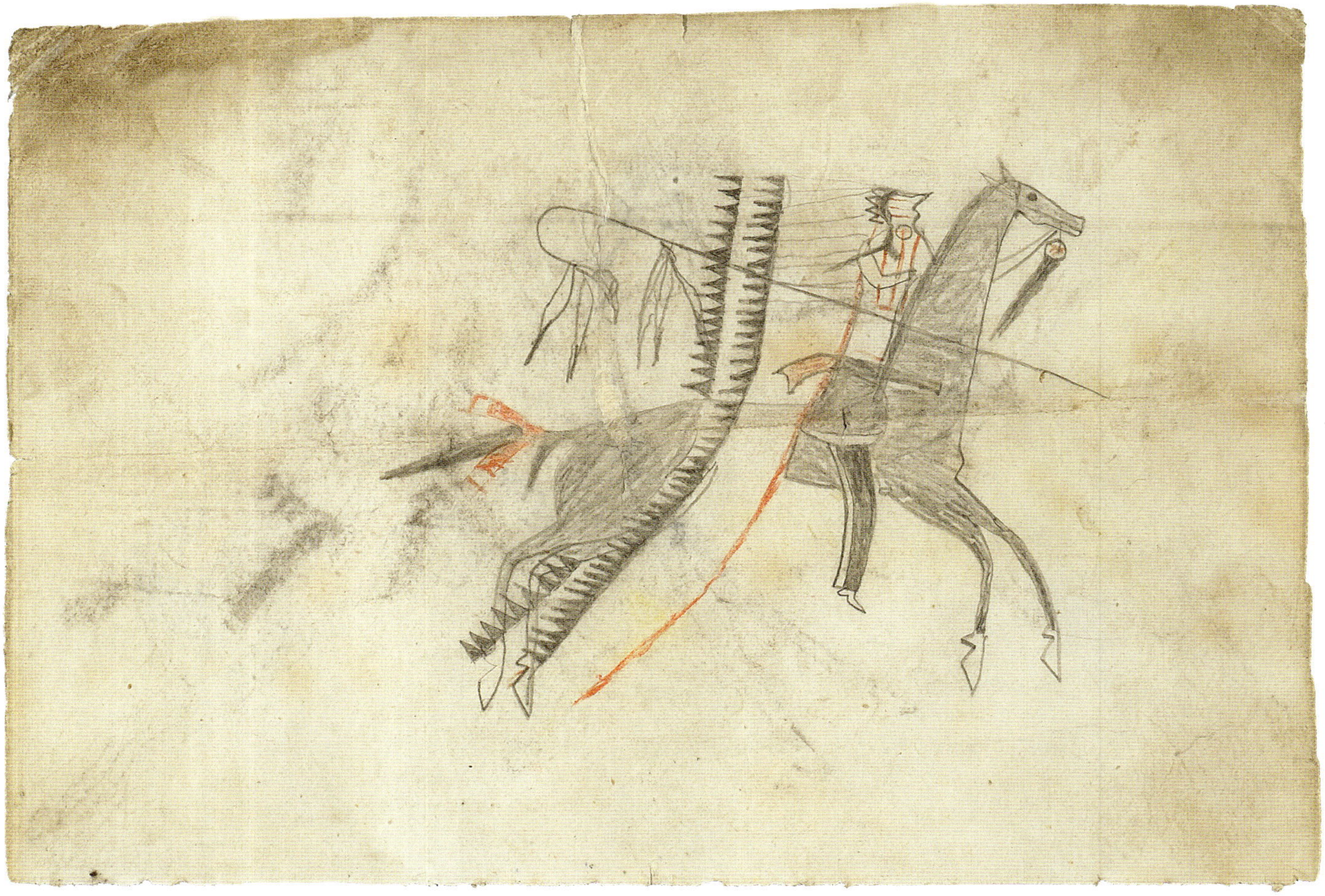

PLATE 12

Unknown artist, possibly Tsistsistas (Cheyenne), active mid- to late nineteenth century, ***Untitled [A Tsistsistas (Cheyenne) Crooked Lance Society warrior],*** from an unidentified sketchbook, late 1860s–early 1870s, graphite and colored pencil on wove paper, reverse: (2007.65.83), sheet: 6 × 8 ¾ in. (15.3 × 22.2 cm); 2007.65.84.

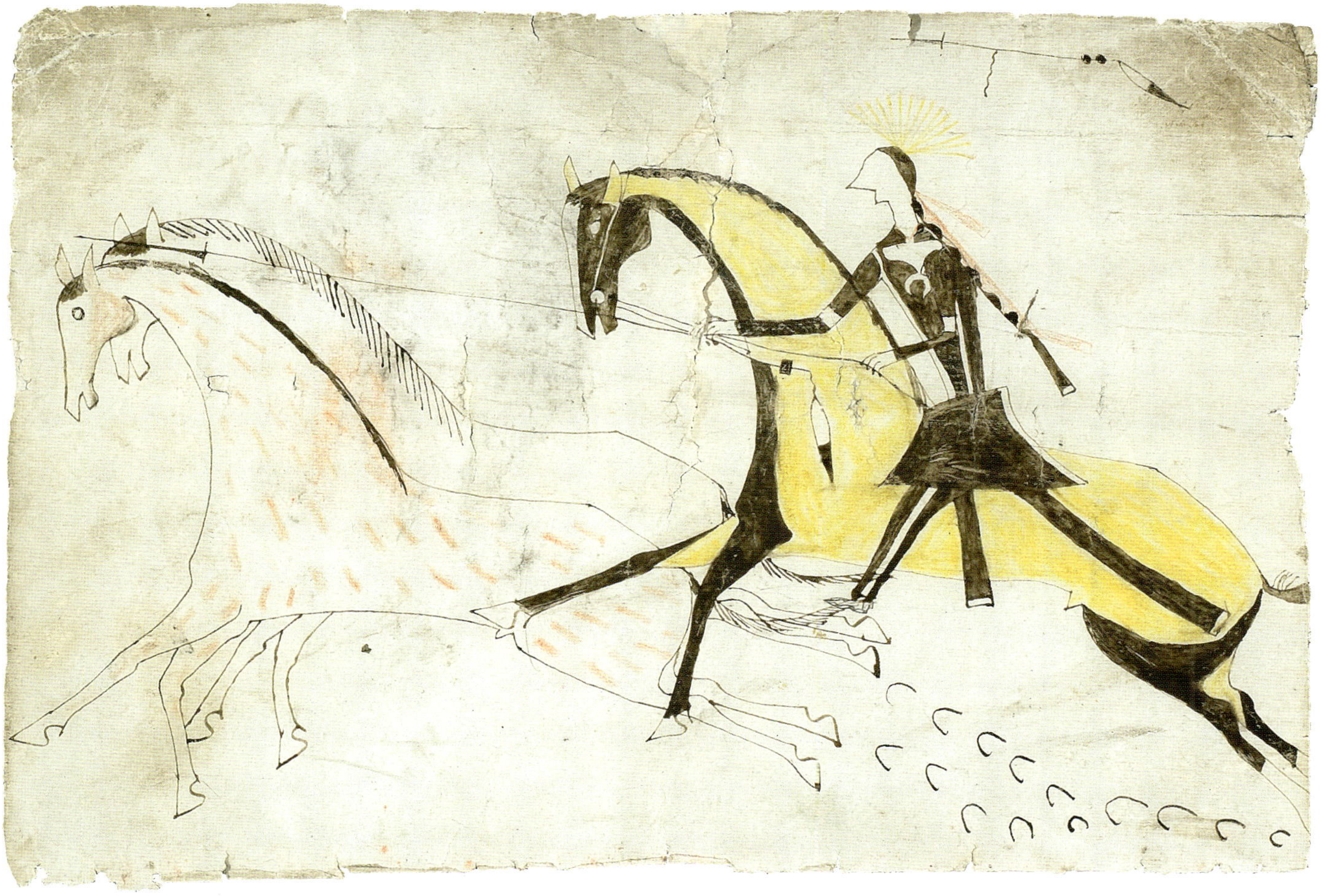

PLATE 13

Unknown artist, possibly Tsistsistas (Cheyenne), active mid- to late nineteenth century, ***Untitled [A Tsistsistas (Cheyenne) warrior raiding two horses]***, from an unidentified sketchbook, late 1860s–early 1870s, ink, colored pencil, and ink wash on paper, reverse: (2007.65.88), sheet: 6 ⅛ × 8 ¾ in. (15.5 × 22.0 cm); 2007.65.87.

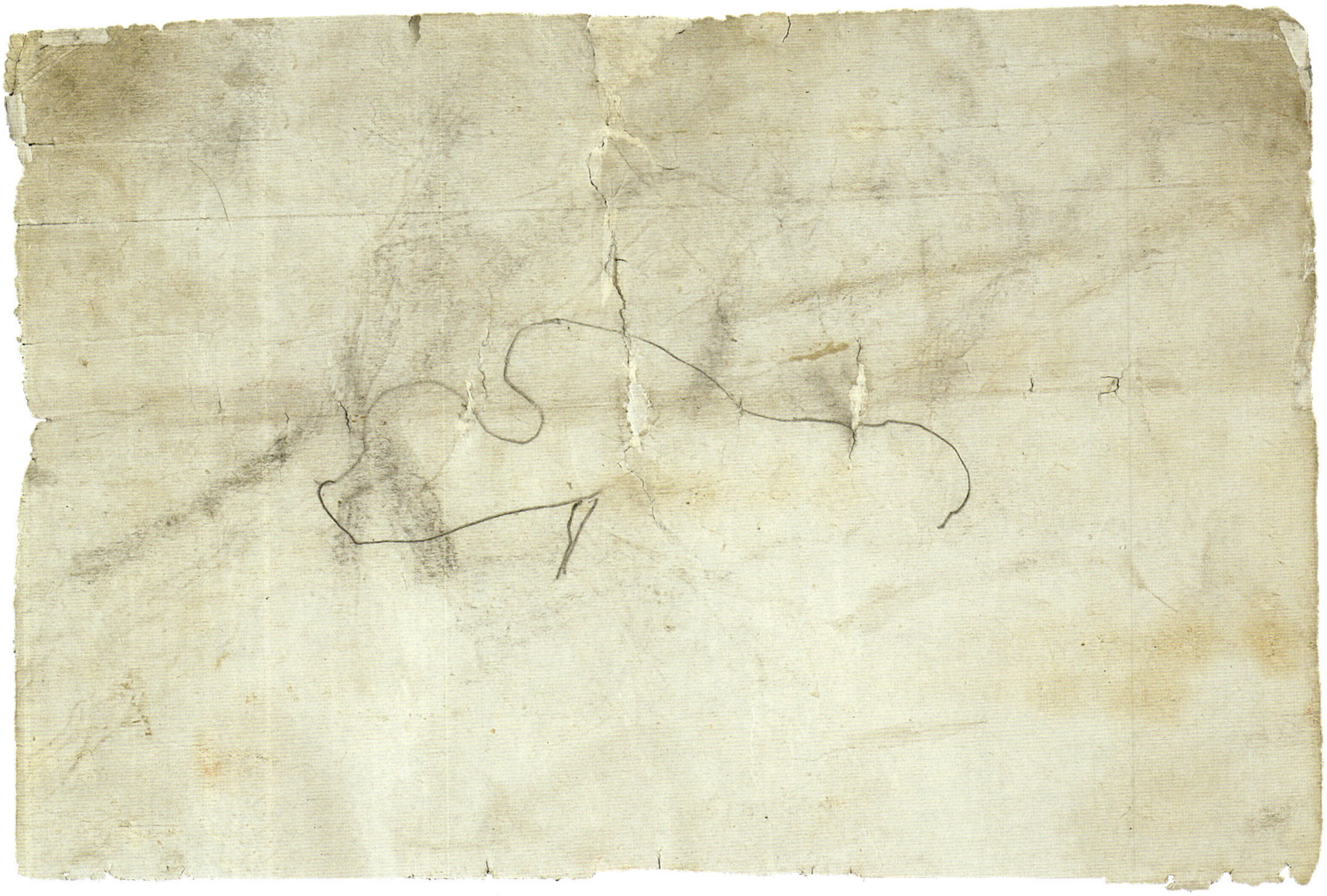

PLATE 14

Unknown artist, possibly Tsistsistas (Cheyenne), active mid- to late nineteenth century, ***Untitled [An unfinished sketch of a buffalo],*** from an unidentified sketchbook, late 1860s–early 1870s, graphite on wove paper, reverse: (2007.65.87), sheet: 6 ⅛ × 8 ¾ in. (15.5 × 22.0 cm); 2007.65.88.

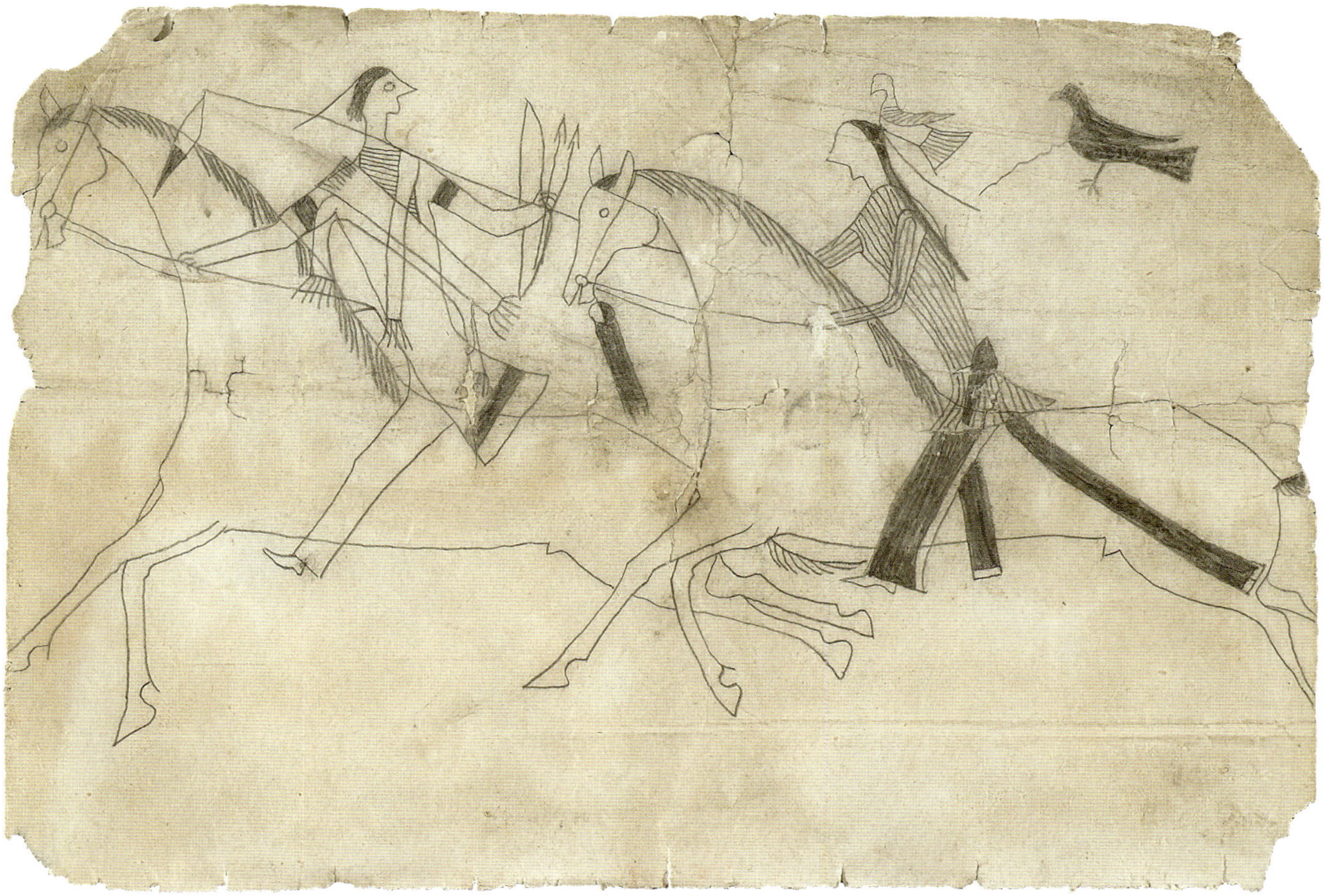

PLATE 15

Unknown artist, possibly Tsistsistas (Cheyenne), active mid- to late nineteenth century, ***Untitled [A Tsistsistas (Cheyenne) warrior counts coup]***, from an unidentified sketchbook, late 1860s–early 1870s, graphite on wove paper, reverse: (2007.65.82), sheet: 6 × 8 ¾ in. (15.1 × 22.0 cm); 2007.65.81.

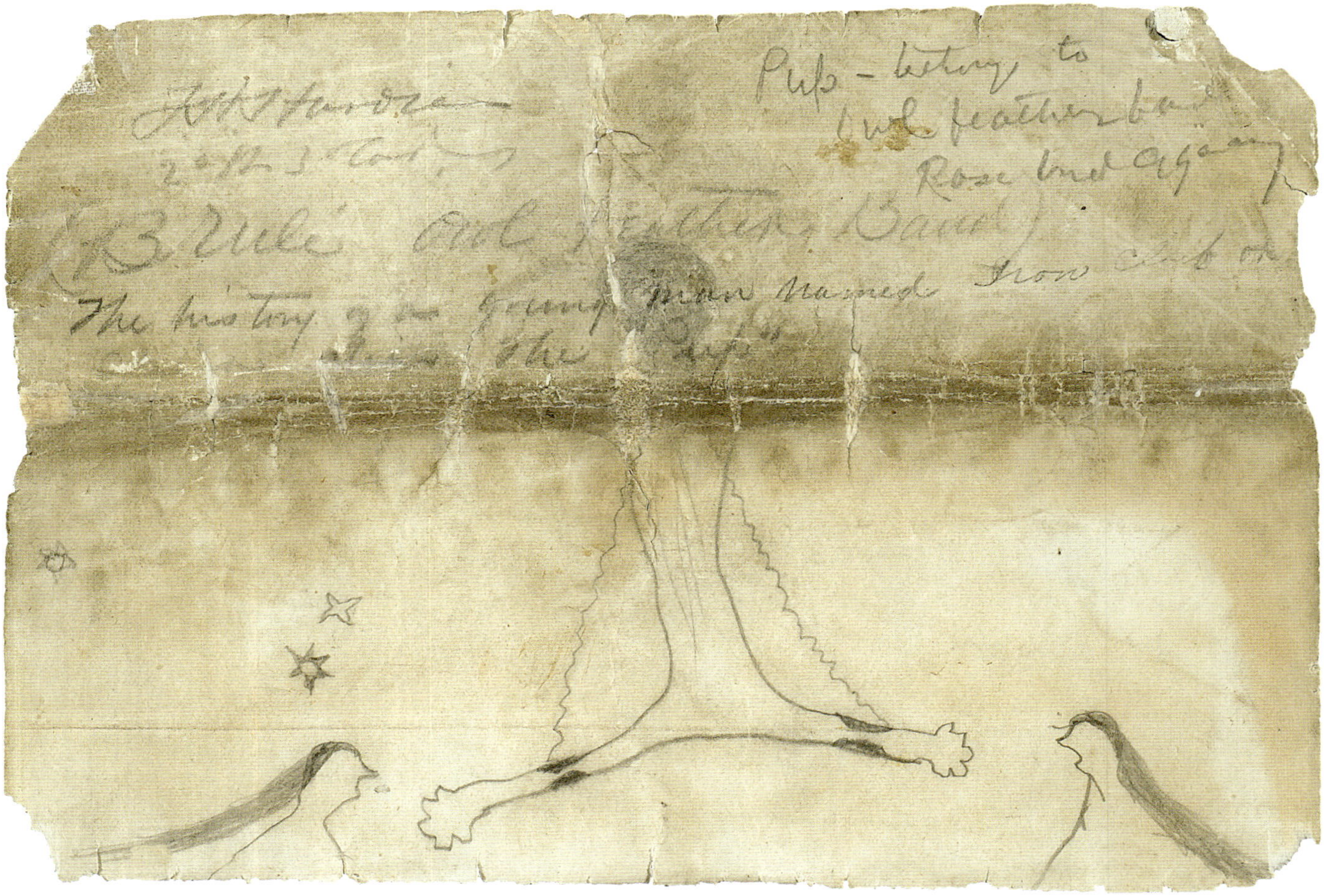

PLATE 16

Unknown artist, possibly Tsistsistas (Cheyenne), active mid- to late nineteenth century, ***Untitled [Two partial figures and a hide],*** from an unidentified sketchbook, late 1860s–early 1870s, graphite on wove paper, reverse: (2007.65.81), sheet: 6 × 8 ¾ in. (15.1 × 22.0 cm); 2007.65.82.

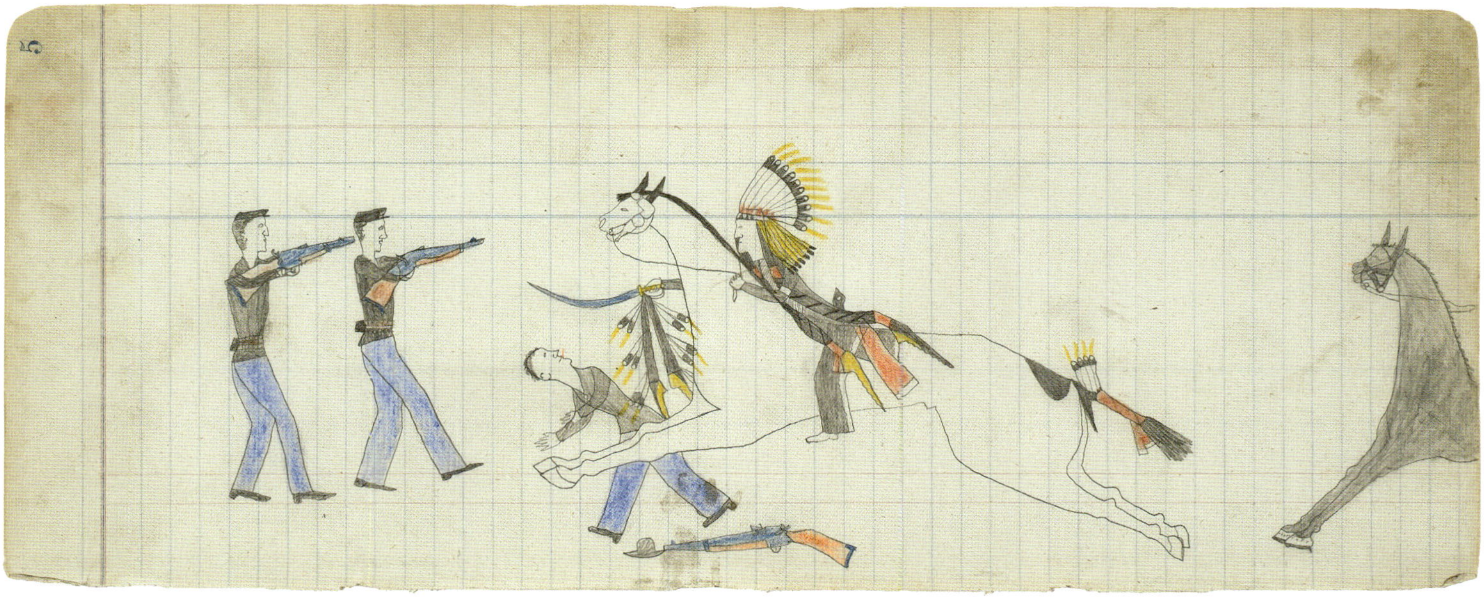

PLATE 17

Unknown artist, Southern Tsistsistas (Cheyenne), active late nineteenth century, ***Untitled [Tsistsistas (Cheyenne) warrior on horseback fighting U.S. soldiers],*** page 5 from the "Arrow's Elk Society Ledger," c. 1874–75, graphite and colored pencil on laid ledger paper, reverse: page 6 (no drawing), sheet: 6 1/8 × 4 7/8 in. (15.5 × 37.7 cm); 2007.65.30.

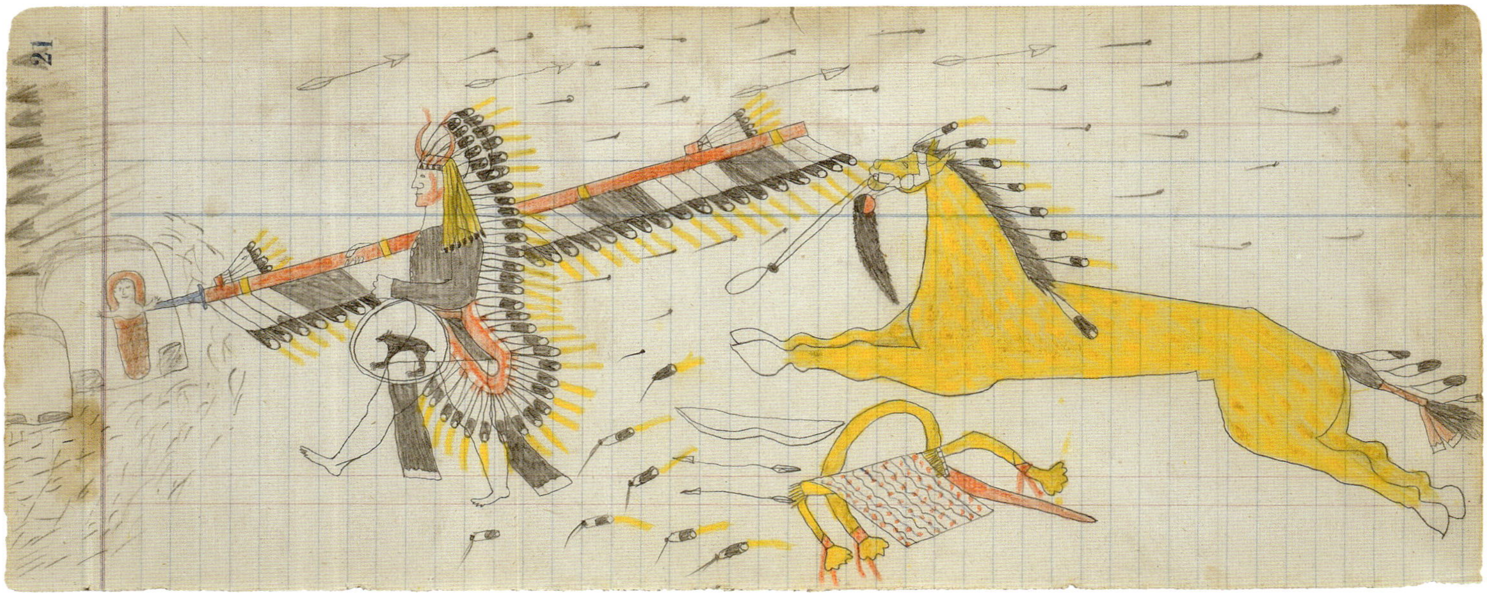

PLATE 18

Unknown artist, Southern Tsistsistas (Cheyenne), active late nineteenth century, ***Untitled [A Tsistsistas (Cheyenne) warrior counting coup on a baby],*** page 21 from the "Arrow's Elk Society Ledger," c. 1874–75, graphite, colored pencil, crayon on laid ledger paper, reverse: page 22 (no drawing), sheet: 6 ⅛ × 14 ⅞ in. (15.4 × 37.7 cm). Gift of Mark Lansburgh, Class of 1949, in honor of James Wright, 16th President of Dartmouth College; 2008.75.

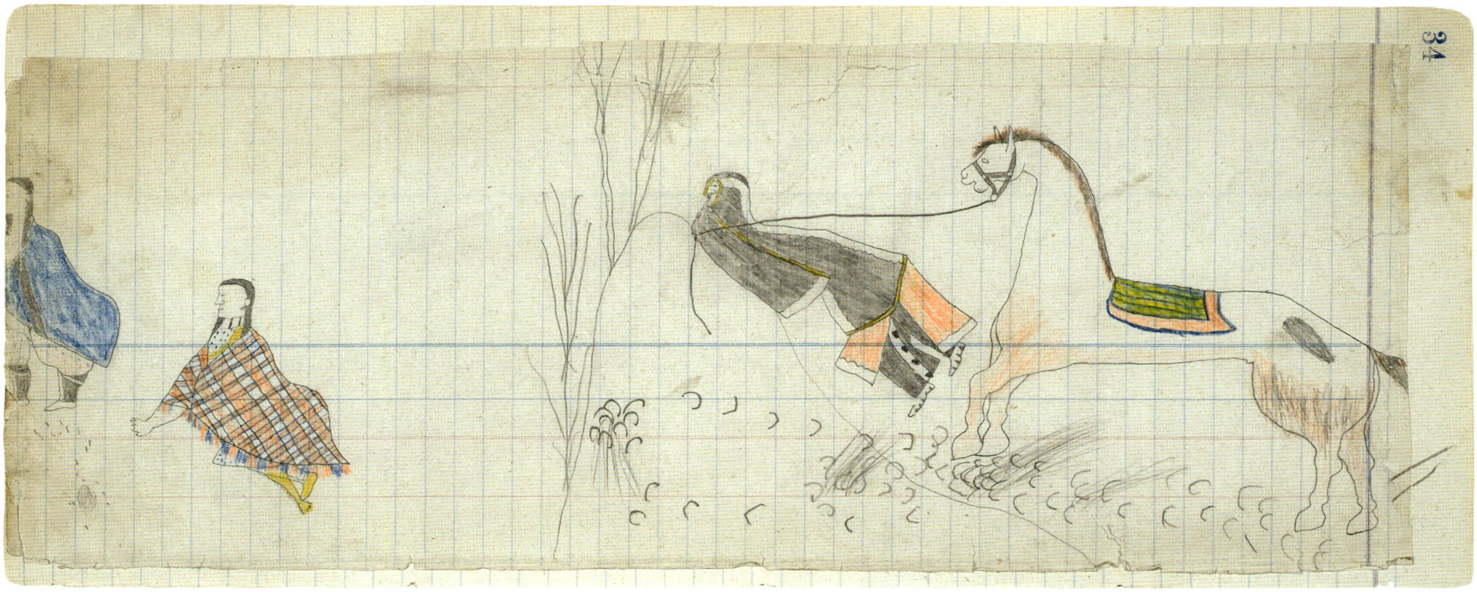

PLATE 19

Unknown artist, Southern Tsistsistas (Cheyenne), active late nineteenth century, ***Untitled [A Tsistsistas (Cheyenne) man watching two women].*** page 34 from the "Arrow's Elk Society Ledger," c. 1874–75, graphite and colored pencil on laid ledger paper mounted on laid ledger paper, reverse: page 33 (no drawing), sheet: 6 ⅛ × 14 ⅞ in. (15.5 × 37.7 cm); 2007.65.23.

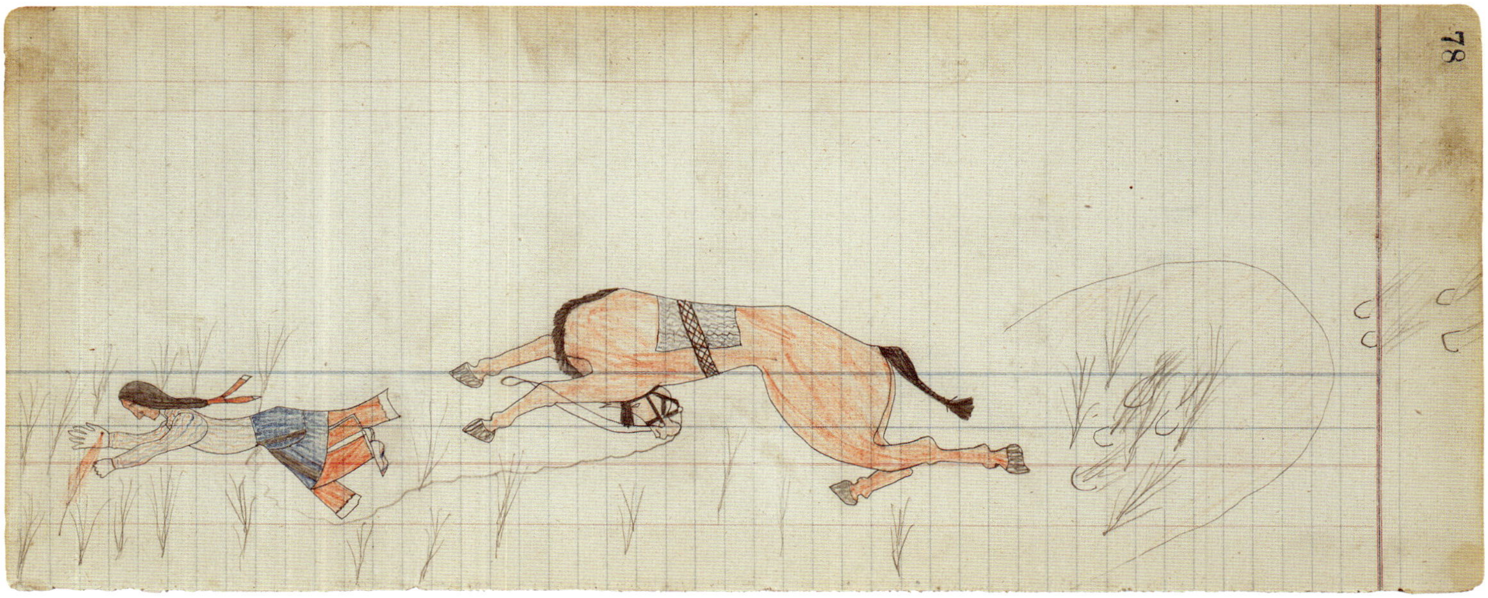

PLATE 20

Unknown artist, Southern Tsistsistas (Cheyenne), active late nineteenth century, ***Untitled [A wounded Tsistsistas (Cheyenne) warrior and a falling horse],*** page 78 from the "Arrow's Elk Society Ledger," c. 1874–75, graphite and colored pencil on laid ledger paper, reverse: page 77 (no drawing), sheet: 6 ⅛ × 14 ⅞ in. (15.5 × 37.8 cm); 2007.65.52.

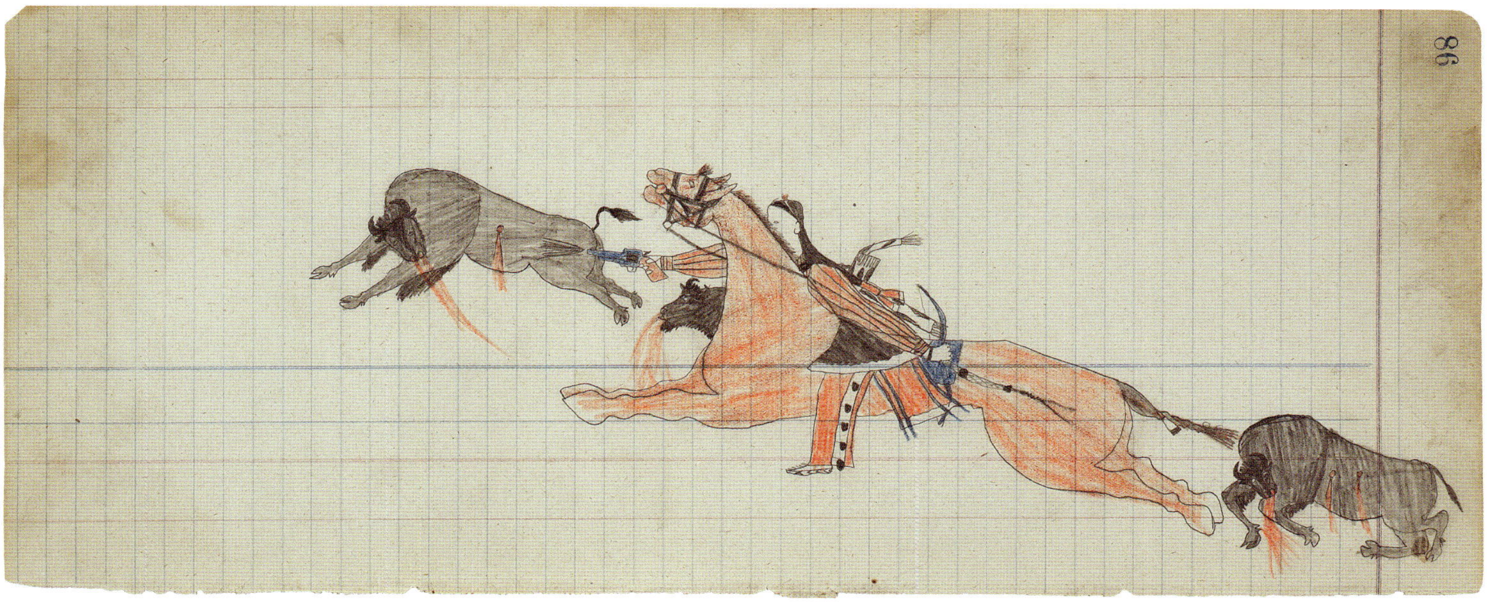

PLATE 21

Unknown artist, Southern Tsistsistas (Cheyenne), active late n neteenth century, ***Untitled [A buffalo hunt],*** page 86 from the "Arrow's Elk Society Ledger," c. 1874–75, graphite and colored pencil on laid ledger paper, reverse: page 85 (no drawing), sheet: 6 1/8 × 14 7/8 in. (15.6 × 37.7 cm); 2007.65.26.

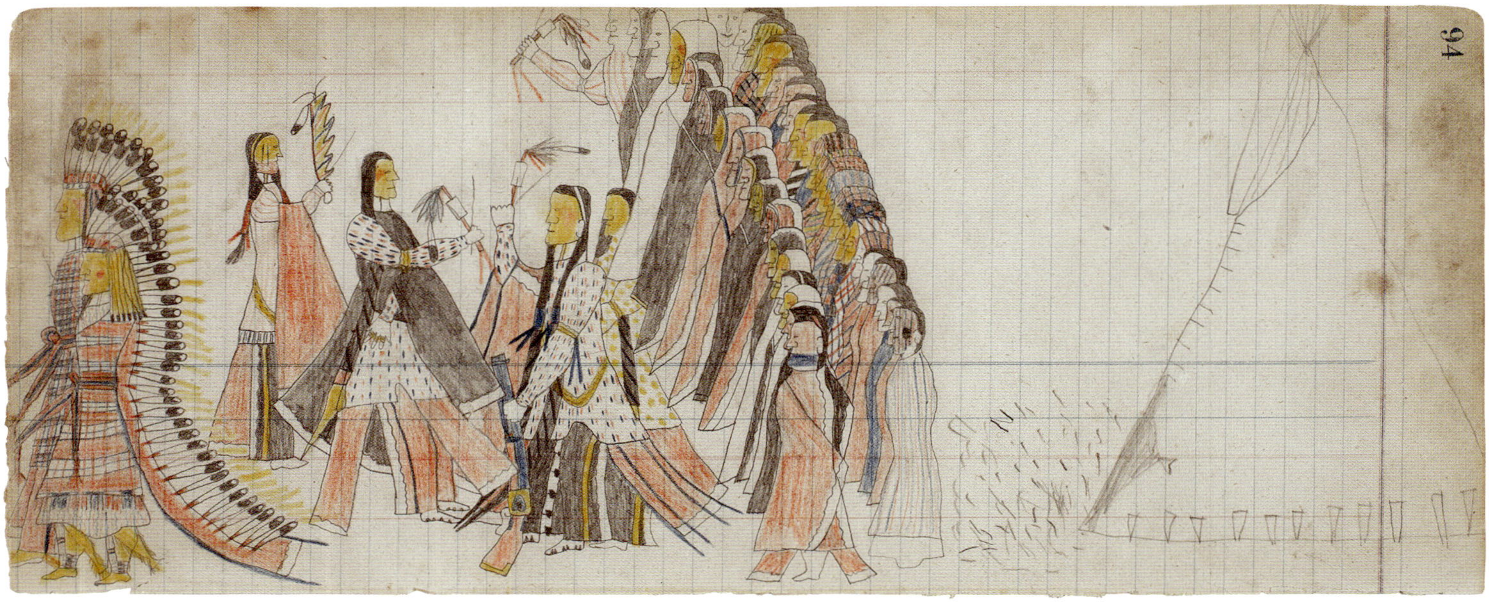

PLATE 22

Unknown artist, Southern Tsistsistas (Cheyenne), active late nineteenth century, ***Untitled [Honoree in the Tsistsistas (Cheyenne) Kit Fox Society social dance],*** page 94 from the "Arrow's Elk Society Ledger," c. 1874–75, graphite and colored pencil on laid ledger paper, reverse: page 93 (no drawing), sheet: 6 ⅛ × 14 ⅞ in. (15.4 × 37.7 cm). Gift of Mark Lansburgh, Class of 1949, in honor of Jim Yong Kim, 17th President of Dartmouth College; 2009.45.

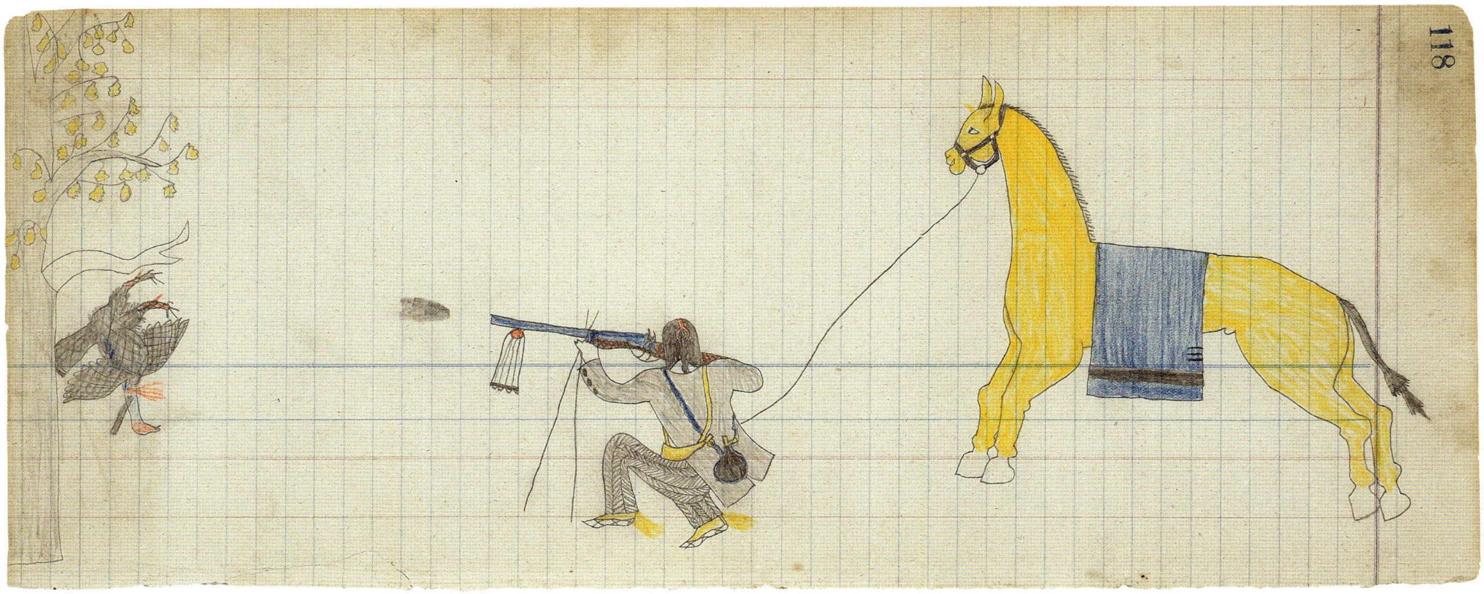

PLATE 23

Unknown artist, Southern Tsistsistas (Cheyenne), active late nineteenth century, ***Untitled [Hunting turkey],*** page 118 from the "Arrow's Elk Society Ledger," c. 1874–75, graphite and colored pencil on laid ledger paper, reverse: page 117 (no drawing), sheet: 6 ⅛ × 14 ⅞ in. (15.5 × 37.7 cm); 2007.65.25.

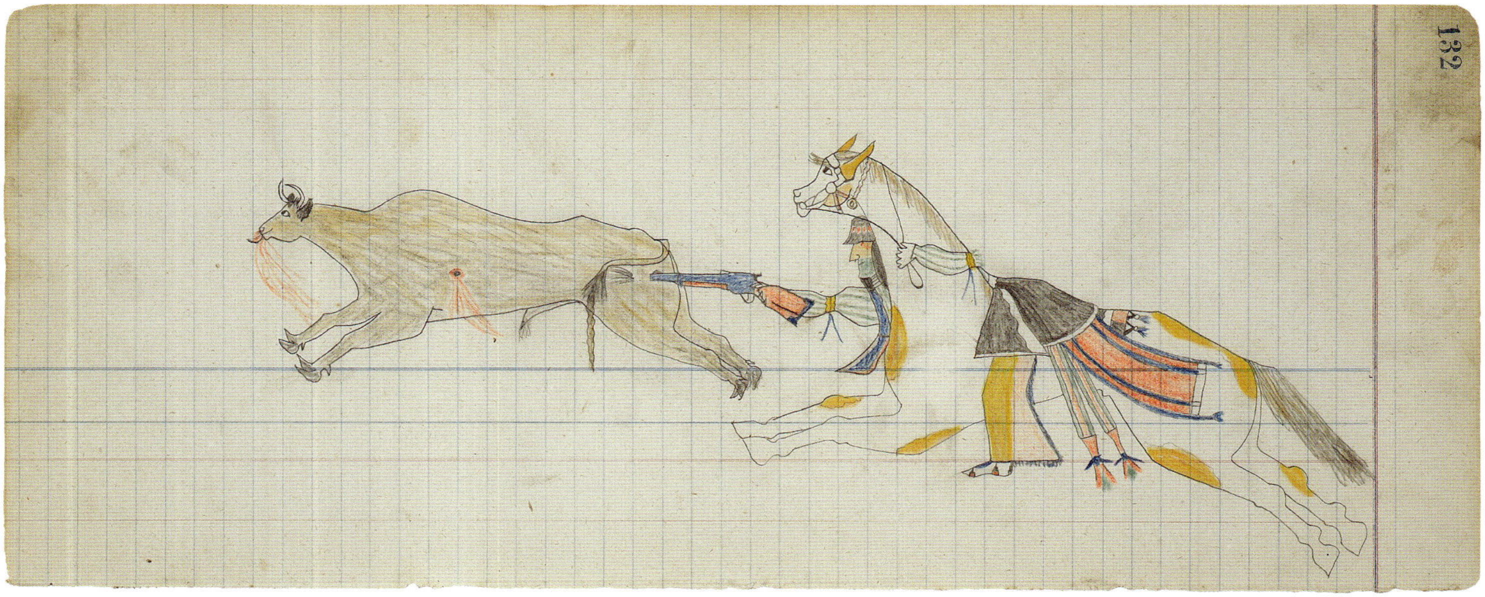

PLATE 24

Unknown artist, Southern Tsistsistas (Cheyenne), active late nineteenth century, ***Untitled [Hunting a bull],*** page 132 from the "Arrow's Elk Society Ledger," c. 1874–75, graphite and colored pencil on laid ledger paper, reverse: page 131 (no drawing), sheet: 6 1/8 × 14 7/8 in. (15.5 × 37.7 cm); 2007.65.27.

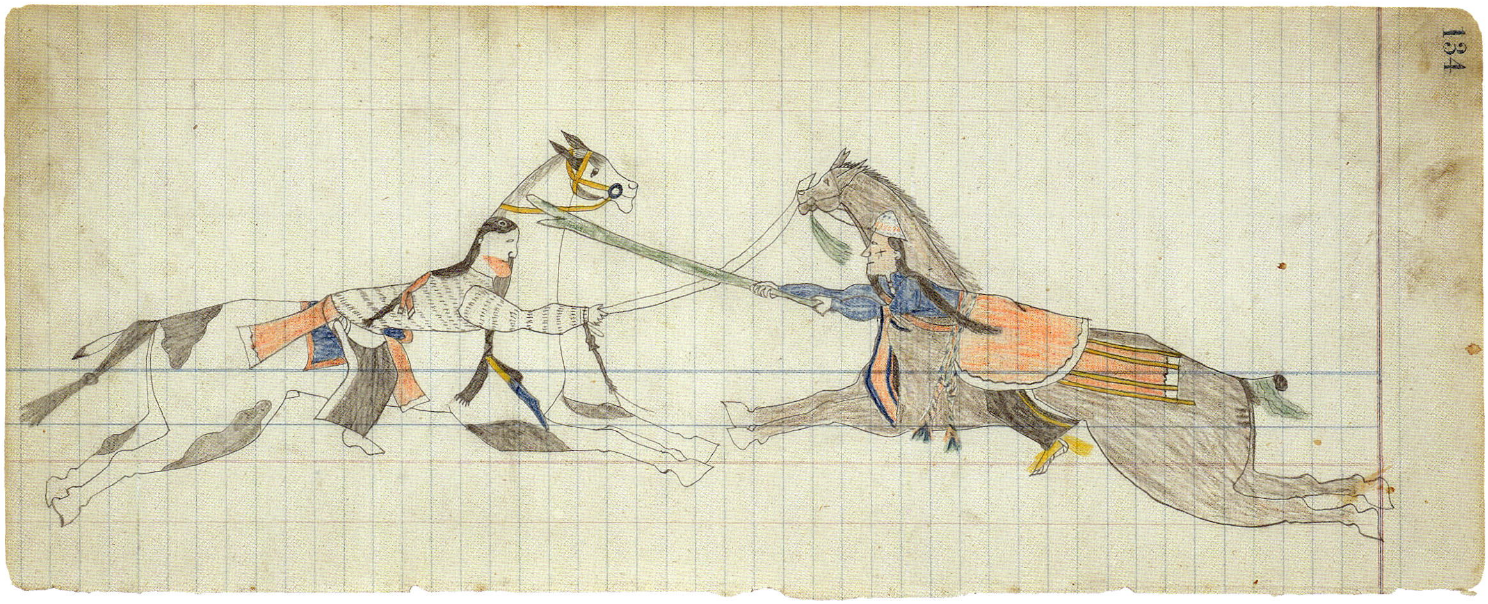

PLATE 25

Unknown artist, Southern Tsistsistas (Cheyenne), active late nineteenth century, ***Untitled [Two different Tsistsistas (Cheyenne) warrior societies in a sham battle prior to a medicine lodge ceremony],*** page 134 from the "Arrow's Elk Society Ledger," c. 1874–75, graphite and colored pencil on laid ledger paper, reverse: page 133 (no drawing), sheet: 6 ⅛ × 14 ⅞ in. (15.5 × 37.7 cm); 2007.65.28.

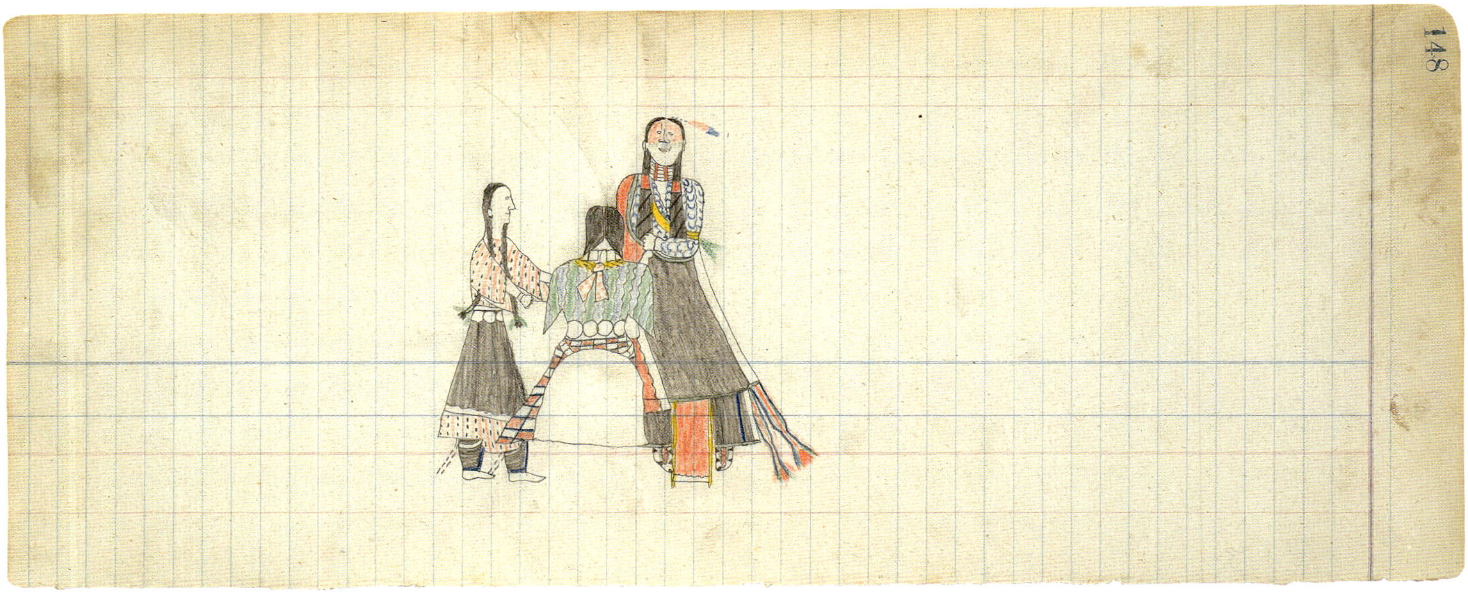

PLATE 26

Unknown artist, Southern Tsistsistas (Cheyenne), active late nineteenth century, ***Untitled [Three Tsistsistas (Cheyenne) people],*** page 148 from the "Arrow's Elk Society Ledger," c. 1874–75, graphite and colored pencil on laid ledger paper, reverse: page 147 (no drawing), sheet: 6 ⅛ × 14 ⅞ in. (15.5 × 37.7 cm); 2007.65.24.

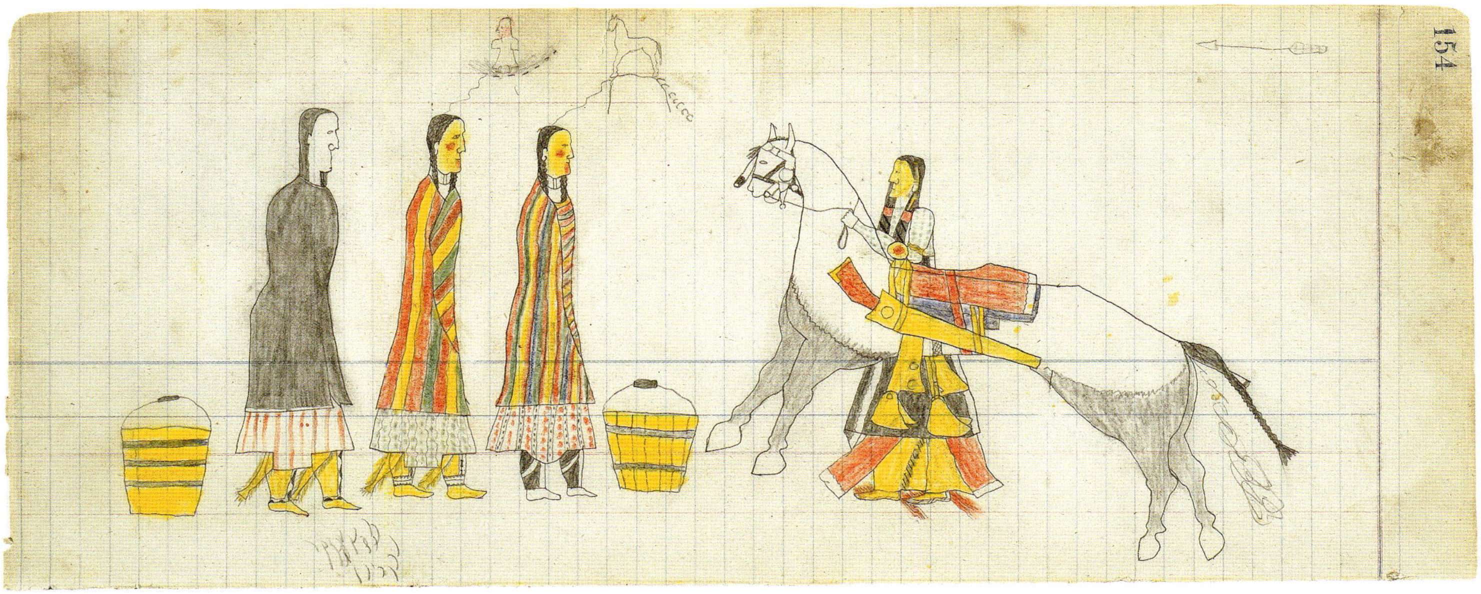

PLATE 27

Unknown artist, Southern Tsistsistas (Cheyenne), active late nineteenth century, ***Untitled [Three Tsistsistas (Cheyenne) women and a man and c horse],*** page 154 from the "Arrow's Elk Society Ledger," c. 1874–75, graphite and colored pencil on laid ledger paper, reverse: page 153 (no drawing), sheet: 6 × 14 ¾ in. (15.4 × 37.5 cm). Purchased with a gift from Mary Alice Kean Raynolds and David R. W. Raynolds, Class of 1949, in honor of Susan and James Wright, 16th President of Dartmouth College; 2008.71.3.

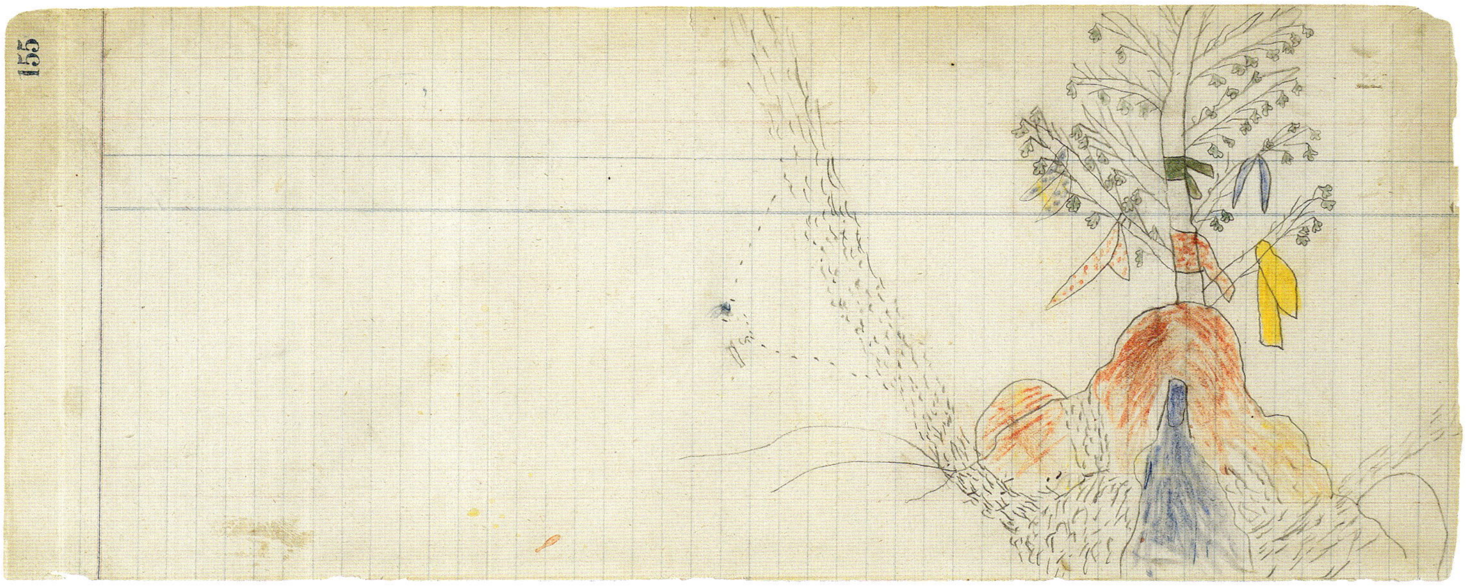

PLATE 28

Unknown artist, Southern Tsistsistas (Cheyenne), active late nineteenth century, ***Untitled [Sacred spring and tree],*** page 155 from the "Arrow's Elk Society Ledger," c. 1874–75, graphite and colored pencil on laid ledger paper, reverse: page 156 (2008.76.2), sheet: 6 × 14 ¾ in. (15.4 × 37.5 cm). Gift of Mark Lansburgh, Class of 1949, in honor of Brian P. Kennedy, Director, Hood Museum of Art, 2005–10; 2008.76.1.

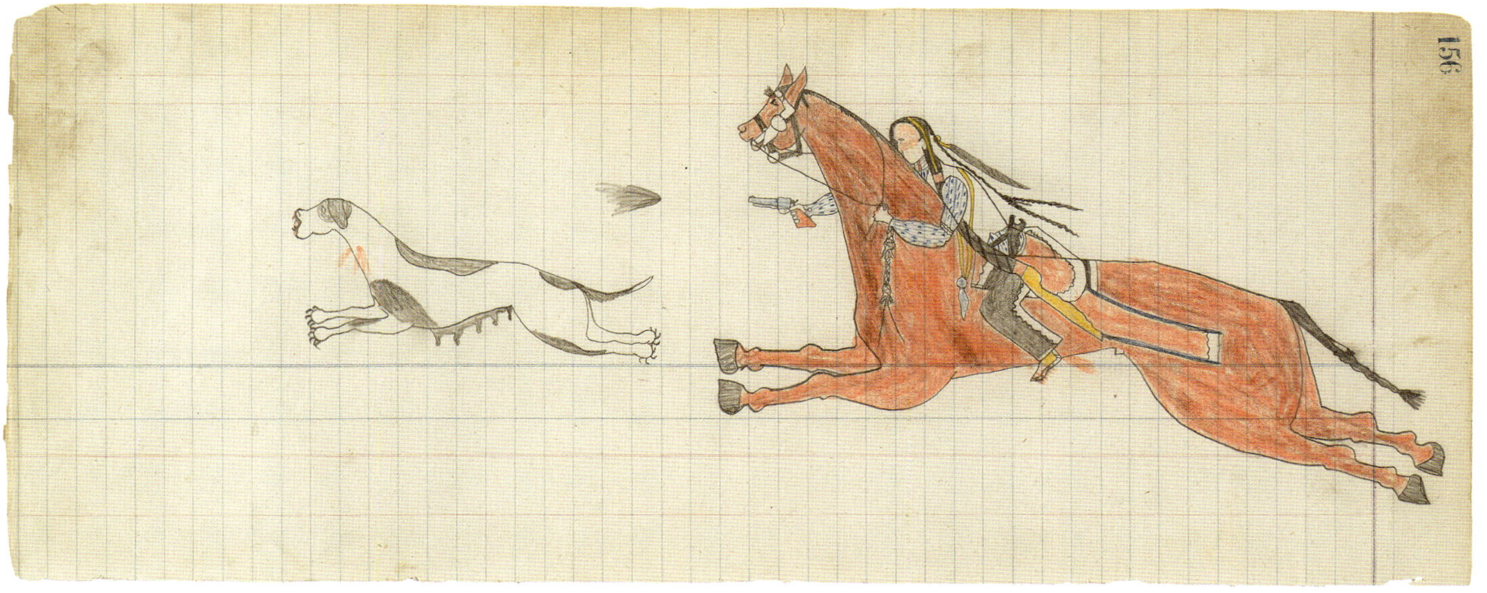

PLATE 29

Unknown artist, Southern Tsistsistas (Cheyenne), active late nineteenth century, ***Untitled [Tsistsistas (Cheyenne) warrior shooting a female dog],*** page 156 from the "Arrow's Elk Society Ledger," c. 1874–75, graphite and color pencil on laid ledger paper, reverse: page 155 (2008.76.1), sheet: 6 × 14 ¾ in. (15.4 × 37.5 cm). Gift of Mark Lansburgh, Class of 1949, in honor of Brian P. Kennedy, Director, Hood Museum of Art, 2005–10; 2008.76.2.

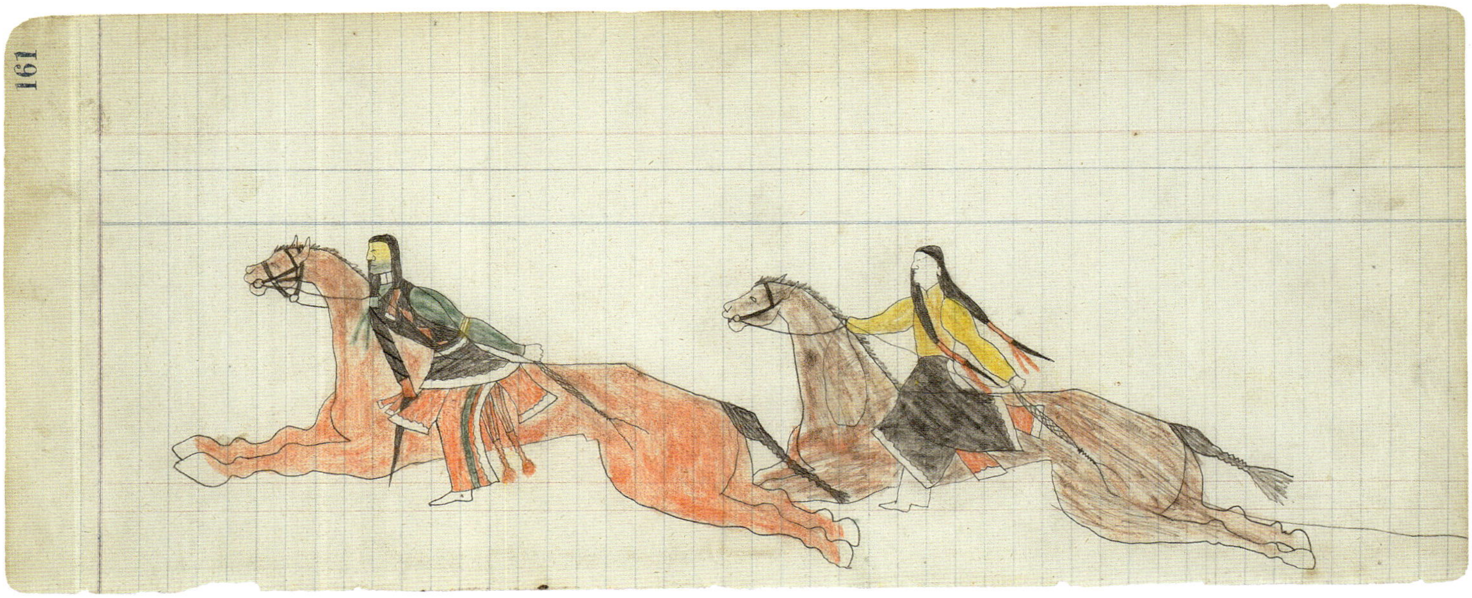

PLATE 30

Unknown artist, Southern Tsistsistas (Cheyenne), active late nineteenth century, ***Untitled [Tsistsistas (Cheyenne) warriors on horseback],*** page 161 from the "Arrow's Elk Society Ledger," c. 1874–75, graphite and colored pencil on laid ledger paper, reverse: page 162 (2008.70.4), sheet: 6 ⅛ × 14 ⅞ in. (15.5 × 37.7 cm). Purchased through the Mrs. Harvey P. Hood W'18 Fund; 2008.70.3.

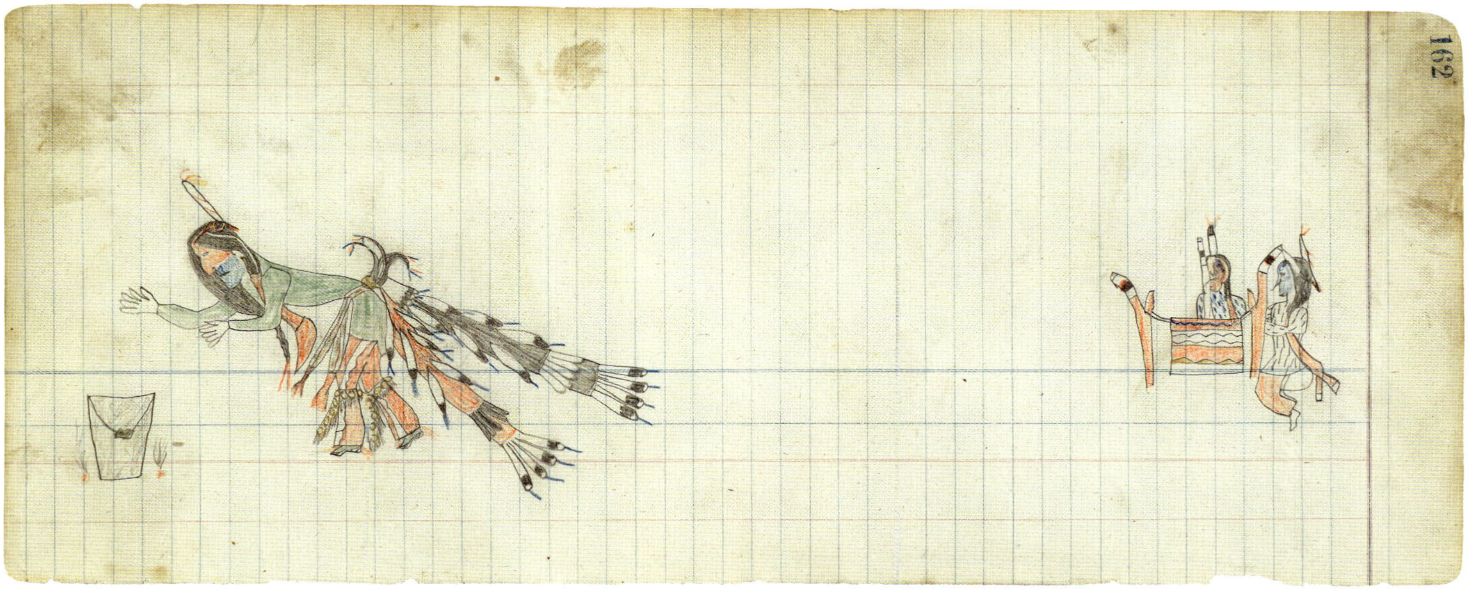

PLATE 31

Unknown artist, Southern Tsistsistas (Cheyenne), active late nineteenth century, ***Untitled [Tsistsistas (Cheyenne) dancer and drummers],*** page 162 from the "Arrow's Elk Society Ledger," c. 1874–75, graphite and colored pencil on laid ledger paper, reverse: page 161 (2008.70.3), sheet: 6 ⅛ × 14 ⅞ in. (15.5 × 37.7 cm). Purchased through the Mrs. Harvey P. Hood W'18 Fund; 2008.70.4.

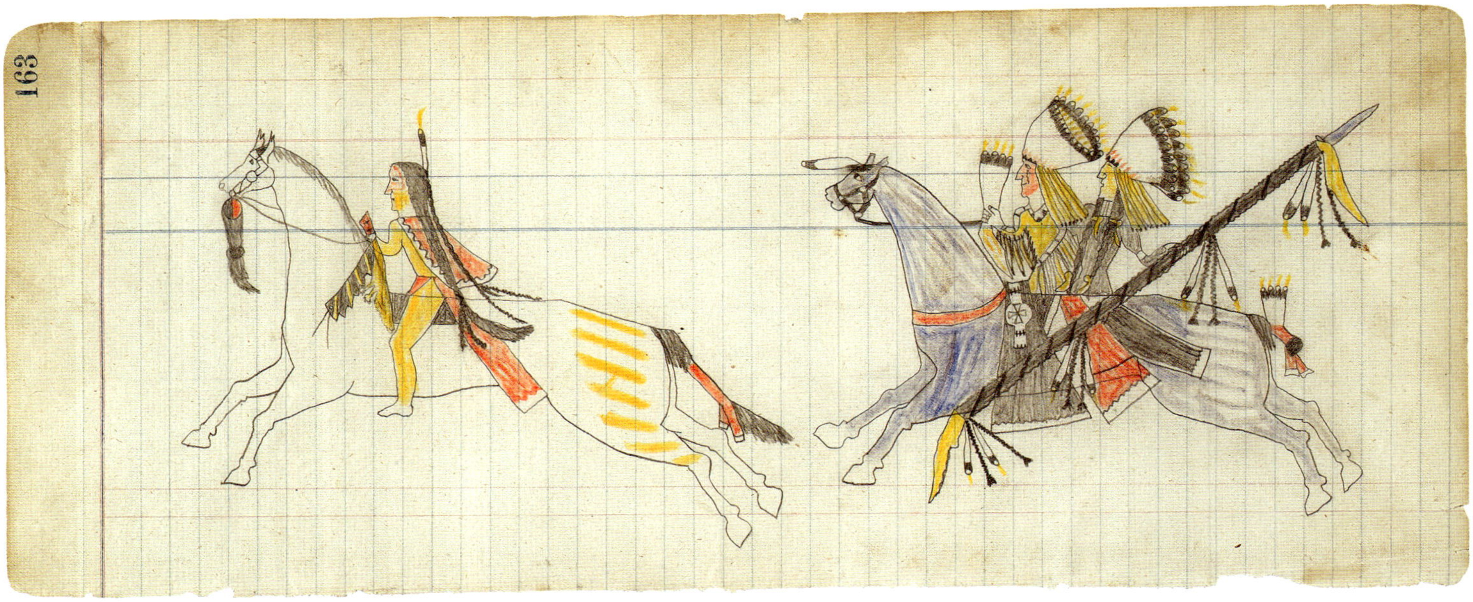

PLATE 32

Unknown artist, Southern Tsistsistas (Cheyenne), active late nineteenth century, ***Untitled [Tsistsistas (Cheyenne) Elk Society warriors],*** page 163 from the "Arrow's Elk Society Ledger," c. 1874–75, graphite and colored pencil on laid ledger paper, reverse: page 164 (2008.71.2), sheet: 6 ⅛ × 14 ⅞ in. (15.5 × 37.7 cm). Purchased through the Mrs. Harvey P. Hood W'18 Fund; 2008.71.1.

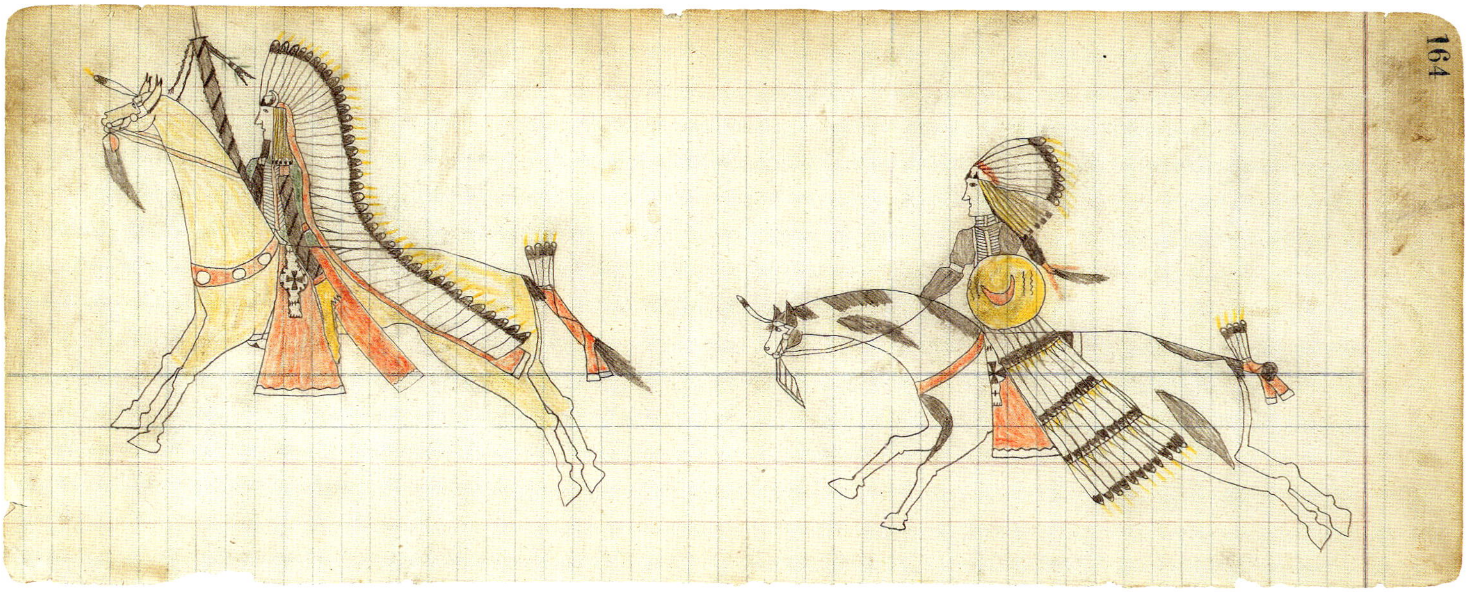

PLATE 33

Unknown artist, Southern Tsistsistas (Cheyenne), active late nineteenth century, ***Untitled [Tsistsistas (Cheyenne) Elk Society warriors],*** page 164 from the "Arrow's Elk Society Ledger," c. 1874–75, graphite and colored pencil on laid ledger paper, reverse: page 163 (2008.71.1), sheet: 6 ⅛ × 14 ⅞ in. (15.5 × 37.7 cm). Purchased through the Mrs. Harvey P. Hood W'18 Fund; 2008.71.2.

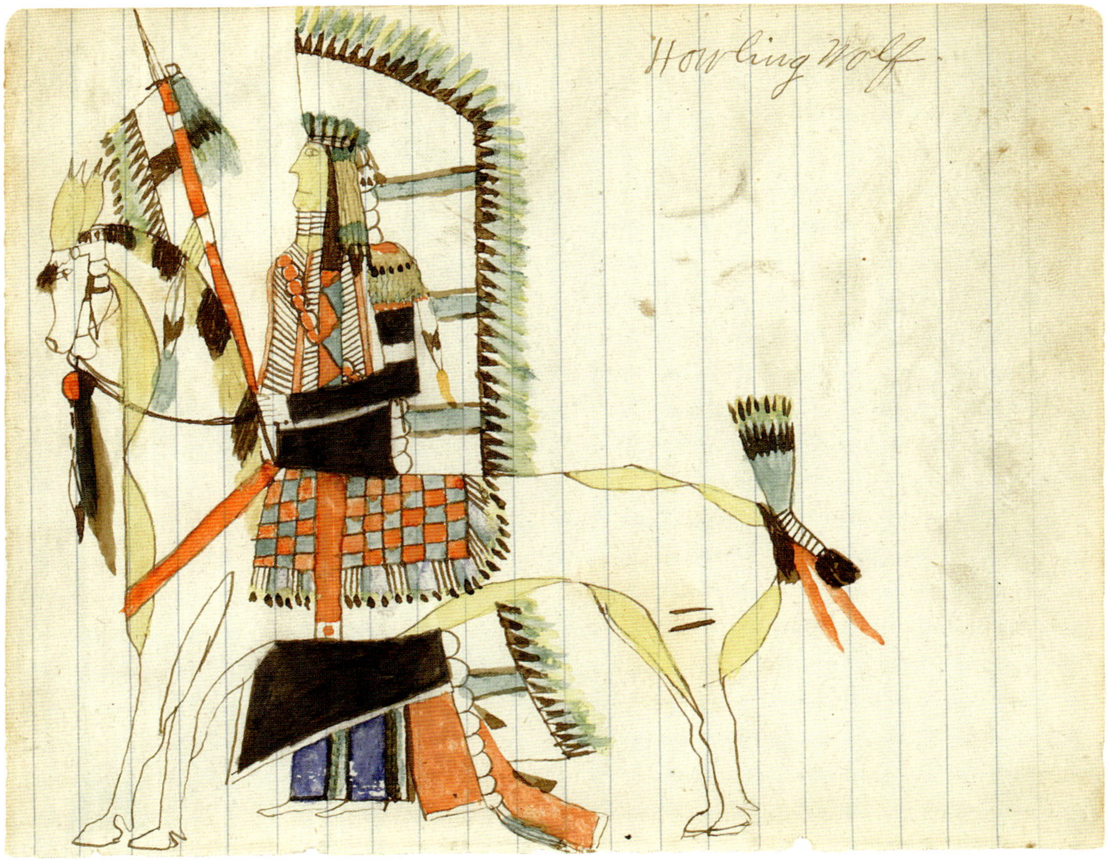

PLATE 34

Howling Wolf (Ho-na-nist-to), Southern Tsistsistas (Cheyenne), 1849–1927, ***Untitled [Howling Wolf with his war horse],*** from the "Robert Allen Guthrie Notebook," c. 1874–75, ink, colored pencil, watercolor, and graphite on wove blue-lined notebook paper, reverse: (no drawing), sheet: 5 ¾ × 7 ¼ in. (14.5 × 18.2 cm). Purchased through the Julia L. Whittier Fund; 2006.51.

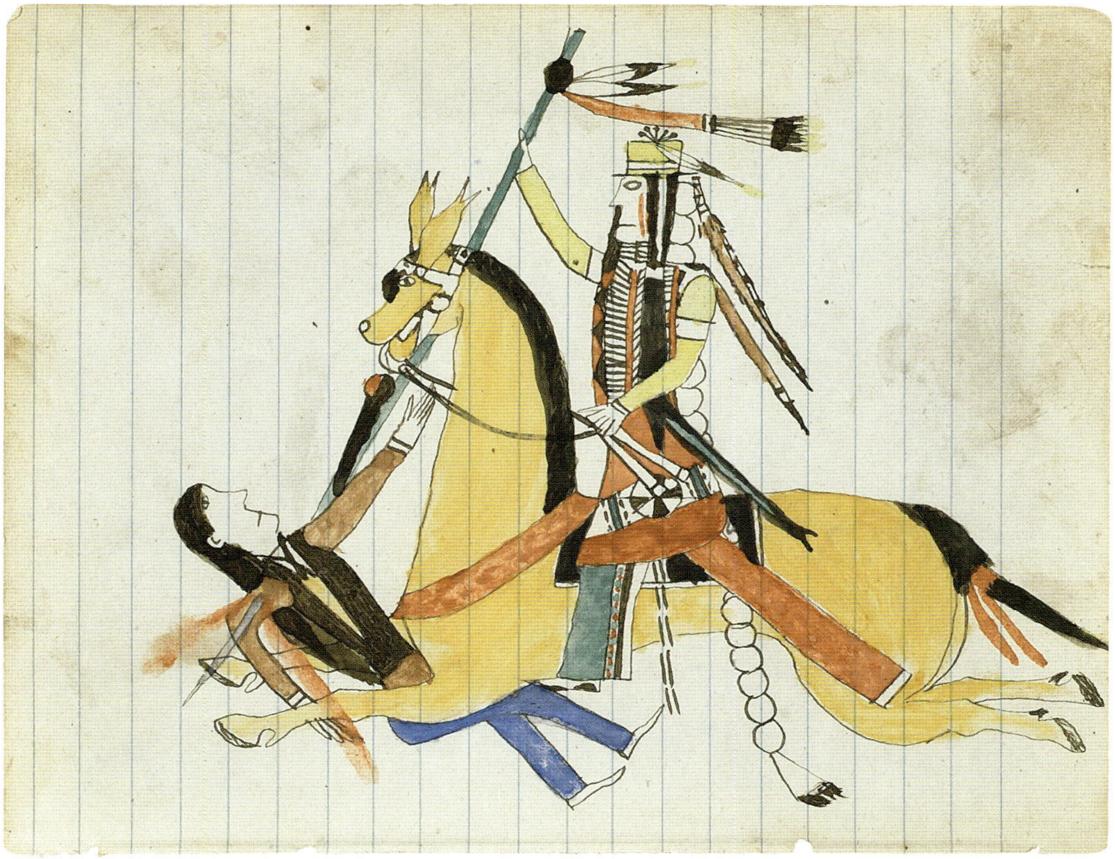

PLATE 35

Howl ng Wolf (Ho-na-nist-to), Southern Tsistsistas (Cheyenne), 1849–1927, ***Untitled [Warrior in battle],*** from the "Robert Allen Guthrie Notebook," c. 1874–75, ink and transparent and opaque watercolor on wove blue-lined notebook paper, reverse: (no d-awing), sheet: 5 ¾ × 7 ¼ in. (14.5 × 18.2 cm); 2007.65.8.

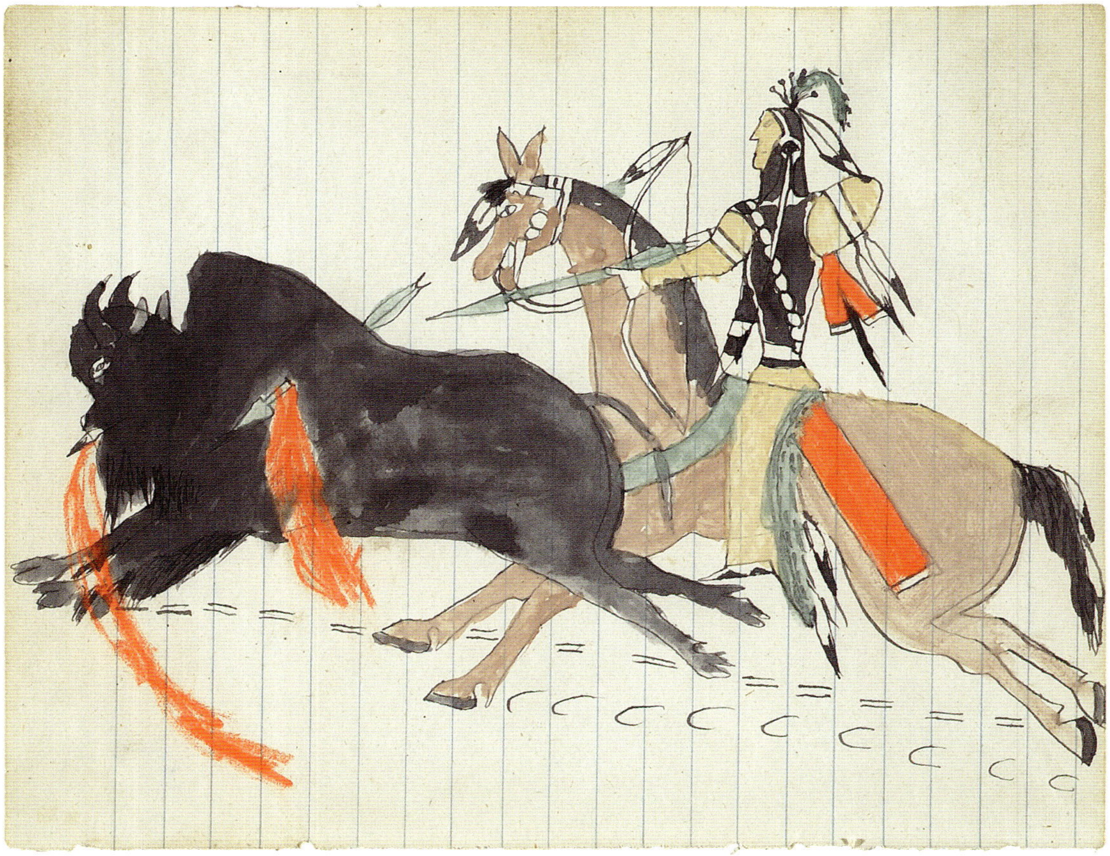

PLATE 36

Howling Wolf (Ho-na-nist-to), Southern Tsistsistas (Cheyenne), 1849–1927, ***Untitled [Warrior on a buffalo hunt],*** from the "Robert Allen Guthrie Notebook," c. 1874–75, watercolor, ink, and crayon on wove blue-lined notebook paper, reverse: (no drawing), sheet: 5 ¾ × 7 ¼ in. (14.5 × 18.2 cm); 2007.65.9.

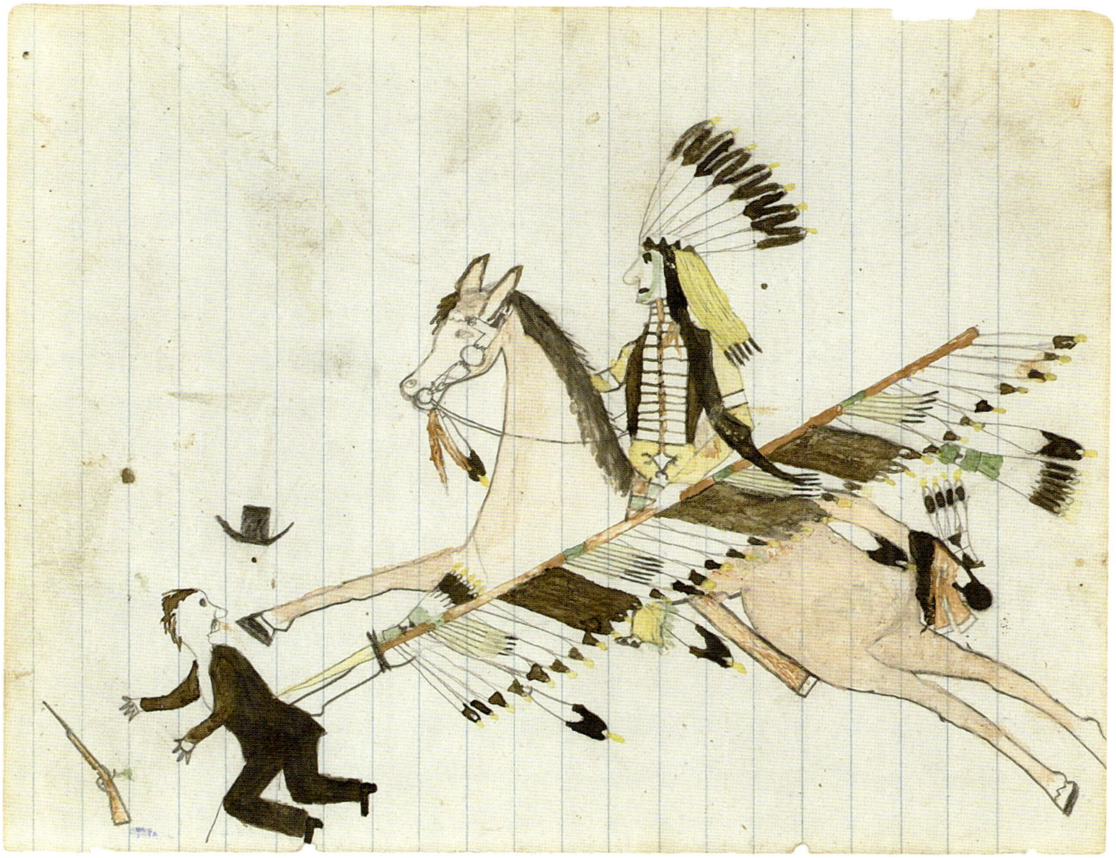

PLATE 37

Unknown artist, Tsistsistas (Cheyenne), active late nineteenth century ***Untitled [A Tsistsistas (Cheyenne) Bowstring Society warrior counts coup on a non-Native enemy],*** from the "Robert Allen Guthrie Notebook," c. 1874–75, graphite and transparent and opaque watercolor on wove blue-lined notebook paper, reverse: (no drawing), sheet: 5 ¾ × 7 ¼ in. (14.5 × 18.2 cm); 2007.65.10.

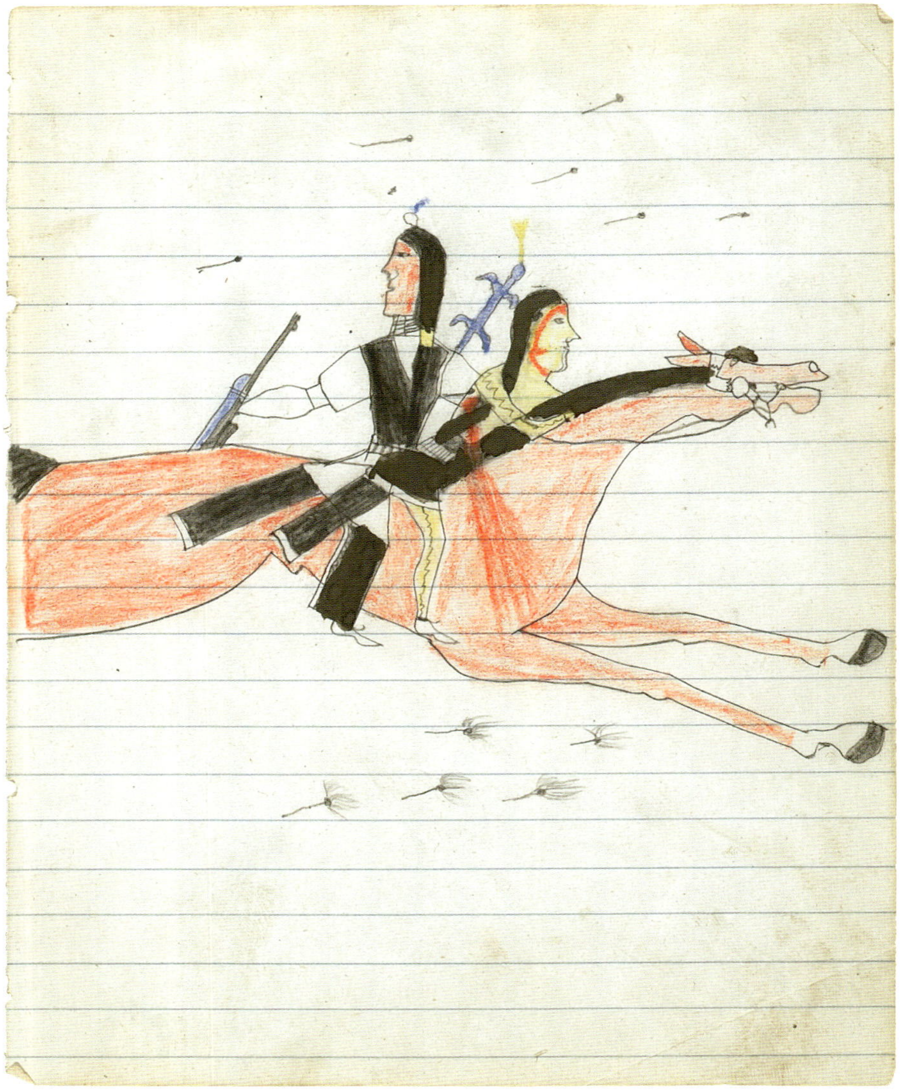

PLATE 38

Unknown artist, Tsistsistas (Cheyenne), active late nineteenth century, ***Untitled [Tsistsistas (Cheyenne) warrior rescuing a wounded comrade],*** from the "Robert Allen Guthrie Notebook," c. 1874–75, graphite, colored pencil, watercolor on wove blue-lined notebook paper, reverse: (no drawing), sheet: 7 ¼ × 5 ¾ in. (18.2 × 14.5 cm); 2007.65.89.

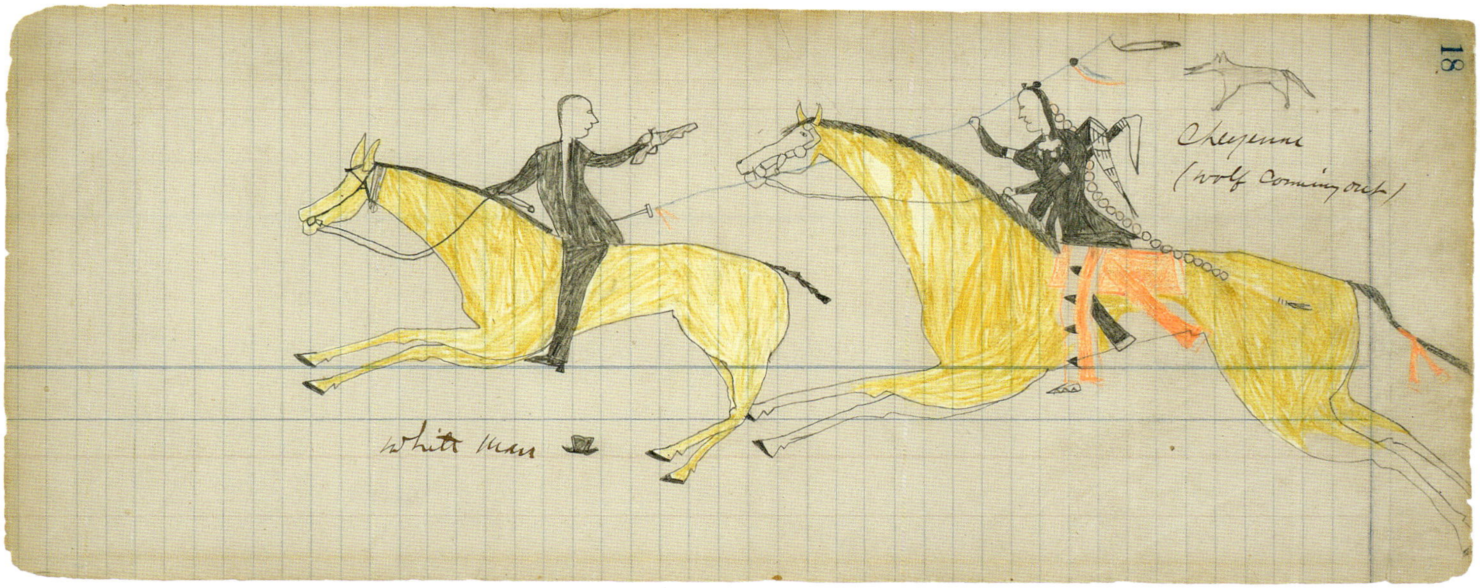

PLATE 43

Unknown artist, Southern Tsistsistas (Cheyenne) and/or Southern Inunaina (Arapaho), active late nineteenth century, ***Untitled [A Tsistsistas (Cheyenne) or Inunaina (Arapaho) warrior counts coup on a non-Native enemy],*** page 18 from the "Carl S. Dentzel Ledger," c. 1875–78, graphite and colored pencil on laid ledger paper, reverse: page 17 (no drawing), sheet: 6 × 14 7/8 in. (15.3 × 37.7 cm); 2007.65.12.

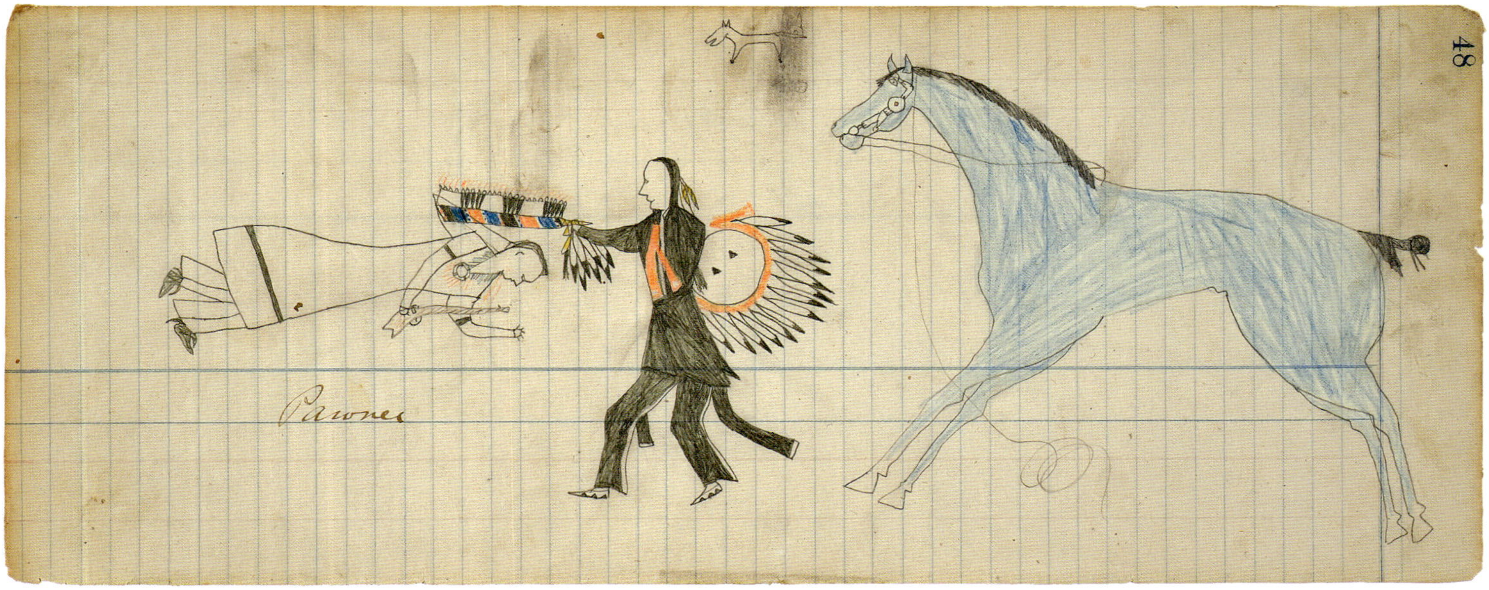

PLATE 44

Unknown artist, Southern Tsistsistas (Cheyenne) and/or Southern Inunaina (Arapaho), active late nineteenth century, ***Untitled [Inunaina (Arapaho) warrior counts coup on an enemy, possibly a Chaticks Si Chaticks (Pawnee) warrior],*** page 48 from the "Carl S. Dentzel Ledger," c. 1875–78, graphite and colored pencil on laid ledger paper, reverse: page 47 (no drawing), sheet: 6 × 14 ⅞ in. (15.3 × 37.7 cm); 2007.65.13.

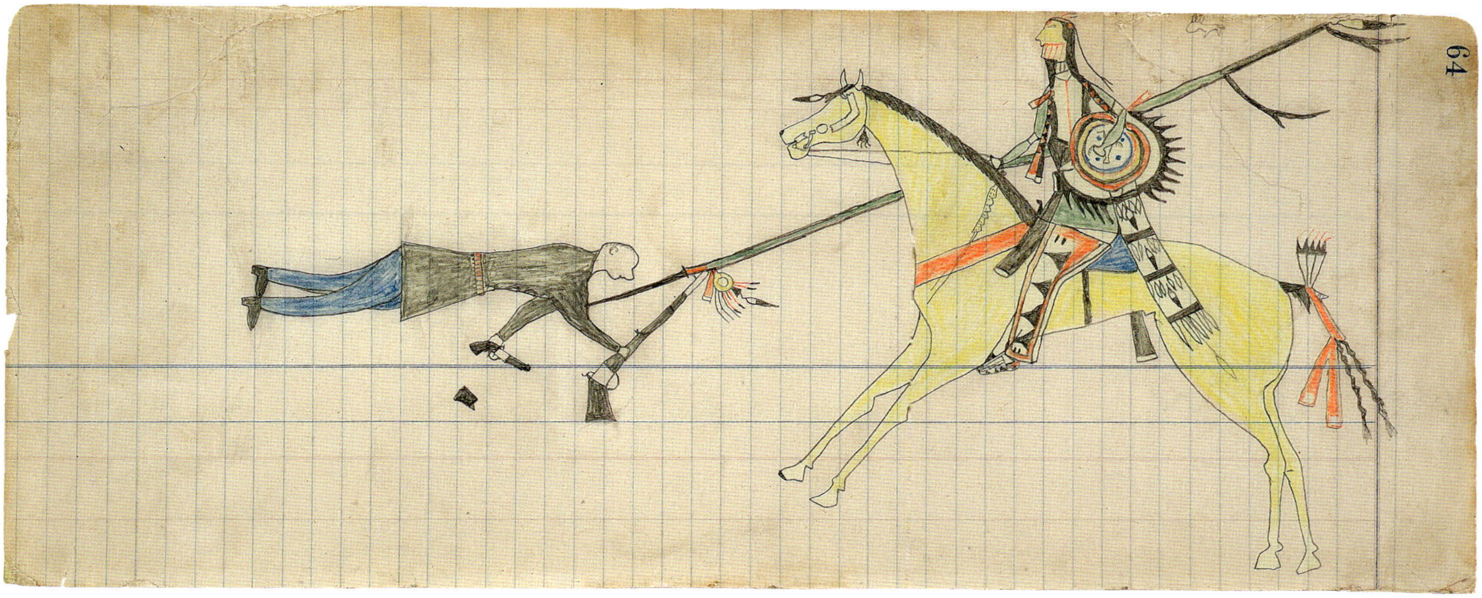

PLATE 45

Unknown artist, Southern Tsistsistas (Cheyenne) and/or Southern Inunaina (Arapaho), active late nineteenth century, ***Untitled [A Tsistsistas (Cheyenne) warrior counts coup on a soldier],*** page 64 from the "Carl S. Dentzel Ledger," c. 1875–78, graphite and colored pencil on laid ledger paper, reverse: page 63 (no drawing), sheet: 6 1/8 × 14 7/8 in. (15.4 × 37.6 cm); 2007.65.11.

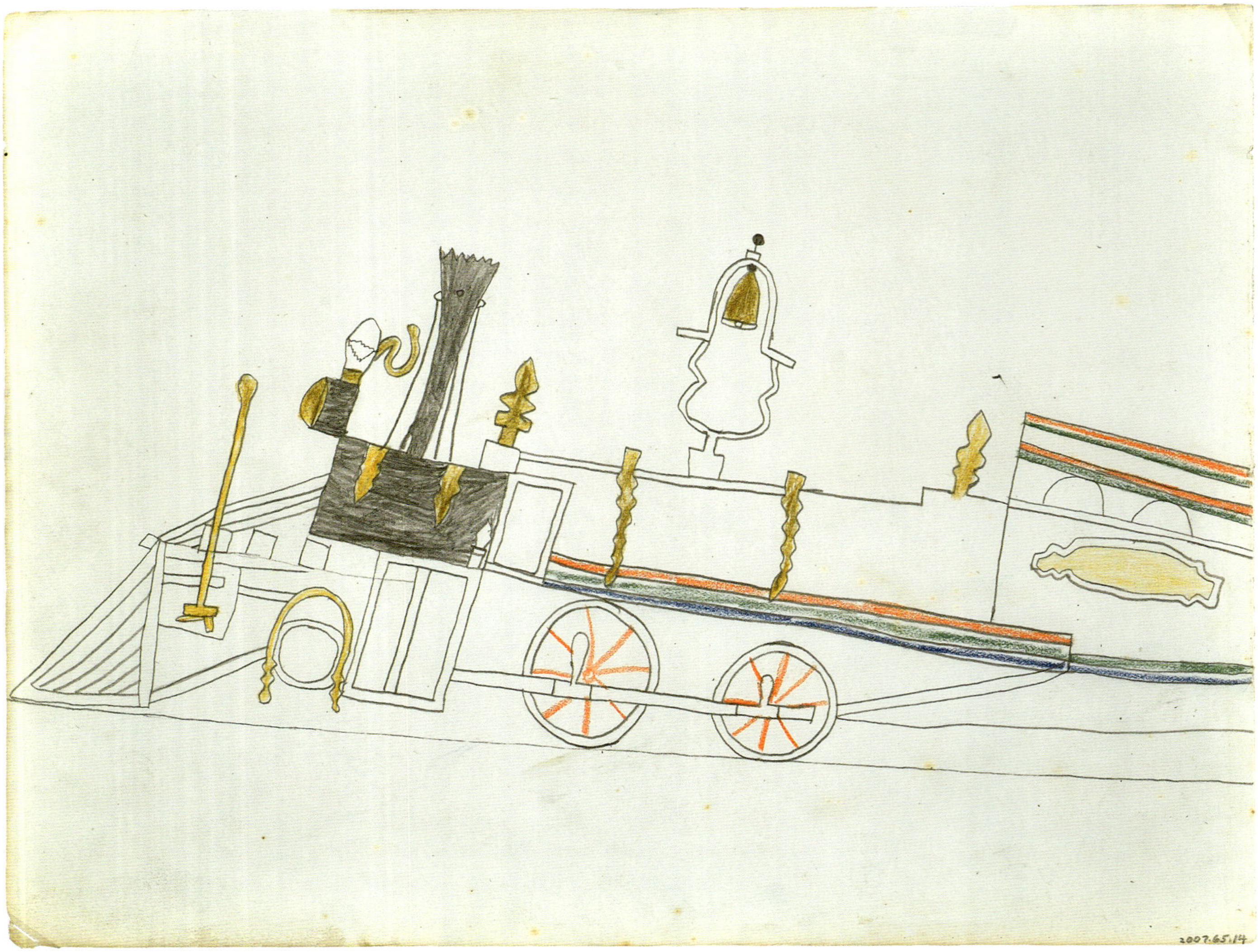

PLATE 46

Ohettoint, Kiowa, 1852–1934, ***Untitled [Steam locomotive],*** from an Ohettoint sketchbook, mid-1875–mid-1878, graphite and colored pencil on wove sketchbook paper, reverse: (2007.65.15), sheet: 8 ¾ × 11 ¼ in. (22.2 × 28.5 cm); 2007.65.14.

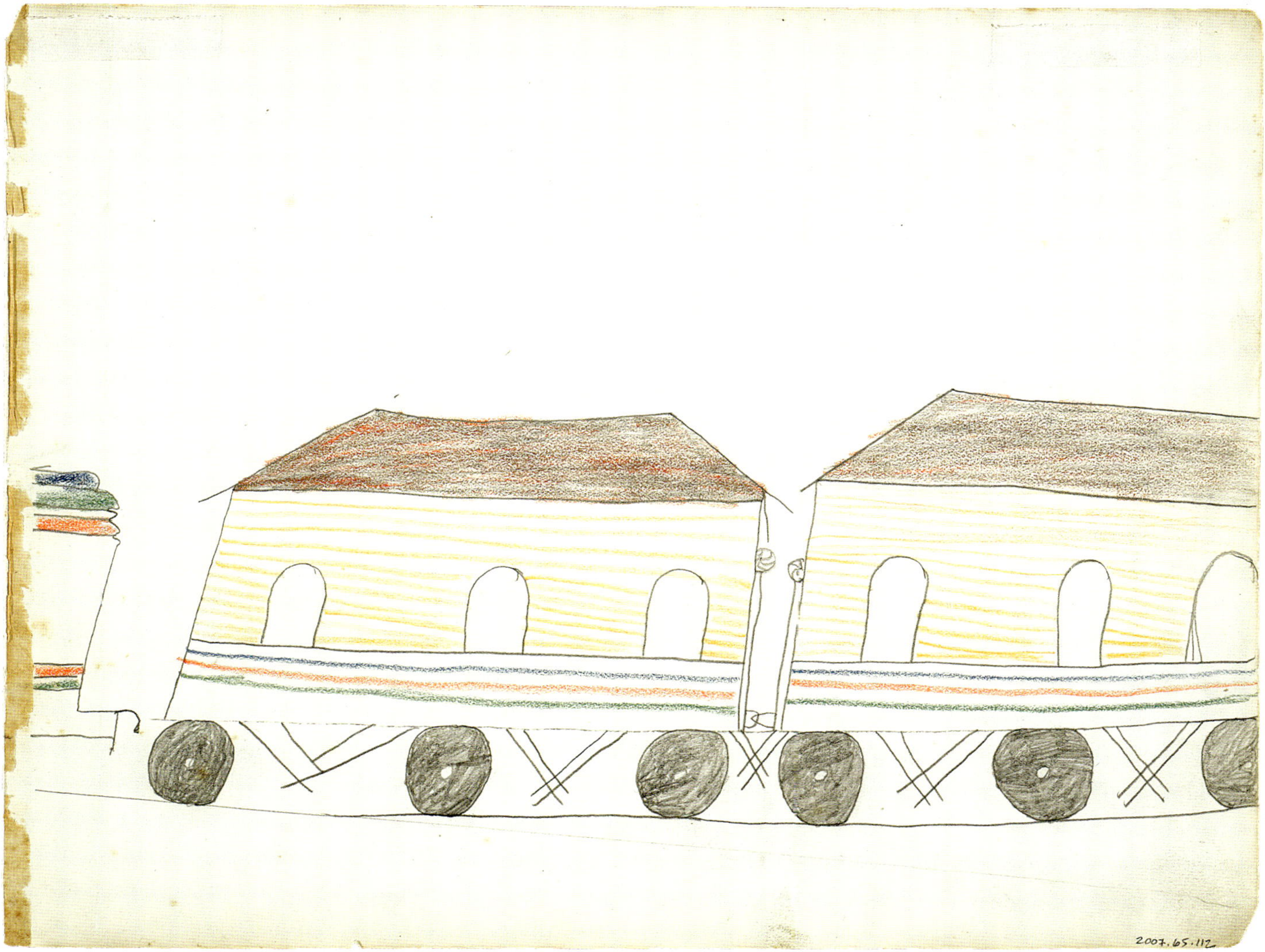

PLATE 47

Ohettoint, Kiowa, 1852–1934, ***Untitled [Train cars],*** from an Chettoint sketchbook, mid-1875–mid-1878, graphite and colored pencil on wove sketchbook paper; reverse: (2007.65.19); sheet: 8 ¾ × 11 ¼ in. (22.2 × 28.5 cm); 2007.65.112.

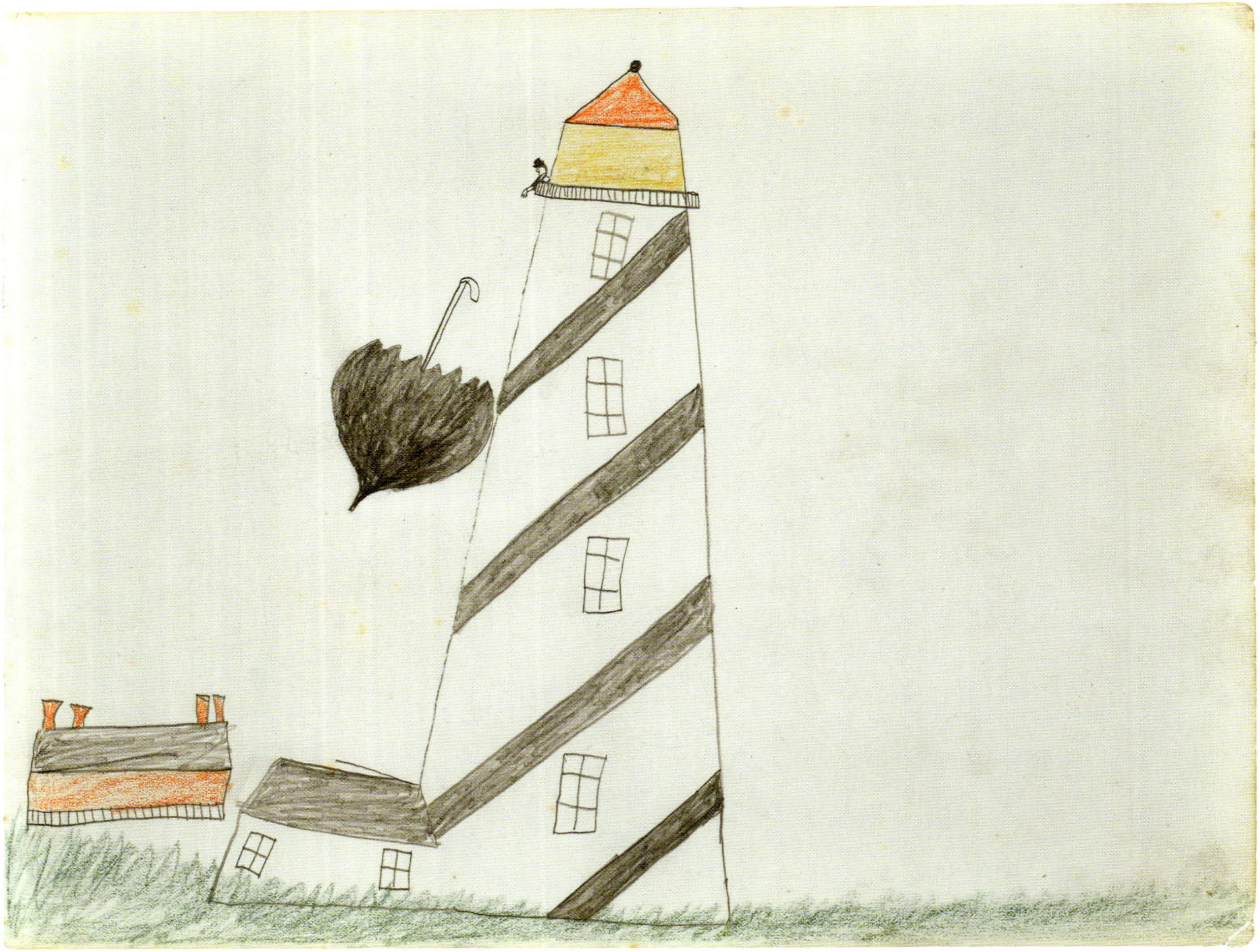

PLATE 48

Ohettoint, Kiowa, 1852–1934, ***Untitled [A man dropping an open umbrella from the top of a lighthouse],*** from an Ohettoint sketchbook, mid-1875–mid-1878, graphite and colored pencil on wove sketchbook paper, reverse: (2007.65.14), sheet: 8 ¾ × 11 ¼ in. (22.2 × 28.5 cm); 2007.65.15.

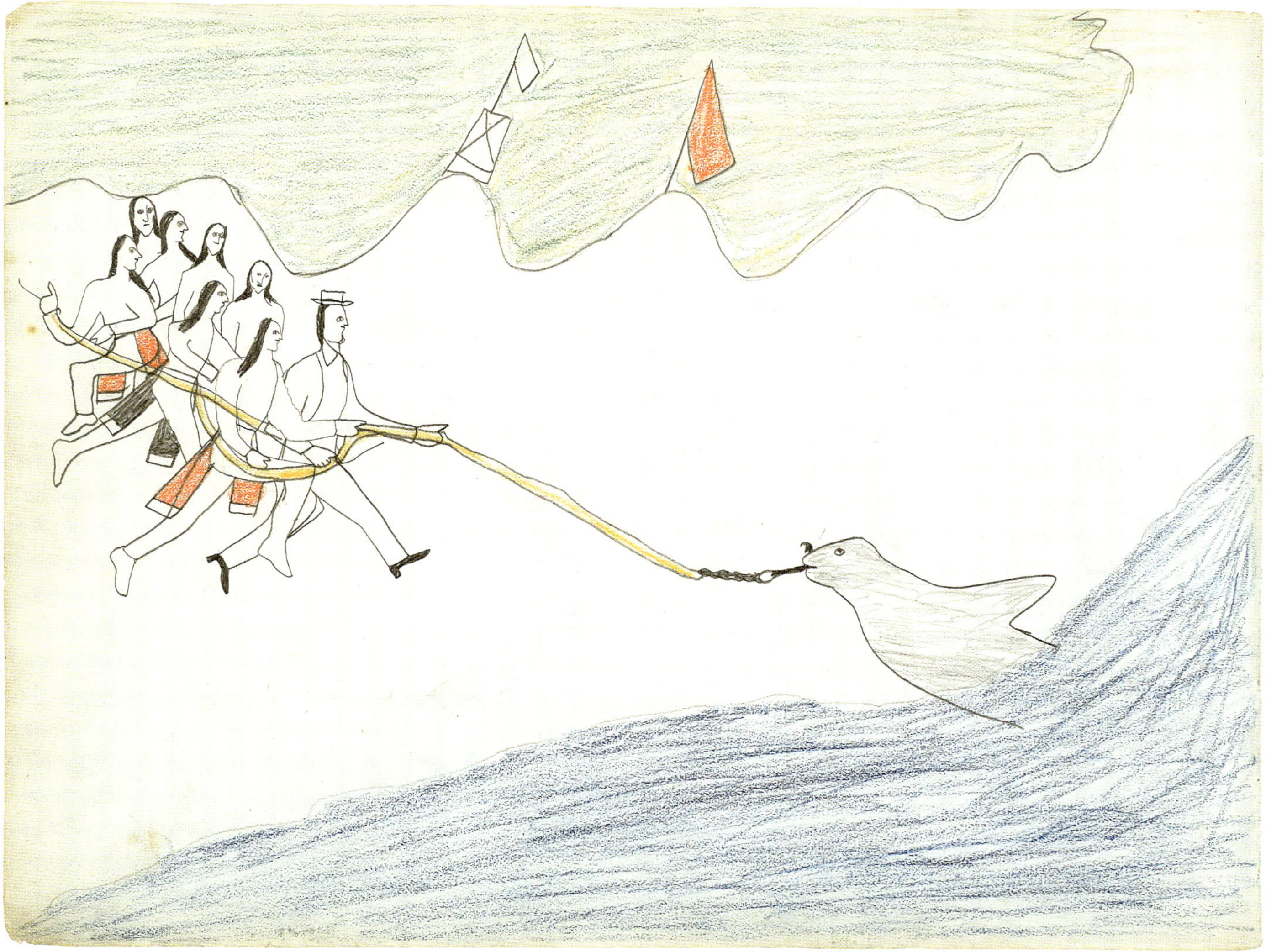

PLATE 49

Ohettoint, Kiowa, 1852–1934, ***Untitled [Fort Marion prisoners and a non-Native man catch a shark],*** from an Ohettoint sketchbook, mid-1875–mid-1878, graphite and colored pencil on wove sketchbook paper, reverse: (2007.65.17), sheet: 8 ¾ × 11 ¼ in. (22.2 × 28.5 cm); 2007.65.16.

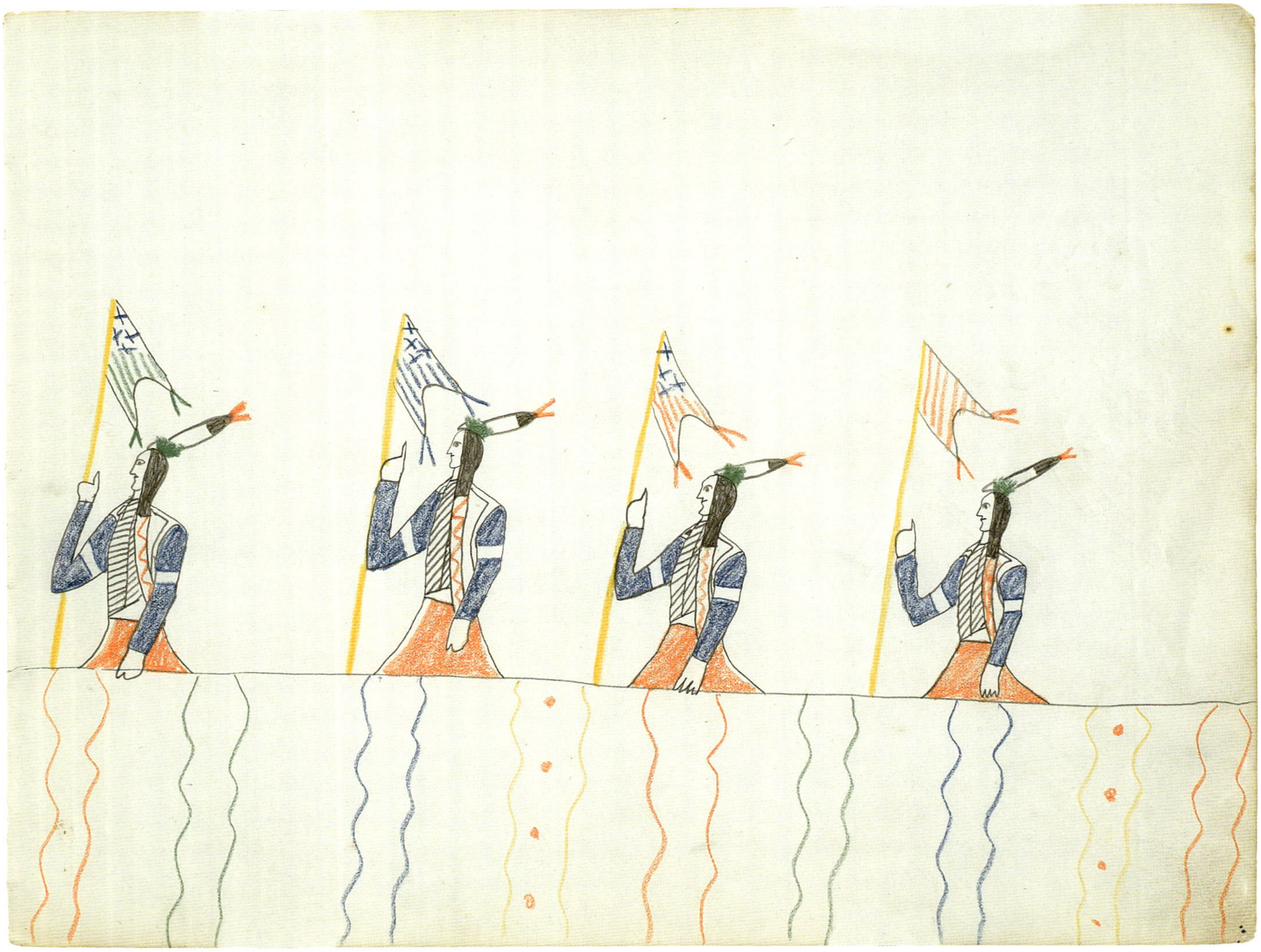

PLATE 50

Ohettoint, Kiowa, 1852–1934, ***Untitled [Kiowa warriors in procession],*** from an Ohettoint sketchbook, mid-1875–mid-1878, graphite and colored pencil on wove sketchbook paper, reverse: (2007.65.16), sheet: 8 ¾ × 11 ¼ in. (22.2 × 28.5 cm); 2007.65.17.

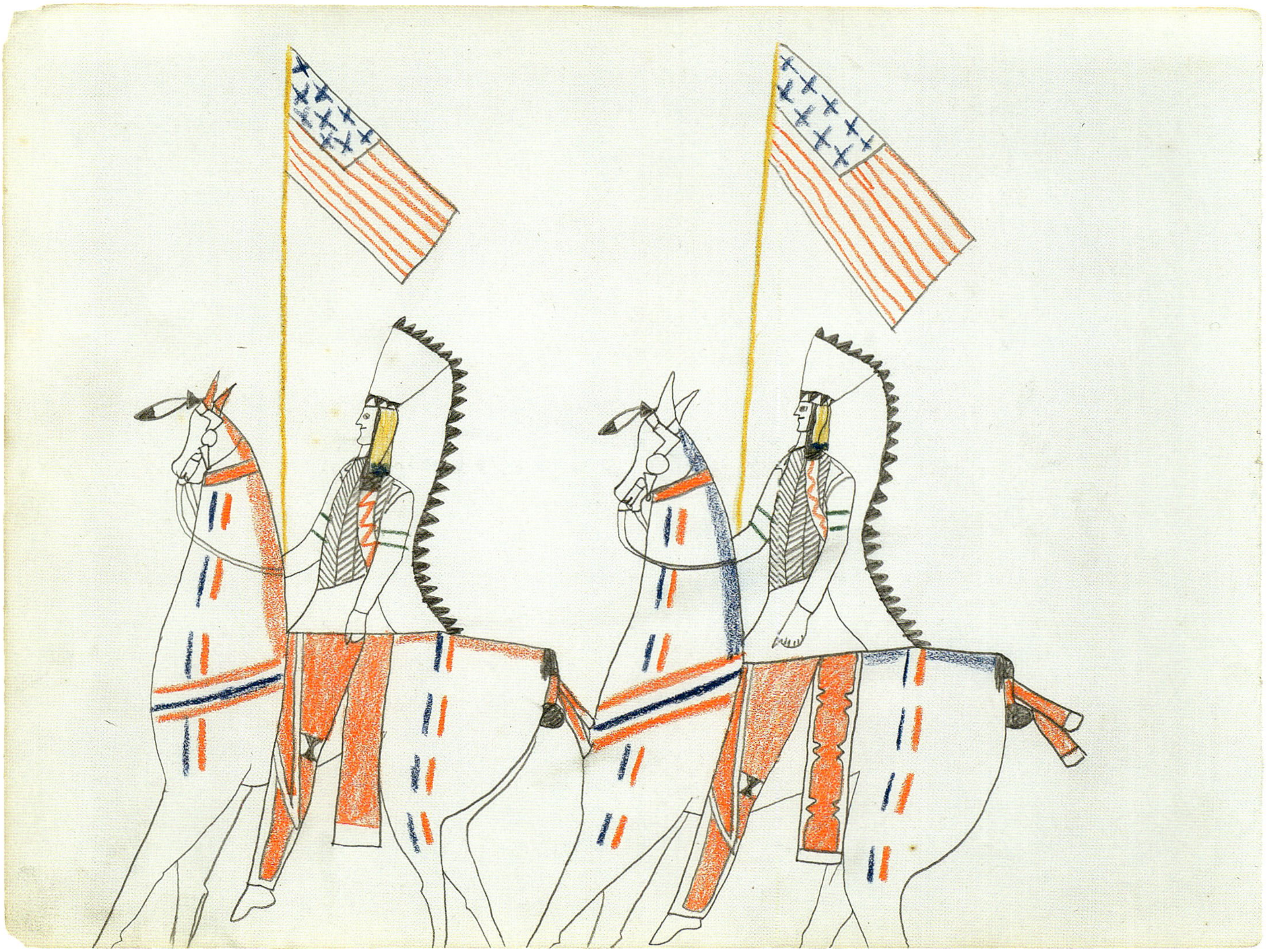

PLATE 51

Ohettoint, Kiowa, 1852–1934, ***Untitled [Kiowa warriors mounted procession],*** from an Ohettoint sketchbook, mid-1875–mid-1878, graphite and colored pencil on wove sketchbook paper, reverse: (2007.65.111), sheet: 8 ¾ × 11 ¼ in. (22.1 × 28.5 cm); 2007.65.18.

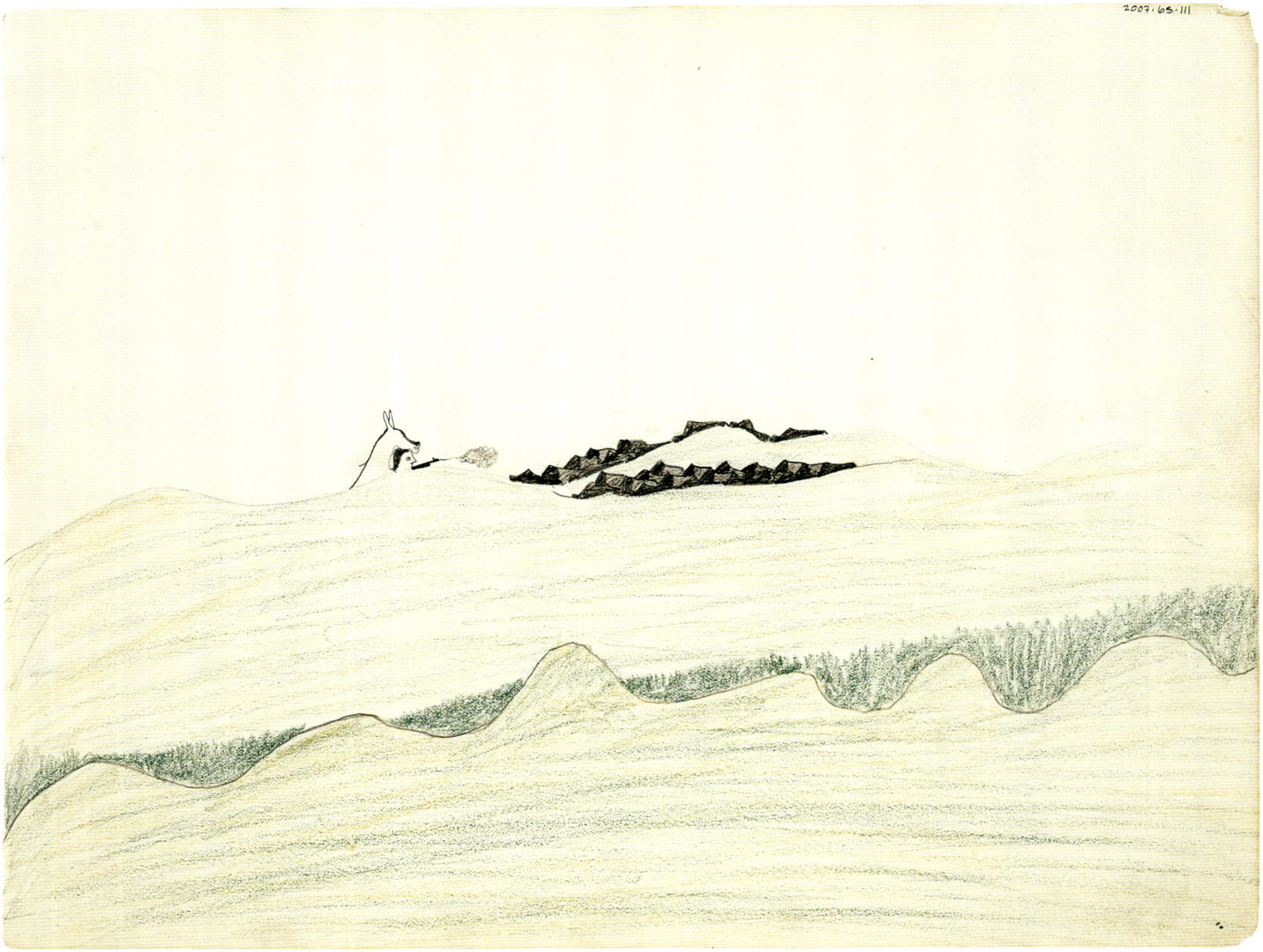

PLATE 52

Ohettoint, Kiowa, 1852–1934, ***Untitled [A warrior shooting a gun]***, from an Ohettoint sketchbook, mid-1875–mid-1878, graphite and color pencil on wove sketchbook paper, reverse: (2007.65.18), sheet: 8 ¾ × 11 ¼ in. (22.1 × 28.5 cm); 2007.65.111.

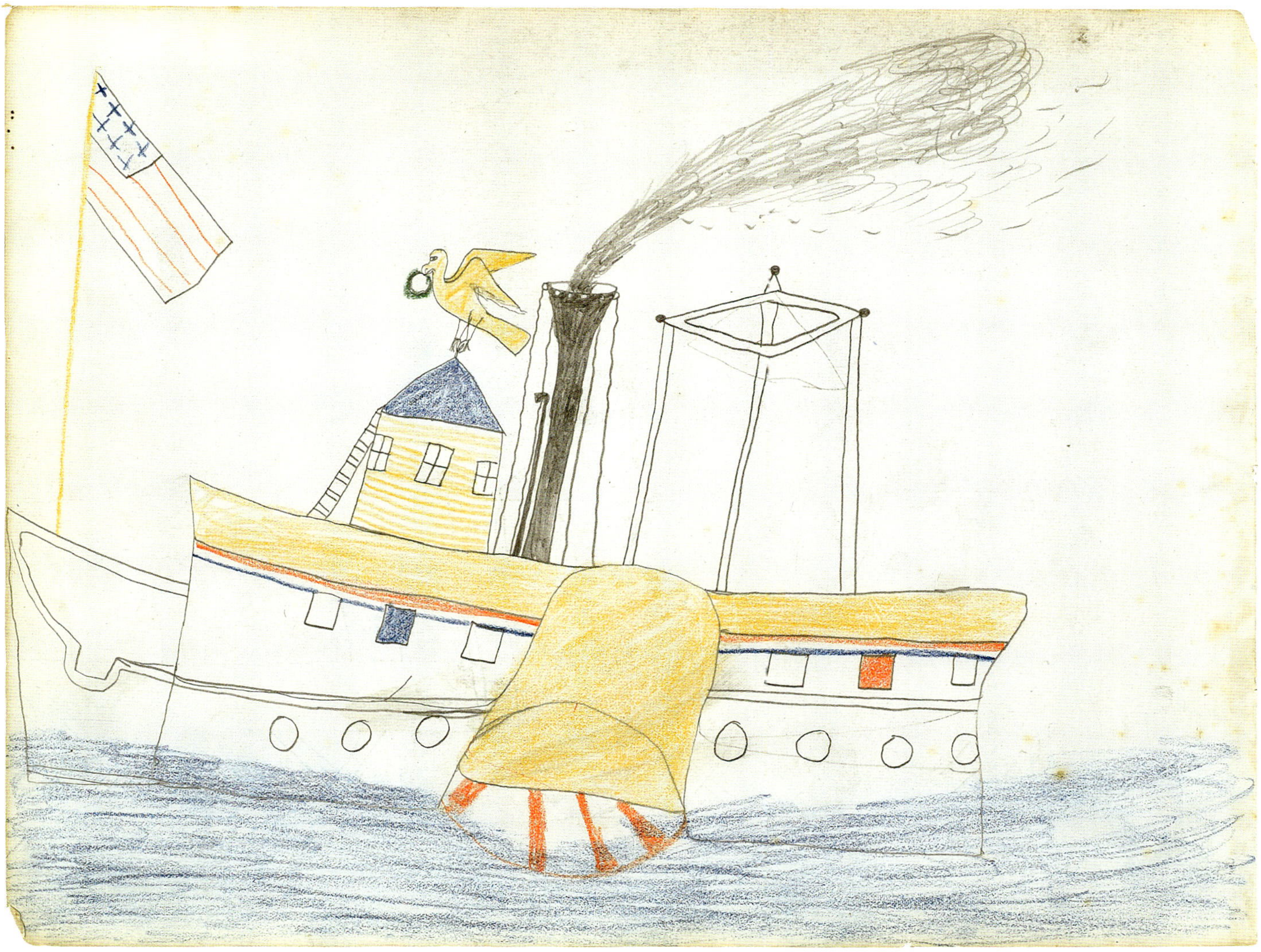

PLATE 53

Ohettoint, Kiowa, 1852–1934, ***Untitled [Paddlewheel steamboat],*** from an Ohettoint sketchbook, mid-1875–mid-1878, graphite and colored pencil on wove sketchbook paper, reverse: (2007.65.112), sheet: 8 ¾ × 11 ¼ in. (22.2 × 28.5 cm); 2007.65.19.

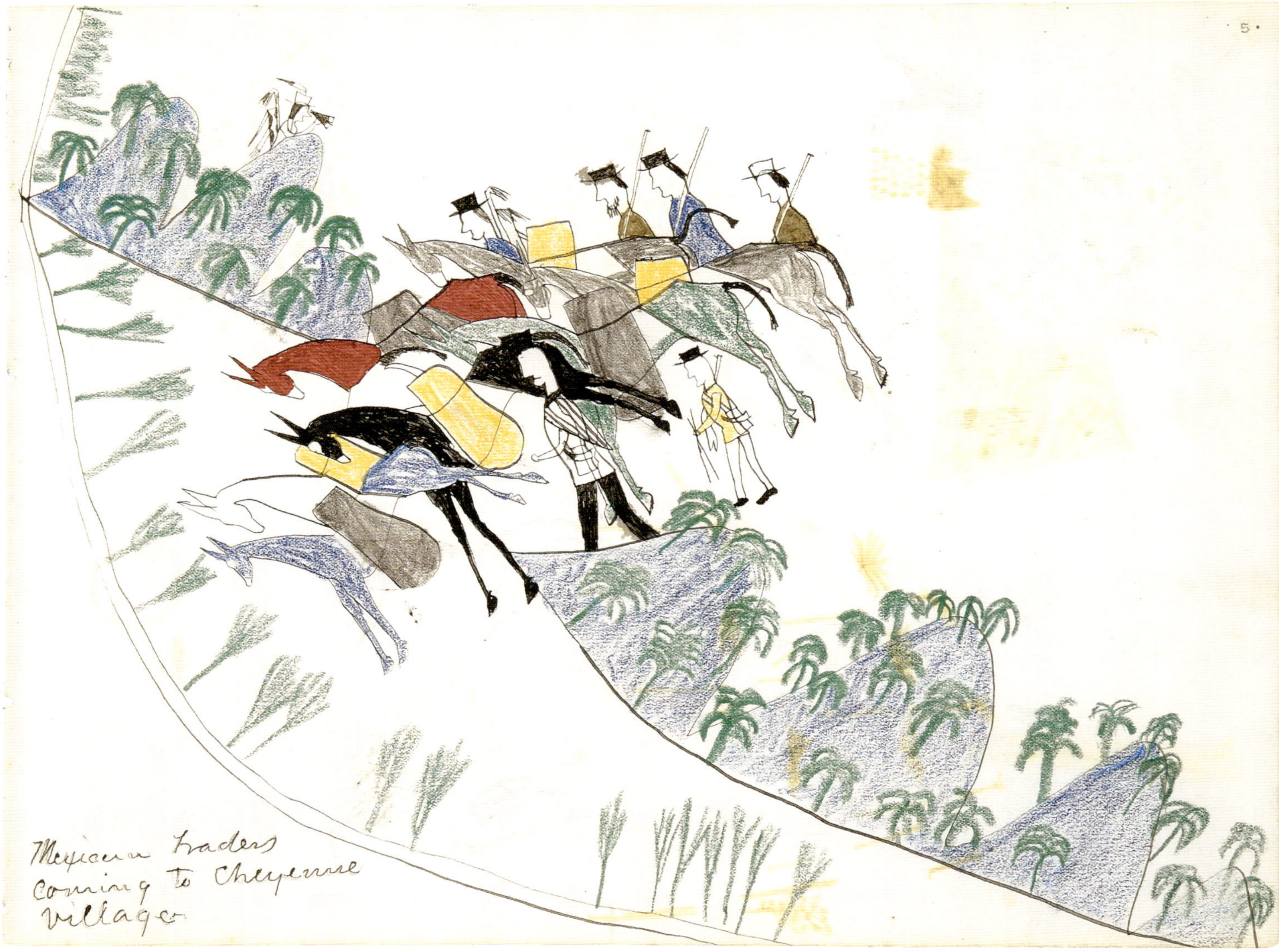

PLATE 54

Chief Killer (Noh-hu-nah-wih), Southern Tsistsistas (Cheyenne), 1849–1922, ***Untitled ["Mexican traders Coming To Cheyenne village"]***, page 5 from a Chief Killer sketchbook, mid-1875–mid-1878, colored pencil, crayon, graphite, ink, and watercolor on wove sketchbook paper, reverse: page 6 (2007.65.21), sheet: 8 ⅝ × 11 ¾ in. (21.9 × 28.6 cm); 2007.65.20.

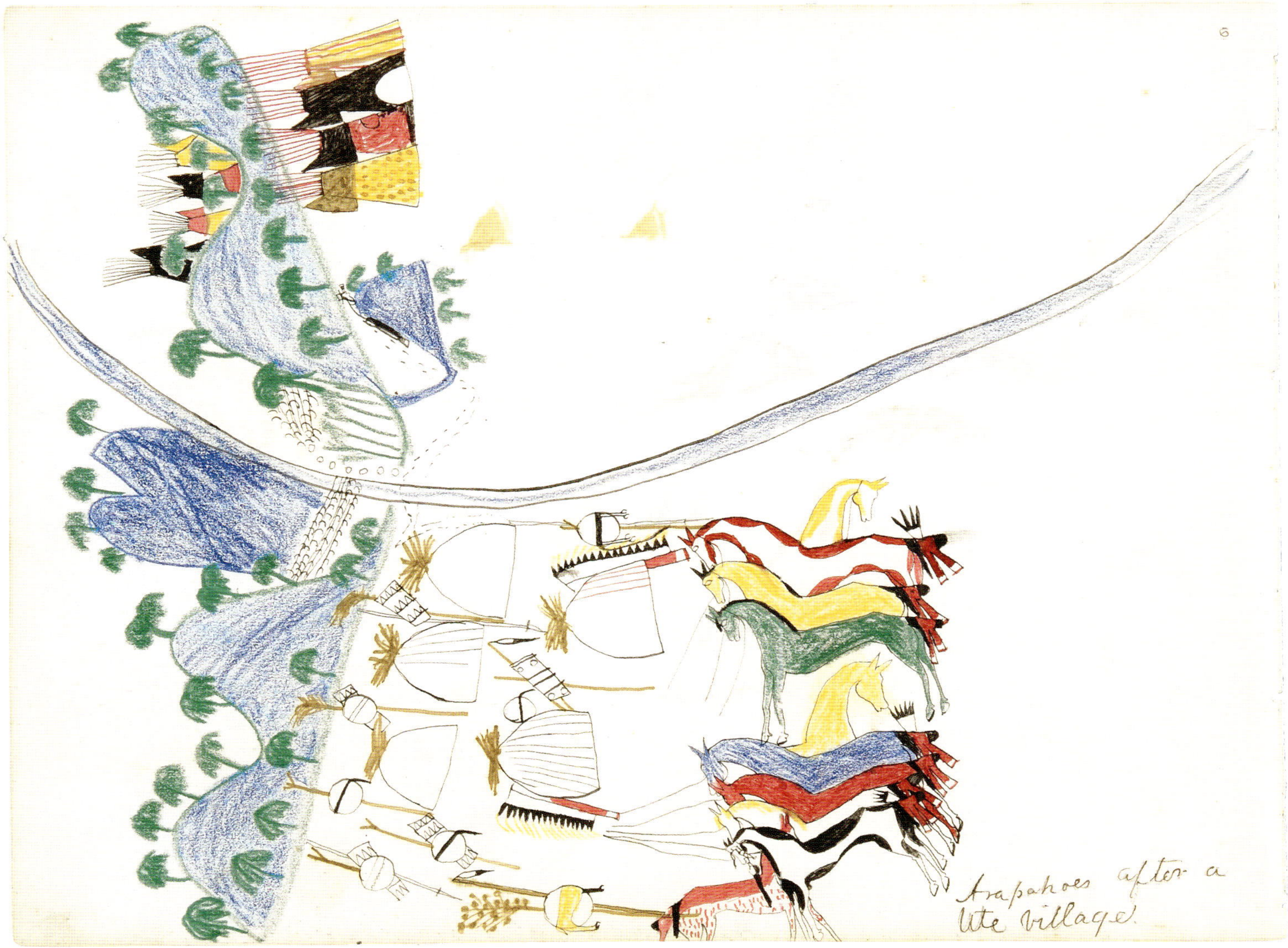

PLATE 55

Chief Killer (Noh-hu-nah-wih), Southern Tsistsistas (Cheyenne), 1849–1922, ***Untitled ["Arapahoes after a Ute village"],*** page 6 from a Chief Killer sketchbook, mid-1875–mid-1878, graphite, colored pencil, ink, crayon, and watercolor on wove sketchbook paper, reverse: page 5 (2007.65.20), sheet: 8 5/8 × 11 1/4 in. (21.9 × 28.6 cm); 2007.65.21.

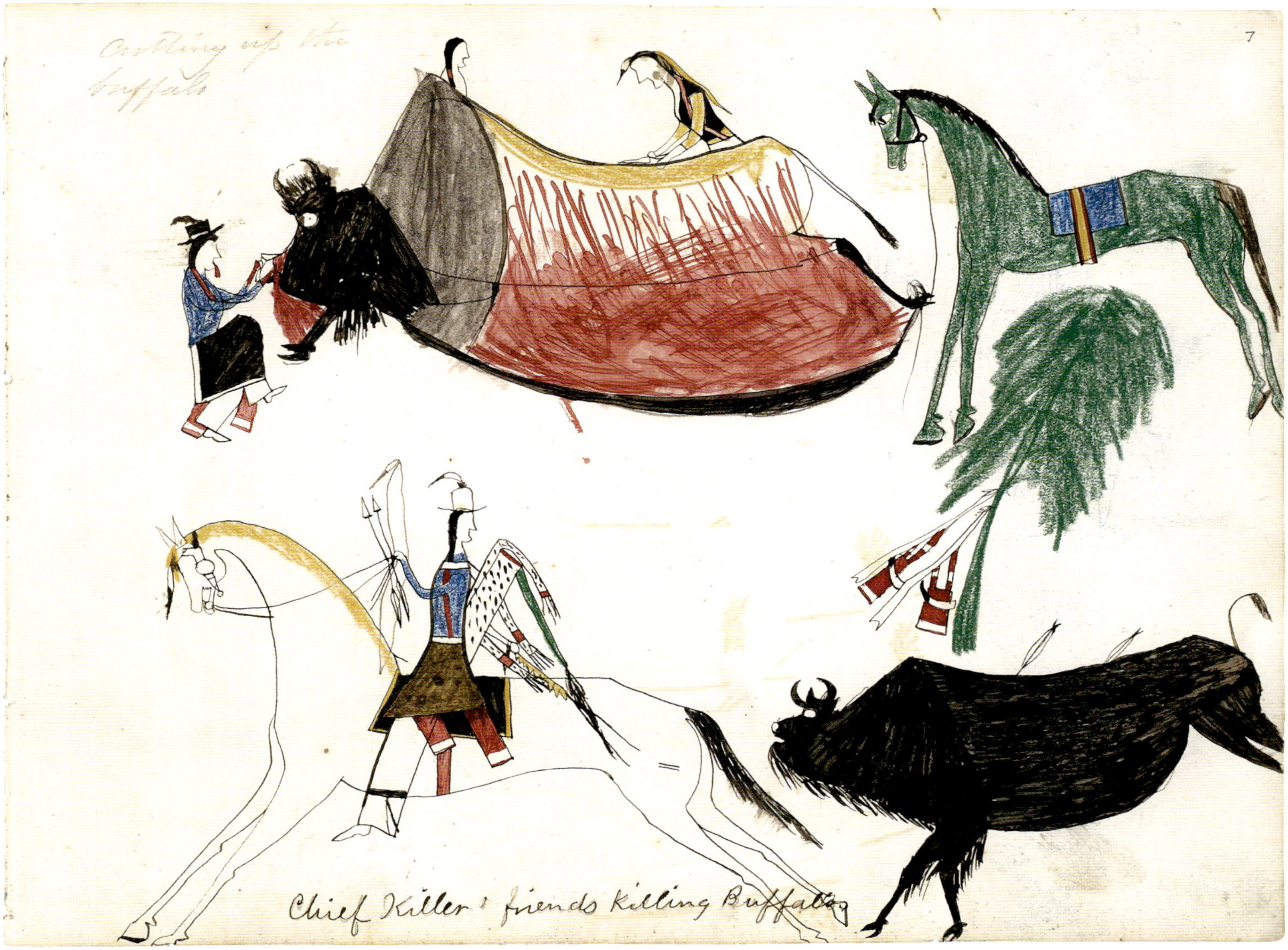

PLATE 56

Chief Killer (Noh-hu-nah-wih), Southern Tsistsistas (Cheyenne), 1849–1922, ***Untitled ["Chief Killer and Friends Killing Buffalos*** (*sic*)***"],*** page 7 from a Chief Killer sketchbook, mid-1875–mid-1878, colored pencil, crayon, graphite, and ink on wove sketchbook paper, reverse: page not numbered (no drawing), sheet: 8 ½ × 11 ¼ in. (21.7 × 28.6 cm). Purchased through the Mrs. Harvey P. Hood W'18 Fund; 2008.70.2.

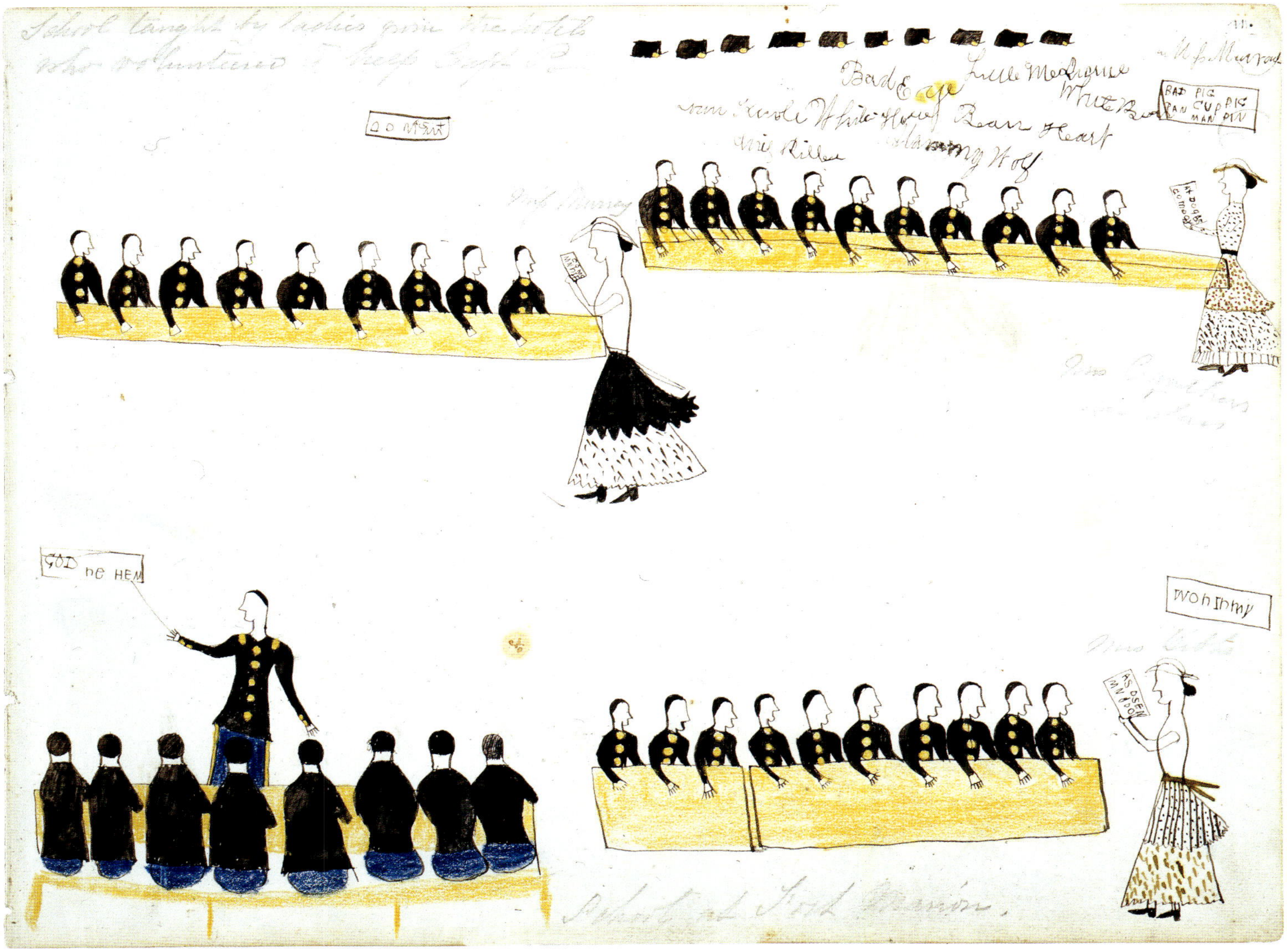

PLATE 57

Chief Killer (Noh-hu-nah-wih), Southern Tsistsistas (Cheyenne), 1849–1922, ***Untitled [“School taught by ladies from the hotels who volunteered to help Capt. P.”]***, page 11 from a Chief Killer sketchbook, mid-1875–mid-1878, pen, ink, colored crayon, and graphite on wove sketchbook paper, reverse: page 12 (D.2003.18.2), sheet: 8 5/8 × 11 1/4 in. (21.9 × 28.6 cm). Purchased through the Robert J. Strasenburgh II 1942 Fund; D.2003.18.1.

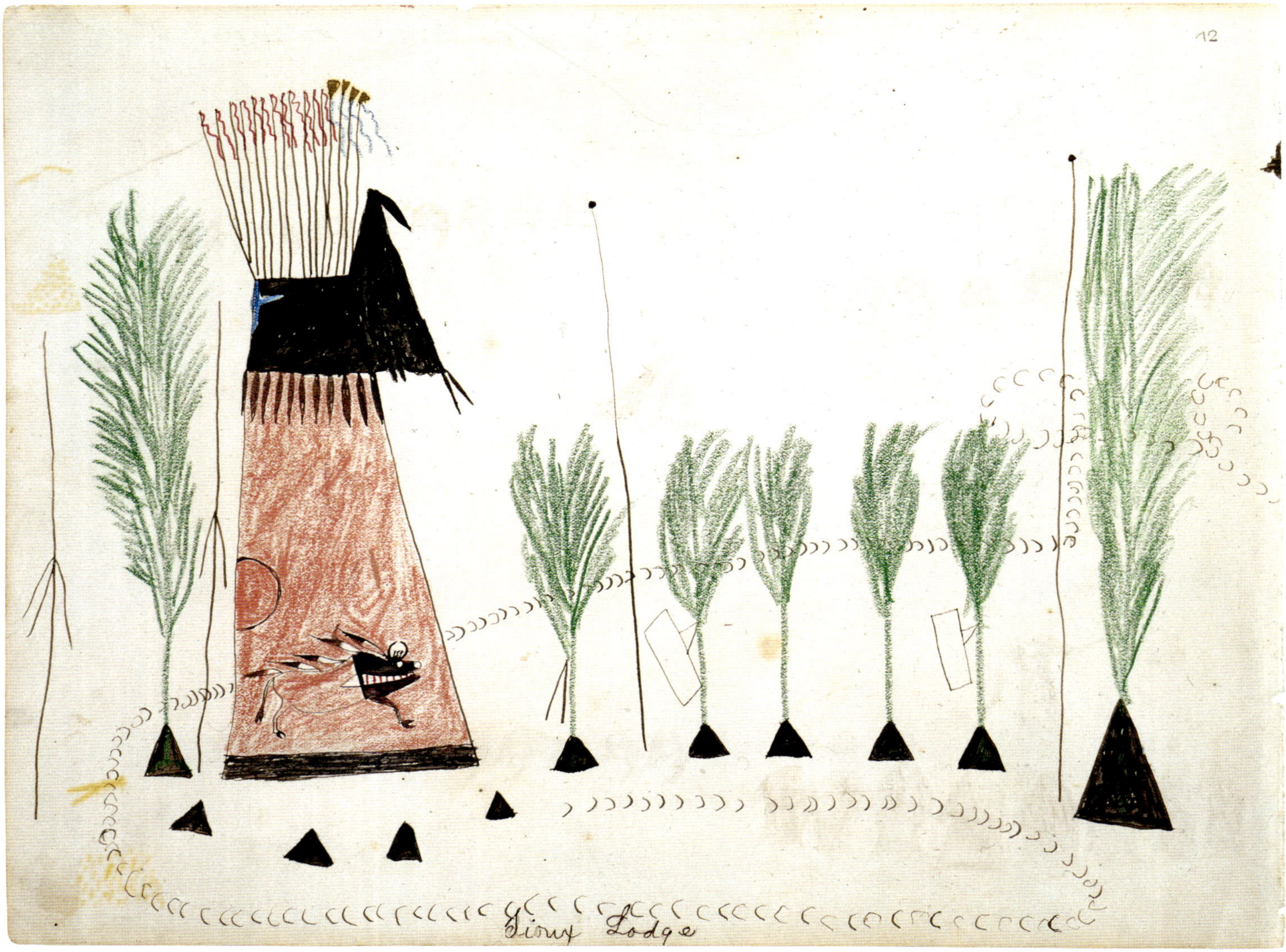

PLATE 58

Chief Killer (Noh-hu-nah-wih), Southern Tsistsistas (Cheyenne), 1849–1922, ***Untitled ["Sioux Lodge"],*** page 12 from a Chief Killer sketchbook, mid-1875–mid-1878, pen, ink, colored crayon, and graphite on wove sketchbook paper, reverse: page 11 (D.2003.18.1), sheet: 8 ⅝ × 11 ¼ in. (21.9 × 28.6 cm). Purchased through the Robert J. Strasenburgh II 1942 Fund; D.2003.18.2.

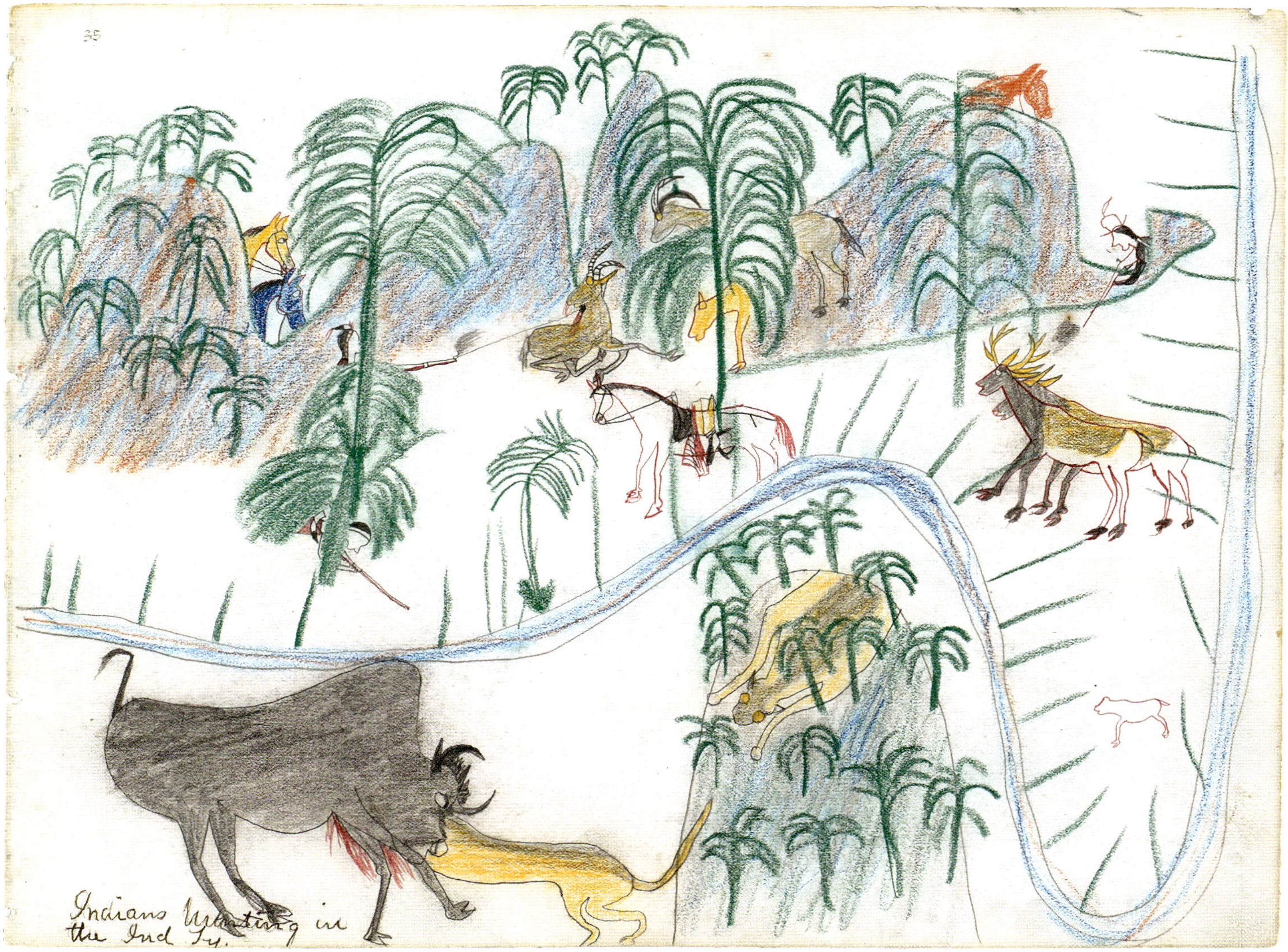

PLATE 59

Chief Killer (Noh-hu-nah-wih), Southern Tsistsistas (Cheyenne), 1849–1922, ***Untitled ["Indians Hunting in the Ind. Terr."],*** page 35 from a Chief Killer sketchbook, mid-1875–mid-1878, colored pencil, graphite, and red ink on wove sketchbook paper, reverse: page not numbered (no drawing), sheet: 8 5/8 × 11 3/8 in. (21.9 × 28.7 cm). Purchased through the Mrs. Harvey P. Hood W'18 Fund; 2008.70.1.

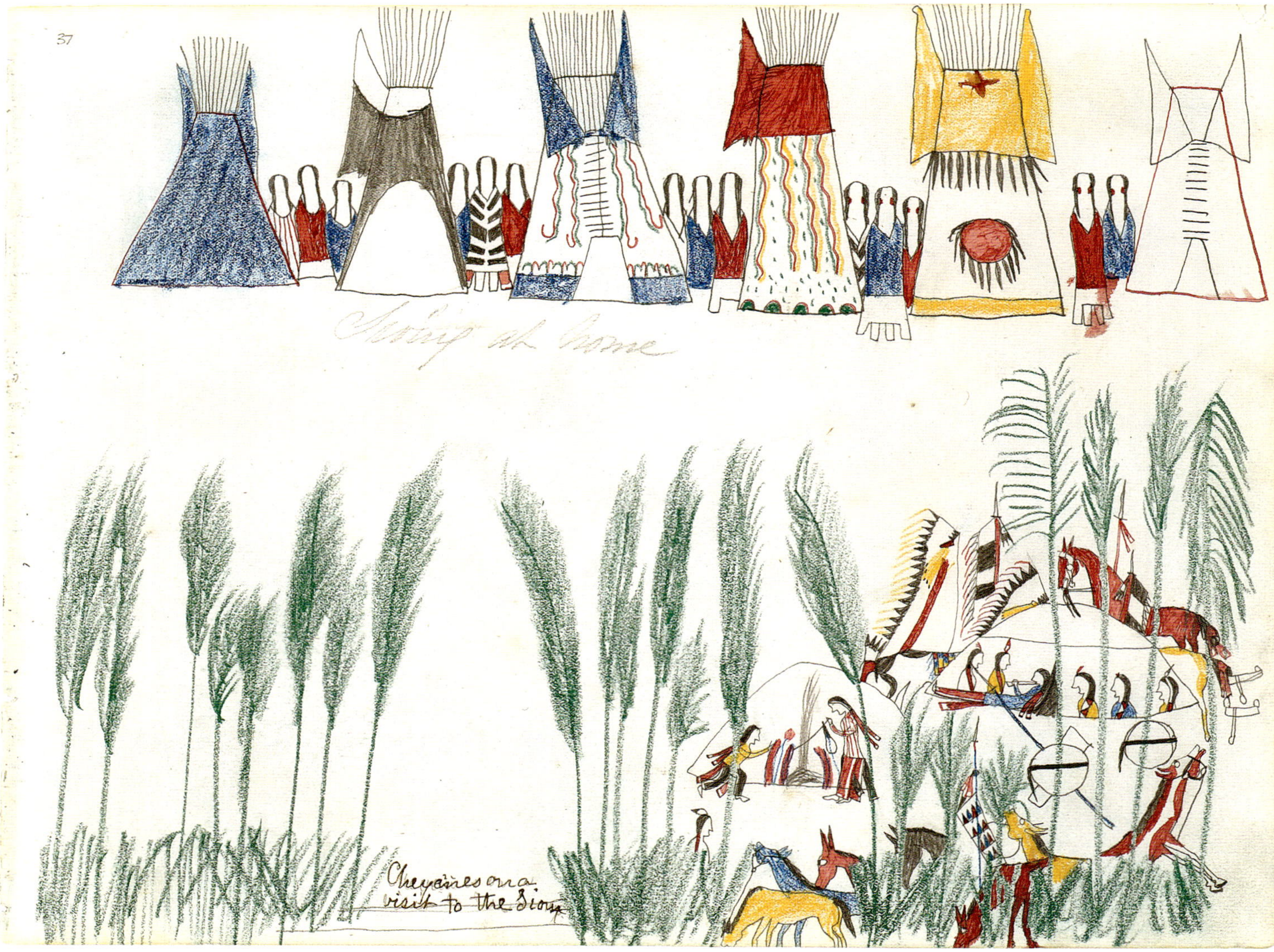

PLATE 60

Chief Killer (Noh-hu-nah-wih), Southern Tsistsistas (Cheyenne), 1849–1922, ***Untitled [“Cheyennes on a visit to the Sioux”],*** page 37 from a Chief Killer sketchbook, mid-1875–mid-1878, graphite, colored pencil, and red ink on wove sketchbook paper, reverse: page not numbered (no drawing), sheet: 8 ⅝ × 11 ¼ in. (21.9 × 28.6 cm); 2007.65.22.

"VINCENT PRICE LEDGER"

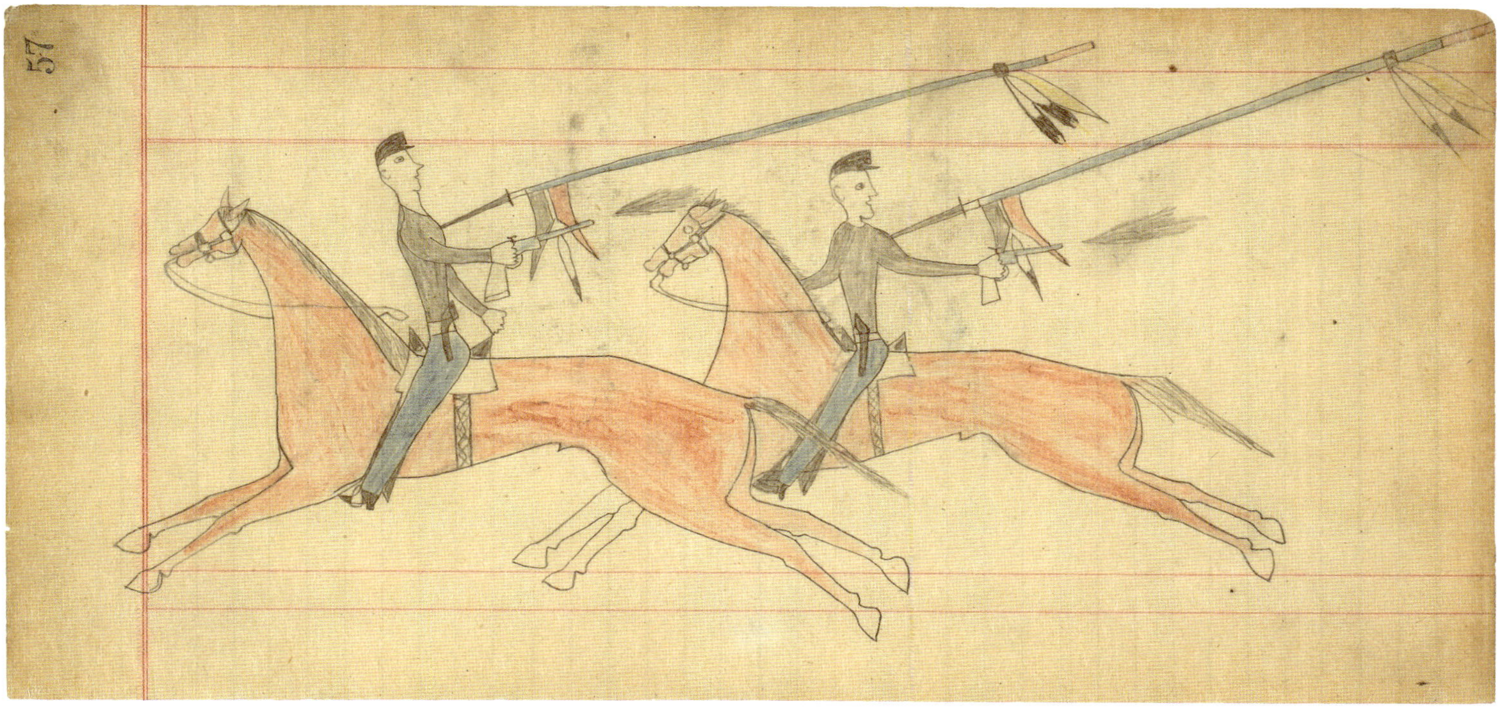

PLATE 61

Unknown artist, Tsistsistas (Cheyenne) and/or Inunaina (Arapaho), active late nineteenth century, ***Untitled [Counting coup on two U.S. soldiers],*** page 57 from the "Vincent Price Ledger," late nineteenth century, graphite and colored pencil on laid ledger paper, reverse: page 58 (2007.88.9), sheet: 5 ⅝ × 11 ¾ in. (14.3 × 29.7 cm). Gift of Mark Lansburgh, Class of 1949; 2007.88.8.

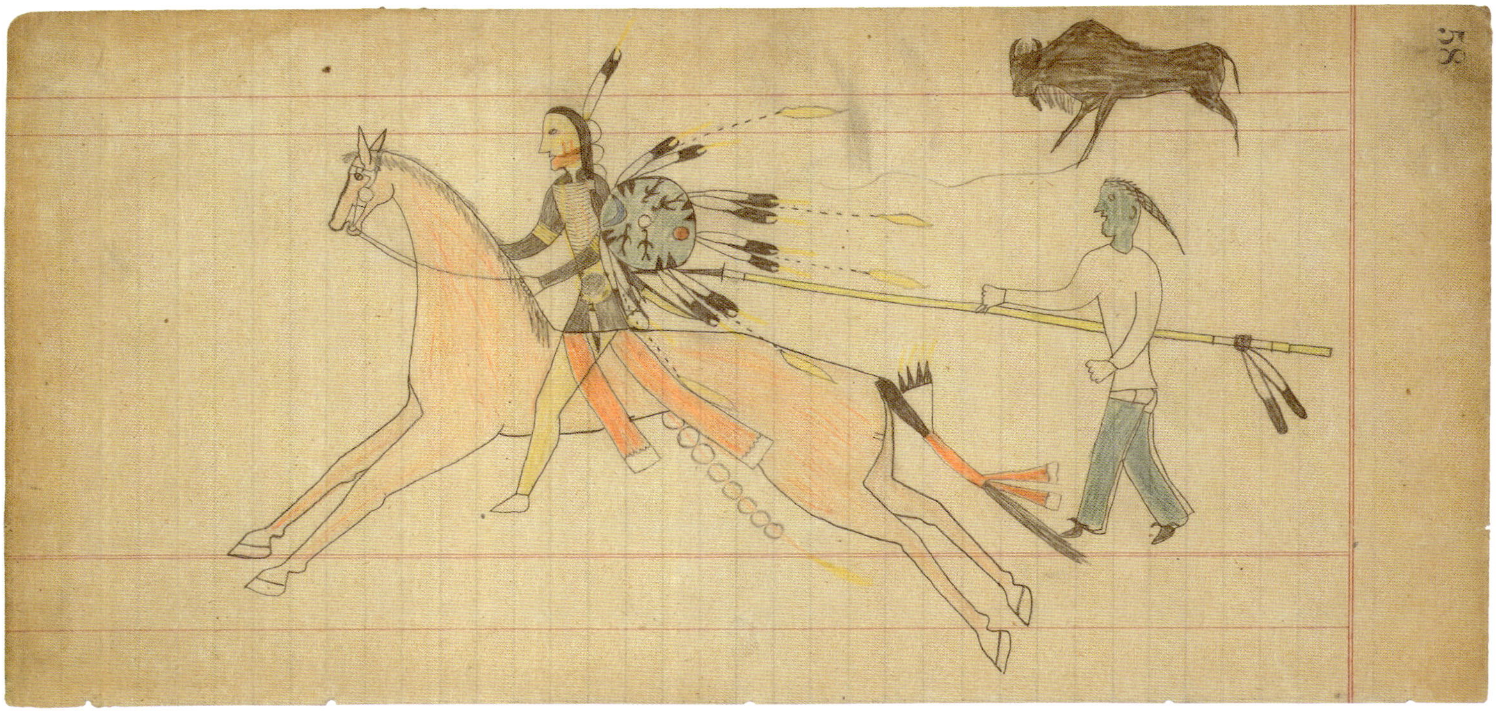

PLATE 62

Unknown artist, Tsistsistas (Cheyenne) and/or Inunaina (Arapaho), active late nineteenth century, ***Untitled [Chaticks Si Chaticks (Pawnee) warrior counts coup on enemy],*** page 58 from the "Vincent Price Ledger," late nineteenth century, graphite and colored pencil on laid ledger paper, reverse: page 57 (2007.88.8), sheet: 5 5⁄8 × 11 3⁄4 in. (14.3 × 29.7 cm). Gift of Mark Lansburgh, Class of 1949; 2007.88.9.

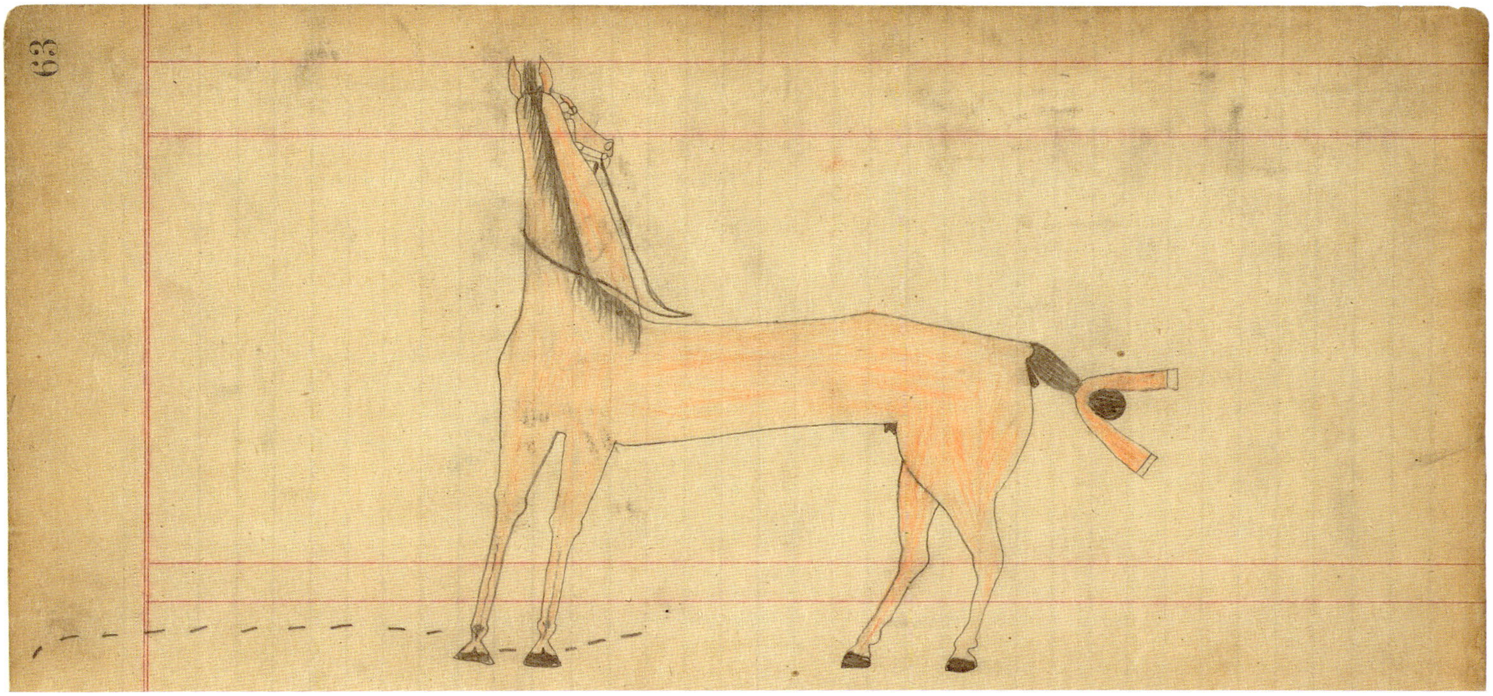

PLATE 63

Unknown artist, Tsistsistas (Cheyenne) and/or Inunaina (Arapaho), active late nineteenth century, ***Untitled [A horse],*** page 63 from the "Vincent Price Ledger," late nineteenth century, graphite and colored pencil on laid ledger paper, reverse: page 64 (2007.65.46), sheet: 5 ⅝ × 11 ¾ in. (14.3 × 29.7 cm); 2007.65.45.

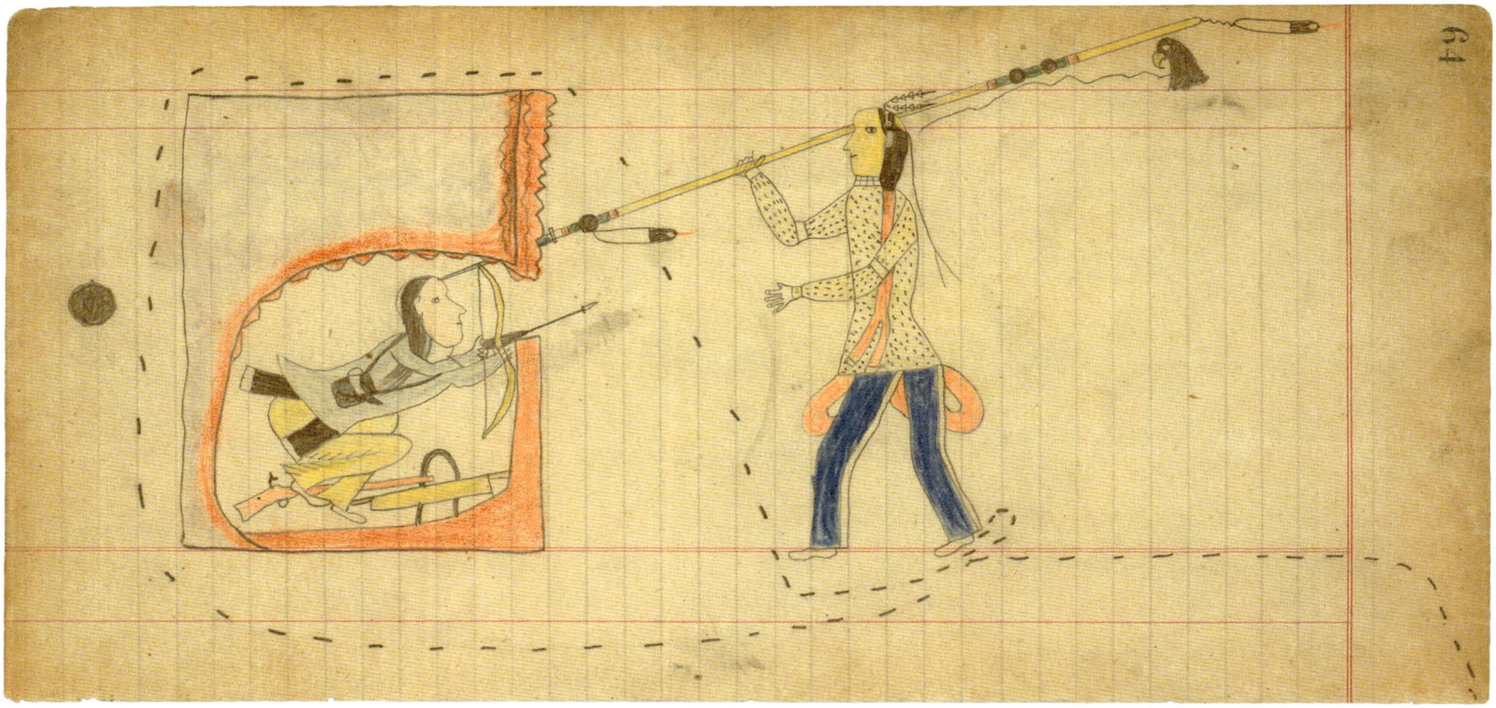

PLATE 64

Unknown artist, Tsistsistas (Cheyenne) and/or Inunaina (Arapaho), active late nineteenth century, ***Untitled [An Inunaina (Arapaho) warrior counts coup on an enemy],*** page 64 from the "Vincent Price Ledger," late nineteenth century, graphite and colored pencil on laid ledger paper, reverse: page 63 (2007.65.45), sheet: 5 ⅝ × 11 ¾ in. (14.3 × 29.7 cm); 2007.65.46.

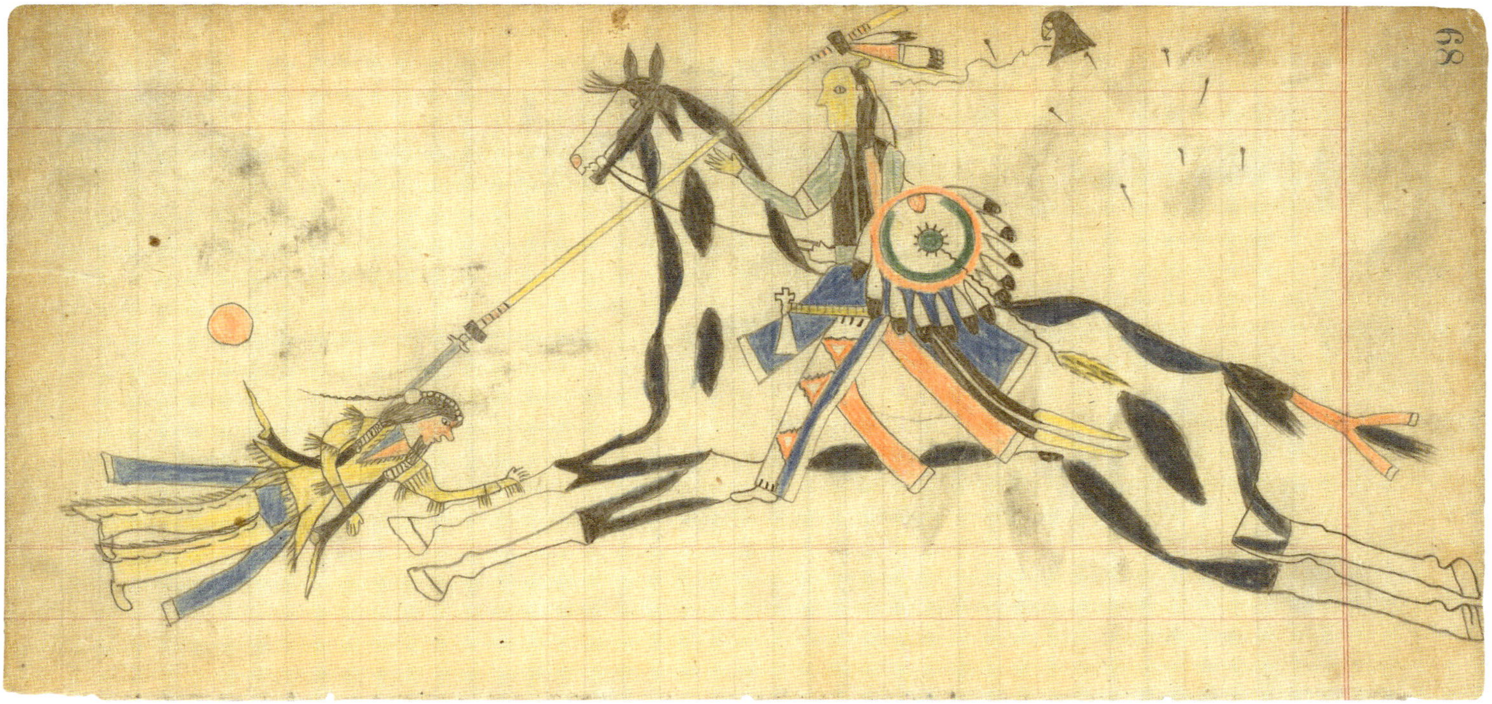

PLATE 65

Unknown artist, Tsistsistas (Cheyenne) and/or Inunaina (Arapaho), active late nineteenth century, ***Untitled [A Tsistsistas (Cheyenne) or Inunaina (Arapaho) warrior counts coup on an enemy],*** page 68 from the "Vincent Price Ledger," late nineteenth century, graphite and colored pencil on laid ledger paper, reverse: page 67 (no drawing), sheet: 5 ¾ × 11 ¾ in. (14.5 × 29.7 cm); 2007.65.39.

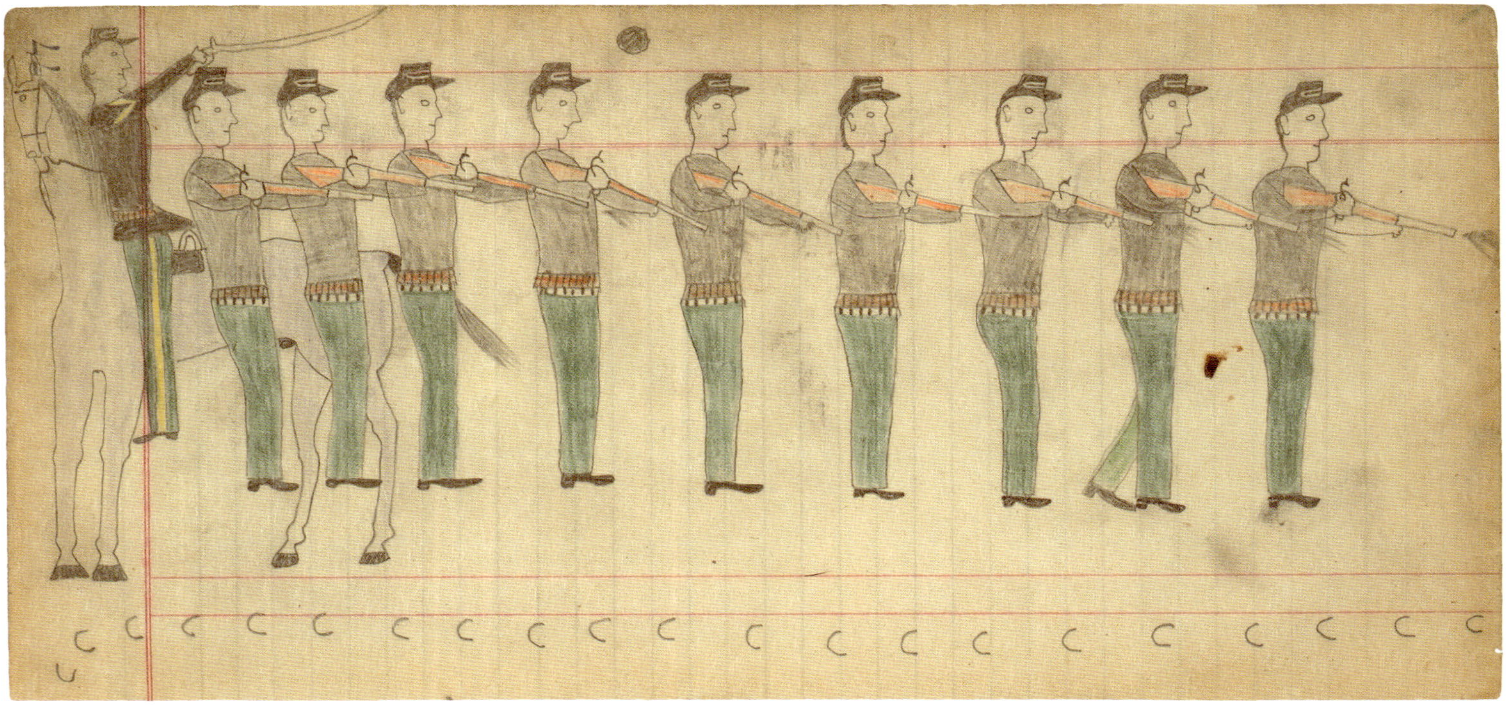

PLATE 66

Unknown artist, Tsistsistas (Cheyenne) and/or Inunaina (Arapaho), active late nineteenth century, ***Untitled [A formation of U.S. infantry soldiers firing in battle],*** page 77 from the "Vincent Price Ledger," late nineteenth century, graphite and colored pencil on laid ledger paper, reverse: page 78 (2007.65.41), sheet: 5 ¾ × 11 ¾ in. (14.5 × 29.7 cm); 2007.65.42.

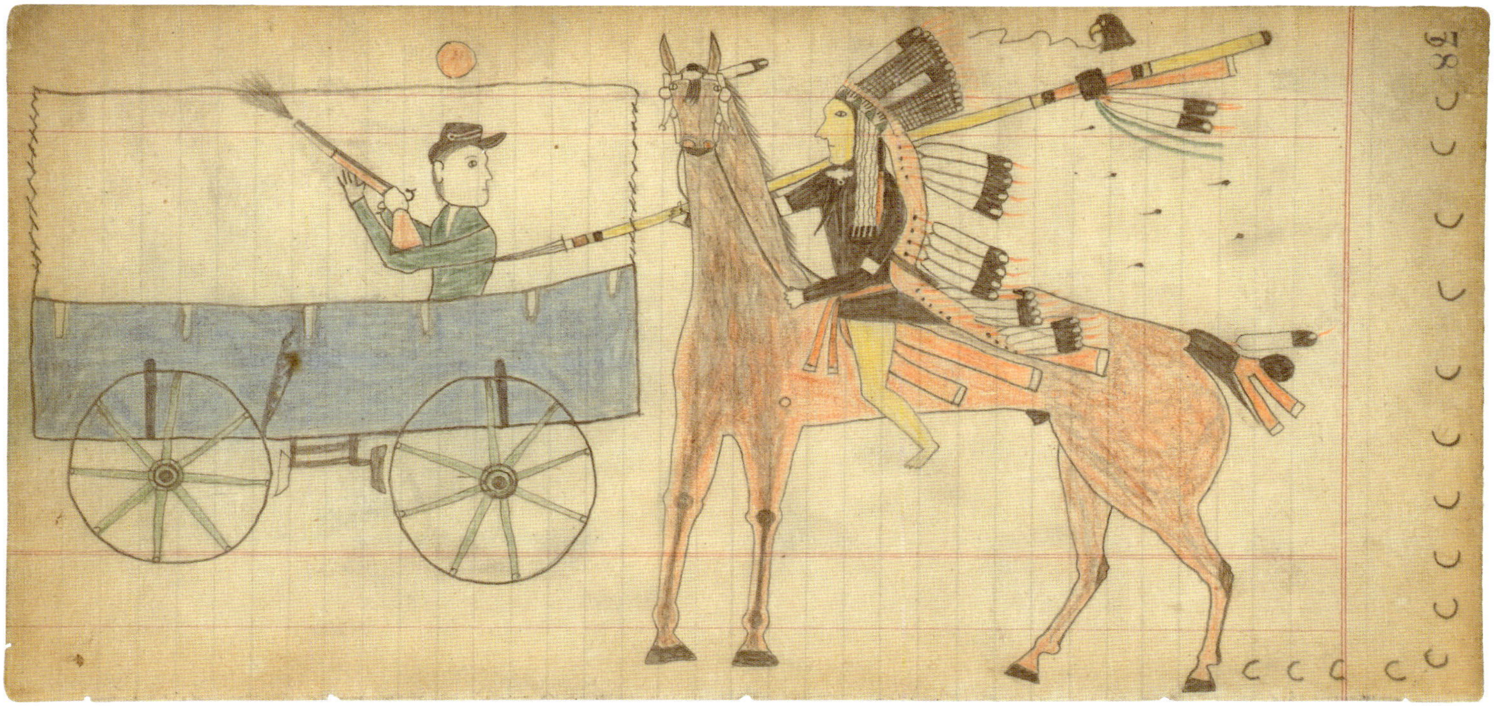

PLATE 67

Unknown artist, Tsistsistas (Cheyenne) and/or Inunaina (Arapaho), active late nineteenth century, ***Untitled [An Inunaina (Arapaho) warrior counts coup on a U.S. soldier],*** page 78 from the "Vincent Price Ledger," late nineteenth century, graphite and colored pencil on laid ledger paper, reverse: page 77 (2007.65.42), sheet: 5 ¾ × 11 ¾ in. (14.5 × 29.7 cm); 2007.65.41.

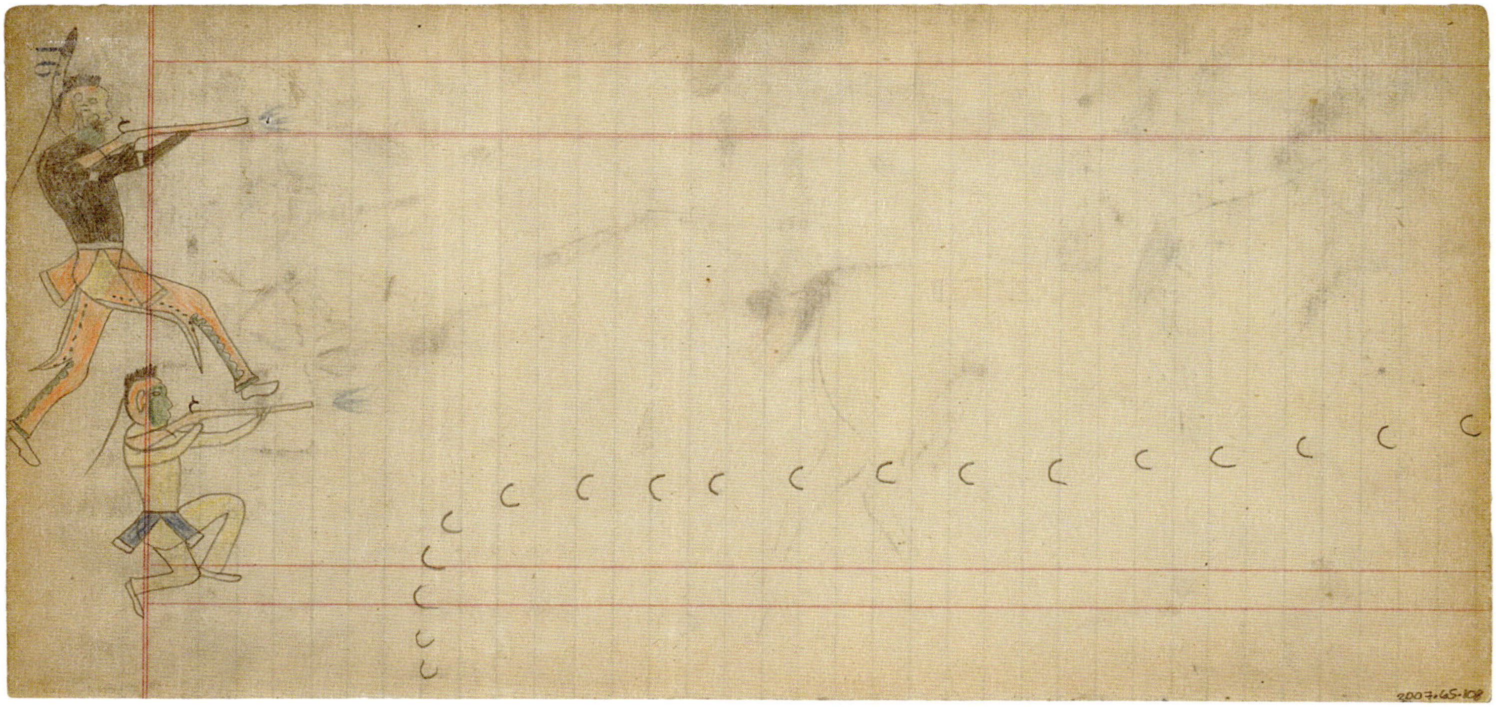

PLATE 68

Unknown artist, Tsistsistas (Cheyenne) and/or Inunaina (Arapaho), active late nineteenth century, ***Untitled [Two warriors in battle],*** page 91 from the "Vincent Price Ledger," late nineteenth century, graphite and color pencil on laid ledger paper, reverse: page 92 (2007.65.40), sheet: 5 ¾ × 11 ¾ in. (14.5 × 29.7 cm); 2007.65.108.

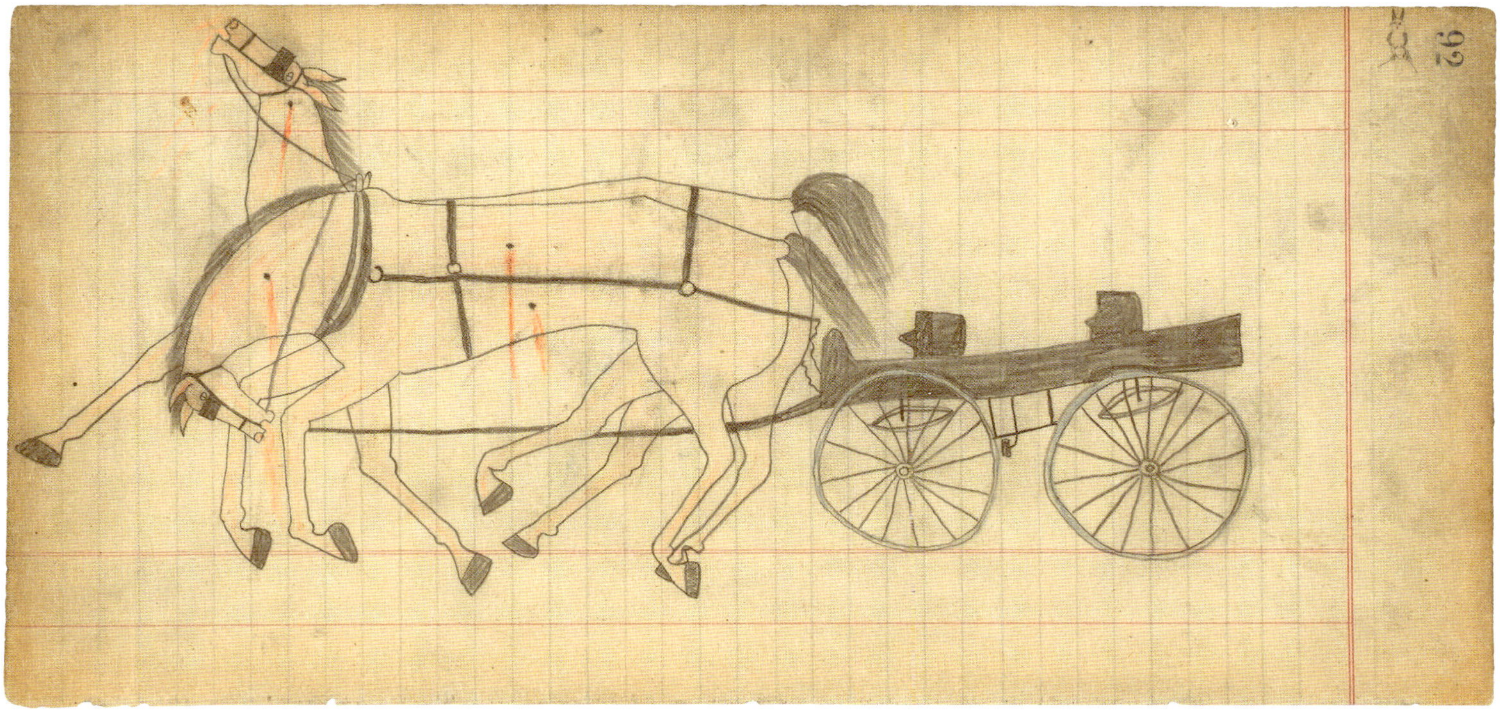

PLATE 69

Unknown artist, Tsistsistas (Cheyenne) and/or Inunaina (Arapaho), active late nineteenth century, ***Untitled [Two wounded horses hitched to a buckboard],*** page 92 from the "Vincent Price Ledger," late nineteenth century, graphite and colored pencil on laid ledger paper, reverse: page 91 (2007.65.108), sheet: 5 ¾ × 11 ¾ in. (14.5 × 29.7 cm); 2007.65.40.

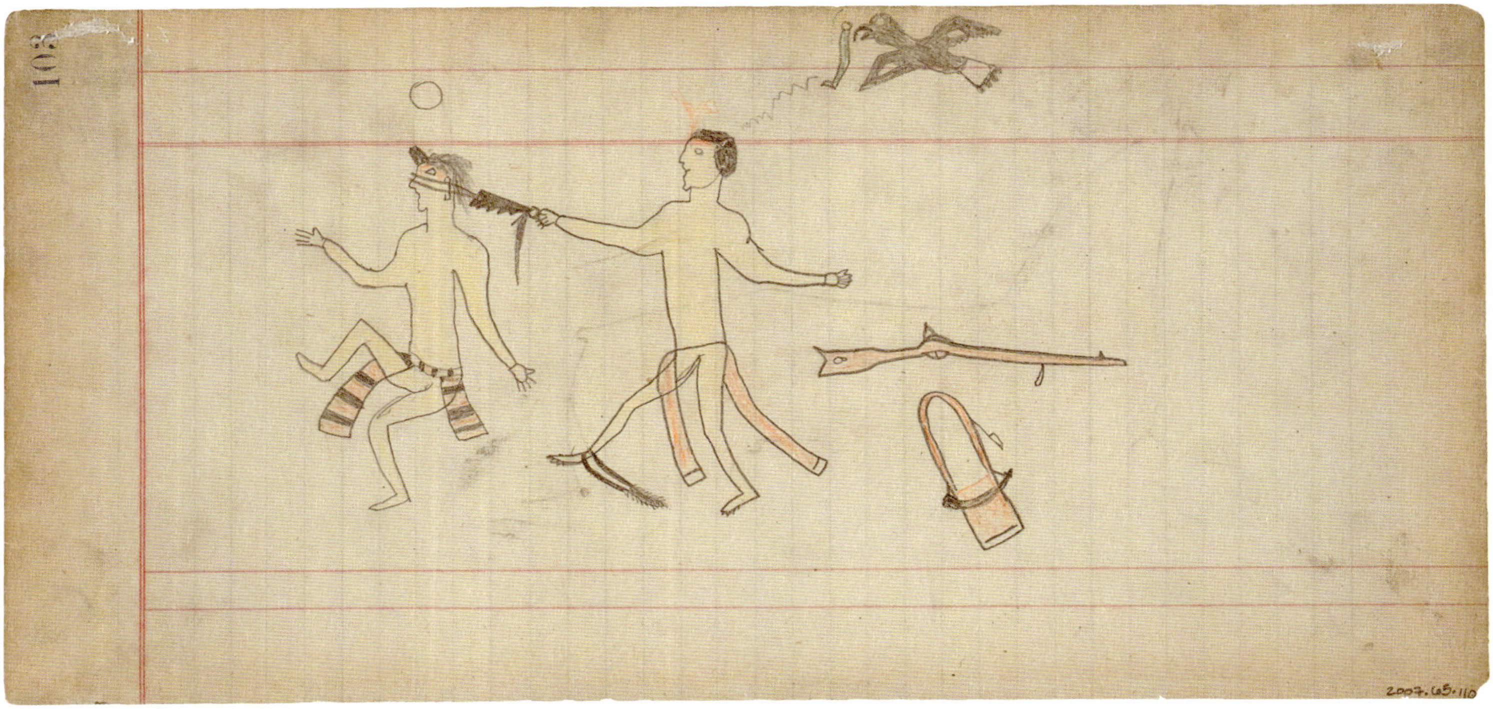

PLATE 70

Unknown artist, Tsistsistas (Cheyenne) and/or Inunaina (Arapaho), active late nineteenth century, ***Untitled [Two warriors in hand-to-hand combat],*** page 103 from the "Vincent Price Ledger," late nineteenth century, graphite and colored pencil on laid ledger paper, reverse: page 104 (2007.65.37), sheet: 5 ¾ × 11 ¾ in. (14.6 × 29.7 cm); 2007.65.110.

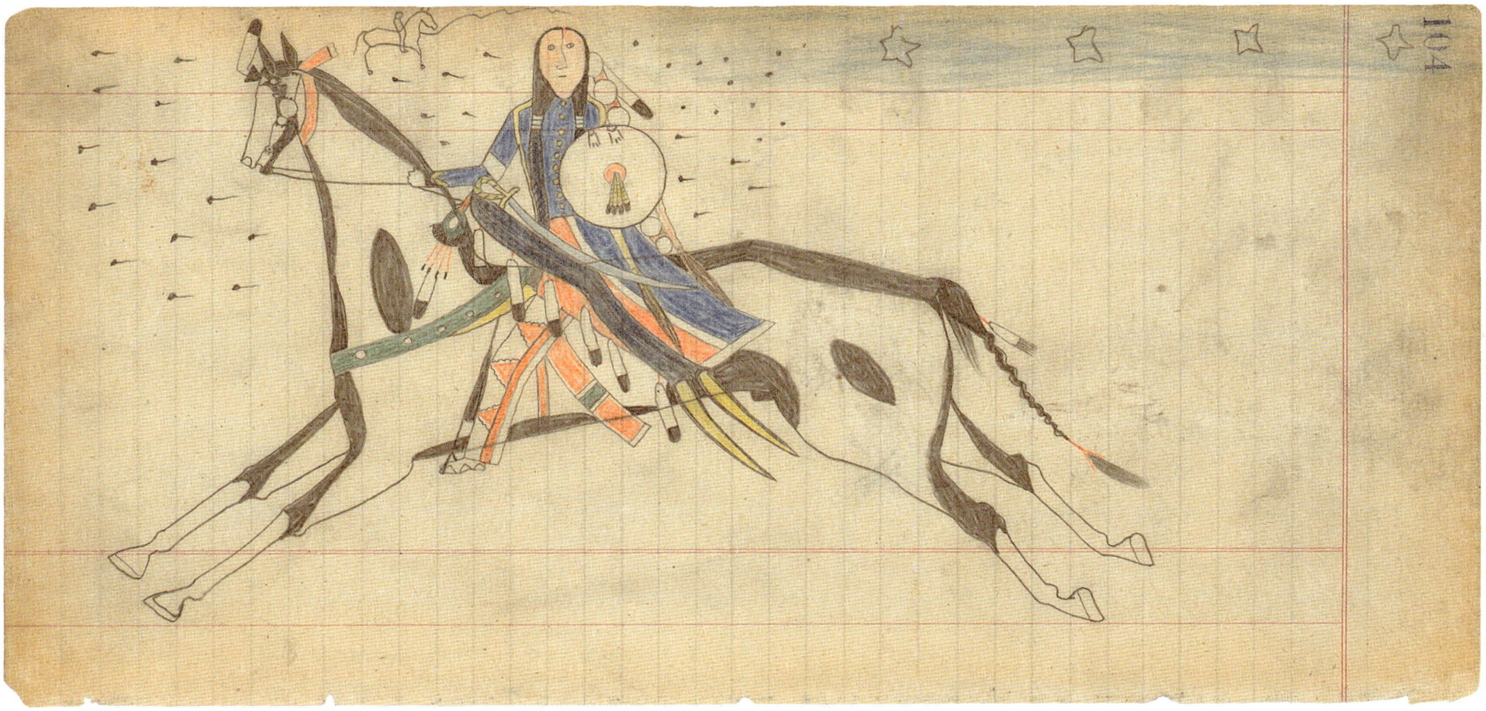

PLATE 71

Unknown artist, Tsistsistas (Cheyenne) and/or Inunaina (Arapaho), active late nineteenth century, ***Untitled [An Inunaina (Arapaho) warrior in the midst of gunfire],*** page 104 from the "Vincent Price Ledger," late nineteenth century, graphite and colored pencil on laid ledger paper, reverse: page 103 (2007.65.110), sheet: 5 ¾ × 11 ¾ in. (14.6 × 29.7 cm); 2007.65.37.

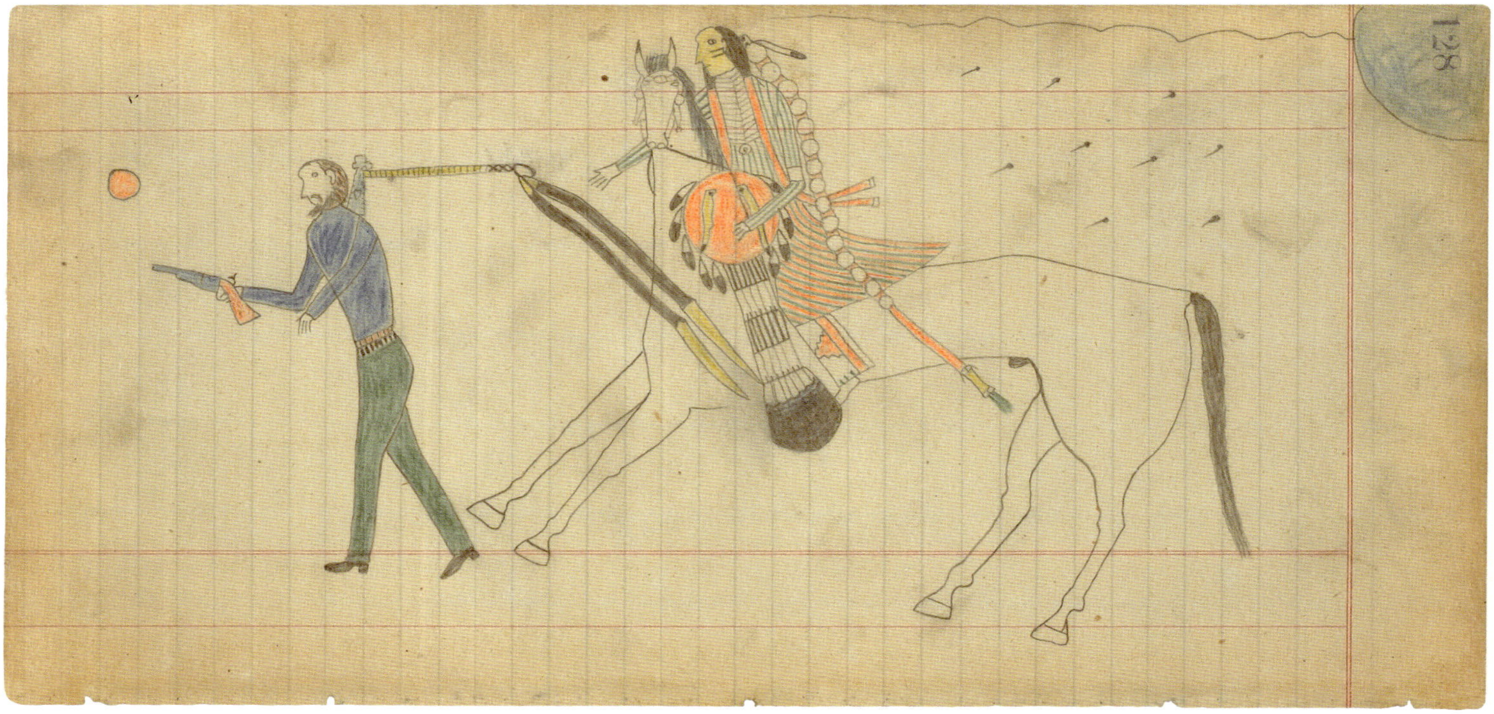

PLATE 72

Unknown artist, Tsistsistas (Cheyenne) and/or Inunaina (Arapaho), active late nineteenth century, ***Untitled [An Inunaina (Arapaho) warrior counts coup on a non-Native enemy],*** page 128 from the "Vincent Price Ledger," late nineteenth century, graphite and colored pencil on laid ledger paper; reverse: page 127 (no drawing); sheet: 5 ¾ × 11 ¾ in. (14.6 × 29.7 cm); 2007.65.29.

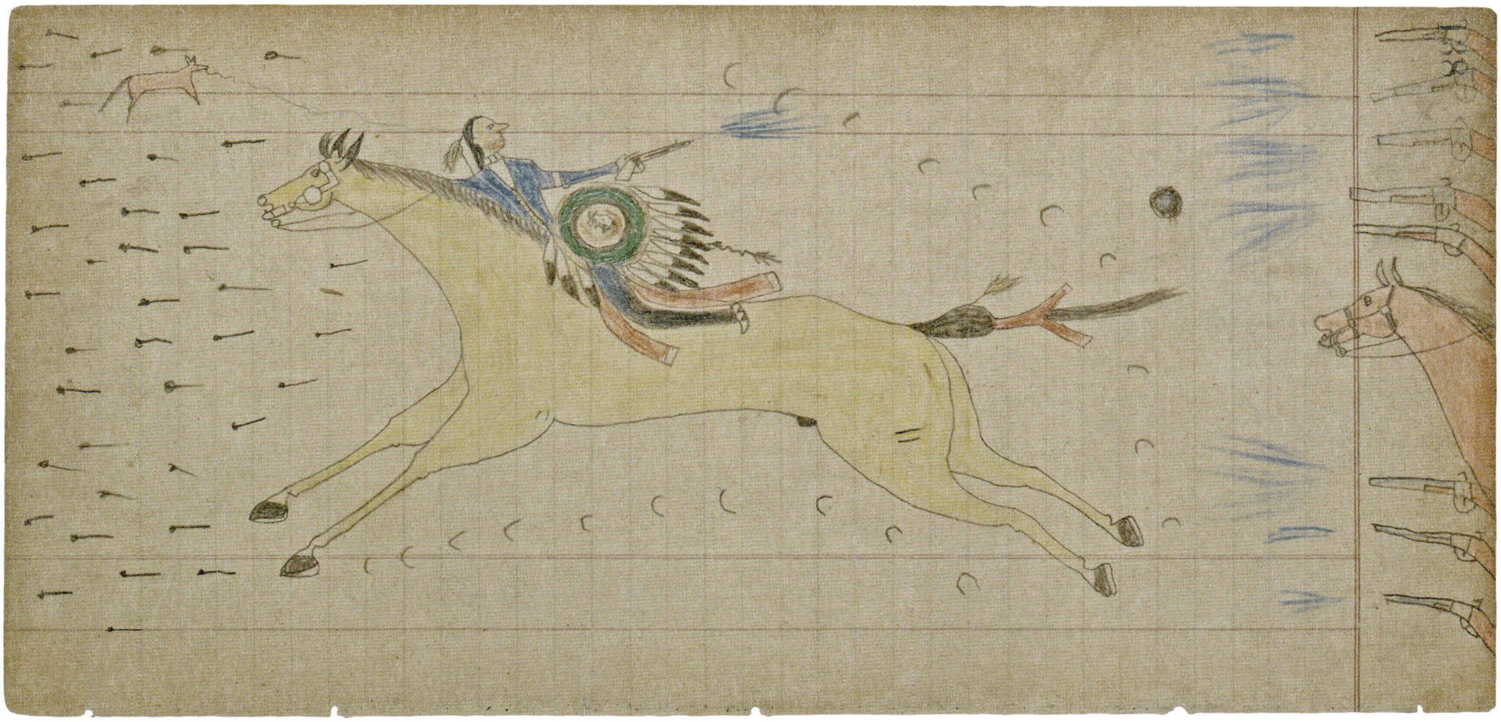

PLATE 73

Unknown artist, Tsistsistas (Cheyenne) and/or Inunaina (Arapaho), active late nineteenth century, ***Untitled [An Inunaina (Arapaho) warrior fires back at U.S. soldiers]***, page 138 from the "Vincent Price Ledger," late nineteenth century, graphite and colored pencil on laid ledger paper, reverse: page 137 (no drawing), sheet: 5 ¾ × 11 ¾ in. (14.6 × 29.7 cm). Purchased through the Hood Museum of Art Acquisitions Fund; D.2004.9.

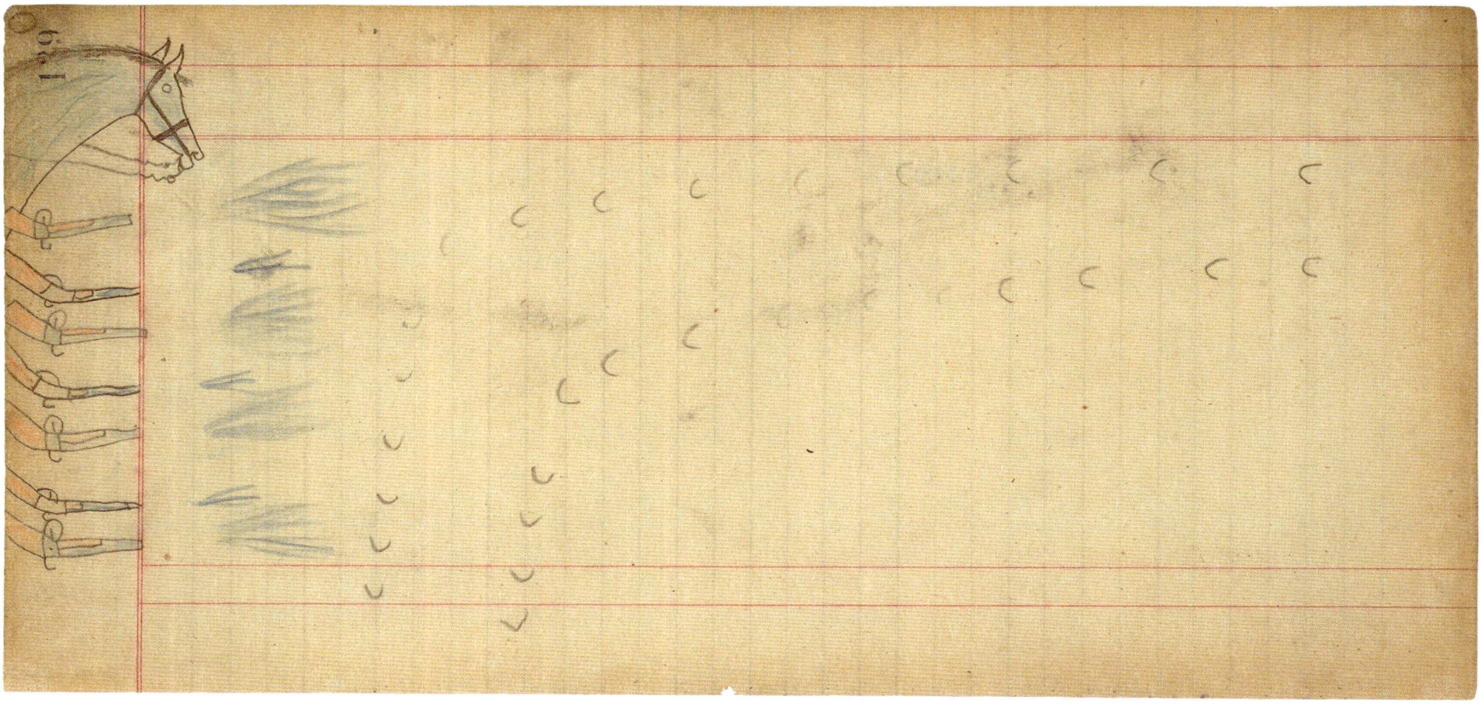

PLATE 74

Unknown artist, Tsistsistas (Cheyenne) and/or Inunaina (Arapaho), active late nineteenth century, ***Untitled [A formation of U.S. soldiers in battle],*** page 139 from the "Vincent Price Ledger," late nineteenth century, graphite and colored pencil on laid ledger paper, reverse: page 140 (2007.88.7), sheet: 5 ¾ × 11 ¾ in. (14.4 × 29.7 cm). Gift of Mark Lansburgh, Class of 1949; 2007.88.6.

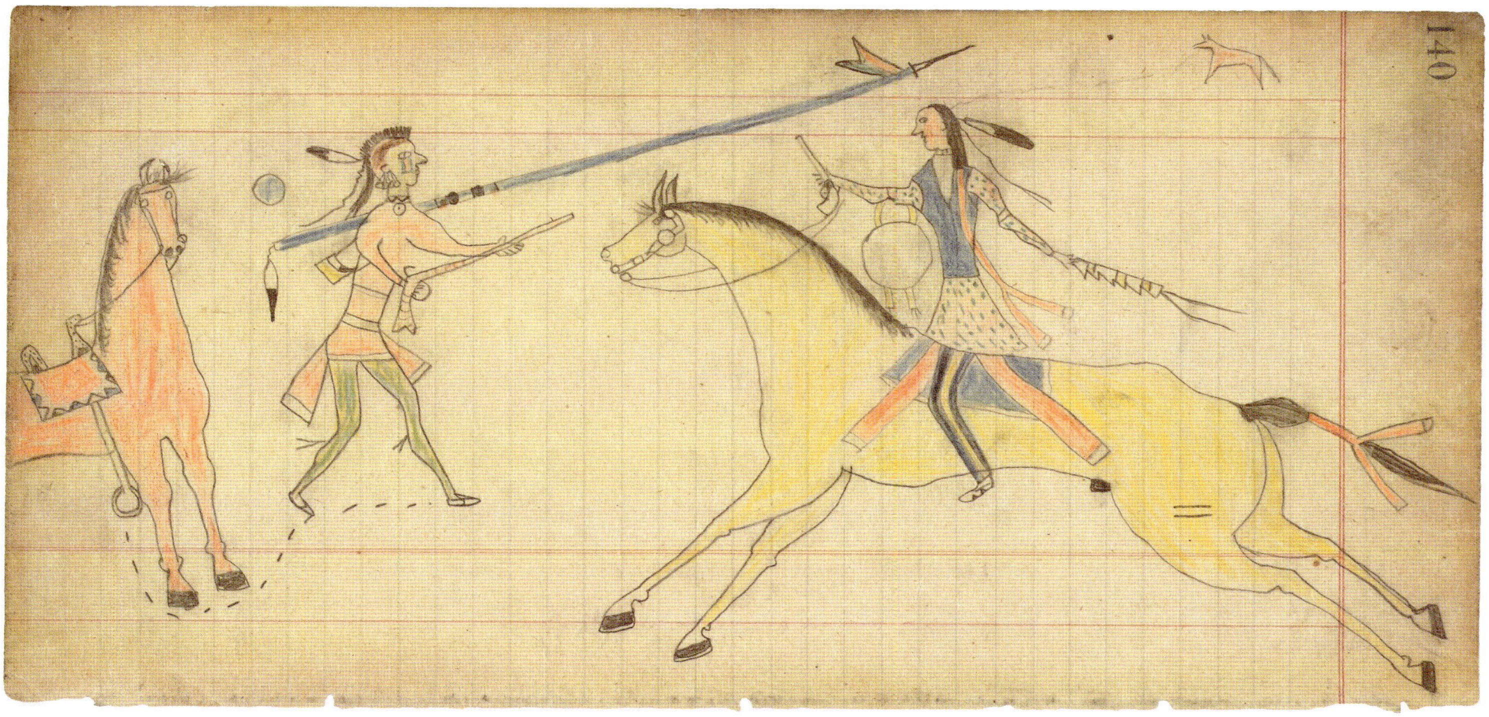

PLATE 75

Unknown artist, Tsistsistas (Cheyenne) and/or Inunaina (Arapaho), active late nineteenth century, ***Untitled [A warrior counts coup on an enemy],*** page 140 from the "Vincent Price Ledger," late nineteenth century, graphite and colored pencil on laid ledger paper, reverse: page 139 (2007.88.6), sheet: 5 ¾ × 1˗ ¾ in. (14.4 × 29.7 cm). Gift of Mark Lansburgh, Class of 1949; 2007.88.7.

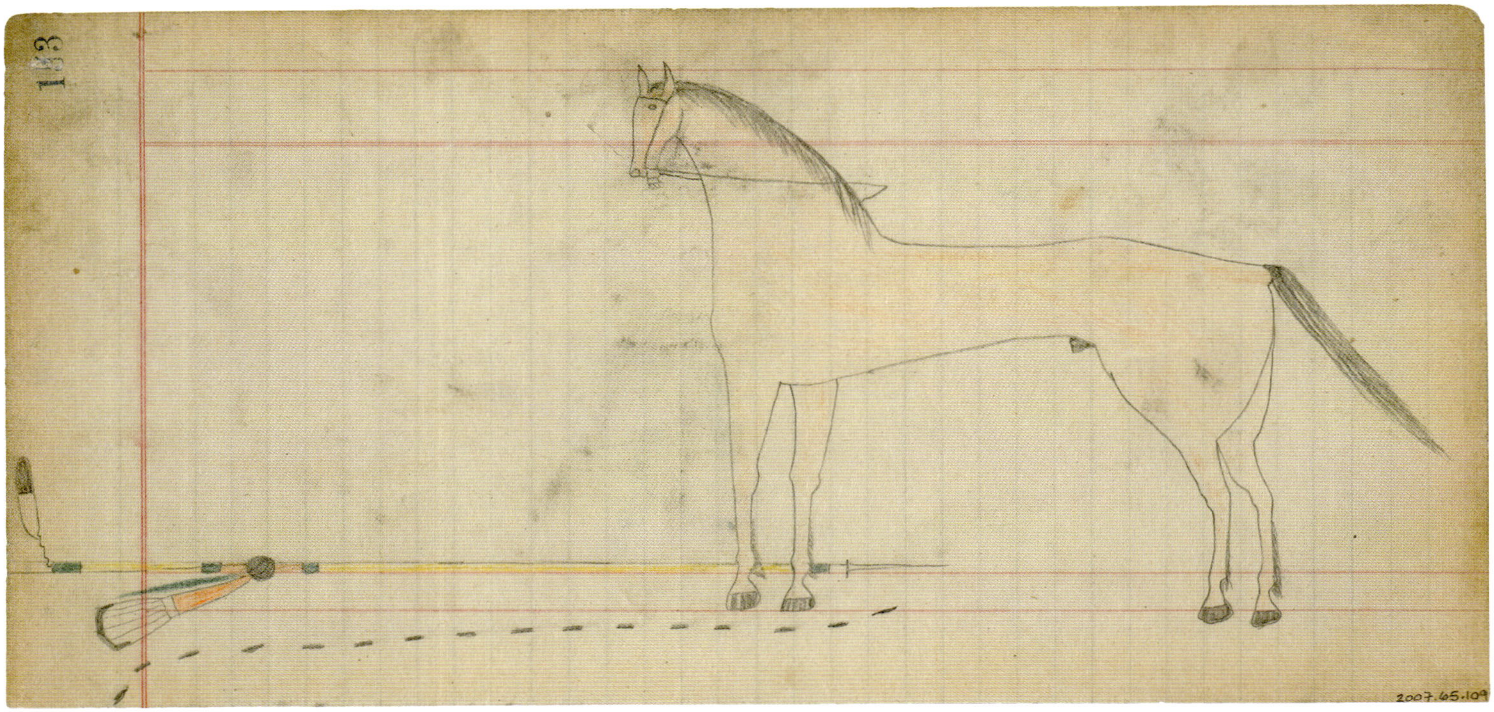

PLATE 76

Unknown artist, Tsistsistas (Cheyenne) and/or Inunaina (Arapaho), active late nineteenth century, ***Untitled [Horse, war lance, and footprints],*** page 153 from the "Vincent Price Ledger," late nineteenth century, graphite and colored pencil on laid ledger paper, reverse: page 154 (2007.65.38), sheet: 5 ¾ × 11 ¾ in. (14.6 × 29.7 cm); 2007.65.109.

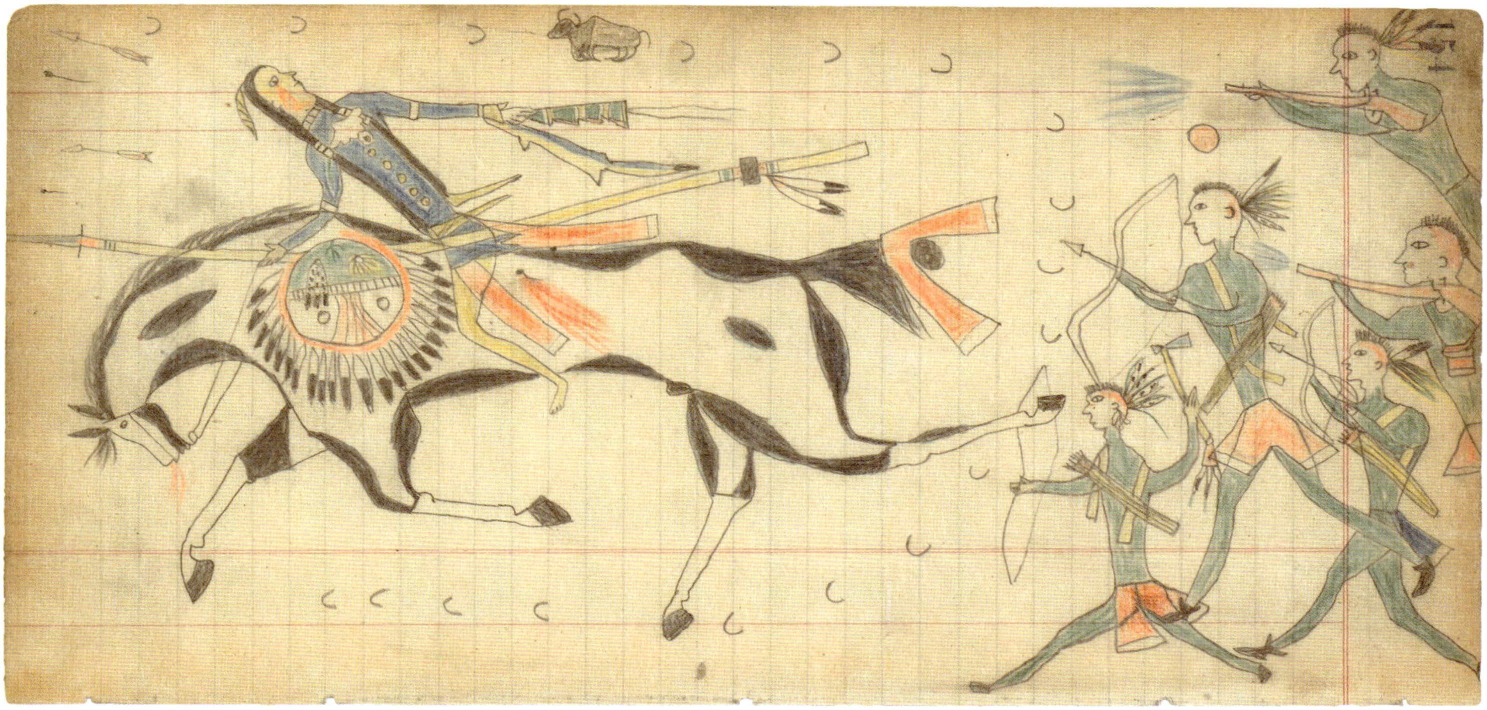

PLATE 77

Unknown artist, Tsistsistas (Cheyenne) and/or Inunaina (Arapaho), active late nineteenth century, ***Untitled [Warrior fleeing Chaticks Si Chaticks (Pawnee) warriors]***, page 154 from the "Vincent Price Ledger," late nineteenth century, graphite and colored pencil on laid ledger paper, reverse: page 153 (2007.65.109), sheet: 5 ¾ × 11 ¾ in. (14.6 × 29.7 cm); 2007.65.38.

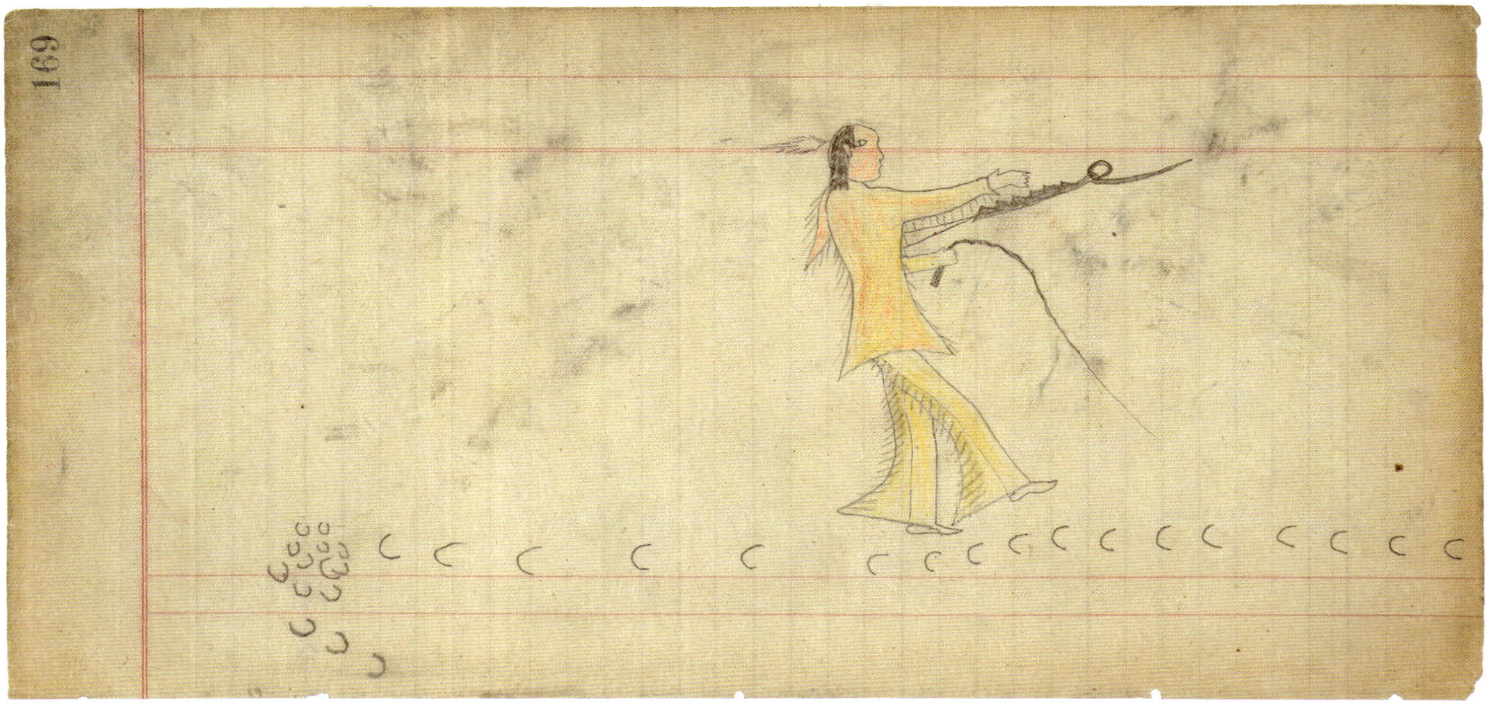

PLATE 78

Unknown artist, Tsistsistas (Cheyenne) and/or Inunaina (Arapaho), active late nineteenth century, ***Untitled [Counting coup with a quirt],*** page 169 from the "Vincent Price Ledger," late nineteenth century, graphite and colored pencil on laid ledger paper, reverse: page 170 (2007.88.5), sheet: 5 ¾ × 11 ¾ in. (14.4 × 29.7 cm). Gift of Mark Lansburgh, Class of 1949; 2007.88.4.

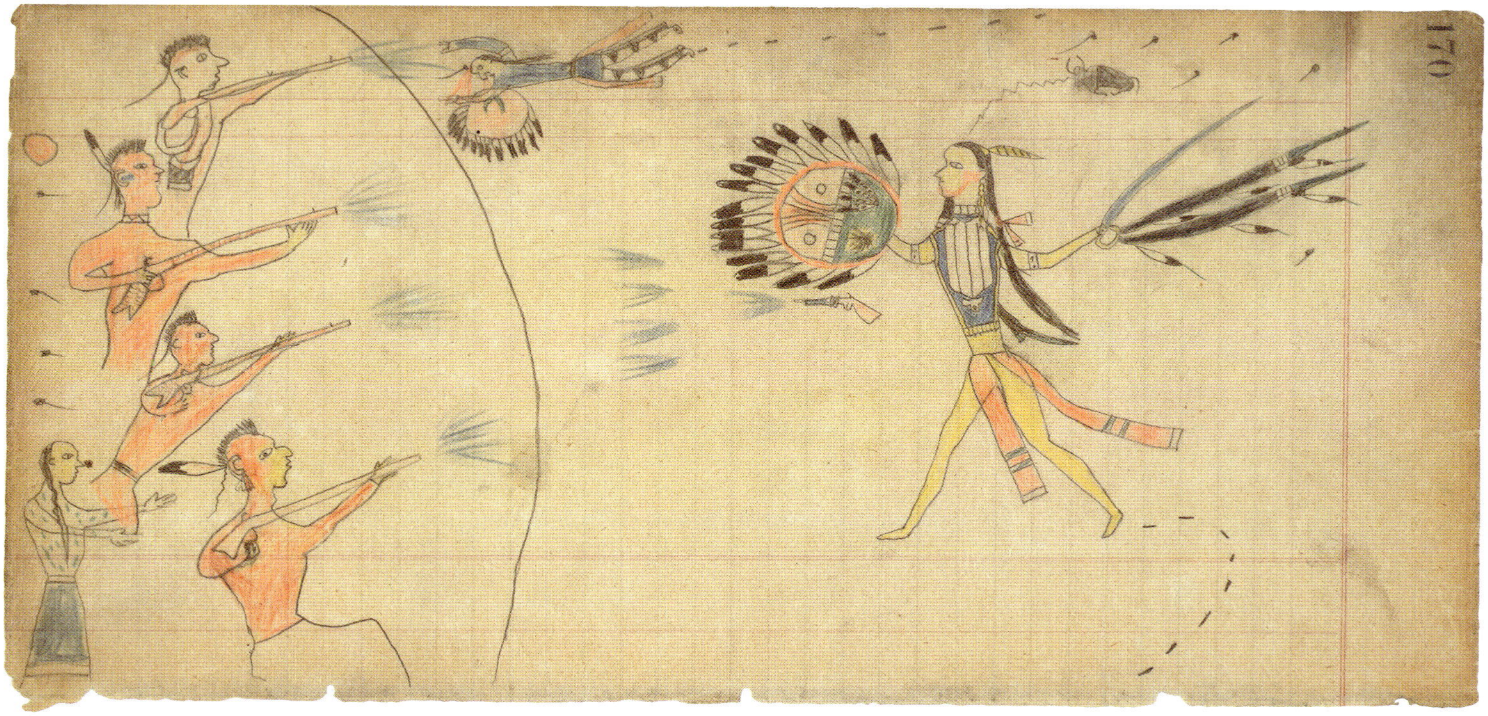

PLATE 79

Unknown artist, Tsistsistas (Cheyenne) and/or Inunaina (Arapaho), active late nineteenth century, ***Untitled [A warrior battles enemies while a fellow warrior has fallen]***, page 170 from the "Vincent Price Ledger," late nineteenth century, graphite and colored pencil on laid ledger paper, reverse: page 169 (2007.88.4), sheet: 5 ¾ × 11 ¾ in. (14.4 × 29.7 cm). Gift of Mark Lansburgh, Class of 1949; 2007.88.5.

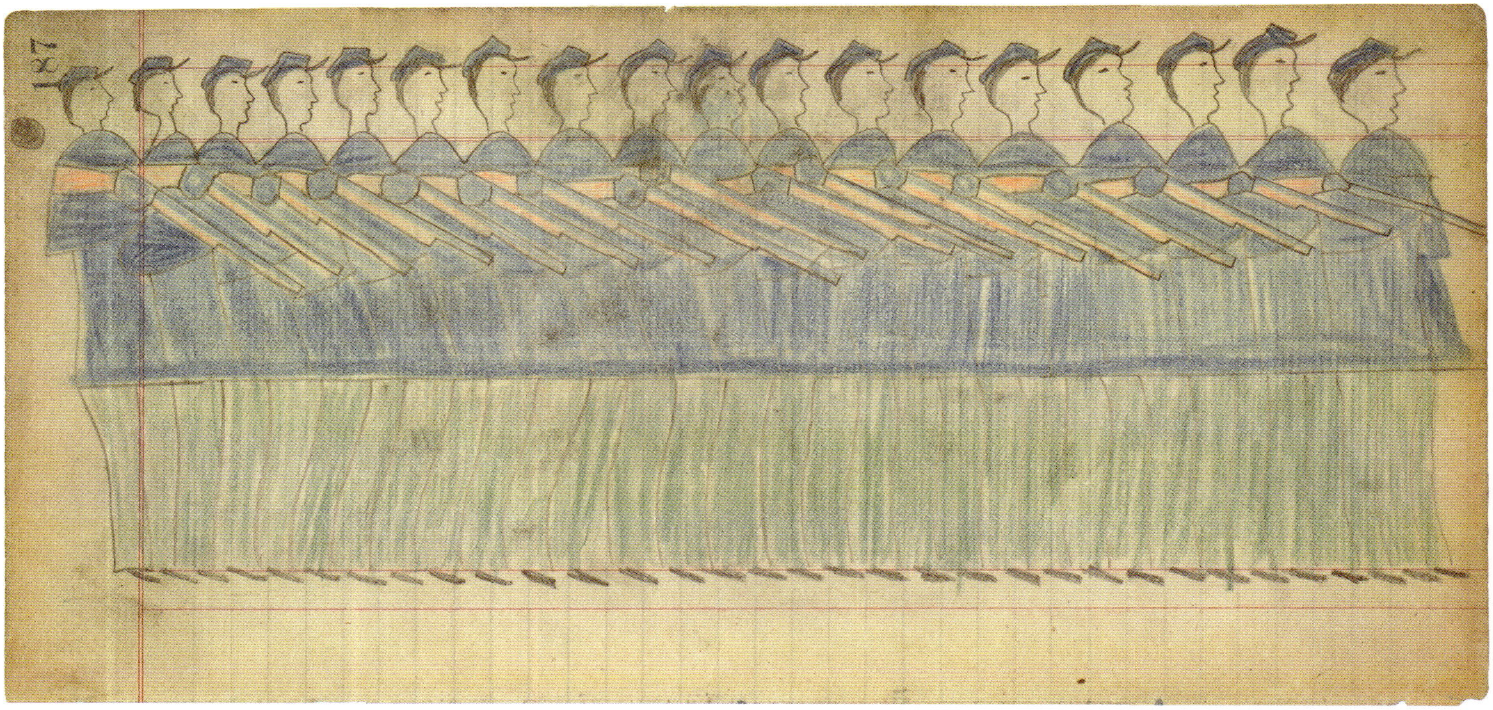

PLATE 80

Unknown artist, Tsistsistas (Cheyenne) and/or Inunaina (Arapaho), active late nineteenth century, ***Untitled [A formation of U.S. soldiers]***, page 187 from the "Vincent Price Ledger," late nineteenth century, graphite and colored pencil on laid ledger paper, reverse: page 188 (2007.65.43), sheet: 5 ¾ × 11 ¾ in. (14.7 × 29.7 cm); 2007.65.44.

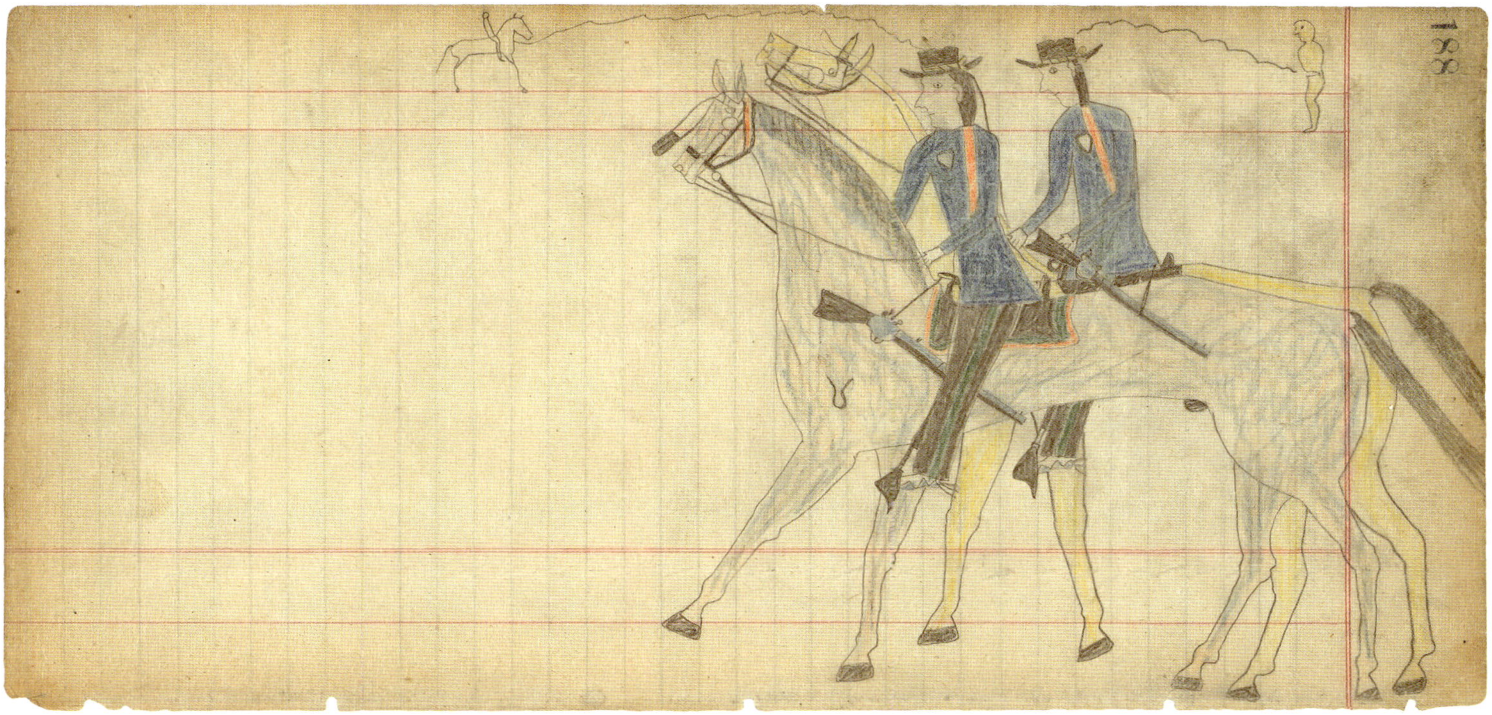

PLATE 81

Unknown artist, Tsistsistas (Cheyenne) and/or Inunaina (Arapaho), active late nineteenth century, ***Untitled ["Indian Police" on patrol],*** page 188 from the "Vincent Price Ledger," late nineteenth century, graphite and colored pencil on laid ledger paper, reverse: page 187 (2007.65.44), sheet: 5 ¾ × 11 ¾ in. (14.7 × 29.7 cm); 2007.65.43.

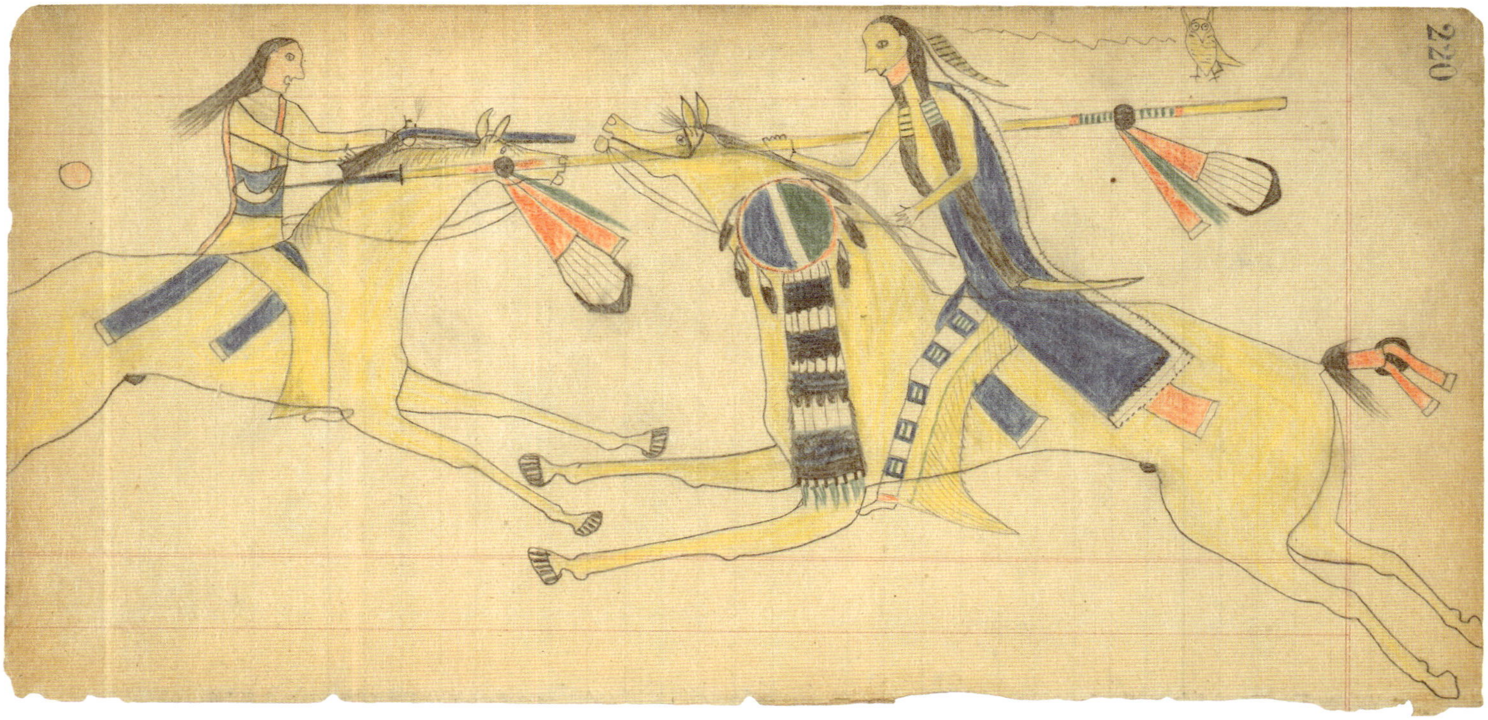

PLATE 82

Unknown artist, Tsistsistas (Cheyenne) and/or Inunaina (Arapaho), active late nineteenth century, ***Untitled [A warrior counts coup on an enemy],*** page 220 from the "Vincent Price Ledger," late nineteenth century, graphite and colored pencil on laid ledger paper, reverse: page 219 (no drawing), sheet: 5 ¾ × 11 ¾ in. (14.6 × 29.7 cm); 2007.65.48.

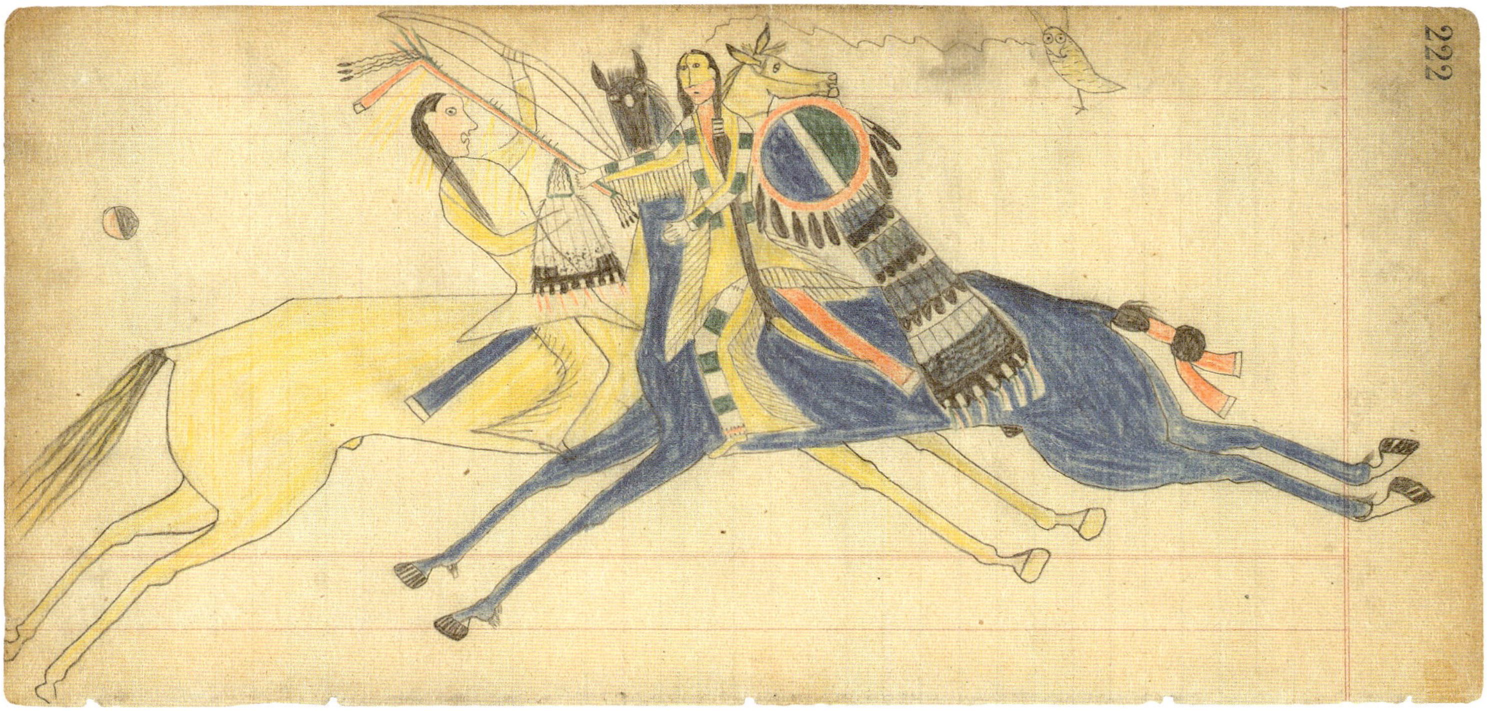

PLATE 83

Unknown artist, Tsistsistas (Cheyenne) and/or Inunaina (Arapaho), active late nineteenth century, ***Untitled [An Inunaina (Arapaho) or Tsistsistas (Cheyenne) warrior counts coup on an enemy],*** page 222 from the "Vincent Price Ledger," late nineteenth century, graphite and colored pencil on laid ledger paper, reverse: page 221 (no drawing), sheet: 5 ¾ × 11 ¾ in. (14.6 × 29.7 cm); 2007.65.49.

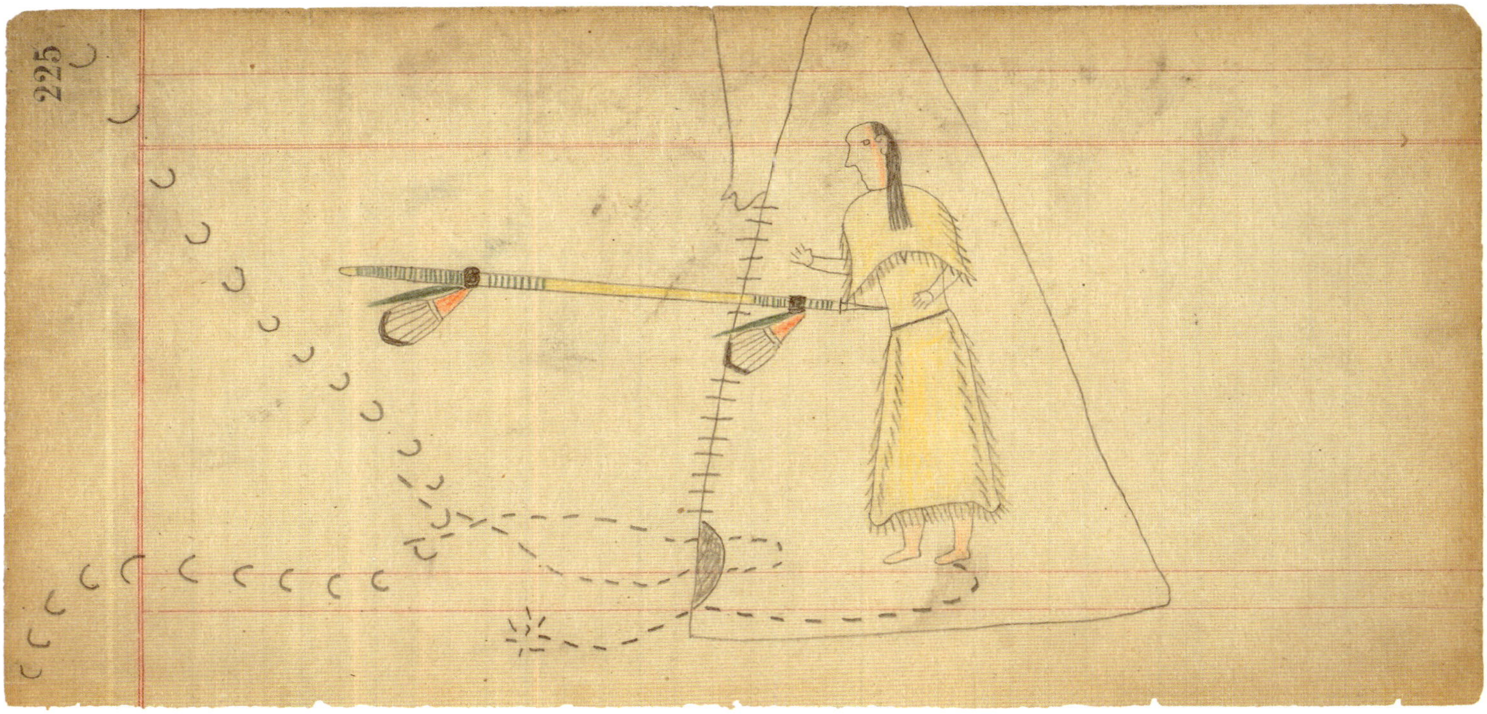

PLATE 84

Unknown artist, Tsistsistas (Cheyenne) and/or Inunaina (Arapaho), active late nineteenth century, ***Untitled [Counting coup on a woman],*** page 225 from the "Vincent Price Ledger," late nineteenth century, graphite and colored pencil on laid ledger paper, reverse: page 226 (2007.65.96). sheet: 5 ¾ × 11 ¾ in. (14.6 × 29.7 cm); 2007.65.97.

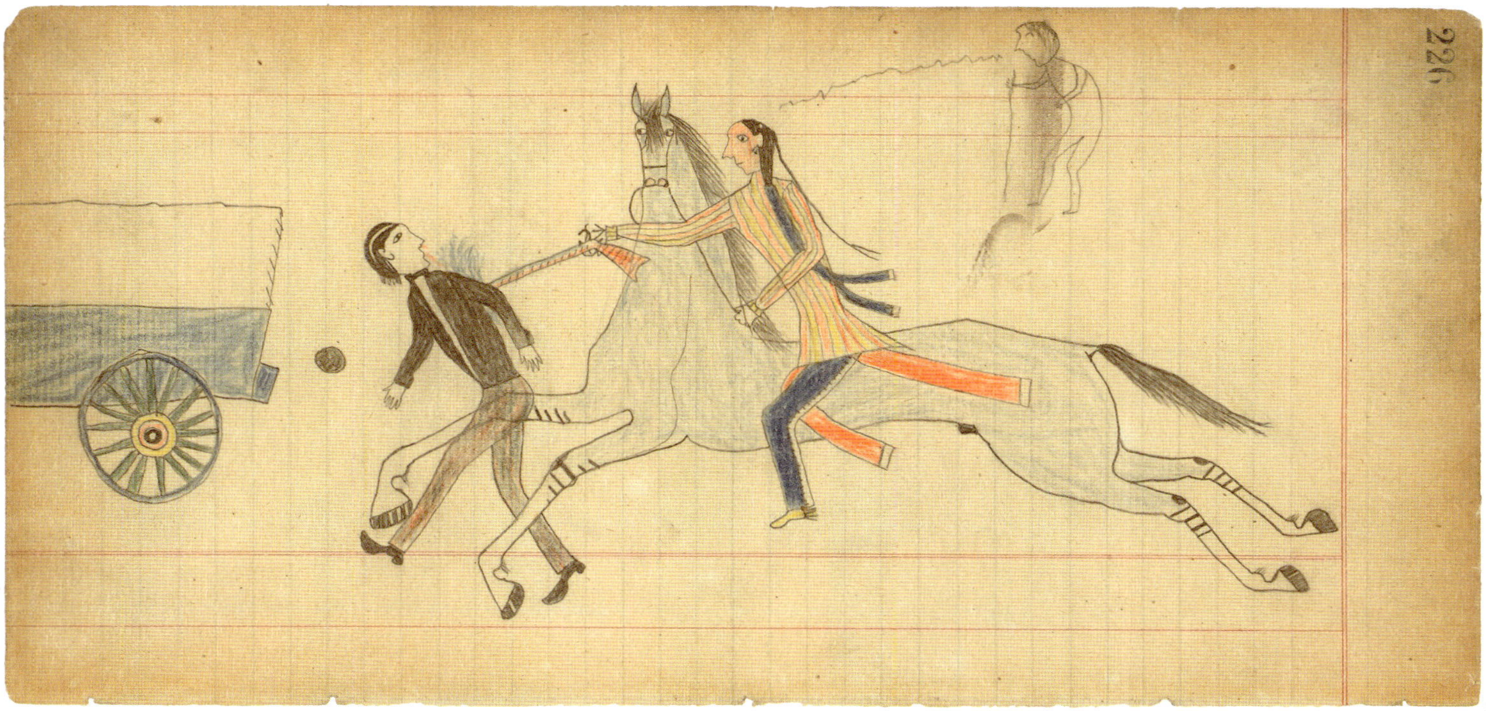

PLATE 85

Unknown artist, Tsistsistas (Cheyenne) and/or Inunaina (Arapaho), active late nineteenth century, ***Untitled [A warrior shoots a non-Native man],*** page 226 from the "Vincent Price Ledger," late nineteenth century, graphite and colored pencil on laid ledger paper, reverse: page 225 (2007.65.97), sheet: 5 ¾ × 11 ¾ in. (14.6 × 29.7 cm); 2007.65.96.

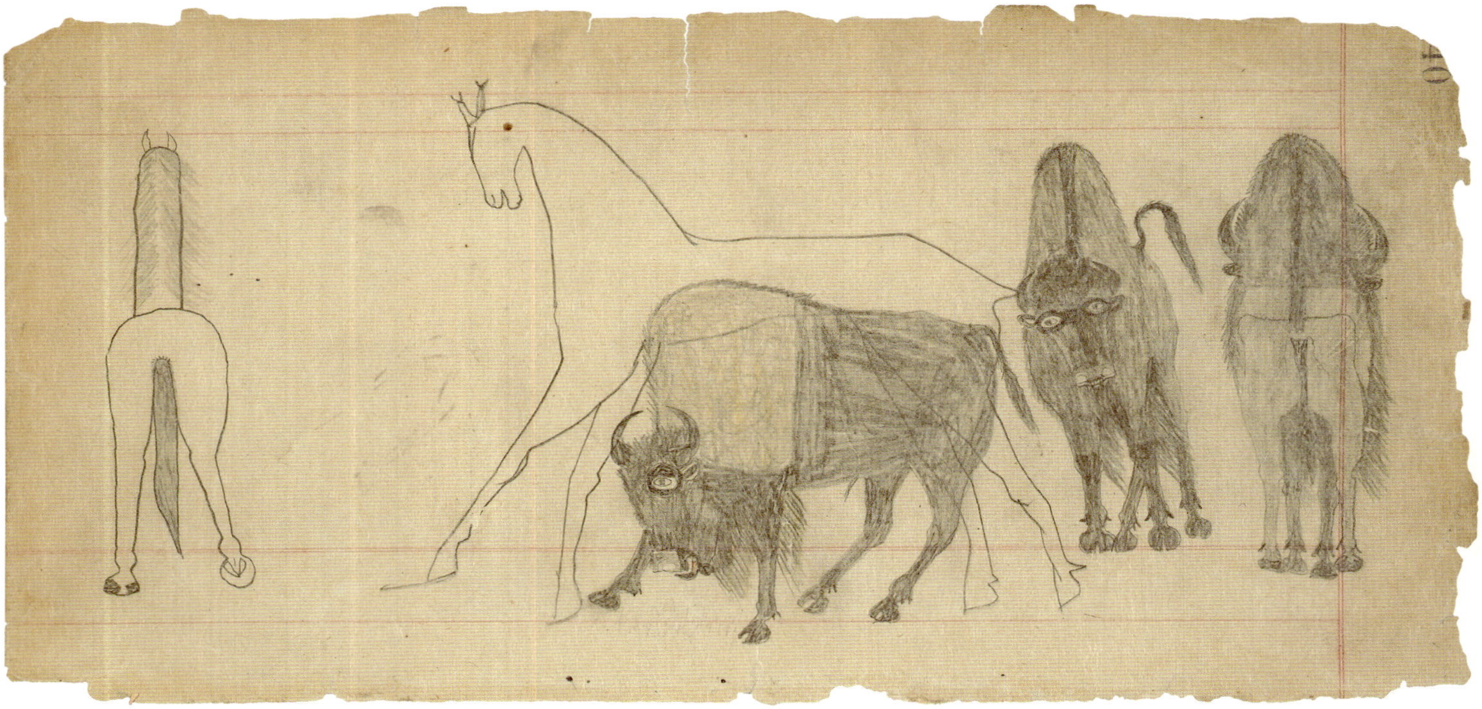

PLATE 86

Unknown artist, Tsistsistas (Cheyenne) and/or Inunaina (Arapaho), active late nineteenth century, ***Untitled [Horses and buffalo],*** page 240 from the "Vincent Price Ledger," late nineteenth century, graphite on laid ledger paper, reverse: page 239 (no drawing), sheet: 5 ¾ × 11 ¾ in. (14.6 × 29.6 cm); 2007.65.104.

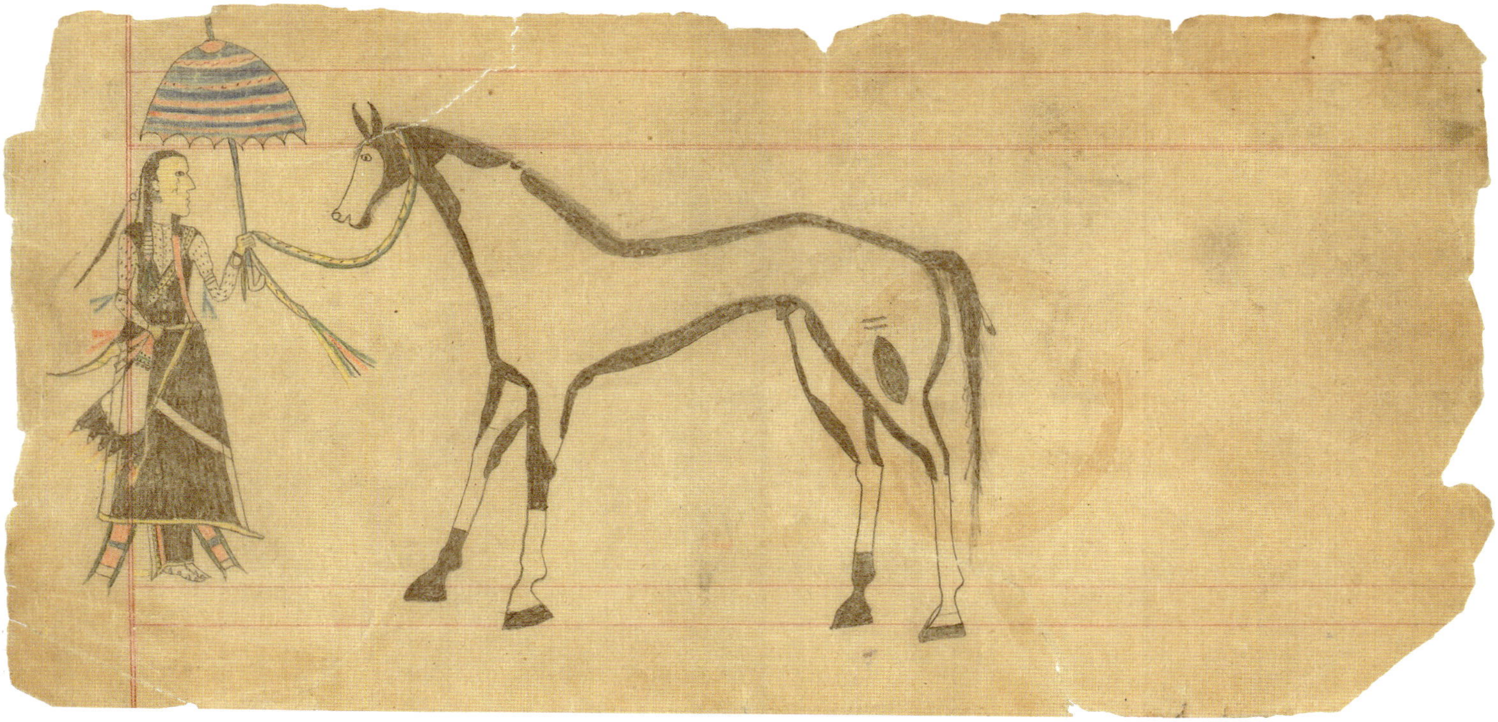

PLATE 87

Unknown artist, Tsistsistas (Cheyenne) and/or Inunaina (Arapaho), active late nineteenth century, ***Untitled [A man holding a parasol leads a horse],*** from the "Vincent Price Ledger," late nineteenth century, page number broken off, graphite and colored pencil on laid ledger paper, reverse: no page number (2007.88.2), sheet: 5 ¾ × 11 ⅜ in. (14.5 × 28.9 cm). Gift of Mark Lansburgh, Class of 1949; 2007.88.3.

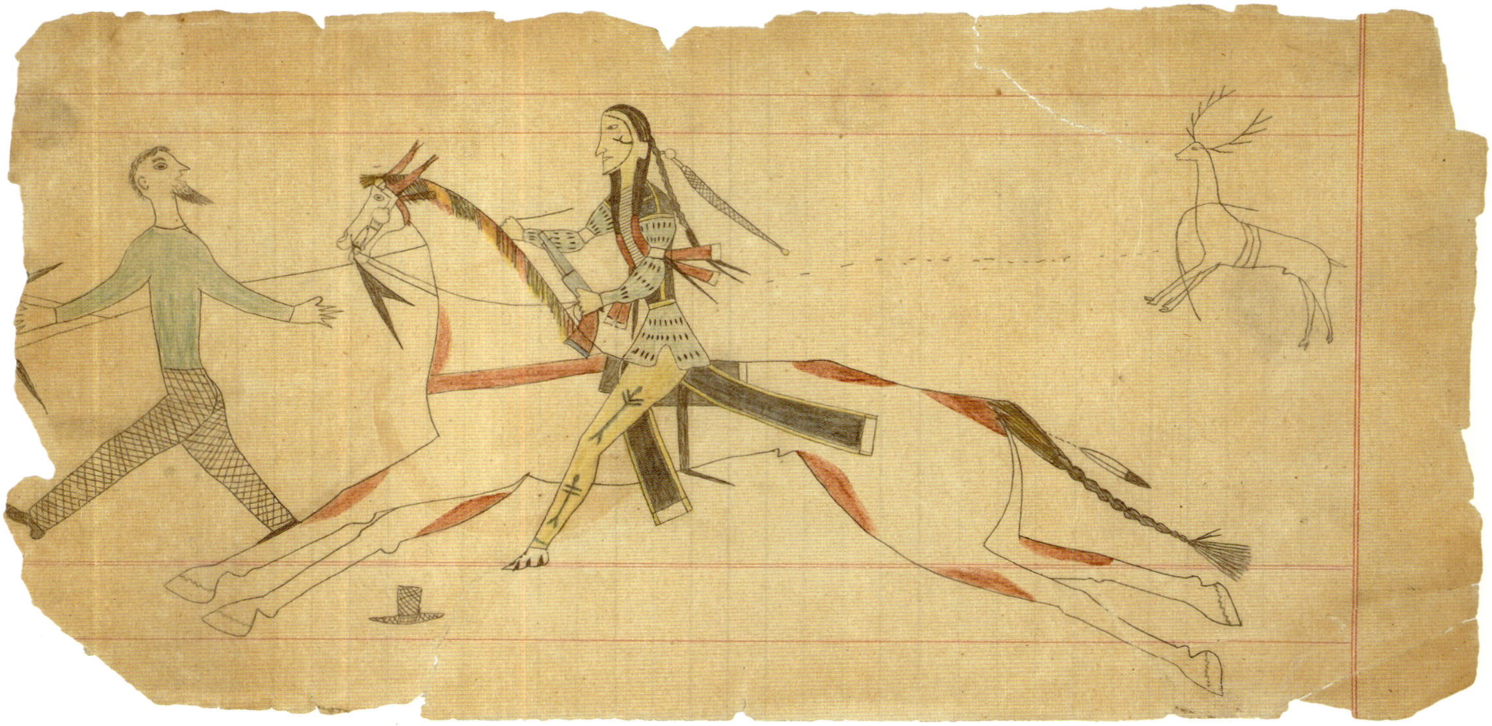

PLATE 88

Unknown artist, Tsistsistas (Cheyenne) and/or Inunaina (Arapaho), active late nineteenth century, ***Untitled [A warrior counts coup on a non-Native enemy],*** from the "Vincent Price Ledger," late nineteenth century, page number broken off, graphite and colored pencil on laid ledger paper; reverse: no page number (2007.88.3); sheet: 5 ¾ × 11 ⅜ in. (14.5 × 28.9 cm). Gift of Mark Lansburgh, Class of 1949; 2007.88.2.

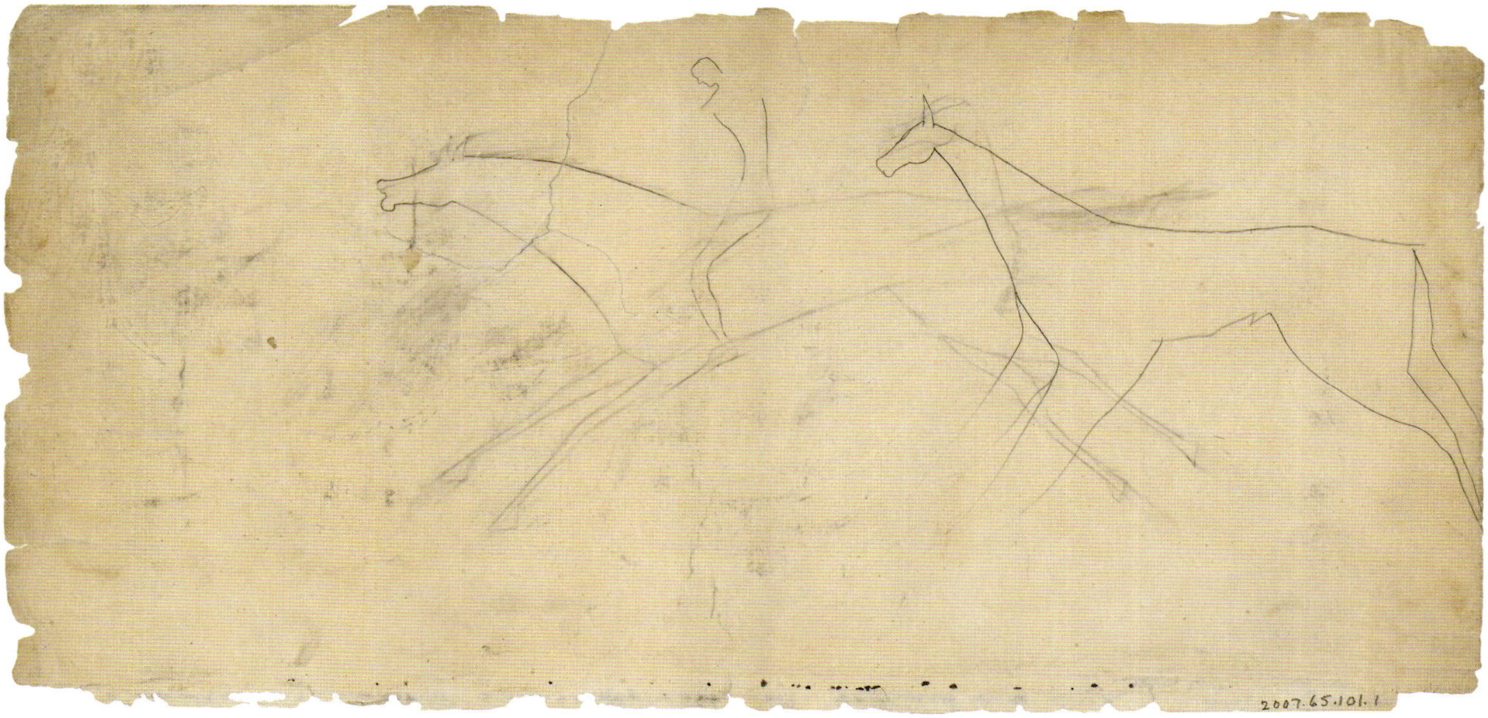

PLATE 89

Unknown artist, Tsistsistas (Cheyenne) and/or Inunaina (Arapaho), active late nineteenth century, ***Untitled [Sketch of two horses and a man],*** from the "Vincent Price Ledger," late nineteenth century, graphite on unlined wove paper (ledger endpaper), reverse: no page number (2007.65.102), sheet: 5 ¾ × 11 ¾ in. (14.4 × 29.6 cm); 2007.65.106.

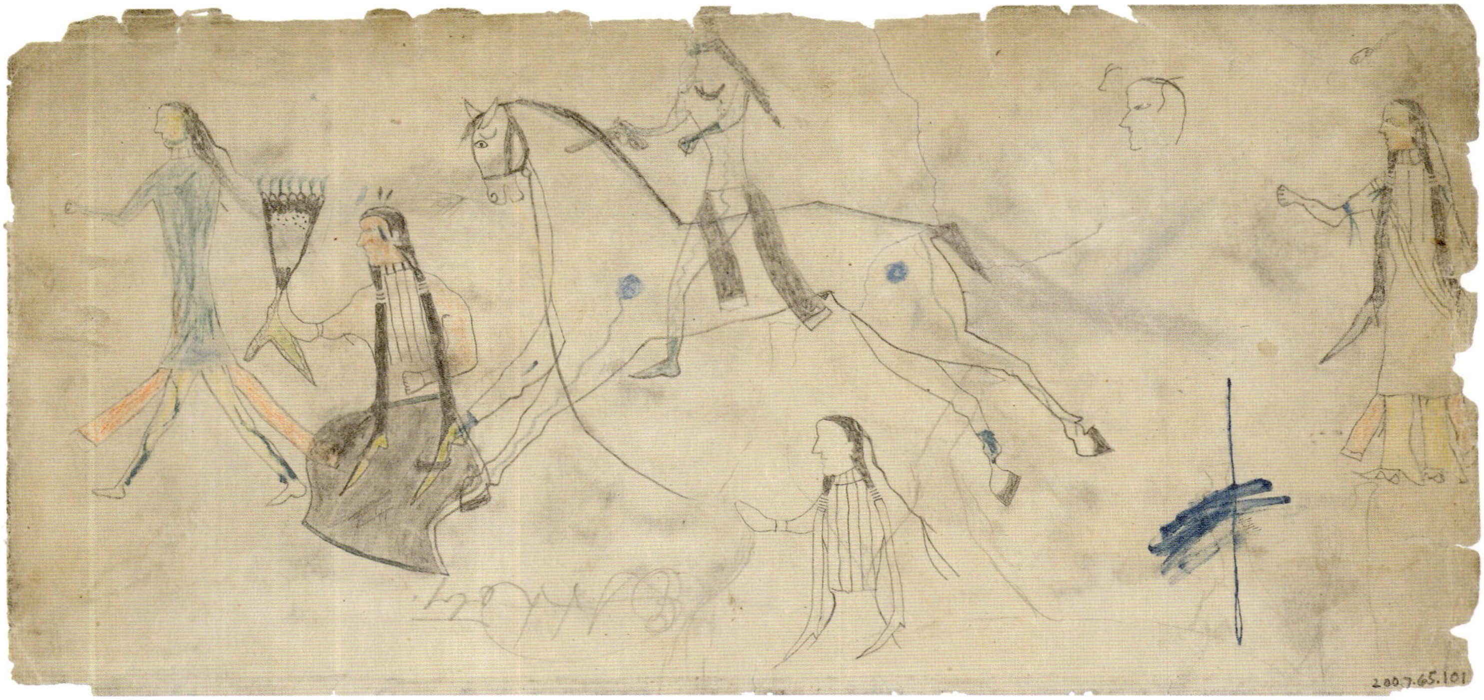

PLATE 90

Unknown artist, Tsistsistas (Cheyenne) and/or Inunaina (Arapaho), active late nineteenth century, ***Untitled [Sketches of warriors and a horse],*** from the "Vincent Price Ledger," late nineteenth century, graphite, colored pencil, and ink on wove paper (ledger endpaper), reverse: no page number (2007.65.106), sheet: 5 ¾ × 11 ¾ in. (14.4 × 29.6 cm); 2007.65.102.

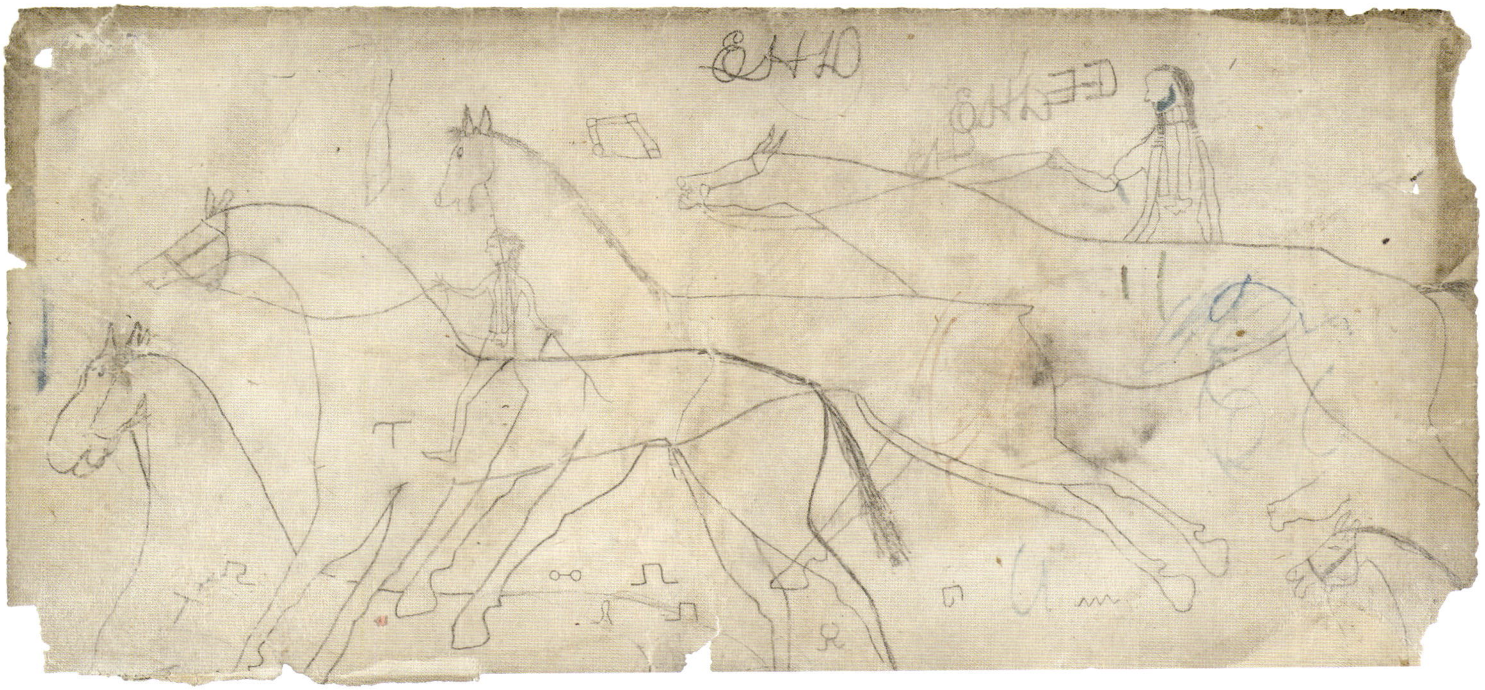

PLATE 91

Un<nown artist, Tsistsistas (Cheyenne) and/or Inunaina (Arapaho), active late nineteenth century, ***Untitled [Sketch of warriors and horses],*** from the "Vincent Price Ledger," late nineteenth century, graphite and colored pencil on wove paper (ledger endpaper), reverse: no page number (no drawing), sheet: 5 5⁄8 × 11 7⁄8 in. (14.1 × 29.6 cm); 2007.65.103.

AN UNIDENTIFIED SKETCHBOOK

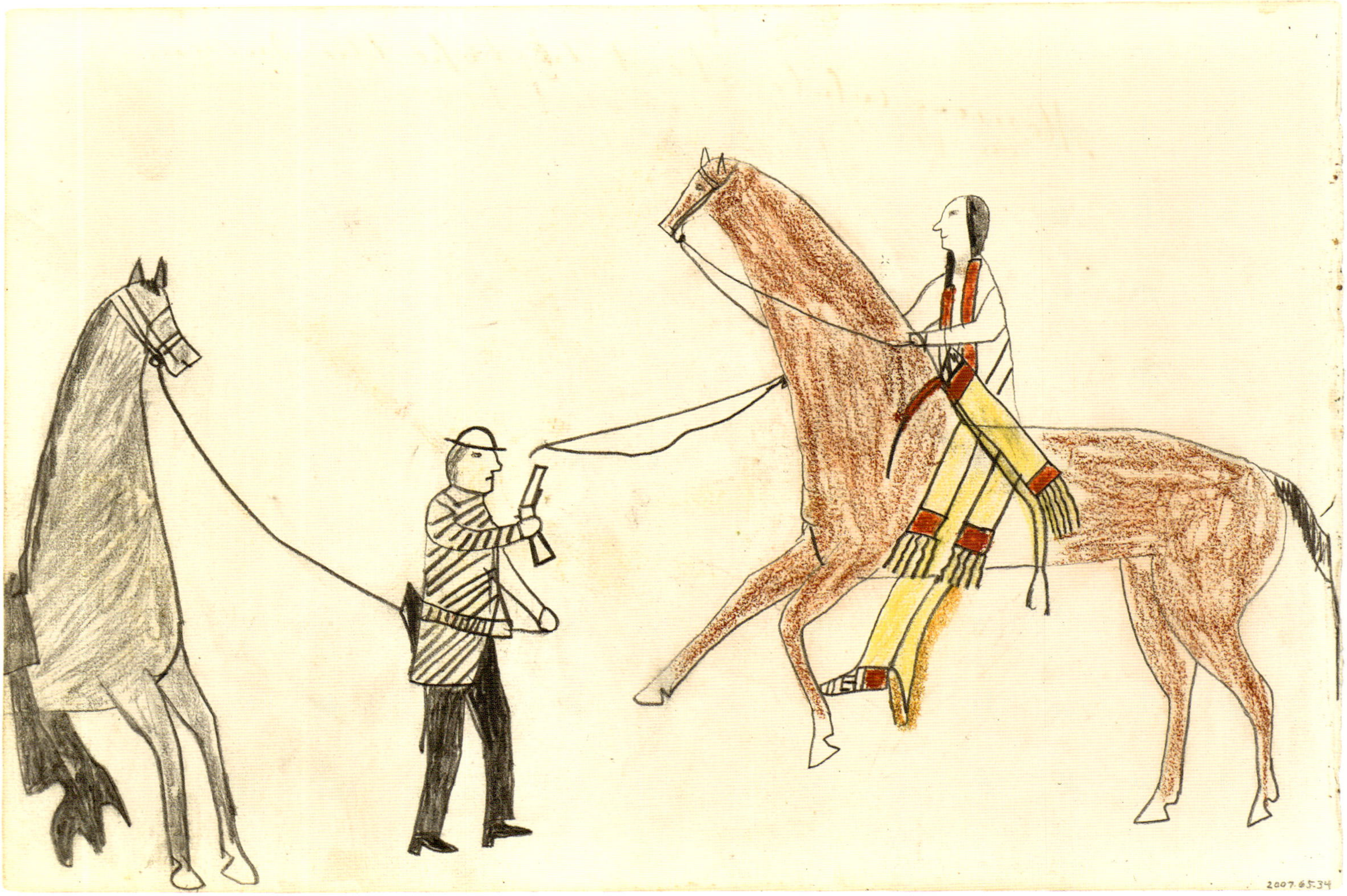

PLATE 92

Unknown artist, Kiowa and/or Mexican, active late nineteenth century, ***Untitled [A Kiowa warrior counts coup on a non-Native man],*** from an unidentified sketchbook, late nineteenth century, graphite and crayon on wove sketchbook paper, reverse: (2007.65.33), sheet: 9 × 13 ¼ in. (22.9 × 33.5 cm); 2007.65.34.

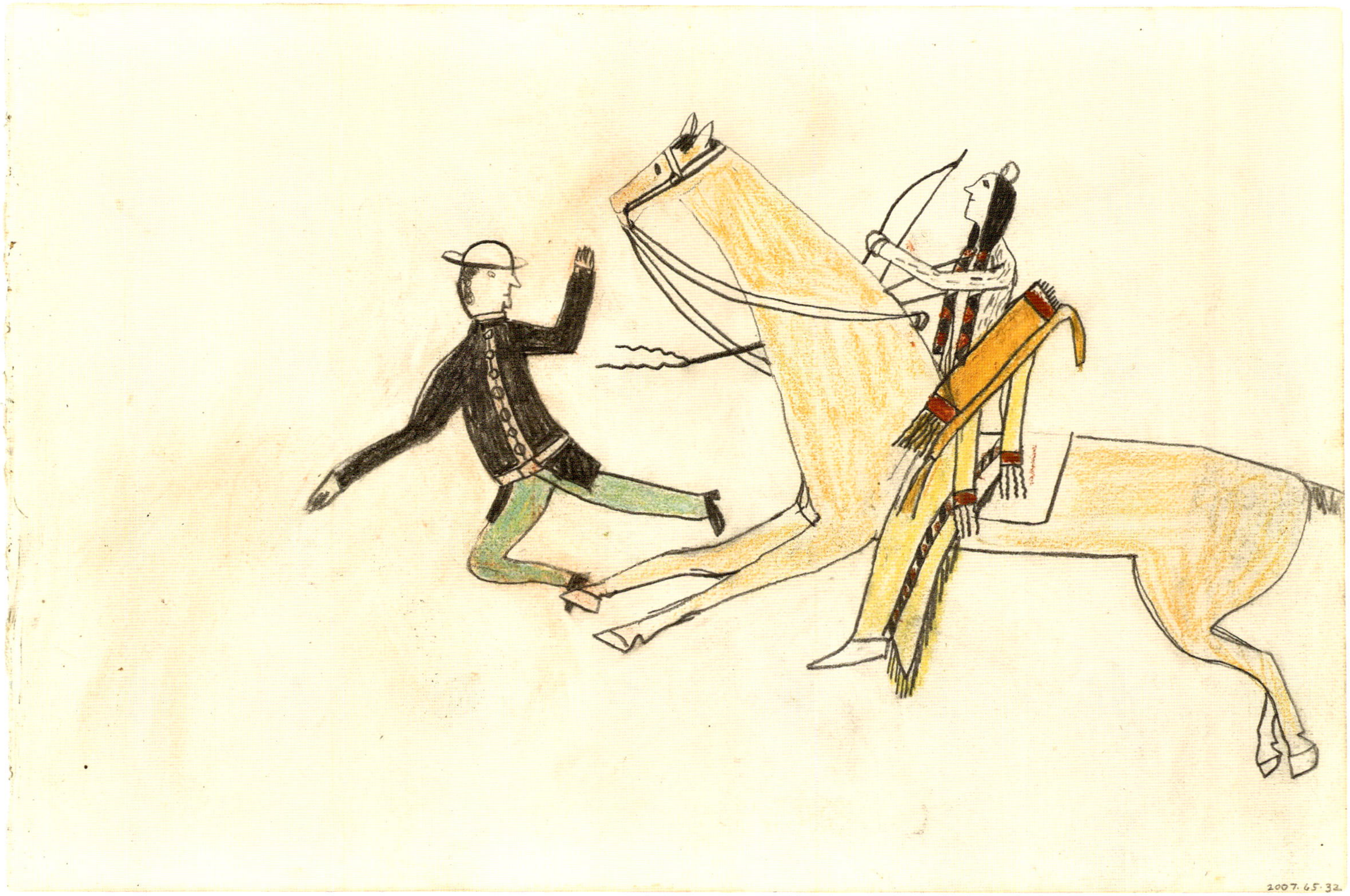

PLATE 93

Unknown artist, Kiowa and/or Mexican, active late nineteenth century, ***Untitled [A Kiowa warrior counts coup on a non-Native man],*** from an unidentified sketchbook, late nineteenth century, graphite and crayon on wove sketchbook paper, reverse: (2007.65.31), sheet: 9 × 13 ¼ in. (22.9 × 33.4 cm); 2007.65.32.

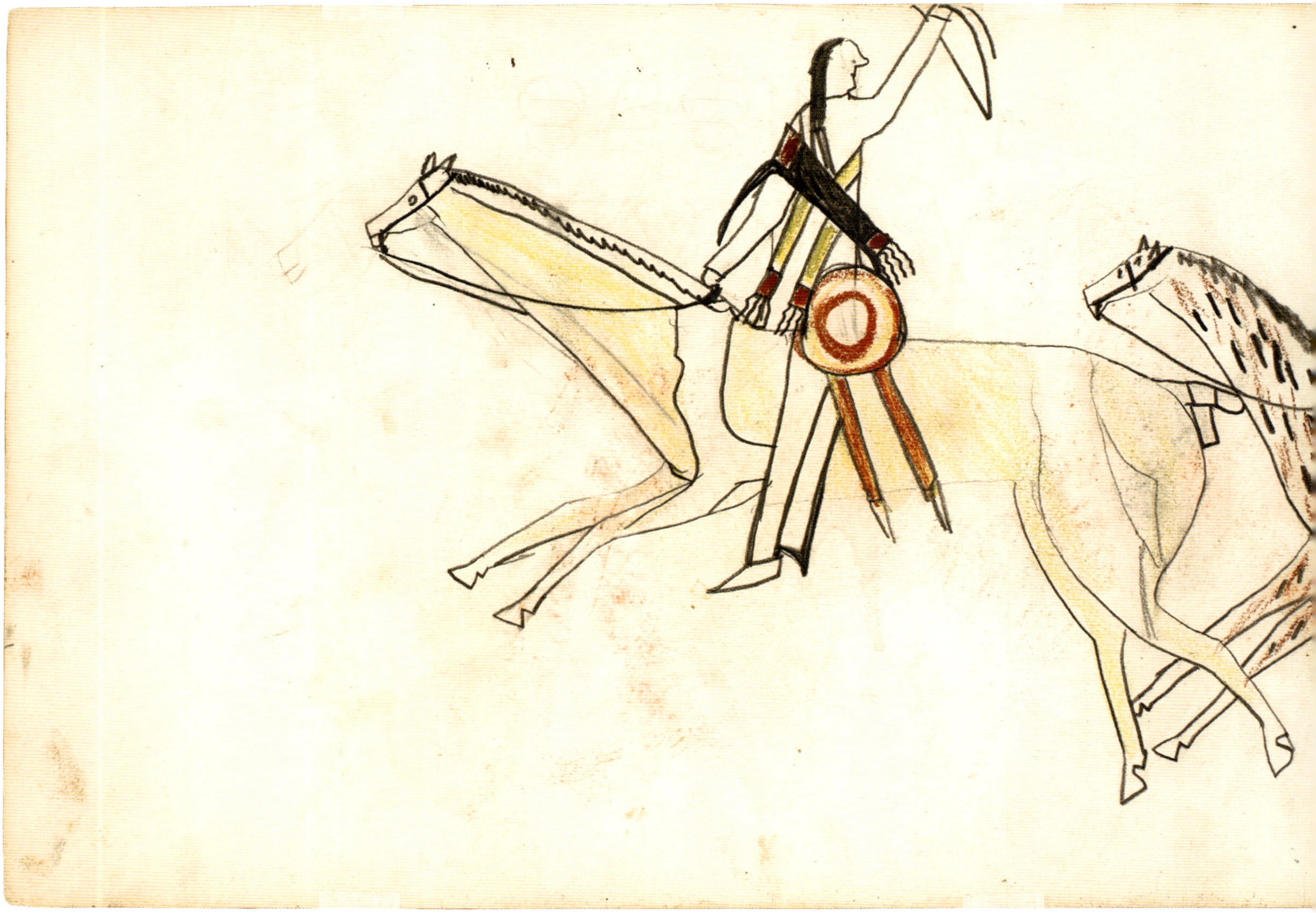

PLATE 94A

Unknown artist, Kiowa and/or Mexican, active late nineteenth century, ***Untitled [A Kiowa warrior],*** from an unidentified sketchbook, left side of a two-page composition, late nineteenth century, graphite and crayon on wove sketchbook paper, reverse: (2007.65.101), sheet: 9 × 13 ¼ in. (22.9 × 33.5 cm); 2007.65.100.

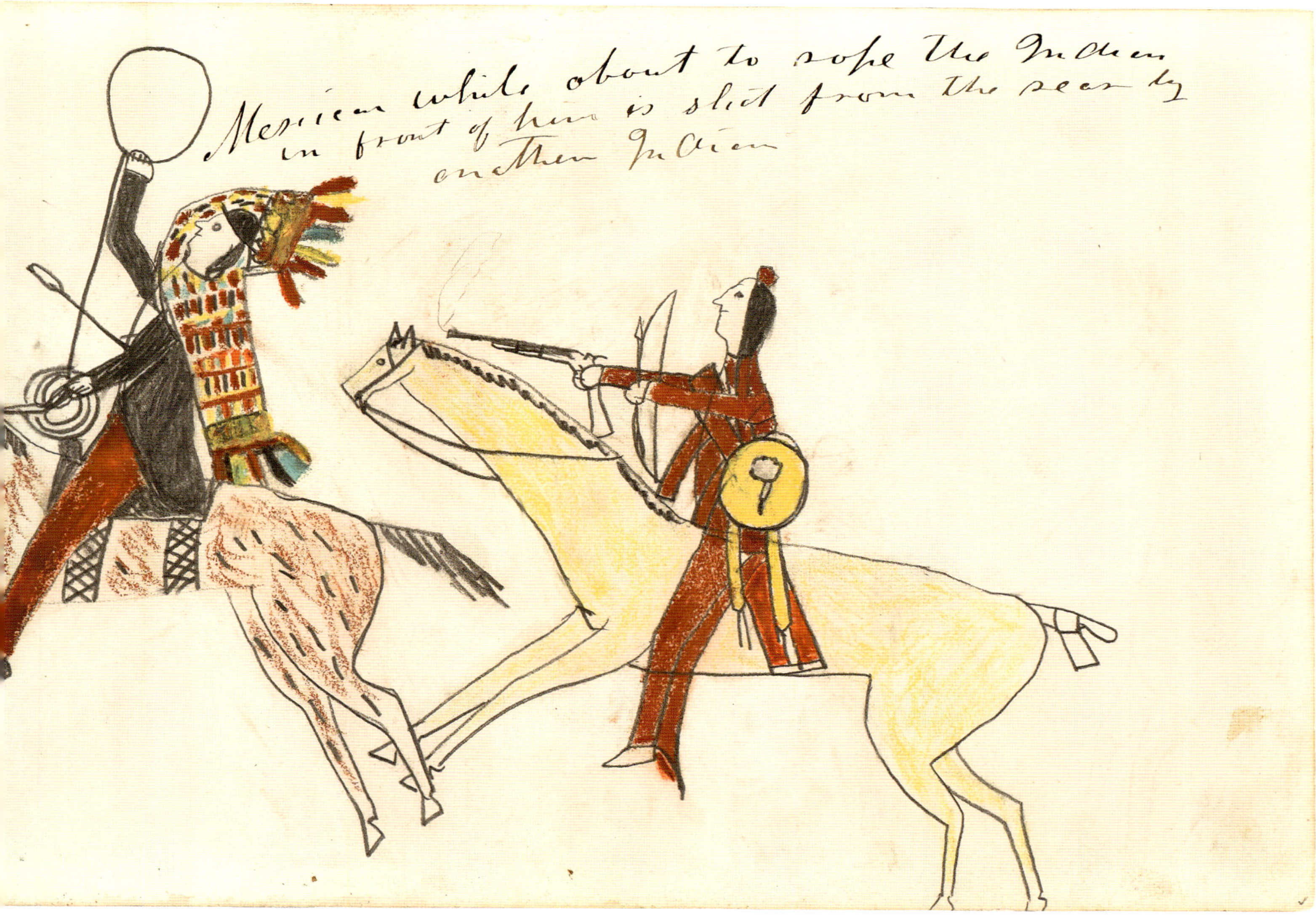

PLATE 94B

Unknown artist, Kiowa and/or Mexican, active late nineteenth century, ***Untitled [A Kiowa warrior fires upon a Mexican],*** from an unidentified sketchbook, right side of a two-page composition, late nineteenth century, graphite, colored pencil(?), crayon, and ink on wove sketchbook paper, reverse: (2007.65.34), sheet: 9 × 13 ¼ in. (22.9 × 33.5 cm); 2007.65.33.

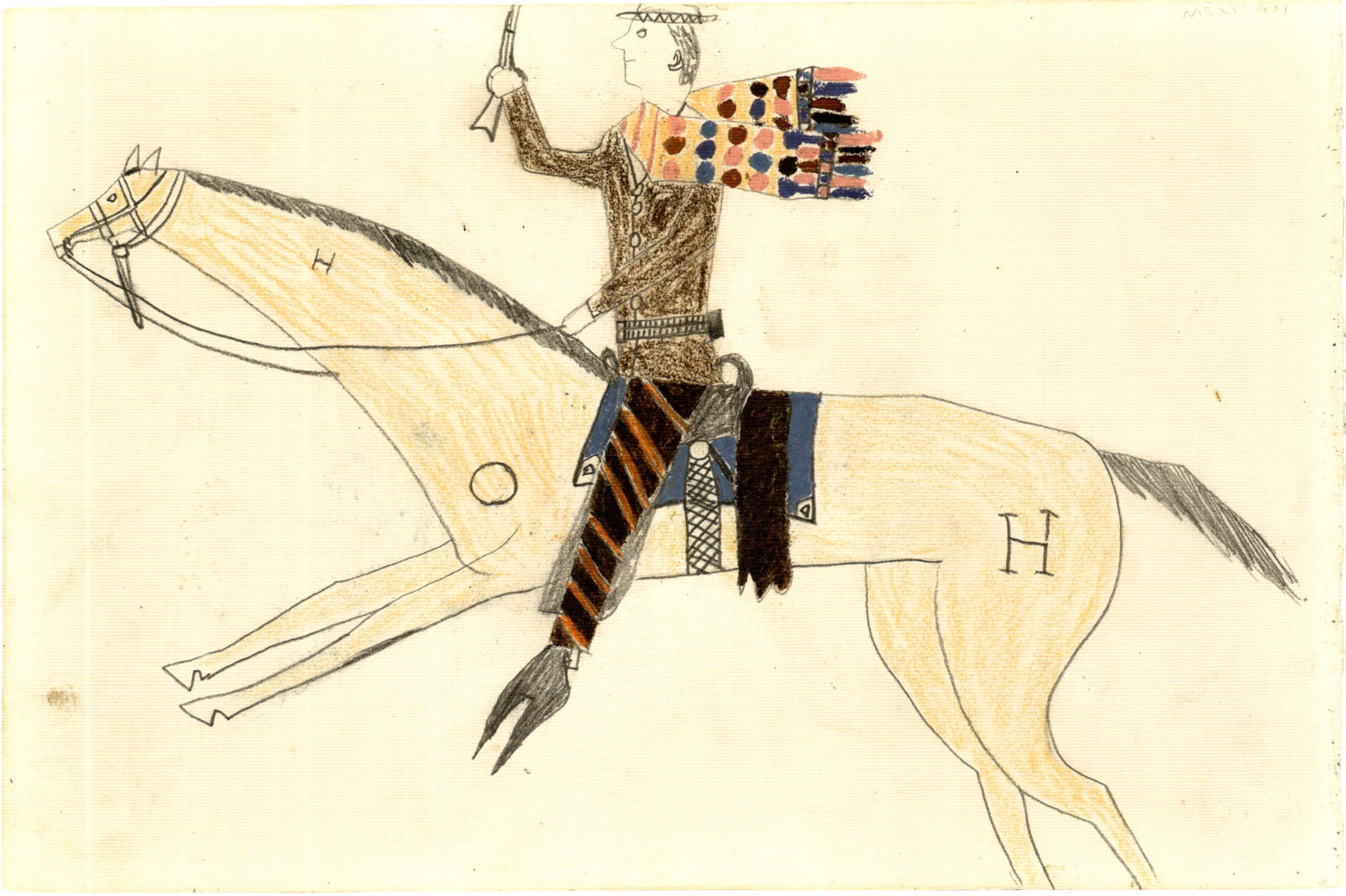

PLATE 95

Unknown artist, Kiowa and/or Mexican, active late nineteenth century, ***Untitled [A Mexican horseman],*** from an unidentified sketchbook, late nineteenth century, graphite, colored pencil, and crayon on wove sketchbook paper, reverse: (2007.65.32), sheet: 9 × 13 ¼ in. (22.9 × 33.4 cm); 2007.65.31.

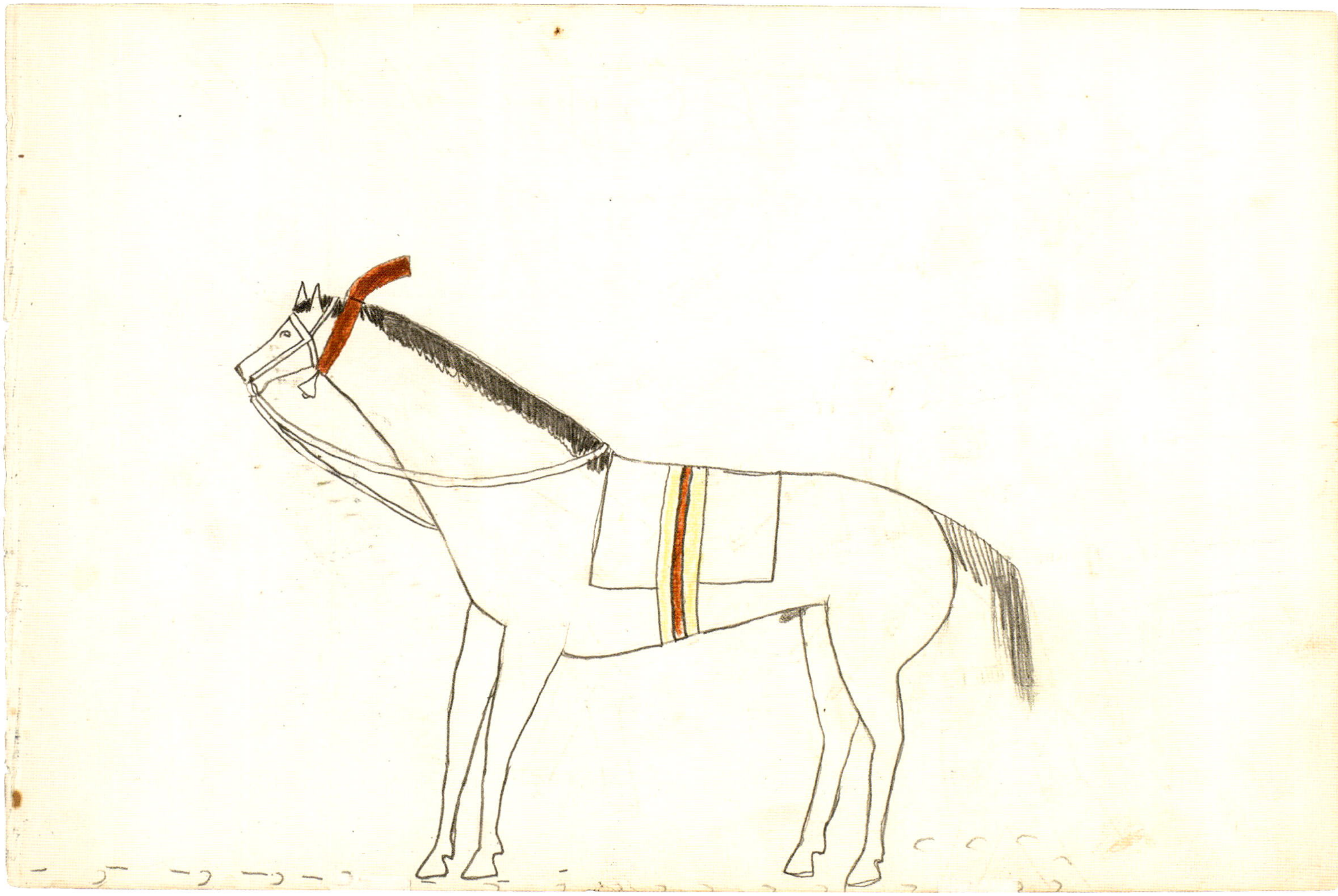

PLATE 96

Unknown artist, Kiowa and/or Mexican, active late nineteenth century, ***Untitled [A horse],*** from an unidentified sketchbook, late nineteenth century, graphite and crayon on wove sketchbook paper, reverse: (2007.65.99), sheet: 9 × 13 ¼ in. (22.9 × 33.5 cm); 2007.65.98.

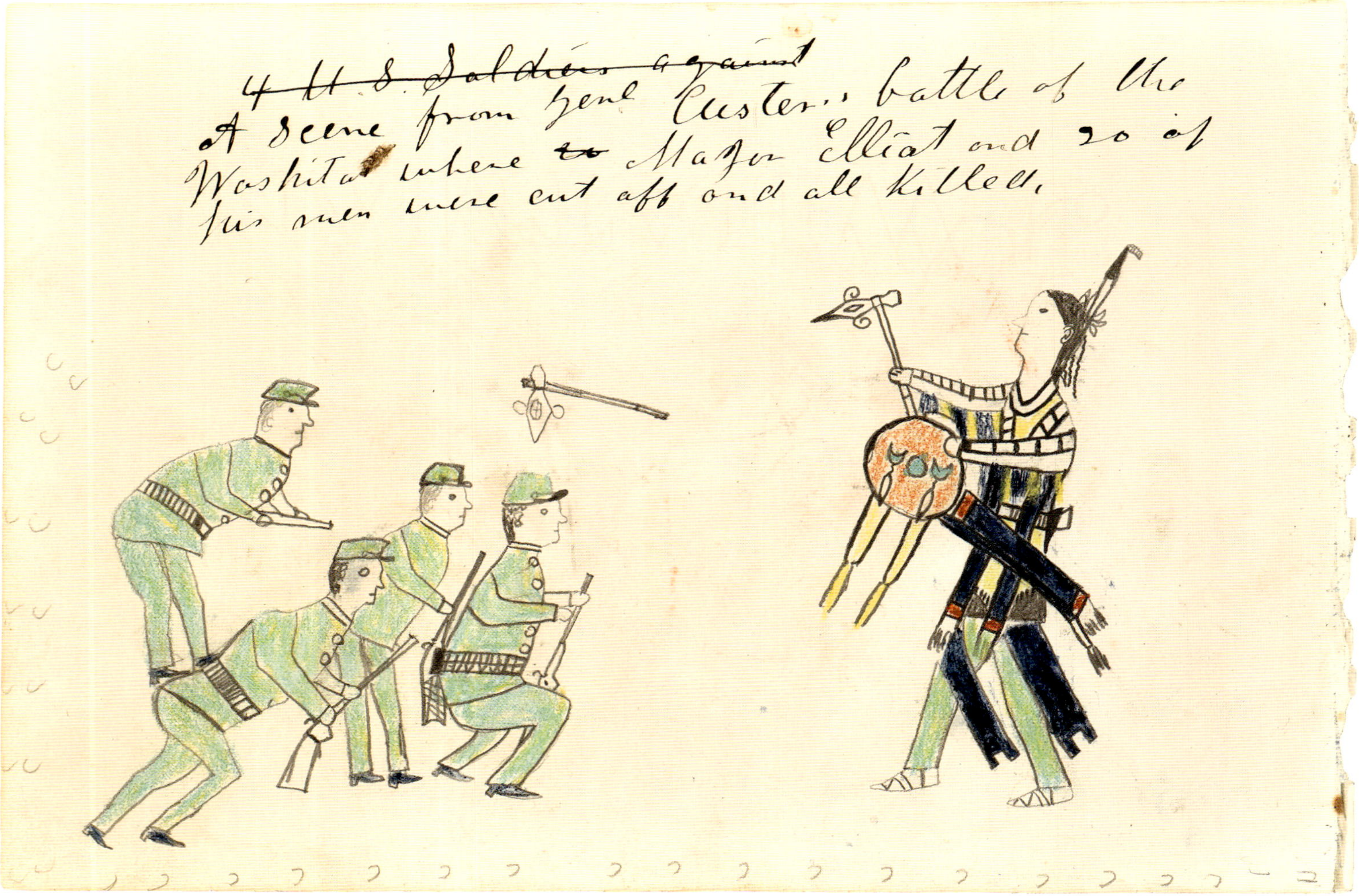

PLATE 97

Unknown artist, Kiowa and/or Mexican, active late nineteenth century, ***Untitled [A Kiowa warrior counts coup on the cavalry]***, from an unidentified sketchbook, late nineteenth century, graphite, colored pencil, crayon, and ink on wove sketchbook paper, reverse: (2007.65.36), sheet: 9 × 13 ¼ in. (22.9 × 33.5 cm); 2007.65.35.

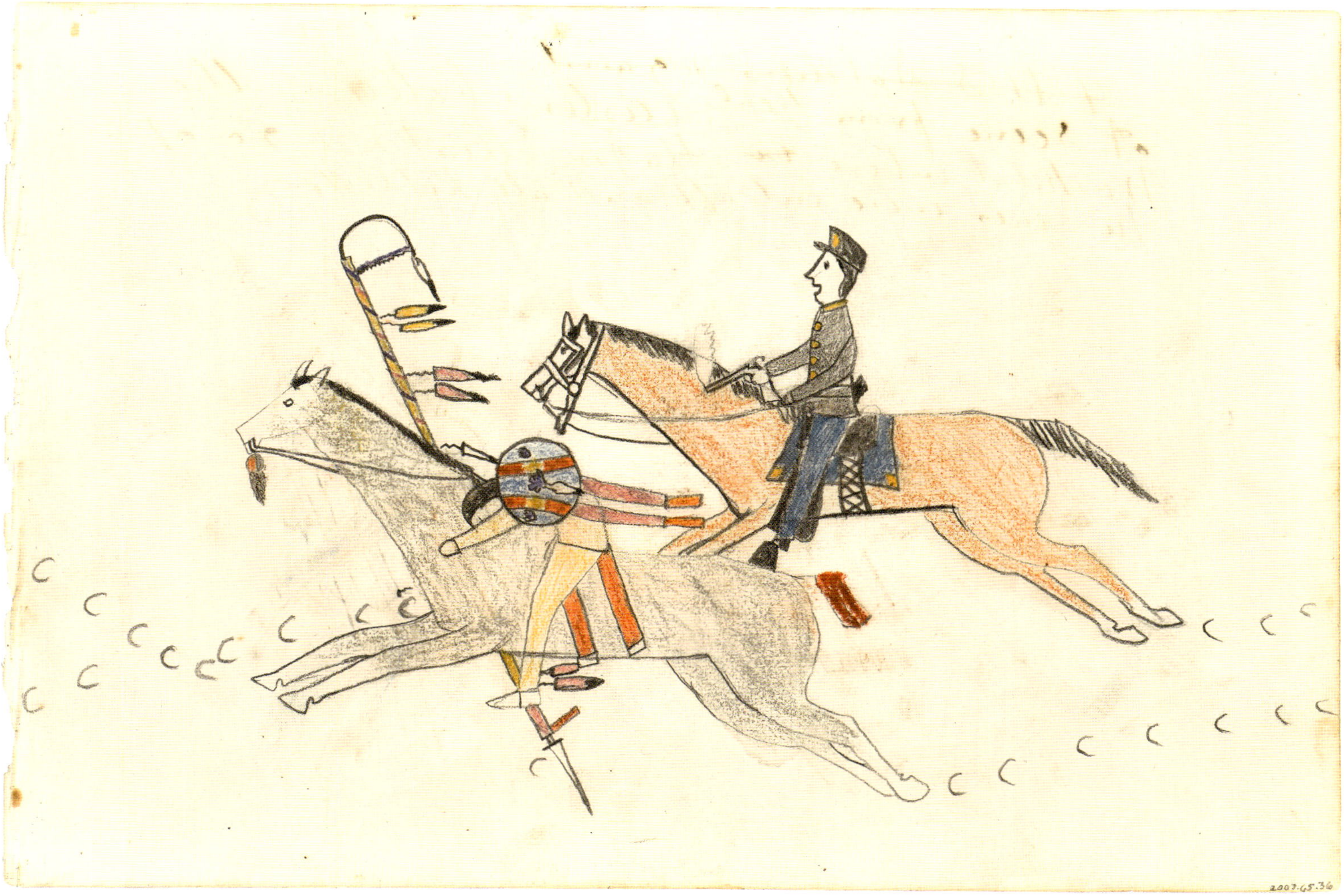

PLATE 98

Unknown artist, Kiowa and/or Mexican, active late nineteenth century, ***Untitled [A soldier in battle with Kiowa warrior]***, from an unidentified sketchbook, late nineteenth century, graphite, colored pencil, and crayon on wove sketchbook paper, reverse: (2007.65.35), sheet: 9 × 13 ¼ in. (22.9 × 33.5 cm); 2007.65.36.

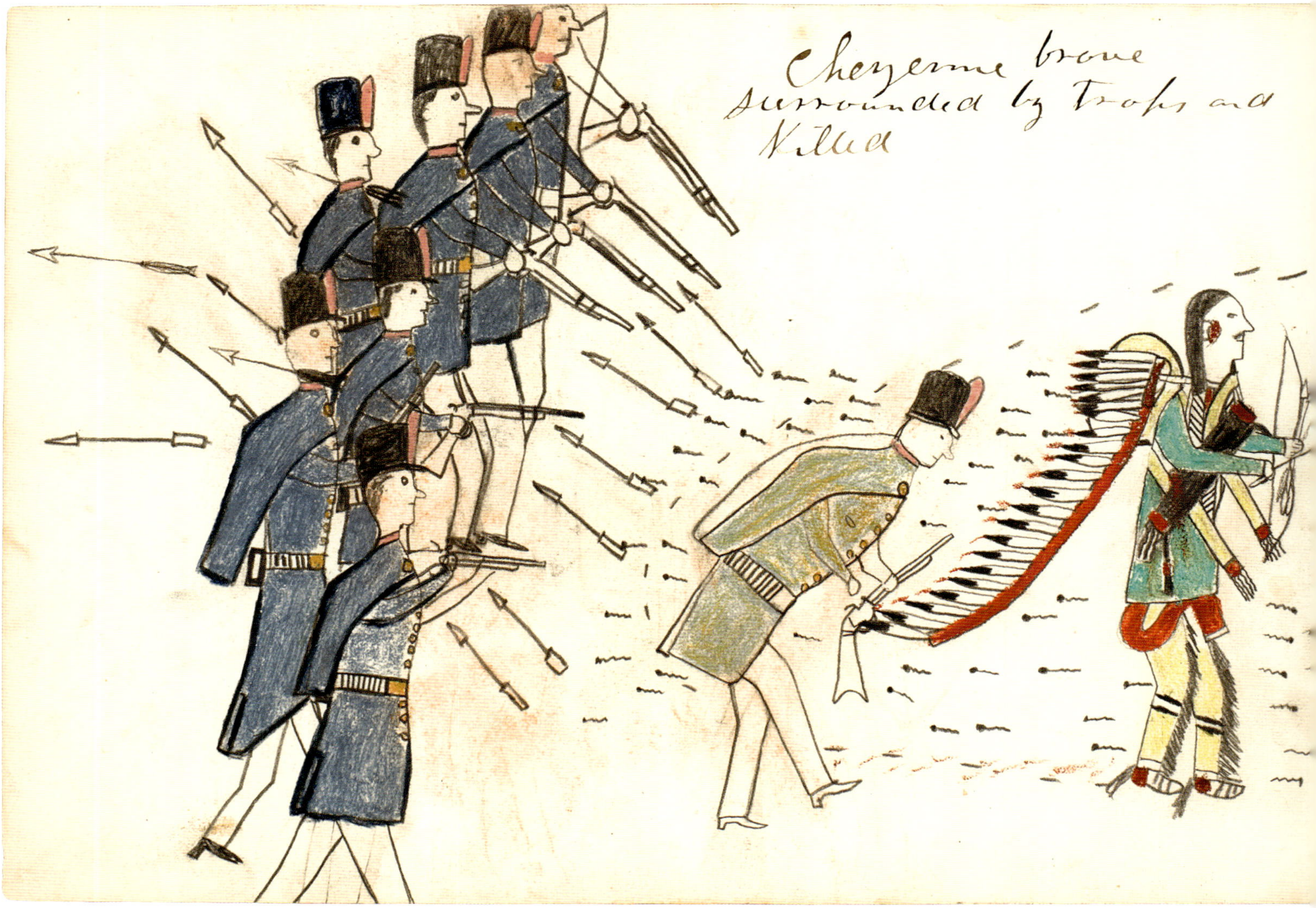

PLATE 99A

Unknown artist, Kiowa and/or Mexican, active late nineteenth century, ***Untitled [Kiowa warrior in battle with Mexican soldiers],*** from an unidentified sketchbook, left side of a two-page composition, late nineteenth century, graphite, crayon, and ink on wove sketchbook paper, reverse: (2007.65.98), sheet: 9 × 13 ¼ in. (22.9 × 33.5 cm); 2007.65.99.

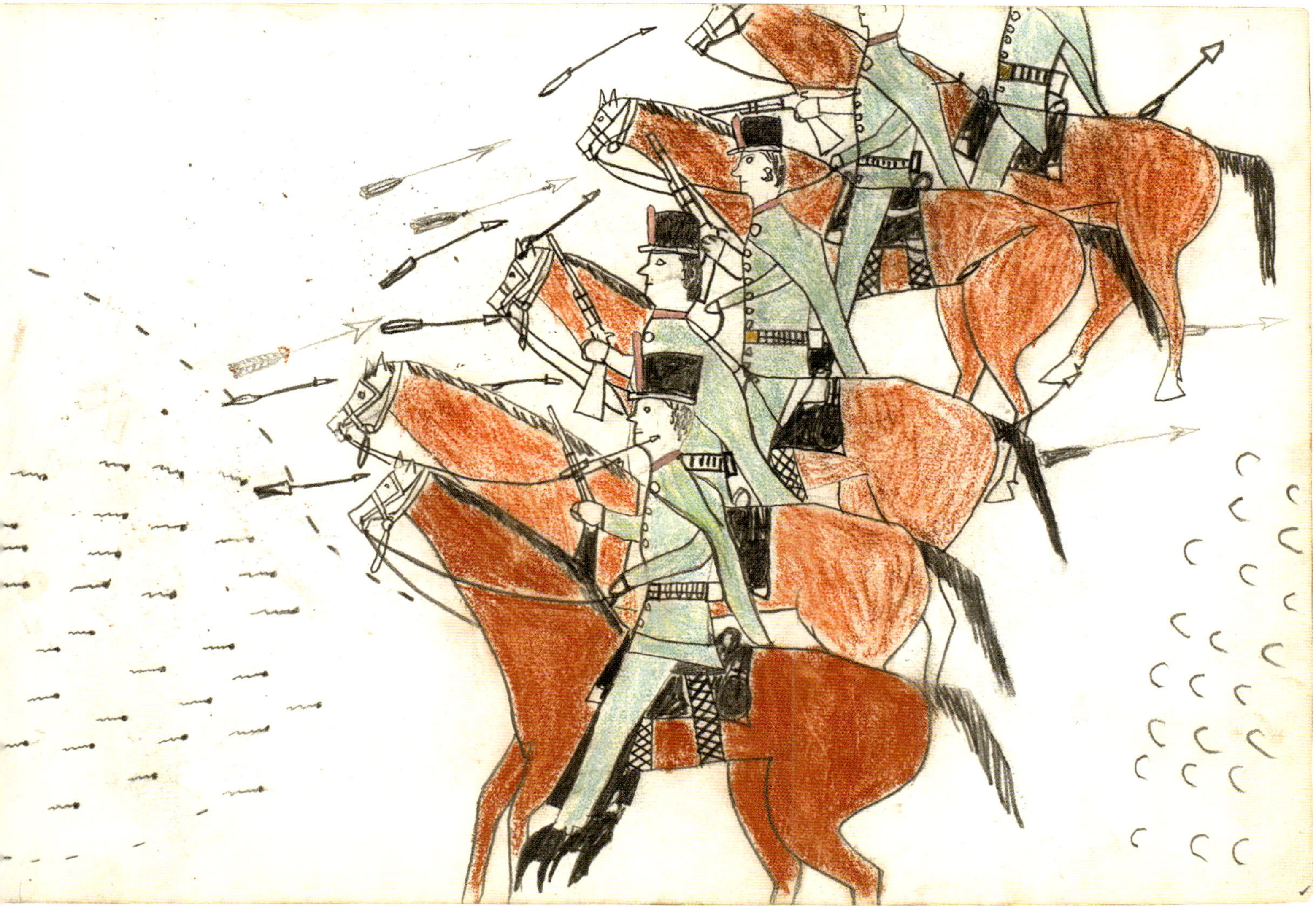

PLATE 99B

Unknown artist, Kiowa and/or Mexican, active late nineteenth century, ***Untitled [Mexican soldiers in battle],*** from an unidentified sketchbook, right side of a two-page composition, late nineteenth century, graphite and crayon on wove sketchbook paper, reverse: (2007.65.100), sheet: 9 × 13 ¼ in. (22.9 × 33.5 cm); 2007.65.101.

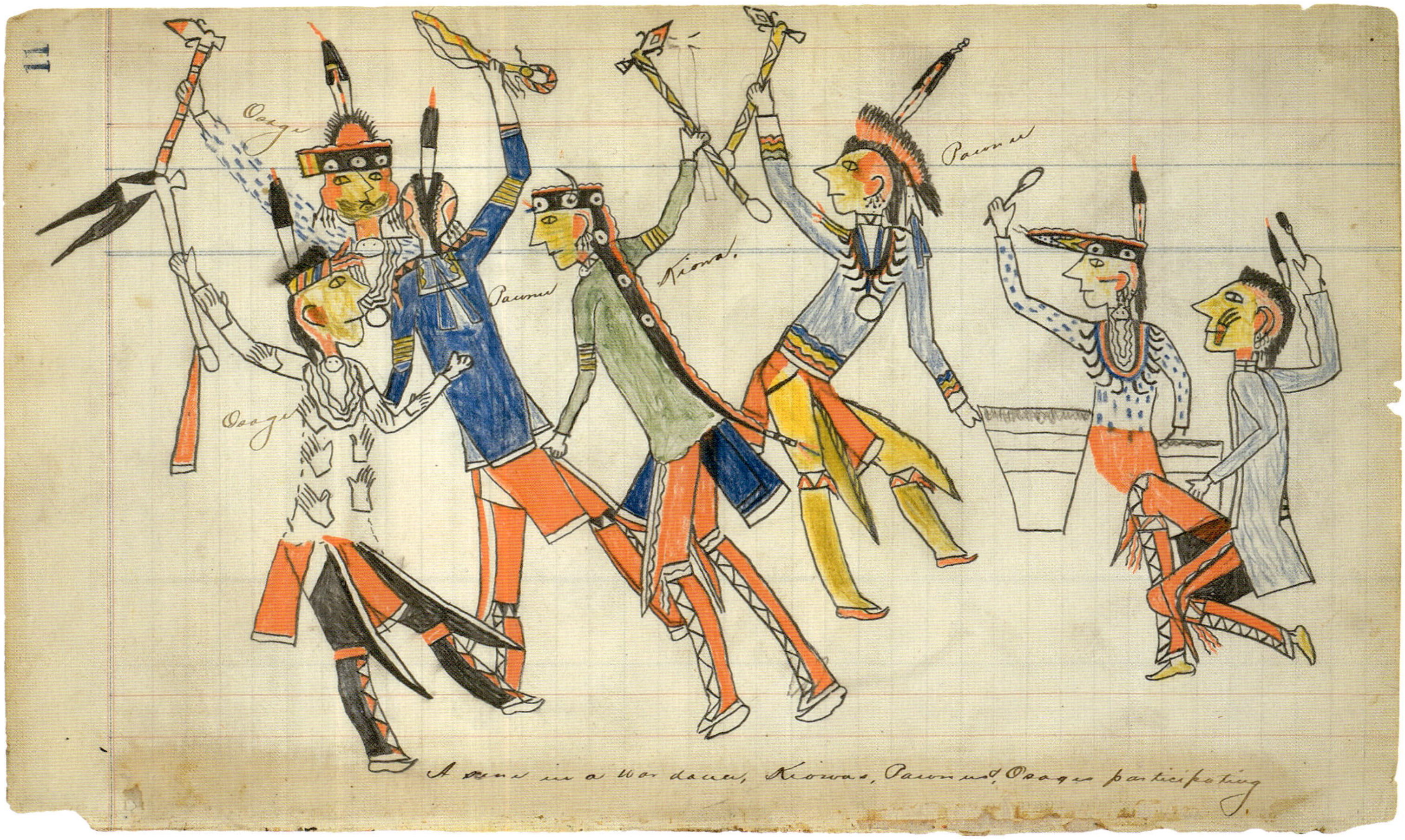

PLATE 100

Unknown artist, Kiowa, active late nineteenth century, ***Untitled [Osage war dance],*** page 11 from the "Julian Scott Ledger," 1880, graphite, colored pencil, watercolor, crayon, and ink on laid ledger paper, reverse: page 12 (no drawing), sheet: 7 ½ × 12 ¼ in. (19.2 × 31.1 cm). Purchased through the Robert J. Strasenburgh II 1942 Fund; D.2003.18.3.

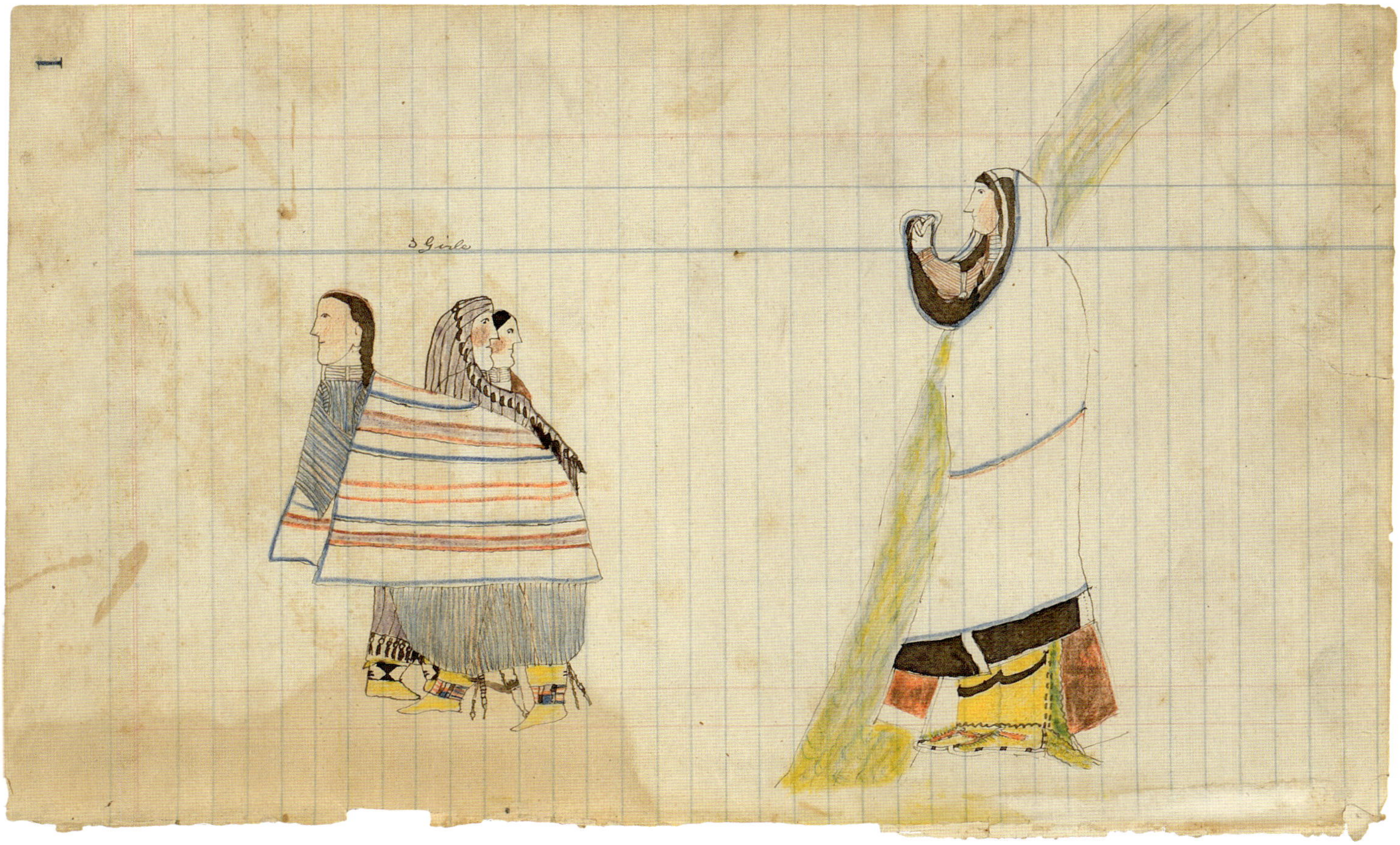

PLATE 101

Unknown artist, Tsistsistas (Cheyenne), active late nineteenth century, ***Untitled [A Tsistsistas (Cheyenne) man and three women],*** page 1 from the "Old White Woman Ledger," c. 1880–90, colored pencil, watercolor, and ink on wove ledger paper, reverse: page 2 (no drawing), sheet: 7 3/8 × 11 7/8 in. (18.7 × 30.0 cm); 2007.65.68.

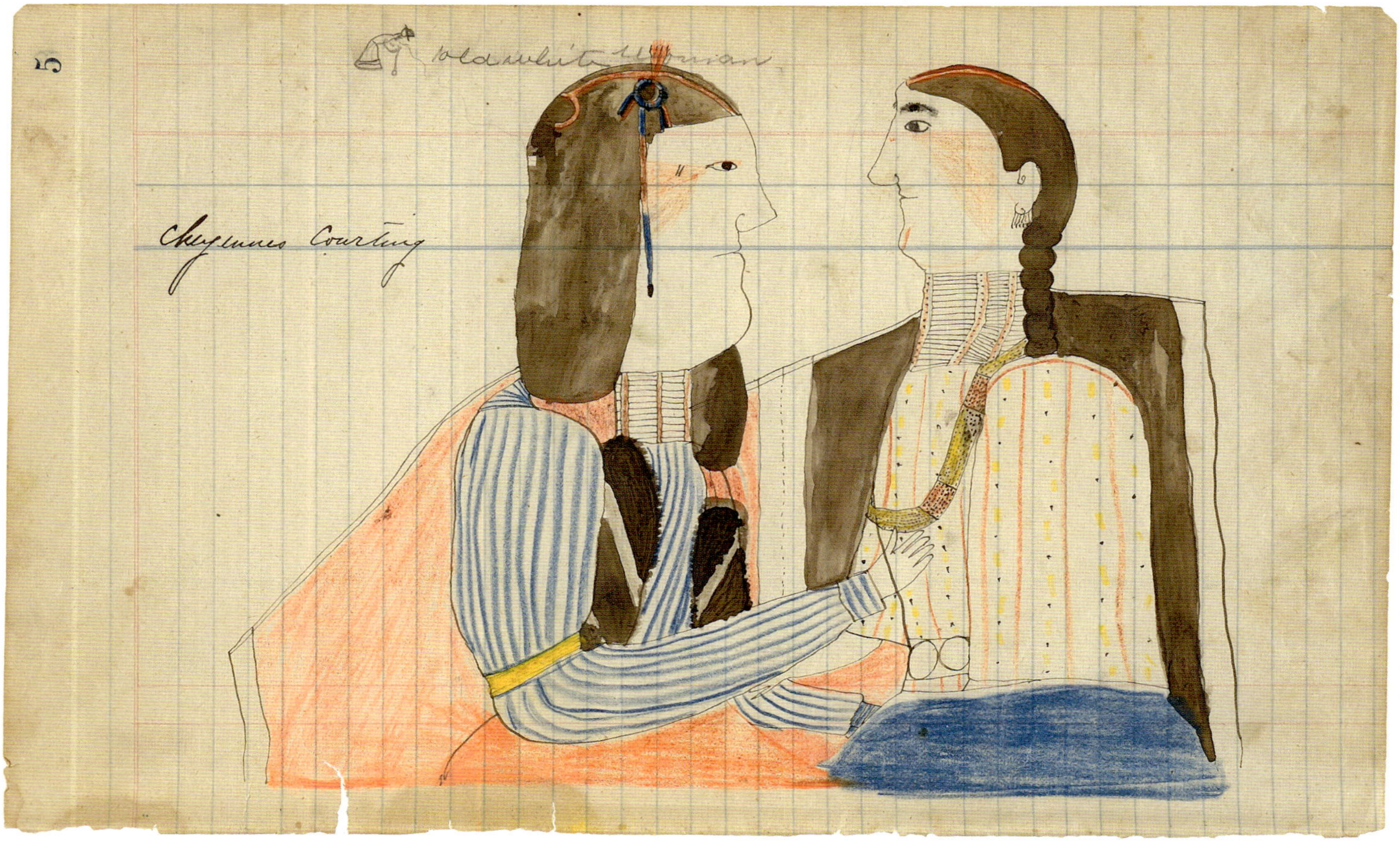

PLATE 102

Unknown artist, Tsistsistas (Cheyenne), active late nineteenth century, ***Untitled ["Cheyennes Courting"],*** page 5 from the "Old White Woman Ledger," c. 1880–90, graphite, colored pencil, watercolor, and ink on wove ledger paper, reverse: page 6 (no drawing), sheet: 7 3/8 × 11 7/8 in. (18.7 × 30.0 cm); 2007.65.70.

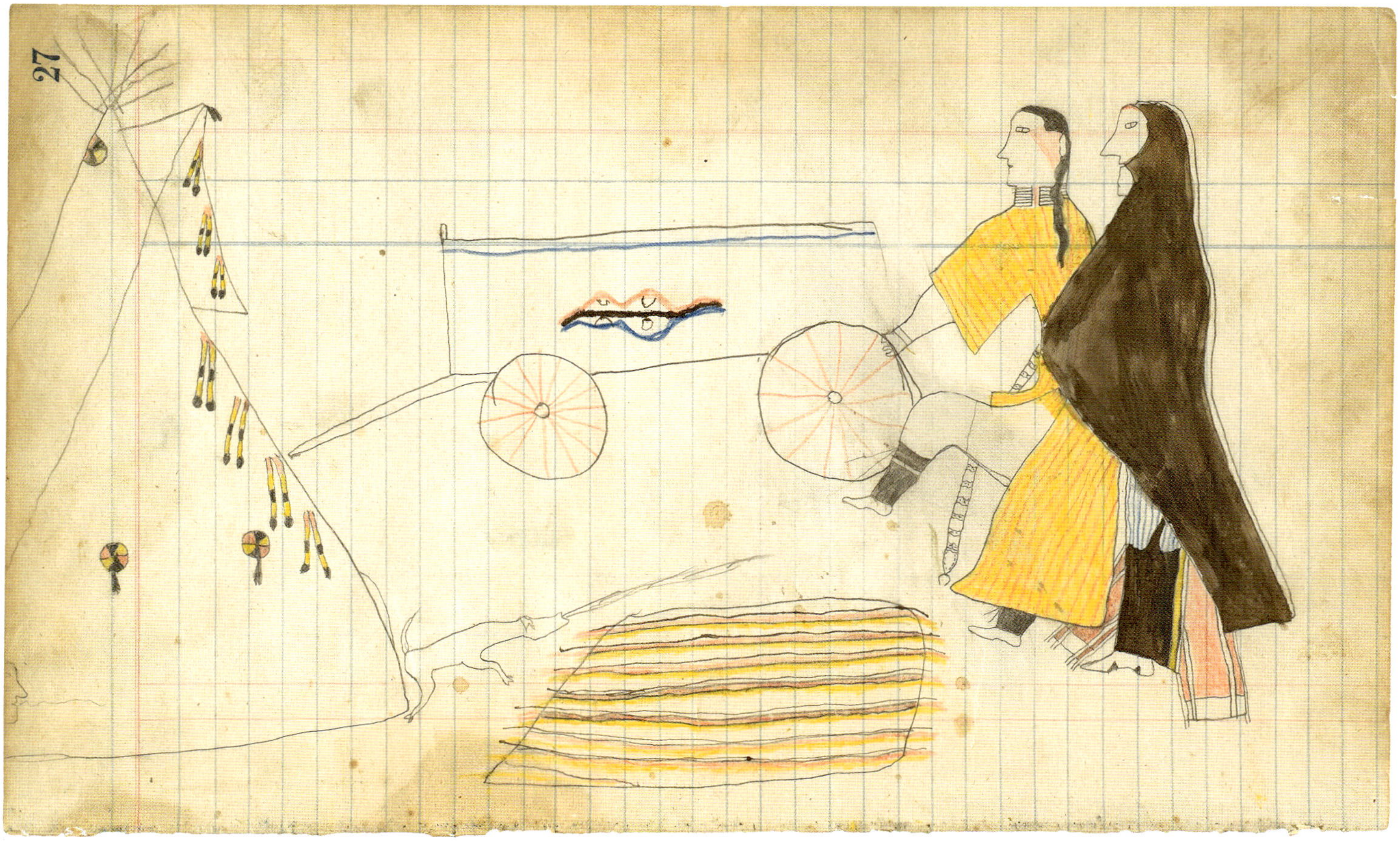

PLATE 103

Unknown artist, Tsistsistas (Cheyenne), active late nineteenth century, ***Untitled [A Tsistsistas (Cheyenne) couple],*** page 27 from the "Old White Woman Ledger," c. 1880–90, graphite, colored pencil, watercolor, and ink on wove ledger paper, reverse: page 28 (no drawing), sheet: 7 3/8 × 11 7/8 in. (18.6 × 30.0 cm). Gift of Mark Lansburgh, Class of 1949; 2007.88.11.

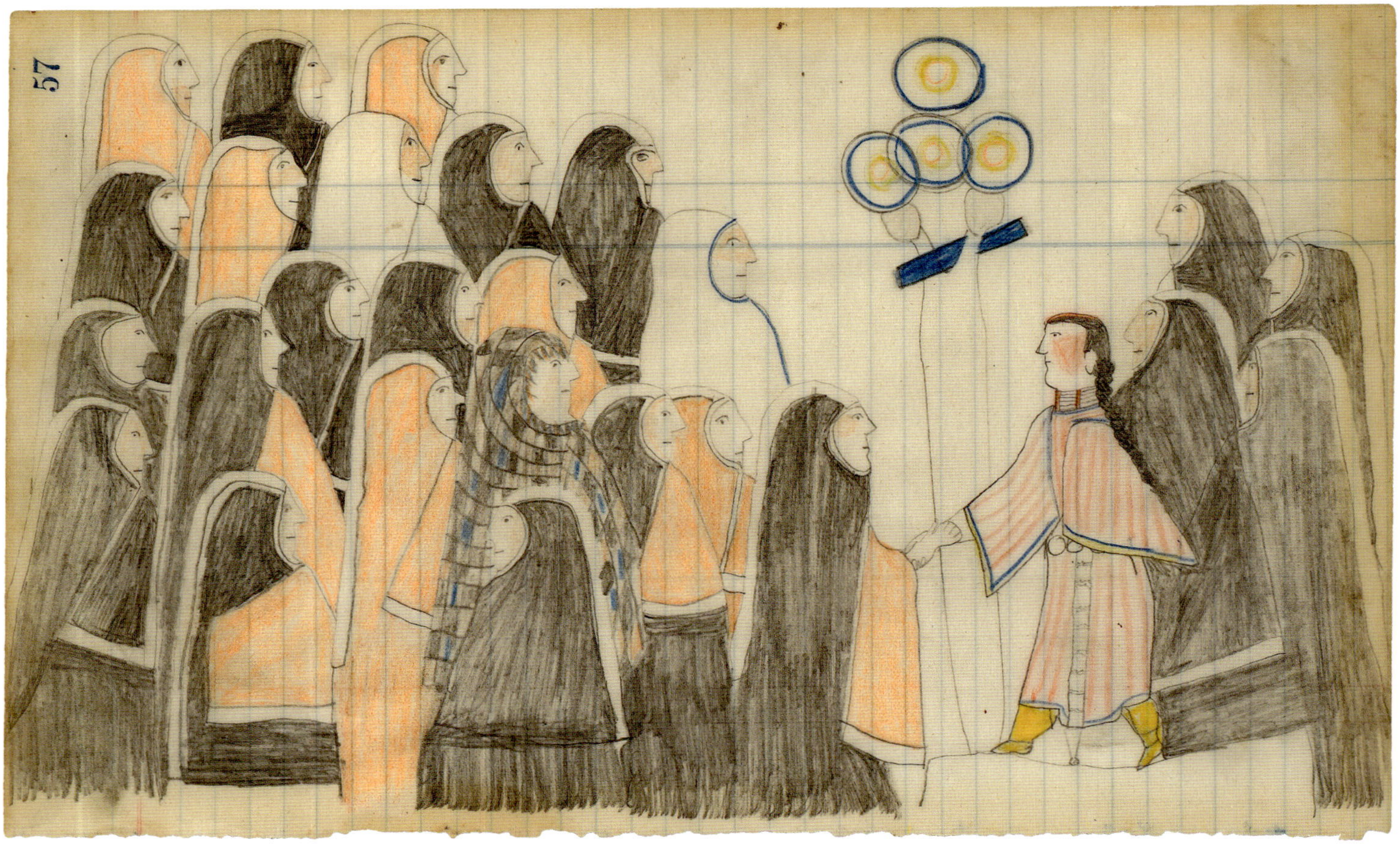

PLATE 104

Unknown artist, Tsistsistas (Cheyenne), active late nineteenth century, ***Untitled [A young Tsistsistas (Cheyenne) initiate with women at a sun dance]***, page 57 from the "Old White Woman Ledger," c. 1880–90, graphite and colored pencil on wove ledger paper, laminated, reverse: page 58 (no drawing), sheet: 7 3/8 × 11 7/8 in. (18.6 × 30.0 cm); 2007.65.75.

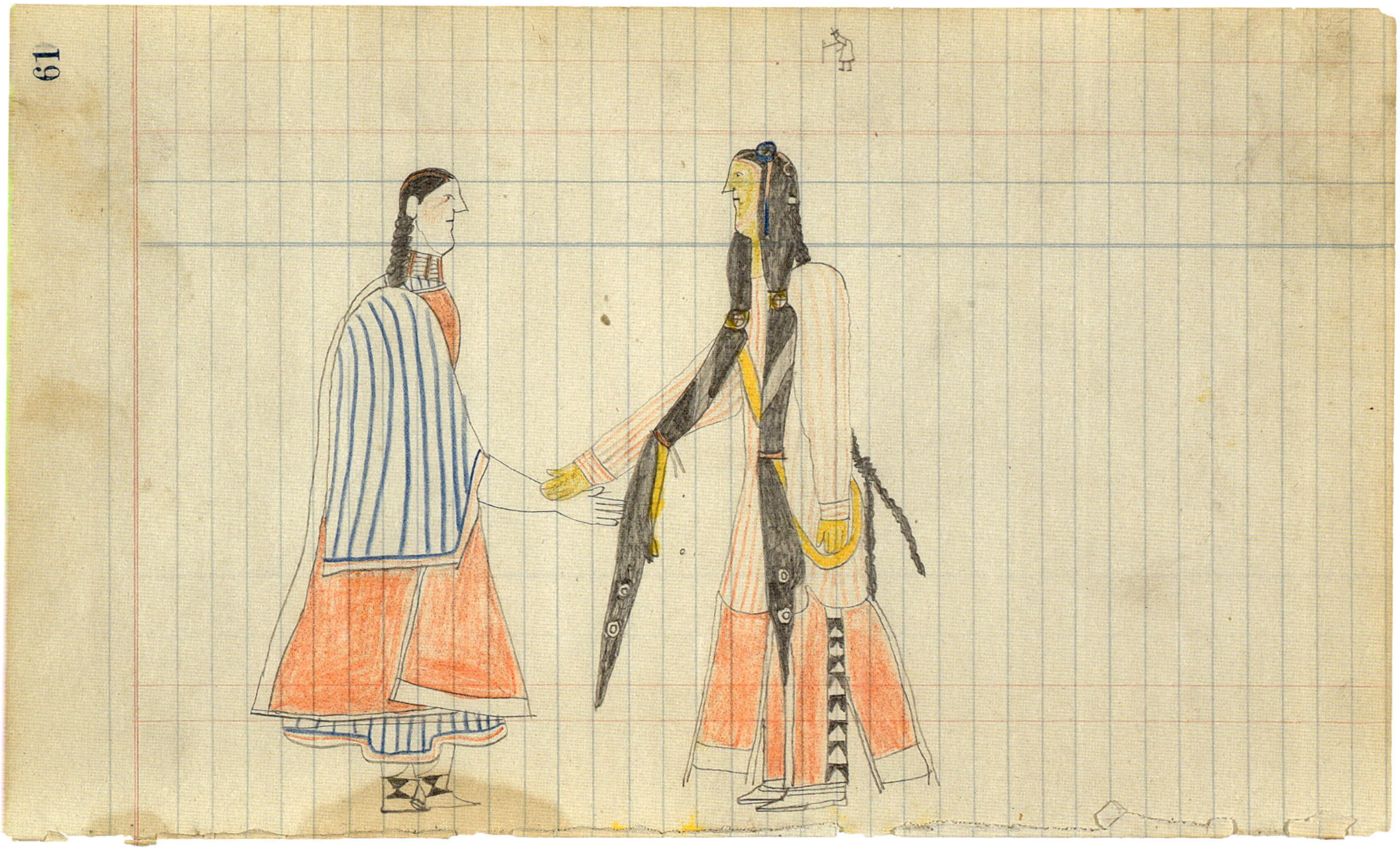

PLATE 105

Unknown artist, Tsistsistas (Cheyenne), active late nineteenth century, ***Untitled [A Tsistsistas (Cheyenne) courting couple meet],*** page 61 from the "Old White Woman Ledger," c. 1880–90, graphite and colored pencil on wove ledger paper, reverse: page 62 (no drawing), sheet: 7 ⅜ × 11 ⅞ in. (18.6 × 30.0 cm); 2007.65.69.

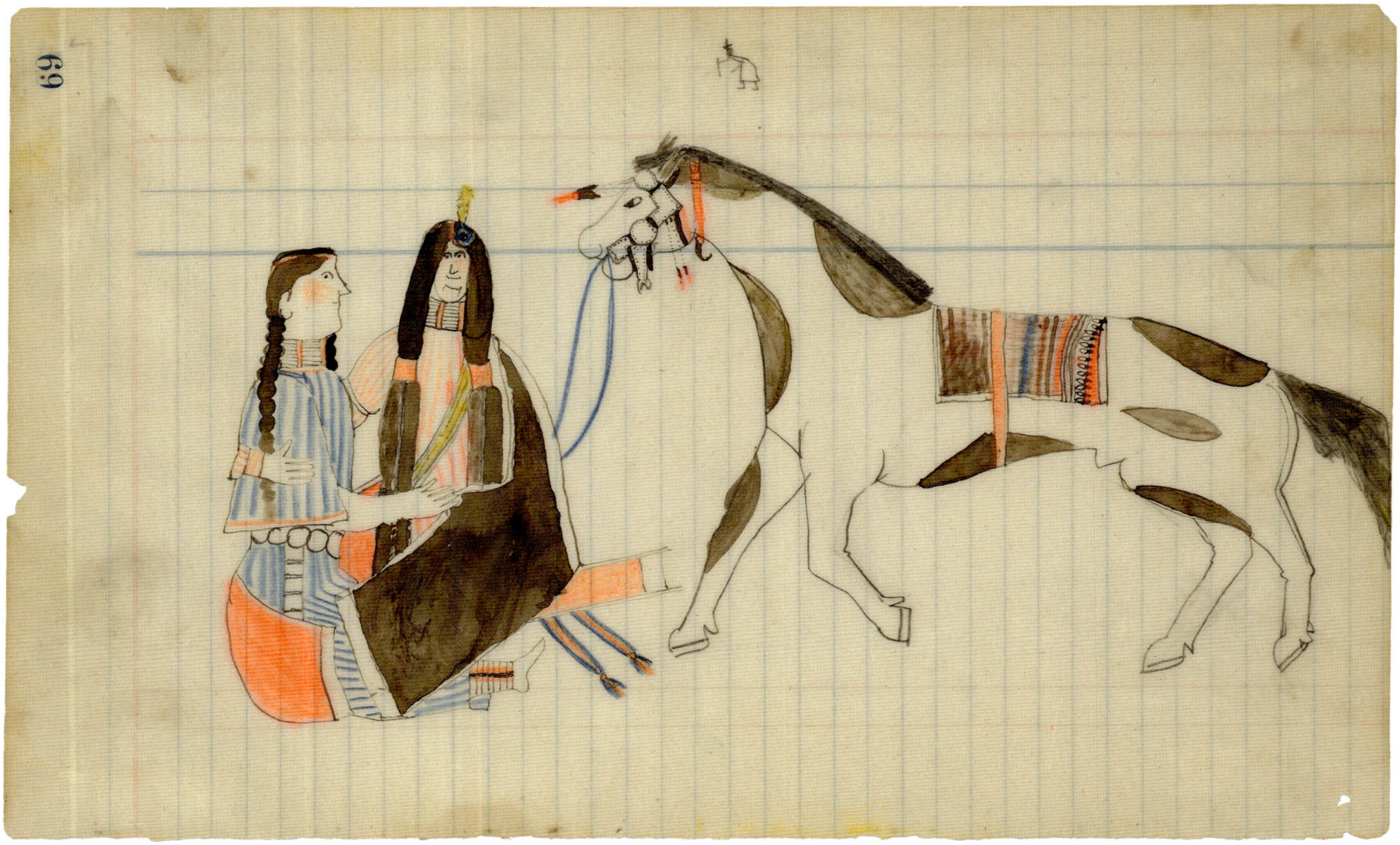

PLATE 106

Unknown artist, Tsistsistas (Cheyenne), active late nineteenth century, ***Untitled [A Tsistsistas (Cheyenne) courting couple],*** page 69 from the "Old White Woman Ledger," c. 1880–90, graphite, colored pencil, watercolor on wove ledger paper, laminated, reverse: page 70 (no drawing), sheet: 7 3/8 × 11 7/8 in. (18.7 × 30.0 cm). Gift of Mark Lansburgh, Class of 1949; 2007.88.10.

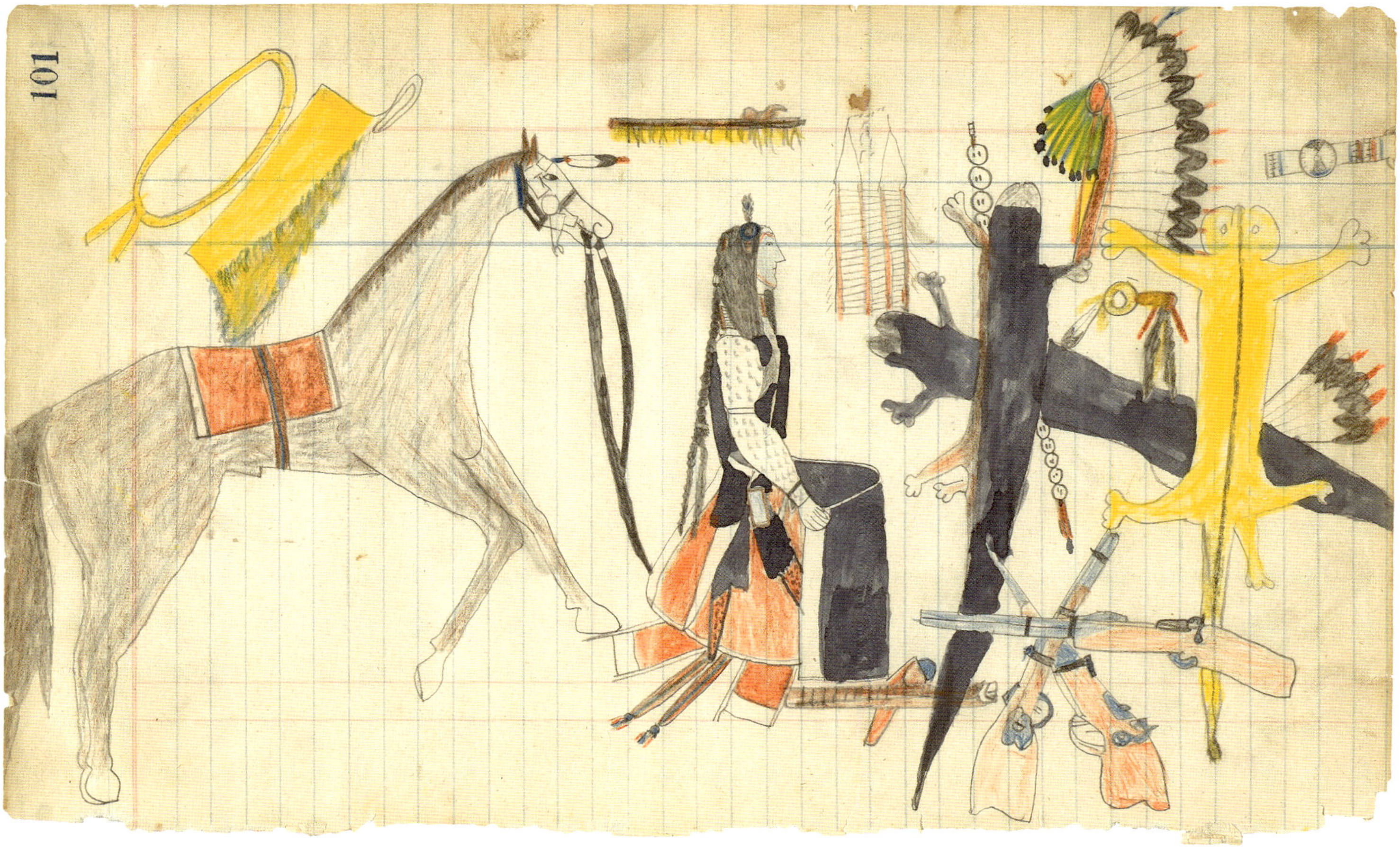

PLATE 107

Unknown artist, Tsistsistas (Cheyenne), active late nineteenth century, ***Untitled [A Tsistsistas (Cheyenne) Bowstring Society warrior with his possessions],*** page 101 from the "Old White Woman Ledger," c. 1880–90, graphite, colored pencil, and watercolor on wove ledger paper, reverse: page 102 (partial s<etch of an arm and head), sheet: 7 3/8 × 11 7/8 in. (18.8 × 30.0 cm); 2007.65.53.

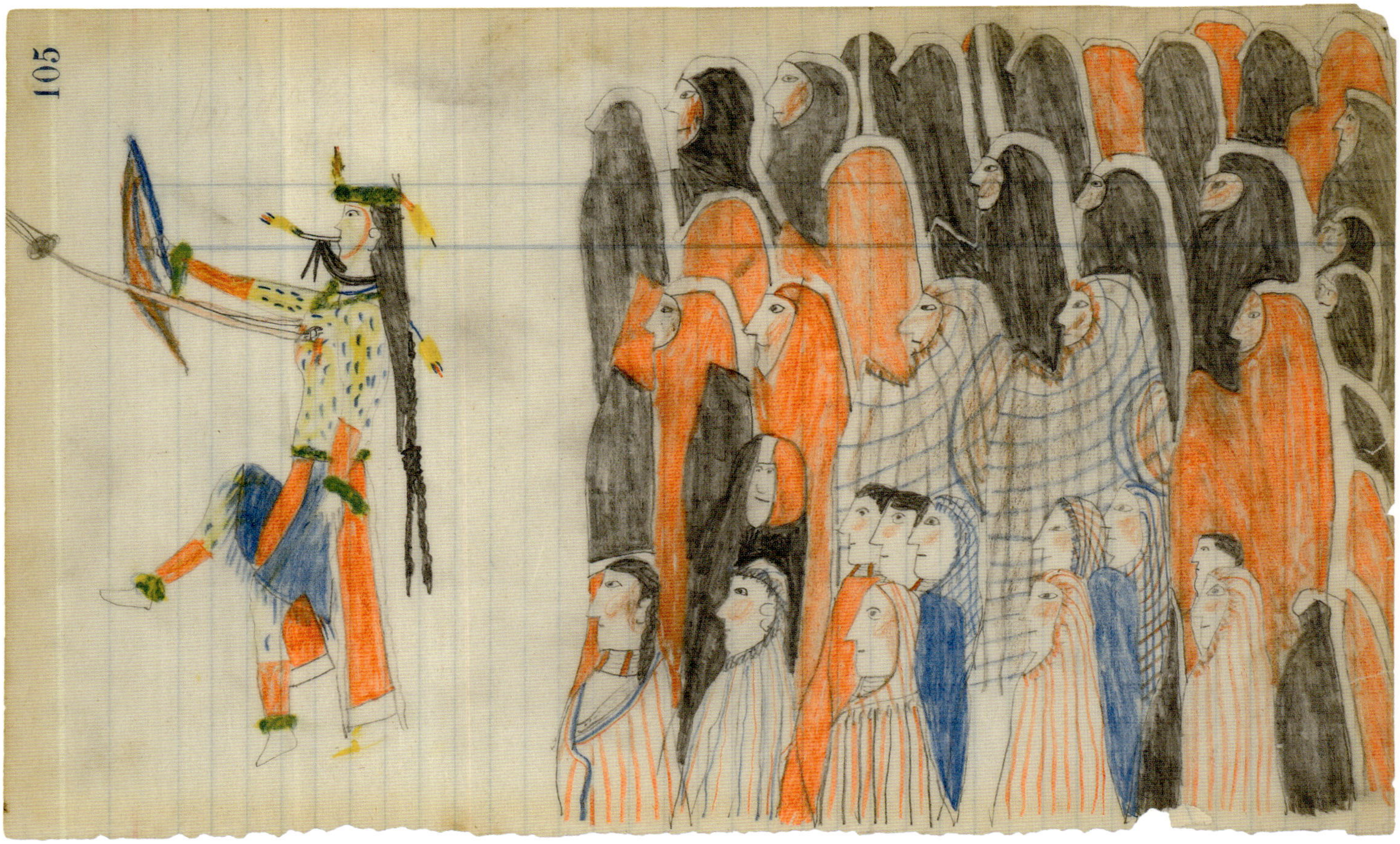

PLATE 108

Unknown artist, Tsistsistas (Cheyenne), active late nineteenth century, ***Untitled [Undertaking the sacred Tsistsistas (Cheyenne) sun dance],*** page 105 from the "Old White Woman Ledger," c. 1880–90, graphite and colored pencil on wove ledger paper, laminated, reverse: page 106 (2007.65.77), sheet: 7 3⁄8 × 11 7⁄8 in. (18.6 × 30.0 cm); 2007.65.76.

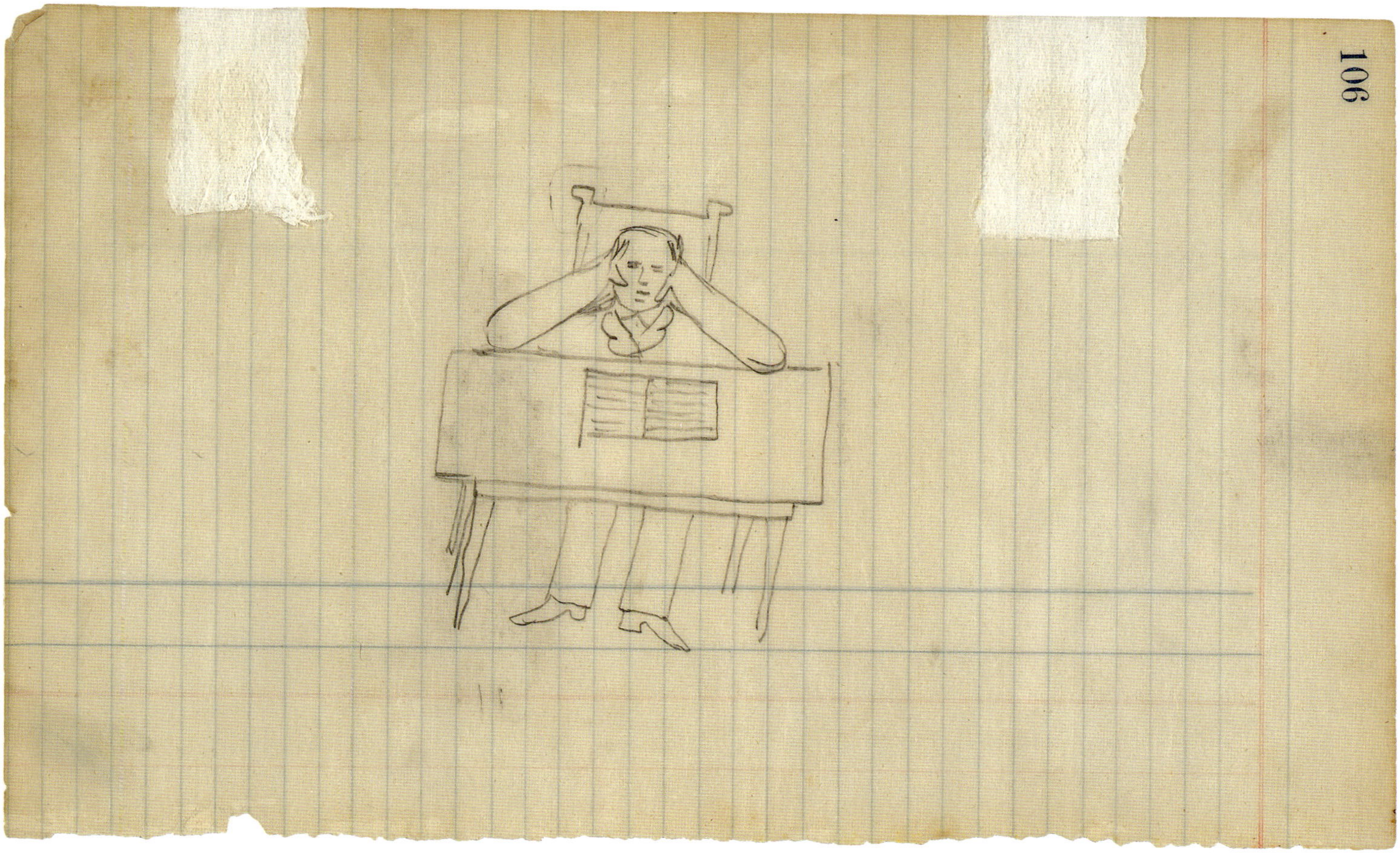

PLATE 109

Unknown artist, Tsistsistas (Cheyenne), active late nineteenth century, ***Untitled [Sketch of a man reading at his desk],*** page 106 from the "Old White Woman Ledger," c. 1880–90, graphite on wove ledger paper, laminated, reverse: page 105 (2007.65.76), sheet: 7 3⁄8 × 11 7⁄8 in. (18.6 × 30.0 cm); 2007.65.77.

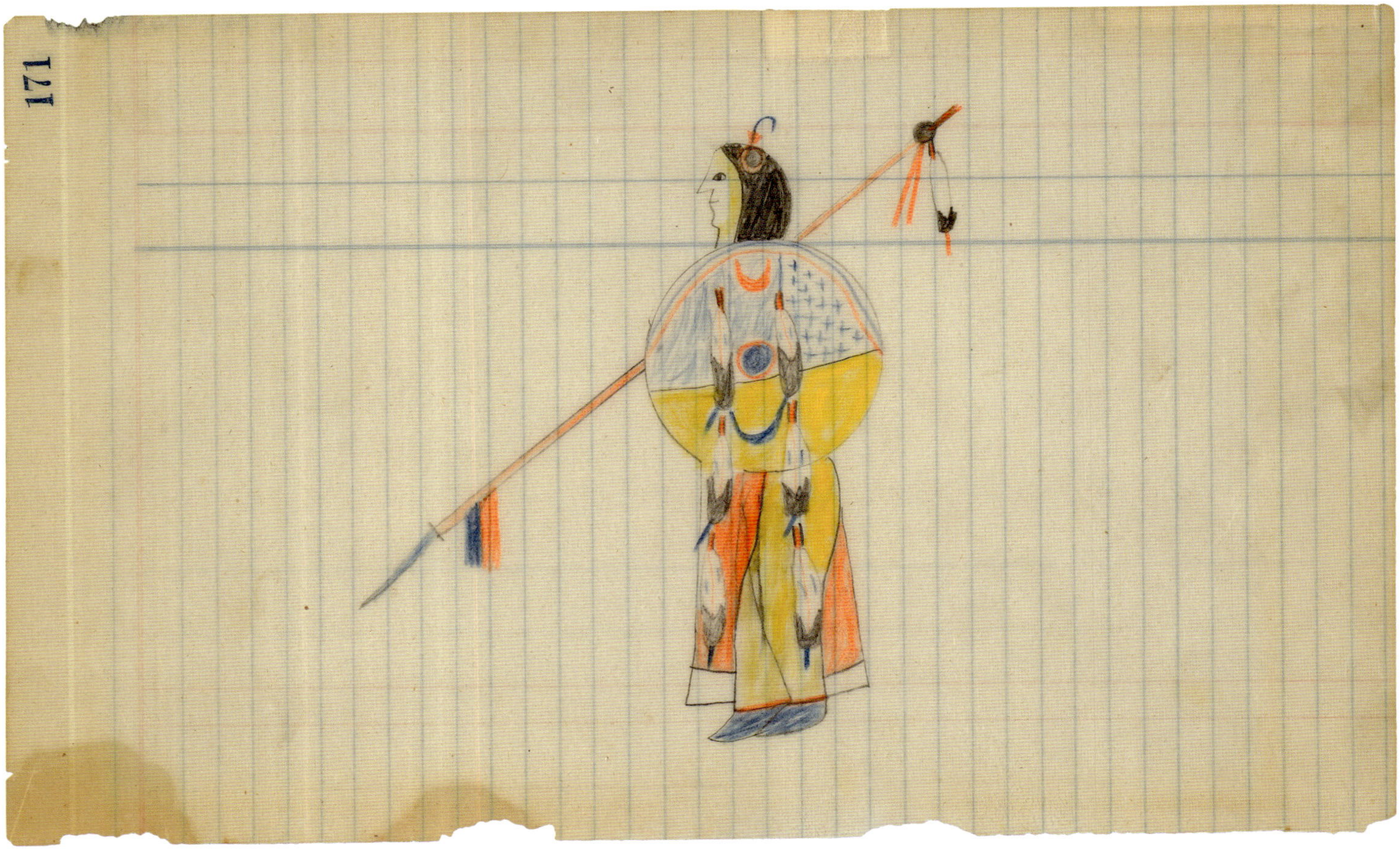

PLATE 110

Unknown artist, Tsistsistas (Cheyenne), active late nineteenth century, ***Untitled [A Tsistsistas (Cheyenne) warrior carrying his shield and lance],*** page 171 from the "Old White Woman Ledger," c. 1880–90, graphite, colored pencil on wove ledger paper, laminated, reverse: page 172 (no drawing), sheet: 7 ¼ × 11 ⅞ in. (18.5 × 30.0 cm); 2007.65.73.

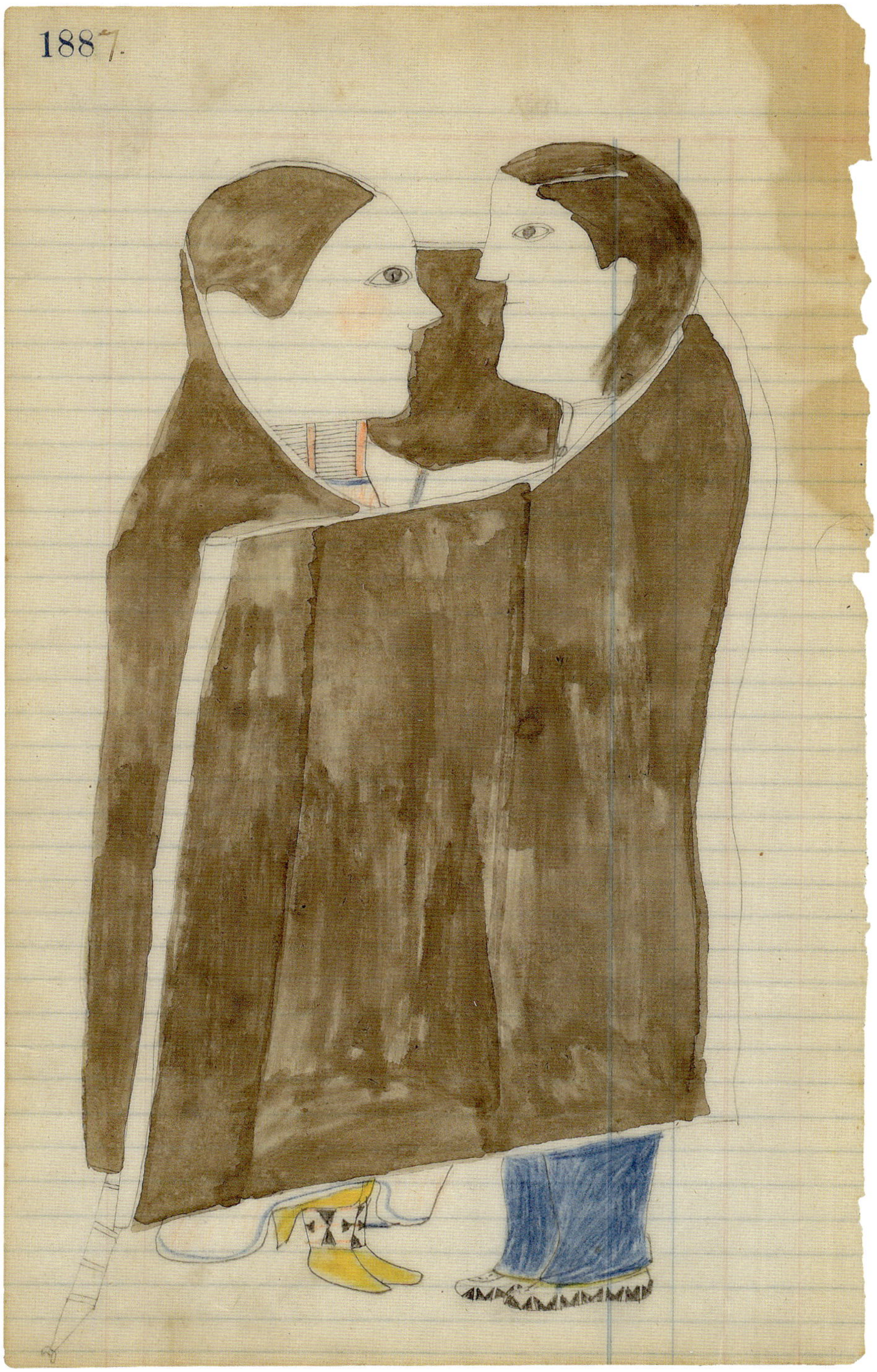

PLATE 111

Unknown artist, Tsistsistas (Cheyenne), active late nineteenth century, ***Untitled [A Tsistsistas (Cheyenne) standing couple wrapped in a courting blanket],*** page 188 from the "Old White Woman Ledger," c. 1880–90, graphite, colored pencil, ink, and watercolor on wove ledger paper, laminated, reverse: page 187 (no drawing), sheet: 11 7/8 × 7 1/4 in. (30.0 × 18.5 cm); 2007.65.72.

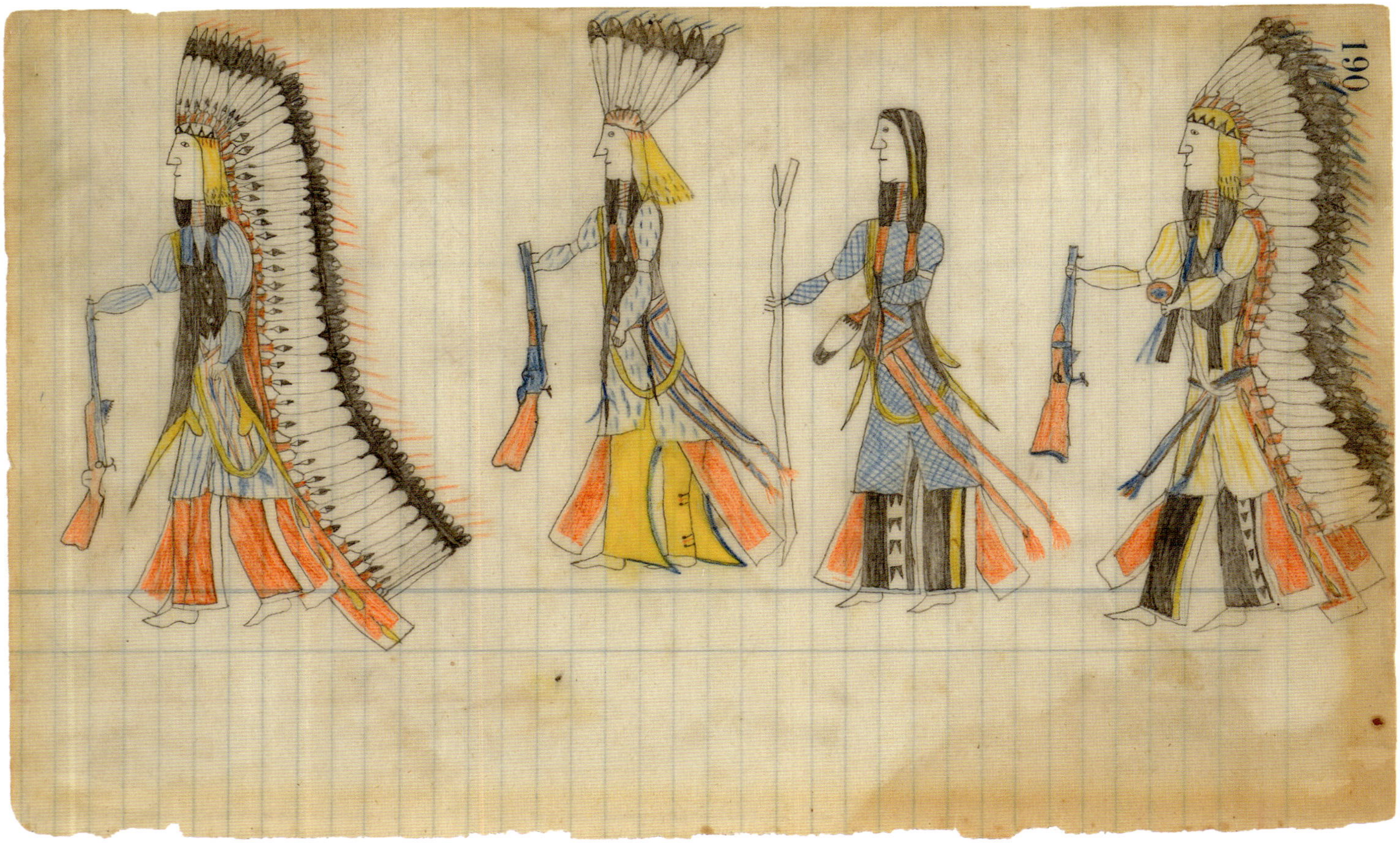

PLATE 112

Unknown artist, Tsistsistas (Cheyenne), active late nineteenth century, ***Untitled [A procession of Tsistsistas (Cheyenne) warriors],*** page 190 from the "Old White Woman Ledger," c. 1880–90, graphite, colored pencil on wove ledger paper, laminated, reverse: page 189 (no drawing), sheet: 7 3/8 × 11 7/8 in. (18.6 × 30.0 cm); 2007.65.74.

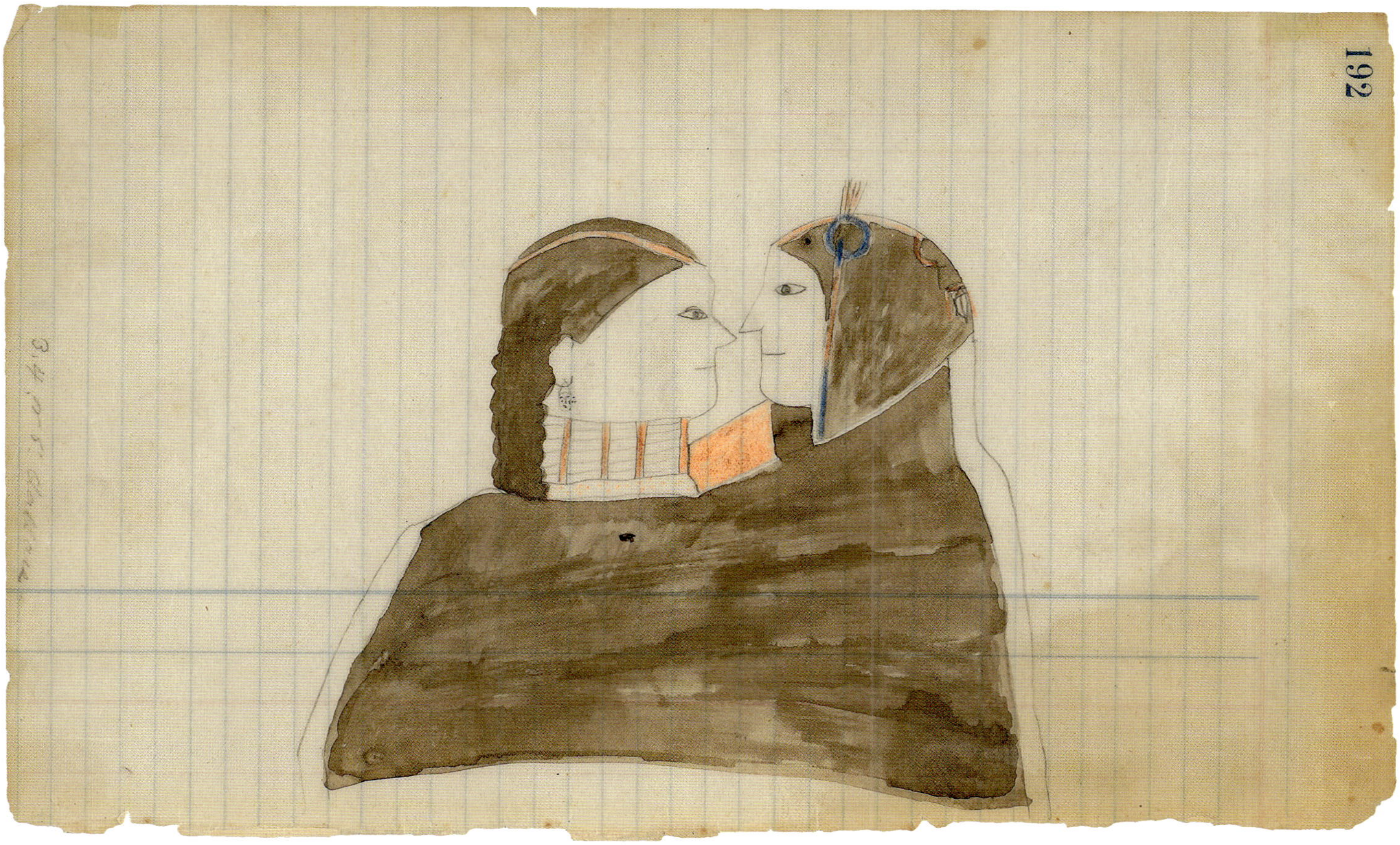

PLATE 113

Unknown artist, Tsistsistas (Cheyenne), active late nineteenth century, ***Untitled [A Tsistsistas (Cheyenne) couple wrapped in a courting blanket],*** page 192 from the "Old White Woman Ledger," c. 1880–90, graphite, colored pencil, watercolor on wove ledger paper, laminated, reverse: page 191 (no drawing), sheet: 7 3/8 × 11 7/8 in. (18.6 × 30 cm); 2007.65.71.

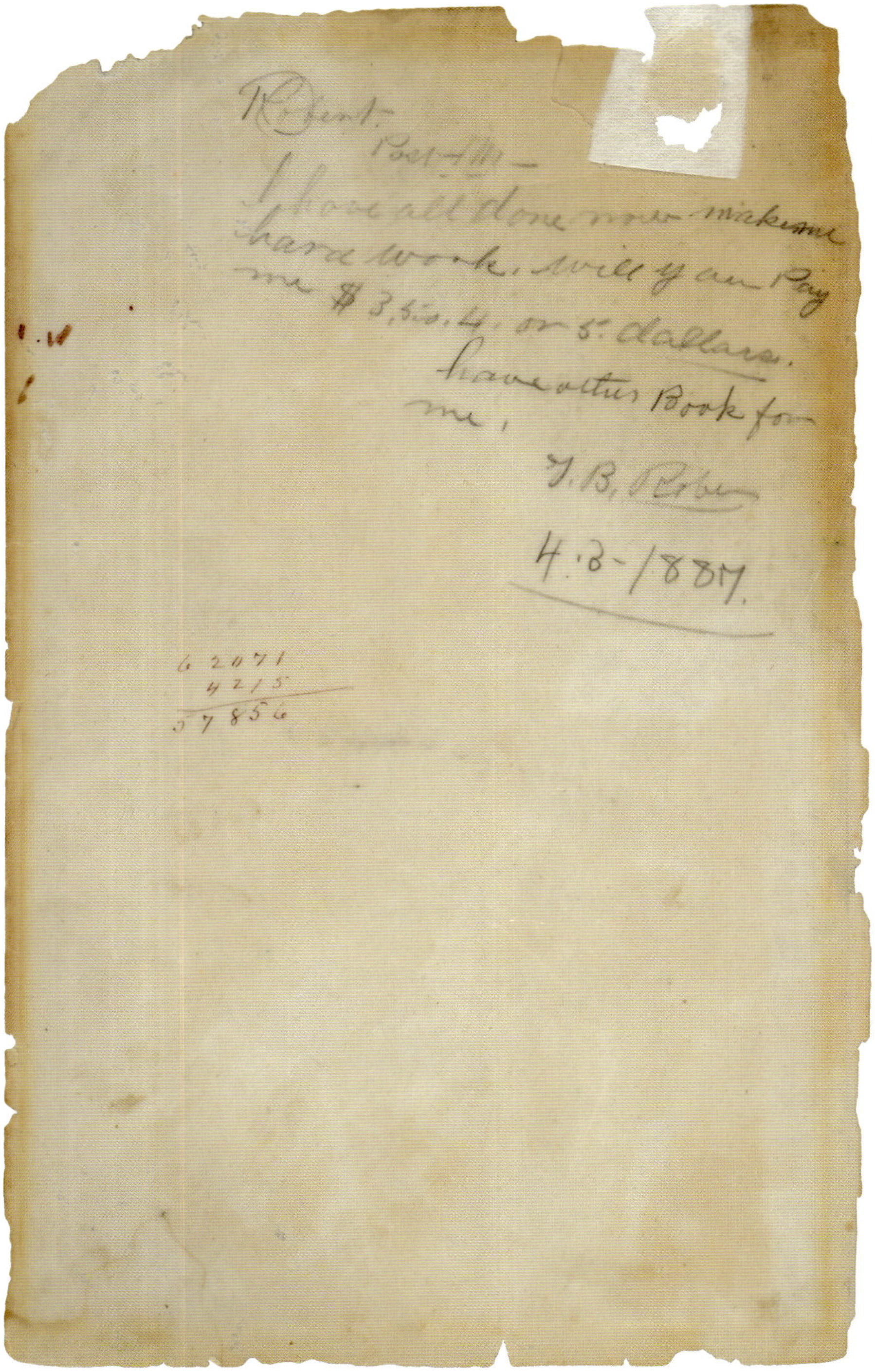
Post-M—
I have all done now make me
hard work. will you Pay
me $ 3,50. 4. or 5. dallars.
have other Book for
me,
T. B, Rober
4.3-1887.
62071
4215
57856

PLATE 114

Unknown artist, Tsistsistas (Cheyenne), active late nineteenth century, ***Untitled [An 1887 dated invoice]***, from the "Old White Woman Ledger," c. 1880–90, graphite and ink on wove paper (ledger endpaper), reverse: (2007.65.67), sheet: 7 ½ × 11 ⅞ in. (18.5 × 30.0 cm); 2007.65.66.

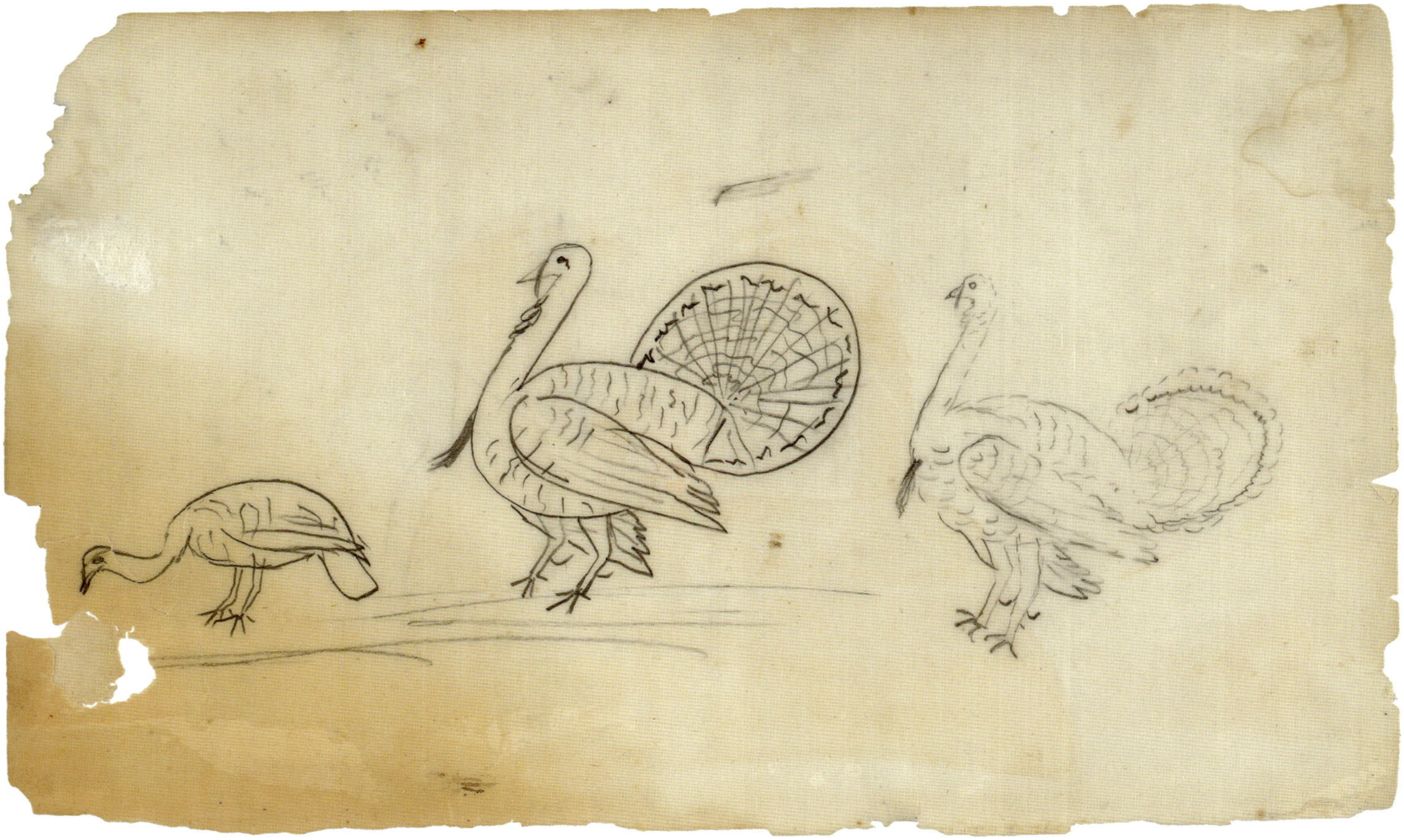

PLATE 115

Unknown artist, Tsistsistas (Cheyenne), active late nineteenth century, ***Untitled [Sketch of three turkeys],*** from the "Old White Woman Ledger," c. 1880–90, graphite on wove paper (ledger endpaper), reverse: (2007.65.66), sheet: 7 ½ × 11 ⅞ in. (18.5 × 30.0 cm); 2007.65.67.

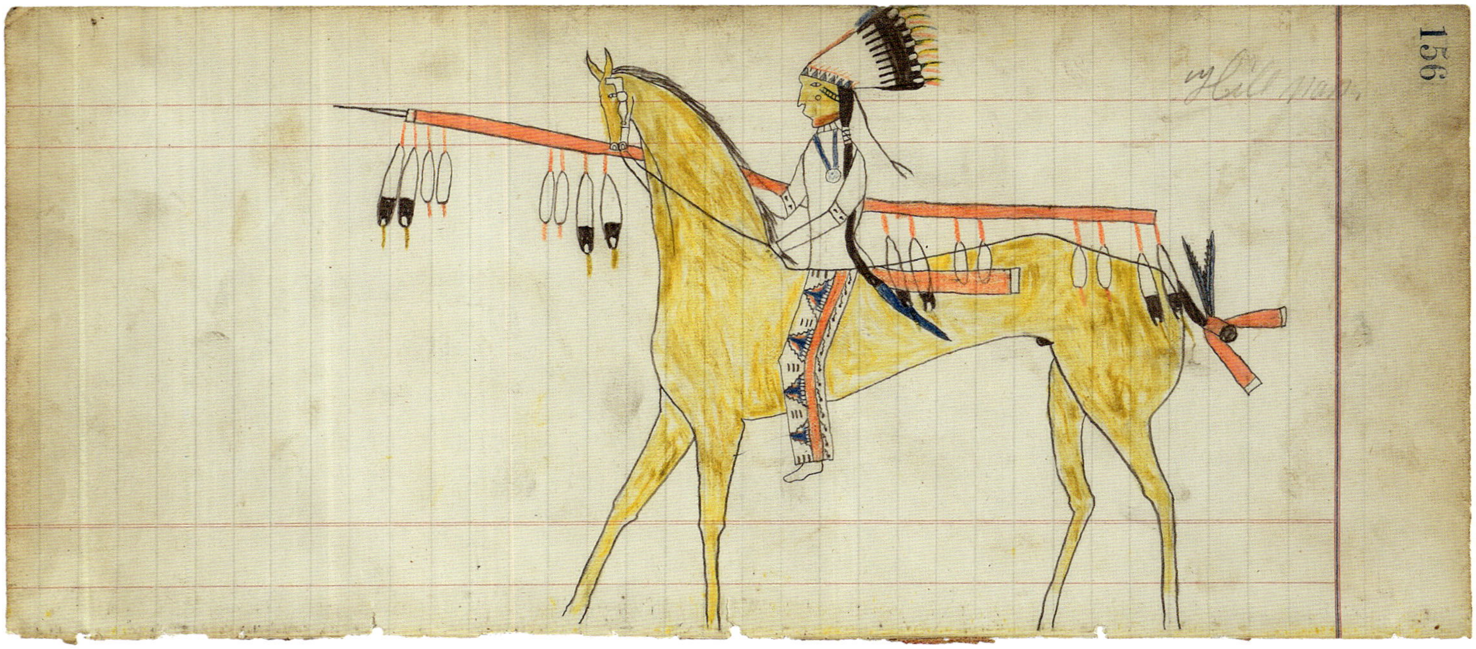

PLATE 116

Unknown artist, Southern Inunaina (Arapaho) and/or Southern Tsistsistas (Cheyenne), active late nineteenth century, ***Untitled [An Inunaina (Arapaho) warrior],*** page 156 from the "Frank Henderson Ledger," June 1881–December 1882, graphite and colored pencil on laid ledger paper, reverse: page 155 (no drawing), sheet: $5\frac{3}{8} \times 11\frac{7}{8}$ in. (13.6 × 30.0 cm); 2007.65.50.

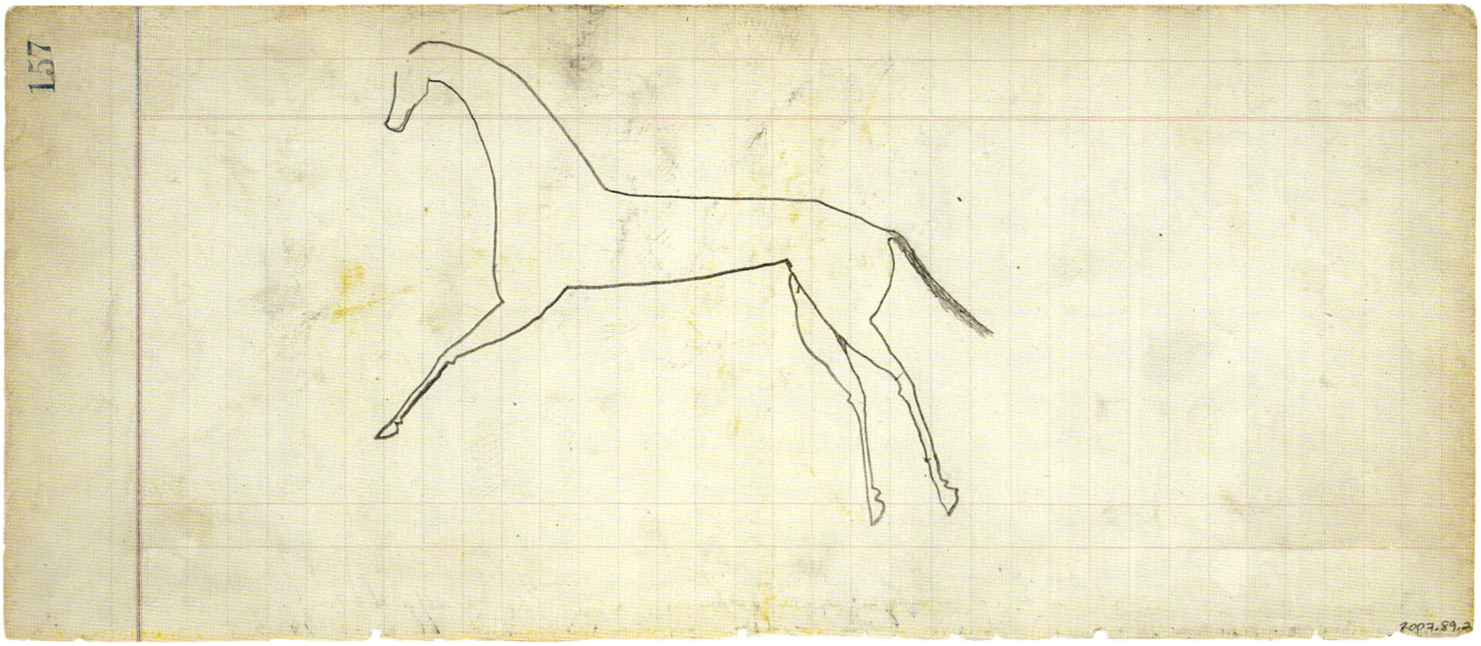

PLATE 117

Unknown artist, Southern Inunaina (Arapaho) and/or Southern Tsistsistas (Cheyenne), active late nineteenth century, ***Untitled [Sketch of a horse],*** page 157 from the "Frank Henderson Ledger," June 1881–December 1882, graphite on laid ledger paper, reverse: page 158 (2007.89.1), sheet: 5 ⅜ × 11 ⅞ in. (13.5 × 30.0 cm). Gift of Mark Lansburgh, Class of 1949, in honor of Barbara Thompson, Curator of African, Oceanic, and Native American Collections, Hood Museum of Art, 2002–2008; 2007.89.2.

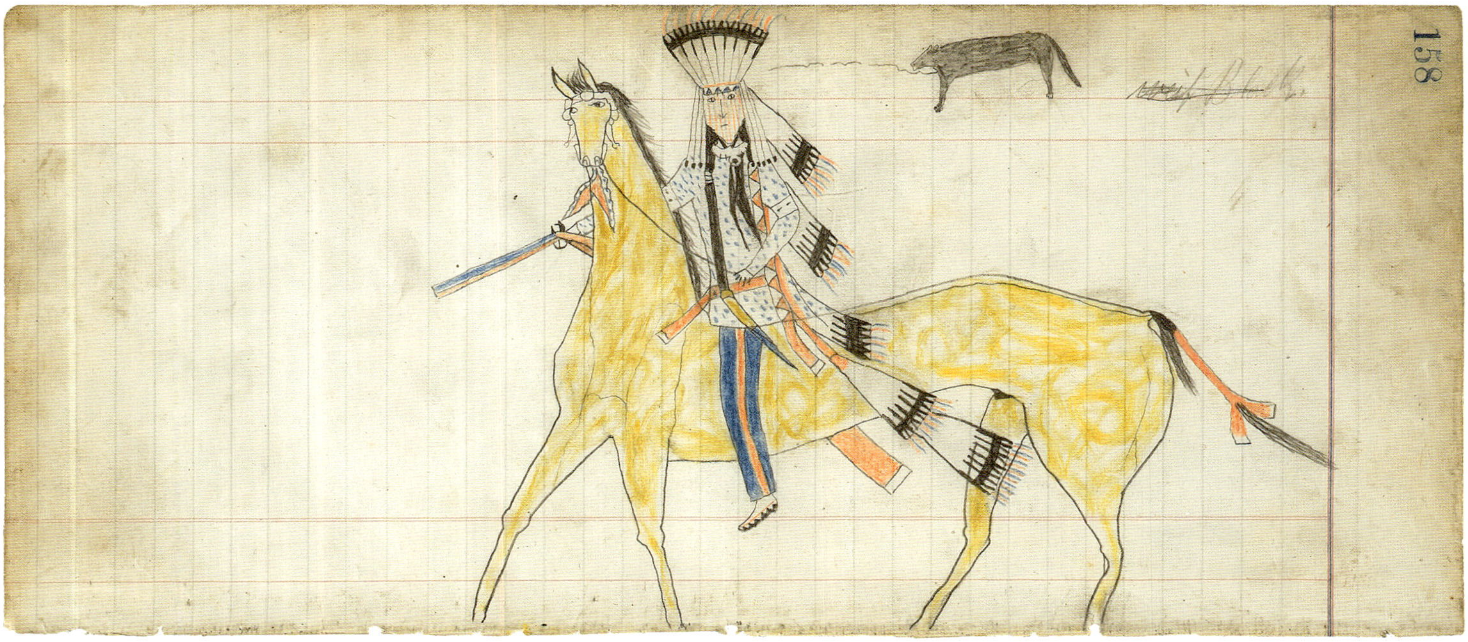

PLATE 118

Unknown artist, Southern Inunaina (Arapaho) and/or Southern Tsistsistas (Cheyenne), active late nineteenth century, ***Untitled [An Inunaina (Arapaho) warrior],*** page 158 from the "Frank Henderson Ledger," June 1881–December 1882, graphite, colored pencil, and watercolor on laid ledger paper, reverse: page 157 (2007.89.2), sheet: 5 3/8 × 11 7/8 in. (13.5 × 30.0 cm). Gift of Mark Lansburgh, Class of 1949, in honor of Barbara Thompson, Curator of African, Oceanic, and Native American Collections, Hood Museum of Art, 2002–2008; 2007.89.1.

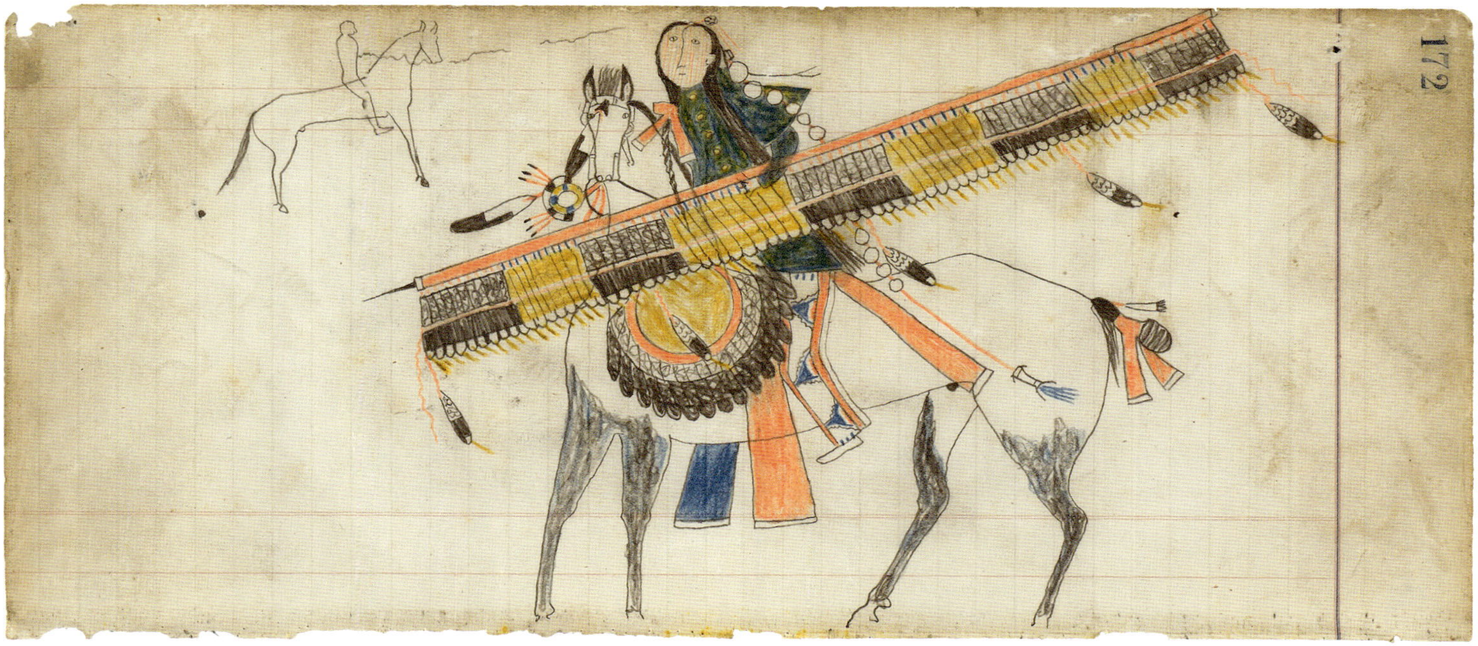

PLATE 119

Unknown artist, Southern Inunaina (Arapaho) and/or Southern Tsistsistas (Cheyenne), active late nineteenth century, ***Untitled [A Crazy Dog Society warrior],*** page 172 from the "Frank Henderson Ledger," June 1881–December 1882, graphite and colored pencil on laid ledger paper, reverse: page 171 (no drawing), sheet: 5 ⅔ × 11 ⅞ in. (13.5 × 30.2 cm); 2007.65.51.

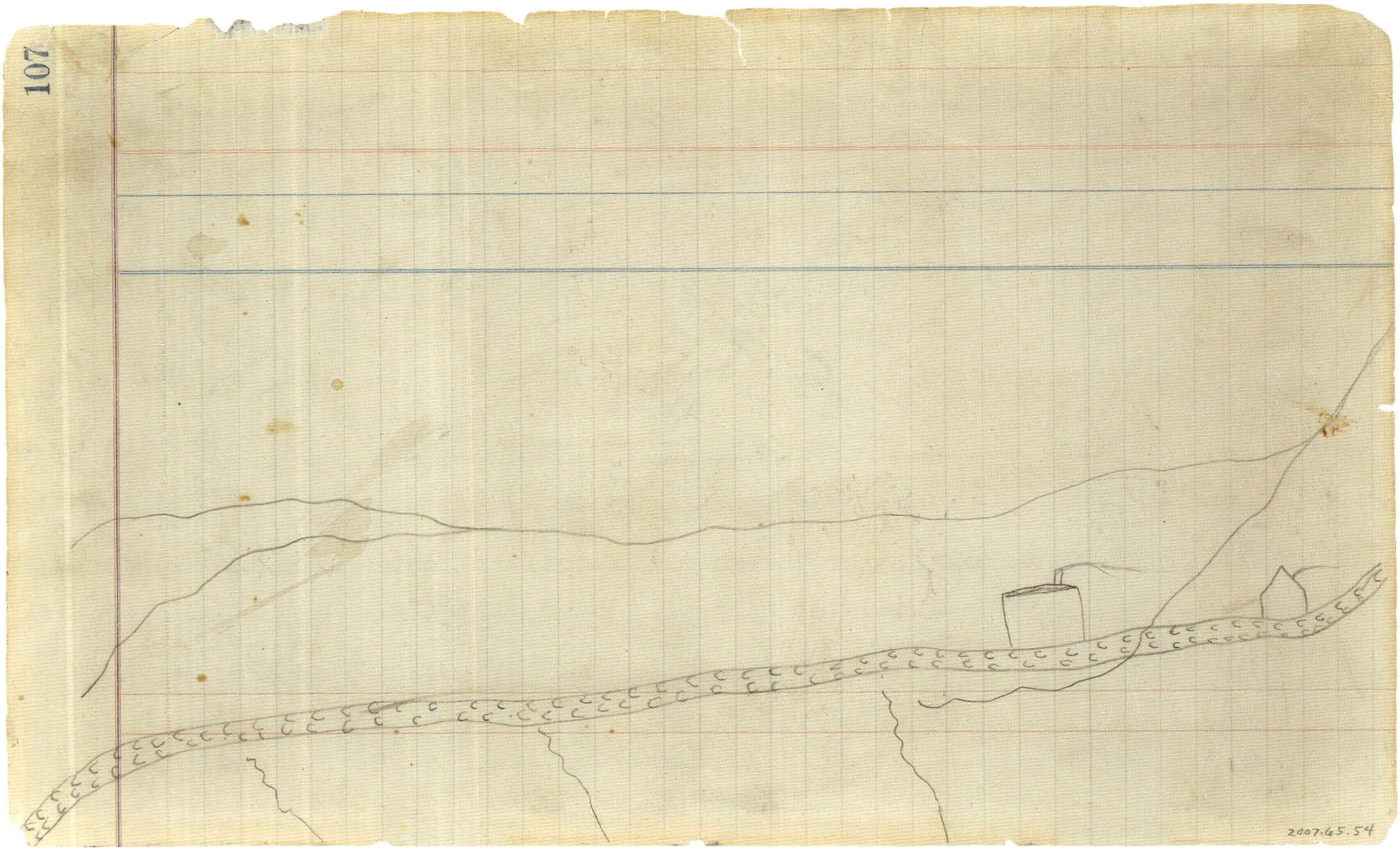

PLATE 120

Unknown artist, Southern Inunaina (Arapaho) and/or Southern Tsistsistas (Cheyenne), active late nineteenth century, ***Untitled [An Inunaina (Arapaho) warrior's map],*** page 107 from an unidentified ledger, early 1880s, graphite on laid ledger paper, reverse: page 108 (2007.65.55), sheet: 7 ¾ × 12 ⅜ in. (19.6 × 31.4 cm); 2007.65.54.

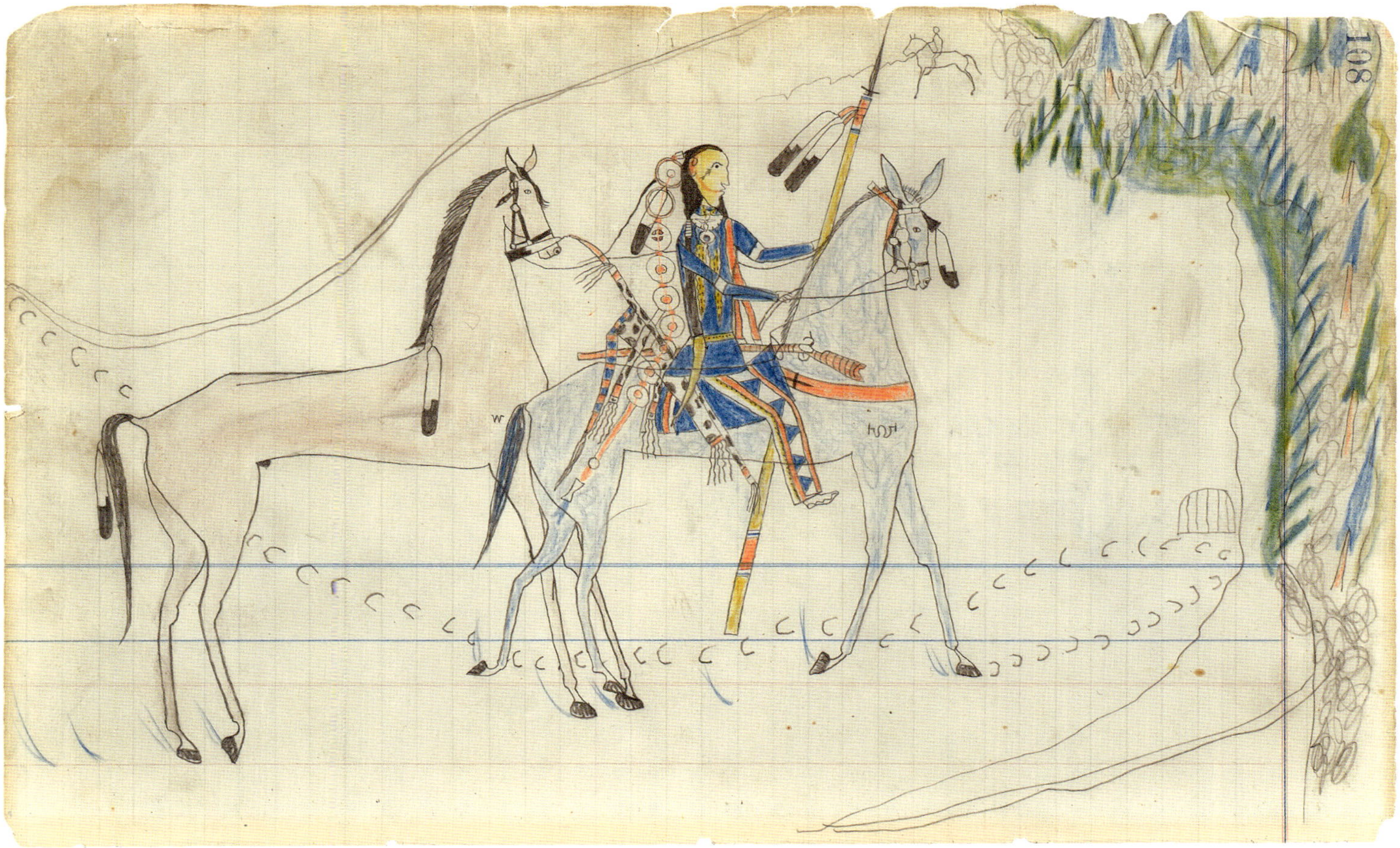

PLATE 121

Unknown artist, Southern Inunaina (Arapaho) and/or Southern Tsistsistas (Cheyenne), active late nineteenth century, ***Untitled [An Inunaina (Arapaho) warrior traveling],*** page 108 from an unidentified ledger, early 1880s, graphite and colored pencil on laid ledger paper, reverse: page 107 (2007.65.54), sheet: 7 ¾ × 12 ⅜ in. (19.6 × 31.4 cm); 2007.65.55.

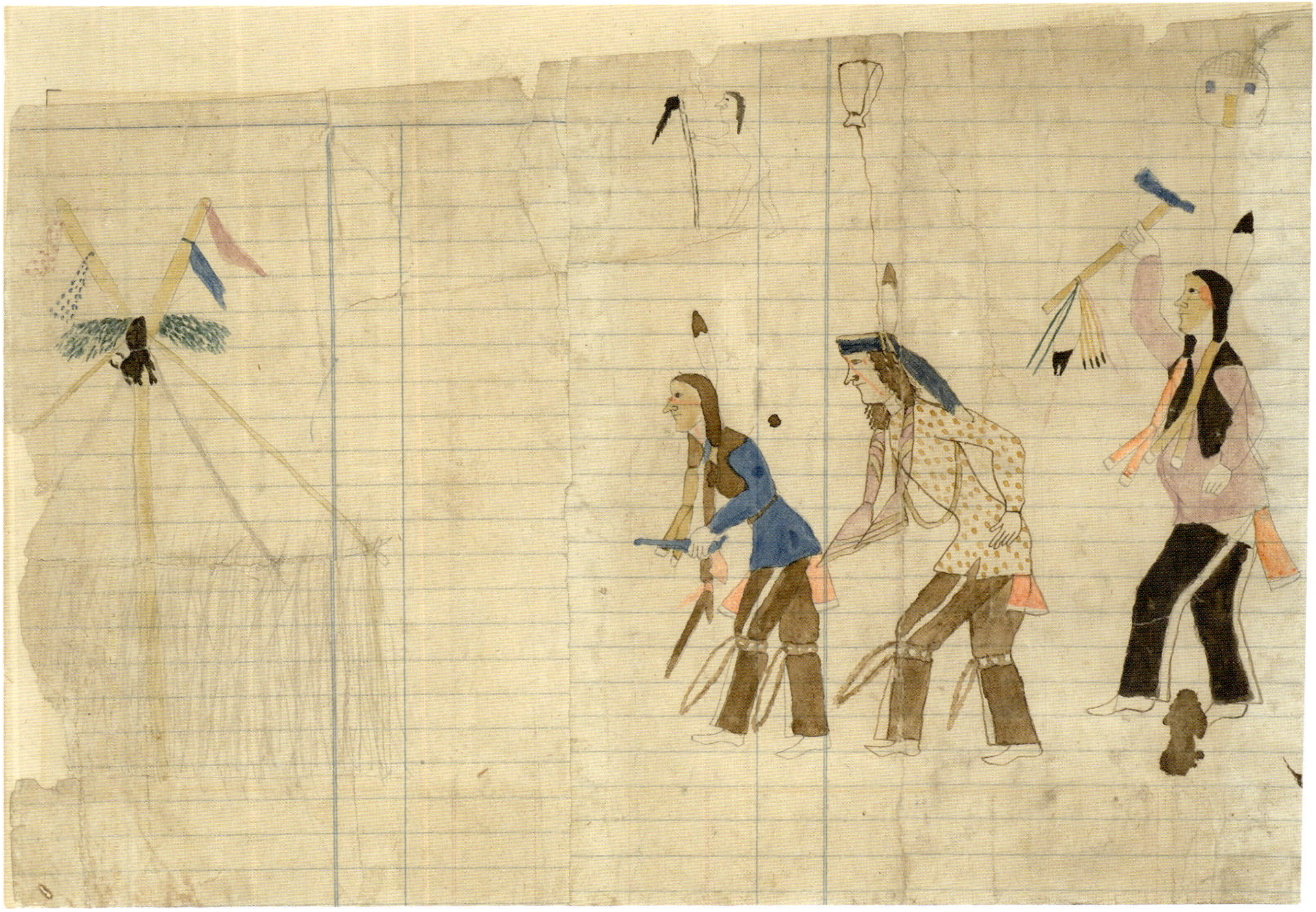

PLATE 122

Wooden Leg (Kum-mok-quiv-vi-ok-ta), Northern Tsistsistas (Cheyenne), 1858–1940. ***Untitled [Joined ledger pages: sun dance medicine lodge/social dancers]***, from an unidentified ledger, c. 1882, graphite, ink, and watercolor on laid ledger paper mounted on wove paper, mount: 7 ½ × 10 ½ in. (19.0 × 26.5 cm) [irregular], 2007.65.56.

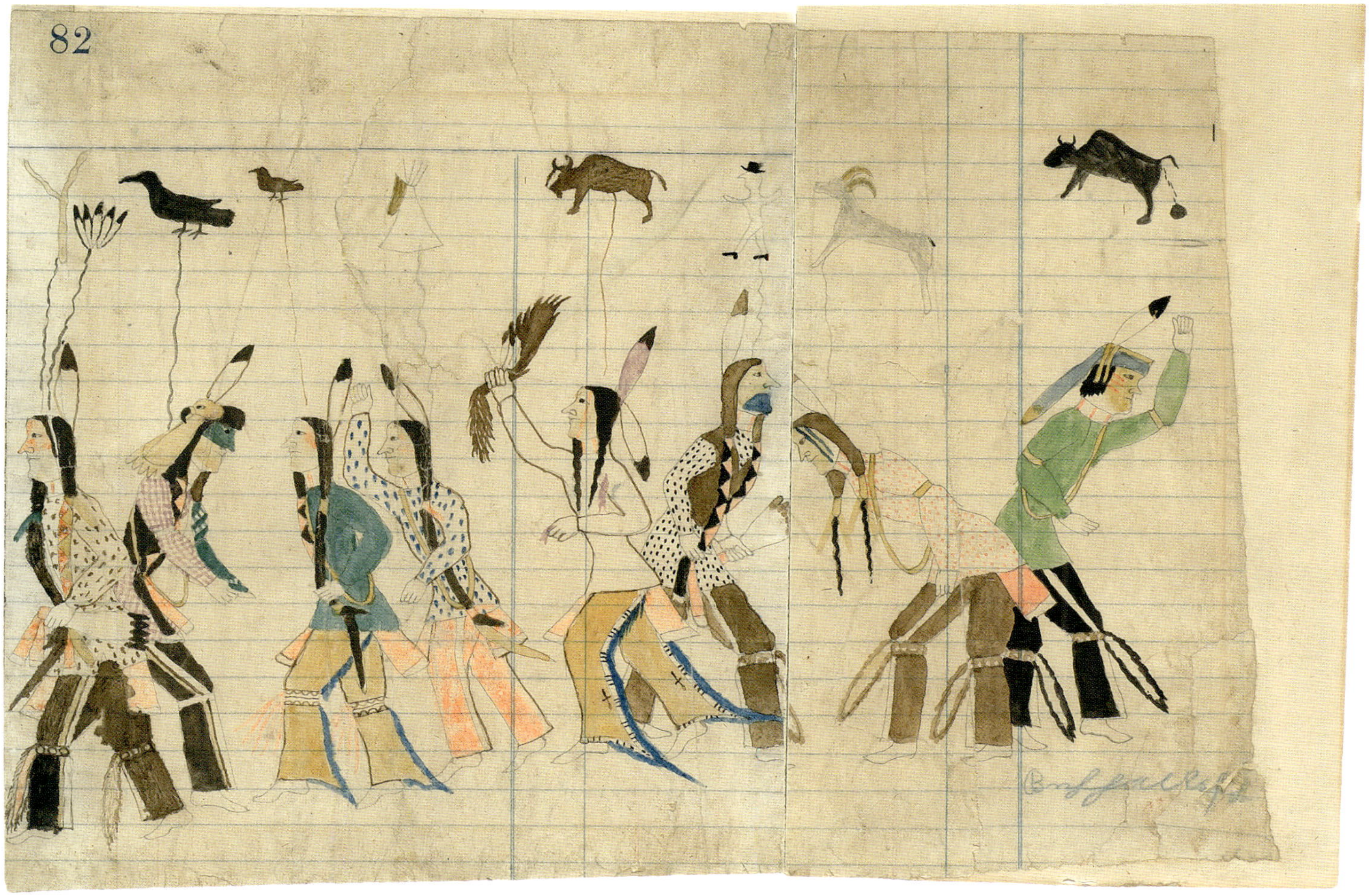

PLATE 123

Wooden Leg (Kum-mok-quiv-vi-ok-ta), Northern Tsistsistas (Cheyenne), 1858–1940. ***Untitled [Joined ledger pages: social dancers, including part of page 82],*** from an unidentified ledger, c. 1882, graphite, colored pencil, ink, and watercolor on wove ledger paper mounted on wove paper, mount: 7 × 10 ¼ in. (17.6 × 26 cm), 2007.65.57.

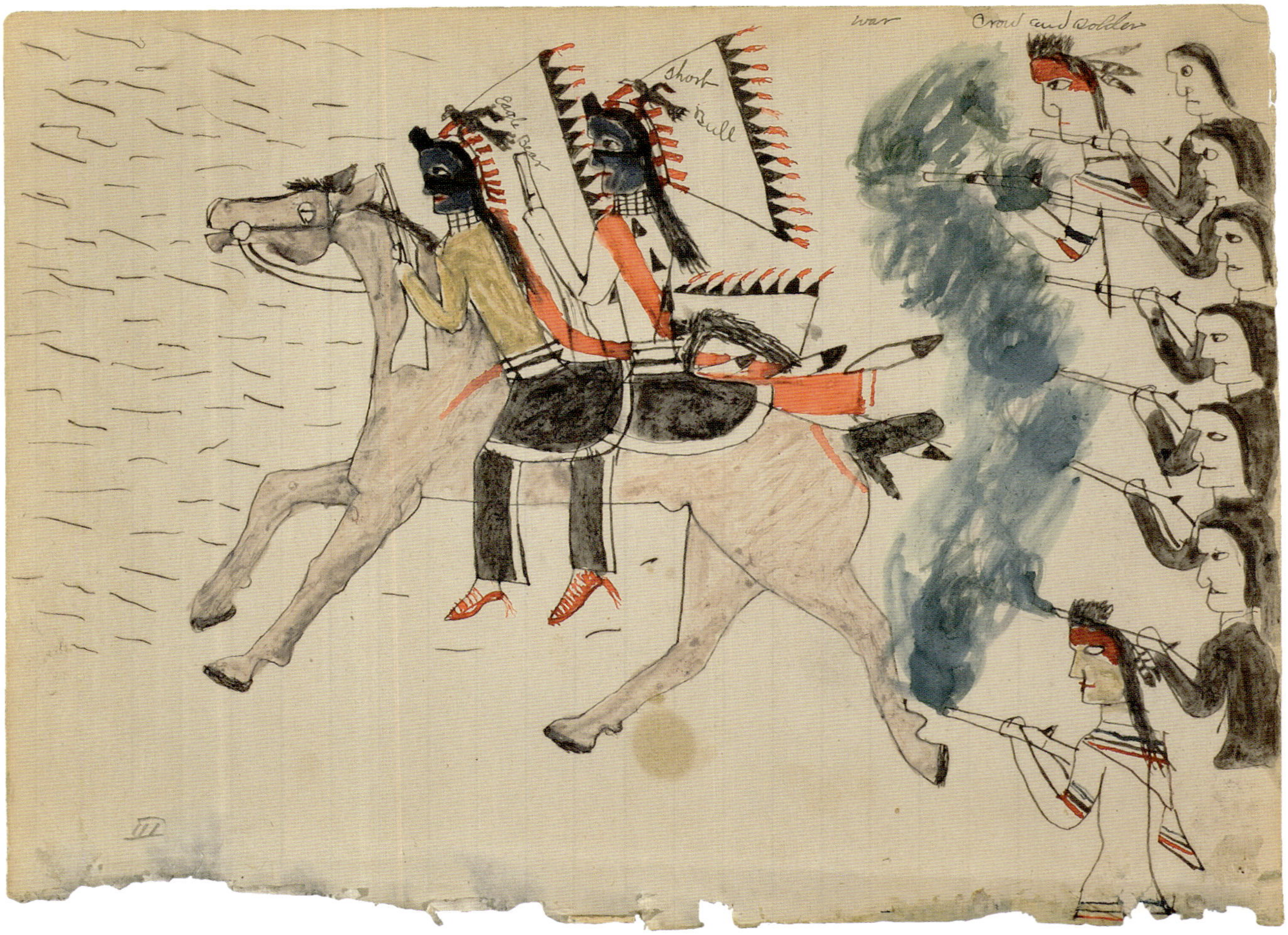

PLATE 124

Short Bull (Tatanka Ptecela), Lakota (Sioux), c. 1845–1915, ***Untitled ["Short Bull" and "Eagle Bear" fleeing gunfire from Apsáalooke (Crow) scouts and U.S. soldiers],*** page III from a Short Bull notebook, c. 1885–90, ink and watercolor on wove blue-lined notebook paper, reverse: page not numbered (no drawing), sheet: 7 ½ × 10 in. (19.0 × 25.4 cm); 2007.65.62.

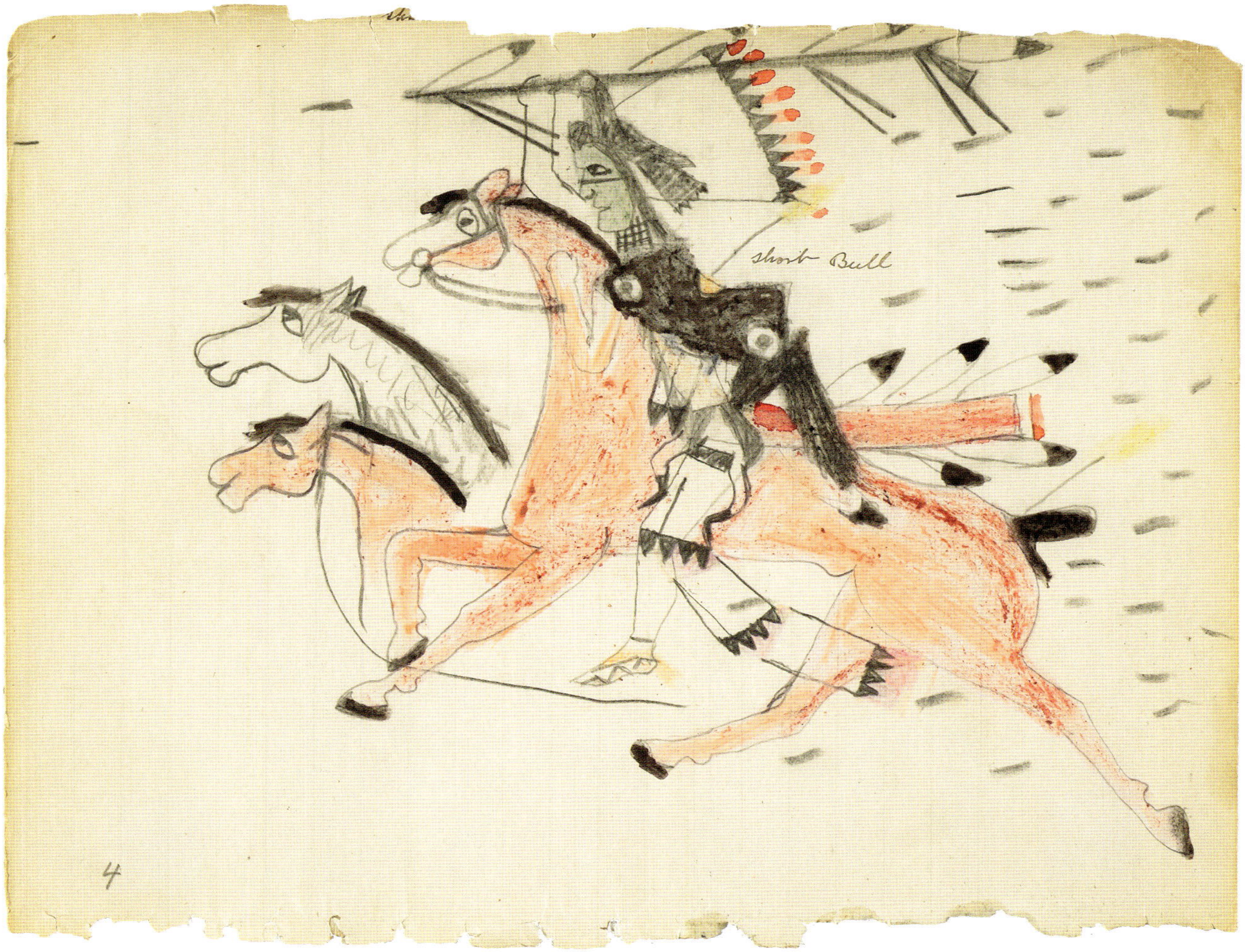

PLATE 125

Short Bull (Tatanka Ptecela), Lakota (Sioux), c. 1845–1915, ***Untitled [Short Bull raiding two horses],*** page 4 from a Short Bull notebook, c. 1885–90, graphite, colored pencil, and watercolor on wove blue-lined notebook paper, reverse: page not numbered (no drawing), sheet: 7 7/8 × 10 in. (20.0 × 25.4 cm). Gift of Mark Lansburgh, Class of 1949; 2007.88.1.

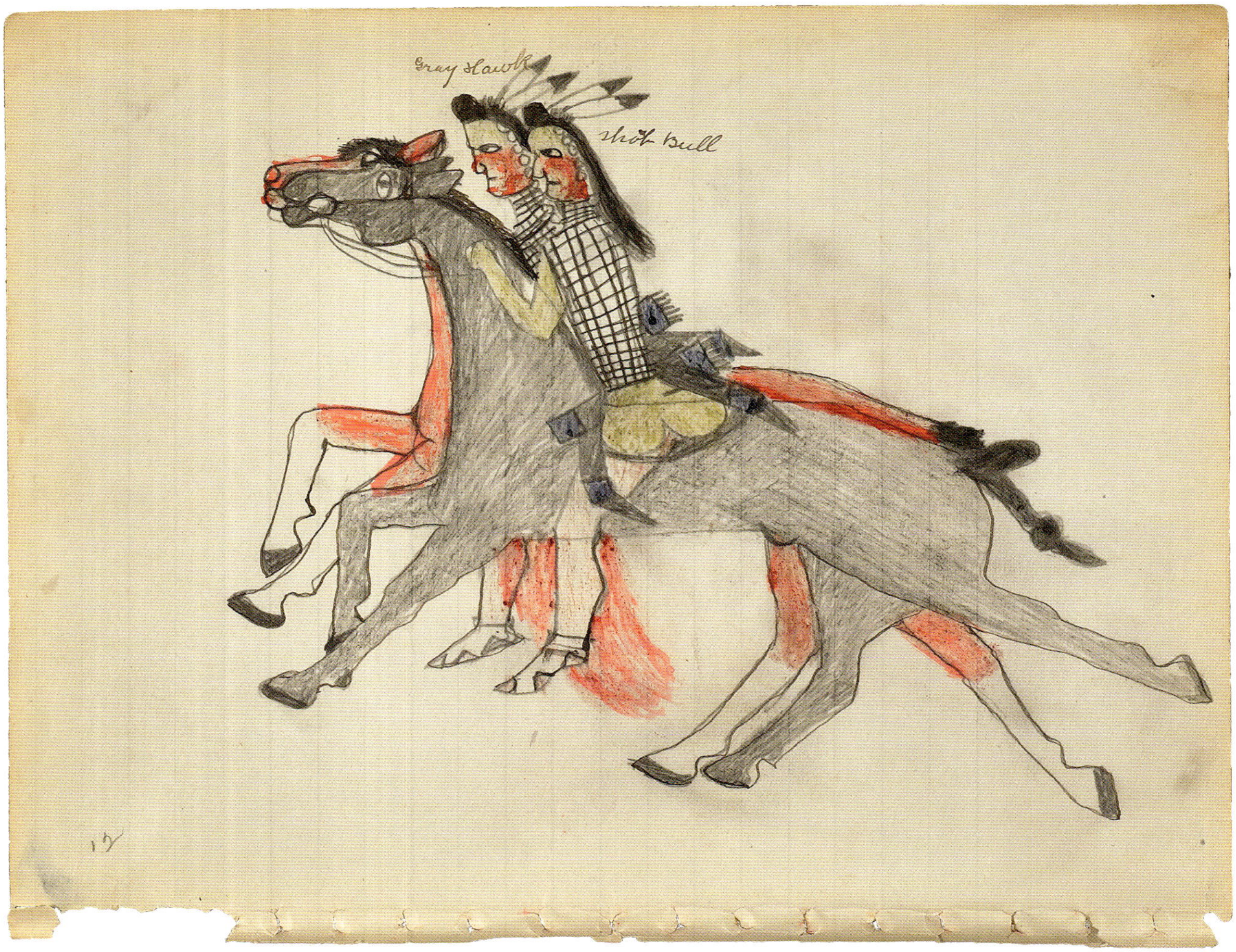

PLATE 126

Short Bull (Tatanka Ptecela), Lakota (Sioux), c. 1845–1915, ***Untitled ["Short Bull" and "Gray Hawk" at a gallop],*** page 12 from a Short Bull notebook, c. 1885–90, graphite, colored pencil, ink, and watercolor on wove blue-lined notebook paper, reverse: page not numbered (no drawing), sheet: 8 × 10 in. (20.2 × 25.4 cm); 2007.65.58.

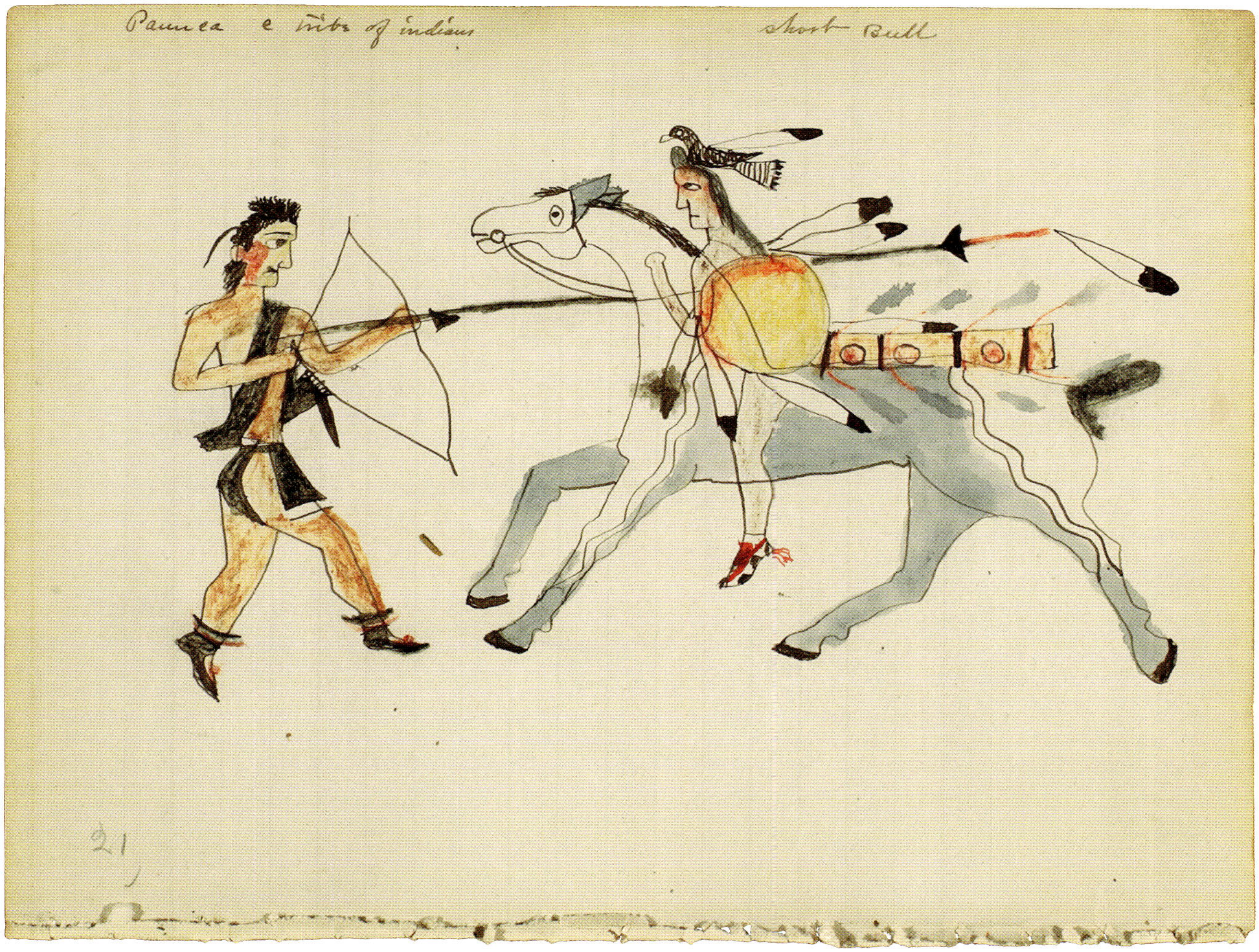

PLATE 127

Short Bull (Tatanka Ptecela), Lakota (Sioux), c. 1845–1915, ***Untitled [Short Bull counting coup on a Chaticks Si Chaticks (Pawnee) warrior]***, page 21 from a Short Bull notebook, c. 1885–90, watercolor, graphite, ink, and colored pencil on wove blue-lined notebook paper, reverse: page not numbered (no drawing), sheet: 7 ¾ × 10 in. (19.7 × 25.4 cm). Gift of Ann H. and Harte C. Crow; 2005.28.

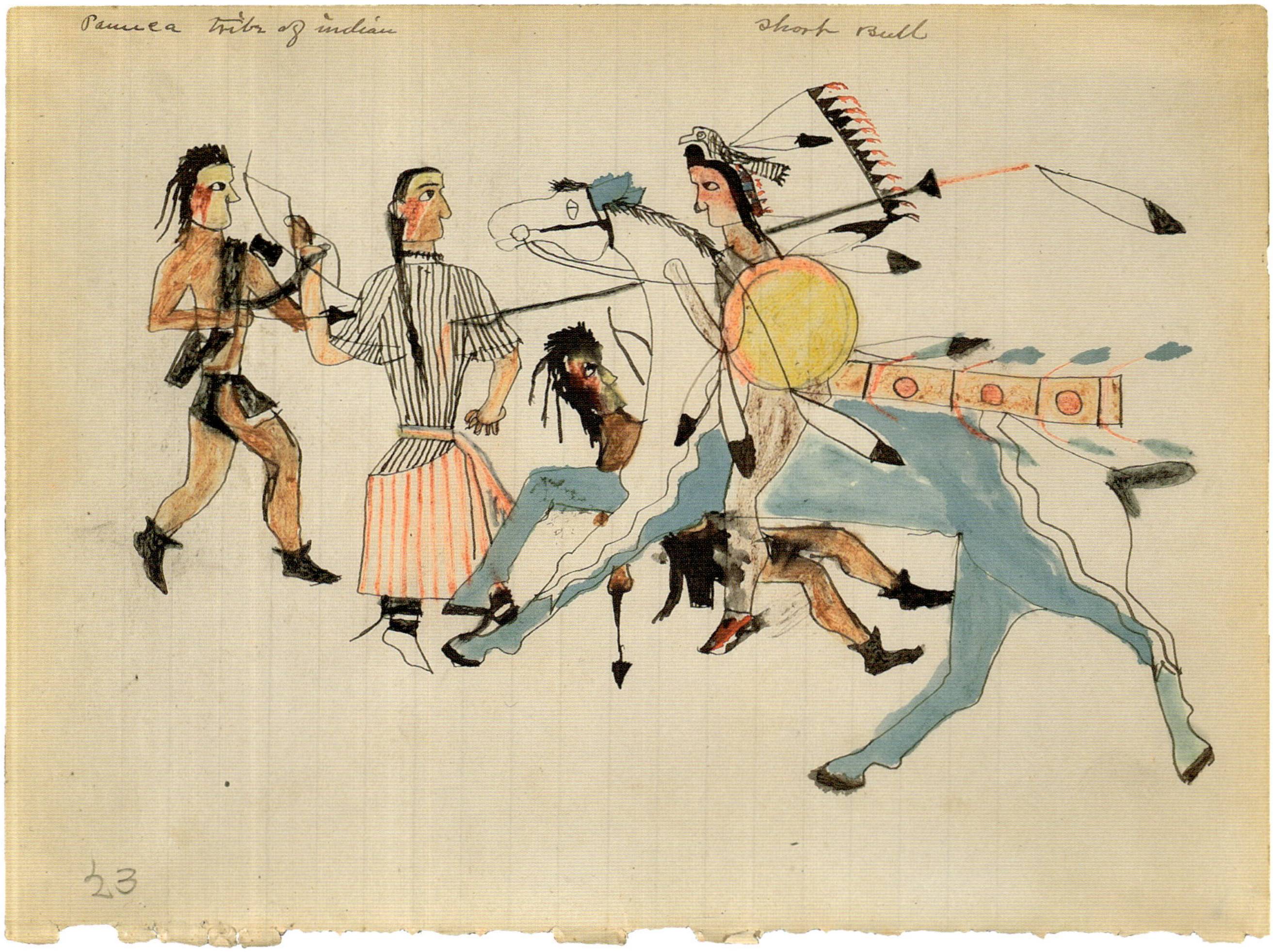

PLATE 128

Short Bull (Tatanka Ptecela), Lakota (Sioux), c. 1845–1915, ***Untitled [Short Bull in battle against the Chaticks Si Chaticks (Pawnees)],*** page 23 from a Short Bull notebook, c. 1885–90, colored pencil, ink, watercolor, and graphite on wove blue-lined notebook paper, reverse: page not numbered (no drawing), sheet: 7 ¾ × 10 in. (19.6 × 25.4 cm); 2007.65.64.

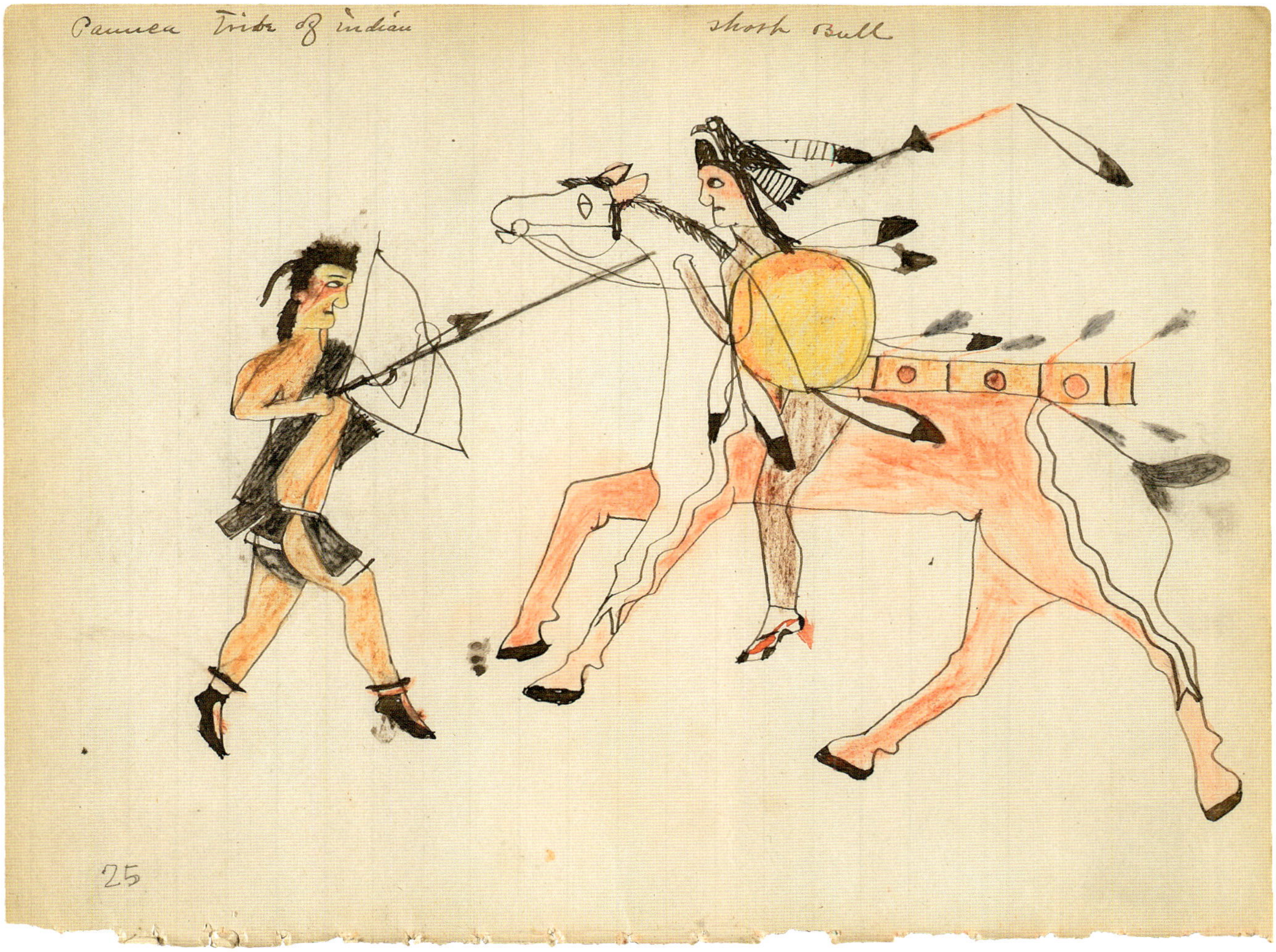

PLATE 129

Short Bull (Tatanka Ptecela), Lakota (Sioux), c. 1845–1915, ***Untitled [Short Bull lancing a Chaticks Si Chaticks (Pawnee) warrior],*** page 25 from a Short Bull notebook, c. 1885–90, ink, watercolor, colored pencil, and graphite on wove blue-lined notebook paper, reverse: page not numbered, (no drawing), sheet: 7 ¾ × 10 in. (19.5 × 25.4 cm); 2007.65.59.

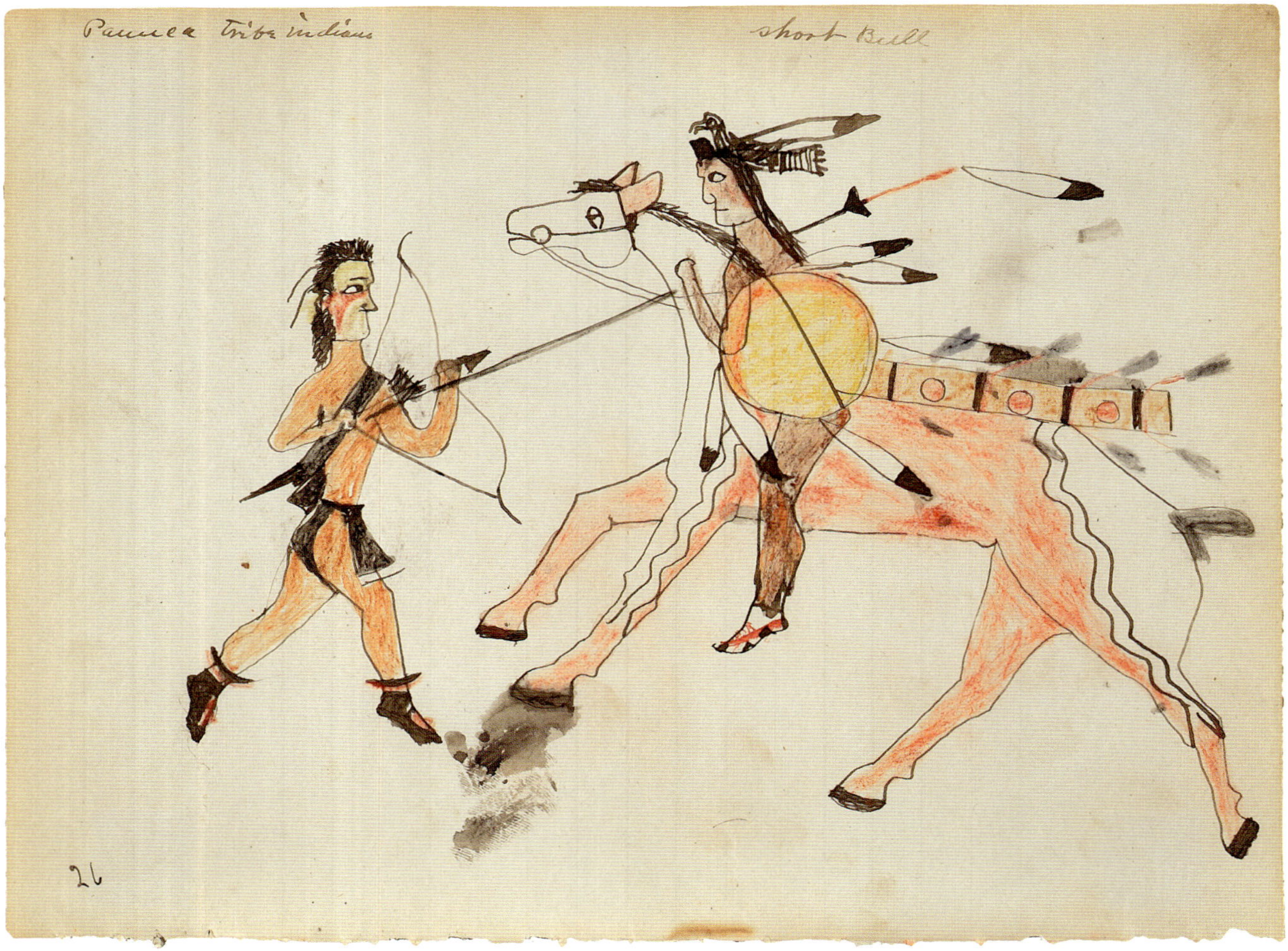

PLATE 130

Short Bull (Tatanka Ptecela), Lakota (Sioux), c. 1845–1915, ***Untitled [Short Bull lancing a Chaticks Si Chaticks (Pawnees) warrior],*** page 26 from a Short Bull notebook, c. 1885–90, ink, colored pencil, and watercolor on wove blue-lined notebook paper, reverse: page not numbered (no drawing), sheet: 7 ⅝ × 10 in. (19.2 × 25.4 cm); 2007.65.60.

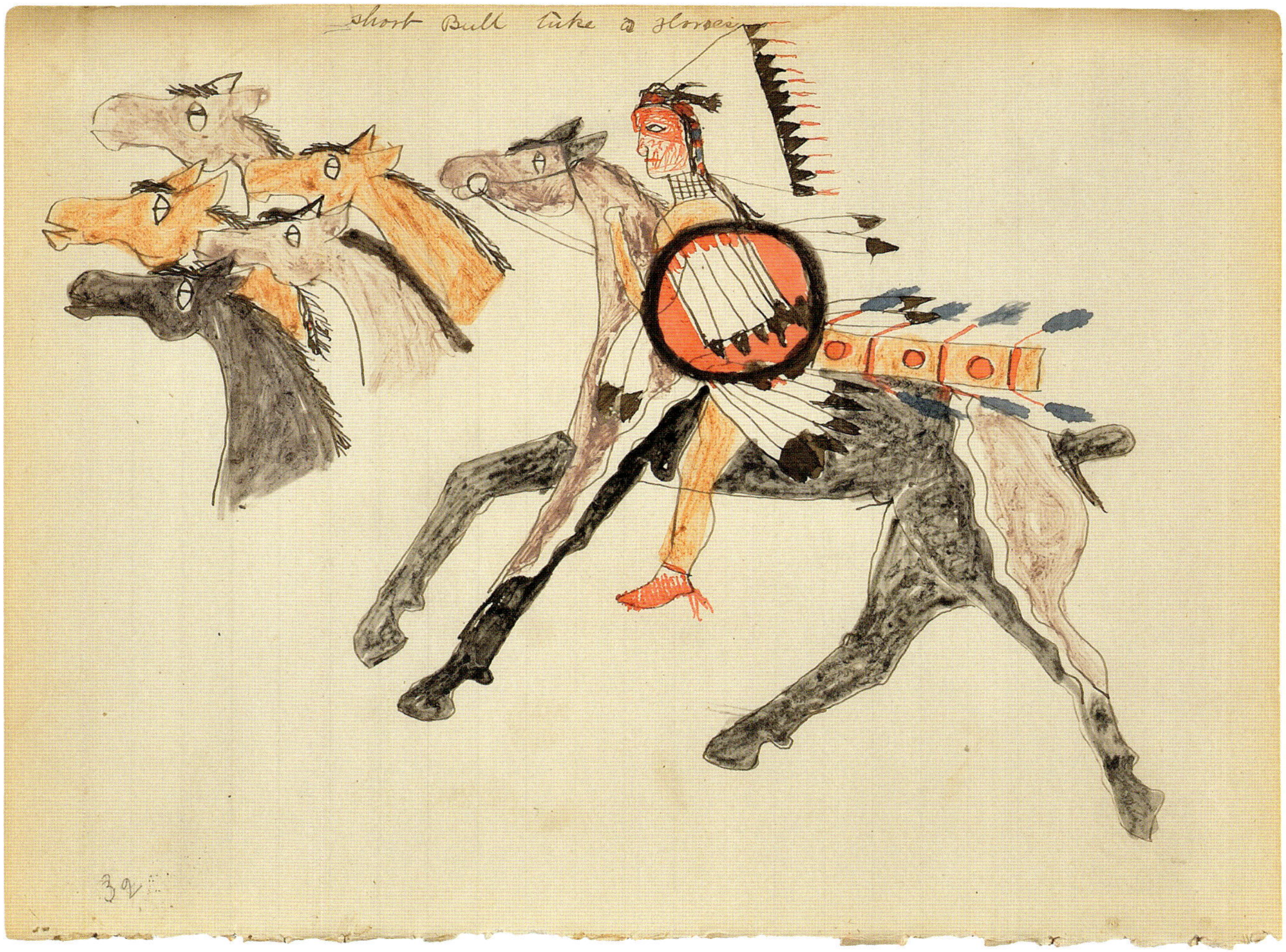

PLATE 131

Short Bull (Tatanka Ptecela), Lakota (Sioux), c. 1845–1915, ***Untitled [Short Bull raiding five horses],*** page 32 from a Short Bull notebook, c. 1885–90, ink, watercolor, and graphite on wove blue-lined notebook paper, reverse: page not numbered (no drawing), sheet: 7 ⅝ × 10 in. (19.4 × 25.4 cm); 2007.65.61.

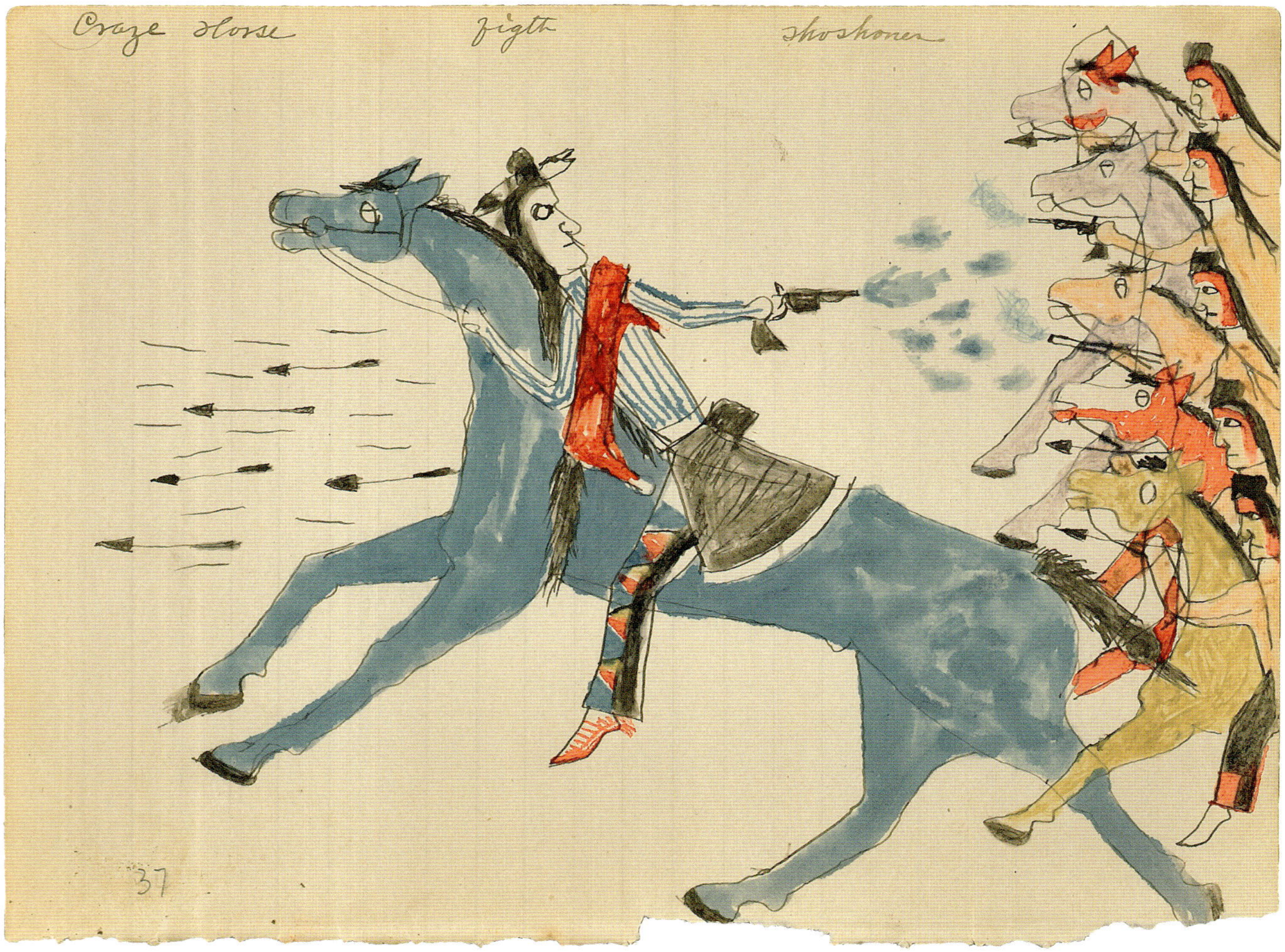

PLATE 132

Short Bull (Tatanka Ptecela), Lakota (Sioux), c. 1845–1915, ***Untitled [Crazy Horse fighting the Apsáalooke (Crow)],*** page 37 from a Short Bull notebook, c. 1885–90, graphite, ink, and watercolor on wove blue-lined notebook paper, reverse: page not numbered (no drawing), sheet: 7 5/8 × 10 in. (19.3 × 25.4 cm); 2007.65.65.

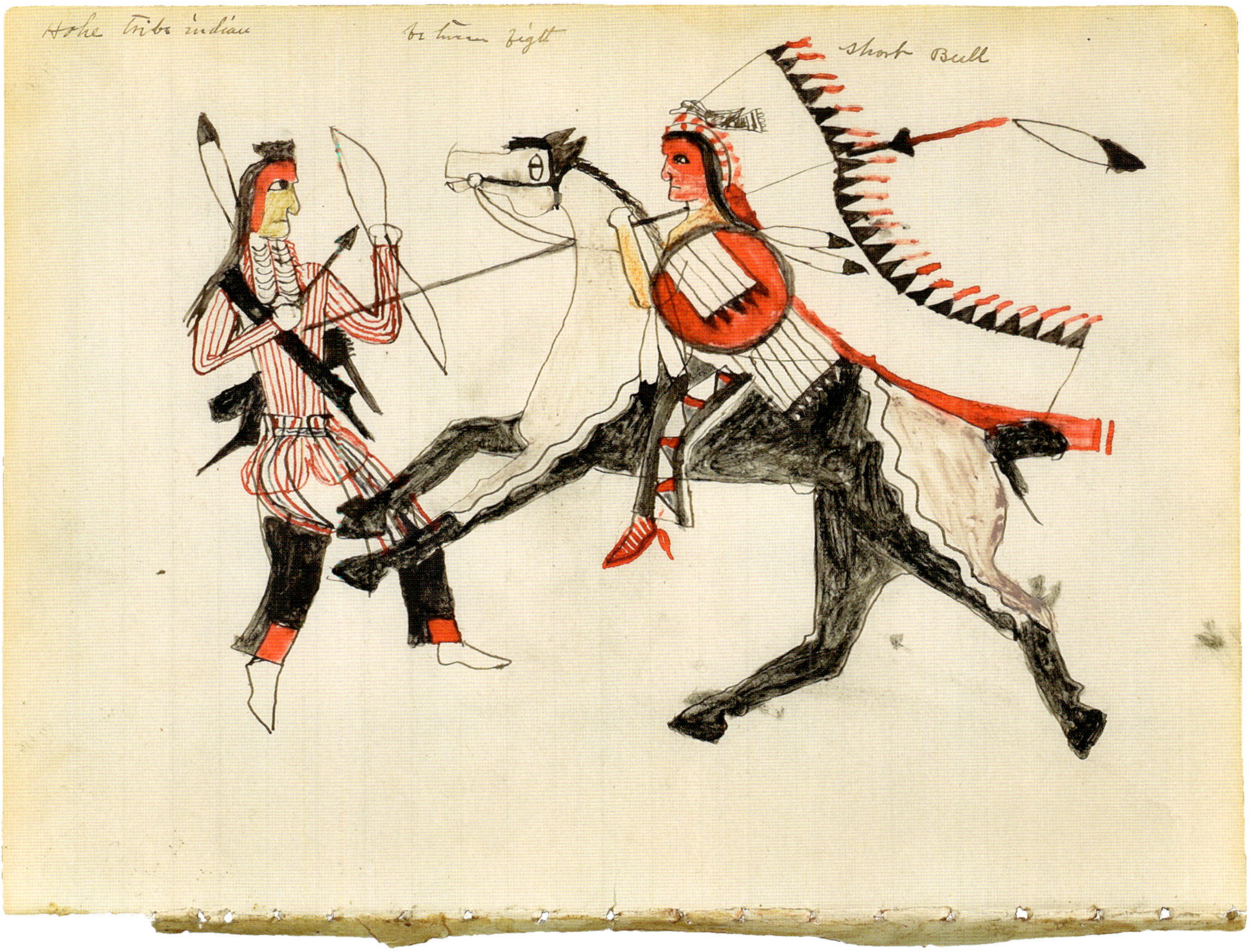

PLATE 133

Short Bull (Tatanka Ptecela), Lakota (Sioux), c. 1845–1915, ***Untitled [Short Bull lancing an Apsáalooke (Crow) warrior],*** from a Short Bull notebook, c. 1885–90, colored pencil, ink, and watercolor on wove blue lined notebook paper, reverse: page not numbered (no drawing), sheet: 8 × 10 in. (20.2 × 25.4 cm); 2007.65.63.

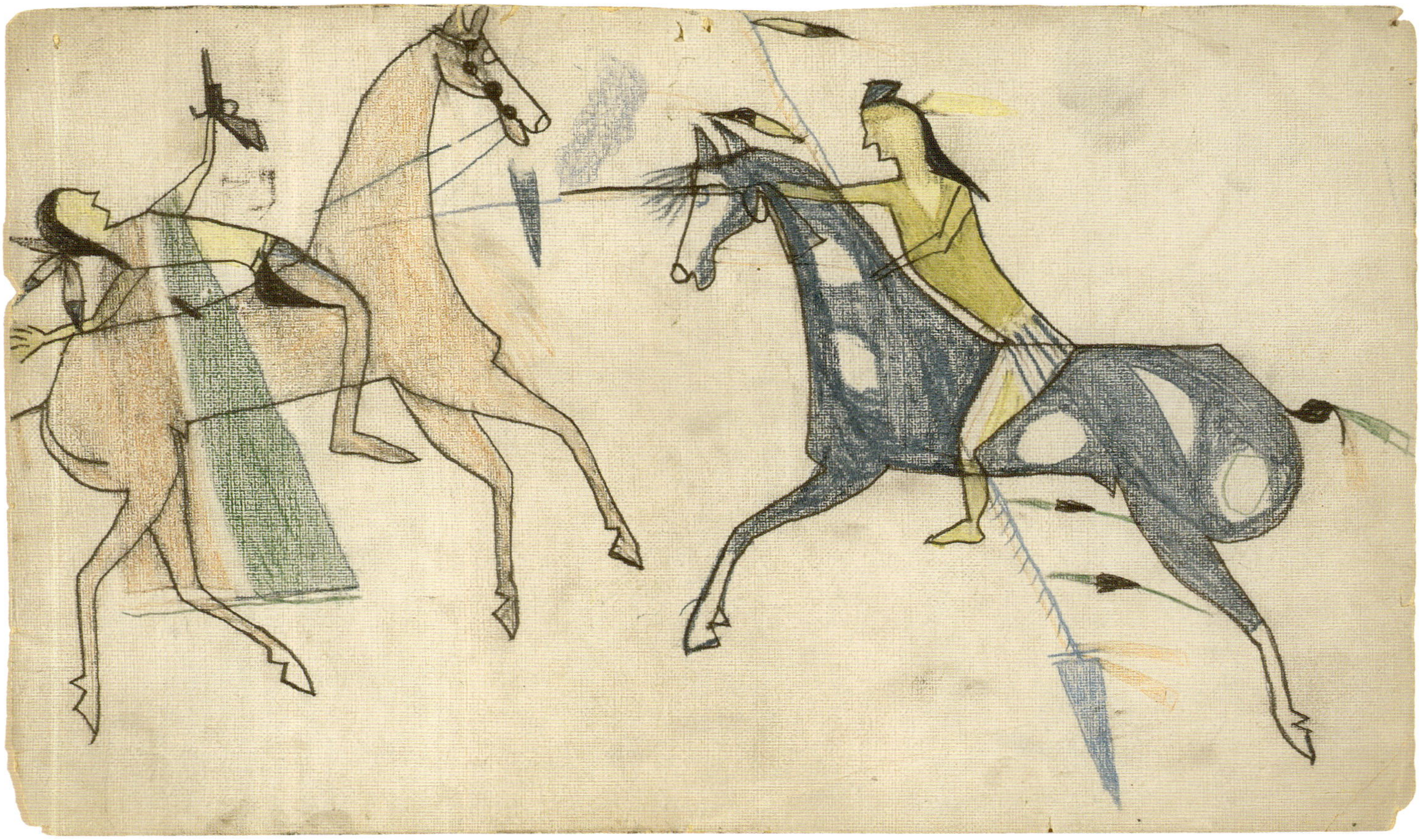

PLATE 134

White Swan, Apsáalooke (Crow), 1851–1904, ***Untitled [White Swan in battle with an Apsáalooke (Crow) warrior]***, c. 1890, graphite and colored pencil on linen-textured, commercially prepared wove paper, coated on one side (possibly wallpaper), reverse: (no drawing), sheet: 7 ½ × 12 ⅜ in. (19.0 × 31.3 cm); 2007.65.47.

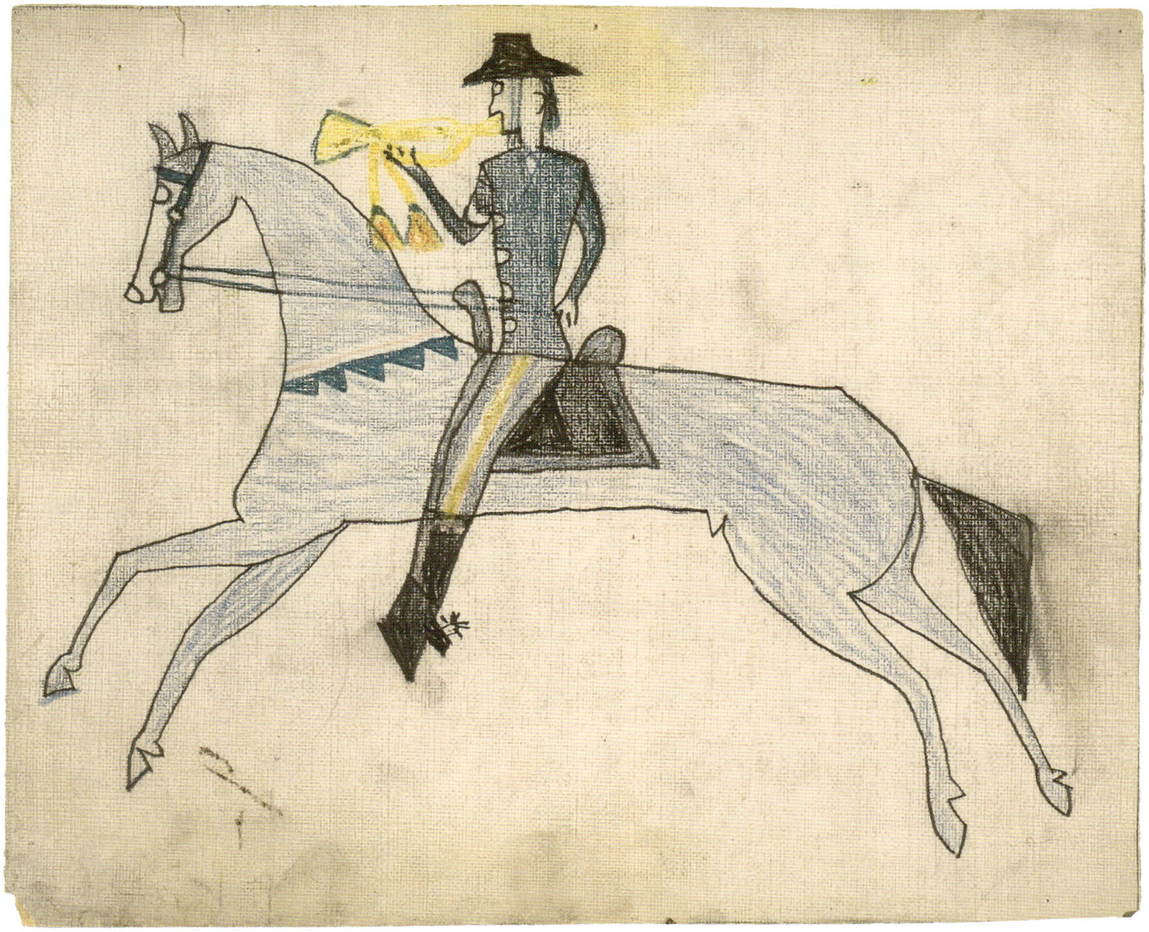

PLATE 135

White Swan, Apsáalooke (Crow), 1851–1904, ***Untitled [A regiment bugler],*** c. 1890, graphite and colored pencil on linen-textured, commercially prepared wove paper, coated on one side (possibly wallpaper), reverse: (no drawing), sheet: 7 ⅝ × 9 ⅛ in. (19.4 × 23.1 cm); 2007.65.92.

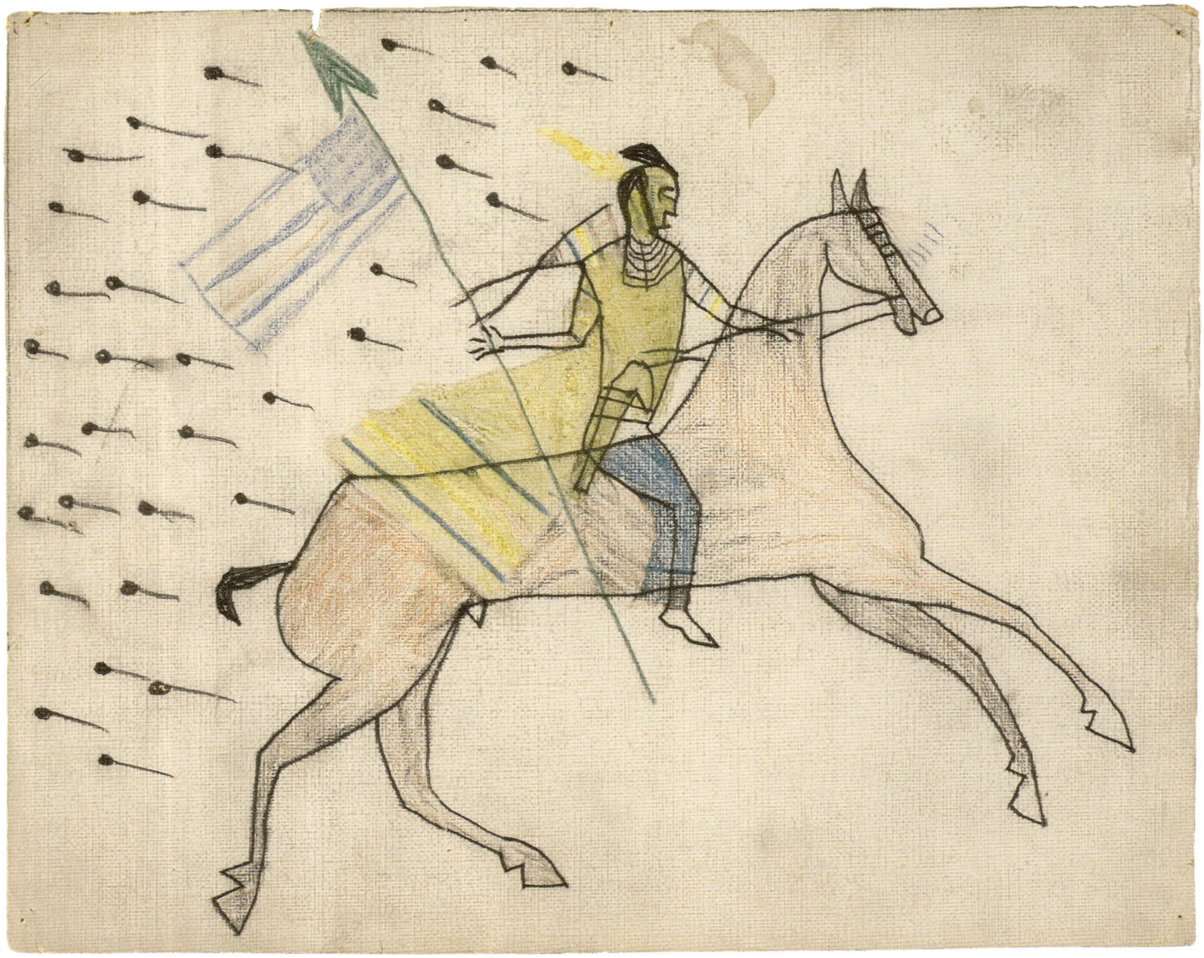

PLATE 136

White Swan, Apsáalooke (Crow), 1851–1904, ***Untitled [White Swan riding through gunfire]***, c. 1890, graphite and colored pencil on linen-textured, commercially prepared wove paper, coated on one side (possibly wallpaper), reverse: (no drawing), sheet: 7 ⅝ × 9 ¼ in. (19.3 × 23.4 cm); 2007.65.93.

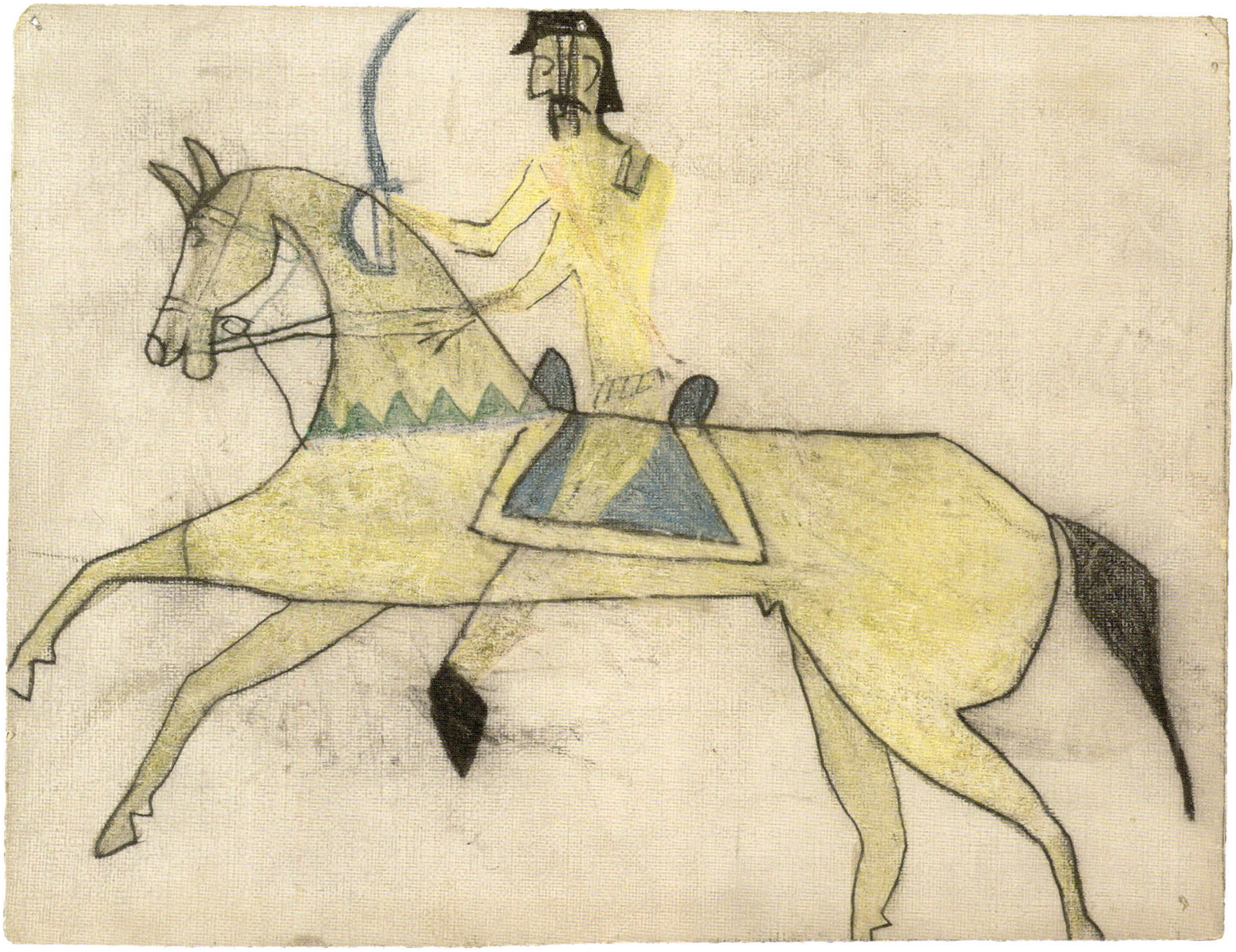

PLATE 137

White Swan, Apsáalooke (Crow), 1851–1904, ***Untitled [A U.S. cavalry officer],*** c. 1890, graphite and colored pencil on linen-textured, commercially prepared wove paper, coated on one side (possibly wallpaper), reverse: (no drawing), sheet: 7 ¼ × 9 ⅛ in. (18.2 × 23.0 cm); 2007.65.94.

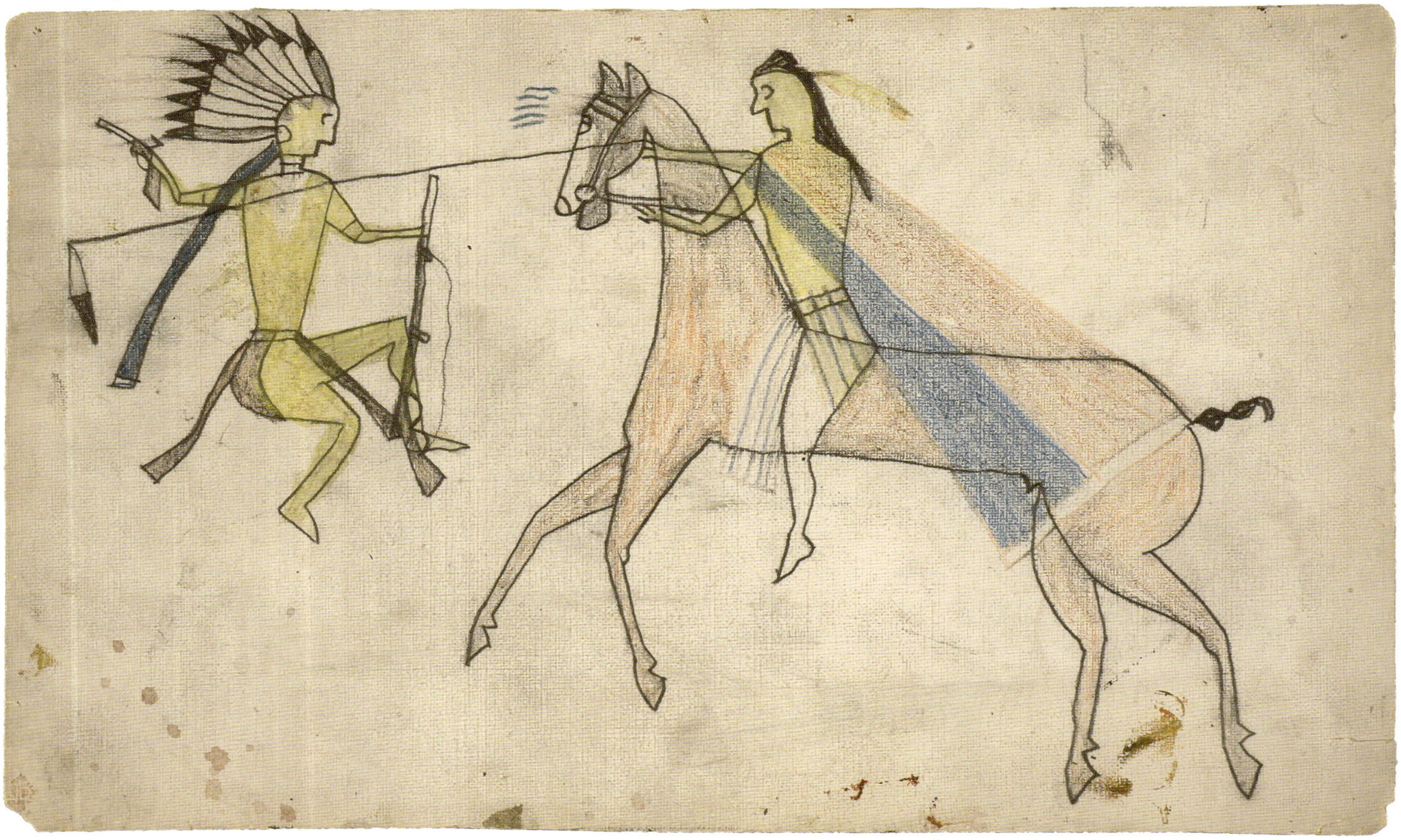

PLATE 138

White Swan, Apsáalooke (Crow), 1851–1904, ***Untitled [White Swan counting coup on a warrior, possibly Lakota],*** c. 1890, graphite and colored pencil on linen-textured, commercially prepared wove paper, coated on one side (possibly wallpaper), reverse: (no drawing), sheet: 7 ⅞ × 12 ⅜ in. (19.3 × 31.5 cm); 2007.65.95.

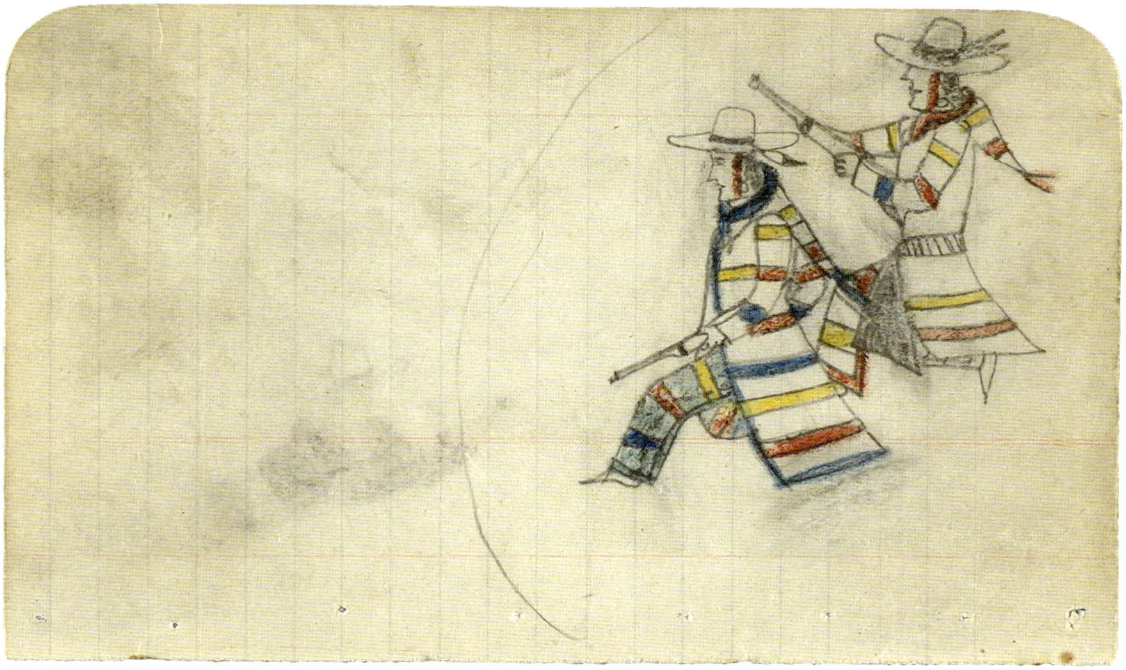

PLATE 139

Robert Ridge Walker, Northern Tsistsistas (Cheyenne), c. 1870–before 1959, ***Untitled [Two Northern Tsistsistas (Cheyenne) men],*** from a Robert Ridge Walker ledger, 1901, graphite and colored pencil on small wove ledger paper, reverse: (2007.65.79), sheet: 3 ½ × 5 ¾ in. (8.9 × 14.6 cm); 2007.65.78.

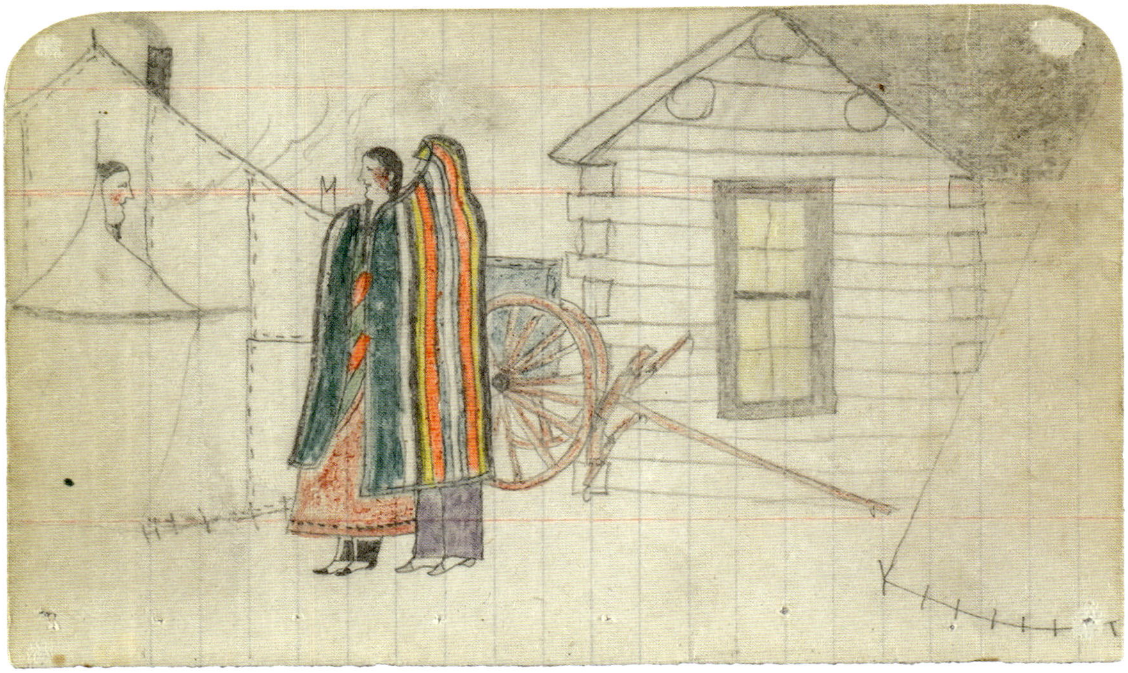

PLATE 140

Robert Ridge Walker, Northern Tsistsistas (Cheyenne), c. 1870–before 1959, ***Untitled [A Northern Tsistsistas (Cheyenne) courting couple],*** from a Robert Ridge Walker ledger, 1901, graphite and colored pencil on small wove ledger paper, reverse: (2007.65.78), sheet: 3 ½ × 5 ¾ in. (8.9 × 14.6 cm); 2007.65.79.

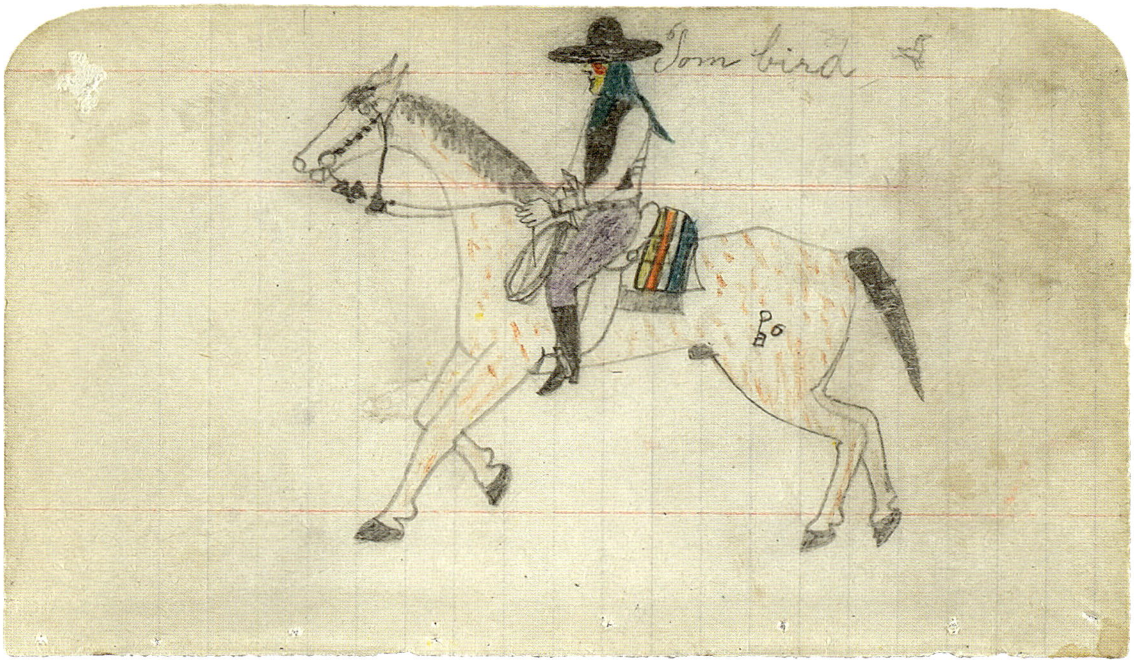

PLATE 141

Robert Ridge Walker, Northern Tsistsistas (Cheyenne), c. 1870–before 1959, ***Untitled ["Tom bird"],*** from a Robert Ridge Walker ledger, 1901, graphite and colored pencil on small wove ledger paper, reverse: (2007.65.80), sheet: 3 ½ × 5 ¾ in. (8.8 × 14.6 cm); 2007.65.105.

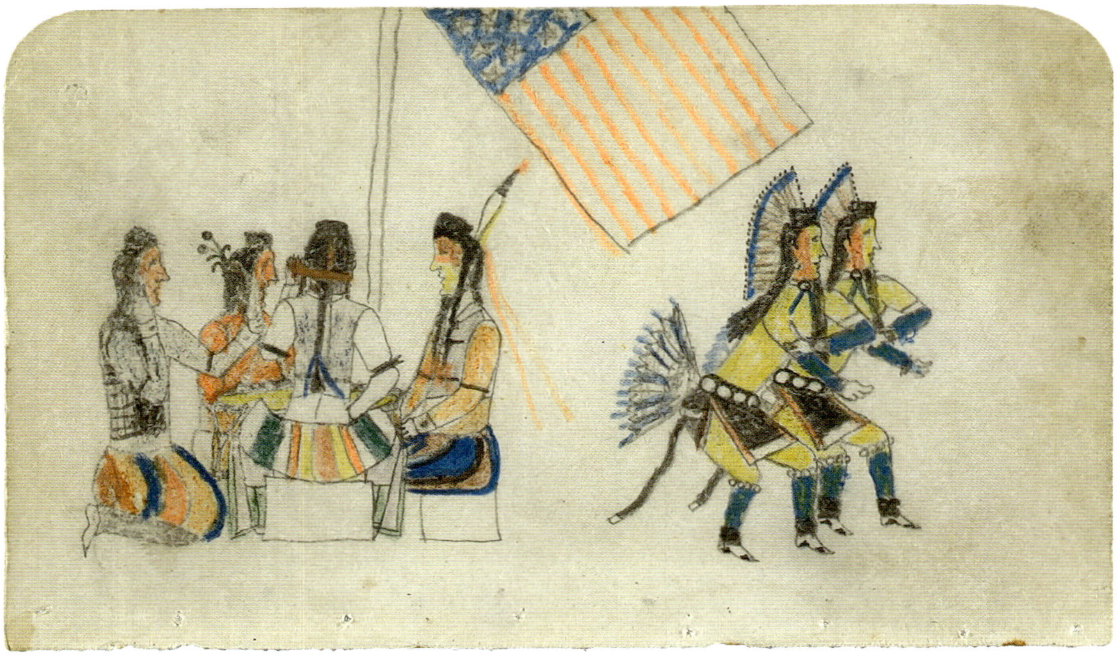

PLATE 142

Robert Ridge Walker, Northern Tsistsistas (Cheyenne), c.1870–before 1959, ***Untitled [Social dancers and drummers],*** from a Robert Ridge Walker ledger, 1901, graphite and colored pencil on small wove ledger paper, reverse: (2007.65.105), sheet: 3 ½ × 5 ¾ in. (8.8 × 14.6 cm); 2007.65.80.

CHAPTER 4

Unsettling Accounts

THE VIOLENT ECONOMIES OF THE LEDGER

MELANIE BENSON TAYLOR

Ledger books, with their drawings by Native Americans, exist in the interstices between writing, drawing, and violence; their production is a metaphor for history in the Great Plains itself.

ANNA BLUME, "IN A PLACE OF WRITING"

Among the multiple conversations taking place in the wake of Plains Indian ledger art's relatively recent canonization, one theme has been strikingly consistent: the presumption that these drawings constitute vital artifacts of resistance. Images of a culture poised in dramatic crisis, they depict world-shattering transition and compulsory assimilation while somehow managing to safeguard tribal memory and tradition in bold, striking, and defiant lines on the intrusive surfaces of enemy paper. As Anna Blume puts it, "Native Americans would draw over this space of foreign calculations, thereby transforming the nature of their own drawing and the ledger book itself, creating a middle place, an in-between place, in a place of writing . . . as part of the process of their own interpretation and survival."[1] In the simultaneous quest for political, economic, and creative sovereignty, ledger art has become a clarion example and inspiration for the generations of Native artists working in its wake and for those critics (Native and non-Native) eager to support and sustain the cultural vibrancy and tenacity it announces. Not coincidentally, contemporary Native writers such as James Welch, N. Scott Momaday, Gerald Vizenor, and Thomas King began to use ledger books as frequent tropes in their fiction. At this critical moment in efforts to uphold Native sovereignty in meaningful ways, ledger art inspires us to look forward—as the artists themselves did—even as we peer backward into a traumatic epoch. Despite the uncommon richness of purview and expression that they bequeath to us, however, these drawings neither settle nor balance the books of colonial-capitalist trauma.

Without question, the importance and influence of ledger drawings has been inestimably vast, and we are only beginning to unravel their manifold impact. For its emergent scholars and students, Native American ledger drawing stands as a metonym for tribal autonomy and survival under protracted assault. Not just the domain of art historians, these images have presented scholars of history and literature with crucial pictographic narratives that address a variety of gaps in the colonial record. Writer and scholar Denise Low categorizes ledger drawings as forms of literary narrative—indeed, an "alternative literature of unbroken cultural integrity."[2] Accordingly, the material form of the ledger itself offers an irresistible opportunity to read these narratives as explicit collisions between the tools of western colonial calculus and Natives' "alternative," resistant notions of cultural specificity and distinction. For some, such as Anishinaabe writer and critic Gerald Vizenor, these statements are fundamentally resistant and transcendent: they represent "the artistic *transmotion* of native sovereignty."[3] For Vizenor, "transmotion" embodies the pragmatic ideal of moving forward in an increasingly hybrid postcolonial reality. Certainly, ledger art promises to help us see those paths, and in doing so, it satisfies a widespread hunger for indigenous stories from indigenous perspectives. Yet the question remains: are these drawings visionary testaments of "sovereignty" or more sober capitulations to the escalating hegemony of economic desire and desperation?

What I would urge us to explore—and the Lansburgh collection's diverse array of drawings and artists facilitates this examination immensely—is the extent to which these drawings signify not just coercion but complicity, not a writing *over* but a writing inextricably tangled *within* all that the ledger represents. What we need to investigate are the unsatisfying indications that the ledger's violent economies were neither very new nor wholly strange in anything other than language and material, and, moreover, the unsettling degree to which "survival" in "post"-colonial America has meant demonstrating an intimacy and a mastery of the very language of the ledger.

LEDGER ART IN COMPARATIVE COLONIAL CONTEXT

Exposing the broader import and darker implications of ledger drawings requires viewing them in comparative historical context. It is not mere happenstance that the conclusion of the Civil War in 1865 transitioned seamlessly into the violent, ongoing crusade to eradicate the Great Plains of the Natives impeding the settlement of the American West. Yet we rarely see the two conflicts in concert: as Elliott West argues, historical epochs regularly attach themselves to salient events and themes, and the story of nineteenth century America has simply become the saga of the Civil War. The ongoing assault on Indian territories and nationhood recedes to the margins of this narrative, despite the fact that it was clearly part of a critical period that redefined and reconstructed the nation. West points instead to a "Greater Reconstruction" that includes western expansion throughout the century in a narrative usually limited to the rebuilding of the South from 1865–77.[4] Similarly in *West from Appomattox* (2007), Heather Cox Richardson argues that "Reconstruction" was a sweeping federal agenda to forcibly remake the nation into an industrial-capitalist organism, a project that required the dispossession of both the plantation South and Indian territories.[5] Despite these compelling correlations, however, western expansion is rarely considered as pivotal as—or even as related to—the Civil War's objectives and significance. Partly, this can be explained by routine processes of imperial repression: the Civil War is remembered as a mission of ethical deliverance, while the Indian wars betray the dark casualties of nation-building and industrial progress.

Nonetheless, an uncanny kinship emerges through the material coincidence of the ledger—the literal and metaphorical emblem onto which both defeated southerners and dispossessed Indians persistently projected their anxieties and anger about the intrusion of a calculating, capitalist order. As the Greater Reconstruction upended and reshaped both worlds, those unseated reacted to their encompassing impoverishment in strikingly analogous ways; for both, part of this process involved not rejecting outright but in fact harnessing the tools of material recovery and empowerment. The effect is as stunning as it is disconcerting, and it reminds us of the power of economic mechanisms to subsume and seduce without regard for politics, probity, or preference. As the objective correlative for this experience—the fetish or the symbol through which both cultures express the horror of defeat—the trope of the ledger signifies the fine, furious balance of colonial theft *and* remuneration.

We know exactly how white southerners responded to their conversion into an American capitalist mainstream, because they bemoaned and descried their "Lost Cause" loudly in political rhetoric and artistic effusions lasting well into the twentieth century; but we can also see the hypocrisy of those protests fairly immediately. For example, in an essay called "The Hind Tit," written in about 1930, the Tennessee writer Andrew Nelson Lytle employed the specter of the ledger to argue that the imposition of capitalism on the South's agrarian arcadia would have disastrous consequences; he laments "the numbering of a farm's resources . . . and as the only reason to number them is to turn them into cash . . . the agrarian South is bound to go when the first page is turned and the first mark crosses the ledger."[6] Writing more than half a century after emancipation, he incoherently casts this disaster as a still-potential event and not a process well underway; moreover, he cleverly veils the fact that ledgers were commonplace features in the antebellum economy, recording the array of a plantation's "resources," the most vital of which was its human chattel. This is the genealogy of the ledger that also haunts Faulkner's Ike McCaslin in *Go Down, Moses* (published just ten years later, in 1940). McCaslin discovers in a dusty plantation ledger the dreadful miscegenation and violence suppressed in his own family history; Faulkner tells us that Ike "would never need to look at the ledgers again nor did he; the yellowed pages in their fading implacable succession were as much a part of his consciousness and would remain so forever, as the fact of his own nativity" (259). This legacy is the southerner's birthright, but one that he needs to reject and repress as Andrew Lytle does: the overt reality and incontrovertible offenses of a "cash" economy—all there in plain view in the columns and figures of the ledger—must remain absolutely antithetical to a simpler, kinder, more humane, and mythical past. As global market commerce

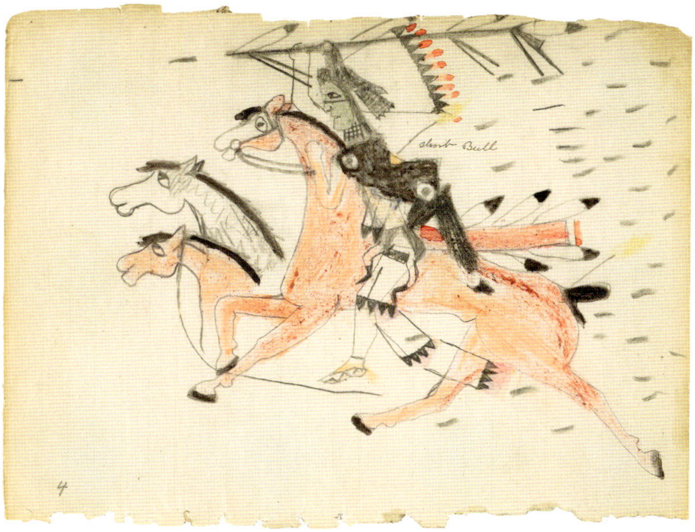

FIGURE 4.1
Short Bull (Tatanka Ptecela), Lakota (Sioux), c. 1845–1915, ***Untitled [Short Bull raiding two horses],*** c. 1885–90, Hood Museum of Art (plate 125).

expanded and the South felt the strictures of its role as an economic colony, white southerners famously retreated even further into this nostalgia.

In Plains Indian ledger art, the discursive confrontation with the ledger and all that it represents seems even more explicit and emphatic: in striking visual dissonance, Natives drew defiantly over the lined and gridded pages of account book paper, very literally *writing over* the enemy's economic balance sheets. As Anna Blume explains, as Natives "witnessed their lives being affected in part by the technology of writing," the warrior-artists explicitly "chose ledger books as places to draw images of their perceptions and exploits. The bound book or lined pages where writing was done was like a silent rifle that, once possessed, even without the necessary ammunition, could potentially give the warrior some of the power of his opponents."[7] These skirmishes occur not just on the pages of ledgers but in autograph books, military target-shooting records, and small notebooks or drawing pads, all of which collectively constitute the western "technology" of writing and colonial accounting; yet regardless of the precise medium, scholars homogenize all of these emergent instances of paper-based drawing as "ledger art"—a selective and seductive rubric for tacitly interpreting them as silent attacks on an economic opponent. In keeping with Blume, most scholars of ledger art see the paper itself as an ideological battlefield. Yet our well-intentioned historical hindsight compels us to see only Natives' *resistance* of a corrosive capitalist invader in these de facto gestures of subversion[8]; what the ledger itself actually introduces, as it did for the modern southerner, is an opportunity to cathect complicated anxieties and ambivalences already simmering in the cultural body—one where the damage of the ledger had been irrevocably wrought long before these outcries against its tyranny. Far more than an incidental surface for hungry artists, the instrument of the ledger itself matters, as a material force to be reckoned *with* and not simply reckoned away.

Indian grievance hasn't been nearly as noisy nor as compromised as southerners' laments, but it has resounded regularly and increasingly to the tune of anticapitalist nostalgia. This skewed historicism has actually increased in the wake of the Civil Rights era and the New Age fascination with Native lifeways, partly as an imagined antidote to the corrosive materialism and consumerism infecting global culture. Certainly, there are seeds of accuracy in the idea that many indigenous tribes functioned harmoniously and generously within subsistence economies and that there were principles of reciprocity for centuries before colonial contact. Yet new scholarship is beginning to probe the extent to which capitalist energies have always energized Native societies struggling to survive colonial incursions. In *Rich Indians* (2010), Alexandra Harmon insists that Indians have long been embroiled in systems of capitalist accumulation and prosperity, despite terrific controversy within their own communities and surrounding white society. An additional, thriving body of scholarship has begun to excavate the little-discussed fact of slave ownership among Native American tribes of the antebellum South (particularly Cherokee and Creek).[9]

Despite this rich and increasing evidence that Native Americans shifted more fluidly to systems of capitalism than we generally believe, the tremendous damage wrought upon indigenous cultures by colonial-capitalism nonetheless explains and often excuses our continued historical hyperbole and reactionary revisionism. Ledger

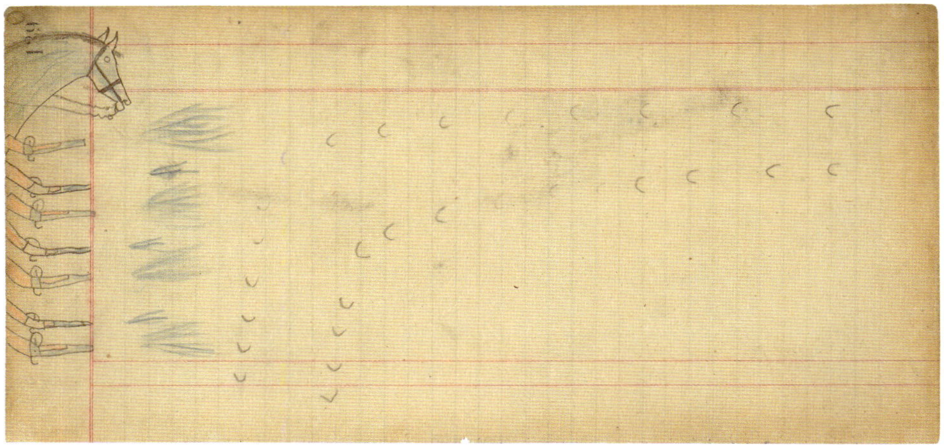

FIGURE 4.2
Unknown artist, Tsistsistas (Cheyenne) and/or Inunaina (Arapaho), active late nineteenth century, ***Untitled [A formation of U.S. soldiers in battle],*** late nineteenth century, Hood Museum of Art (plate 74).

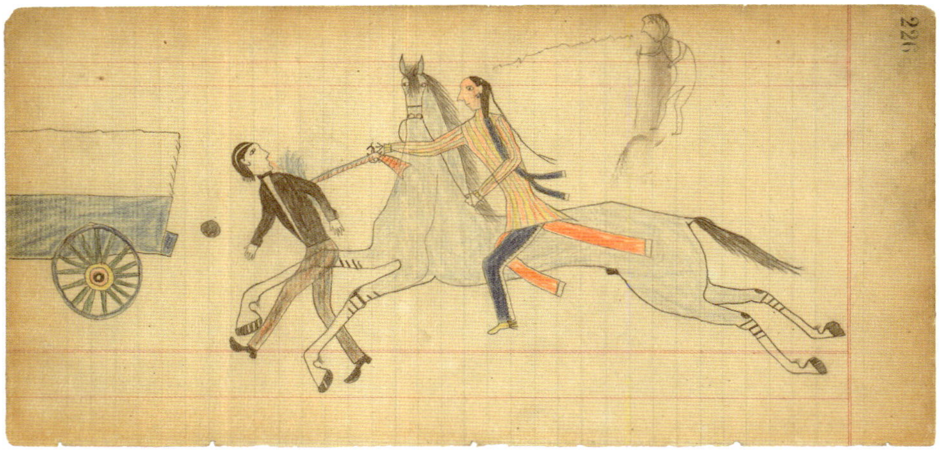

FIGURE 4.3
Unknown artist, Tsistsistas (Cheyenne) and/or Inunaina (Arapaho), active late nineteenth century, ***Untitled [A warrior shoots a non-Native man],*** late nineteenth century, Hood Museum of Art (plate 85).

art seems an obvious expression of our desires to see colonial injuries avenged; and yet, the drawings themselves inevitably contain not just anxiety but ambivalence about the manner of survival and opportunity offered by and through capitalism. It seems dangerously unproductive to celebrate an anticapitalist ethos under conditions and economies that make mere resistance a trivial conceit; in doing so, we confuse agency with affect. A sturdy ethical position in global affairs is vital, but pretending to defy capitalism in any consequential way runs the risk of overlooking the myriad, destructive ways in which we are already imbricated practically, psychologically, and emotionally, and in ways we can hardly begin to comprehend, much less escape. Put another way, simply rejecting the ledger and all that it signifies cannot so easily uncoil one from its dominion.

While we generally don't like to admit it in just these terms, economies of cruelty and avarice plagued many tribal communities long before the introduction of American capitalism. As anthropologist Morris Foster puts it, "Plains scholars have . . . been as reluctant as Anglo politicians to treat explicitly the economic bases for [Plains] warfare . . . [and so] The pre-reservation era became an ideal that was not part of historical time."[10] Bernard Mishkin was among the first scholars to rigorously explore the economic motivations of Plains society, where wealth was rooted not in a cash but a horse economy. According to Mishkin, the vital "economic importance" of the horse simply "cannot be exaggerated,"[11] a fact corroborated by the Lansburgh collection's great preponderance of images containing horses—which comprise probably 90 percent of the set. Such insistence in subject matter might indicate a desire to fill the pages of books *intended* to catalog riches with what constituted wealth for a Plains man, along with the exploits that would result in an individual adding to his store of equine possessions (figure 4.1). The ledger in fact becomes a supremely appropriate container for such bookkeeping: what is new is simply the ledger's novel materiality and the coercive means of its entry into the Plains economy.

Ledger art thus seems to convey the endemic violence not just of dispossession but of imagined recompense, a

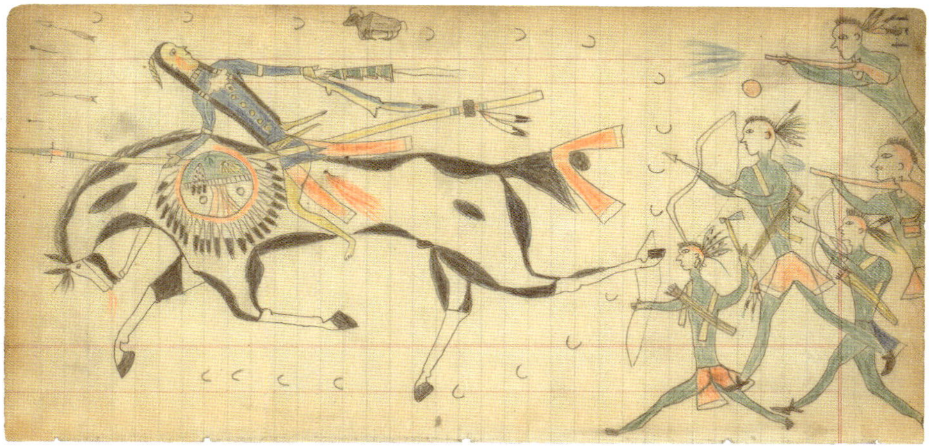

FIGURE 4.4
Unknown artist, Tsistsistas (Cheyenne) and/or Inunaina (Arapaho), active late nineteenth century, ***Untitled [Warrior fleeing Chaticks Si Chaticks (Pawnee) warriors]***, late nineteenth century, Hood Museum of Art (plate 77).

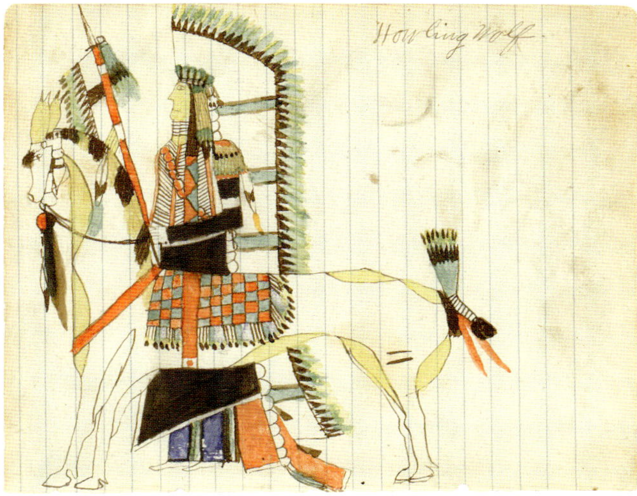

FIGURE 4.5
Howling Wolf (Ho-na-nist-to), Southern Tsistsistas (Cheyenne), 1849–1927, ***Untitled [Howling Wolf with his war horse]***, c. 1874–75, Hood Museum of Art (plate 34).

striking credit imposed upon a column of mounting debits. Both the violence and the priority of wealth are emphatic, but neither is entirely new. In numerous drawings in the Lansburgh collection (especially those by several artists in the "Vincent Price Ledger"), horses and weapons share conceptual and visual space as integral components of a violent economy. In many, panoramic scenes of battle overwhelm and exceed the limits of the bounded ledger terrain, as bullets and hoofprints imply dynamic narratives of action continuing well beyond the borders of the page (see plate 73).[12] One drawing in particular (figure 4.2) features just the head of a horse and the barrels of guns charging through the left-hand border of the page, as if exploding onto a battlefield already evacuated of its fleeing foes. While such depictions are in many ways consistent with earlier illustrations and pictographs, in the new space of the ledger they demonstrate a fluid confrontation with the conscripted planes of these account books and the assaults they signified. In one drawing (figure 4.3), a white settler is plainly shot—not simply "counted coup" upon, as in many similar images—which may suggest the dramatic heightening of violence and the sharpening of its retaliatory target as both territory and mobility were being steadily co-opted from the Plains tribes. The subject matter chosen by the artists during this period seems to correlate stridently with the world they most wanted to memorialize and preserve, one being persistently undone by unparalleled, acquisitive violence.

Increasingly, then, the drawings reveal a greater emphasis on the trappings of wealth and status, as Michael Jordan notes in his contribution to this volume. In many of these drawings, men depict themselves pursuing prey (human or animal) while festooned in brilliant regalia normally reserved for combat or ritual (figure 4.4); these scenes thus eschew the actual accoutrements of warfare or hunting in favor of grand spectacles of wealth, possession, and status. In other instances, both horses and warriors appear together outfitted in excessive finery (figure 4.5) or otherwise surrounded by evidence of ample possessions. To be a warrior always meant negotiating a complicated fusion of honor, status, wealth, tradition, and accumulation—a narrative of possession that the ledger invites easily into its pages, a space to treasure a memory of wealth and triumph. To put it another way, these artists do not reject the principle of ownership and acquisition so much as they angrily and persistently mourn its loss and imagine extravagant restitution.

FORT MARION: THE DISPOSSESSED IN THE LAND OF THE DISPOSSESSED

Elaborate representations like those discussed above suggest a complex desire to preserve the traditional metrics of status in a time when such measures and the freedom to obtain them were under persistent and devastating attack. Some of the most difficult years of this period were endured by seventy-two Plains warriors deemed "hostile" to reservation settlement and imprisoned at Fort Marion from 1875 to 1878; not coincidentally, these years also constitute some of the most transformative and fertile for the development of ledger art. Most critics have marveled at the profound changes in worldview and method evident in the drawings from this period. But another revealing comparative context looms in the background of these analyses and stands to tell us much more about the art and the anxieties produced in this context. Indeed, the Fort Marion environment places the Reconstruction South and the settled Plains in geographic and ideological juxtaposition. St. Augustine, Florida, was a prized and rapidly developing tourist destination in the post-war South, well known for its semitropical climate and apparent healthful properties; yet it was also a typical scene of Reconstruction volatility, transitioning rapidly into institutionalized apartheid—which happened officially in 1877, during the warriors' period of incarceration. We need to begin exploring just what the warrior-artists learned at Fort Marion about the difficult algorithms of race and economics in the resurgent South.

Florida may have been uniquely appealing to many, as it represented a kind of "frontier country" lagging behind the rest of the South's grudging capitulation to social and economic reform.[13] The perceived outlaw principles of the state, along with its supposed health benefits, contributed to its appeal as a destination for ailing consumptives, wealthy northerners, and well-heeled southerners seeking a retreat into an encompassing curative space. As historian Susan A. Eacker notes, "For many travelers, writers, and readers, the lure of the South, the land of the 'Lost Cause,' was that it appeared to be a lost civilization as well—medieval, anachronistic, and untainted by the crass commercialism that permeated the industrialized North."[14] The Connecticut-born writer and abolitionist Harriet Beecher Stowe, for instance, chose to spend significant portions of the year in Florida aiding in its Reconstruction and education efforts (including a stint volunteering in a classroom at Fort Marion[15]), and finding inspiration for her anticapitalist novel, *Oldtown Folks* (1869), which she penned there and long declared her "magnum opus."[16] The unfettered, unspoiled spirit of the South clearly evokes the mythic opportunities of the West. Yet both landscapes and histories eventually expose their enabling fictions: among other despoilers was the fact that much of the tourism and development along the coast had been financed by Henry Morrison Flagler—New York tycoon, railroad magnate, and partner to John D. Rockefeller. In short, many Americans were already beginning to elide southerners and Native Americans as malleable entities to be alternately romanticized and feared according to their own needs and anxieties.

Romanticizing the Indian proved an effective method of insuring civic and racial order. Richard Henry Pratt facilitated this by organizing "authentic" cultural demonstrations performed by the Indians at Fort Marion regularly—about "twice each week." With the blessings and encouragement of their keepers, the Natives "held grand powwows, conducted war dances, and sang traditional songs for audiences. The performers seemed to entertain guests with relish," as Brad D. Lookingbill notes in *War Dance at Fort Marion*, "though at times observers discerned that they were merely acting for public amusement" and undoubtedly for profit as well (they were regularly paid around two dollars, and occasionally significantly more, for each show). Indeed, there is ample evidence that the men deliberately embellished their performances in order to tease and pique the curiosity of the crowds; as Lookingbill puts it, "the Indians were playing Indians for the crowds" in their frequent theatrical performances.[17] Such safe, controlled displays were echoed eerily in the spectacles of black docility and inferiority that became common soon after Reconstruction was abandoned in Florida. "Beginning in the 1890s," David R. Colburn reports, St. Augustine's well-to-do "whites invited blacks to take part in an annual cake walk. The leading black people dressed in their finest clothes for the occasion and paraded before a white audience. Other blacks sang Negro spirituals, and the waiters performed a variety of dances. Whites apparently used the event to render approval for certain patterns of black behavior and dress."[18]

Yet it also seems undeniable that the rewards of participation are often simple and satisfying, and that the pleasures of material possession can trump principled resistance. Indeed, we know that the Fort Marion prison-

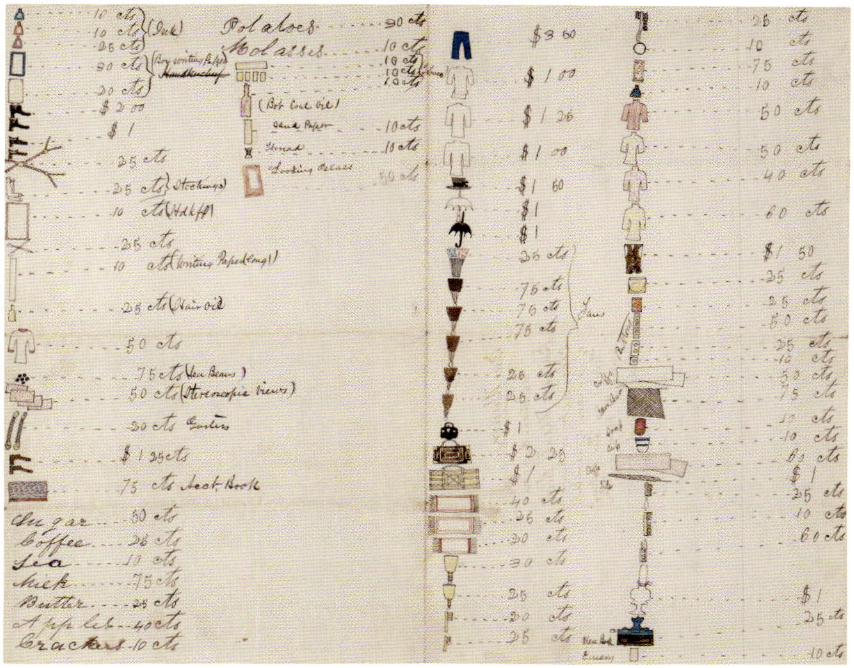

FIGURE 4.6
Buffalo Meat, Cheyenne, ***Buffalo Meat's Price Menu***, Richard Henry Pratt Papers, Yale Collection of Western Americana, Beinecke Rare Book and Manuscript Library, Yale University.

ers did apparently find great pleasure in earning money from their drawings, jewelry, and physical labor. Being able to send funds home to their abandoned families was one driving motivation; however, another was apparently to simply partake in the accumulation of small comforts and private possessions. A Cheyenne prisoner named Buffalo Meat produced a pictographic price list that became one of the more popular items at Fort Marion, both for use by fellow prisoners and for purchase by curious tourists (figure 4.6). The novelty of the items available to them on the market (see, for instance, plate 48, Ohettoint's striking image of an umbrella being dropped from a lighthouse) seems trumped only by the appeal of being able to purchase and possess them. Harriet Beecher Stowe relates the sight of "Manimic, or Eagle's Head, a Cheyenne chief of great influence . . . [who] stood before us in the garments of civilization. . . . Over his United States uniform he wore a long linen coat, bought with his own money, and in which, for that reason, perhaps, he seems to take special pleasure. . . . 'We like the white ways,' he said, 'We like the dress,' and here he stroked his linen robe complacently."[19] Stowe's account implies even further that the trappings of white society had become not just treasured costumes to don, but rather internalized instincts and desires. Upon helping to build their own barracks and a brick oven for cooking, two Indians were apprenticed to a baker who instructed them in making bread for the inmates; one disciple, Charley (Ohettoint), soon became an accomplished head-baker for the fort, at which he announced proudly, "'Me make. By and by, out there, will make bread, and get money.'" At this, Stowe observed approvingly, "Already the idea of a profitable trade has opened before him."[20]

Perhaps what is ultimately most compelling and fraught about the Fort Marion drawings—and the way we have come to value and judge them in retrospect—is their complicated status as both cultural artifacts and market commodities. As items composed primarily for consumption by local tourists and visiting dignitaries, the works become calculated expressions of cultural authenticity often composed to meet the demands and tastes of individual buyers. Janet Berlo relates the numerous instances of "self-censorship" in which artists intentionally obscured or altered details in order to please (or simply not offend or alarm) their buyers.[21] Nostalgia seems also to play a significant role in the production of many drawings that return to scenes and customs from their prior lives on the plains. Such imaginative returns influence the seeming demise of the tenets of realism and honor that once governed the genre, as nostalgia breeds a noticeable sleight of the mimetic hand. In a drawing of a shark hunt by Ohettoint (figure 4.7), for example, the Natives working together to pull ashore the sea creature are depicted in traditional loincloths rather than the military uniform in which they would have been dressed, and which their warden is pictured wearing. The only time the men were permitted to wear traditional dress would have been

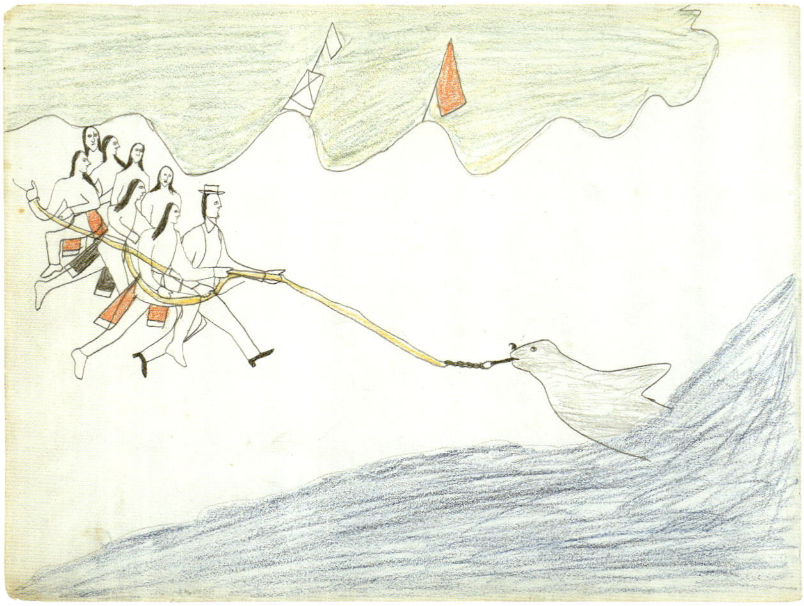

FIGURE 4.7
Ohettoint, Kiowa, 1852–1934, ***Untitled [Fort Marion prisoners and a non-Native man catch a shark],*** mid-1875–mid-1878, Hood Museum of Art (plate 49).

in the staged theatrical performances, an anomaly that makes it difficult not to see Ohettoint's picture as a kind of pageantry as well. Given the alterations and exaggerations that we know of, could there be more, less evident oddities and fabrications that we have not yet considered, simply because we don't know what they might look like?

Berlo suggests that "the act of making even those drawings intended for sale also held profound meaning for those who made them. It is an act of resistance to chronicle the old ways and keep them alive."[22] My intention here is not to discredit the power of these efforts nor to deny that they are often intentional gestures of resistance; I only want to recognize that they are also acts of participation, in the manner that capitalism compels us to either compete or surrender, and to be aware that wealth purchases autonomy. The more one is foreclosed from the game, as it were, the more vitriol that attends the process; but it also works the other way. Just as white southerners eventually benefited from industrial and economic developments, so too have many tribal communities solidified their sovereignty *through* capitalist mechanisms like gaming and tourism. And while these measures obviously buttress and sustain, they also distort and discompose in often uncanny ways. As Rosalind Krauss argues, following similar ideas proposed by Fredric Jameson, this ideological conflict—between resisting capitalism and being conditioned by it—typifies the very character of art in the age of late capitalism: she says, "in its very resistance to a particular manifestation of capital . . . the artist produces another version . . . although possibly more ideated or rarefied . . . of the very thing against which he or she was reacting."[23] What gets produced is thus often a cultural object indissoluble from its market purpose.

Still more sobering is the reminder that the Indians' peddling of their artistic wares did not ensure them true fiscal or practical independence. Their incarceration most obviously stood in the way; but more than that, Pratt was careful to preserve the distinction of their status as subordinate entities in a hierarchical economy. When a local church failed to secure the necessary funds to move its Sunday school building closer to town and worship, Pratt agreed to lend out the Indians' labor at a pittance: "the job was undertaken and successfully carried out, only Indians doing the heavy work. The balance of funds gave what was to them acceptable pay and it was a valuable object lesson."[24] Pratt seems tacitly aware that "acceptable pay" meant something entirely different to the prisoners, yet he values the "object lesson" more than the equity of their wage. The "lesson" indeed seems twofold: first, that a salary earned by physical labor is the bedrock of American initiative and citizenry; and secondly, within that system, certain individuals can ineluctably be exploited and undervalued with impunity. Indeed, what the prisoners at Fort Marion surely learned through such experiences was that although it was vitally important to adopt white ways, they might never fully profit from the effort.

The profound anxiety activated by these enterprising, mobile Indians quickly becomes apparent in reports from locals and visitors. In a particularly critical period for the simultaneous formation of national identity and the achievement of material prosperity, racial distinction and separation becomes an issue of pronounced significance. Like many African Americans of the period, Natives were thus considered threats to both racial and economic stability. Beyond the fort walls, the Indians' relative freedom and mobility in fact proved incongruous and threatening to local citizens. As Lookingbill tells us, the Indians were often permitted to contract themselves out in the community, engaging not just in performance capacities but in physical day labor; consequently, their competition in these spaces was protested vehemently by working-class whites who eventually appealed to Washington to intercede in the affair. According to Lookingbill, "they complained that the low wages paid to gang laborers undermined their own capacities as family breadwinners. They wanted no competition for jobs from the Indians."[25] Moreover, the warriors' dark presence in town—and especially their contact with the chaste Victorian ladies who volunteered their time as teachers in the prison classroom—seemed implicitly threatening. In 1876, a Florida senator even introduced legislation intended to scrutinize and curtail the "liberty" of the prisoners. Although the resolution was ultimately tabled in Congress, Pratt nonetheless responded by limiting the prisoners' ability to go into town unsupervised or without explicit business.[26]

Visitors to the town continued to look upon the prisoners warily. Take for instance the southern (Georgian) poet, musician, and ex-Confederate soldier Sidney Lanier, who visited Fort Marion briefly while composing a travelogue for a local railroad company (perhaps the railroad owned by Henry Flagler). After rhapsodizing about the austere beauty and peacefulness of the defunct fort—which the Indians apparently ruined with their "shuffling chains and strange tongues and barbaric gestures"[27]—Lanier goes on to condemn the base character of the prisoners. "They seem excessively fond of trying their skill in drawing," he observes, "and are delighted with a gift of pencil and paper. Already, however, the atmosphere of trade has reached into their souls: I am told they now begin to sell what they were ready enough to give away when I saw them a few weeks ago; and one fancies it will not be long before they are transformed from real Indians into those vile things, watering-place Indians."[28] The "watering-place Indian" was already a well-known and much-detested type in the nineteenth-century United States, akin to the "hang-around-the-fort" Indian who sets up camp near the reservation agency and appears first in line for every distribution of goods and services.[29] Other visitors to Fort Marion were provoked to similar responses: in her own travelogue *Petals Plucked from Sunny Climes*, Abbie Brooks (writing as "Silvia Sunshine") remarks dyspeptically that "these red men" were invulnerable to the betterment efforts of their captors, little more than "predatory" savages hungering for the blood and possessions of others and utterly incapable of being reformed. She was unimpressed by their "rude system of representing their ideas by picture-writing," which she interpreted as proof of substandard language skills, rather than evidence of any innate intellectual and creative gifts.[30]

To Joyce Szabo, Lanier epitomizes the broader "romantic view that Native people should continue in a way of life untouched by non-Native practices" with little awareness that "trade had been a part of Native cultures from the archaeological past forward."[31] Still, Lanier's reflection seems to have less to do with the Indians' perceived primitivism than with his own anxiety about participating in this artistic marketplace himself. After all, Lanier was peddling his own artwork in the same way that these warriors were: at about the same time that he accepted the travelogue contract, Lanier was selling his most famous poems to magazines in order to support his family; and just a year after publishing his *Florida* book (1875), Lanier produced another travelogue called *Sketches of India* (1876) despite never having set foot on the continent. Lanier's inability to view the American Indians as purveyors of their own creativity suggests, on the one hand, his unwillingness to deem the "savage" capable of either producing real art or deigning to seek payment for it; further, though, he seems palpably uneasy about keeping company with these "sell-outs" and thereby admitting an unsavory fact about the corruption of his own creative industry and regional character. In the process, Lanier betrays his own anxieties about economics, race, and social hierarchy as a white Confederate man taxed by the pressures and threats of Reconstruction and the assimilation of dark others into the white populace and economy. Like so many similarly hysterical critiques of Indians, Lanier's and Brooks's comments expose their personal ambivalence about the "degenerating" forces of dependency and consumerism that southerners themselves were forced to engage in.

In complicated ways, the Fort Marion context constitutes just one of many pivotal moments in the long American tradition of posing the Indian as ideological foil and pivot point for national anxieties and crises. The Reconstruction-era South, battling invasive economic and social dictates from without, amplifies its anticapitalist rhetoric even as it was forced to engage fully in those very economic mechanisms in order to recover and thrive. The southern experience simply turns a magnifying glass on a national crisis of scrupulous and inequitable capitalist

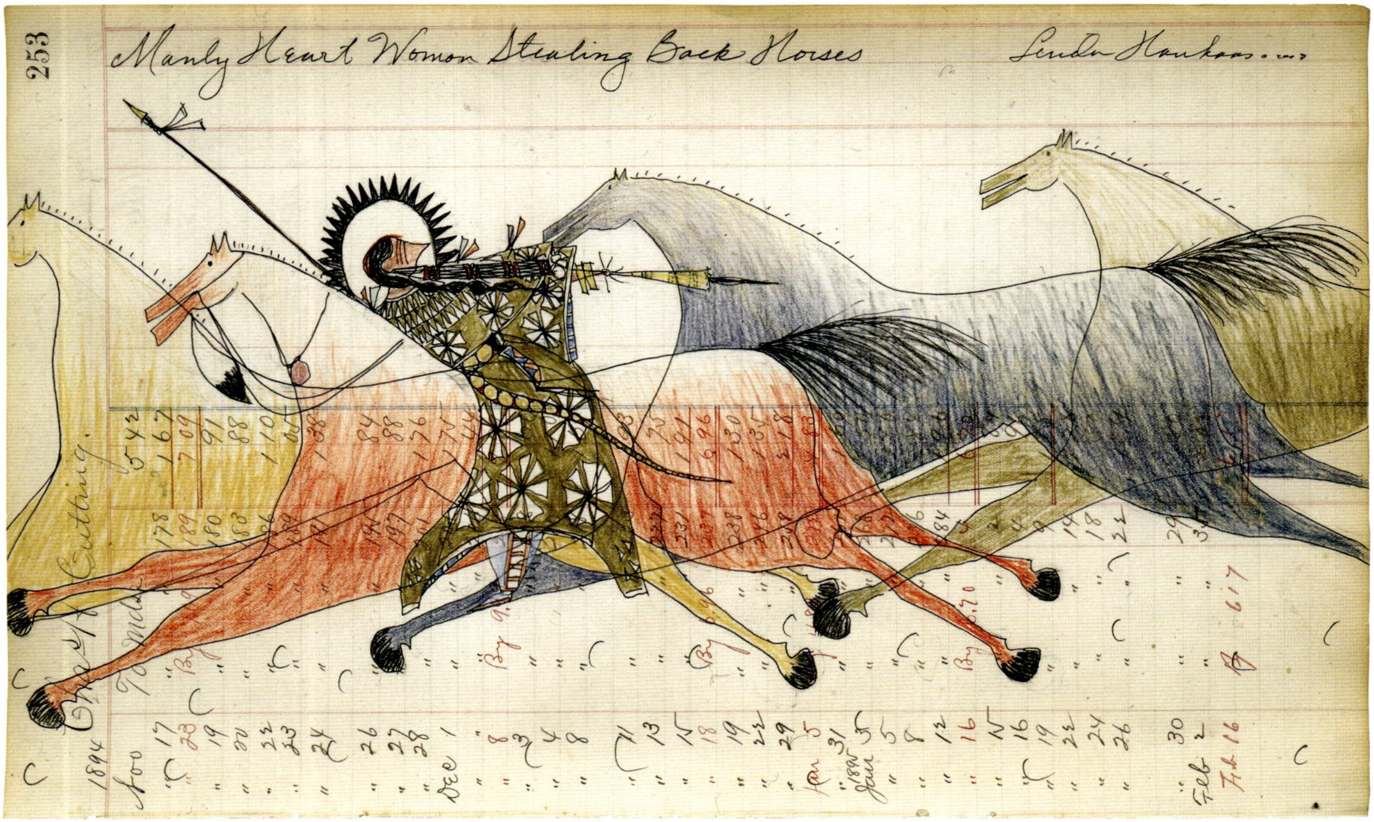

FIGURE 4.8
Linda Haukaas, Sicanju (Rosebud Sioux), born 1957, ***Manly Heart Woman Stealing Back Horses,*** 2003. Hood Museum of Art, purchased through the Hood Museum of Art Acquisitions Fund, D.2004.30.

development, one that obviously remains with us today; and in that ongoing calamity, the Native American remains *both* kindred trope of noble resistance *and* threatening competition. This is a caricature that even Indians have internalized in their own struggles to recuperate sovereign status. The Indians imprisoned at Fort Marion were enfolded directly into this incipient cultural logic, and we have yet to shed its myth of radical difference: today, battles between traditional and progressive individuals splinter and often shatter tribes. And yet, the truth now is the same as it always has been: sovereignty, status, and survival are fungible quotients, but they are rooted essentially in shifting and often violent economies.

AFTER FORT MARION: CONTEMPORARY ART AND CRITICAL NOSTALGIA

A direct line from the Fort Marion warrior-artists to contemporary practitioners has proven seductive; of the few art historians who have begun seriously to study these early drawings, most have emphasized their seminal importance to indigenous art's persistent attempts to resist the pressures of assimilation and preserve traditional memory and narrative at all costs.[32] Contemporary artists producing their own updated forms of ledger art acknowledge this by overtly invoking and recreating the genre as a vehicle of resistance: Arthur Amiotte, an Oglala Lakota artist, explains "I was exploring the tradition of ledger art, but I was also thinking of the other, original meaning of ledger: a place for keeping track of sums. . . . It is sort of a bittersweet notion—the whole idea of ledgers, and accounting for what was taken from Indians and what we were given in exchange."[33] Significantly, Amiotte and others, such as the Rosebud Sioux artist Linda Haukaas (see figure 4.8), demonstrate their plain intentions by choosing to write over actual used account book pages, a gesture that appears in contemporary art far more explicitly and frequently than in any of their predecessors' versions. Making a virtual palimpsest of these "antique" documents endows the enterprise of ledger art with an explicit, subversive, and defiant purpose that exaggerates the seeds of defiance they—and we—would like to see dawning in the works made by their artistic predecessors.

And yet, in many ways, Native art produced since Fort Marion has never escaped its ambivalent purpose as both reservoir of tradition and market commodity. While the marketing of ledger drawings was most fully organized and pronounced in the Fort Marion context, it predated and long outlived those three years. In the Mark Lansburgh collection in particular, the Southern Cheyenne "Old White Woman Ledger" is notable for its many scenes of courting and more quotidian affairs. The violence and showmanship of earlier drawings seem absent, but anxieties about wealth and honor do not: one drawing in particular depicts a warrior surrounded by an impressive cache of possessions and finery (see plate 107). Indeed, the book as a whole betrays the conditions of both its production and its priorities on the final page, which features a short hand-written appeal to whomever has commissioned it: "I have all done now making hard work. Will you pay me 3.50 4. or 5. dollars. Have other book for me. J.B. [?] 4-3-1887" (*sic*) (see plate 114). Looking more critically at the revealing and troubling contexts surrounding ledger art's emergence and commercialization might help us to complicate the reductive binarisms that continue to plague our broader discussions of Native artistic expression. Because of all that ledger art seems to signify and substantiate, we are in danger of letting it stand as unmediated truth or triumphant subversion in keeping with our current cultural discontents, as much as recognizing the precise colonial contexts in which they were produced. The production of community—indeed, the *re*production of community—arises in response to these commercial threats from without; however, it is also intimately affected and conditioned by those very forces. Put another way, in the effort to regain worlds and values lost, Natives often find themselves ineluctably entangled in the very economies they mean to resist, and they in fact reconstitute communities along distinctly material lines. In the process, they remind us of the unsettling complexities of our own origins, and the very deep and human impulse to survive and sustain community at any and all costs.

These revelations matter, because we are at a moment when it has become nearly impossible to extricate anything—least of all tribal sovereignty—from the means and mechanisms of global capitalism.[34] This is not a phenomenon limited to southerners and Indians, of course. In an age where we realize the terrific hegemony of capitalism, we are anxious to exercise our contrary values and will—an alternative for which indigenous culture frequently becomes a signifier, not only for New Age spiritualists but for esteemed political economists (see, for instance, David Blaney and Naeem Inayatullah's *Savage Economics*, 2010). Recognizing the inherent brutality of both pre- and post-settlement economies is vital in our ability to translate the stories left us by the Plains ledger art and, in turn, to focus productively on our own crises of late capitalism. Adopting a comparative view seems the best (and perhaps the only) way to fruitfully engage the coeval experience of our vast economic interpellation, along with all the cruelties and violence it inspires. Ledger art constitutes a period and a phenomenon most vulnerable to hopeful but damaging revisionism because it *seems* to speak its protest so plainly. Collections like Lansburgh's give us the opportunity and the courage to attend much more closely not just to what the ledger represents but to what it betrays: not just the unwelcome changes wrought by the introduction of American colonial-capitalism, but the sublimation of acquisitive energies and violence *already* integral to Plains societies; not the antithesis of indigeneity but the uncanny connections, convergences, and conversions from which none of us are immune if we hope to survive in this world.

NOTES

1. Blume, "In a Place of Writing," 40.

2. Low, "Composite Indigenous Genres," 102. See also Hertha Dawn Wong's *Sending My Heart Back across the Years*, which was the first to consider ledger drawings and Plains autobiographical narratives in the same study.

3. Vizenor, *Fugitive Poses*, 179. Italics added for emphasis.

4. West, *Last Indian War*, xvii–xxiii.

5. See also H. Craig Miner, *The Corporation and the Indian*, which aligns the beginning of corporate dominance in America with the decline of Indian sovereignty after the Civil War.

6. Lytle, "The Hind Tit," 234. This volume of essays, composed and collected by a group of southern scholars known as the Vanderbilt Agrarians, represents the height of regional discontent with the increasing industrialization and mechanization of the rural South in the early twentieth century. The views expressed throughout the book tend to be conservative defenses of a more humane, productive, and culturally rich way of life, which they felt had existed in the antebellum era.

7. Blume, "In a Place of Writing," 42.

8. Additionally, as Janet Berlo notes, the aftermath of the identity politics of the 1980s and '90s "led us all to search for an ennobling historical narrative that foregrounded resistance. This was, itself, a resistance to an earlier anthropological and art historical narrative that saw hybrid forms as debased and not 'authentic'." Janet Berlo, personal communication to author, July 2011.

9. See, for example, Tiya Miles, *The Ties that Bind*, and, more recently, her *The House on Diamond Hill*; Etheridge and Shuck-Hall, eds., *Mapping the Mississippian Shatter Zone*; Snyder, *Slavery in Indian Country*; and Hudson, *Creek Paths and Federal Roads*.

10. Foster, "Introduction" to Mishkin, *Rank and Warfare*, v, vi.

11. Mishkin, *Rank and Warfare*, 8.

12. Joyce Szabo notes a similar effect in Howling Wolf's drawings, and she assays a connection to earlier pictographic conventions in which action "carried well beyond the arbitrary limits of time and space presented by the single ledger page." Szabo, *Howling Wolf*, 171.

13. Hedrick, *Harriet Beecher Stowe*, 330.

14. Eacker, "Gender in Paradise," 496n. Similarly, Anne Rowe agrees that "nonsouthern writers were released from their obligations to criticize southern ways and institutions and became free to praise the South and to capitalize upon its variety and exoticism." Rowe, *The Enchanted Country*, xx.

15. Lookingbill, *War Dance*, 124–25.

16. Eacker, "Harriet Beecher Stowe," 501.

17. Lookingbill, *War Dance*, 88, 105.

18. Colburn, *Racial Change*, 19.

19. Pratt, *Battlefield and Classroom*, 159.

20. Stowe quoted in Pratt, *Battlefield and Classroom*, 160.

21. Berlo, "Drawing and Being Drawn In," 17–18.

22. Ibid., 61.

23. Krauss, "Cultural Logic," 3–17, 11.

24. Stowe quoted in Pratt, *Battlefield and Classroom*, 130.

25. Lookingbill, *War Dance*, 104.

26. Ibid.

27. Lanier, *Florida*, 51.

28. Ibid., 52–53.

29. I am grateful to Colin Calloway and Joyce Szabo for this interpretation.

30. Sunshine (Abbie Brooks), *Petals Plucked from Sunny Climes*, 194, 195, 197.

31. Szabo, *Art from Fort Marion*, 29.

32. See Rushing, "Legacy of Ledger Book Drawings," 56–57.

33. Quoted in Rushing, "Legacy of Ledger Book Drawings," 61.

34. Central to economic thought from Karl Marx to Justus Möser, Edmund Burke, and Jürgen Habermas has been the anxiety over capitalism's "spillover" properties—that is, how market principles are likely to contaminate and erode essential human relationships.

CHAPTER 5

New Geographies and Surveying Eyes

The Landscapes of Noh-hu-nah-wih (Chief Killer)

Mary Peterson Zundo

Throughout the drawings in the Mark Lansburgh collection colorful horses, their legs outstretched, rock and glide across the lines printed for the accounting of Anglo money and goods as they transport their heroic riders through peril and victory. Riders in detailed regalia count coup and dispatch enemies, Native and non-Native, who vie for the precious resources of the western plains. Figures travel from right to left, the powerful against the weak—the compositional format privileged in Plains depictions of action—sometimes across one side of the page, over and around to the opposite, leaving a trail of footprints in their wake. Pictorial stories, once rendered upon the organic shapes of animal skins, now travel over rectangular picture planes, tails and noses streaming off the pages to continue their narrative beyond the conceptual bounds of the paper's edge. Such compositions customarily focused on action and relationships between figures and ignored the depiction of a landscape setting—or even a ground line on which the protagonists might perform.[1]

Although most ledger art does not qualify as landscape in any general sense of the word, one set of drawings in the Lansburgh collection stands apart and addresses the physical environment as a subject worthy of attention—the Tsistsistas or Southern Cheyenne landscape drawings of the warrior Noh-hu-nah-wih, also known as Chief Killer.[2] His treatment of pictorial space and choice of subjects distinguish these drawings from the others and evidence a new understanding of the functions of art. To the customary repertoire of dynamic warriors on horseback and the vocabulary of identifying regalia, Chief Killer added rugged hills, winding rivers surrounded by trees in full leaf, and trails lined with golden grasses. In three of his drawings from the collection, Mexican traders traverse a mountain range, a river separates Ute wickiups from Plains tipis, and wild animals populate a western habitat rife with vegetation (figures 5.1, 5.2, and 5.3). While imprisoned at Fort Marion in the seacoast town of St. Augustine, Florida, the young warrior turned his attention to geography—the visual transcription of the physical landscape and the description of place—as a new means through which to express his Native identity and understanding of the world, and in the process his work marked an extraordinary transformation in Plains pictorial composition.

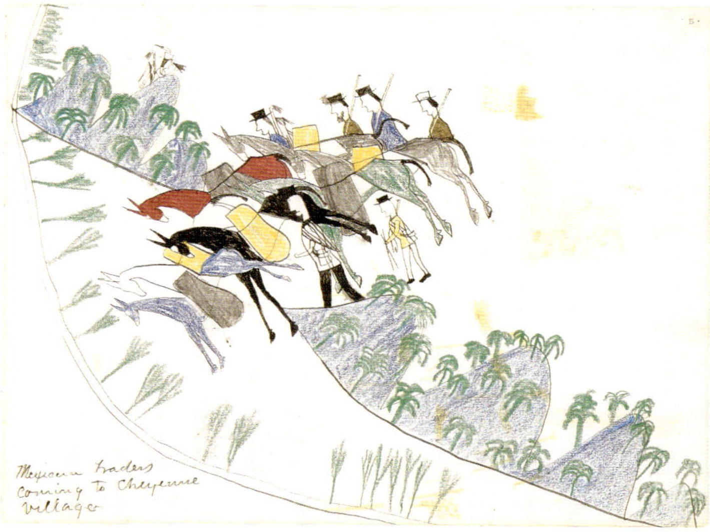

FIGURE 5.1
Chief Killer (Noh-hu-nah-wih), Southern Tsistsistas (Cheyenne), 1849–1922, ***Untitled ["Mexican traders Coming to Cheyenne village"],*** mid-1875–mid-1878, Hood Museum of Art (plate 54).

THE IMPERIAL LANDSCAPE

Within the fragile papers of the ledger, Plains picture-makers came face-to-face, page by page, materially and metaphorically, with an alien society obsessed with geometric measurement, mathematical calculation, and

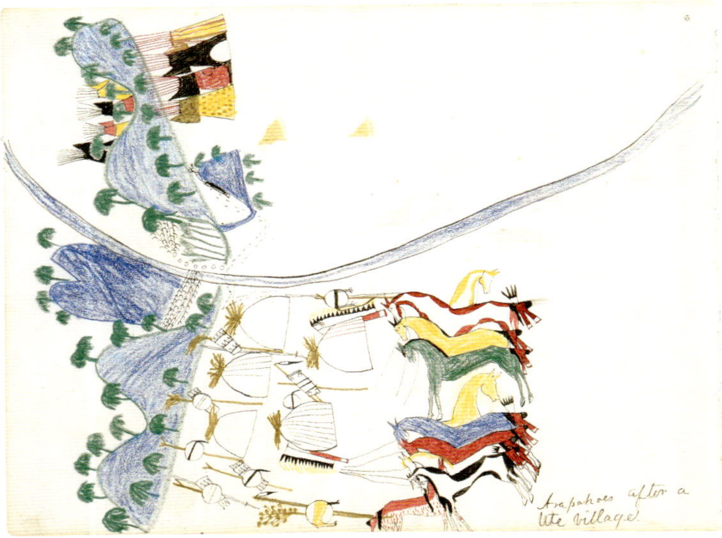

FIGURE 5.2
Chief Killer (Noh-hu-nah-wih), Southern Tsistsistas (Cheyenne), 1849–1922. ***Untitled [“Arapahoes after a Ute village],*** mid-1875–mid-1878, Hood Museum of Art (plate 55).

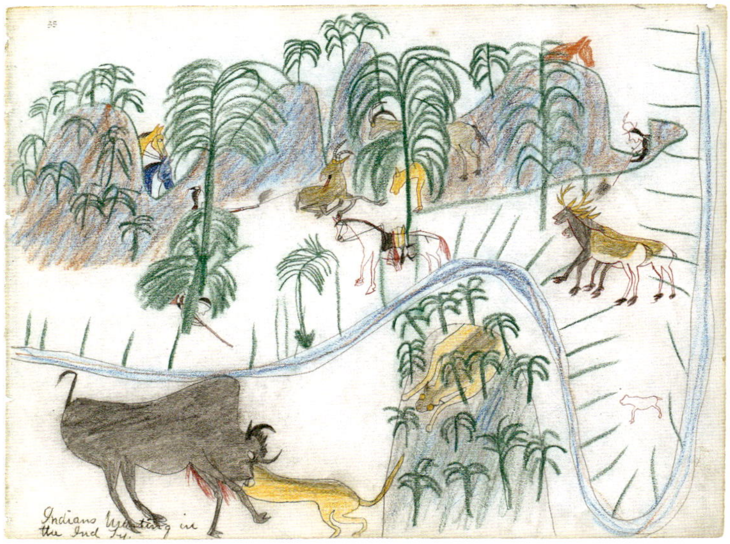

FIGURE 5.3
Chief Killer (Noh-hu-nah-wih), Southern Tsistsistas (Cheyenne), 1849–1922, ***Untitled [“Indians Hunting in the Ind. Terr.”],*** mid-1875–mid-1878, Hood Museum of Art (plate 59).

lined white rectangles. This Euro-American culture regularly and aggressively commandeered the rhetoric of nineteenth-century science into the service of imperial ambition to justify westward expansion into the Great Plains. While mounted Indian warriors dashed across the compressed, attenuated surfaces of the ledger in seeming disregard of mechanically printed lines, white surveyors were measuring the plains into thousands upon thousands of quadrangles for the production of maps and the sale of Native homelands. Just as their pictures, once rendered on hide, adapted to the narrower confines of the rectangular page, communities of Cheyennes, Kiowas, and their allies found themselves squeezed into ever shrinking territories. After the Civil War, the enormous pressures they experienced at the hands of the Americans and their Indian allies rose to fever pitch as the United States returned its military forces to the service of surveying land for sale and patrolling its western frontiers for the protection of emigration and railroad building. It was during these decades that ledger art flourished and recorded the violent encounters then taking place on the plains.[3]

Euro-Americans largely viewed the land as a commodity that could be divided, owned, and sold, a rich resource for one’s progeny and the future prosperity of the nation-state. But for Plains peoples the land was a crucial link to one’s ancestors and cultural history— its meaning even embedded in Native linguistic expression—not a “thing” that one could own, but the very source of communal identity.[4] Most of the drawings in the Lansburgh collection reject the depiction of landscape features or even a ground line; landscape art and mapmaking are, after all, customarily the dominant genre of imperial societies bent upon land acquisition. Not surprisingly, Euro-American landscape art had risen to prominence during the very period that marked the most rapid United States western expansion and the efflorescence of ledger art. Monumental panoramic canvases by painters such as Albert Bierstadt, for example, drew crowds by the thousands in New York City throughout the 1860s, and lithographs of the western landscape circulated prolifically throughout the country. But these pictures, which capitalized upon the demands of a public familiar with the formal conventions of the European-derived genre of landscape painting, conveniently sanitized the violence and degradation experienced by peoples of the plains, who increasingly faced starvation, diseases brought by new interlopers, and repeated military aggression. The mimetic quality of these paintings lent credence to their messages about a harmonious Eden in faraway places like the American West, as did the artists’ eyewitness claims to scientific accuracy in the rendering of geology and plant life. Such images presenting the land as untouched and unoccupied were, of course, ideological fictions—in the words of landscape theorist W. J. T. Mitchell, the utopian "dreamwork of imperialism."[5] And while the "magisterial gaze" upon the pictured terrain signified present and future white dominion over the land below, the Native figures in such images—often seen surveying white settlements or an encroaching locomotive—symbolized instead the loss of that land.[6] Thus, Euro-American landscape representation was ultimately harnessed to the discourses of Manifest Destiny and massive land acquisition.

At the same time, territorial expansion spurred a golden age in American cartography, which grew exponentially to meet the demand for ever newer, more "accurate" maps of the nation's western fringes. Year by year, maps of the plains diminished Native presence in the land, erasures that "spoke as loudly of calculated hegemony" as did the lined grids that provided a sense of order to white Americans who struggled to orient themselves within the vast, unfamiliar spaces.[7] But while the U.S. government assigned Plains tribes to the confines of reservations sectioned in square miles, Native drawings reveal the utter porosity of these invisible borders that appeared only as ink on the American maps. Throughout the paper pages of the Lansburgh drawings, Southern Cheyennes visit Sioux allies to the north, Kiowas travel to Mexico, and enemies encounter one another from east to west, north to south.

More than any other artist represented in the Lansburgh collection, Chief Killer paid close attention to landscape representation as a subject and demonstrated the resourcefulness of one individual in coming to terms with survival in new cultural circumstances through art-making. On the surface it might seem that he in some way capitulated to his captors—that he rejected the depiction of violence so integral to warrior life on the plains and adopted only subjects and styles acceptable to Euro-American eyes—but, in fact, his art-making continued to serve as a means through which he was able to express a Native point of view in response to disorienting circumstances far from home. Within the walled rectangle of the Fort Marion prison he continued his work as a warrior-artist, adding new compositional strategies to his arsenal as he adapted to life in an alien world.[8]

CHIEF KILLER'S STORY

Chief Killer was twenty-six or twenty-seven when he was sent to Fort Marion for his participation in deadly insurgent attacks on the western Kansas plains.[9] As a member of the Himatanohis, or Bowstring Warrior Society, he had joined his comrades in riding great distances to fight enemies and capture horses, whereby he earned the privilege to depict his deeds and recount the events to his listeners. The Bowstrings, like other Plains warrior societies, gained renown for their valor as fighting men and willingness to sacrifice their lives to defend and secure rights to game and homeland, the sustenance of their people. These courageous actions, and the drawings they made of them, constituted a crucial part of the fabric that knit their communities together and ensured survival.[10] But as the U.S. cavalry began to wage some of the most notorious battles in the history of the American plains, the massive loss of innocent Native lives, including many women and children, at Sand Creek and the Washita River was seared into the memories of the Cheyenne resistance leaders.

Perhaps not surprisingly it was, in part, a deadly encounter with a party of surveyors that landed Chief Killer in prison alongside his stepfather, the Bowstring Society leader Mi-huh-heu-i-mup, or Medicine Water.[11] In August 1874 a band of nineteen Cheyenne warriors attacked Captain Oliver Short and his crew as they prepared to measure section lines near Meade in western Kansas—the officer's compass, papers, and surveyor's chains later found in Medicine Water's camp were reported as incriminating evidence.[12] A few weeks later the group fired upon the emigrant family of John and Lydia German (Germain) traveling through the Smoky Hill River region of Kansas en route to Colorado. They leveled their attack after surveying the morning activities about the wagon and carried off four of the daughters, leaving the rest for dead.[13]

Sensational news accounts of the attacks and the reported abuse of the girls fueled an all-out effort by the U.S. Army to apprehend the men responsible. Though the girls were found gaunt, reports indicate that their captors experienced a similar state of starvation. George Bent, the son of trading post owner William Bent and a Cheyenne mother, later recalled, "Naturally, the lot of the girls was not a pleasant one; but that they suffered any greater hardships than the rest of the party the Cheyennes positively deny."[14] The sisters subsequently identified their assailants, and eight members of the war party, including Chief Killer and Medicine Water, were sentenced to prison along with other warriors accused of various war crimes from allied Kiowa, Arapaho, Caddo, and Comanche bands. At Fort Marion, in faraway St. Augustine, Florida, the new prisoners found themselves under the tutelage of Lieutenant Richard Henry Pratt, who would remain their jailer and teacher for the next three years.

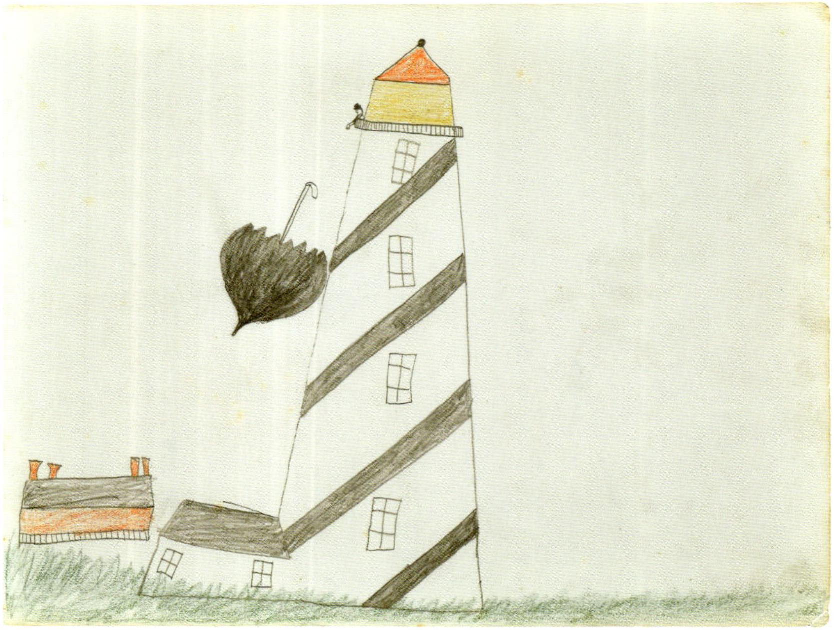

FIGURE 5.4
Ohettoint, Kiowa, 1852–1934, ***Untitled [A man dropping an open umbrella from the top of a lighthouse]***, mid-1875–mid-1878, Hood Museum of Art (plate 48).

FORT MARION

Chief Killer and his fellow prisoners were, of course, subject to a constant regime of surveillance while on the grounds at Fort Marion, and even on outings they could not escape the eyes of curious tourists and townspeople. From the time they arrived with their long hair and Native clothing, they were, in Pratt's words, a "curio class."[15] As they traveled from the train station through the crowded town plaza in horse carts, they shielded their faces with blankets to avoid the stares of onlookers who pushed to catch a glimpse of the new arrivals, but even after shearing their hair and donning U.S. army issue uniforms, they continued to attract attention—at first fear, but soon as celebrated tourist attractions.[16] Their notoriety as warrior-killers and their surprising "transformation" under Pratt eventually boosted the sales of their drawings and other items they made. They also garnered popularity and money through performances of Indian dances, mock buffalo hunts, and parades in Native dress for white audiences. The men posed in various activities around the Fort Marion environs under the scrutinizing lenses of professional photographers who sold the stereographs to the public, but perhaps the most objectifying and humiliating event was a visit by Smithsonian zoologist Spencer Baird and the renowned sculptor Clark Mills, who subjected the men to plaster castings of their heads. The resulting models were to be measured and examined "scientifically" in the interests of making a "contribution to Indianology."[17] The continual visual assault on the men was likely as coercive as any physical punishment would have been, and more insidious.[18] Frustrated by the fact that the public voyeurs expected to see the warriors on display round the clock like "caged tigers," Pratt began to limit the number of visitors and complained the prisoners "are simply objects of curiosity here."[19]

However, Chief Killer and the other prisoners also engaged in a fair amount of looking back, as their drawings attest. Noting the artistic proclivity of his wards and their initial inability to express themselves in written words, Pratt supplied the men with art supplies and encouraged them to make pictures of their experiences. From their arrival, the warriors were afforded a commanding view of St. Augustine and the surrounding shore from the fort's high terreplein and parapet, and over the next few years they augmented their artistic repertoire with scenes of new experiences and people in faraway places, often giving attention to the representation of the land itself. To the familiar depictions of warriors in regalia and courting scenes Chief Killer added pictures of the journey from Fort Sill in Indian Territory (present-day Oklahoma) and of his new surroundings in the East, as did a number of the other artist-prisoners.

The Kiowa warrior Ohettoint, for example, rendered the black-and-white striped lighthouse in St. Augustine, the very same structure that appears in a town view made by Chief Killer (figures 5.4 and 5.5). The locomotive that carried the Fort Marion artists cross-country spanned multiple pages in Ohettoint's sketchbook (figure 5.6). In his version of the journey, Chief Killer depicted two engines streaming horizontally through a town conveyed by tiers of block-shaped houses (figure 5.7).

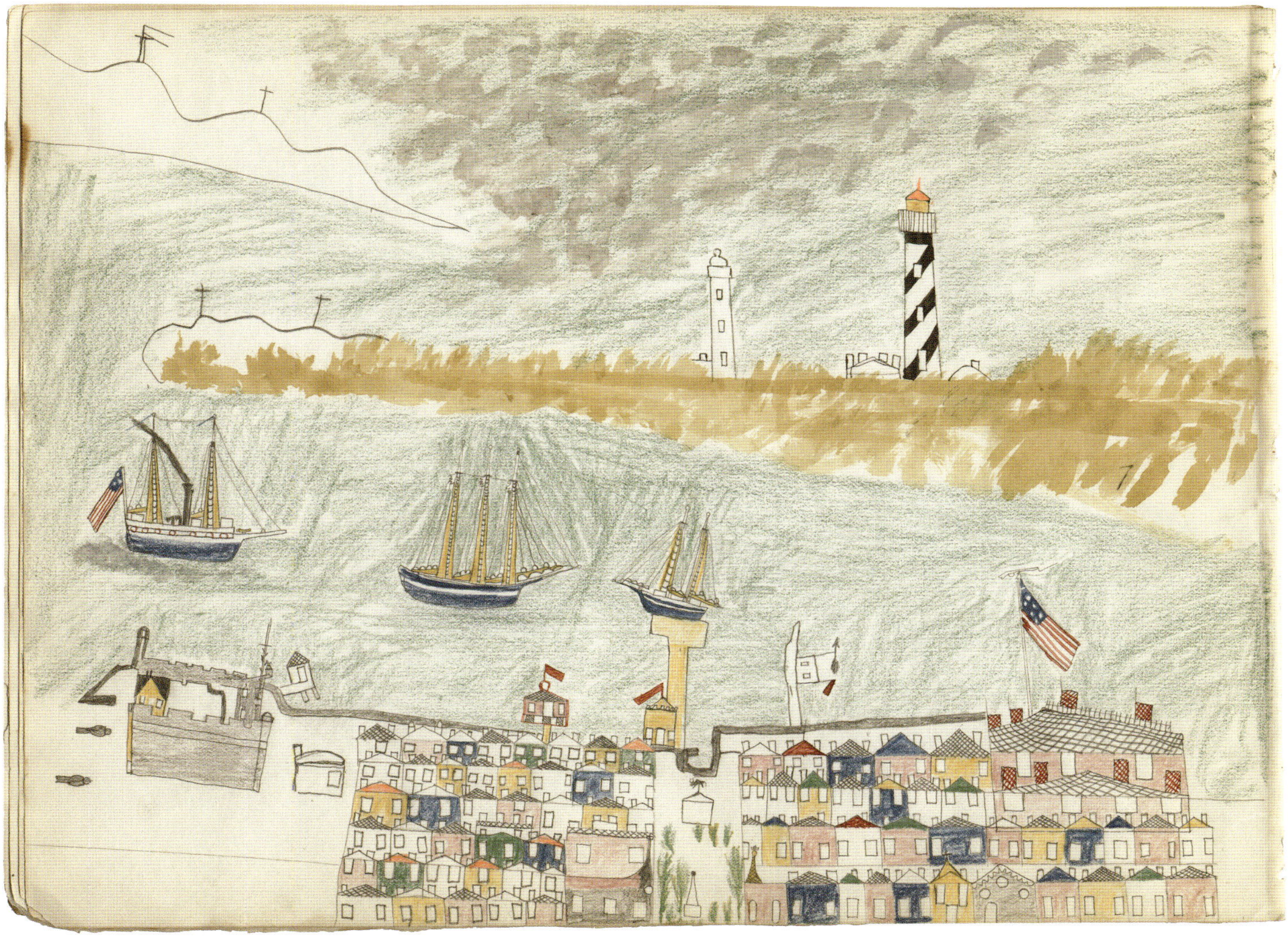

FIGURE 5.5
Chief Killer, ***St. Augustine***, Anne S. K. Brown Military Collection, Brown University Library.

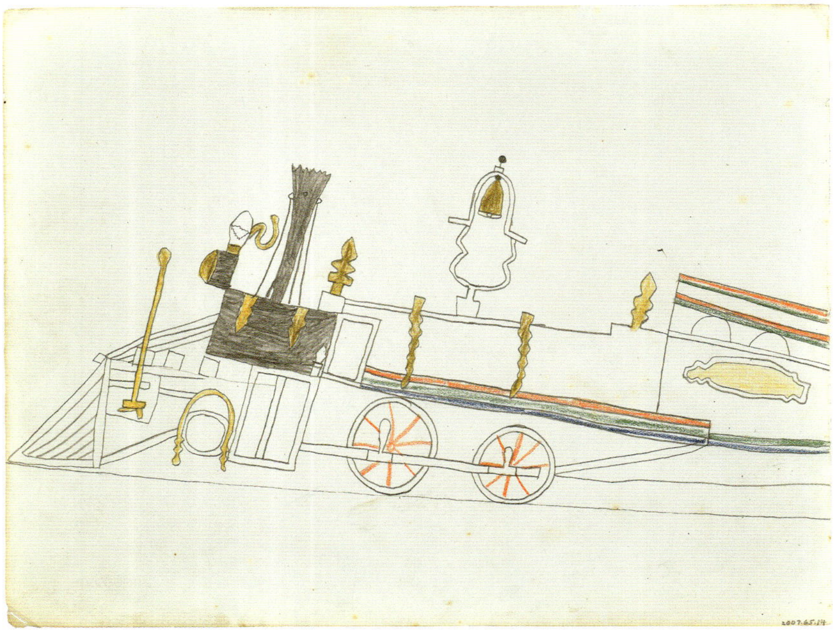

FIGURE 5.6
Ohettoint, Kiowa, 1852–1934, ***Untitled [Steam locomotive],*** mid-1875–mid-1878, Hood Museum of Art (plate 46).

Unlike many earlier ledger drawings, which often leave a fair amount of white negative space, Chief Killer's town drawings fill the picture plane with great attention to detail across the surfaces, enabling the viewer to identify specific types of buildings and landforms. In both drawings (figure 5.5 and figure 5.7), his interest lies more in the broad topographical view, unlike Ohettoint, who focuses primarily on the rendering of large objects like the lighthouse and engine—even a large steamer upon the water—with less regard for the terrain itself. But Ohettoint's drawing of shark fishing (see plate 49)—one of the warriors' many remarkable adventures on the seacoast—necessitated the suggestion of sand dunes and water in order to support the pictorial anecdote. A number of other artists, such as Howling Wolf, Bear's Heart, and Etahdleuh Doanmoe, who were skilled at reproducing the new images they saw, created a number of drawings that approximated some traditional European landscape views and panoramic vistas. In other words, the men experimented with a variety of ways to represent the physical environment as they grappled with new modes of visually conceiving the land and compositional space.[20]

Pratt believed that through proper exposure to a white education and immersion in the Anglo community he might teach his wards how to be "good American citizens" and prepare them for survival in the wider world. Chief Killer documented this classroom experience at Fort Marion, where interested educators introduced the prisoners to English, reading, writing, and arithmetic. Here linear rows of uniformed students sit at yellow rectangular tables within an undefined blank space, yet in this picture Chief Killer still retains the Cheyenne preference for right to left compositional structure.[21] The teachers, Mrs. Murray, Mrs. Carruthers, and Mrs. Gibbs, each identified by name in pencil, address their pupils from the right as they deliver the daily lessons from books. A list of students, some of whom made drawings of their own, appears on the upper right edge: Chief Killer, Howling Wolf, and Bear's Heart, for example. Some basic primer words, such as "RAN" "CUP" "PIG," are legible and, not surprisingly, given the Christianizing mission of the school—"GOD" in capital letters. The words, some recognizable, others random and unintelligible, reflect the process of one who is learning a foreign sign system and language, but the picture of a visionary buffalo and tipi on the obverse of the page reveals that the uniformed veneer of assimilation in the classroom was only paper thin (figures 5.8 and 5.9).

Geography loomed large as a subject, and a wall map of the United States was added to the old fort chapel, alongside large spelling cards, a blackboard, and tapestries of the Ten Commandments.[22] In the nineteenth century, geography had, in fact, become central in the education of American youth, who from their geography texts learned histories of each region, topographical features of the earth's surface, and the characteristics and classification of flora, fauna, and peoples of the world. Above all, they learned to read and draw maps as a second language through which they might visually locate and identify themselves as American citizens. Geography books and drawing manuals alike advocated the drawing of maps

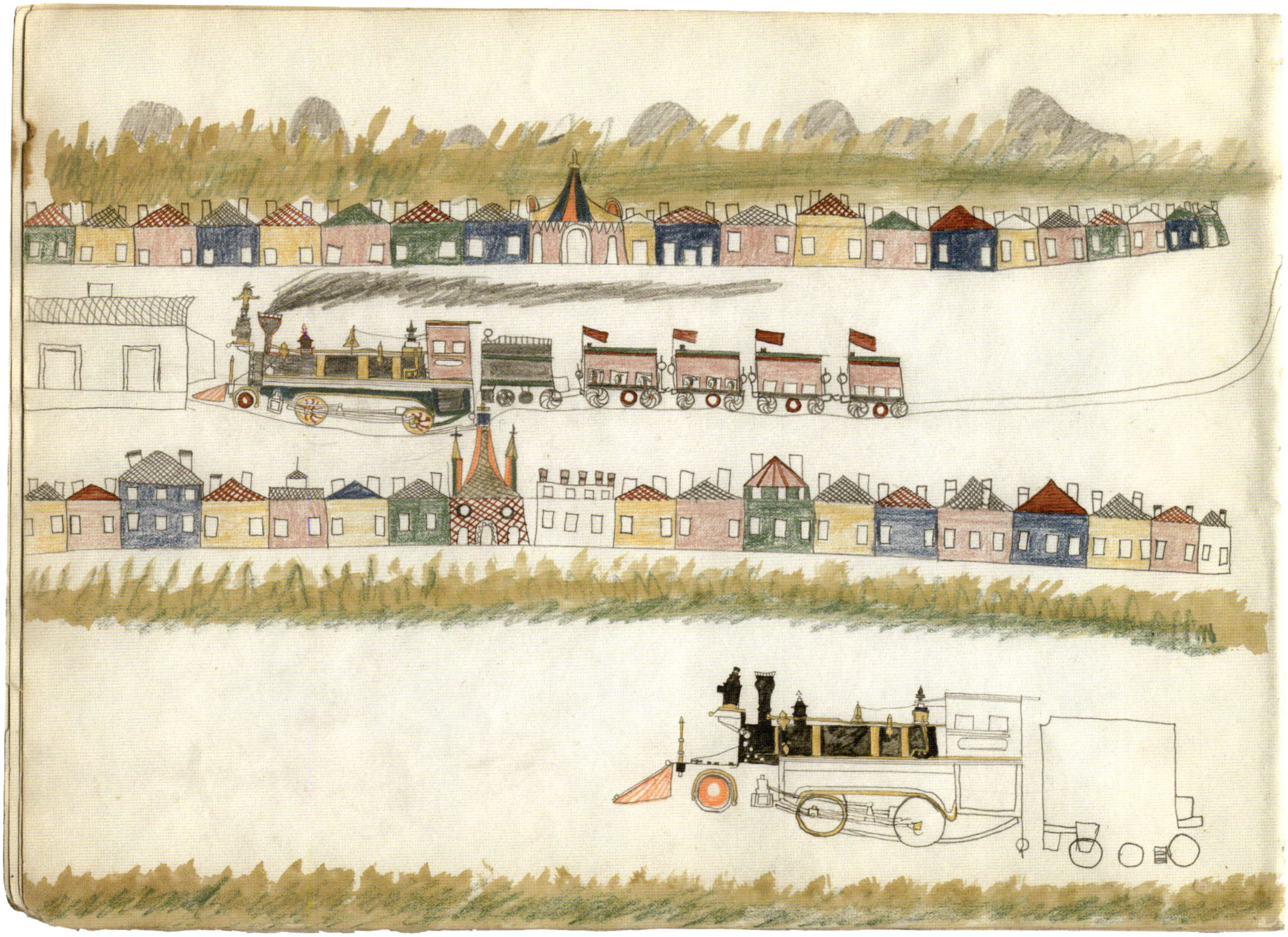

FIGURE 5.7
Chief Killer, ***Town and Steam Engines***, Anne S. K. Brown Military Collection, Brown University Library.

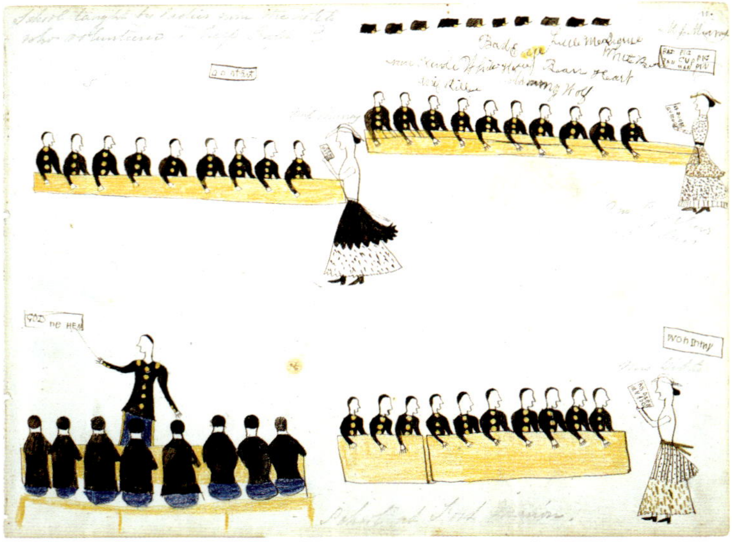

FIGURE 5.8
Chief Killer (Noh-hu-nah-wih), Southern Tsistsistas (Cheyenne), 1849–1922, ***Untitled ["School taught by ladies from the hotels who volunteered to help Capt. P. "],*** mid-1875–mid-1878, Hood Museum of Art (plate 57).

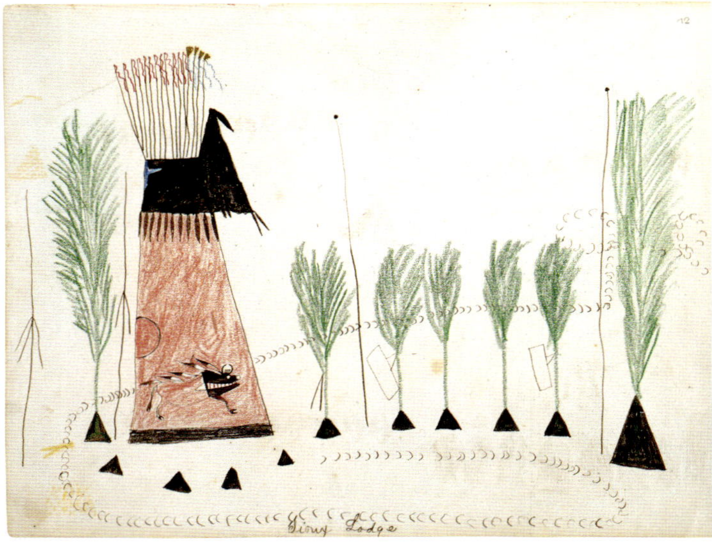

FIGURE 5.9
Chief Killer (Noh-hu-nah-wih), Southern Tsistsistas (Cheyenne), 1849–1922, ***Untitled ["Sioux Lodge"],*** mid-1875–mid-1878, Hood Museum of Art (plate 58).

as a means by which to create a broad class of productive Americans in a democratic society where every man could draw and "plow a straight line" in rectangular acres.[23] Likewise, through their geography lessons the Fort Marion prisoners learned how to locate their own homelands on the Euro-American map, and received sermons on the "civilizing" benefits of agriculture. White surveyors had already divided the western prairies into rectangular sections, and before long each reservation would be remeasured into grids of smaller, squared allotments for farming. As in other nineteenth-century American classrooms, maps and pictures were used to teach the prisoners their place within the expanding non-Indian nation surrounding them.

But the freedom to make pictures and the knowledge gleaned from their captors' geography lessons may have provided new ways for at least some of the Fort Marion warriors to exercise resistance to the assimilationist objectives of their captors. In the spring of 1876, Pratt noticed suspicious behavior among some of the Kiowas, and after one pressed individual divulged the plot, it was discovered that Lone Wolf and White Horse had been organizing a breakout to be executed under the next full moon. Historian Brad Lookingbill has speculated that, given ready access to drawing materials and the latitude to wander about the adjacent grounds, the men may have sketched the facilities and even made maps of the local environs to help them carry out the scheme.[24] Chief Killer and the other Cheyennes were intent on maintaining order at the fort and were not implicated in the plot, but the incident nonetheless illuminates the fact that drawing the surrounding geography might have yielded potential strategic advantages beyond mere artistic and cultural expression.

In the end, Pratt's educational experiment at Fort Marion was such a success that within a year of the prisoners' release, he set up a model off-reservation boarding school in the former army barracks at Carlisle, Pennsylvania. Some of the younger men had already decided to continue their education in the East and were accepted at Hampton Institute, a school recently opened for African Americans, but a number of the others followed Pratt to Carlisle and for a short time may have passed their artistic traditions along to a younger generation of pupils. At first, colorful pictures of mounted warriors and buffalo hunting appeared in Carlisle student sketchbooks and on class blackboards, but with the arrival of white art teachers in the years immediately following the departure of the Fort Marion artists, the traditional European genres of landscape, still life, and portraiture came to predominate student art work there.[25]

At agency and boarding schools across the country, globes, geography lessons, and map-drawing served as educational tools with which to break and replace the environmental and cosmological threads that bound and sustained Native Plains societies—spiritually, historically, and psychologically. Noted Dakota physician Charles Eastman (ironically, also grandson of American topographer and army officer Seth Eastman, who abandoned his Native wife), remembered how Anglo geography lessons at the Santee School challenged his Native comprehension of space and place: "It seemed now that everything must be measured in time or money or distance. And when the teacher placed before us a painted globe, and said that our world was like that—as it whirled and danced around the sun in space—I felt my foothold was deserting me."[26] At a number of schools, model farm plots measured and mapped in right angles and squares—and plowed in straight lines—underscored the notion of land as agricultural commodity and reinforced the imposed physical arrangement of the government reservation allotment system, as did the careful accounting of seeds and sales in student ledgers. The goal of such a multipronged educational attack was to alter visual and cognitive worldviews to the extent that new generations might march in step with Euro-American notions of progress and societal improvement. This was the new world that would face Chief Killer and his fellow warriors in the ensuing decades.

NEW PICTURES, OLD TERRITORIES, AND SURVEILLANCE

While at Fort Marion, Chief Killer added description of place and views of landscape features to the existing battery of narrative subjects typically found in Cheyenne drawings. For example, his renderings of eastern towns reflect the linear arrangement of ordered Anglo streets and box-shaped buildings. Though somewhat skewed, his view of St. Augustine maintains a relatively consistent orientation to the borders of the page, as does his town view of engines (figures 5.5 and 5.7). The slightly drooping island sand dunes in the upper left of figure 5.5 likely resulted from the angle of the sketch pad upon the artist's lap, as suggested by a photograph of an unnamed inmate sketching atop a stone ledge (now in the Richard H. Pratt Papers). Besides the maps and pictures in their classrooms, the men at Fort Marion had access to a wide variety of images and even bought stereograph views, those products of the nineteenth-century Euro-American passion for parlor gadgetry and scientific viewing. Views of the fort and the town were popular with tourists, and the prisoners could buy them, along with many other items, with money they earned.[27]

Chief Killer's western landscapes from the Lansburgh collection contrast sharply with his town views, however, in their rejection of a stationary point of view or any consistent compositional relationship to the pictures' edges. For all purposes, they are landscapes, with fully articulated topographical features—hills, rivers, and trees. Unlike the flat coloration found in other warriors' drawings, his are marked by an interest in rendering forms and textures with multiple shades, applying various amounts of pressure with the pencil. Chief Killer's rendering of Indians hunting in the Indian Territory recalls a land abundant with game, wherein elk, wild goats, and mountain lions populate a vibrant landscape unified by energetic line, bold color, and repeated form (figure 5.3). A flowing river echoes the mounded forms of hills and divides the terrain into two parts. In the lower foreground a yellow mountain lion attacks a buffalo, while another pictured from above waits in the underbrush to the right. As our eyes are drawn upward to the second cat we spy, across the river, a yellow buffalo calf at the base of a hill, a seated goat beside him, and the heads of two horses—one bright gold, another blue—watching from behind the rugged terrain at left. The hunters' kill lies draped across the back of the white horse at center, its slim carcass and ribs delineated in ultrathin lines of yellow and red ink. From behind the promontory on the upper right a hunter in a plumed hat shoots at two elk, his red horse tethered largely out of sight. Only after intense looking do we espy, hidden among the trees on the left, two more hunters, one of whom has just downed a wild goat. As in other ledger art, this view of a hunt is not a snapshot of a single moment in time but a narrative repository of multi-temporal events, a kind of episodic hunting "tally."

The camouflaged mountain lion's luminous eyes hint that this picture is not just about hunting. It is ultimately about the act of *looking*, about who gets to look, and what the artist—the one who has visual mastery over the land from within—allows us to see. It reenacts the very act of hunting, for which skillful surveillance is a requirement—the art of seeing but not *being* seen. While distracted by colorful animals and dancing trees, we eventually trace the trajectory of the bullet that killed the goat back to discover the two human predators partially cloaked by the tree at center. With subtle irony, Chief Killer subverts the gaze of his audience, reverses expectations, and deftly shifts the narrative from the Anglo as surveyor to the Native master of the land and all that walks it.[28]

Through art-making Chief Killer confirms his knowledge of the western landscape and his prowess as a hunter, one who can stalk his prey—embedded until almost invisible within the geography—without being seen. With superior vision he skillfully takes aim through the sights of his gun. Through hunting the warrior sustains his people

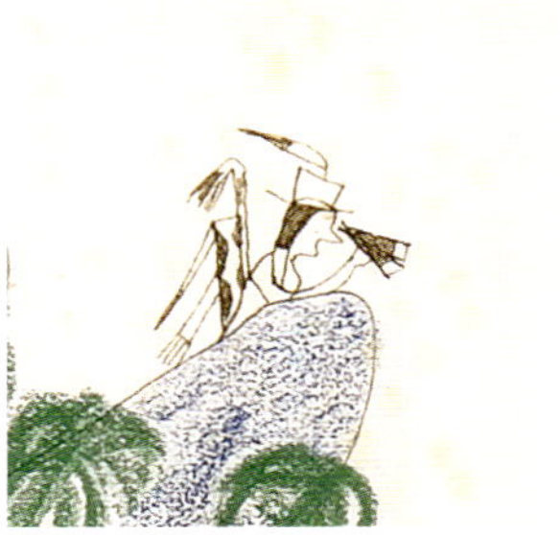

FIGURE 5.10
Detail, Chief Killer, *Untitled ["Mexican traders Coming to Cheyenne village"].* A close-up of the figure with binoculars in the upper left. (figure 5.1, plate 54).

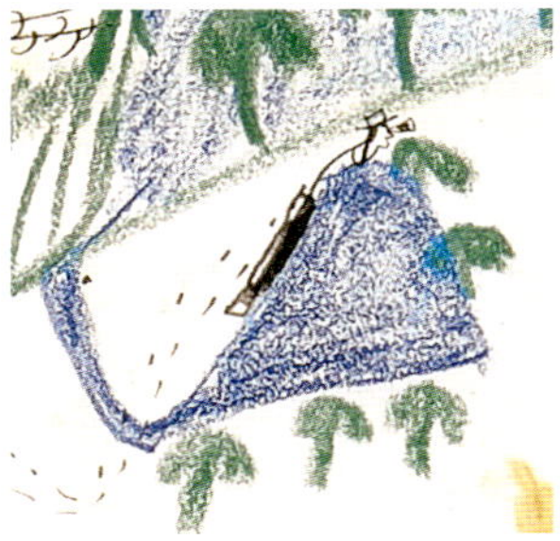

FIGURE 5.11
Detail, Chief Killer, *Untitled ["Arapahoes after a Ute village].* A close-up of the figure with binoculars in the upper right on the small blue hill. (figure 5.2, plate 55).

and affirms his status as an important member of the Bowstring society, for whom certain animals embodied sacred powers. The second cat bears a resemblance to the gold mountain lion skin in another Cheyenne drawing of Bowstring trophies in the collection (see plate 107) and in another incomplete pencil sketch of sacred visions (see plate 16). Among other species, this powerful mountain cat might appear in a hunter's dream and was believed to endow him with powers to perform certain supernatural acts. In sacred rites, such as the Massaum Ceremony, participants reenacted the behavior of the animal with which each identified—in the case of the mountain lion, for example, one would imitate a feline hunting by stalking and making a long leap, with a young boy serving as its prey, a buffalo calf.[29] The skins of these prized predators could be crafted into special objects associated with hunting, such as quiver covers. Undoubtedly, each animal in Chief Killer's drawing generated a host of meaningful associations inaccessible to non-Native eyes.

A similar theme of "looking" or surveillance emerges in Chief Killer's rendering of the Ute village and that of the Mexican traders crossing the mountains (figures 5.2 and 5.1, and detail figures 5.10 and 5.11). This time our protagonists come armed with second sight, a pair of binoculars, to aid them in scrutinizing potential enemies and targets. In the former, we see a small figure perched just behind the crest of a hill, spying upon a neighboring village. We can trace his steps back to the camp across the river—and a series of hoofprints in the distance tell of the many horses that have crossed the same water toward another camp behind the large blue hills in the background. Again, the colorful, kaleidoscopic patterns of the lodges, lively trees, and tethered horses entertain the eye, allowing the tiny Indian figure to go momentarily undetected. The Utes had already been competing with the Cheyennes and the Arapahos in the region, and in the interest of battling a common enemy, had allied themselves with the United States military. Mexicans also formed an important part of the Southern Plains trade network (see chapter 3), but they, too, had been subject to the hungry raiding parties of their northern neighbors as plains resources dwindled. The complex and often dangerous intersocietal dynamics of the region required strategic intelligence made possible through keen visual observation. The hair-fine lines of ink that define the small figures in Chief Killer's drawings evidence the young artist's own visual acuity and manual dexterity, in this case as a master of the pen and brush.

Whereas a picture of Indians hunting animals would have had tremendous cachet with the Euro-Americans who frequented Fort Marion—hunting other humans would not. Chief Killer substitutes technologies—binoculars for gun—each of which aided practical survival on the hotly contested and potentially violent terrain. In all three pictures, the Indian figure is partially hidden—we only have visual access to the parts that can shoot or see. Chief Killer, living under constant supervision in exile, thwarts his viewer's ability to look upon the Native body, which in these drawings is no longer objectified. In the context of Chief Killer's works, it is clear that his hunting pictures, with their regime of looking and similar actors, are conceptually linked to his binocular drawings. We might then think of these as his battle pictures, his resistance to visual subjugation in an Anglo world.[30]

VIEWS FROM ABOVE

In essence, all of Chief Killer's landscapes are bird's-eye views that suspend the viewer above the terrain. But they are neither landscapes nor views in the European sense. Chief Killer's bird is not stationary; it capably turns and swoops to the whim of the artist. And the objects in his pictures for the most part remain in profile. I would offer that these drawings share certain features with, and possibly operate compositionally, like maps—not the Euclidean maps printed by faraway Philadelphian cartographers, but maps that reflect a Native understanding of space and place based upon personal, lived experience in that land. This is not meant to suggest that the small slices of topography in Chief Killer's drawings were intended for

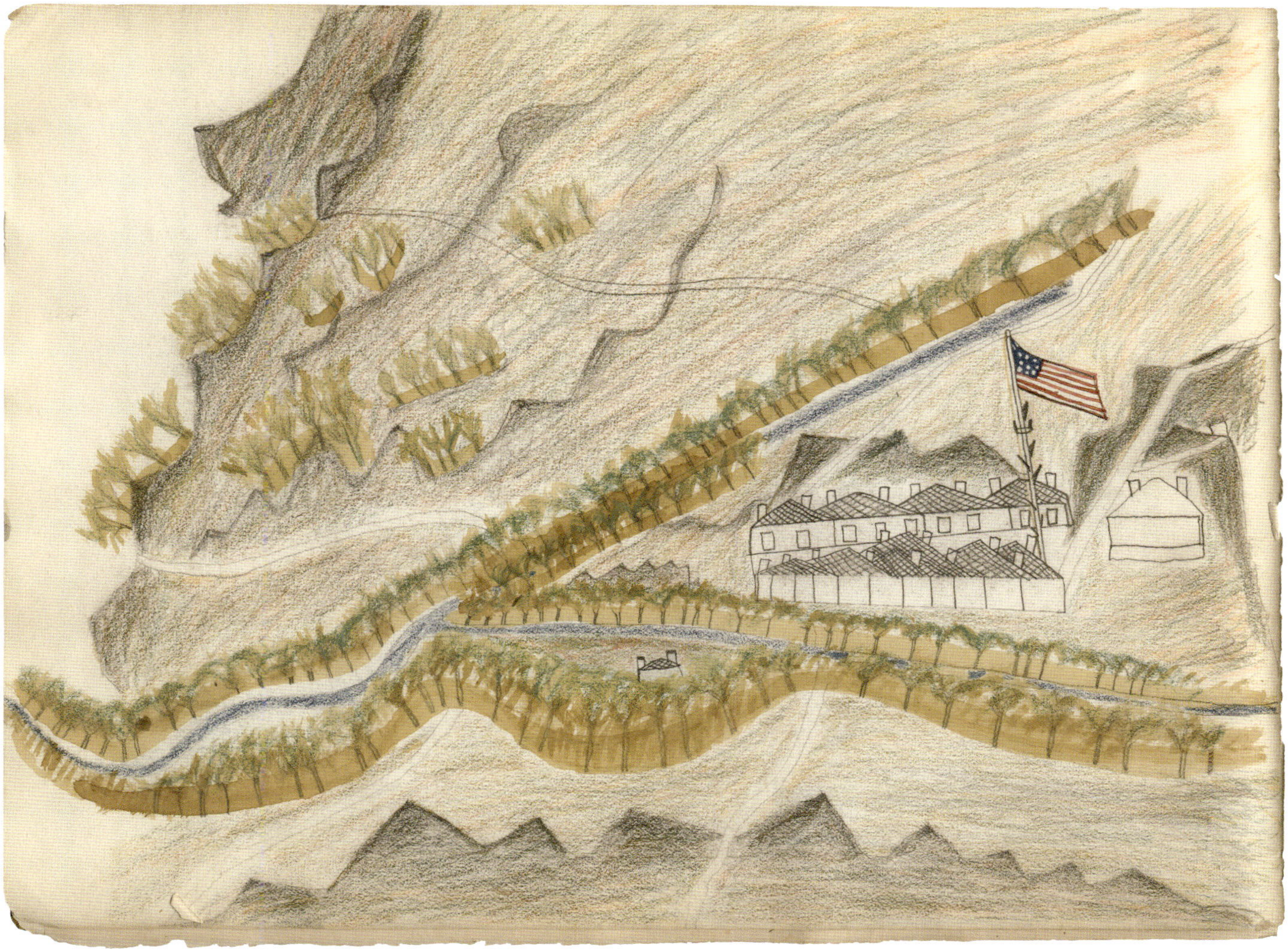

FIGURE 5.12
Chief Killer, ***Fort in the Mountains,*** Anne S. K. Brown Military Collection, Brown University Library.

navigation—rather that they drew from his knowledge of how to represent the land upon which all worldly activity transpired. In the Cheyenne conceptual toolbox, this knowledge would have likely come from Native maps, which were ephemeral and drawn for purposes other than record keeping. While the expert geographic knowledge of the Plains Indians, like that of many other Native peoples, was largely oral, physical maps were sometimes created to assert land claims in treaty negotiations or at the request of travelers needing navigational information. Native informants were ultimately crucial to white exploration and cartographic enterprise throughout the century, and their knowledge was consequently subsumed in thousands of printed Anglo maps. Native plains maps of the physical environs were generally executed upon temporary surfaces to meet immediate navigational needs and are, therefore, extremely rare, but the few extant examples lead scholars to believe that ledger art and plains maps grew from similar roots in pictographic conventions.[31]

Chief Killer's arrangement of figures and topographical elements within the landscape exhibits a rejection of the stationary rectangular plane that we see in most contemporaneous Euro-American maps and pictures, and instead suggests adherence to Native mapping conventions. For example, rather than rendering trees and bushes vertically parallel to the sides of the frame as in European linear perspective, trees project perpendicularly from the contours of hillsides, resulting in a kind of "stubbled chin" appearance. Correspondingly, hills along the course of rivers or ridges show similar disregard of a single, stationary viewpoint. In other words, in order to take in all of the elements in the composition, the viewer must rotate the page much as one might do with a trail map while walking and acquiring one's bearings. It is especially

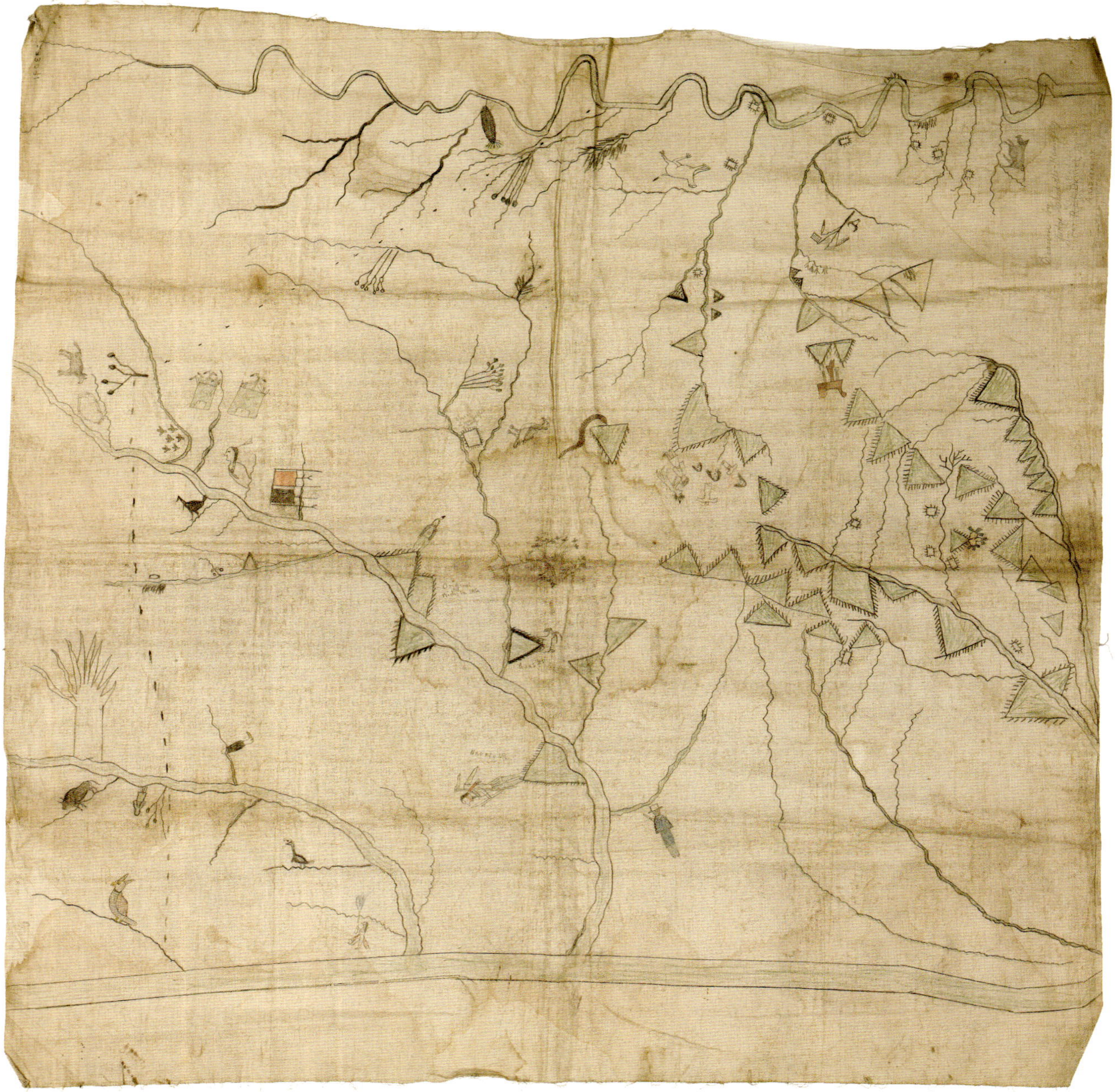

FIGURE 5.13

Map Drawn by Chaddle-Kaungy-Ky or Black Goose. Washita River at top (north), Red River at bottom (south), Department of Anthropology, National Museum of Natural History, Smithsonian Institution, catalogue no. 233,091.

taxing, for example, to visually comprehend all of the features in his picture of the Ute village (figure 5.2) without turning the page ninety-five degrees. If we view the image with the hills at the top, the horses lie on their sides, and if we turn it so that we can see the horses, the hills are now "wrong." It is somewhat easier to grasp the Mexican trader drawing (figure 5.1) as a whole, because the artist has angled the composition in a cross shape, allowing us to see from both angles at the same time. The Mexicans and their mules literally and metaphorically cross the hills, but their orientation runs perpendicular to the hills and to the Indian who watches them. A similar topsy-turvy configuration appears in another of Chief Killer's pictures in which garrisons lie perpendicular to the mountain ridge (figure 5.12). Pictures such as these defy the rectangular border as an organizing structure.

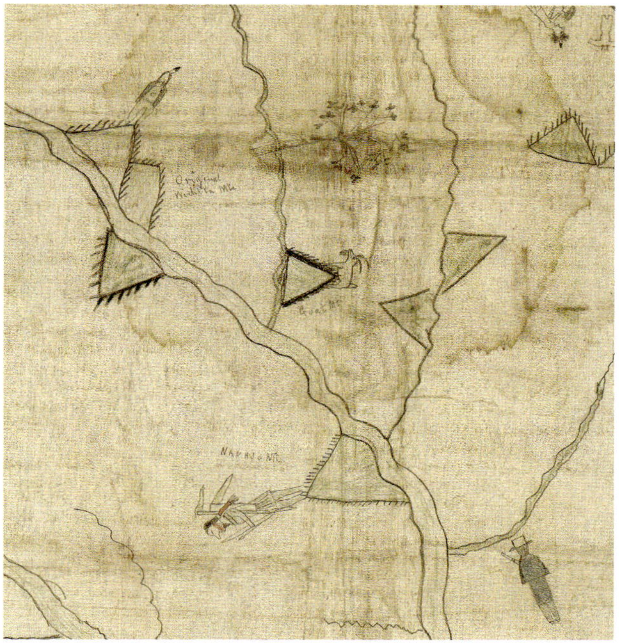

FIGURE 5.14
Detail, ***Map Drawn by Black Goose,*** south-central portion.

In fact, the arrangement of hills and figures along the contours of lines appears in some of the few extant physical maps produced by Native Plains artists. The map of the Kiowa-Comanche-Apache reservation in Indian Territory made by Chaddle-kaungy-ky, or Black Goose, evidences similar features: mountains point upwards from the edges of rivers and ridges regardless of the viewpoint of the audience, and pictographs of events and objects show no allegiance to a stationary frame. In the center of the map, for example, human figures and a mountain goat project from the tops of triangular mountains that point in various directions. A detailed figure with quiver, bow and arrow, red face paint, and a Navajo hair tie identifies Navajo Mountain, so named by the Kiowas after discovering a Navajo spy watching them from the promontory. His head points to the lower left, whereas a wild goat atop Goat Mountain faces the top of the drawing. Likewise, the single feather of a Wichita figure aims northeast from a peak designated as representing the so-called original Wichita Mountains. Projecting eastward from a creek, north of Goat Mountain, a sacred tree displays attached offerings—similar to a tree depicted in the Lansburgh collection (see plate 28) In order to see each element right side up, one must turn the map, much as in Chief Killer's landscapes. Perhaps not surprisingly, the contents of the Black Goose map echoed some of Chief Killer's own geographic memories: wild goats and bison, mountains and rivers, and neighbors spying upon neighbors from on high (figures 5.13 and 5.14).

Black Goose's map challenged the implementation of forced allotment and the opening of the Kiowa-Comanche-Apache reservation, which would have greatly diminished the Kiowa's lands as designated in the 1867 Medicine Lodge treaty. With pointed political purpose, the map documents eighty-nine streams and tributaries, fifty-three mountains and hills, fourteen camps, and fourteen locales of significant historic events dating back to the 1830s, many of which are identifiable in pictographs. Name glyphs like those used in ledger art designate the camps of specific individuals. All of the elements in the map identify the historic Kiowa presence in the region, giving special attention to that of the influential Lone Wolf–Black Goose family, to support the Kiowas' claim to the lands, which culminated in the 1903 legal case of *Lone Wolf v. Hitchcock.*[32]

By the time Black Goose drew his map, probably between 1893 and 1895, he and his brother Lone Wolf would have had exposure to a wide array of visual culture, both Euro-American and Native. Historian William C. Meadows has noted that the map's detailed, realistic images more closely resemble ledger-type drawing than the rudimentary pictographic forms found in other maps. And though the map draws from a long tradition in Kiowa picture-writing (particularly calendar-making), geographic knowledge, oral history, and Plains ledger art, Black Goose also crafts it in a way that might make sense to his opponents. For example, the map as a whole conforms to the rectangular muslin surface, framed by the Washita

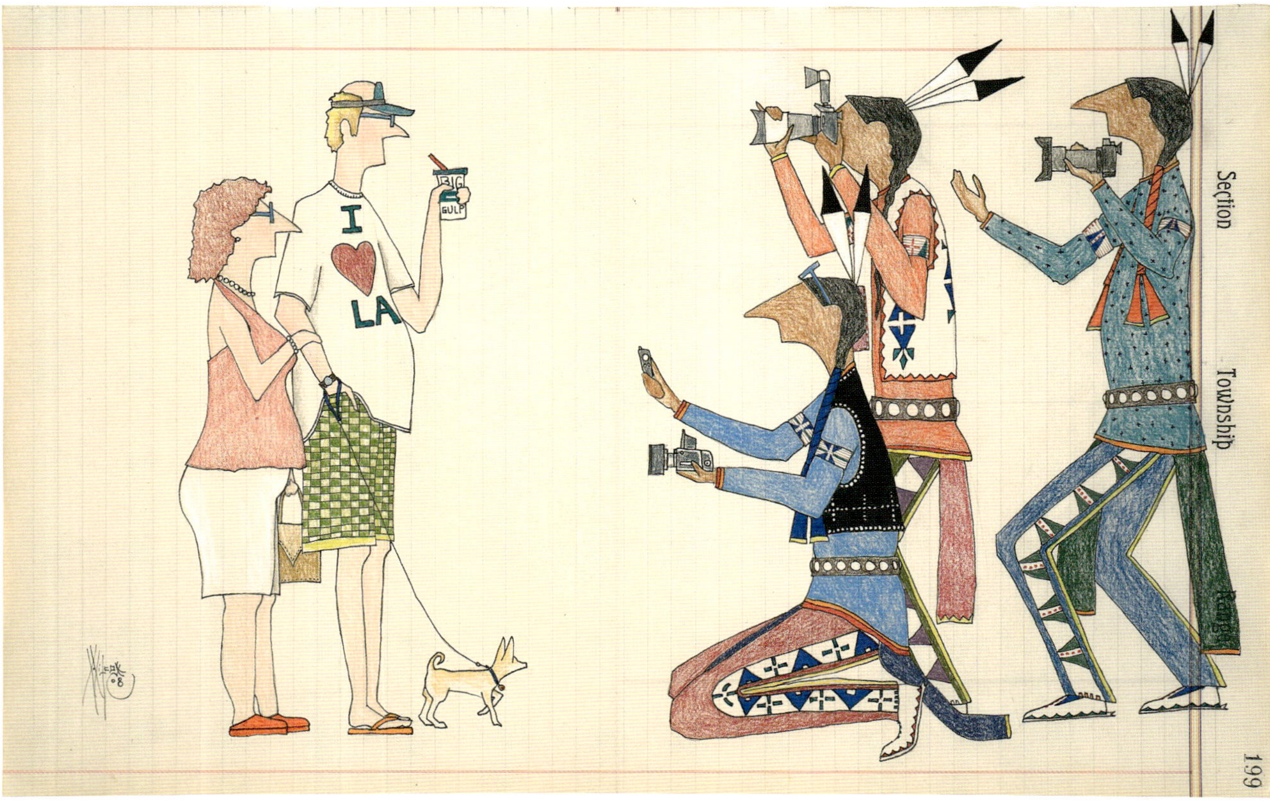

FIGURE 5.15
Dwayne Wilcox, Oglala Lakota, born 1957, ***WOW—Real Full Blooded White People,*** 2008, Hood Museum of Art, purchased through the Guernsey Center Moore 1904 Fund, 2008.59.5.

River at the top, the Red River along the lower edge, and a partial dotted line signifying the Texas–Indian Territory border running vertically along the western edge.[33] Like Chief Killer, who combined Cheyenne and Anglo compositional elements nearly two decades earlier, Black Goose reconfigures the rectangular picture plane to reassert Native identity and sovereign mastery over the land and its contents. Chief Killer's landscapes were not maps per se, but reflect a Native understanding of landscape representation that persists within the drawings he created during his own dislocating circumstances of exile.

RETURN TO INDIAN TERRITORY

Jubilant families gathered near the Darlington Agency in Indian Territory on April 22, 1878, to celebrate the return of their beloved soldier-veterans from Fort Marion.[34] Because game was scarce and rations were very poor, due in part to agency corruption, the former prisoners found few opportunities. Though they recognized the many injustices in reservation life, the men were empowered by the education they had received in the East and, for the most part, had positive regard for Pratt and their former teachers. In 1879 Chief Killer wrote to Pratt, "We all still love you and your family and have not forgotten you." He explained, "I have nothing, no horses and no money, but I am going to work to get some." He promised that by the time the captain planned his visit to the reservation, "I want to have four horses, and show you how I can make corn." He was working as a butcher for twenty dollars a month when Pratt's teenage son, Mason, at his father's behest, visited the former prisoners three years later. The younger Pratt reported that Chief Killer "was anxious to come to Carlisle now, that he would do anything Papa would give him."[35] Chief Killer does not appear in the Carlisle records, but he did send his daughter Maud, who subsequently returned with her husband Colonel Horn to work together at the agency school.[36] Though he knew Pratt's disdain of the custom, Chief Killer celebrated Maud's homecoming in the traditional manner, by bestowing gifts upon the community. Pratt, his former jailer-teacher, admonished him in a letter: "I am sorry that you are so foolish as to give away horses and spend money because Maud came home. It is a very foolish Indian way. . . . You must not only learn

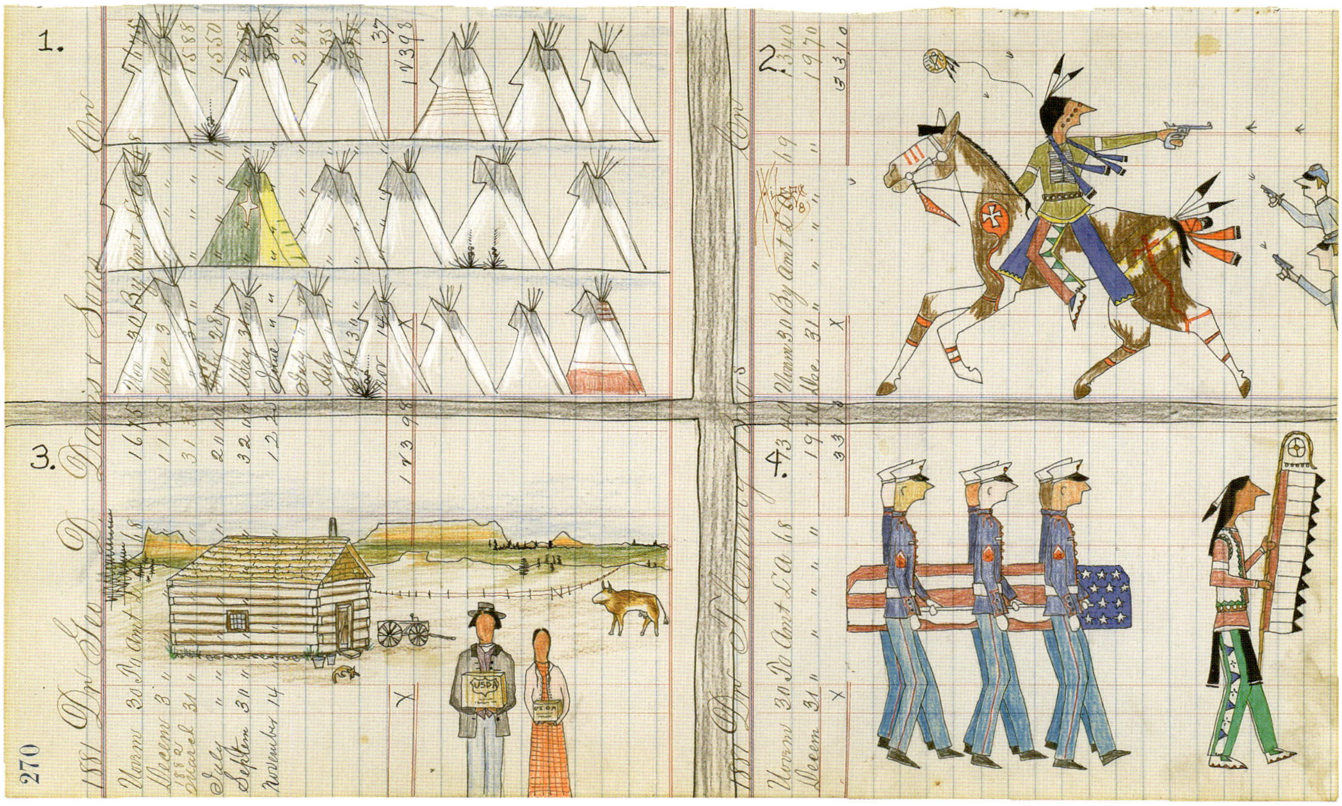

FIGURE 5.16
Dwayne Wilcox, Oglala Lakota, born 1957, ***From Here to Eternity***, 2008, Hood Museum of Art, purchased through the Guernsey Center Moore 1904 Fund, 2008.59.3.

to earn money and increase your cattle, but you must learn to save them. I had always hoped that you would some day be a rich, influential farmer among the Cheyennes."[37] From this letter we know that Chief Killer eventually acquired the horses that signified wealth among his people in his generation, and while he deemed a white education essential for his daughter's success and survival, he was not prepared to relinquish the lifeways central to Cheyenne society.

GEOGRAPHIC LEGACIES

For a number of contemporary Native American artists, the visual interface of maps, landscapes, and ledgers continues to provide fertile metaphorical visual grounds upon which to reinscribe history and reassert Native presence in the land. Themes of visual surveillance and geographic memory in their work creatively address contemporary issues, both personal and political. Dwayne Wilcox presses contemporary pop culture onto the fabric of the past by imposing outlined ledger-like figures on antique land accounting papers. In *WOW—Real Full Blooded White People*, Lakota paparazzi in full regalia defend their rectangular space through the lens of the camera—their "weapon" of choice—not unlike Chief Killer's binocular-wielding characters (figure 5.15). Literally compressed against the vertical red ledger lines on the right, bearing the headings "section" and "township," Wilcox's Indian photographers control the looking and reverse the tourist gaze as they assess the optimal arrangement of their clueless subjects through hand gestures and scientific meter readings. In *From Here to Eternity* the artist revisits the historic act of forced allotment by further subdividing the ledger page into four rectangles, each containing a "section" of Lakota history, from tipi encampment and war on horseback to farming and the sacrifice of a soldier's life for the United States government. With comedic wit and the metaphorical possibilities of lined paper as land, Wilcox speaks to reservation experience in the present (figure 5.16).

Perhaps the most physical geographic intervention may be found in the work of self-described warrior-artist Hachivi Edgar Heap of Birds, whose great-grandfather was imprisoned at Fort Marion with other Cheyenne resistance

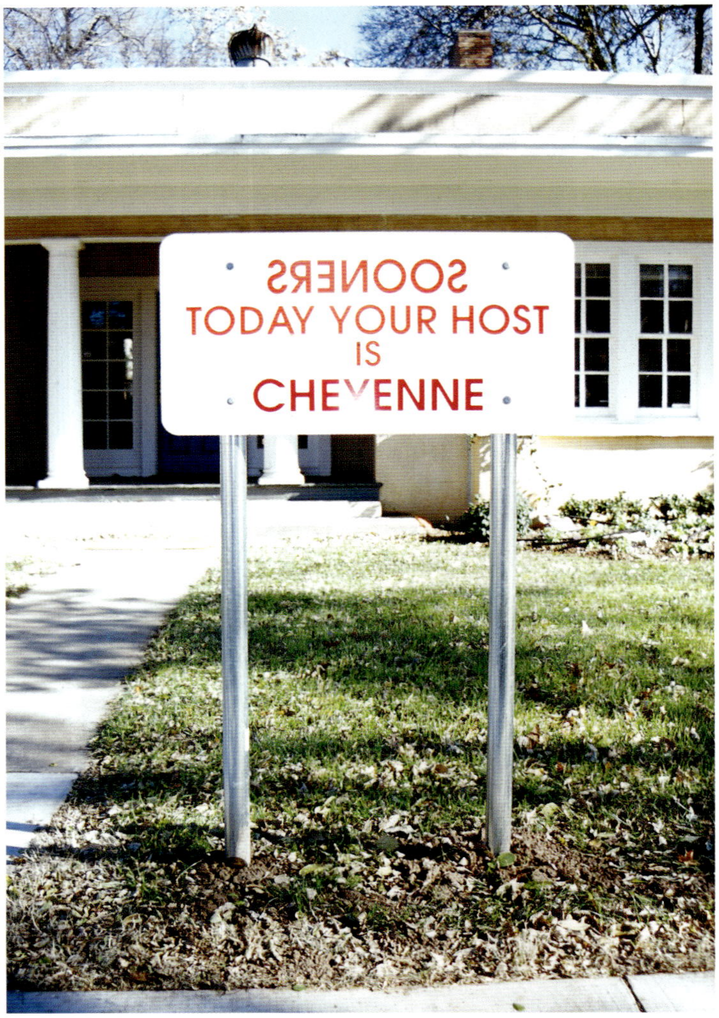

FIGURE 5.17
Hachivi Edgar Heap of Birds, "***Native Hosts: Today Your Host Is Cheyenne.***" One of seven tribal sign panels installed in Norman, Oklahoma, 2000.

leaders.[38] His landscape installations in America and abroad physically restore indigenous presence in the actual soil through the emplacement of Native words and graphic forms upon the colonizer's language of manufactured metal road signs. His *Native Hosts* series asks the viewer to see who came before, the myriad peoples who occupied the sites before intruders inserted their own highways on the map.[39] In an Oklahoma installation, "Sooners"—the name acquired by land-hungry interlopers who raced ahead to gobble up sectioned homesteads (subsequently adopted as state and university moniker)—is here turned back upon itself, as if a foreign idiom. "Cheyenne" reclaims the site (figure 5.17). As agents in the contestation over Native sovereignty, works by these artists and others interrogate the measured survey of Native lands and peoples and challenge the cultural construction of American geography and maps.

Likewise, Chief Killer and his fellow prisoners at Fort Marion used art forms, new and old, for the reaffirmation of Native identity. Having lived through the most catastrophic cultural assault in Cheyenne history, Chief Killer lived past the age of seventy, survived in death by his two daughters and five grandchildren.. To grandson John Swallow he bequeathed his bay horse, branded I. D. T. Twelve years before, he had been baptized in the Re-organized Church of the Latter Day Saints and was declared to be "a devoted father and a good Christian."[40] The Fort Marion warriors' creative reconfiguration of art-making helped them to foster personal and cultural resilience in the face of intense pressure to assimilate and forget who they were. By addressing the geography of the land and its representation in their artistic enterprise, they added a second language to their artworks without forgetting the old. The strategic choices they made, to adopt some forms and deny others and to renegotiate their circumstances as soldier-artists in a non-Native culture, continue to survive in the artistic practices of new generations. The cultural and personal narratives embedded with their drawings are, indeed, manifold.

NOTES

1. For this essay I am deeply indebted to the generosity and groundbreaking scholarship of Janet Catherine Berlo, Candace S. Greene, Joyce M. Szabo, and Hachivi Edgar Heap of Birds. On Native Plains compositional structure, see Greene, "Structure and Meaning in Cheyenne Ledger Art," in Berlo, ed., *Plains Indian Drawings,* 26–33; Szabo, *Howling Wolf,* 30–38.

2. Unless otherwise noted, in this essay the word "landscape" is intended in its broadest sense, i.e., features and forms upon the physical land, or representations thereof, as opposed to the highly formalized genre of landscape painting in its varied forms from the European art historical canon. Likewise, unless otherwise specified, the term "geography" is used here primarily to signify an understanding of the earth, of particular topography, and of its contents, which are, of course, conceptually contingent upon cultural worldview, as opposed to geography as strictly an academic discipline.

3. Calloway, *One Vast Winter Count*; Moore, *The Cheyenne*; Berthrong, *Southern Cheyennes.*

4. See, for example, Basso, *Wisdom Sits in Places.*

5. Mitchell, "Imperial Landscape," in *Landscape and Power,* 5–46.

6. Boime, *Magisterial Gaze*; For the Native figure surveying the land as trope of loss, see Dippie. "The Moving Finger Writes," in Prown, et al., *Discovered Lands, Invented Pasts,* 89–115.

7. For the ideological function of silences in maps, see Harley, *New Nature of Maps.*

8. Szabo, *Howling Wolf,* 26–33. Szabo has identified forty-four pictures that could be attributed to Chief Killer. Szabo, "Chief Killer and a New Reality."

9. Pratt, *Battlefield and Classroom,* 140.

10. Grinnell, *Cheyenne Indians,* vol. 2: 48–86.

11. Pratt, *Battlefield and Classroom,* 140. Pratt's list from 1878 identifies Chief Killer as age twenty-eight.

12. A three-mile-long trail of bullets and prints indicated a desperate fight, and the compass pressed into Short's forehead suggested the Cheyennes well understood the significance of the instrument. Montgomery, "United States Surveyors Massacred," 266–72; Pratt, *Battlefield and Classroom,* 138–39; Berthrong, *Southern Cheyennes,* 393–94.

13. The girls were subsequently recovered; the younger sisters were given to another band in November, and the older two set free in March of the following year. Szabo, "Chief Killer and a New Reality," 51; Lookingbill, *War Dance,* 22–23; Berthrong, *Southern Cheyennes,* 392–400; Pratt, *Battlefield and Classroom,* 138–40.

14. Hyde, *Life of George Bent,* 363.

15. Lookingbill, *War Dance,* 83.

16. Ibid., 55.

17. Ibid., 126–27; Pratt, *Battlefield and Classroom,* 136–46.

18. A number of post-colonial writers have applied Michel Foucault's writings on the coerciveness of visual surveillance in prisons and asylums to explicate the relationship between colonizer and colonized—theories especially relevant to any discussion of the Fort Marion prison experience. Foucault, *Discipline and Punish.*

19. Lookingbill, *War Dance,* 85.

20. On landscape representation and Plains pictures see, for example, Berlo, "A Kiowa's Odyssey," in Earenfight, ed., *A Kiowa's Odyssey,* 178–80; Szabo, *Howling Wolf,* 74–76, 135–37.

21. Lookingbill, *War Dance,* 116.

22. Pratt, *Battlefield and Classroom,* 118. Also cited in Lookingbill, *War Dance,* 107.

23. On geographic education, see Bruckner, *Geographic Revolution in America*; citation for "plow a straight line," Brainerd, *Elementary Principles,* 1–4; for geographic textbooks typical of the period, see J. H. Colton, *Colton and Fitch's Modern School Geography* (New York: J. H. Colton, published from the 1840s through the 1880s); on American drawing manuals, education and national rhetoric, see Marzio, *Art Crusade.*

24. Lookingbill, *War Dance,* 97–101. Later, Edmund Nequatewa, a Hopi at the Phoenix Indian School, also paid close attention to geography lessons, "because it is the only way that I can find my way out. I put my whole mind on . . . studying rivers and mountains in order to find the road that I am going to use to get away from here." Adams, *Education for Extinction,* 143–44.

25. Witmer, *Indian Industrial School*; Witmer, *Changing Images.*

26. Adams, *Education for Extinction,* 143.

27. Szabo, *Howling Wolf,* 76, 80–81. Photograph, Richard H. Pratt Papers, Western Americana Collections, Beinecke Rare Book and Manuscript Library, Yale University.

28. Unlike romantic Euro-American pictures that depict the Native observer in terms of land loss (see Dippie, "The Moving Finger," 99–101), Chief Killer's "surveillance" images speak instead of Native mastery over the contents of this land and, in this case, animals and other people. On the interchangeablity of gun vision and looking, see Alan C. Braddock, "Shooting the Beholder: Charles Schreyvogel and the Spectacle of Gun Vision," *American Art,* vol. 20, no. 1 (Spring 2006), 36–59; also "The Art of Predatory Looking," in Kenneth Haltman, *Looking Close and Seeing Far: Samuel Seymour, Titian Ramsay Peale and the Art of the Long Expedition, 1818–1823* (University Park: Pennsylvania State University Press, 2007).

29. Grinnell, *Cheyenne Indians,* 334–35; Moore, *The Cheyenne,* 228–31.

30. Contemporary Cheyenne artist Edgar Heap of Birds says of the Fort Marion artists: "They made pastoral paintings and the ones about war were the ones about hunting." Hachivi

Edgar Heap of Birds, "Hachivi Edgar Heap of Birds," in Abbott, ed., *I Stand in the Center of the Good,* 50.

31. Here I am not referring to expressions of Native American cosmological concepts of place and space, which customarily privilege the four directions and an originary center, but rather to concepts of space as related to navigation and the recording of movement. Maps such as these were produced on a wide variety of ephemeral materials, such as soil, snow, tree bark, or other arrangements of natural materials on the ground. See Woodward and Harley, eds., *History of Cartography,* vol. 2, pt. 3; Lewis, ed., *Cartographic Encounters*; Belyea, *Dark Storm Moving West*; and Warhus, *Another America.*

32. Meadows, "Black Goose's Map," 265–82.

33. Ibid., 270–76.

34. Lookingbill, *War Dance,* 174–98; *John Sipes Cheyenne Family Oral Histories—Standing Bird Family,* Oklahoma Historical Society. Interview with Measure Woman Standing Bird, the daughter of Medicine Water and Buffalo Calf.

35. Lookingbill, *War Dance,* 187.

36. *Indian Helper,* Carlisle Indian School newspaper (August, 11, 1893).

37. Adams, *Education for Extinction,* 282; Richard H. Pratt to Chief Killer, July 5, 1887, Pratt Papers. Beinecke Rare Book and Manuscript Library, Yale University.

38. Heap of Birds, also called Many Magpies, succumbed to heart disease while at Fort Marion. *Weekly Floridian,* October 23, 1877; Lookingbill, *War Dance,* 153–54, 158.

39. Hachivi Edgar Heap of Birds, *Beyond the Chief/Native Hosts* lectures at the University of Illinois, Spring 2009.

40. Sipes/Berthrong Cheyenne Collection, Fort Marion POWs Section. Fort Marion and Darlington Agency, Indian Territory Sections, file numbers 42–56. Oklahoma Historical Society. Will of Chief Killer, June 1, 1921. Copy at Oklahoma Historical Society. Also, *Calumet Chieftain,* August 3, 1922; Lookingbill, *War Dance,* 194.

CHAPTER 6

Tracing the Schoolhouse/Big House Legacy

LEDGER ART AND PRISON WORK

VERA B. PALMER

By 1879, my people were no longer free, but were subjects confined on reservations under the rule of agents. One day there came to the agency a party of white people from the East. Their presence aroused considerable excitement when it became known that these people were school teachers who wanted some Indian boys and girls to take away with them to train as were white boys and girls. . . . I could think of no reason why white people wanted Indian boys and girls except to kill them, and not having the remotest idea of what a school was, I thought we were going East to die. . . . Back on the train the older boys sang brave songs in an effort to keep up their spirits and ours too. In my mind I often recall that scene—eighty-odd blanketed boys and girls marching down the street surrounded by a jeering, unsympathetic people whose only emotions were those of hate and fear; the conquerors looking upon the conquered. And no more understanding us than if we had suddenly been dropped from the moon.

At last at Carlisle the transforming, the "civilizing" process began. . . . The task before us was not only that of accepting new ideas and adopting new manners, but actual physical changes. . . . Everything was queer, and it took a few months to get adjusted to the new surroundings.[1]

LUTHER STANDING BEAR (*Oglala Lakota*)

FROM HIS WRITTEN ACCOUNTS, Luther Standing Bear, a young Oglala Lakota from the Pine Ridge Indian Agency in South Dakota, experienced Lieutenant Richard Pratt's newly minted Carlisle Indian School to be frightening, confining, and alienating in ways that only Pratt's *first* group of "hostile" Plains Indian prisoner-students could have understood, based on their Fort Marion incarceration and subsequent tutelage in "civilization." The objective of Pratt's social experiment with the Fort Marion warrior-prisoners, and later with young Indian children conscripted to Carlisle, was to "kill the Indian, save the man"—all within an environment of military discipline, conformity, and close monitoring. In its day, and in light of most Euro-American settlers' antipathies toward Indians, this was considered a radically progressive (read: much *too* humane) notion. For it was Pratt who removed the shackles and prevailed upon the government to free the Fort Marion captive-students after three years, and a number of those released went to Hampton Institute for Freedmen in Virginia. Furthermore, Pratt's appeal for government funds to establish Carlisle Indian School was prompted by a worry that "his" Fort Marion Indians would experience the same level of prejudice at Hampton Institute that was so prevalent against black freedmen after the Civil War. His protectiveness of the Fort Marion captives' welfare was singular.[2]

But despite the individual efforts of this well-meaning reformer, the ensuing conjunction of prison and school has left a deep and wounding intaglio upon the legacy of Native American education in America. The discussion in this essay is situated at the historical intersection of school and prison, and it attempts to locate some perspectives on ledger art within a landscape of colonial power relations and institutions. The meaning of creativity in the conditions of captivity is the common theme here in juxtaposing selected historical ledger work, with ledger-inspired expressions by contemporary Native American prisoners. Both expressive forms reveal fertile sites for the (re)constitution of tribal subjectivity and relationships, despite operating in the midst, or in the wake of personal and cultural trauma.

Over time, the cumulative Indian experiences of this institutional mix of school and prison have continued to profoundly compromise tribal integrities through the loss of cultural treasures: fluency in one's own Native language; social, political, and spiritual literacy in one's own tribal traditions; and, among the most critical, a physical displacement from homelands that are understood to be sacred, replete with ancestral signifiers, and sources of physical sustenance and environmental knowledge—all core to individual and collective tribal identity. Such crucial and staggering losses create the conditions for despair to flourish, a legacy enduring from colonial times into the present day. Without spilling into a discussion here of urgent and current social trends, suffice it to say that in Luther Standing Bear's Dakota homelands, for example, today's ACLU (American Civil Liberties Union) of the Dakotas and the attorney general of the Rosebud Sioux Tribe have brought a class-action law suit against a local school district as part of the ACLU's national challenge to address the "school to prison pipeline." In one local elementary school, approximately 30 percent of the students are Native American (mostly Sioux), but only 1 percent of them complete high school. These students—often suspended or dropped-out—are ten times more likely to become wards of state and federal correctional facilities.[3]

For American Indians, the historical blending of prison and school has woven long, strong threads into a fabric of meanings more often somber than inspirational. Historically, the projection of deviancy upon American Indian bodies, tribes, and customs provided a central rationale for the creation of the Indian residential schools. It also gave cause for oppressive U.S. Indian policies, and it certainly justified rounding up the original "hostile" group of seventy-two Fort Sill–to–Fort Marion prisoners in the first place. The common source of grievance among this captive band of Cheyenne, Kiowa, Comanche, Caddo, and Arapaho warriors and ledger artists—the grievance that precipitated their crimes against encroaching settlers—was their armed resistance to expanding settlement into their ancient homelands and their adamant objection to their people's forced confinement to reservations. The *amour propre* motivating their tribe- and self-preserving actions was turned into grounds for their "criminality."

This historical intersection in the Native American experience of school and prison brought into focus for me a way to integrate my years of volunteer work with Native American prisoners with an exploration of their unique relationships with the very idea of ledger art and its visual impact upon their individual and tribal identities. While many historical ledgers came about as novel expressions emerging from a field of radical disruption and change, the following narrative of my deployment of the genre somewhat reverses that sequence; the ledger became the catalyst within an environment of enforced routine and stasis.

BRINGING A NINETEENTH-CENTURY LEDGER INTO A CONTEMPORARY PRISON COMMUNITY

The Native American Prisoner Support Programs situated at Auburn Correctional Facility, New York, the country's oldest maximum security prison, and Cayuga Correctional Facility in Moravia, New York, were conceived during my doctoral studies at Cornell University. I had already been involved in outreach programs to Native prisoners for over a decade beginning the late 1980s, along with the late Ojibway prison activist, Barbara Owl, who recruited me to join her group visiting Native inmates at the supermax correctional facility at Lewisburg, Pennsylvania. After the initial Cornell funding came through to set up a Native inmate outreach program in the New York State Department of Corrections system, the program continued for several years of weekly visits lasting three hours each. (Reportedly, this program at Cornell continues.) The guiding principles of the Native American Prisoner Support Program are to affirm Native community across prison walls and to acknowledge this gesture of solidarity as an act of Native sovereignty affecting those on both sides of prison ramparts. While the prison institution may control the space confining these Native men, they remain our Native relations on the outside. So volunteer visitations are not acts of charity, they are acts of reclamation that perform and continue that relationship.

A noteworthy caveat deserves reprise here: sentimental illusions about prisoners, Native or otherwise, that would trivialize the hideous nature of some of the crimes

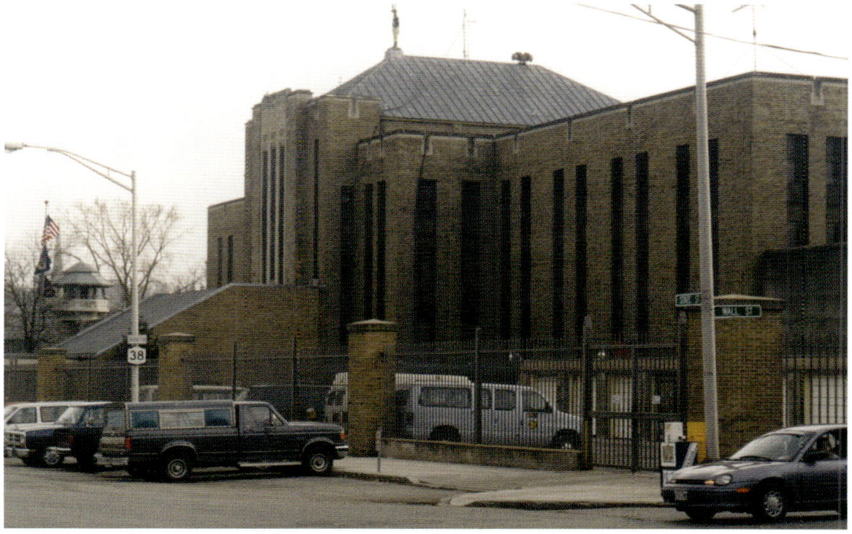

FIGURE 6.1
Auburn Prison façade, Auburn, New York, April 1999.

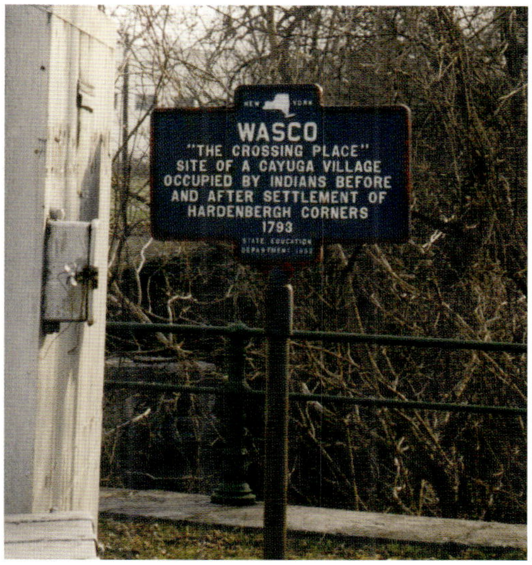

FIGURE 6.2
New York State historic marker indicating "Wasco," former Cayuga village, as the site of today's Auburn Correctional Facility, April 1999.

for which they are held, or gloss the necessity of legal redress for their offenses would be grossly inappropriate. Discussion about ledger art's role in the context of this prison project is not intended to minimize criminality, or to deflect attention away from the seriousness of crime and the accountability of these Native men as offenders. The transgressions of Pratt's warrior-students at Fort Marion are not conflated here within the same moral category as the crimes of those Native inmates in Auburn or Cayuga correctional facilities with whom I worked. But also relevant to this discussion is the fact that indigenous people of the Americas have always had their own specific tribal protocols to deal with those who broke faith with the community—those whose actions betrayed or violated the life and welfare of the tribal group. Among these remedies were consequences like banishment, temporary exile, or sometimes service, indenture, or adoption into the family who was aggrieved by the crime, or even death. "Rick"[4] was one Mohawk member of the Auburn prisoner group who fully owned up to his crime, but he expressed a form of historical regret that the current prison system, and not Mohawk tradition, dictates his penalty. In his view, even if death might be his tribal community's ultimate verdict, he deemed it better than a numbing prison sentence in which he pays an abstracted debt to a disembodied, anonymous public, with no specific amends to the people his crime actually harmed. A host of traditional systems of tribal accountability have been nearly lost; overtaken by punitive methods and theories derived from Europe's long history with prisons. Certainly English legal and social reformer Jeremy Bentham's innovations brought a great improvement: that the prison's goal and even its architecture should elicit inmates' self-assessment and penance. But having long abandoned this nineteenth-century reform goal for the penitentiary as a place of remorse and reeducation of the offender, the modern prison system makes little pretense to restore lives or to "heal the broken hoop." As illustrated in "Rick's" response, the dialectic inherent in the ledger art form became a catalyst for quickening his perspective of tribal and historical consciousness as well as his own ledger-inspired creative work. My work with the men of Auburn and Cayuga Correctional Facilities bears witness to many examples of the ledger's catalytic role within these places of confinement.

Auburn is an old prison currently in use to full- and usually over-capacity. Its physical plant evokes medieval imagery. And lest one lose track of the role colonialism plays here, the thick-stoned structure has a tall, painted statue of an American colonial sentry perched high atop the façade's entrance. It was built in 1813, and it's the oldest maximum security prison in the country to be in continuous use since its opening. It also has the dubious distinction of housing and using the first electric chair in U.S. penal history. It has another claim of unique interest to the Native inmates housed there: It was built on the very site of a former Cayuga tribal village named "Wasco" (trans., "The Place of Crossing"). The irony of this geographical palimpsest was very affecting to the Native men of the Auburn group. Most were not aware of this historical information about the very land under their prison-home. It appeared to provide them with a meaningful and alternative narrative of what Keith Basso calls, "place making,"[5] and afforded the men a unique sense of indigenous and historical connection to Native land, even within their delimited space inside the prison walls.

After a department of corrections' state and federal background check, fingerprint registration, DOC registration photo, and tuberculosis shots and lab tests, I became authorized to enter any of New York State's many maximum and medium security prisons as a volunteer and to begin meeting with Native prisoners. As a female planning to enter these venues alone, I preferred to have a willing male join the project. The presence of a Cherokee colleague, Sean Teuton, helped to diffuse the starkly gendered disproportionality in walking past the razor-wired entrance and multiple sets of solid steel doors, gates, and bars, across the open prison yard, surrounded at the perimeter by floors of stacked and warehoused human souls in cellblocks, to arrive at the building deep inside the prison complex where the Native men waited each week to greet us. I will never forget the feelings and thoughts I had during so many somber treks past the prison's steeled entrance and across the interior, metal thresholds of control. It felt like a privilege to forge a path across those barriers to meet with the men who are my Indian brothers, but at times hearing the collective pain of their storied lives was almost too much to brave. The experience continues to be for me a unique pedagogy of tribal consciousness, as much as the culminating "Art Across Walls" project proved later to be a breakout of human and tribal expression for the Native American men living behind the walls of those institutions. The historical and conceptual influence of the ledger art pieces that we shared helped to inspire these weekly encounters in a way that brought the men a degree of tribal selfhood inside a crushing machine of constraint and under the relentless gaze of institutional surveillance.

During these weekly visits we also shared with the men various pieces of Native literature and poetry, and Native-produced films and documentaries. The opening prayer and honoring drum were very important to the men during these occasions, as was the Talking Circle. These visits were the only times the men were allowed to bring out the drum and sing traditional tribal songs together. They said that hearing their own voices joined together in traditional songs was a powerful experience for them—one of unity and mutual support in an environment designed to promote mostly ruthless, bare-life survival. They reported to me that even this privilege had to be earned; they were frequently obliged to first sit through a Christian mass or service earlier in the week, since Native spiritual matters, and even ceremonial objects such as the group's eagle feather, their drum, and their one Sacred Pipe with tobacco, were all under the control and whim of the prison's Christian chaplain, a penal system cleric the men sardonically dubbed "Black Robe." This bit of religious tyranny exerted over cherished tribal objects sacred to the Native men of Auburn Prison invigorated their viewing of Chief Killer's ledger that depicts the Fort Marion warriors uniformed, seated on benches, and being regaled with sermons and scripture by local missionaries. The men recognized elements of their own Auburn experience in this ledger, and the unavoidable irony brought them some humor and perspective (see plate 57).

None of the Native men in either the Auburn or the Cayuga group were previously aware of the history or significance for Native people of the ledger art tradition. When they began to learn more about it, they expressed a desire to contribute in their own way to this genre, as they understood it. With funds awarded from another grant, we took modern-day, commercial ledger books, markers, colored pencils and other "approved" art materials into the prison each week for the men to work with, much as the Fort Marion prisoner-artists had done before them. Each Native inmate bearing the institutional mark of his identity—an inventoried prison number tattooed on his forearm—embraced with gusto the signifying practice of making his own version of ledger art as an expression of humanity, of familial ties and homeland memories, of his indigenous consciousness, and as a humanizing counterpoint to prison exigencies. After a number of months working together, the multimedia results of their collective creativity were striking; the men had produced poetry, personal narratives and reverie, songs, drawings, shields, some amazingly fashioned paper and wood sculptures created from poster board, popsicle sticks, and sheer resourcefulness—all products of their deeply personal expression. These were creative acts performed under the conditions of lost freedom and a captive future, separated (for some, terminally) from tribal community and family. Their work bears a sense of dignity, and it begged to be shared outside the confines of prison—to be mounted as a showcase of Native prisoners' voices and vision. The exhibit in Cornell University's Willard Straight Gallery titled, "Art Across Walls: Expressions of Native American Prisoners," was the result and the showcase of their humanity and identities to an audience outside the walls.

Following are some images of their creative work done

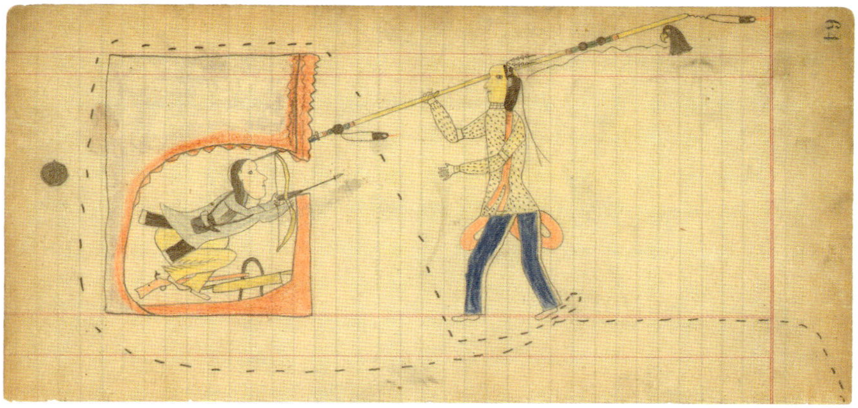

FIGURE 6.3

Unknown artist, Tsistsistas (Cheyenne) and/or Inunaina (Arapaho), active late nineteenth century, ***Untitled [An Inunaina (Arapaho) warrior counts coup on an enemy]***, late nineteenth century, Hood Museum of Art (plate 64).

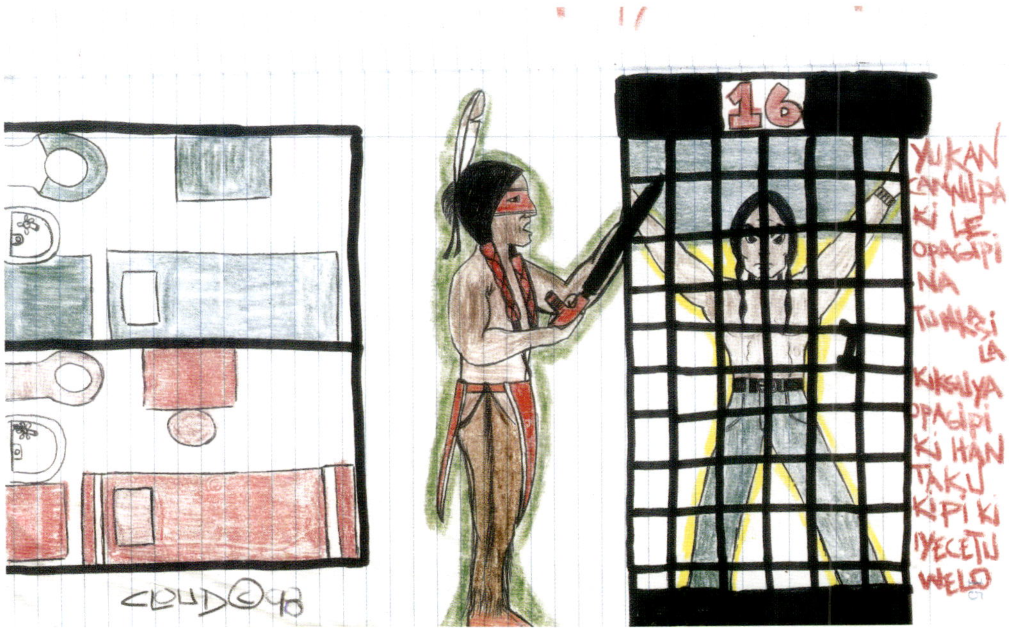

FIGURE 6.4

"Ray," Lakota. ***Two images of Self***, multiple views of his prison cell, and Chanupah (Sacred Pipe), 1998.

in the spirit of the historical ledger art tradition, as these contemporary Native American prisoners conceived it. Their art provided an outlet for expressing their voices and experience.[6] I have paired several pieces of their work with selected ledger pieces from the Mark Lansburgh collection, plus some examples from other historical ledger collections, to illustrate the dynamic and antiphonal exchange that this historical genre inspired for the Native men who were part of the project. Opening their awareness and imaginations to the forms and the legacy of nineteenth-century ledger artwork gave rise to their own newfound notions of meaning in this richly decorated and uniquely Indian visual genre. In the following examples, a traditional ledger drawing is juxtaposed with an example drawn by an inmate. I have chosen the specific pairings for their mutual resonance across time and circumstance. These are connections that I traced years after the art exhibit at Cornell of the men's artwork. Accompanying each set of drawings is a brief commentary offering a possible interpretation of the visual tensions and congruencies that surface in the space and time between the two images.

An unknown artist in the "Vincent Price Ledger" depicts a warrior in stealthy apprehension of his enemy and poised to count coup while his enemy hides, crouched in a tiny enclosed space (see figure 6.3). In many of "Ray's" conversations, he spoke about the Native prisoner's desire to conquer the greatest enemy of all: the "enemy within," as he put it. His ledger shows one image of a Native self, imprisoned by his own rage, while his alter ego brings solace and strength, offering the Sacred Pipe through the bars (see figure 6.4). The pipe-bearer self appears "free" compared to the confined self of pent up anger. The aerial view of side-by-side prison cells suggests that the two "selves" endure identical circumstances, but their

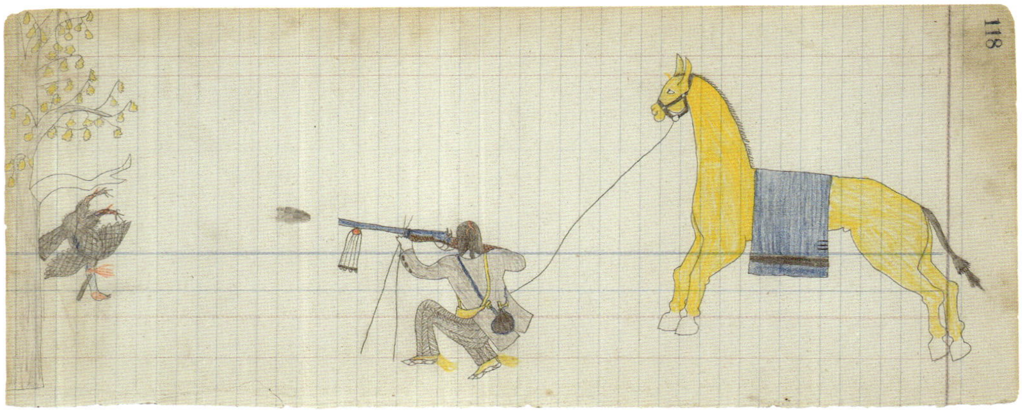

FIGURE 6.5
Unknown artist, Southern Tsistsistas (Cheyenne), active late nineteenth century, ***Untitled [Hunting turkey],*** c. 1874–75, Hood Museum of Art (plate 23).

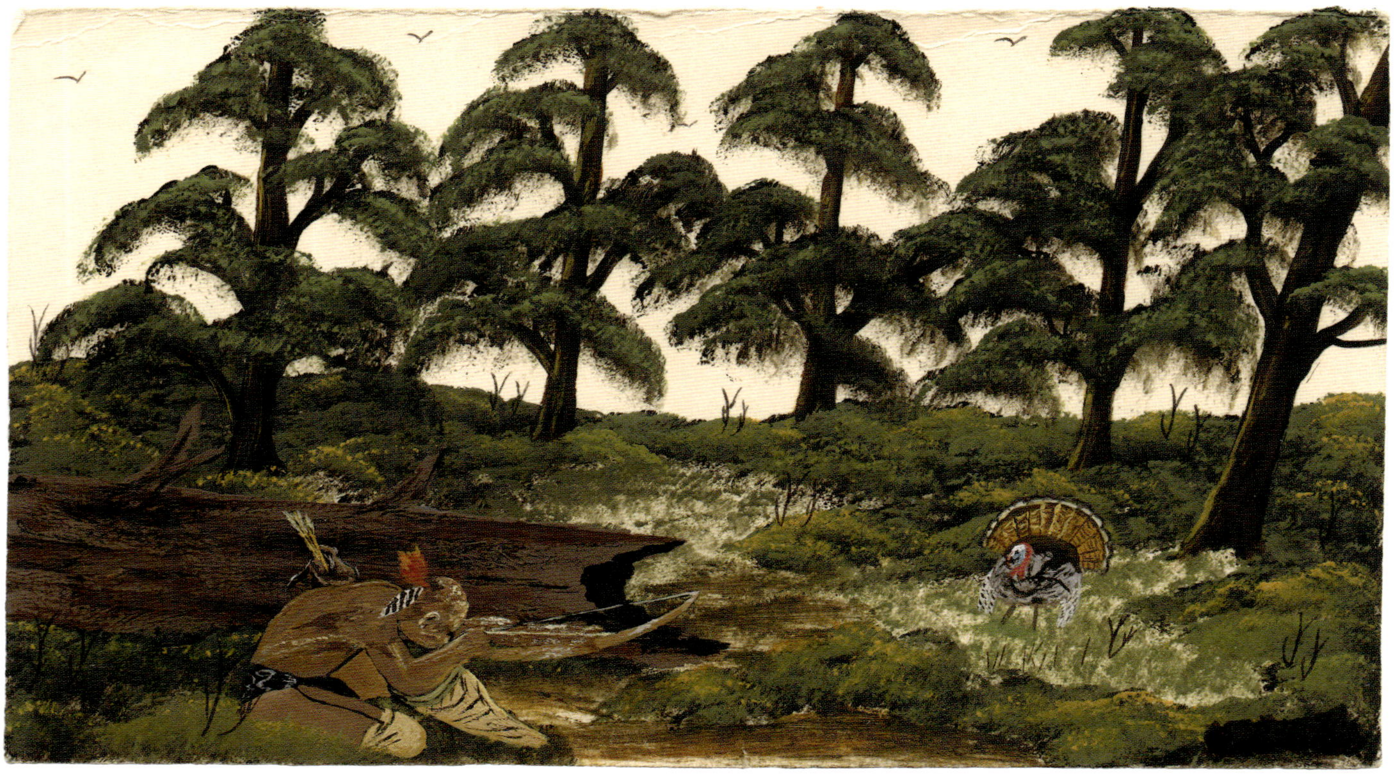

FIGURE 6.6
"Isaiah," Cherokee. ***Isaiah's turkey hunt down South.*** Pen-and-ink drawing on manila folder, 1999.

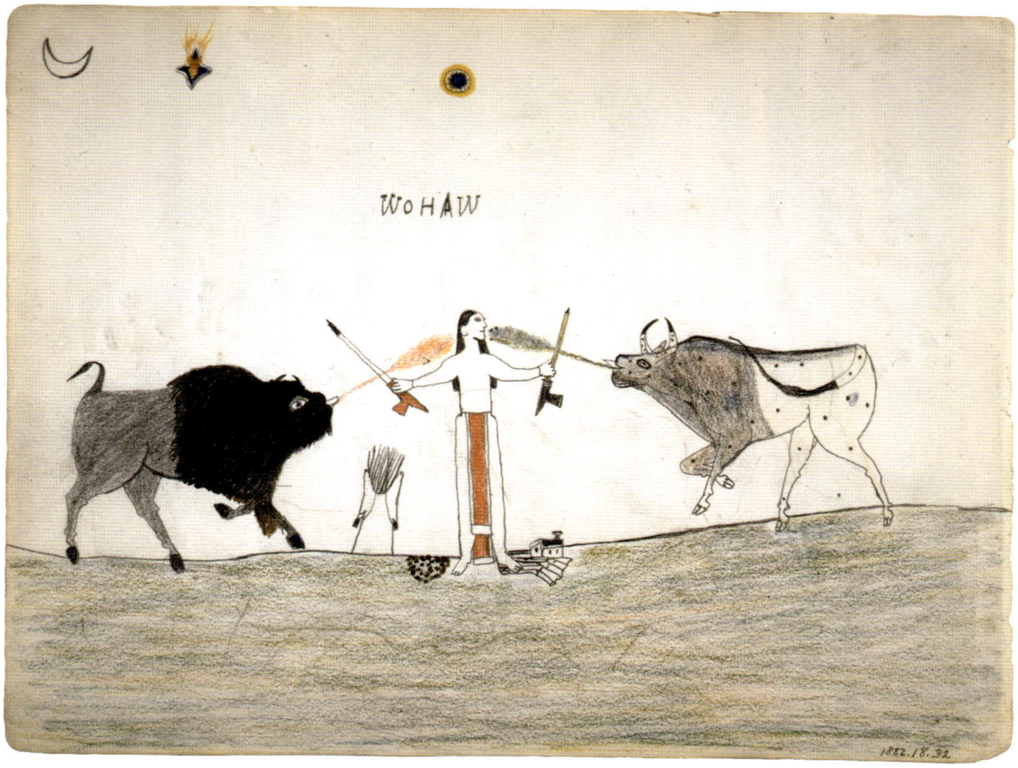

FIGURE 6.7
Wohaw, Kiowa. ***Untitled [Wohaw between two worlds]***, c. 1876–77. Missouri Historical Society, no. 1882.18.32.

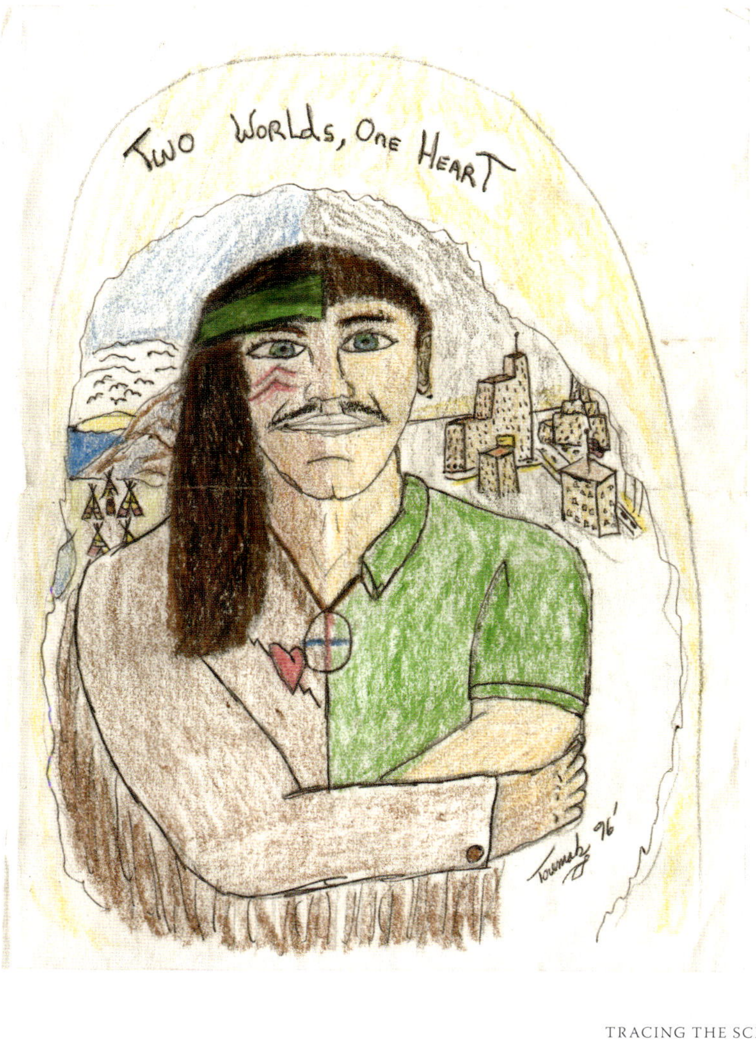

FIGURE 6.8
"Tom," Choctaw. ***Two Worlds, One Heart.*** Pen-and-crayon drawing on journal paper, 1998.

responses to the same conditions are completely different. From another viewpoint, considering sheer, physical logistics, "Ray's" Auburn drawing chronicles an interior prison architecture of dominance and conformity—features more conducive to rampage than to spiritual growth.

The ledger drawing, thought by some to portray George Bent hunting, seems simple and straightforward (see figure 6.5). A warrior turns hunter, and takes aim at a wild turkey. George Bent was a well-known Cheyenne and the grandson of an Arrow Keeper, an important role in Cheyenne society. A mere ten years before this ledger was drawn, George Bent had survived the Sand Creek Massacre, an assault executed under the command of Colonel John Chivington, who is also famous for the epithet "Nits make lice," uttered as an explanation for his ordering that Cheyenne and Arapaho women and children be slaughtered, along with their warriors. In contrast to this torturous event in Bent's past, this ledger conveys a quotidian, nearly pastoral quality. The detailed drawing done by "Isaiah," a Cherokee prisoner-artist at Auburn, shares the same tone of normalcy in depicting his own memory of hunting to provide food for his family (figure 6.6). "Isaiah" pined for his home, and the time he spent trekking and hunting in the verdant landscapes of his southern home, a scene that he artfully recreates in his ledger. Sometimes a turkey hunt is just a turkey hunt. But the common reverie these Cheyenne and Cherokee drawings share across time of life lived in an abundant landscape is a poignant example of lush memory surviving against the backdrop of personal loss and anguish.

Wohaw's sketchbook drawing from around 1876–77 (figure 6.7) famously evokes the "two worlds" trope that today has become a rather worn cliché of Native identity: living in two worlds. It is the expanded but destabilizing experience of occupying a liminal space that crests and shifts between two or more realms of social or cultural identity. However, Wohaw's self-representational position in the drawing appears lodged at a fault-line of time, rather than of space. He holds up two pipes, one extended toward the sacred buffalo whose numbers dwindle, and the other pipe toward a steer. He faces the cow, as he faces the approaching changes to Plains tribal life; beef will eventually replace the buffalo as a food staple on the plains, but would never achieve the buffalo's status as an honored, sacred being and relative among the Kiowa. The tiny square prairie house to the right of Wohaw's figure is another presage of an unavoidable future. Though it is unlikely that Wohaw was employing Western conventions of visual depth perspective, which would make the cabin's comparatively small size on the page imply distance, most certainly its miniaturization relative to the size of the tipi reveals Wohaw's prioritized values. And while Wohaw faces toward the steer and a new and inevitable future, the other half of his ledger is loaded with Kiowa signifiers: the sky is full on the left with sacred and storied celestial bodies, and the plains tipi is prominent. By using the same saffron color in his loincloth, the buffalo's breath (or spirit), and the pipe bowl, Wohaw chromatically unites his identity with Kiowa semiotics of spiritual value. As for all the Native men of the Auburn and Cayuga prisons, the concept and history of ledgers were new to Choctaw inmate, "Tom," who had never viewed or known of any ledger art, and certainly did not know Wohaw's drawing. Yet his self-portrait bears striking resemblance to the expressive motifs apparent in Wohaw's, with perhaps one major difference. While Wohaw's drawing is linked to an awareness of changing temporal conditions, "Tom" orients his self-representation in relation to space. To lean on the metaphor, "Tom" is in fact, "doing time." Time is the very substance of his debt to society and, ironically, time is what he has in abundance. Space and place are the rarities. "Tom" depicts the effect of this spatial deprivation in his violently split self-image. Unlike Wohaw's image that is merely turned toward an uncertain future, "Tom's" body appears irreparably severed, with even his heart transplanted from its normal placement on the left of his body, to the right side—the side that he aligns with the space that home and identity occupy in his consciousness.

These examples and comparisons underscore the capacity of Native American ledger art to animate and reveal experiences and perceptions that were submerged, and those that history has tended to ignore. From settler society's point of view—motivated as it was to obliterate Indian presence from the frontier landscape in order to satisfy greedy appetites for cheap property and expanded ownership—Pratt's project of the prison-turned-school for Indians who were "hostile" to settlement seems generous. His plan even appears to comply with some of the best intentions of nineteenth-century prison reforms. Pratt's assumption that a disciplined curriculum of Indian assimilation would erase the "Indian part" of his captive warrior-charges seemed reasonable enough in its day—it had the efficient common sense of business arithmetic: take one Indian savage, subtract the Indian part, add the pedagogy of Euro-American civilization, and a civilized man (or some facsimile) emerges as the outcome. Reportedly, nothing made Pratt angrier than Indian recidivism, meaning one of his students who "went back to the blanket." Backsliding Indian students betrayed more than

Pratt's hard work, they violated his colonial logic. Pratt regarded students who left Carlisle Indian School and returned to their reservations and traditional ways with a level of disgust second only to the general reaction to white settlers on the western frontier who "went native." But aside from the error in Pratt's lobotomous scheme to amputate human identity, how can we unpack exactly *why* Pratt's experiment would ultimately fail in achieving its intended result on the bodies, and in the hearts and minds, of Native people?

CONCEPTUAL IMAGES OF NATIVE AMERICAN PRISON EXPERIENCE

The prison art project was designed to respectfully engage the lives and the artwork shared by each Native American man, and to treat each of their narratives with the dignity one would afford to a relative. Their experiences cannot be reduced to serve some external goal; nor was the prison project a vehicle to commodify their creative expressions into artifacts for intellectual consumption only. These are ethical concerns that require particular attention and are especially salient from a tribal perspective. Accordingly, the human and cultural complexities of this work with Native prisoners and its use of the ledger art genre calls for some integration of the extreme context of historical change and losses, structural conditions, and personal experience represented in the historical ledgers, with the changes, conditions, and experiences of the modern-day prisoners themselves.

Foucault's exploration of deviancy helps explain and negotiate these topics. In *Madness and Civilization,* Foucault cites the development of confinement beginning in the mid-seventeenth century as a phenomenon that assigned "the same homeland to the poor, to the unemployed, to prisoners, and to the insane. . . . [Thus] madness was linked with this *country of confinement*, and with the act which designated confinement as its natural abode."[7] Within an incipient lexicon of colonial settlement, Indian people and tribes represented not one, but all of the categories appearing on Foucault's list: the poor, the unemployed, the insane, and the imprisoned. Applied to Indian experience, his terms "homeland" and "country of confinement" are particularly apt to this discussion, evoking the physical space of tribal homelands lost and limited, either due to a tribe's removal or to confinement within the enclosure of reservation borders.

Ideas first articulated and argued by John Locke became a consensus of Euro-American views of Indians: "the several nations of the *Americans* [Indian tribal nations] who are rich in land, and poor in all the comforts of life . . . with the materials of plenty . . . yet for *want of improving it by labour* [they] have not one hundredth part of the convenience [the material value] we enjoy. . . . Thus in the beginning all the world was *America*, and . . . no such thing as *money* was any where known"[8] These definitions of Indian poverty ("rich in land and poor in life's comforts," they apparently have plenty of nothing), and their lack of market style labor that is seen as idleness, were viewed as evidence of Indian deviancy. Indians were deemed "poor" because they didn't "labor," converting "state of nature" wilderness into private agricultural property. Furthermore, Indians didn't use money in the continental sense of symbolic exchange. Locke's term for this rationale of Indian deficits is "natural logic." Using this Euro-American logic, Indian values and lifeways gave evidence of an irrational mind. Thus insanity entered the colonial diagnosis of America's indigenous people. Because they didn't make "rational" use of the land as Locke and others prescribed, the American Indians appeared to settlers' to be mentally inferior.

Accordingly, Natives who merely resisted or openly objected to government policies that further encroached upon their homelands, or those who spoke out against treaty violations or mass slaughter of the buffalo—a main food source for Plains tribes—often found themselves forcibly committed to various insane asylums. The U.S. Congress eventually established the infamous Canton Indian Insane Asylum in Canton, South Dakota, the only asylum exclusively designated for "patients" who were tribal Indians.[9] In most cases, the only "clinical symptom" for these individuals was their objection to abusive government policies, resistance to encroaching land speculators and settlers, or their activism against the confinement of their tribe to a reservation. Marginalizing those deemed "abnormal" recalls Foucault's model of power; the assignment of deviance, in the language of derogation and exclusion, provides the logic for setting up institutions to contain, manage, and monitor those considered markedly aberrant. Whether these Native Americans were forced onto reservations or committed to an institution like Canton Asylum—either way they were isolated and confined.

Parallel examples abound of a hegemonic reach that normalizes race-specific oppression by using the language of deviancy as pathology. Dr. Samuel Cartwright, a physician in 1851 at the University of Louisiana, without irony coined the term, *drapetomania*, referring to the psychiatric "disease" whose symptom was "the slave's incurable urge to run away." Similarly, *dyesthaesia Aethiopica* was another racist "diagnosis" of nineteenth-century psychiatry that validated a perverted normalcy by cobbling a definition of racial deviancy. It posited "the slave's 'healthy' behavior to be happy-go-lucky in his daily life of *subordination* . . . [and accordingly, it identified a 'disease'] which allegedly caused the slave to begin to slack off in his work, or to incite rebellion against the master/overseer."[10] Within an ordered colonial logic of power and confinement, the institutional image of the prison fills the bill to contain those labeled deviant—a moniker for Indians' behavior that today we recognize as acts of human survival and resistance to oppression. Salish and Kootenai tribal scholar, Luana Ross points out that the ideology of Native deviance "was used to justify both genocide *and* attempts [like Indian residential schools] to supposedly assimilate Natives into the dominant society."[11] Even colloquial usage in American popular culture of the derivative term, "going off the reservation," exposes the double bind that the controlled "deviancy" of Indian people has come to signify. Political arguments to forcibly contain "wild" Indians on reservations were *predicated* on the "deviant" status assigned to them. Yet the term, "off the reservation" has come to mean "going rogue," or engaging in unauthorized speech or activities. Before and after restraint, inside or outside the designated field of confinement, Indians' identities are, to the policy makers of the day, marked by de facto and official exclusion.

Native American Indians shut out in this way, then forced into carceral conditions—whether in the confinement of reservations or as actual prison inmates—suggest the figure of *homo sacer,* an ancient designation revived by philosopher Georgio Agamben. This Latin term, meaning "sacred man," refers to an arcane concept in the political life of ancient Rome. "Sacred" in this instance connotes an outlawed status of exclusion and isolation. However, it is a paradoxical status that both sanctifies and condemns the outcast; the homo sacer figure is protected from being sacrificed in (Roman) religious ritual, but at the same time his life lacks all political meaning. He is even deprived of civil protection that would outlaw his murder. This liminal, ambiguous state renders him paranormal in one sense, and in another sense he is subhuman and extremely vulnerable. Agamben uses the term to explore the characteristics of exceptional power over human biological life. The sovereign is able to act both inside and outside the law. If we turn for clarification to Hegel's notion of *Aufhebung,* the sovereign's power simultaneously *destroys* the condemned by reducing his human life to a cipher and excluding him from the polis, while it also *preserves* the condemned by forbidding that his life be sacrificed in rituals.

Agamben's term is significant to this discussion of the social and political effects upon Indians of their assigned deviancy from an Anglo norm, in that the homo sacer figure is criminalized and isolated, and his identity and very existence are paradoxically defined *by way of his exclusion* from social and political bodies. His biological life (*zoë*) is acknowledged, but that life has no affirmative political value (*bios*).[12] This schema bifurcates the "self" along a fault-line that Pratt attempted to delineate with his prison-school. He honestly thought he could separate Indians from their Indianness. His assimilative theory reckoned that a martial, curricular drubbing would eventually cleave "the Indian" from all of his Fort Marion tribal hostage-students, and later those at Carlisle Indian School as well. What remained would be reconstituted, more civilized and human candidates of at least some social and economic value, if not political significance (Indian suffrage did not occur until 1924). Pratt thought he could foreground Natives' humanness by eradicating all traces of their intimate cultural, cognitive, and spiritual affiliation with nature. For them to remain as "Indian," to Pratt meant they would have little more significance than the "bare life" shared with fauna in the venatic wilderness. The rationale for excluding Indians from the body politic and targeting some for Pratt's prisoner roundup, was rooted in a familiar philosophical notion dating from seventeenth-century Europe, that indigenous people exist in a "state of nature." Thought to be a feral condition, the notion operates rhetorically as a conceptual space outside of civilization and history, and certainly apart from a political life of human agency and intellect. Again, this "state of nature" recalls Agamben's discussion of a biology-only, "bare life" (zoë).

Engaging Agamben's work, Caleb Smith picks up on this point of *civil death* and applies it to conditions of modern imprisonment:

> Banishing the criminal from the protective circle, the community redefines him as a creature less than human. A "wolf' belonging to the state of nature and encountered in a state of war, he is exposed to unlimited violence. Yet his human life divested of its humanity is never absolutely "a piece of animal nature without any relation to law;". . . the outlaw or bandit represents [a liminal space] between animal and man. The person "dead in law" dwells at the boundary between inside and outside, between the human and the haunting other.[13]

Smith goes on to elide this state of civil (living) death with the physical dehumanization of the prison, which he declares "is no excess or exception; it is the very premise of the American prison. The inmate in the penitentiary is not only a subject in the making; he is also a figure of exclusion and decay, inspiring both pity and terror."[14]

Within the history of colonialism these harsh terms of foreclosure have applied *doubly* to American Indians. The "hostile" conduct of so many nineteenth-century tribal Natives was really their efforts to reject settler incursions and the government's theft and fragmentation of their homelands. Their battles against America's military were waged in defense of their aboriginal lands and people. While clearly, the historical narratives of these indigenous freedom-fighters who refused colonial domination bear no resemblance to criminal accounts of Native Americans sentenced to America's modern penal system, the same, preset mark of deviancy and otherness inscribed upon American Indians adheres, uninterrupted then and now. Foucault's work again comes to bear here; the reservation system as panopticon is a literal and figurative operative of power over Indian peoples. Much like Jeremy Bentham's penitentiary architecture, the panopticon is a potent metaphor for the hegemonic mechanisms, policies, and institutions that control the discrete "cells" of reservation land and, in turn, Indian lives, all from a distant and central locus of government oversight.

In terms of power relations, the symbolism of the ledger book is itself historically ambiguous. It can be seen as merely a mundane artifact of market culture and a concept born of economic necessity to efficiently trace capital and property. Ledger books are used less today, but perhaps a modern counterpart might be the spreadsheet, listing inventories, commodities, expenditures, or the calculation of profit and loss. The ledger book had become a coveted and sometimes accessible canvas for Native drawings long before the Fort Marion prisoners began to draw their images. However, a significant part of the ledger's symbolism is also its use as a colonizing device, organizing human beings into categories, reckoning accounts that reduce their humanity to a set of particular characteristics, features, and functions that are deemed relevant to the purposes and economies of containment and control. In these uses the ledger purports to identify significant markers of the things it lists; it singles out particular features for their utility and commodification. It defines and orders the terms under which people and objects are viewed, valued, and managed. Government tribal rolls, commodity rations assigned to starving or displaced tribes, the blood-quantum calculus of the Dawes Allotment Act rolls, and, in the broader history of colonial experience, the slave ship's cargo inventory and human labor-units of the plantation, and catalogs of the work-camp—all these historical examples convene in the iconic image of the ledger book, whose semiotics in these contexts is far from morally neutral. The Dawes Roll as a mechanism of forced assimilation remains a vivid historical example of the way individual Indians' humanity was reduced to homogenizing categories that were significant to colonial imperatives of Indian removal and land seizure. Each person's name was listed across the ledger page according to: percentage of Indian blood, tribe of origin, Dawes enrollment number, name, age, and gender. Christian names were often assigned just as arbitrarily as the number sequence of the Dawes Roll.

Upon his arrival at Carlisle Indian School as one of Pratt's younger generation of drafted students, Luther Standing Bear recounts how he was required to choose a new, Christian name for himself from a random list of names written on a blackboard. He says that he chose the name "Luther," pointing at it, "as if I were about to touch an enemy."[15] Within his resolve to assert his Oglala identity, and his deliberate gesture to prophylactically isolate his newly assigned Christian name from his personal, tribal identity Ota K'Te (or Plenty Kill), is an act that anticipates an indigenous, Foucauldian understanding of exactly how the power to name operates in a colonial context. As Foucault states in "The Subject and Power":

> I would like to suggest another way to go further toward a new economy of power relations, a way which is more empirical, more directly related to our present situation, and which *implies more relations between theory and practice*. It consists of taking the forms of resistance against different forms of power as a starting point. To use another metaphor, it consists of using this resistance as a chemical catalyst so as *to bring to light power relations*, locate their position, and find out their point of application and the methods used. Rather than analyzing power from the point of view of its internal rationality, it consists of analyzing power relations through the *antagonism of strategies*.[16]

Obviously, Luther Standing Bear was not consciously placing his gesture within a historical critique of colonial power. But the creative act of affirming his tribal subjectivity in the midst of the (re)naming event is within *a range* of possible expressions that indelibly perform and demonstrate what Foucault conveys: an empirical illumination of power relations that conjugates practice with theory. After all, Standing Bear's father did send his young son to Carlisle, where "Luther" continued his Western education for several years before returning permanently to live with his people at Pine Ridge. But his unyielding act of agency in the schoolroom that first day opens a tertiary space—a space shared with many works of ledger art—that neutralizes the false interpretive choice pointed out in Melanie Benson Taylor's essay: the binary logic of expecting the art of the ledger to represent either resistance to colonial power, or complicity with it (see chapter 4). I came to witness and experience the dynamic implications of this third space during some of my work with Native American prisoners.

LEDGERS, NATIVE SELF, AND HOME

In a general but foundational way, nothing so sharply distinguishes Native American worldviews from Euro-American perspectives as their variant understandings of human relationship to land—homeland in particular. A nearly universal indigenous perspective of the self includes a thick assumption of the Native individual's *coextension* with a particular homeland—with its specific geography and its human and nonhuman inhabitants. Native subjectivity experienced in this way permeates individual and tribal identity. A Native person's sense of identity is not an arbitrary choice, but an *inalienable relationship* with a specific homeland that entails reciprocal care and obligation. Rather than experiencing land possession as an outer extension of the self through private property possession, *indigenous* land possession inheres to a palpable sense of unity with the land to which one belongs. This deeply ontological perspective shapes cultural meaning and endows metaphors of self and place with a bias toward material, corporeal references. So, in the case of Indians forced away from cherished homelands, or faced with the temporal dissolution of social structures and cultural lifeways—as in conditions faced by the prisoners at Fort Marion—a traumatic loss at this level is analogous to the somatic experience of a severed limb.

Maurice Merleau-Ponty's work in perceptions that reveal themselves through the human body as well as in the mind is useful to reckon the effects of mutilation and amputation. This phenomenon understood in physiological terms is no less affectively experienced and no less devastating when applied to the situation of aboriginal losses of land and cultural structures. In his text, *The Phenomenology of Perception*, Merleau-Ponty discusses the familiar syndrome of phantom pain following amputation; the experience of pain in a limb that no longer appears as part of the physical body. While contemporary work in neuroscience provides a new idiom through which to consider the embodied features of phantom pain, Merleau-Ponty's examples remain relevant in assessing the deep effect on Natives traumatically separated from their homelands. For American Indians this cultural severance is tantamount to losing part of the physical self, but with an interesting inversion. In the case of clinical amputation, the loss is visible to an outside observer, while the pain to the aggrieved is often felt in the absent limb. In the case of Natives' rupture from their sacred homelands, the human body may appear to be intact, but the subjective, nostalgic pain is experienced out of sight, inwardly, as if a vital body part has been hacked away. Merleau-Ponty's ideas lay out the symbolic dilemma:

> [The phantom limb] is the representation of an actual absence. . . . Proust can recognize the death of his grandmother, yet without losing her *as long as he can keep her on the horizon of his life*. [Similarly, the] phantom arm is not a representation of the arm, but the ambivalent presence of an arm. The *refusal of mutilation* in the case of the phantom limb . . . [is] not a deliberate decision and does not take place at the level of positing consciousness . . . after considering various possibilities. . . . This phenomenon, distorted equally by physiological and psychological explanations is . . . *understood in the perspective of being-in-the-world*. What it is in us which refuses mutilation and disablement is an "*I*"committed to a certain physical and inter-human world, who continues to tend toward his world despite handicaps and amputations and who, to this extent, does not recognize [the amputation] *de jure*.[17]

Merleau-Ponty's analogy here illustrates this category of loss as not merely contemplated loss, but loss that affects one's very *being and way of being* in the physical world. An ineluctable tropism toward *wholeness* persists in the amputee's consciousness and therefore in practice, even after the loss. Natives displaced from their homelands, reacting much as the human dismembered body, refuse disunity with a sense of this extended "self" that deeply identifies with place. The self of Native identity is constituted in land-based knowledge, local phenomena, aesthetic form, enduring place names and stories, traditional commissaries and apothecaries, and sacred fastnesses. In the face of losses and separations in all these categories, the desire to keep integral a relationship to homelands "on the horizon of life" abides, often ferociously, and this urge for completeness is felt no less for lost homelands than it would be for a lost limb. The pain consists of an embodied memory of lost wholeness. The locus of pain persists at the intersection of spiritual synecdoche and soma.

Philosopher, Alva Noë, explores the theory of perception and the philosophy of mind. His research interests have drawn him to the phantom-limb pain phenomenon and how relief might be found. He notes that the challenge is in addressing an absence or loss that manifests spectrally in both physical and perceptual ways. He and a colleague speculated a therapy for the condition that was later evidenced in experiments by neuroscientist, V. S. Ramachandran. The experiments revealed that "the use of *mirrors* to create sensory feedback could provide a therapy for phantom-limb pain. . . . What Ramachandran and others have done is allow somebody who experiences phantom-limb discomfort to look at a mirror and move his *good* arm but get visual feedback as if he is moving the *bad* [absent] arm. They find that through moving the good arm it's possible to work out [pain] in what is in fact an absent arm."[18]

So, how might we translate these ideas into a language useful to the traumatic wounds of American Indians' cultural and historic losses, and the visual impact and potential of the ledger's legacy? In one sense, the men I came to know during the ledger project in these two prisons were seeking a mnemonic for tribal identity and community. But I eventually realized that their reward for embracing the project was less an occasion for nostalgic musings of a distant tribal history than it was a poignant affirmation of their humanity and homeland, especially from behind the thick stone walls of confinement that would deny them both. The phantom-pain mirror remedy holds a strong metaphor for the ledger's important function for Natives—on either side of the reservation boundary, or even across the prison wall. By way of the now-archival ledger images created and consumed by those first Native warrior-artists in Pratt's school, through ledger-inspired art by many contemporary Native artists, or through the creative work of today's Native prisoner-artists, losses can be addressed—(re)peopled and (re) storied into Native subjectivity and consciousness. In this way, the ledger may operate like Ramachandran's mirror device. And although the process cannot recover the material losses of the past, nor palliate the anguish of broken lives, it can inaugurate an imaginative, "third space" of perception in which the narratives of history, experience, and vision nourish Native subjectivity—beyond survival and toward thrivance.

A number of Native prisoners from New York's Auburn and Cayuga prisons opted to create essays, poems, songs, and stories, rather than drawings, for their contributions to the Art Across Walls project. I'll conclude with a passage written by someone I will call, "Manny," a Lakota inmate "doing time" in New York State, too far and costly a distance for his family in South Dakota to travel for visits. "Manny" speaks eloquently about shared humanity across cultures, across individual histories, and most emphatically across prison walls. The passages appear here as written, without the intrusive editorial designator [*sic*] to point out errors in spelling and grammar. The corrections would not improve on the meaning or spirit of the words. This text is his ledger:

> **"How I Keep the Strength of 'Our' Hoop in this Iron House of 'There's'"**
> To my little brothers and sister's out-there where life is so beautiful and sacred. Even though you may feel its not so! . . . Behind these walls where life is dark and ugly, the sun still shines, the wind still blows, the birds fly over-head, the insect's still buzz. Even some-thing so ugly as a cockroach, which is one of the oldest living life's on our Mother keeps me stronge. I think of all the ways people have tried to kill, to wipe out, exterminate, "like us," them. And there still here. How stronge a breath the Mother, the Great Spirit blew into such a stronge little ugly creature. . . .When I walk this Iron House yard and see a sparrow or crow fly over. Or look down and see a small ant or spider. To look at a piece of grass growing or a weed. I feel the sun on my face, the wind in my hair, the rain, the snow. Without a doubt in my mind, my hart, my body and my spirit I know I am one with our Great Spirit Grandfather and our Mother. Yes, these people denie me some of our Sacred Item's that would make the feeling on Oneness even stronger. But that Oneness will never leave this Brother as long as theres breath in this body. And little brothers and Sisters, it's the same sun shining on your faces, the same wind in your hair! The same rain and snow! And from my Hart to Yours, the same great love and care and strengthe. Reach out, reach within You'll feel them both our Mother's, our Great Spirit Grandfather's for us there Children!

Despite his prison confinement, Manny's narrative voice ascends from a "third space" of perception that nineteenth-century ledgers helped open. This outcome is a far cry from what Pratt had in mind for his prisoner-warriors when he first handed them colored pencils and paper. But it offers promise for the wholeness of American Indian consciousness and, in turn, for tribal restoration even across daunting boundaries—consequences that Pratt's well-intentioned plan so ardently sought to destroy.

NOTES

Vera Palmer thanks the trustees of the Robinson-Appel Award Committee for funding all art materials used by the inmates of the Native American Prisoner Support Program to create artwork for the gallery exhibit "Art Across Walls: Expressions of Native Amerian Prisoners" in Cornell University's Willard Straight Hall in April 1999.

1. Standing Bear, *Land of the Spotted Eagle*, 230–32.
2. Viola, *Warrior Artists*, 14–15.
3. Pember, "Graduating to Prison."
4. All names of the prisoners who participated in the Native American Prisoner Support Program have been changed, in this essay, to protect their privacy.
5. Basso, *Wisdom Sits in Places*.
6. Again, the men's names in the art program at the Auburn and Cayuga prisons have been changed in this essay to protect their identities. While they are prohibited from making individual profit in an outside market from their artwork produced while incarcerated, some of them opted to keep originals of their work with them inside the prison, as a memento of the project.
7. Foucault, "The Great Confinement," 124–25. Italics added for emphasis.
8. Locke, *Second Treatise of Government*, 25–26, 29.
9. Leahy, *They Called It Madness*.
10. Mama, "Enslaving the Soul of the Other," 17–42. Italics added for emphasis.
11. Ross, *Inventing the Savage*, 16–17. Italics added for emphasis.
12. Heller-Roazen, *Homo Sacer*.
13. Smith, *Prison and the American Imagination*, 30.
14. Ibid., 29.
15. Standing Bear, *My People, The Sioux*, 137.
16. Foucault, "Subject and Power," 208. Italics added for emphasis.
17. Merleau-Ponty, *Phenomenology of Perception*, 93–94. Italics added for emphasis.
18. Noë, "Life Is the Way the Animal Is in the World." Italics added for emphasis.

CHAPTER 7

Reconstructing History from a Fragmented Past

JOYCE M. SZABO

KNOWLEDGE OF HISTORY IS ALWAYS fragmentary, full of glaring absences. The Mark Lansburgh collection of Plains drawings illustrates yet another kind of fragmented past, as the individual drawings exist detached from their context as parts of complete books. They are also divorced from their original uses within the societies that made them. Even Fort Marion drawings, created when their artists were separated from homes and families, had additional cultural associations formed in Florida from which these pages have been disconnected.

All of these drawings, whether dating from the pre-reservation era, the Fort Marion confinement of mid-1875 to mid-1878, or the reservation period, were made in difficult circumstances. This is most apparent for those created during the Florida incarceration, but it applies equally to works from the period of the restriction of American Indians to reservations. Even drawings created as part of the pre-reservation lifestyle were made under the duress of fighting an expanding variety of enemies in order to maintain control of lifeways and homelands. Information recorded in Plains drawings was vital to their creators and users, and attempts to unlock some of those diverse messages can allow contemporary viewers greater understanding of a fragmented history. Interrogating multiple sources of evidence—some visual, some written, and some oral—can add new meanings to Plains drawings and make apparent at least some of their complexity.

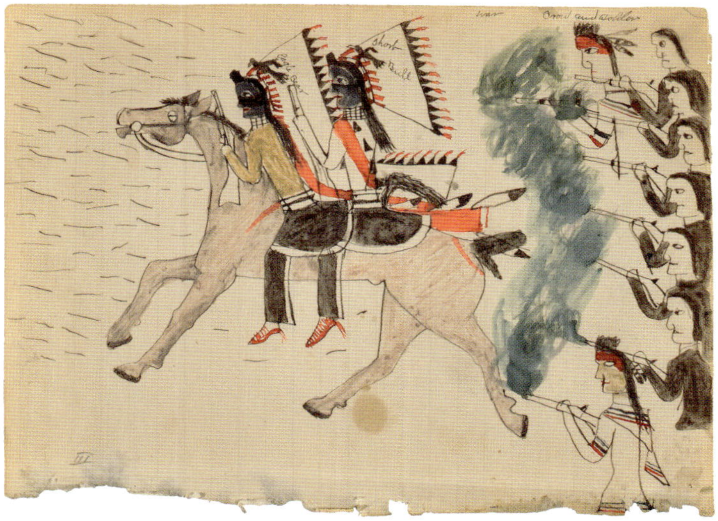

FIGURE 7.1
Short Bull (Tatanka Ptecela), Lakota (Sioux), c. 1845–1915, Untitled *["Short Bull" and "Eagle Bear" fleeing gunfire from Apsáalooke (Crow) scouts and U.S. soldiers]*, c. 1885–90, Hood Museum of Art (plate 124).

FORT MARION: VARIED INTERPRETATIONS AND THE LANSBURGH COLLECTION

Many of the Lansburgh drawings encourage immediate appreciation as works of art. Artistic skill and experimental nature, sure draftsmanship, and careful attention to detail are clear. Others, while not as meticulously rendered, are works of art with emphases and affective power revealed in different ways. The strength of the Short Bull drawings from the reservation era is clear (figure 7.1) even if the delicacy of drawing differs from the kind of precision found in some other examples.

Only 15 of the 144 works in the Lansburgh collection are from Fort Marion. Drawings from the Florida prison have received extensive attention from the collective body of people who have done research on Plains drawings. Fort Marion is a distinct period in the history of ledger-style art. Its parameters are clear; the prisoners arrived in Florida in May 1875 and left three years later. While no one knows when the first drawings were made there, even the full three years offer a seemingly manageable time frame. In addition, the number of potential artists at the fort was limited. If all of the men drew, the coterie of artists would, at the maximum, have been 70. The Cheyenne chief Grey Beard was killed during the journey east when he tried to escape from the train on which the prisoners traveled.[1] One of the original 72 prisoners was a woman, and there are no known drawings by her. The lone Caddo and nine Comanche prisoners apparently also did not draw. There is also no firm evidence that the older men drew. This would certainly follow Cheyenne cultural practices, in which younger warriors recorded their battle prowess to help establish their positions, while older, recognized leaders, especially chiefs like Eagle Head and Heap of Birds who were both exiled in Florida, would not. Thirty-three Cheyennes were taken as prisoners and thus constitute the largest potential body of artists, so the age distinction is an important one; the Cheyenne prisoners whose birth dates appear on government lists ranged in age at the time of their incarceration from 53 to 20.[2] The vast majority of currently known Cheyenne Fort Marion drawings were created by men in their twenties and the first half of their thirties. Cultural practices among the Arapahos concerning the creation of battle exploit imagery are not as clear, but only two Arapahos went to Florida. Kiowa practices would have a potentially greater impact on Fort Marion art because there were 27 Kiowa prisoners.[3] The Kiowa artists who created the majority of known Fort Marion drawings were in their twenties. However, discussion of who created drawings at what ages is impossible without known examples of pre-reservation Kiowa battle imagery, and the association of younger men with drawing and painting may not have applied to Kiowa culture.

The Fort Marion environment and the art created there are both extremely complex. In that complexity rich possibilities for interpretation occur. Viewers of these drawings undoubtedly feel that they can *know more* about them and the forces at work that encouraged their creation than they can about drawings created on the plains, whether during the pre-reservation or reservation eras. Fort Marion drawings are unique documents in many ways. Prisoners made them, at least in part, for sale. Drawings were created while the men were incarcerated and isolated from their homes, families, and friends. They reflect memories of the life from which the inmate-artists were separated, and they record some aspects of the new lives they experienced in Florida. Richard Pratt's autobiography and personal papers provide further information. Although limited in number, there are also letters and recorded comments by some Fort Marion prisoners after they returned to their homes. Descendants, of course, have many family memories.

Fort Marion drawings are so multilayered that it seems almost impossible to go wrong in whatever approaches we take. Because the prisoner-artists were removed from their cultures and placed in another world, issues of colonialism and acculturation are apparently closer to the fore, and we seek their presence in the drawings. Likewise, we look for evidence of resistance to that colonialism and acculturation. Here Gerald Vizenor's sometimes overused term "survivance" is clearly applicable, as survival, too, was paramount at Fort Marion; drawing was a means of survival as well as resistance.[4]

Ohettoint's shark hunting scene is intriguing because it connects the prisoners to their former lives as hunters on the plains, even though the animal pursued is vastly different from those generally found in reservation ledger art or in the few examples of pre-reservation drawings that depict hunts; even in drawings made at Fort Marion, hunters more frequently pursue buffalo. Ohettoint's drawing is a syncretic image because of the way in which the men are dressed, as if they were still free as hunters on the plains, but their prey is a strange new one indicative of their lives in Florida. The non-Native man presented here is probably not Richard Pratt, because the prisoners were extremely conscious of status and social position; Pratt appears, in their rather frequent representations of him, dressed in military uniform with markers of his rank. This man may be George Fox, the interpreter at the fort, or Mr. Pacetti, the man who took the men to Mantanzas Inlet to troll for sharks (see plate 49).[5]

Ohettoint's drawing of the lighthouse on Anastasia Island is also captivating for its bold, graphic presentation of the black-and-white striped lighthouse, the lighthouse keeper's home, and the man on the platform above who has either intentionally or unintentionally let his umbrella fall. We feel comfortable suggesting that this might be a whimsical drawing, given its apparent focus. Alternatively, it could illustrate an experiment in aerodynamics. It is also a unique representation among extant drawings that depict the lighthouse the men saw daily from Saint Augustine (see plate 48).

Some of the other Lansburgh Fort Marion drawings appear to offer less opportunity for interpretation. Ohettoint's two views of men on horseback and men behind a tipped sunshade are interesting compositions. They potentially reflect new ways of visualizing space that the men encountered in Florida, such as house façades with balconies that allowed people to stand on another level, elevated above the people and actions below. But these drawings are not narrative like most other Fort Marion drawings in the collection. It is an inability to draw stories

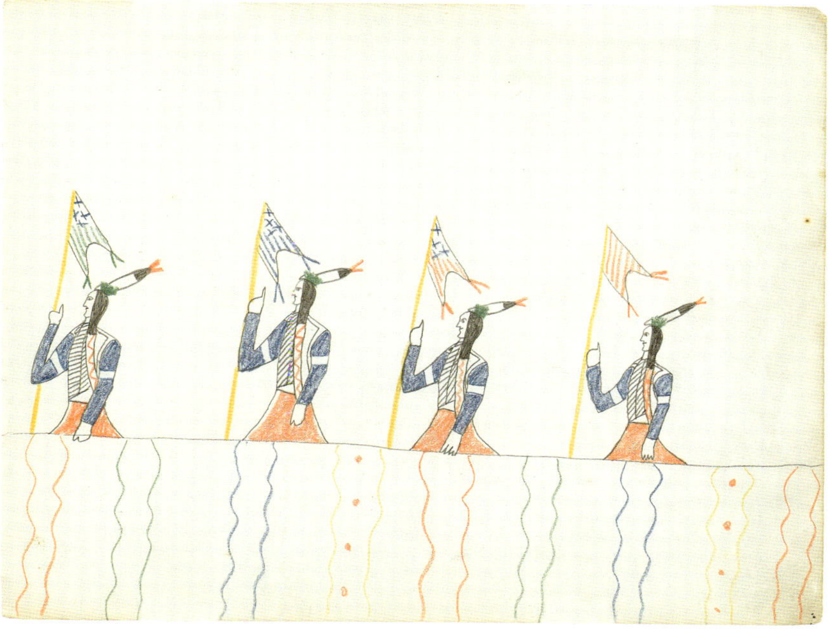

FIGURE 7.2
Ohettoint, Kiowa, 1852–1934, *Untitled [Kiowa warriors in procession],* mid-1875–mid-1878, Hood Museum of Art (plate 50).

from these images that makes them less accessible, but their inclusion of flags or pennants does offer potential for further analysis (see figure 7.2 and plates 50 and 51).

Flags had played important roles for Native people as diplomatic gifts presented by various non-Native delegations well before the nineteenth century, and they continued to be used in this manner during the era leading to the Southern Plains wars.[6] Although not consistently read as signs of peaceful intentions by the army,[7] flags were used by various Plains people to indicate neutrality. They were also seen by some as signs of power, appearing in medicine bundles or worn as protection in battle.[8] Flags were, of course, captured in battle and used as indications of prowess, even employed in the same way coup sticks were—to touch and, therefore, achieve dominion over enemies. That flags appear in great numbers and in various art forms during the 1870s, both at Fort Marion and on the plains, was probably influenced by the July 4, 1876, Centennial, when a profusion of flags appeared throughout the nation. Flag designs are also graphically interesting, but the continued appearance of flags in Fort Marion art may suggest that some of the connections to power and battle known from life on the plains continued to be shown in Florida in ways not readily apparent to non-Native viewers.

Other drawings like Chief Killer's view of a classroom suggest multiple narratives. One involves the text that appears in various places on the drawing.[9] Both the choice of words, such as "God," with their indication of acculturation, and the names or signatures of various prisoners in the classroom raise additional questions. While the classroom scene offers striking evidence of colonialism and attempts at assimilation, it also relays other messages. Recording their names was a way for the prisoners not only to demonstrate their success in mastering some aspects of the English language, but also to declare their identity in a new system, one now open to them as a substitute for others impossible to maintain in Florida, at least through obvious external means. Chief Killer's drawing includes several recognizable names and one that has yet to be deciphered; the names of Howling Wolf, Bear's Heart, White Horse, White Bear, Chief Killer, Little Medicine, and Bad Eye appear. The inclusion of Bad Eye, a Kiowa prisoner, is perplexing (see plate 57).

Bad Eye, an established warrior and Kiowa chief, was also known as Bird Chief. If the ages are correct as listed on official documents from the 1870s, Bad Eye was 43 at the time of his imprisonment. No known drawings have come to light that have been attributed to any of Bad Eye's age group, yet an inscription inside a book of drawings now at the Fairbanks Museum and Planetarium in St. Johnsbury, Vermont, reads "Made by Bad Eye Kiowa." The book of drawings has been at the museum since 1917, when the daughter of the museum's founder gave it to the museum.[10] There is no evidence that it came from Fort Marion except for the tantalizing association of Bad Eye's name. This book differs in several ways from the majority of known Fort Marion books. First, while it is a relatively small-scale book, measuring 11.5 by 8.5 inches,

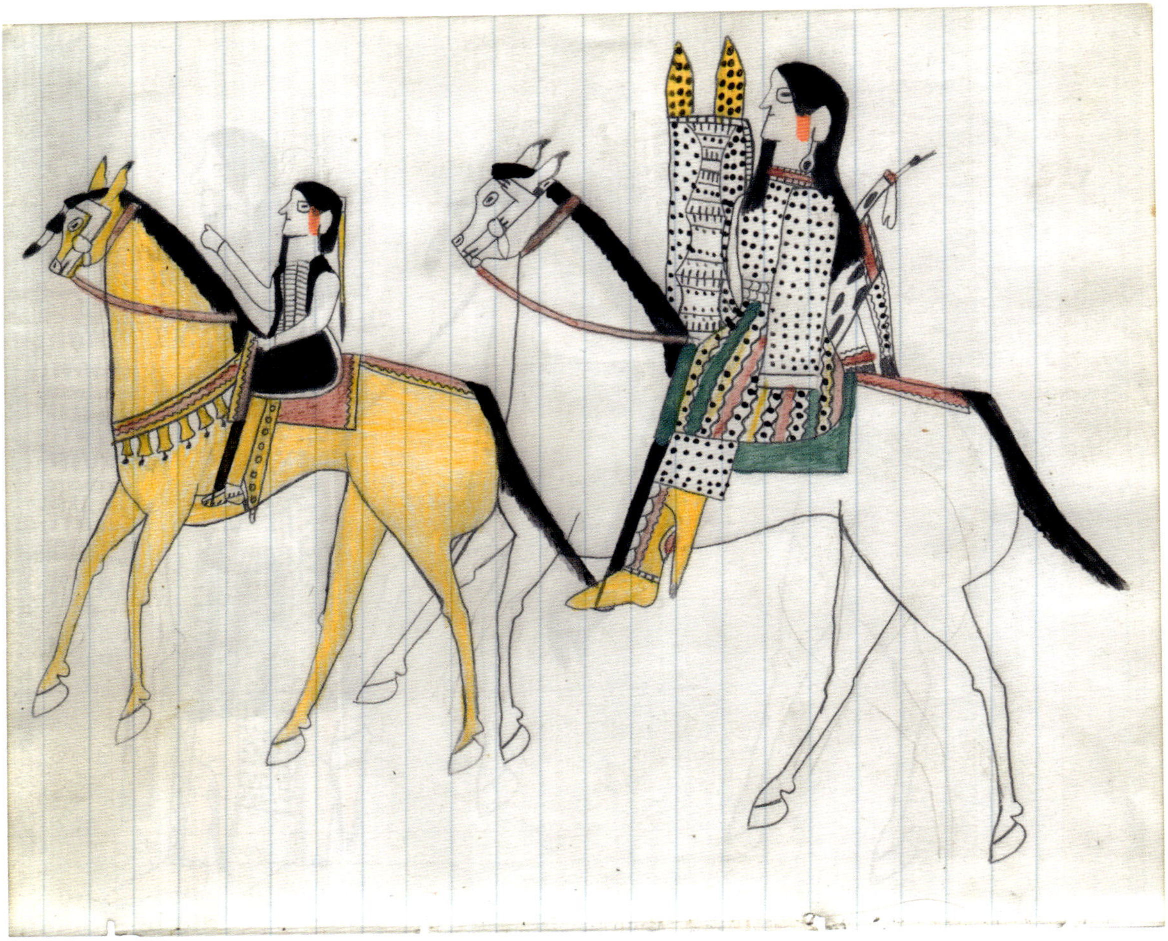

FIGURE 7.3
Bad Eye, Kiowa, p. 17. Fairbanks Museum and Planetarium (plate 15, https://plainsledgerart.org).

it is an extremely large book in the number of pages; Fort Marion books typically have 16 or 18 pages at the most, but there are 57 drawings here. And it is a book of lined paper, not the kind of unlined drawing book that the men generally used at Fort Marion (figure 7.3). While there are exceptions, a book as large as that attributed to Bad Eye is not the norm. Questions remain, then, about whether the drawings are from Fort Marion or if they were even made by a former Fort Marion prisoner.

However, the Fort Marion inmate Bad Eye seems to have defied the basic suppositions people have had about life at the prison in another way. Conventional discussion of the Florida period holds that the students who were learning to read and write at the fort were the younger prisoners; if the names or signatures on Chief Killer's drawing are accurate, then Bad Eye did not fit this convenient profile. While he was 43 at the time of his incarceration, the other prisoners named in the drawing were much younger: Howling Wolf was 27, Chief Killer 28, Bear's Heart 26, White Horse 30, and White Bear 25. Little Medicine, the closest in age to Bad Eye, was only 35, eight years Bad Eye's junior. Men from multiple Plains societies are identified in Chief Killer's drawing, but if we compare the only two named Kiowas, White Horse who was 30 and Bad Eye at 43, the same age discrepancy is apparent. There are various other figures depicted without names, and thus specific identification of students in the classroom is not definitive, but Chief Killer's representation does locate Bad Eye within a space previously denied to older prisoners.[11]

The prolific reservation-era Kiowa artist Silver Horn (1860–1940) is credited with creating more than a thousand illustrations from the 1870s to 1920, many depicting Kiowa trickster stories and genre scenes.[12] If Silver Horn did continue to draw until approximately 1920, he would have been an active artist until he was sixty. Some of Silver Horn's reservation-era works offer the closest comparison

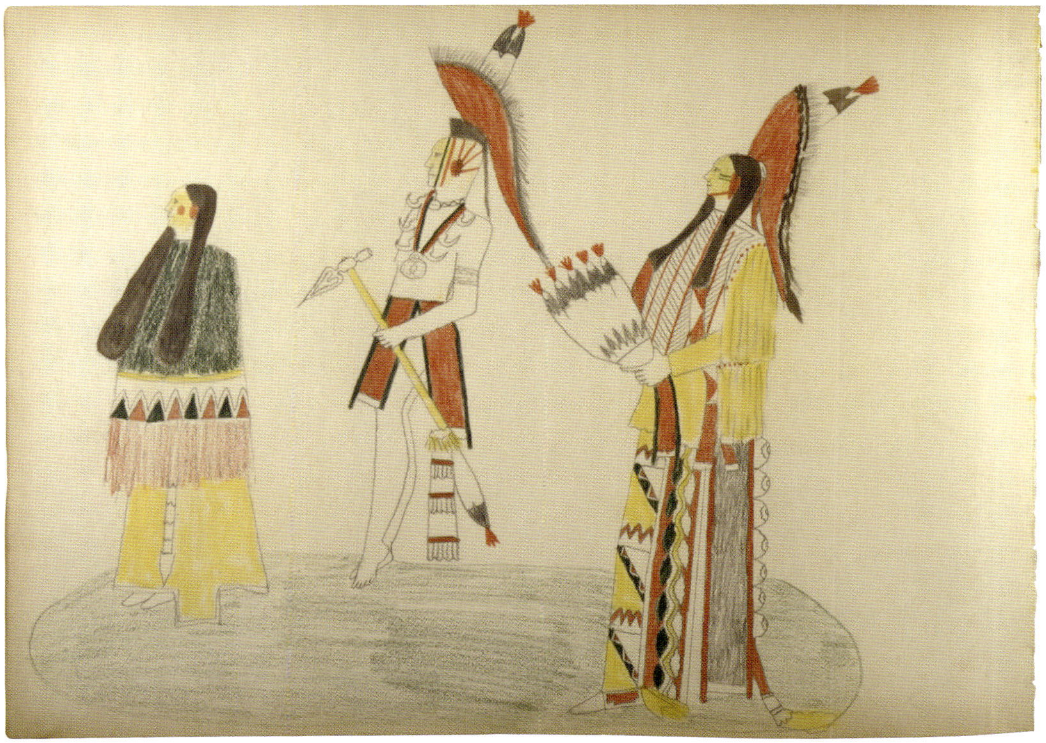

FIGURE 7.4
Silver Horn (1860–1940), Kiowa, p. 54. Field Museum of Natural History, Chicago 67719.4.

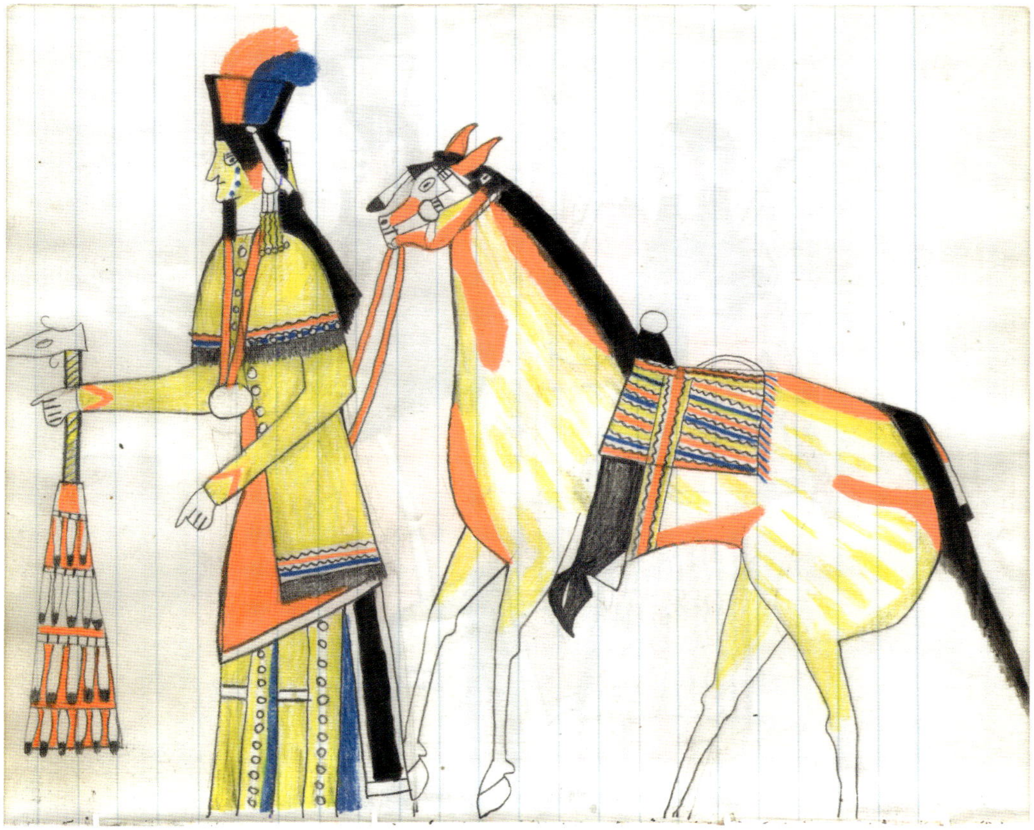

FIGURE 7.5
Bad Eye, Kiowa, p. 27. Fairbanks Museum and Planetarium (plate 25, https://plainsledgerart.org).

to those in the Fairbanks Museum's Bad Eye book (figure 7.4). Yet, the Bad Eye drawings differ dramatically from most other Plains drawings, both those created at Fort Marion and those from the plains. Bad Eye's focus was heavily on the activities of women, not to the exclusion of men but certainly far more than in most ledger drawings. These are more than courting scenes, although various examples of that subject do appear. He rendered painstaking details of clothing and other objects such as cradles (figure 7.3). Women hunt, they carry men's shields, guns, and warrior society paraphernalia, and they engage in other activities with men, women, and children. In addition, his depictions of non-Kiowa people are also startling in their intricacy (figure 7.5). If the Fairbanks Museum book is from Fort Marion, it is unique in many ways.

Fort Marion drawings have been treated as rich sources of many kinds of information. While ledger drawings created on the plains continue to be mined for ethnographic evidence, historic alignments with other types of records, and artists' identities, Fort Marion art is explored from angles not frequently pursued for pre-reservation and reservation-era drawings. Art from the three-year Florida period has been ripe for its indications of assimilation, evidence of colonialism, and suggestions of sovereignty, but cannot those concepts also be posited for drawings found in the Lansburgh collection that were created on the plains? To do so requires examining other sets of information or finding different ways in which to formulate questions.

EXPANDING THE HISTORIC RECORD

While the identification of specific people and events may not be possible in many Plains drawings, there are some concrete approaches to gathering such information. Inscriptions can be questioned, and the leads they provide tracked. In the event that the entire, or nearly entire, book of drawings from which individual pages in the Lansburgh collection came has been published, the facsimile may provide additional information to help interpret specific images. Drawings from other books that appear to depict the same subjects or individuals offer another possibility. As creations from specific times and places, pre-reservation and reservation drawings can be interrogated concerning why certain subjects were explored and why others apparently were not. The latter is, of course, an open-ended problem, because we do not have the complete corpus of drawings that were originally created before the reservation era, after the enforcement of the reservation system, or even during the three-year Fort Marion confinement; we can only discuss what we have, using the extant drawings as a microcosm of what the whole might have been.

While the Lansburgh drawings exist as single sheets separated from their original context, the collection does include works that came from the same books, allowing us to examine them as part of a larger whole. Howling Wolf's drawings and several others by unknown artists came from the same small drawing book that, given its inscription, was probably filled with drawings just prior to the Fort Marion exile. Elsewhere, I have suggested a date of 1874 or early 1875 for the drawings, because handwriting within the book included the name Robert Allen Guthrie of Topeka, Kansas, and the date 1874.[13] Guthrie's educational experience was also recorded: "six weeks scoolen to Ben Shoemake, two weeks to Mrs. Sharp in Topeka, Kansas, and one month to Mr. Burns in Great Bend, Kansas." An additional inscription notes that the Guthries moved to Indian Territory.[14]

The small, 4-by-6-inch drawing book offers the opportunity to suggest how one warrior artist might have learned from other men sharing the same volume. Howling Wolf's drawings in the Lansburgh collection are earlier than works the artist made that now reside at the Allen Memorial Art Museum of Oberlin College.[15] Drawings in the Oberlin book reflect a practiced, skilled artist who drew well-proportioned horses and figures (figure 7.6). A caption identifies the figure in one of the Lansburgh images as Howling Wolf (see plate 34). While this is no proof that Howling Wolf was the artist of the drawing, his often repeated manner of representing horses' heads and human faces makes that identification secure. The Lansburgh self-portrait must predate the Oberlin drawings, given the elongated nature of the horse and the relative scale of the standing figure and the horse. The artist's portrayal of human and animal figures changed dramatically as he gained more experience drawing.[16] Howling Wolf's images in the Lansburgh collection came from a book that included the work of perhaps six different artists, at least one of whom was a particularly adept draftsman. Sharing a drawing book, whether during war expeditions or later, allowed men the opportunity to observe how others rendered their images and, undoubtedly, to learn from other warriors with whom they went to war or those who were members of the same warrior society. Books such as these were opened and shared, and stories were told about the events depicted, with the drawings functioning as ongoing history.

Artistic individuality is apparent in ledger art, within Southern Cheyenne or Arapaho cultures, for example, but clear visual evidence for cultural styles of representation

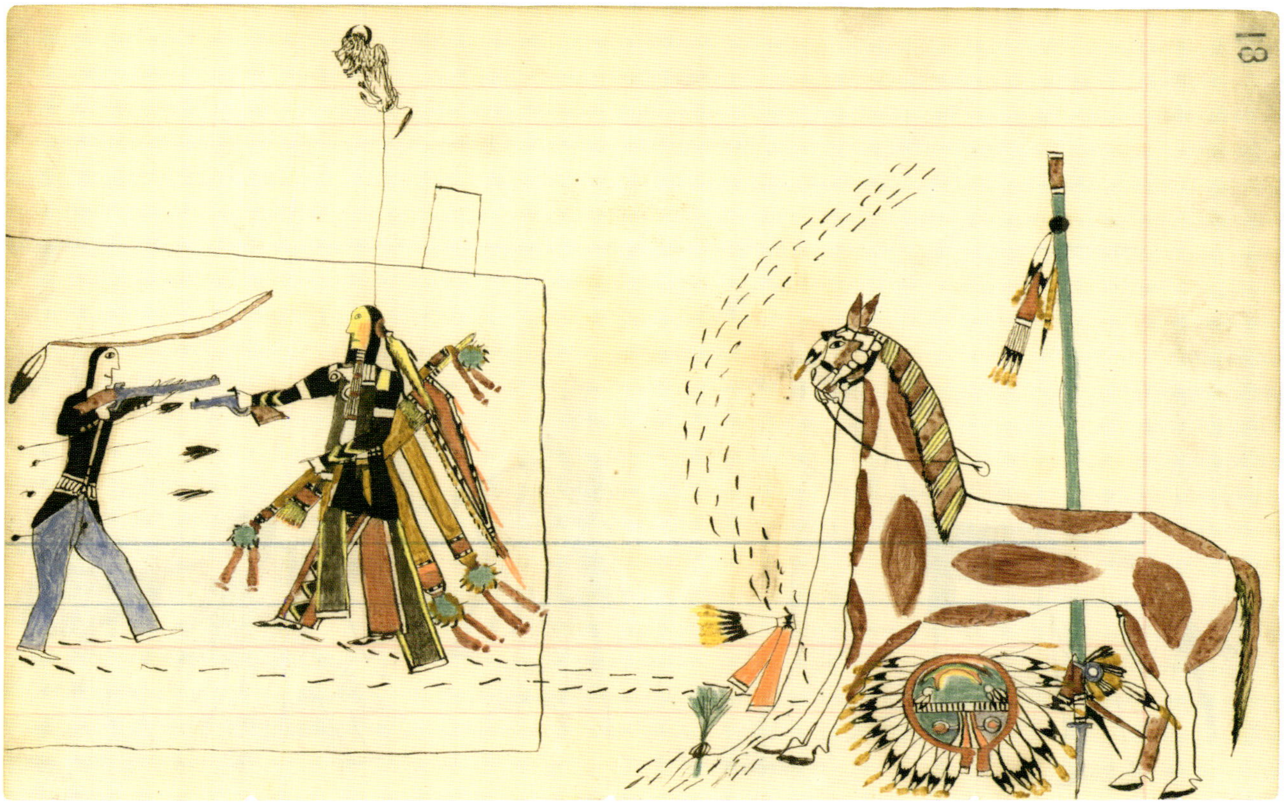

FIGURE 7.6
Howling Wolf (1849–1927), Southern Cheyenne, c. 1874–75. p. 18. Allen Memorial Art Museum, Oberlin College, 04.1180.

is lacking. Choice of subjects may be a different matter. Extant drawings evince a comparative abundance of courting scenes among Cheyenne artists, both reservation-era works and those drawn at Fort Marion; there are, however, more Cheyenne drawing books known than those from any other Southern Plains group. Cheyenne and Arapaho men also shared various books. While such Arapaho drawings are not as frequent, they, too, at least during the reservation era, provide numerous representations of courting, as do examples of Lakota ledger drawings. Kiowa artists drew courting images, particularly in Florida, but, given the lack of Kiowa works on paper prior to the Fort Marion exile and relatively few examples afterward (with some notable exceptions like the Kiowa artist Silver Horn and the Bad Eye drawings previously discussed) observations concerning Kiowa courting images are difficult if not impossible.

Many Lansburgh drawings suggest, on first examination, that they were made during the reservation era. The diversity of subject matter, a large number of courting scenes, and some ceremonial representations argue for a date later than the active years of the Plains wars. However, most of these subjects, by themselves, are no guarantee of the date of creation. This diversity of subjects and a lack of concrete dates offer another line of investigation concerning the potential reasons for the creation of these non war-like images and the expansion of subject matter portrayed. As Michael Jordan argues in chapter two, wealth was an important indicator of social position for many Plains groups during the late nineteenth and early twentieth centuries. Representing oneself with signs of wealth became, if not as important as battle prowess, then a close second. Among some Plains cultures, men would not be considered for membership in specific warrior societies if they did not have this kind of wealth, not only because moving through the society's organizational system required gifting to receive new knowledge, but also because a man who did not have wealth to give away was considered lazy. Such a man would have been seen as unconcerned with bettering his position and would not be able to be generous to the community at large, as was expected of leaders in warrior societies.[17]

Inquiries about what Plains warrior-artists represented and what they did not are central to a wider understanding

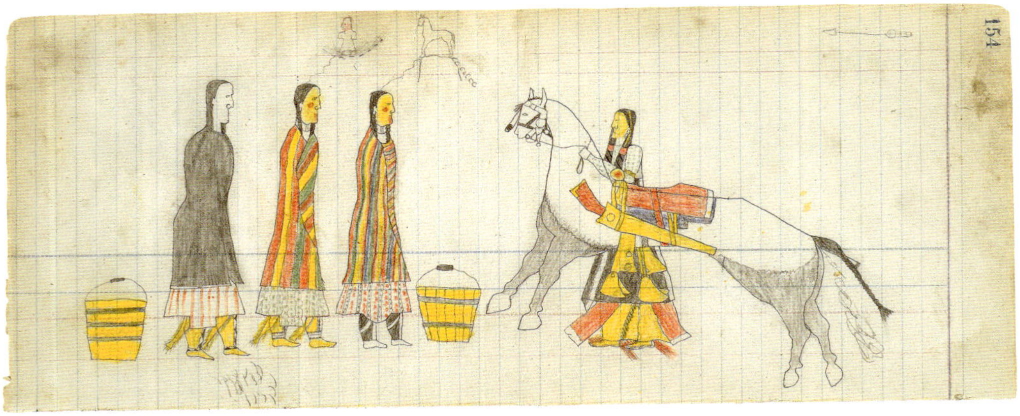

FIGURE 7.7
Unknown artist, Southern Tsistsistas (Cheyenne), active late nineteenth century, ***Untitled [Three Tsistsistas (Cheyenne) women and a man and a horse]***, c. 1874–75, Hood Museum of Art (plate 27).

of Plains drawings. However, these questions are, in an overall sense, impossible to pursue. Not only do we have a limited number of extant drawings from which to explore ideas of inclusion and exclusion, but the very manner in which these separate pages came to the collectors offers another stumbling block. Collectors collect what appeals to them, what is available, and what they can afford. Mark Lansburgh's collection is, therefore, idiosyncratic. The subjects to which he was drawn include those that would be of obvious interest for collectors of this material—battle and hunting scenes. Genre subjects are also here, of course, particularly colorful dances and courting scenes.

EXPANDING INTERPRETATIONS OF RESERVATION DRAWINGS

Yet, if we take the Lansburgh collection as representative of the larger whole of ledger art, we can ask what is here and what is not, why these particular courting subjects are present, and why other subjects are absent. The answer to these questions may be, at least in part, related to the aftermath of the Plains wars. This goes beyond the fact that there were no more battles in which young men could prove themselves and that the subject matter depicted in ledger art expanded to fill a void; battle images did continue to be drawn during the reservation era. But there are additional possible effects that stem from how the wars affected Plains cultures. One significant result of the wars was a change in the ratio of Plains men to women. The overall populations of Plains tribes diminished not only from the diseases that had long been rampant but also due to fatalities from battles with both Native and non-Native enemies. Certainly women and children died, but more Plains men were lost. Some statistics underscore that the reduced number of available men encouraged the expansion of polygamy during the reservation era among some cultures, as Loretta Fowler's recent in-depth study of Southern Arapaho history demonstrates.[18] In Arapaho and various other Plains cultures a man, should he be of sufficient means, might marry second and even third wives, often the sister or sisters of his first wife. Comparable practices were in place for the Cheyennes prior to the end of the Plains wars and a similar loss of male population must have impacted marriage patterns. John Moore's examination of 1880 census records for the Cheyennes indicates that the number of men with multiple wives was then roughly equivalent to the number of men who would have been council chiefs, thus underscoring the need for men in such marital relationships to have both means and social position.[19] Fowler also records that, among the Arapaho people, women in polygamous or even in monogamous relationships often married older men during the early years of reservation life, again perhaps due to altered demographics and more limited access to wealth.

Moore notes that the 1880 census, occurring shortly after the end of the Plains wars, was one taken before polygamy became a major issue for non-Natives who exercised some measure of control over Native people on reservations.[20] Agents and missionaries discouraged polygamy, but Native people resisted forced change on reservations and some men and women found ways around prohibitions. At the same time, Arapaho leaders in the first years after the Plains wars pursued a less confrontational path, adhering in good faith to what they saw as treaty agreements even if the United States government and Army did not.[21] Because agents saw the Arapaho leadership as more cooperative than their more confrontational Cheyenne neighbors, they tended to look the other way when Arapahos continued to practice multiple marriages.[22] For the Arapahos, as may well have been the case for some of their Southern Plains neighbors, the imbalance in numbers of men and women made polygamy a necessity during the early reservation years.[23]

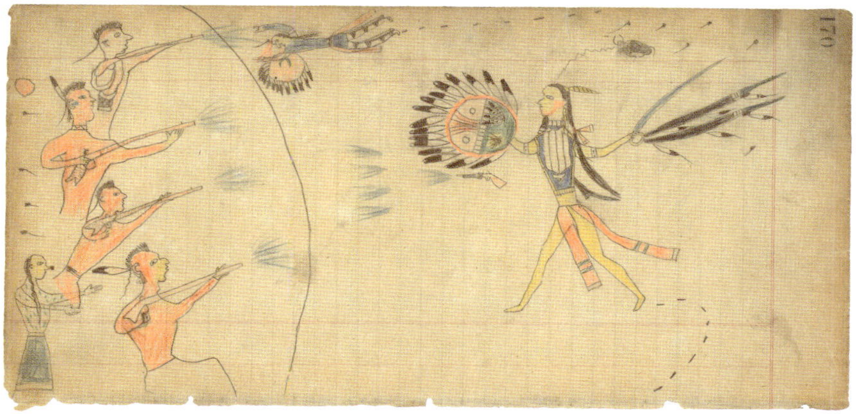

FIGURE 7.8
Unknown artist, Tsistsistas (Cheyenne) and/or Inunaina (Arapaho), active late nineteenth century, ***Untitled [A warrior battles enemies while a fellow warrior has fallen],*** late nineteenth century, Hood Museum of Art (plate 79).

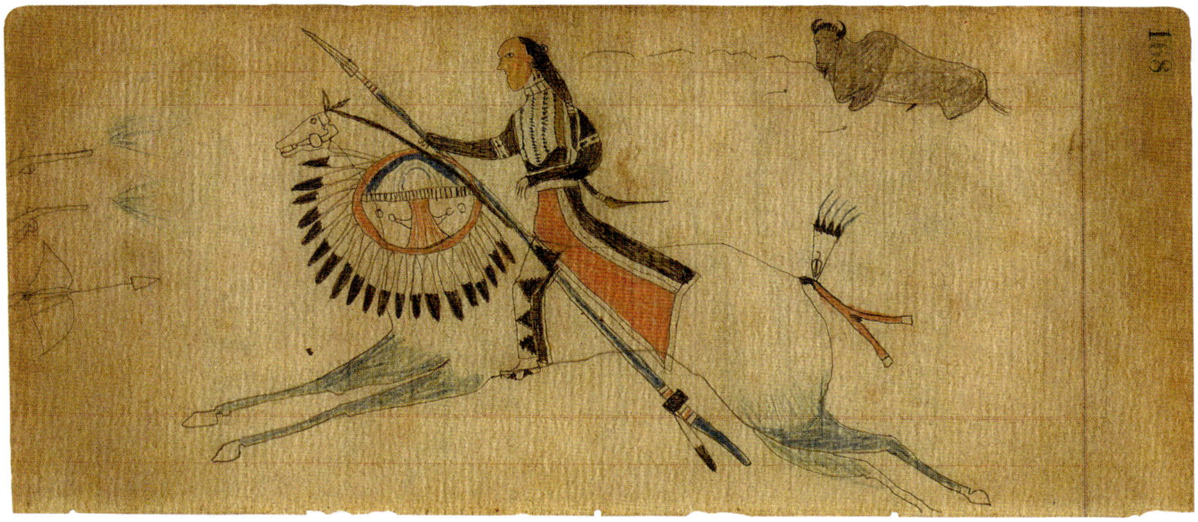

FIGURE 7.9
Unknown artist ("Frank Henderson Ledger"), Southern Arapaho/Southern Cheyenne, 1881–1882. ***Untitled***, p. 168. Morning Star Gallery, Santa Fe, New Mexico.

Representations of men who might be courting two women simultaneously, then, may be the result of a basic demographic fact (see figure 7.7). Even in times of increased poverty that came with reservation life, courting required goods to bring to the woman's family. Horses were primary sources of wealth, however other presents were also given. Horse ownership was more limited with reservation life, but men of standing—chiefs and their children as well as leaders of warrior societies—still had horses. Men depicted providing attention to multiple women are probably from those leadership groups, because they could afford to successfully court more than one woman. While few extant drawings depict men with cattle, these animals might also be used as part of a successful courting gift; younger men who had been to school and worked well, in the eyes of the school superintendents, were often given cattle as a sign of approval.[24] Returning students could, then, bring home an alternate indication of wealth.

CELEBRATING RENOWNED WARRIORS

Male fatalities in the Plains wars also would have left a smaller potential pool of warrior-artists to draw their own battle exploits, and whether a man killed in battle could be represented by someone else may have varied by culture. At least among some societies, a warrior might render his own battle exploits during his lifetime or he might ask others to do so for him. Looking for representations of the same individuals by different warrior-artists offers another potential area of investigation.

The Lansburgh collection includes two drawings from the "Vincent Price Ledger" of a man whose name sign is that of a buffalo bull either sitting or lying down or lame (see figure 7.8 and plate 77). His shield has a distinctive two-part design. The "Frank Henderson Ledger" also includes two representations of a man with this same name sign and shield (figure 7.9),[25] but, while the Lansburgh collection does contain some drawings

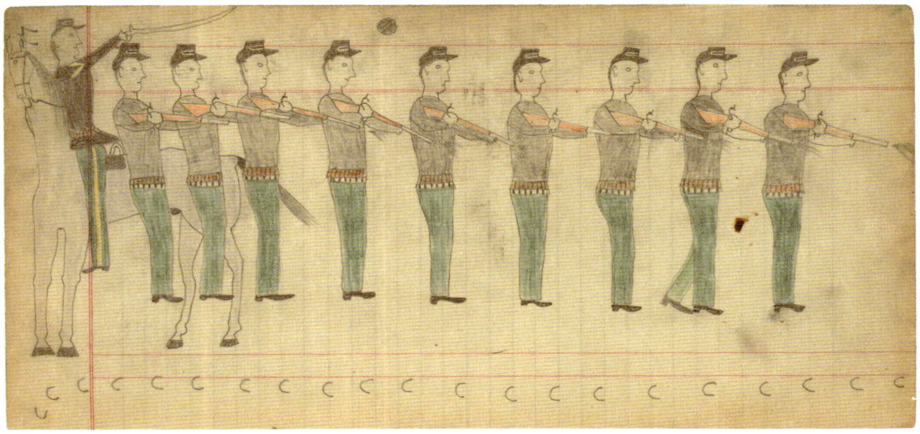

FIGURE 7.10
Unknown artist, Tsistsistas (Cheyenne) and/or Inunaina (Arapaho), active late nineteenth century, ***Untitled [A formation of U.S. infantry soldiers firing in battle],*** late nineteenth century, Hood Museum of Art (plate 66).

from the Henderson Ledger, these are not among them. It is apparent, however, that at least one of the artists who rendered images in the Henderson Ledger also drew in the book now known as the "Vincent Price Ledger."

Some of the artists in the Henderson book may have been Cheyennes while others were Arapahos, given that the two tribes were closely allied and shared a reservation in Indian Territory. The warrior society regalia portrayed and a lack of known cultural authorship indicate that the "Vincent Price Ledger" may also contain works by both Cheyenne and Arapaho artists. Various men who would have been active during the Southern Plains wars among both the Cheyennes and Arapahos had names that were some variant of buffalo or bull.

The buffalo-glyph, shield-bearing man was an important warrior no matter what his cultural identity. One of Howling Wolf's Oberlin drawings includes a very similar shield and a warrior whose name sign is that of a buffalo bull upright on its haunches; a handwritten addition to the drawing suggests that his name was Sitting Bull (see figure 7.6.)

Several men might own or at least use the same shield among both the Southern Cheyennes and the Arapahos. Such was the case with a shield owned by both the Arapaho warrior Sitting Bull, born in 1853, and his half-brother Scabby Bull. Sitting Bull initially went to war against the Pawnees when he was not yet a teenaged youth,[26] but he soon became a widely recognized, successful warrior as did his brother. Given their status, both men would probably have become members of the Arapaho Tomahawk or Spear Society by the late 1860s.[27] Members of this warrior society were men in their middle years who had the greatest responsibilities in battle.

Some of the depictions of the warrior with the buffalo name glyph have him clothed in a military jacket, German silver pectoral, and armbands. While the Lansburgh drawings, the additional drawings from the Henderson Ledger, and the Oberlin drawing were obviously created by different artists and have variations, they also share distinct similarities and may represent the same protagonist. One difference is in the use of blue and green in the shield's design. The artist of the drawings from the "Vincent Price Ledger" apparently alternated his use of blue and green, not just on the shield but also on the bodies of the figures he depicted battling the protagonist; the men the warrior fights wear the flared cuff moccasins generally associated with Pawnee enemies. This same artist from the "Vincent Price Ledger" sometimes depicted soldiers wearing blue uniforms, while in other instances the soldiers are clothed, at least partially, in green (see figure 7.10 and plate 61).

Various drawings in the Lansburgh collection raise questions about why it was important for the artist to depict what appears in them. For example, why was it apparently notable for a warrior to count coup on a baby who was, obviously, not fighting back (see figure 7.11)? Acts of bravery that required close potential encounters in enemy space were celebrated. For example, stealing a horse that was tied outside an enemy's lodge was recognized by the Arapaho as a braver action than stealing one further from the village.[28] The protagonist from the book now known as "Arrow's Elk Society Ledger," for the frequency with which a man with the name sign of an arrow appears,[29] had to enter the enemy's camp to reach the child just as the unseen but understood protagonist who has counted coup on an enemy woman had to come into the village; footprints make the path of entry and exit clear (see figure 7.12). Even though neither the baby nor apparently the woman rendered in the Arrow ledger offered the resistance an armed enemy might, their location far behind enemy lines makes the actions depicted important and heroic.

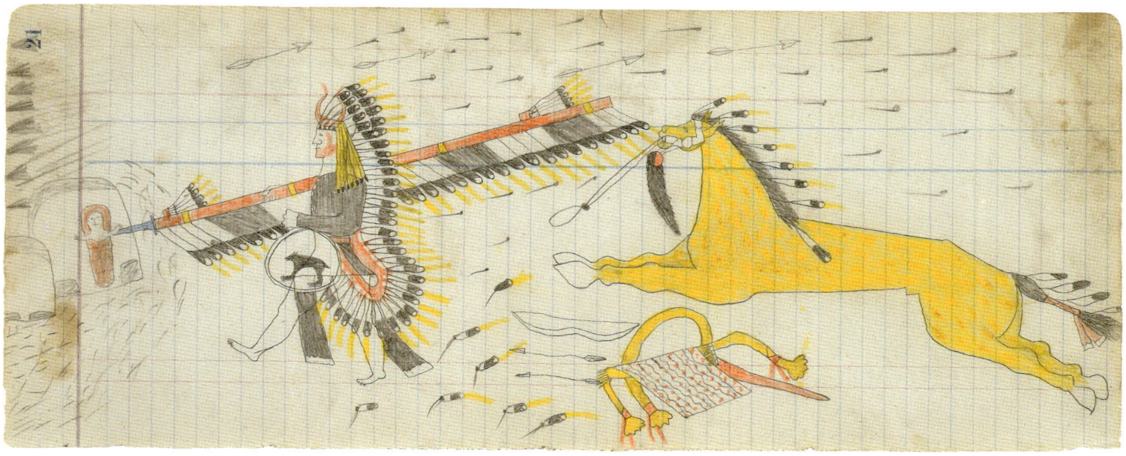

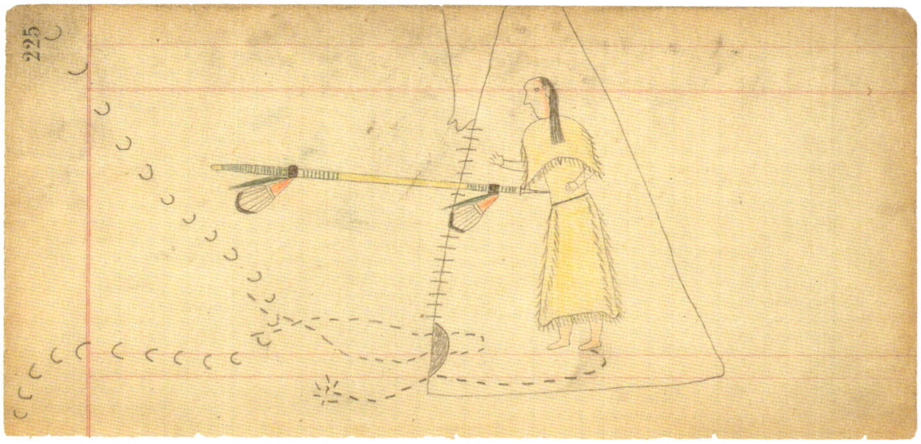

FIGURE 7.11
Unknown artist, Southern Tsistsistas (Cheyenne), active late nineteenth century, ***Untitled [A Tsistsistas (Cheyenne) warrior counting coup on a baby]***, c. 1874–75, Hood Museum of Art (plate 18).

FIGURE 7.12
Unknown artist, Tsistsistas (Cheyenne) and/or Inunaina (Arapaho), active late nineteenth century, ***Untitled [Counting coup on a woman]***, late nineteenth century, Hood Museum of Art (plate 84).

AN ALTERNATE POSITION OF STATUS: ARMY SCOUTS

A page from the Peter Edwards book (see figure 7.13) depicts a mounted warrior in battle with a Pawnee. The protagonist has a name sign comprised of a bear glyph with various slash marks in front of it which could be interpreted as Many Bears or Heap of Bears, as two sets of handwriting suggest. The Pawnee has no name sign; he is clearly Pawnee by the flared cuffs of his moccasins and his hairstyle, but his individual identity is not important.

Various representations of Pawnees in Plains drawings depict the warriors in blue dress which is probably a reference to Pawnee scouts who served with the United States Army from 1864 forward during the Plains wars.[30] Scouts were given uniforms but often did not wear full army dress, instead refashioning the trousers into leggings or only wearing the shirt or jacket with their own loincloths.[31] If they had time, some men would remove most of what must have seemed like cumbersome clothing to fight more freely in battle, being certain to leave enough army attire on to allow the army to distinguish them from the enemies they fought.[32] While the drawings of Pawnees in blue are not literal portraits, they make obvious references to these double enemies through the use of blue color. For the Cheyenne, Arapaho, Lakota, Gros Ventre and various other Plains warriors, their Pawnee foes of the 1860s and 1870s were the worst kind of enemies—they maintained their distinction as tribal enemies of long standing and they also represented the army and encroaching non-Native forces entering the Plains.

That Pawnee scouts were not required to constantly wear a full military uniform but were allowed to retain some of their own cultural signifiers, including hair style and face paint, is important to how they are portrayed in Plains drawings. Pawnees appear as enemies both in uniform (colored blue) and without uniforms, underscoring the distinction being made between scouts and Pawnees who were not scouts. Such distinctions were important to the events portrayed and help place each event more securely in Plains history. From the Pawnees' standpoint,

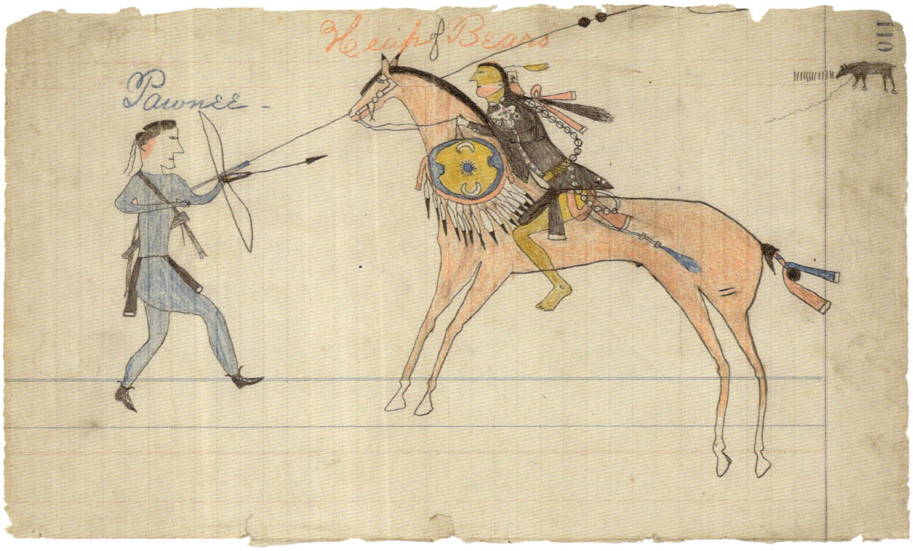

FIGURE 7.13
Unknown artist, Southern Inunaina (Arapaho) and/or Southern Tsistsistas (Cheyenne), active mid- to late nineteenth century, ***Untitled [A warrior counts coup on a Chaticks Si Chaticks (Pawnee) warrior],*** 1860s, Hood Museum of Art (plate 8).

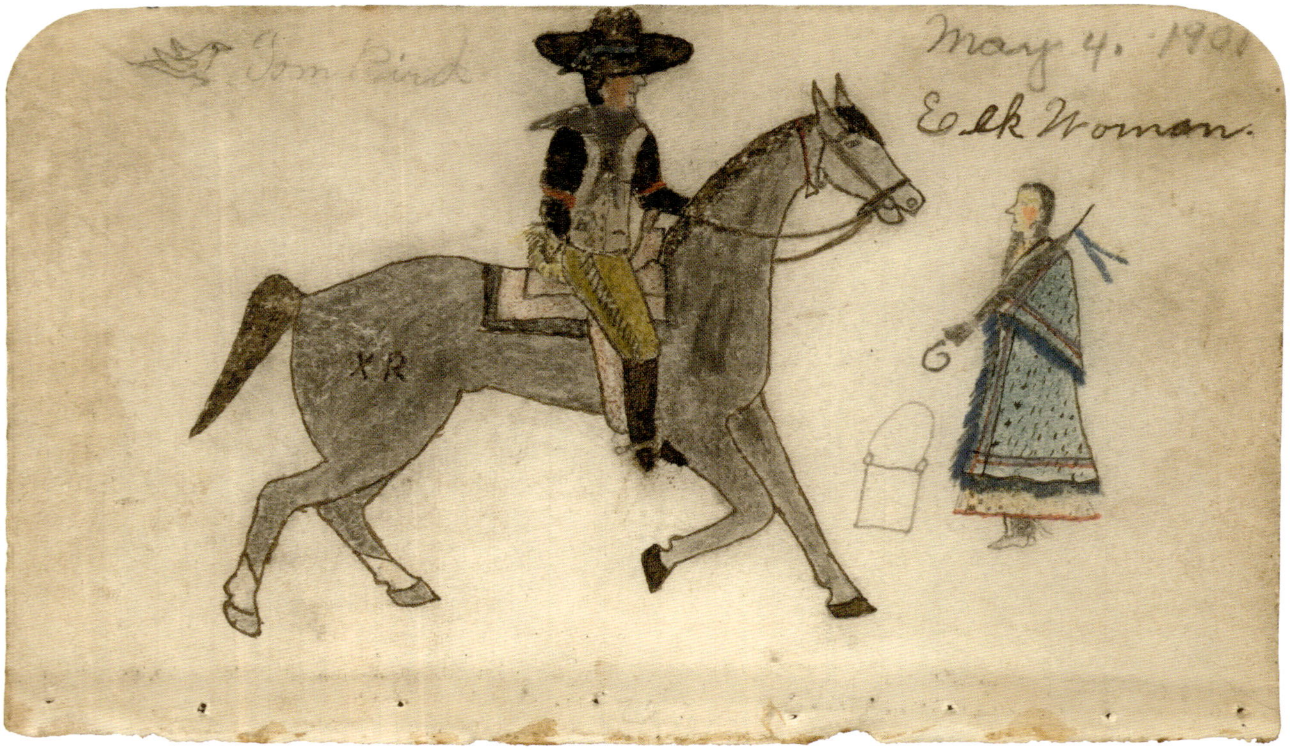

FIGURE 7.14
Robert Ridge Walker (c. 1870–before 1959), Northern Cheyenne, c. 1901. Thaw Collection, Fenimore Art Museum, T376.

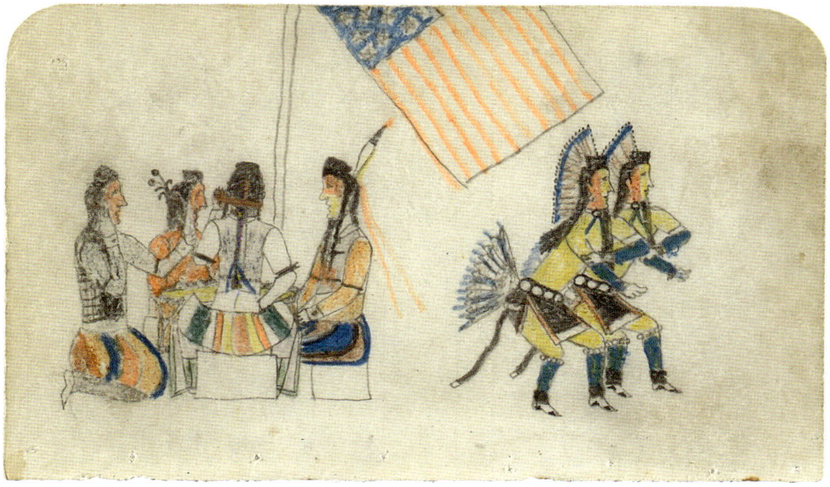

FIGURE 7.15
Robert Ridge Walker, Northern Tsistsistas (Cheyenne), c.1870–before 1959, ***Untitled [Social dancers and drummers]***, 1901, Hood Museum of Art (plate 142).

their positions as scouts allowed them the opportunity to fight their long-time enemies, particularly the Cheyennes and Arapahos, with the strong support of the army. During the early 1870s, Pawnee scouts were less frequently employed by the army, specifically due to the influence of Quaker agents who saw the practice as antithetical to acculturation; the agents underscored that the practice of employing Pawnees as scouts supported and continued their culturally embedded militaristic traditions. The latter is certainly true and explains, in part, why Pawnee men were so willing to serve with the army. Later another factor motivated Pawnees to enlist as scouts when called upon to do so. Some of the younger men had been to schools, and they returned to their homes feeling out of place within their cultural setting. Serving as scouts allowed them to establish themselves as brave men in battles, as their fathers, uncles, and grandfathers had done.[33]

The smallest drawings in the Lansburgh collection, only 3 1/2 by 5 3/4 inches, are from what is known as the Robert Ridge Walker ledger, tentatively dated 1901 from a note on a drawing from the volume (see figure 7.14). That drawing was previously owned by Mark Lansburgh but is now in the Thaw Collection at the Fenimore Art Museum in Cooperstown, New York.[34] Robert Ridge Walker, a Northern Cheyenne man, was twenty years old when he enlisted in the army as a scout on September 18, 1890; he was honorably discharged in 1891.[35]

Two pages from the book remain in the Lansburgh collection, but each page has a drawing on both the obverse and the reverse for a total of four images. The artist of these tiny drawings was extremely adept at employing the small area available to maximum advantage. One of the drawings is of two dancers, four seated or kneeling drummers, and an American flag (see figure 7.15). This is the kind of activity that might have been encouraged during the reservation era as part of a Fourth of July celebration, for example, when Plains people continued their own celebrations under the apparent guise of acceptable U.S. holidays. That Ridge Walker was Northern Cheyenne adds weight to this interpretation, because the Lakota were well known for maintaining their cultural traditions masked as Fourth of July celebrations.[36] While both the Northern and Southern Cheyennes fought alongside the Lakotas in the Plains wars, the Northern Cheyennes had closer relationships with the Lakotas given their relative geographic locations. They were so alike that, when the government moved some of the Northern Cheyennes to Indian Territory in 1877 to unite them with their Southern Cheyenne relatives, the Southern Cheyennes taunted their northern counterparts for having become "too Sioux."[37] Given Ridge Walker's employment as a scout with the army, the appearance of the flag in the drawing might also be a reference to that position and the status associated with it. A potentially late date for the drawing may also reflect the replacement of meetings of warrior societies with other dances that had ritual and ceremonial ties. The Omaha Society, or the Grass Dance, known by different names in Plains cultures, carried an association with veterans. Introduced late to various Plains cultures, it was a central part of reservation-era life for many.[38] The artist of the dance image in the Ridge Walker book emphasized the feather bustle worn by the dancers and the roach in the men's hair; both were signs of military prowess. As the Omaha Society or Grass Dance complex developed, it retained, for many, an association with warriors reflected not only by regalia but also by the manner of dancing itself. For some Plains people, skill as dancers and singers became

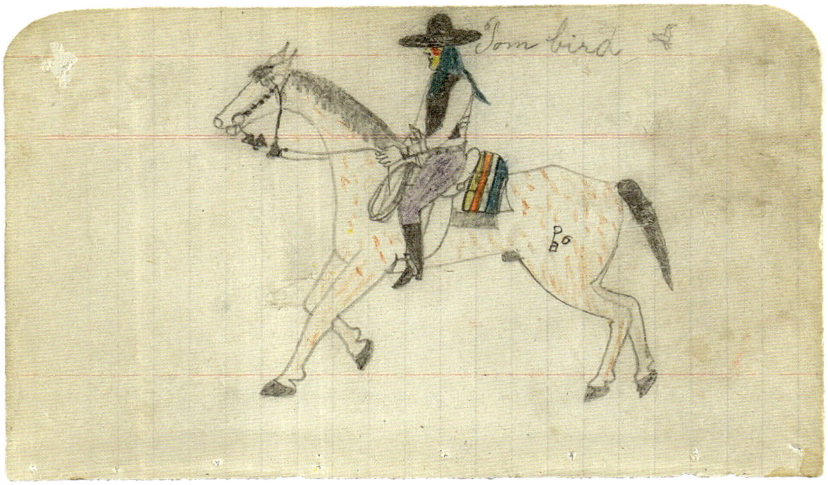

FIGURE 7.16
Robert Ridge Walker, Northern Tsistsistas (Cheyenne), c. 1870–before 1959, ***Untitled ["Tom bird"]***, 1901, Hood Museum of Art (plate 141).

reservation-era ways to obtain public stature previously limited largely to battle prowess.[39]

The reverse of the dancing scene page holds other important information (see figure 7.16). To the right of the mounted figure, the name Tom Bird appears with a bird name glyph. Dressed as a cowboy might be, complete with hat, tall boots, and vest, he also has face paint. His horse has a saddle, and the man carries a lariat. Behind the saddle, a striped object, perhaps a Hudson's Bay blanket, appears. The rider's horse is clearly branded. Other pages from the same small book now at the Fenimore Museum also include Tom Bird's handwritten name and the bird name sign. Several other handwritten names also appear on the pages, including Elk Woman and Katie Hard Robe. Each of these names appears on 1901 census rolls from Tongue River Agency; Robert Ridge Walker and his family are recorded there as well.[40] That the people whose names appear on various pages resided at the same agency in 1901 provides a point of reference for the drawing book. It undoubtedly was not created when Robert Ridge Walker was a scout between 1890 and 1891, because Katie Hard Robe would have been approximately eight years old then and would not have been the subject of Ridge Walker's or Tom Bird's attention. By the 1901 date written on the drawing in the Fenimore Museum and the date of the census, the men and women would have been old enough to have considered marriage. According to the census, Tom Bird was not married in 1901, while Robert Ridge Walker had one wife, named Dora.

Tom Bird also appears in the record of known ledger drawings elsewhere. The Southwest Museum in Pasadena, now part of the Autry National Center of the American West, has a forty-two page account book filled with drawings; two entries dated 1878 appear on its pages.[41] Lieutenant John G. Balance, who was at Fort Keogh in Montana during the 1890s, collected the book; he retired at the rank of brigadier general in 1904.[42] Robert Ridge Walker served as a scout at Fort Keogh, where Lieutenant Edward W. (Ned) Casey had originally developed his troop of Northern Cheyenne scouts in 1890. .

Two separate pages of the Autry/Southwest Museum book include the name Tom Bird (see figure 7.17). The handwritten names from the Autry book and from the Ridge Walker drawings are similar in style, and both sets of drawings also include a bird name glyph. Comparisons of the depictions of horses, horse hooves, human figures, profiles of faces, and the cowboy-style clothing underscore the strong possibility that the same artist created many of the Southwest Museum's drawings and at least some of the drawings that were originally in the Robert Ridge Walker book.

A SECOND OPTION: AGENCY POLICE

The early reservation years were extremely difficult, and employment as scouts brought some American Indians necessary income while simultaneously continuing a cultural focus on bravery, offering a way to increase status within one's community. Agency policemen held similar positions of importance. Early census records list occupations for the men whose names are recorded, and several listings make it apparent that some men moved between employment as Indian police and enlisted scouts.[43]

Policing a reservation agency was perhaps not as dangerous as scouting in combat, but both occupations carried social standing and responsibilities. When some of the Northern Cheyennes who had been moved to Indian Territory in 1877 escaped to return north, Cheyenne

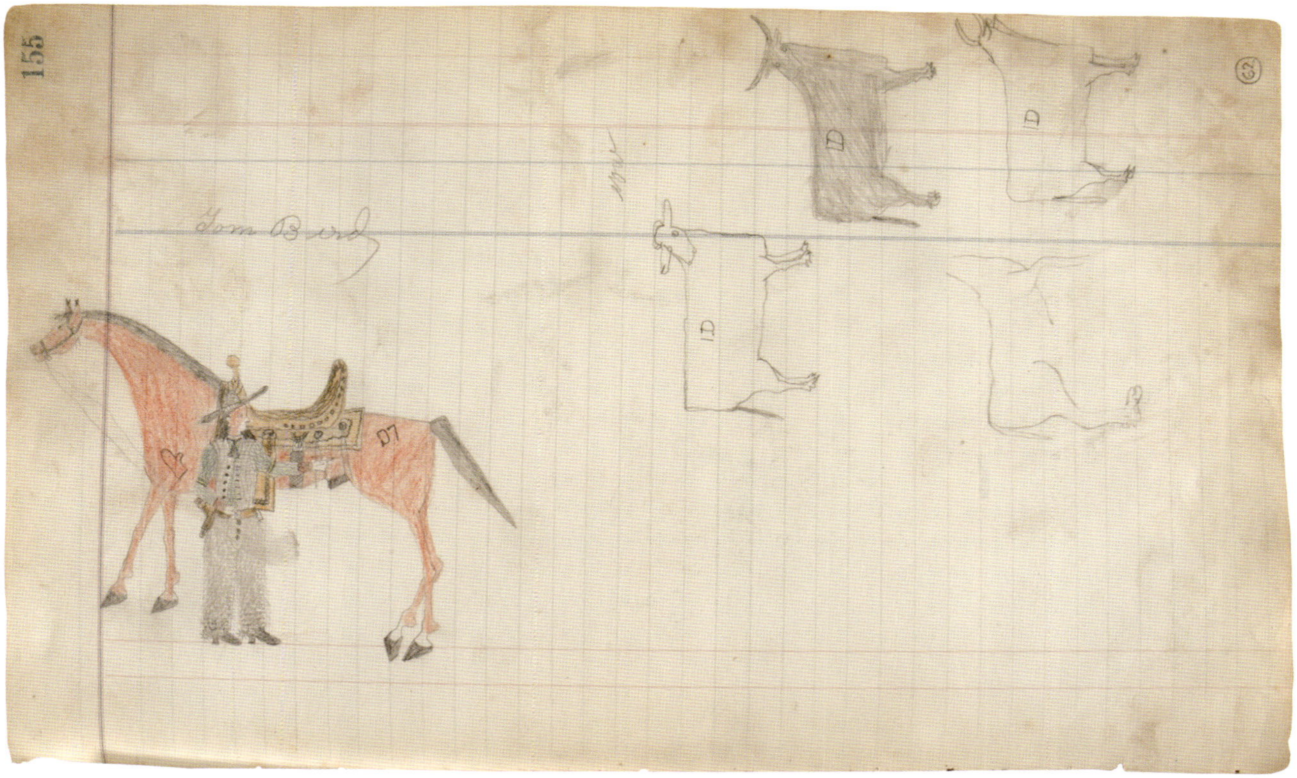

FIGURE 7.17
Northern Cheyenne Ledger Artist, late nineteenth century. Braun Research Library Collection, Autry National Center; 871.G.21.62.

police on the Cheyenne and Arapaho reservation served as scouts to track them.[44] A battle ensued in which the policemen-turned-scouts became combatants, and one Arapaho scout was killed.[45] As problems continued on the southern reservation with the Northern Cheyennes, Agent John D. Miles added five Northern men to the police force with the hope that they would be able "to prevent 'horse stealing, and many little domestic broils.'"[46] By the summer of 1879, the Indian police force at the Cheyenne and Arapaho Agency in Indian Territory included twelve privates, three sergeants, and one lieutenant under the leadership of a non-Native captain.[47] The noted Arapaho warrior Scabby Bull demonstrated his bravery once again when some of the Northern Cheyennes left the agency in 1879; he fought alongside the army against his northern relatives.

Serving as policemen brought not only status but also danger; in addition, the position included the difficulty of potentially fighting one's relatives. Because food rations were perilously meager, some men on the Cheyenne and Arapaho reservation stole cattle to feed their families. During the summer of 1880, Agent Miles ordered the Indian police to arrest three men for stealing or attempting to steal cattle, but the police refused because they knew that the men, stripped as they would have been for war, had the support of some four hundred other men.[48] Not only would the three men have fought to the death but losses would have been far greater. In fact, even Miles feared a massacre. Working as police fit well within long-established cultural practices. Among most Plains groups, men of significant standing or men who were members of specific warrior societies policed villages, ensuring that warriors, particularly younger men anxious to prove themselves in battle, did not disobey the orders of more senior war leaders. They might also hold eager hunters back when larger groups were involved in hunts. On occasion, warriors who acted as agents of social control also became peacemakers when people in camp argued or had altercations in other ways, including those involving marital discord or arguments over who would court a woman or who owned a horse or some cattle. Among the Arapahos, the police also carried out the orders of the council chiefs. While at some agencies this might have raised conflicts, it generally did not among the Arapahos,

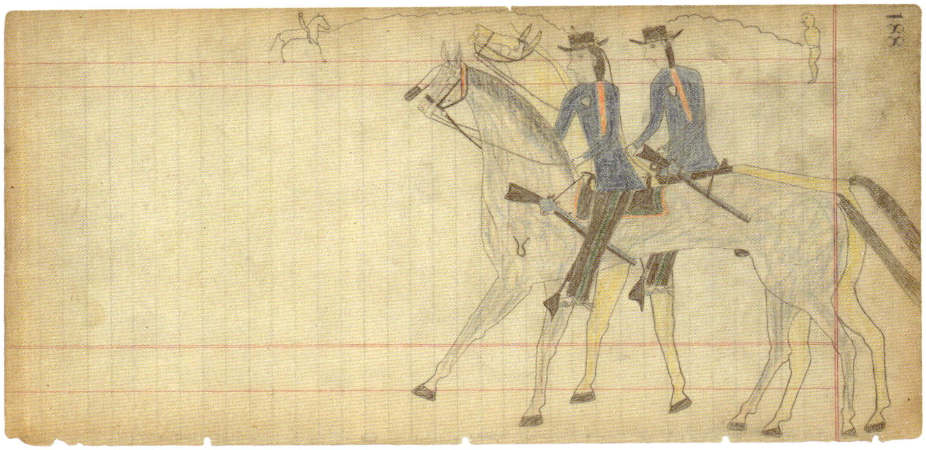

FIGURE 7.18
Unknown artist, Tsistsistas (Cheyenne) and/or Inunaina (Arapaho), active late nineteenth century, ***Untitled ["Indian Police" on patrol],*** late nineteenth century, Hood Museum of Art (plate 81).

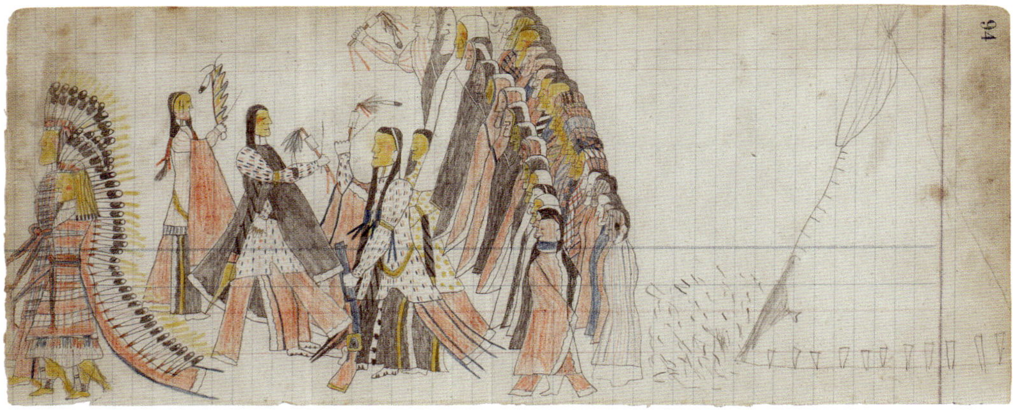

FIGURE 7.19
Unknown artist, Southern Tsistsistas (Cheyenne), active late nineteenth century, ***Untitled [Honoree in the Tsistsistas (Cheyenne) Kit Fox Society social dance],*** c. 1874–75, Hood Museum of Art (plate 22).

especially during the early years of reservation life when the council chiefs were trying to uphold what they saw as treaty agreements and maintain peace.

Unlike warrriors in some cultures like the Cheyennes and Lakotas, Arapaho warrior societies were age graded. All young men, or perhaps boys might be more accurate, entered the Kit Foxes and then, as they increased both in age and knowledge—becoming in the Arapaho view more fully Arapaho—they could move up in the sequence of societies.[49] Such movement required sponsorship from a symbolic grandfather and, along the way, gift giving. The leadership of Arapaho society came from the upper two warrior societies. Social position could also be established through ritual means, by sponsoring and taking part in the annual life renewal ceremonies, for example. But, for the most part, Arapaho men achieved the kind of position that would allow them to have authority in daily circumstances through the age-grade system.

One of the many Lansburgh drawings from the "Vincent Price Ledger" depicts two men on horseback (figure 7.18). Each has a name glyph and each wears a military-style uniform and wide-brimmed hat. Their braids are wrapped in red trade cloth. Both men use saddles with stirrups and have rifles. The man closest to mid-page has affixed a feather to his horse's headstall.

The two men could be scouts but for the clear police badges worn by each. Such insignia, while different from those previously used within Plains cultures, became yet another sign of status. Arapaho men who policed camp and enforced the orders of chiefs during the pre-reservation era came from the middle ranks of the age-grade system, and it seems likely that this cultural practice would have continued during the reservation era. These men had held the most active roles in warfare, with specific obligations during the pre-reservation era; being a policeman would have carried additional responsibilities and would have been seen as comparable, within the new social structure, to more active and potentially dangerous roles in war.

Agents who appointed policemen would have been aware of the esteem in which some of these men were held by their communities, and they undoubtedly soon learned that other men would not follow the orders of someone put in charge if that policeman did not merit the position of power. In a similar manner, Richard Pratt knew when he

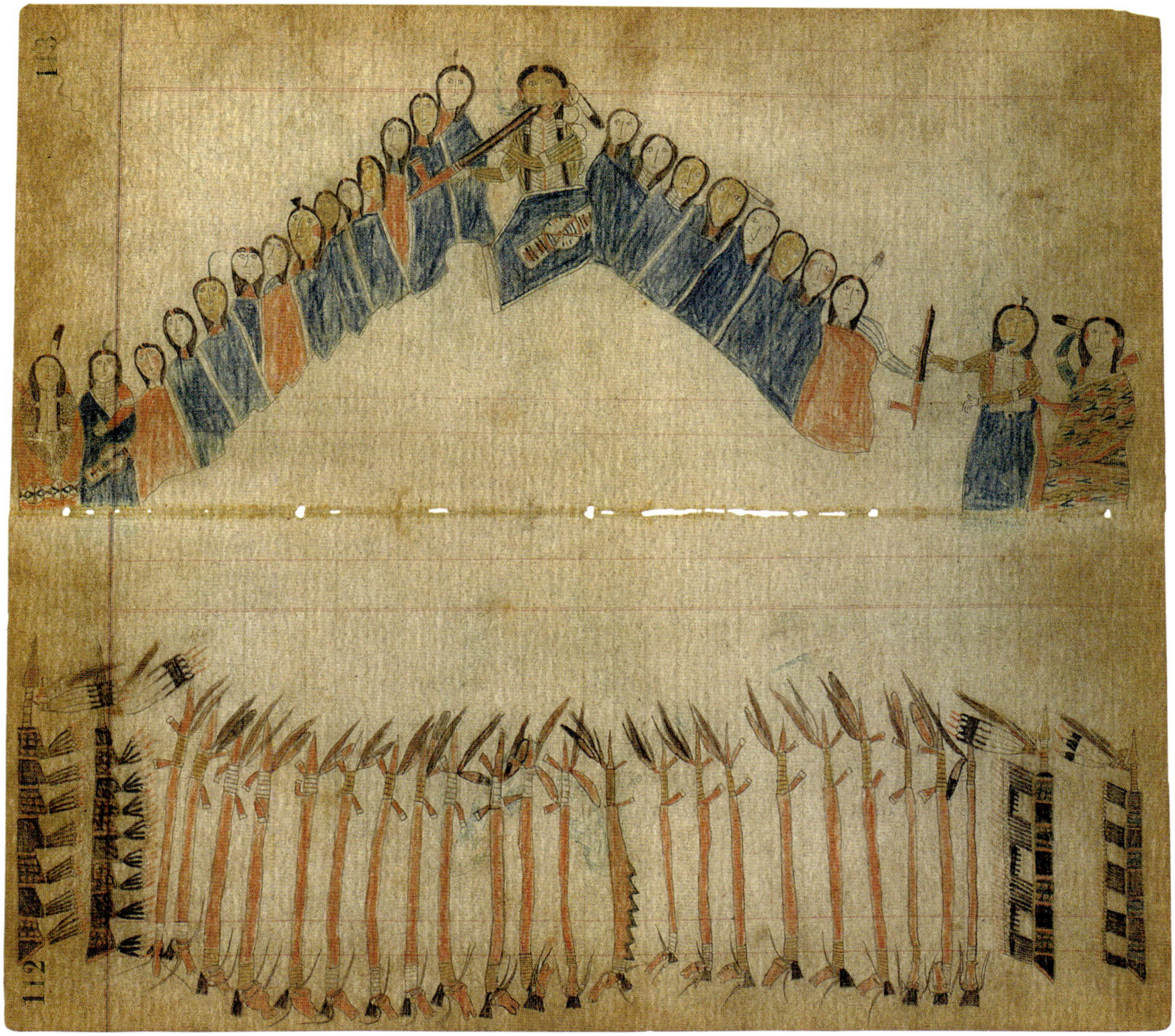

FIGURE 7.20
Unknown artist ("Frank Henderson Ledger"), Southern Arapaho/Southern Cheyenne, c. 1881–1882, pp. 112–14. Courtesy of Morning Star Gallery, Santa Fe, New Mexico.

appointed inmates to serve as guards at Fort Marion that those men had to be established and respected leaders. Arapaho chiefs, who were trying to maintain peaceful relations and hold their younger men in check, may have offered suggestions to the agent concerning appropriate police appointments.

Men who were chosen to serve as policemen at agencies must have ranged in ages and in experience, as the number of years on the reservation increased. For the Arapahos, according to Fowler, younger men in their twenties and even thirties were considered "boys" if they had not been to war.[50] Becoming an agency policeman may well have allowed an opportunity for those without warrior status to prove their worth. In fact, the leaders of the Arapaho warrior society lodges altered the requirements for advancement in the age-grade system during the early reservation era to include community service.[51] Becoming a policeman probably fit the community service category. If so, then the Arapahos employed a position required within the reservation system—a system of containment, acculturation, and removal of many aspects of pre-reservation life—to work within its own culturally established parameters, conflating pre-reservation and reservation practices to maintain tradition.[52]

MAINTAINING CULTURAL CONTINUITY

Many Plains ledger drawings include detailed representations of protagonists with intricate warrior society paraphernalia. In some cases, even warrior society celebrations such as that depicted in a drawing from the Arrow Ledger appear (see figure 7.19).[53] Such gatherings and paraphernalia also appear with some frequency in Fort Marion art. The Lansburgh collection contains four drawings from the Henderson Ledger, three of which present mounted warriors, two with very detailed warrior society lances; the fourth drawing is a sketch of a horse. Within the book, however, other drawings depicting the rich regalia, and in some cases the activities, of Arapaho warrior societies appear, emphasizing the continuing importance of the age-grade societies in the early reservation era (see figure 7.20).

The strength of the Arapaho lodge associations and those of various other Plains cultures defied, in many ways, the assimilationist project that was well underway. Arapaho society, for example, both maintained and adjusted their age-grade system; survival and resistance are both apparent. Some of those continuities and adaptations are suggested by other drawings in the Lansburgh collection, as are celebrations of past brave actions, realities of new lives and new ways of gaining status, and continuing battles with old enemies. All of these subjects provide visual displays of cultural identity. They also indicate reactions to and negotiations within the changing world that profoundly affected Plains people. These pages evidence the resilience of people who moved between opposition and accommodation to allow the survival of cultures. In many ways, the drawings themselves are sites of resistance and adaptation.

Through its breadth of drawings from different cultures, locations, and eras, the Lansburgh collection provides an extremely rich resource. The drawings, in conjunction with other sources of information, can tell us much about Plains Indian societies in the late nineteenth and early twentieth centuries. They demonstrate the very real presence and actions of Plains people throughout eras of great stress, their refusal to simply capitulate to the assimilation being demanded of them, and their struggles to uphold values and maintain sovereignty in the face of dramatic change.

NOTES

1. Two more Cheyenne men, Big Moccasin and Lean Bear, died in captivity in July 1875 and November 1875, respectively; three more died at different times later in Florida.

2. These ages and all others cited here, as well as numbers of prisoners from each culture and death dates for prisoners at Fort Marion, can be found most readily in Richard Henry Pratt, *Battlefield and Classroom: Four Decades with the American Indian, 1867–1904*, 138–44.

3. Two men, Sun and Straightening an Arrow, died in May and October of 1875, respectively.

4. Vizenor discusses survivance in various places, especially his *Manifest Manners: Postindian Warriors of Survivance*. Edwin L. Wade and Jacki Thompson Rand discuss some aspects of these concepts in relation to Fort Marion in "The Subtle Art of Resistance: Encounter and Accommodation in the Art of Fort Marion," in Berlo, ed., *Plains Indian Drawings*, 45–49.

5. Pratt, *Battlefield and Classroom*, 126–27.

6. While various discussions of the prevalence of flags in Plains beadwork and drawings have appeared in print, the most comprehensive to date is Schmittou and Logan, "Fluidity of Meaning," 559–604.

7. At the Sand Creek Massacre of 1864, Cheyenne chief Black Kettle had a large American flag attached to his lodge pole indicating his peaceful stance. When the village was attacked, he told his people not to worry because they would not be hurt. Many Native people died in the ensuing battle. Sand Creek is discussed in various places; of particular importance is Hyde, *Life of George Bent*, 152. The Southern Cheyenne warrior-artist Howling Wolf also drew an image, when he was imprisoned at Fort Marion, depicting a group of Southern Plains people entering a village of another group; the envoy carries an American flag in this image, undoubtedly as a sign that they came in peace to speak with their neighbors. See Szabo, "Medicine Lodge Treaty Remembered," 52–59.

8. Schmittou and Logan, "Fluidity of Meaning," 566–67.

9. Discussions surrounding the representation of the classroom were frequent during the Ledger Art Institute held at Dartmouth in the fall of 2010. I am particularly indebted to Dr. Mary Coffey for observations concerning this drawing.

10. Fairbanks Museum and Planetarium, St. Johnsbury, Vermont, Accession Files, Bad Eye Sketchbook.

11. Following his return to Indian Territory, Bad Eye/Bird Chief became active in the Omaha Society, later O-ho-ma, which was introduced to the Kiowas in 1884 by the Cheyennes; the society and its related associations with the Grass Dance largely replaced warrior societies among the Kiowa until recent revivals. There were approximately twenty-one ceremonial leaders in the Kiowa Omaha Society including two whipmen; Bird Chief held one of these positions. Both he and his fellow whipman Afraid of Bears were veterans

of the Plains wars, while some of the other members of the ceremonial organization were not. Bad Eye/Bird Chief's and Afraid of Bears' positions indicate their standing within Kiowa culture. Meadows, *Kiowa Military Societies*, 268–69. That Bad Eye/Bird Chief was both an established warrior from the pre-reservation era and an honored warrior who fought for survival in other ways as a Fort Marion inmate supports his qualifications for this position in the society.

12. Silver Horn's work is discussed in depth in Candace Greene, *Silver Horn: Master Illustrator of the Kiowas* and Robert G. Donnelley, *Transforming Images: The Art of Silver Horn and His Successors.*

13. Szabo, "Howling Wolf: An Autobiography," 24nn45–46.

14. Examination of census records reveals no Robert Guthrie in either Topeka or Indian Territory, but another reference in the drawing book lists Saint Claire in an unnamed state. Illinois census records, where there is a Saint Claire County, indicate that a Ben Shoemake resided there in 1870.

15. Howling Wolf probably created the Oberlin drawings shortly before his Fort Marion confinement because a Sun Dance appears; the double-page composition includes Bowstring Warrior Society members and their Northern Cheyenne counterparts the Crazy Dogs, who sponsored the annual renewal ceremony during the summer of 1874, the last Sun Dance that the artist would have experienced prior to imprisonment. In addition, the Oberlin drawings are the work of a masterful, skilled artist. During his confinement in Florida, Howling Wolf developed severe vision problems and lost the vision in one eye before he returned to Indian Territory. Thus, he would not have been able to draw with the precision apparent in the Oberlin images. Given the subject matter of the Oberlin book, with its heavy emphasis on battles between Native and non-Native people as well as between Native enemies, it is doubtful that the book was filled with drawings at Fort Marion.

16. The Lansburgh collection also contains a buffalo-hunting image by Howling Wolf. The Southern Cheyenne warrior-artist created a similar but more complex scene in the Oberlin book, again underscoring the later date of the Oberlin drawings. See comparative discussions of the two hunting scenes in Szabo, *Howling Wolf*, 173–75, 193, and plates 27, 32.

17. Meadows, *Kiowa, Apache, and Comanche Military Societies*, 53; Mishkin, *Rank and Warfare*, 24–27, 35–36; Fowler, *Wives and Husbands*, 69–70.

18. Fowler, *Wives and Husbands.*

19. Moore, *The Cheyenne Nation*, 179.

20. Moore, *The Cheyenne Nation*, 178–79.

21. Fowler, *Wives and Husbands*, 96–97, 112, 156, 195.

22. Ibid., 112.

23. Ibid., 172.

24. Ibid., 118.

25. Peterson, *American Pictographic Images*, plates 108, 168.

26. Fowler, *Wives and Husbands*, 39

27. Ibid., 77. The separation of Sitting Bull and Scabby Bull is complex because Sitting Bull had joined the Northern Cheyennes in 1879 and worked as a scout with the army; in return for their service as scouts the Northern Cheyennes were promised a reservation in Wyoming. He remained in the north until 1890, when he returned to the Southern Arapahos bringing with him news of the prophet Wovoka and the Ghost Dance, of which he became a major proponent. His brother Scabby Bull was also named Sitting Bull at that time, but he subsequently changed his name to Scabby Bull. Both brothers were prominent men during the reservation era. Scabby Bull demonstrated his bravery once again when some of the Northern Cheyennes left the agency in 1879; he fought alongside the army against his northern relatives. Fowler, *Wives and Husbands*, 155, 158–59.

28. Ibid., 73–74.

29. Cowdrey, *Arrow's Elk Society Ledger* provides an in-depth examination of the ledger, complete with color illustrations of the drawings.

30. Mark van de Logt's recent *War Party in Blue: Pawnee Scouts in the U.S. Army* is an excellent, in-depth study of the scouts that adds significantly to previously published sources. I am indebted to Colin Calloway who suggested the identity of these blue-clad Pawnees as scouts.

31. See van de Logt, *War Party in Blue*, 121, for example.

32. Ibid., 128, for example.

33. There are several well-known tragic instances that arose from a lack of avenues for young men to prove themselves within their cultures. Most telling are two examples from the Lakotas. In 1890, Headchief killed three white men because he felt it was the only way he could become a man. Liberty, "I Will Play with the Soldiers," 16–26. Plenty Horses, who killed Lieutenant Ned Casey in 1891, had attended Carlisle Indian School, and when he returned home, he was lonely. As he testified, "I shot the lieutenant so I might make a place for myself among my people. Now I am one of them. I shall be hung and the Indians will bury me as a warrior. They will be proud of me." McGillycuddy, *McGillycuddy, Agent*, 272.

34. Morning Star Gallery, *Native American Ledger Drawing Book*; Vincent, Brydon, and Coe, eds., *Arts of the North American Indians*, 165.

35. Registers of Enlistments in the United States Army, Indian Scouts, 1878–1914, National Archives, M-233, roll 71, entry 475.

36. An in-depth study of Lakota practices can be found in Green, "Performance and Celebrations." 37. Northern Cheyennes also criticized their southern relatives for giving in

too readily to non-Native forces. U.S. Congress, Senate, *Testimony Taken by a Select Committee of the Senate Concerning the Removal of the Northern Cheyennes*, S. Rept. 708, 46th Cong., 2d sess., 1880, p. 6; Monthly Report, John D. Miles to Commissioner of Indian Affairs, May 2, 1881, Letters Received by the Office of Indian Affairs, RG 75, National Archives, file 7770; Monthly Report, John Miles to Commissioner of Indian Affairs, June 6, 1881, Letters Received by the Office of Indian Affairs, RG 75, National Archives, file 9624.

38. Ellis, *Dancing People*, 51–52.

39. Flannery, "Changing Form," 64–65.

40. National Archives M-595, roll 574, Census Records, Tongue River Agency, 1888; M-595, roll 575, Census Records, Tongue River Agency 1901 and 1902. Tom Bird was twenty-six in 1901 and Katie Hard Robe was eighteen; Robert Ridge Walker was thirty-five in 1902.

41. These 1878 dates are, of course, not proof that the drawings themselves were made at that time.

42. The book was subsequently given to the Southwest Museum by family members in 1951. Accession Records 871.G.21, Southwest Museum/Autry National Center of the American West.

43. See, for example, National Archives, M-233, roll 71, Registers of Enlistments, 1878–1914, Indian Scouts, entries 1178, 1180, and 1181, for three men at Pine Ridge who moved between these positions; the men listed here are Crow, Charging in Morning, and Chief White Cow. Being scouts was far preferable to serving as agency police. The pay a scout received was three times more than that provided to police, and scouts seemed to have more leisure time and better provisions. Hagan, *Indian Police*, 43–44.

44. Berthrong, *Cheyenne and Arapaho Ordeal*, 33.

45. Berthrong, *Cheyenne and Arapaho Ordeal*, 34.

46. Ibid., 43.

47. Ibid., 348n30.

48. Ibid., 45.

49. Excellent discussions of the Arapaho lodge system can be found in Anderson, *Four Hills of Life* and Fowler, *Wives and Husbands*.

50. Fowler, *Wives and Husbands*, 121.

51. Ibid., 137.

52. The drawing of the policemen from the Vincent Price ledger, created by one of the artists who also worked in the Henderson book, offers no apparent suggestion through the paraphernalia the two policemen carry of their position within Plains warrior societies. However, the information concerning one Arapaho man is telling. Only two Arapaho prisoners went to Fort Marion. One of them, White Bear, who had been an established warrior, as several drawings from Fort Marion make clear, also went to Carlisle but for less than a year. When he returned to Indian Territory, he was appointed a policeman by Agent John Miles at the Cheyenne and Arapaho Agency, according to Fowler, although Karen Petersen records that he was a scout instead. Both would have been positions of authority, but the Cheyenne and Arapaho agent Miles's domain would have included appointing agency police, rather than Army scouts. The agent may have recommended men for scouting positions. In White Bear's case, either position would have been merited. He was an established pre-reservation warrior, a man who had at least reached a level of membership in the Spear Lodge (sometimes also referred to as the Clubboard or Tomahawk Society) as indicated in a drawing now at Hampton Institute in which he holds a clubboard, and a Fort Marion veteran who would have been honored for his bravery there. The Hampton Institute drawing was reproduced in Szabo, "Drawing Life's Changes," 41–51.

53. See Cowdrey, *Arrow's Elk Society Ledger*, 19–22 and 35–39, for example.

Appendix

LEDGER DRAWINGS IN THE MARK LANSBURGH COLLECTION

DRAWINGS IN CHRONOLOGICAL ORDER

"FREDERIC H. DOUGLAS LEDGER"

ARTIST(S):	Unknown artist(s), Tsistsistas (Cheyenne), active mid- to late nineteenth century
ORIGINAL FORMAT:	Ledger book, known as the "Frederic H. Douglas Ledger" (collector's name)
DATE:	1860s
COLLECTOR:	Early collection history unknown; later collected by Dr. Frederic Huntington Douglas (1897–1956), Denver, Colorado, date unknown
BINDING HISTORY:	Unbound about or by 1990
MEDIUM:	Ink, colored pencil, watercolor, graphite
PAPER:	Laid ledger paper
DIMENSIONS:	Sheets approximately 7 ⅜ × 12 ¼ in. (18.7 × 31.2 cm) [irregular]
PAGINATION:	Preprinted numbers; number of pages unknown (up to page number 104 in this collection)
COLLECTION SUMMARY:	5 drawings; 5 sheets (all of them one-sided); ledger page numbers: 53/54, 55/56, 57/58, 61/62, 103/104

"PETER W. EDWARDS LEDGER"

ARTIST(S):	Unknown artist(s), Southern Inunaina (Arapaho) and/or Southern Tsistsistas (Cheyenne), active mid- to late nineteenth century
ORIGINAL FORMAT:	Ledger book, known as the "Peter W. Edwards Ledger" (collector's name)
DATE:	1860s
COLLECTOR:	Collected by Peter W. Edwards (1822/24–1872), Waukegan, Illinois; given to his eldest daughter, Ida Edwards; given to her son, George Williams; given to his son, G. Kent Williams
BINDING HISTORY:	Unbound about 1990
MEDIUM:	Graphite, colored pencil
PAPER:	Laid ledger paper
DIMENSIONS:	Sheets approximately 7 ⅝ × 12 ⅞ in. (19.4 × 31.5 cm) [irregular]
PAGINATION:	116 preprinted ledger page numbers; only 42 pages are extant
COLLECTION SUMMARY:	3 drawings; 2 sheets (1 of them 2-sided, 1 of them 1-sided); ledger page numbers: 47/48, 110/109
REFERENCE:	David A. Schorsch, Karen Daniels Petersen, and Jean Afton, *The Edwards Ledger Drawings: Folk Art by Arapaho Warriors* (New York: David A. Schorsch, 1990)

AN UNIDENTIFIED SKETCHBOOK

ARTIST(S):	Unknown artist(s), possibly Tsistsistas (Cheyenne), active mid- to late nineteenth century
ORIGINAL FORMAT:	Sketchbook, unidentified, formerly known as "Lance Owner Ledger" (a name glyph in ledger)
DATE:	Late 1860s–early 1870s
COLLECTOR:	Unknown
BINDING HISTORY:	Unknown
MEDIUM:	Ink, colored pencil, graphite, ink wash, watercolor
PAPER:	Wove sketchbook paper
DIMENSIONS:	Sheets approximately 6 × 8⅝ in. (152 × 21.9 cm) [irregular]
PAGINATION:	Original number of pages unknown; pages not numbered
COLLECTION SUMMARY:	8 drawings; 4 sheets (all of them 2-sided)

"ARROW'S ELK SOCIETY LEDGER"

ARTIST(S):	Unknown artist(s), Southern Tsistsistas (Cheyenne), active late nineteenth century
ORIGINAL FORMAT:	Ledger book, known as the "Arrow's Elk Society Ledger" (a name glyph in ledger)
DATE:	About 1874–75
COLLECTOR:	Collected by Sallie C. Maffet, Darlington Agency (Cheyenne-Arapaho Reservation), Indian Territory, 1882; in the family by descent until 1997
BINDING HISTORY:	Unbound 1999
MEDIUM:	Graphite, colored pencil, crayon
PAPER:	Laid ledger paper
DIMENSIONS:	Sheets approximately 5¾ × 11⅜ in. (14.5 × 28.9 cm) [irregular]
PAGINATION:	Preprinted ledger page numbers, 168 ledger page numbers
COLLECTION SUMMARY:	17 drawings; 14 sheets (3 of them two-sided, 11 of them one-sided); ledger page numbers: 5/6, 21/22, 33/34, 77/78, 85/86, 93/94, 117/118, 131/132, 133/134, 147/148, 153/154, 155/156, 161/162, 163/164
REFERENCE:	Mike Cowdrey, *Arrow's Elk Society Ledger: A Southern Cheyenne Record of the 1870's* (Santa Fe: Morning Star Gallery, 1999)

"ROBERT ALLEN GUTHRIE NOTEBOOK"

ARTIST(S):	Unknown artist(s), Tsistsistas (Cheyenne), active late nineteenth century, including Howling Wolf (Ho-na-nist-to), Southern Tsistsistas (Cheyenne), 1849–1927
ORIGINAL FORMAT:	Notebook, known as the "Robert Allen Guthrie Notebook" (name from an inscription in the book)
DATE:	About 1874–75
COLLECTOR:	Unknown
BINDING HISTORY:	Unbound about 1981
MEDIUM:	Ink, colored pencil, watercolor, graphite, crayon
PAPER:	Wove blue-lined notebook paper [blue horizontal lines (faded), rounded corners, sewn binding]
DIMENSIONS:	Sheets approximately 5¾ × 7¼ in. (14.5 × 18.2 cm)
PAGINATION:	Approximately 33 drawings; pages not numbered; original sequence not recorded
COLLECTION SUMMARY:	9 drawings; 8 sheets (7 of them one-sided, 1 of them two-sided)

"CARL S. DENTZEL LEDGER"

ARTIST(S):	Unknown artist(s), Southern Tsistsistas (Cheyenne) and/or Southern Inunaina (Arapaho), active late nineteenth century
ORIGINAL FORMAT:	Ledger book, known as the "Carl S. Dentzel Ledger" (collector's name)
DATE:	About 1875–78
COLLECTOR:	Collected in Fort Reno, Indian Territory, 1878; collected by Dr. Carl Schaefer Dentzel (1913–1980), date unknown
BINDING HISTORY:	Unbound possibly around 1972
MEDIUM:	Graphite and colored pencil
PAPER:	Laid ledger paper
DIMENSIONS:	Sheets approximately 6 × 14⅞ in. (15.3 × 37.7 cm) [irreg.]
PAGINATION:	Preprinted ledger page numbers, original number of pages unknown
COLLECTION SUMMARY:	3 drawings; 3 sheets (all of them one-sided); ledger page numbers: 17/18, 47/48, 63/64

AN OHETTOINT SKETCHBOOK

ARTIST:	Ohettoint, Kiowa, 1852–1934, also known as Charley Ohettoint, High Forehead, Charley Buffalo, Padai (Twin)
ORIGINAL FORMAT:	Sketchbook, known by the artist's name
DATE:	Mid-1875–mid-1878
COLLECTOR:	Unknown, drawn at Fort Marion, St. Augustine, Florida
BINDING HISTORY:	Unknown
MEDIUM:	Graphite and colored pencil
PAPER:	Wove sketchbook paper
DIMENSIONS:	Sheets approximately: 8¾ × 11¼ in. (22.2 × 28.5 cm)
PAGINATION:	Original number of pages unknown; pages not numbered
COLLECTION SUMMARY:	8 drawings; 4 sheets (all of them two-sided)

A CHIEF KILLER SKETCHBOOK

ARTIST:	Chief Killer (Noh-hu-nah-wih), Southern Tsistsistas (Cheyenne), 1849–1922
ORIGINAL FORMAT:	Sketchbook, known by the artist's name
DATE:	Mid-1875–mid-1878
COLLECTOR:	Unknown, drawn at Fort Marion, St. Augustine, Florida
BINDING HISTORY:	Unknown
MEDIUM:	Colored pencil, crayon, graphite, ink, watercolor
PAPER:	Wove sketchbook paper
DIMENSIONS:	Sheets approximately 8⅝ × 11¼ in. (21.9 × 28.6 cm) [irregular]
PAGINATION:	About 29 drawings; original number of pages unknown; numbered in graphite [probably at a later date]
COLLECTION SUMMARY:	7 drawings; 5 sheets (2 of them two-sided, 3 of them one-sided); page numbers: 5/6, 7, 11/12, 35, 36

"VINCENT PRICE LEDGER"

ARTIST(S):	Unknown artist(s), Tsistsistas (Cheyenne) and/or Inunaina (Arapaho), active late nineteenth century
ORIGINAL FORMAT:	Ledger book; known as the "Vincent Price Ledger" (collector's name)
DATE:	Late nineteenth century
COLLECTOR:	Early ownership history unknown; purchased by Vincent Leonard Price Jr. (1911–1993), California, early 1960s
BINDING HISTORY:	Unknown, possibly after 1993
MEDIUM:	Graphite, colored pencil, ink
PAPER:	Laid ledger paper
DIMENSIONS:	Sheet approximately 5¾ × 11⅜ in. (14.5 × 28.9 cm) [irreg.]
PAGINATION:	Preprinted ledger page numbers, about 86 drawings
COLLECTION SUMMARY:	31 drawings; 19 sheets (12 of them two-sided, 7 of them one-sided); ledger page numbers: 57/58, 63/64, 67/68, 77/78, 91/92, 103/104, 127/128, 138/139, 139/140, 153/154, 169/170, 187/188, 219/220, 221/222, 225/226, 239/240 [3 drawings on end pages, not numbered; 2 drawings on pages with paper loss, ledger number missing]

AN UNIDENTIFIED SKETCHBOOK

ARTIST:	Unknown artist, Kiowa and/or Mexican, active late nineteenth century
ORIGINAL FORMAT:	Sketchbook; formerly known as the "Mexican-Kiowa" sketchbook (subject matter)
DATE:	Late nineteenth century
BINDING HISTORY:	Unknown
MEDIUM:	Graphite, colored pencil, crayon, ink
PAPER:	Wove sketchbook paper [watermark: J. Whatman/1858]
DIMENSIONS:	Sheets approximately 9 × 13¼ in. (22.9 × 33.5 cm) [irreg.]
PAGINATION:	Not numbered
COLLECTION SUMMARY:	10 drawings; 5 sheets (all of them 2-sided)

"JULIAN SCOTT LEDGER"

ARTIST(S):	Unknown artist(s), Kiowa, active late nineteenth century
ORIGINAL FORMAT:	Ledger book, known as the "Julian Scott Ledger" (collector's name)
DATE:	About 1880
COLLECTOR:	Drawn at Fort Sill, Indian Territory, about 1880; collected by Julian Scott (1846–1901), about 1890; ownership by descent in the Scott family
BINDING HISTORY:	Unbound by 1987
MEDIUM:	Graphite, colored pencil, watercolor, crayon, ink
PAPER:	Laid ledger paper
DIMENSIONS:	Sheet approximately 7½ × 12¼ in. (19.2 × 31.1 cm) [irreg.]
PAGINATION:	Preprinted ledger page numbers; ledger pages up to page number 101; about 50 drawings
COLLECTION SUMMARY:	1 drawing; 1 sheet (one-sided); ledger page numbers 11/12
REFERENCE:	Ronald McCoy, *Kiowa Memories: Images from Indian Territory, 1880* (Santa Fe: Morning Star Gallery, 1987)

"OLD WHITE WOMAN LEDGER"

ARTIST(S):	Unknown artist(s), Tsistsistas (Cheyenne), active late nineteenth century
ORIGINAL FORMAT:	Ledger book, known as the "Old White Woman Ledger" (a name glyph in ledger)
DATE:	About 1880–90
COLLECTOR:	Unknown
BINDING HISTORY:	Unbound by 2000
MEDIUM:	Graphite, colored pencil, watercolor, ink
PAPER:	Wove ledger paper
DIMENSIONS:	Sheets approximately 7 ⅜ × 11 ⅞ in. (18.6 × 30.0 cm) [irreg.]
PAGINATION:	Preprinted, ledger page numbers; approximately 46 pages
COLLECTION SUMMARY:	15 drawings; 13 sheets (2 of them two-sided, 11 of them one-sided); ledger page numbers (some numbers are missing [paper loss]; the end pages do not have numbers): 1/2, 5, 27, 57/58, 61/62, 69, 101/102, 105/106, 171/172, 187/188, 189/190, 191/192

"FRANK HENDERSON LEDGER"

ARTIST(S):	Unknown artist(s), Southern Inunaina (Arapaho) and/or Southern Tsistsistas (Cheyenne), active late nineteenth century, including Frank Henderson, Southern Inunaina (Arapaho), about 1862–1885
ORIGINAL FORMAT:	Ledger book; known as the "Frank Henderson Ledger" [one of the artists in the ledger]
DATE:	June 1881–December 1882
COLLECTOR:	Frank Henderson (artist), Cheyenne and Arapaho Agency, Darlington, Indian Territory, completed 1882; given [sent] to his friend Martha Ker Underwood (?–1890), Carlisle, Pennsylvania, in 1882; to her grandniece, Josephine [Mrs. James B.] Underwood Ritter, Carlisle, Pennsylvania
BINDING HISTORY:	Unbound about 1988
MEDIUM:	Graphite, colored pencil, watercolor
PAPER:	Laid ledger paper
DIMENSIONS:	Sheets approximately 5 ⅜ × 11 ⅞ in. (13.5 × 30.2 cm) [irregular]
PAGINATION:	Preprinted ledger page numbers; about 122 pages
COLLECTION SUMMARY:	4 drawings; 3 sheets (1 of them two-sided, 2 of them one-sided); ledger page numbers: 155/156, 157/158, 171/172
REFERENCE:	Karen Daniels Petersen, *American Pictographic Images: Historical Works on Paper by the Plains Indians* (New York: Alexander Gallery; Santa Fe: Morning Star Gallery, 1988)

AN UNIDENTIFIED LEDGER

ARTIST(S):	Unknown artist(s) Southern Inunaina (Arapaho) and/or Southern Tsistsistas (Cheyenne), active late nineteenth century
ORIGINAL FORMAT:	Ledger book; unidentified
DATE:	Early 1880s
COLLECTOR:	Found in a storage box in the Chilocco Indian School, Oklahoma, by an unidentified man, about 1965
BINDING HISTORY:	Unbound about 1965
MEDIUM:	Graphite, colored pencil
PAPER:	Laid ledger paper
DIMENSIONS:	Sheet approximately 7 ¾ × 12 ⅜ in. (19.6 × 31.4 cm) [irreg.]
PAGINATION:	Preprinted, ledger page numbers; approximately 70–80 pages
COLLECTION SUMMARY:	2 drawings; 1 sheet (two-sided); ledger page numbers: 107/108

AN UNIDENTIFIED LEDGER

ARTIST:	Wooden Leg (Kum-mok-quiv-vi-ok-ta), Northern Tsistsistas (Cheyenne), 1858–1940; also known as Richard Wooden Leg
ORIGINAL FORMAT:	Ledger book; unidentified
DATE:	About 1882
COLLECTOR:	Unknown
BINDING HISTORY:	Unknown
MEDIUM:	Graphite, ink, watercolor
PAPER:	Laid ledger paper, mounted on wove paper
DIMENSIONS:	Mount [sheets irregular]: 7½ × 10½ in. (19.0 × 26.5 cm)
PAGINATION:	Preprinted, ledger page numbers, unknown; at least up to ledger page 82
COLLECTION SUMMARY:	2 drawings; fabricated from about 6 partial pages, joined together, including part of ledger page number 82

A SHORT BULL NOTEBOOK

ARTIST:	Short Bull (Tatanka Ptecela), Lakota (Sioux), about 1845–1915; also known as Arnold Short Bull
ORIGINAL FORMAT:	Notebook known by the artist's name
DATE:	About 1885–90
COLLECTOR:	Given to Natalie Curtis Burlin (1875–1921) by the artist, about 1909
BINDING HISTORY:	Unbound, date unknown
MEDIUM:	Ink, watercolor, graphite, colored pencil
PAPER:	Wove blue-lined notebook paper
DIMENSIONS:	Sheets approximately 8 × 10 in. (20.2 × 25.4 cm) [irreg.]
PAGINATION:	Original number of pages unknown; pages numbered in graphite [probably added at a later date]
COLLECTION SUMMARY:	10 drawings; 10 sheets (all of them one-sided); page numbers (1 drawing is not numbered): Roman numeral III, 4, 12, 21, 23, 25, 26, 32, 37

WHITE SWAN DRAWINGS

ARTIST:	White Swan, Apsáalooke (Crow), 1851–1904
ORIGINAL FORMAT:	Individual sheets (possibly cut from a larger composition) with primarily irregular, hand-cut edges
DATE:	About 1890
COLLECTOR:	Unknown
BINDING HISTORY:	Not applicable
MEDIUM:	Graphite and colored pencil
PAPER:	Linen-textured, commercially prepared wove paper, coated on one side (possibly wallpaper); traces of graphite lines at edges indicate where the paper was ruled before being cut
DIMENSIONS:	Sheets approximately 7½ × 12⅜ in. (19.0 × 31.3 cm) [irreg.]
PAGINATION:	Not applicable
COLLECTION SUMMARY:	5 drawings; 5 sheets (all of them one-sided)

A ROBERT RIDGE WALKER LEDGER

ARTIST:	Robert Ridge Walker, Northern Tsistsistas (Cheyenne), about 1870–before 1959; also known as Robert Ridgewalker
ORIGINAL FORMAT:	Small ledger book; known by the artist's name
DATE:	About 1901
COLLECTOR:	Unknown
BINDING HISTORY:	Unbound, date unknown
MEDIUM:	Graphite, colored pencil, crayon
PAPER:	Small wove ledger paper
DIMENSIONS:	Sheets approximately 3 ½ × 5 ¾ in. (18.9 × 14.6 cm) [irreg.]
PAGINATION:	Original number of pages unknown; pages not numbered
COLLECTION SUMMARY:	4 drawings; 2 sheets (both of them two-sided)

NOTE: The drawings are presented in the catalogue plate section in approximate chronological order, and subsequently in ledger page number order (when possible). Many ledgers are known in the literature by the name of either the artist or the collector, or by their subject matter. When these names are used in this volume, it is for identification purposes only.

DRAWINGS ORGANIZED BY ORIGINAL FORMAT

DRAWINGS FROM LEDGER BOOKS

"Vincent Price Ledger," late nineteenth century, unknown artist(s), Tsistsistas (Cheyenne) and Inunaina (Arapaho), active late nineteenth century (31 drawings)

"Arrow's Elk Society Ledger," about 1874–75, unknown artist(s), Southern Tsistsistas (Cheyenne), active late nineteenth century (17 drawings)

"Old White Woman Ledger," about 1880–90, unknown artist(s), Tsistsistas (Cheyenne), active late nineteenth century (15 drawings)

"Frederic H. Douglas Ledger," 1860s, unknown artist(s), Tsistsistas (Cheyenne), active mid- to late nineteenth century (5 drawings)

A Robert Ridge Walker ledger, about 1901, Robert Ridge Walker, Northern Tsistsistas (Cheyenne), about 1870–before 1959 (4 drawings)

"Frank Henderson Ledger," June 1881–December 1882, unknown artist(s), Southern Inunaina (Arapaho) and/or Southern Tsistsistas (Cheyenne), active late nineteenth century, including Frank Henderson, Southern Inunaina (Arapaho), about 1862–1885 (4 drawings)

"Carl S. Dentzel Ledger," about 1875–78, unknown artist(s), Southern Inunaina (Arapaho) and/or Southern Tsistsistas (Cheyenne), active late nineteenth century (3 drawings)

"Peter W. Edwards Ledger," 1860s, unknown artist(s), Southern Inunaina (Arapaho) and/or Southern Tsistsistas (Cheyenne), active mid- to late nineteenth century (3 drawings)

Unidentified ledger, early 1880s, unknown artist(s), Southern Inunaina (Arapaho) and/or Southern Tsistsistas (Cheyenne), active late nineteenth century (2 drawings)

Unidentified ledger, about 1882, Wooden Leg (Kum-mok-quiv-vi-ok-ta), Northern Tsistsistas (Cheyenne), 1858–1940 (2 drawings)

"Julian Scott Ledger," about 1880, unknown artist(s), Kiowa, active late nineteenth century (1 drawing)

DRAWINGS FROM SKETCHBOOKS

Unidentified sketchbook, late nineteenth century, unknown artist, Kiowa and/or Mexican, active late nineteenth century (10 drawings)

A Chief Killer sketchbook, mid-1875–mid-1878, Chief Killer (Noh-hu-nah-wih), Southern Tsistsistas (Cheyenne), 1849–1922 (9 drawings)

Unidentified sketchbook, late 1860s–early 1870s, unknown artist(s), possibly Tsistsistas (Cheyenne), active mid- to late nineteenth century (8 drawings)

An Ohettoint sketchbook, mid-1875–mid-1878, Ohettoint, Kiowa, 1852–1934 (8 drawings)

DRAWINGS FROM NOTEBOOKS

A Short Bull notebook, about 1885–90, Short Bull (Tatanka Ptecela), Sicangu (Brule) Lakota (Sioux), about 1845–1915 (10 drawings)

"Robert Allen Guthrie Notebook," about 1874–75, unknown artist(s), Tsistsistas (Cheyenne), active late nineteenth century (6 drawings), including Howling Wolf (Ho-na-nist-to), Southern Tsistsistas (Cheyenne), 1849–1927 (3 drawings)

DRAWINGS FROM INDIVIDUAL SHEETS OF PAPER

White Swan drawings, about 1890, White Swan, Apsáalooke (Crow), 1851–1904 (5 drawings)

DRAWINGS ORGANIZED BY ACQUISITION DATE

2003

D.2003.18.1-.3	3 drawings, purchased from Mark Lansburgh: *Purchased through the Robert J. Strasenburgh II 1942 Fund*

2004

D.2004.9	1 drawing, purchased from Price-Dewey Galleries Ltd., Santa Fe, New Mexico: *Purchased through the Hood Museum of Art Acquisitions Fund*

2005

2005.28	1 drawing, given by Ann H. and Harte C. Crow (originally a gift from Mark Lansburgh): *Gift of Ann H. and Harte C. Crow*

2006

2006.51	1 drawing, purchased from Mark Lansburgh: *Purchased through the Julia L. Whittier Fund*

2007

2007.26.1–2	2 drawings, purchased from Mark Lansburgh: *Purchased through the Robert J. Strasenburg II 1942 Fund and the Julia L. Whittier Fund*
2007.65.1–112	112 drawings, partial gift/partial purchase from Mark Lansburgh: *Partial gift of Mark Lansburgh, Class of 1949, and partial purchase through the Mrs. Harvey P. Hood W'18 Fund and the Offices of the President and Provost of Dartmouth College*
2007.88.1–11	11 drawings, given by Mark Lansburgh: *Gift of Mark Lansburgh, Class of 1949*
2007.89.1–2	2 drawings, given by Mark Lansburgh: *Gift of Mark Lansburgh, Class of 1949, in honor of Barbara Thompson, Curator of African, Oceanic, and Native American Collections, Hood Museum of Art, 2002–2008*

2008

2008.70.1–4	4 drawings, purchased from Mark Lansburgh: *Purchased through the Mrs. Harvey P. Hood W'18 Fund*
2008.71.1–2	2 drawings, purchased from Morning Star Gallery, Santa Fe, New Mexico: *Purchased through the Mrs. Harvey P. Hood W'18 Fund*
2008.71.3	1 drawing, purchased from Morning Star Gallery, Santa Fe, New Mexico: *Purchased with a gift from Mary Alice Kean Raynolds and David R. W. Raynolds, Class of 1949, in honor of Susan and James Wright, 16th President of Dartmouth College*
2008.75	1 drawing, given by Mark Lansburgh: *Gift of Mark Lansburgh, Class of 1949, in honor of James Wright, 16th President of Dartmouth College*
2008.76.1–2	2 drawings, given by Mark Lansburgh: *Gift of Mark Lansburgh, Class of 1949, in honor of Brian P. Kennedy, Director, Hood Museum of Art, 2005–2010*

2009

2009.45	1 drawing, given by Mark Lansburgh: *Gift of Mark Lansburgh, Class of 1949, in honor of Jim Yong Kim, 17th President of Dartmouth College*

Bibliography

PRIMARY SOURCES

Accession Records, 871.G.21. Southwest Museum/Autry National Center of the American West, Los Angeles.

Accession Records, Bad Eye Ledger. Fairbanks Museum and Planetarium, St. Johnsbury, Vt.

Battey, Thomas C. *The Life and Adventures of a Quaker Among the Indians.* Norman: University of Oklahoma Press, 1968.

Catlin, George. *Letters and Notes on the Manners, Customs, and Conditions of the North American Indians.* Vol. 2. 1844. Reprint, New York: Dover, 1973.

———. *North American Indians.* Vol. 2. Minneapolis: Ross and Haines, 1965.

Chief Killer. Will of Chief Killer, June 1, 1921. Copy at Oklahoma Historical Society.

Faulkner, William. *Go Down, Moses.* New York; Random House, 1942; reprint, New York: Vintage, 1991.

Hyde, George E. *Life of George Bent: Written from His Letters.* Edited by Savoie Lottinville. Norman: University of Oklahoma Press, 1968.

Indian Helper. Carlisle Indian School Newspaper, August, 11, 1893.

Kelly, Fanny. *My Captivity among the Sioux Indians.* 1871; reprint, New York: Carol Publishing, 1993.

Lanier, Sidney. *Florida: Its Scenery, Climate, and History.* Philadelphia: J. P. Lippincott & Co., 1876.

Locke, John. *Second Treatise of Government.* Edited by C. B. Macpherson. Indianapolis: Hackett, 1980.

Marcy, Randolph B., and McClellan, Captain G. B. *Adventure on the Red River: Report on the Exploration of the Red River by Captain Randolph B. Marcy and Captain G. B. McClellan.* Edited by Grant Foreman. Norman: University of Oklahoma Press, 1937.

Marriott, Alice. Alice Marriott Collection, Western History Collection, University of Oklahoma Libraries.

Methvin, J. J., *Andele, or The Mexican-Kiowa Captive: A Story of Real Life Among the Indians.* 1899; reprint, Albuquerque: University of New Mexico Press, 1996.

Monthly Report, John D. Miles to Commissioner of Indian Affairs, May 2, 1881, Letters Received by the Office of Indian Affairs, RG 75, National Archives, file 7770.

———, June 6, 1881, Letters Received by the Office of Indian Affairs, RG 75, National Archives, file 9624.

Mooney, James. *Calendar History of the Kiowa Indians.* Seventeenth Annual Report of the Bureau of American Ethnology (1895–96). 1898; reprint, Washington, D.C.: Smithsonian Institution Press, 1979.

———. "Unpublished Manuscript 2531." Washington, D.C.: National Anthropological Archives, Smithsonian Institution, n.d.

Morning Star Gallery. *Native American Ledger Drawing Book.* N.p.: PARCO, n.d.

National Archives, M-233, roll 71. Registers of Enlistments, 1878–1914, Indian Scouts.

National Archives M-595, roll 574. Census Records, Tongue River Agency, 1888.

National Archives M-595, roll 575. Census Records, Tongue River Agency 1901 and 1902.

Pratt, Richard Henry. *Battlefield and Classroom, Four Decades with the American Indian, 1867–1904.* Edited with introduction by Robert M. Utley. New Haven: Yale University Press, 1964; reprint, Norman: University of Oklahoma Press, 2003.

Registers of Enlistments in the United States Army. Indian Scouts, 1878–1914. National Archives, M-233, roll 71.

Richard Henry Pratt Papers, 1862–1956. Yale Collection of Western Americana, Beinecke Rare Books Library.

Sipes, John. *John Sipes Cheyenne Family Oral Histories—Standing Bird Family.* Interview with Measure Woman Standing Bird. Oklahoma Historical Society.

Sipes, John. *Sipes/Berthrong Cheyenne Collection*, Fort Marion POWs Section. Fort Marion and Darlington Agency, Indian Territory Sections, File Numbers 42–56. Oklahoma Historical Society.

Standing Bear, Luther. *Land of the Spotted Eagle.* Lincoln: University of Nebraska Press, 1978.

———. *My People, the Sioux.* 1928; reprint, Lincoln: University of Nebraska Press, 1978.

Sunshine, Silvia. *Petals Plucked from Sunny Climes.* Nashville: Southern Methodist Publishing House, 1886.

U.S. Congress. Senate. *Testimony Taken by a Select Committee of the Senate Concerning the Removal of the Northern Cheyennes,* S. Rept. 708, 46th Cong., 2d sess., 1880.

SECONDARY SOURCES AND LEDGER ART

Adams, David Wallace. *Education for Extinction: American Indians and the Boarding School Experience, 1875–1928.* Lawrence: University Press of Kansas, 1995.

Afton, Jean, David Fridtjof Halaas, and Andrew E. Masich. *Cheyenne Dog Soldiers: A Ledgerbook History of Coups and Combat.* Denver: Colorado Historical Society, 1997.

American Pictographic Images: Historical Works on Paper by the Plains Indians. Introduction and captions by Karen Daniels Petersen. New York: Alexander Gallery and Santa Fe, N.Mex.: Morning Star Gallery, 1988.

Anderson, Jeffrey D. *The Four Hills of Life: Northern Arapaho Knowledge and Life Movement.* Lincoln: University of Nebraska Press, 2001.

Appadurai, Arjun. "Introduction: Commodities and the Politics of Value." In *The Social Life of Things: Commodities in Cultural Perspective,* edited by Arjun Appadurai, 3–63. Cambridge: Cambridge University Press, 1986.

Basso, Keith. *Wisdom Sits in Places: Landscape and Language Among the Western Apache.* Albuquerque: University of New Mexico Press, 1996.

Belyea, Barbara. *Dark Storm Moving West.* Calgary, Alberta: University of Calgary Press, 2007.

Berlo, Janet Catherine. "Artists, Ethnographers, and Historians: Plains Indian Graphic Arts in the Nineteenth Century—and Beyond." In *Transforming Images: The Art of Silver Horn and His Successors,* edited by Robert G. Donnelly, 26–45. Chicago: The David and Alfred Smart Museum of Art, University of Chicago, 2000.

———. "Creativitiy and Cosmopolitanism: Women's Enduring Traditions." In *Identity by Design: Tradition, Change, and Celebration in Native Women's Dresses,* edited by Emil Her Many Horses, 97–147.

———. "Drawing and Being Drawn In: The Late Nineteenth-Century Plains Graphic Artists and the Intercultural Encounter." In *Plains Indian Drawings 1865–1935: Pages from a Visual History,* edited by Janet Catherine Berlo, 12–18.

———, ed. *Plains Indian Drawings 1865–1935: Pages from a Visual History.* New York: Harry N. Abrams, in association with the Federation of Arts and the Drawing Center, 1996.

———. "Wheeler Drawings: Catalogue Numbers 38-42." In *Plains Indian Drawings 1865–1935: Pages from a Visual History,* edited by Janet Catherine Berlo, 112–14.

———, and Gerald McMaster. "Encyclopedias of Experience: A Curatorial Dialogue on Drawing and Drawing Books." In *Plains Indian Drawings 1865–1935: Pages from a Visual History,* edited by Janet Catherine Berlo, 19–25.

Berthrong, Donald J. *The Cheyenne and Arapaho Ordeal: Reservation and Agency Life in the Indian Territory, 1875–1907.* Norman: University of Oklahoma Press, 1976.

Berthrong, Donald J. *The Southern Cheyennes.* Norman: University of Oklahoma, 1963.

Blaney, David, and Naeem Inayatullah. *Savage Economics: Wealth, Poverty, and the Temporal Walls of Capitalism.* New York: Routledge, 2010.

Blume, Anna. "In a Place of Writing." In *Plains Indian Drawings 1865–1935: Pages from a Visual History,* edited by Janet Catherine Berlo, 40–44.

Boime, Albert. *The Magisterial Gaze: Manifest Destiny and American Landscape Painting, c. 1830–1865.* Washington, D.C.: Smithsonian Institution Press, 1991.

Bol, Marsha C. "Defining Lakota Tourist Art, 1880–1915." In *Unpacking Culture: Art and Commodity in Colonial and Post-Colonial Worlds,* edited by Ruth B. Phillips and Christopher B. Steiner, 214–28. Berkeley: University of California Press, 1999.

Brainerd, Jehu. *Elementary Principles of Plane and Perspective Drawing.* Cleveland, Ohio: Tooker and Catchell, 1853.

Brooks, James F. *Captives and Cousins: Slavery, Kinship, and Community in the Southwest Borderlands.* Chapel Hill: University of North Carolina Press, 2002.

Bruckner, Martin. *The Geographic Revolution in America: Maps, Literacy, and National Identity.* Chapel Hill: University of North Carolina Press, 2007.

Calloway, Colin G. "Army Allies or Tribal Survival? The 'Other Indians' in the 1876 Campaign." In *Legacy: New Perspectives on the Battle of the Little Bighorn,* edited by Charles E. Rankin, 62–81. Helena: Montana Historical Society Press, 1996.

———. *One Vast Winter Count: The Native American West before Lewis and Clark.* Lincoln: University of Nebraska Press, 2003.

———. "The Only Way Open to Us: Intertribal Warfare and the Crow Struggle for Survival," *North Dakota History* 53 (1986): 24–34.

Clark, William Philo. *The Indian Sign Language.* Lincoln: University of Nebraska Press, 1982.

Colburn, David R. *Racial Change and Community Crisis: St. Augustine, Florida, 1877–1980.* New York: Columbia University Press, 1985.

Coleman, Winfield. "Riders of the Storm: The Shamanic Basis of Cheyenne Horse Decoration." In *American Indian Horse Masks,* edited by Ned Martin, Mike Cowdrey, and Jody Martin. Nicasio, Calif.: Hawk Hill Press, 2006.

Cowdrey, Mike. *Arrow's Elk Society Ledger: A Southern Cheyenne Record of the 1870's.* Santa Fe, N.Mex.: Morning Star Gallery, Ltd., 1999.

DeLay, Brian. *War of a Thousand Deserts: Indian Raids and the U.S.-Mexican War.* New Haven: Yale University Press, 2008.

Dippie, Brian. "The Moving Finger Writes: Western Art and the Dynamics of Change." In *Discovered Lands, Invented Pasts: Transforming Visions of the American West*, by Jules David Prown, et al., 89–115. New Haven: Yale University Press, 1992.

Donnelley, Robert G., Candace S. Green, and Janet C. Berlo, eds. *Transforming Images: The Art of Silver Horn and His Successors.* Chicago: The David and Alfred Smart Museum of Art, University of Chicago, 2000.

Dorsey, George A. *The Cheyenne Indians: The Sun Dance.* Glorieta, N.Mex.: Rio Grande Press, 1971.

Douglas, H. Fredric, and Marriott, Alice. "Metal Jewelry of the Peyote Cult." In *Material Culture Notes: Denver Art Museum, American Indian Art Department.* Denver: Denver Art Museum, 1942.

Dunlay, Thomas W. *Wolves for the Blue Soldiers: Indian Scouts and Auxiliaries with the United States Army, 1860–90.* Lincoln: University of Nebraska Press, 1982.

Eacker, Susan A. "Gender in Paradise: Harriet Beecher Stowe and Postbellum Prose on Florida." *Journal of Southern History* 64, no. 3 (August 1998): 495–512.

Earenfight, Phillip, ed., *A Kiowa's Odyssey: A Sketchbook from Fort Marion.* Seattle: University of Washington Press, 2007.

Ellis, Clyde. *A Dancing People: Powwow Culture on the Southern Plains.* Lawrence: University of Kansas Press, 2003.

Etheridge, Robbie, and Sheri M. Shuck-Hall, eds. *Mapping the Mississippian Shatter Zone: The Colonial Indian Slave Trade and Regional Instability in the American South.* Lincoln: University of Nebraska Press, 2009.

Ewers, John C. "Climate, Acculturation, and Costume: A History of Women's Clothing among the Indians of the Southern Plains." In *Plains Indian History and Culture: Essays on Continuity and Change*, 119–49. Norman: University of Oklahoma Press, 1997.

———. "Images of the White Man in Nineteenth-Century Plains Indian Art." In *The Visual Arts: Plastic and Graphic*, edited by Justine M. Cordwell, 411–29. New York: Mouton, 1979.

———. *Murals in the Round: Painted Tipis of the Kiowa and Kiowa-Apache Indians.* Washington, D.C.: Smithsonian Institution Press, 1978.

Flannery, Regina. "The Changing Form and Functions of the Gros Ventre Grass Dance." *Primitive Man* 20, no. 3 (July 1947): 39–70.

Foster, Morris W. Introduction to *Rank and Warfare among the Plains Indians*, by Bernard Mishkin. Lincoln: University of Nebraska Press, 1992.

Foucault, Michel. *Discipline and Punish: The Birth of the Prison.* Translated by Alan Sheridan. New York: Pantheon Books, 1977.

———. "The Great Confinement." In *Madness and Civilization: A History of Insanity in the Age of Reason*, from *The Foucault Reader*, edited by Paul Rabinow. New York: Pantheon Books, 1984.

———. "The Subject and Power." Afterword to *Michel Foucault: Beyond Structuralism and Hermeneutics*, by Hubert Dreyfus and Paul Rabinow. Chicago: University of Chicago Press, 1982.

Fowler, Loretta. *Wives and Husbands: Gender and Age in Southern Arapaho History.* Norman: University of Oklahoma Press, 2010.

Gell, Alfred. *Art and Agency: An Anthropological Theory.* Oxford: Claredon Press, 1998.

Green, Adriana Greci. "Performance and Celebrations: Displaying Lakota Identity, 1880–1915." PhD diss. Rutgers, New Brunswick, N.J., 2001.

Greene, Candace S. "Artists in Blue: The Indian Scouts of Fort Reno and Fort Supply." *American Indian Art Magazine* 18, no. 2 (1992): 50–57.

———. "Changing Times, Changing Views: Silver Horn as a Bridge to Nineteenth and Twentieth-Century Kiowa Art." In *Transforming Images: The Art of Silver Horn and His Successors*, edited by Robert G. Donnelley, Candace S. Greene, and Janet C. Berlo, 15–25.

———. "From Bison Robes to Ledgers: Changing Contexts in Plains Drawings." *European Review of Native American Studies* 18, no. 1 (2004): 21–29.

———. *One Hundred Summers: A Kiowa Calendar Record.* Lincoln: University of Nebraska Press, 2009.

———. *Silver Horn: Master Illustrator of the Kiowas.* Norman: University of Oklahoma Press, 2001.

———. "Southern Plains Graphic Art before the Reservation." *American Indian Art Magazine* 22, no. 3 (1997).

———. "Structure and Meaning in Cheyenne Ledger Art." In *Plains Indian Drawings 1865–1935: Pages from a Visual History*, edited by Janet Catherine Berlo, 26–33.

———. "The Tepee with Battle Pictures." *Natural History* 102, no. 10 (1993): 68–76.

———. "Women, Bison, and Coup: A Structural Analysis of Cheyenne Pictographic Art." PhD diss., University of Oklahoma, 1985.

———, and Thomas Drescher. "The Tipi with Battle Pictures: The Kiowa Tradition of Intangible Property Rights." *Trademark Reporter* 84, no. 4 (1994): 418–33.

Grinnell, George Bird. *The Cheyenne Indians.* 2 vols. 1923; reprint, Lincoln: University of Nebraska Press, 1972.

———. "The Cheyenne Medicine Lodge." *American Anthropologist* 16, no. 2 (1914): 245–56.

———. "Coup and Scalp among the Plains Indians." *American Anthropologist* 12, no. 2 (1910): 296–310.

———. "The Young Dog's Dance." *Journal of American Folklore* 4, no. 15 (1891): 307–13.

Hagan, William T. *Indian Police and Judges: Experiments in Acculturation and Control.* New Haven: Yale University Press, 1966.

———. *United States–Comanche Relations: The Reservation Years*. New Haven: Yale University Press, 1976; reprint, Norman: University of Oklahoma Press, 1990.

Hail, Barbara, ed. *Gifts of Pride and Love: Kiowa and Comanche Cradles*. Bristol, R.I.: Haffenreffer Museum of Anthropology, Brown University, 2000.

———. *Hau, Kóla!: The Plains Indian Collection of the Haffenreffer Museum of Anthropology*. Providence, R.I..: Haffenreffer Museum of Anthropology, Brown University, 1980.

Hämäläinen, Pekka. "The Western Comanche Trade Center: Rethinking the Plains Indian Trade System." *Western Historical Quarterly* 29, no. 4 (Winter 1998): 485–513.

Hanks, Jane Richardson. *Law and Status among the Kiowa Indians*. 2nd ed. Monographs of the American Ethnological Society. Seattle: University of Washington Press, 1940; reprint, 1966.

Harley, J. B. *The New Nature of Maps: Essays in the History of Cartography*. Baltimore, Md.: Johns Hopkins University Press, 2001.

Harmon, Alexandra. *Rich Indians: Native People and the Problem of Wealth in American History*. Chapel Hill: University of North Carolina Press, 2010.

Harris, Moira F. *Between Two Cultures: Kiowa Art from Fort Marion*. St. Paul, Minn.: Pogo Press, 1989.

Heap of Birds, Hachivi Edgar. "Hachivi Edgar Heap of Birds." In *I Stand in the Center of the Good: Interviews with Contemporary Artists*, edited by Lawrence Abbott, 29–54. Lincoln: University of Nebraska Press, 1994.

Hedrick, Joan D. *Harriet Beecher Stowe: A Life*. New York: Oxford University Press, 1994.

Heller-Roazen, Daniel. *Homo Sacer: Sovereign Power and Bare Life*. Translated by Giorgio Agamben. Palo Alto, Calif.: Stanford University Press, 1998.

Her Many Horses, Emil, ed. *Identity By Design: Tradition, Change, and Celebration in Native Women's Dresses*. New York: HarperCollins, in Association with the National Museum of the American Indian, Smithsonian Institution, 2007.

Hudson, Angela Pulley. *Creek Paths and Federal Roads: Indians, Settlers, and Slaves, and the Making of the American South*. Chapel Hill: University of North Carolina Press, 2010.

Jablow, Joseph. *The Cheyenne in Plains Indian Trade Relations, 1795–1840*. Monographs of the American Ethnological Society. New York: J. J. Augustine, 1950.

Kenner, Charles. *The Comanchero Frontier: A History of New Mexican–Plains Indian Relations*. Norman: University of Oklahoma Press, 1994.

Keyser, James D. "Painted Bison Robes: The Missing Link in the Biographic Art Style Lexicon." *Plains Anthropologist* 41, no. 155 (1996): 29–52.

Kopytoff, Igor. "The Cultural Biography of Things: Commoditization as Process." In *The Social Life of Things: Commodities in Cultural Perspective*, edited by Arjun Appadurai, 64–91. Cambridge: Cambridge University Press, 1986.

Krauss, Rosalind. "The Cultural Logic of the Late Capitalist Museum." *October* 54 (Autumn 1990): 3–17.

Kroeber, Alfred. *The Arapaho*. Lincoln: University of Nebraska Press, 1983.

LaBarre, Weston. "Typescript of Students' Notes [Combined Notes of Wm. Bascom, Donald Collier, W. Labarre, Bernard Mishkin, and Jane Richardson of the 1935 Laboratory of Anthropology Field School, Led by A. Lesser]." In *Papers of Weston LaBarre*. Washington, D.C.: National Anthropological Archives, Smithsonian Institution, 1935.

Lansburgh, Mark. "Foreword." In Ronald McCoy. *Kiowa Memories: Images from Indian Territory, 1880*. Santa Fe, N.Mex.: Morning Star Gallery, 1987.

Leahy, Todd E. *They Called It Madness: The Canton Asylum for Insane Indians 1899–1934*. Frederick, Md.: Publish America, 2009.

Lewis, G. Malcolm, ed. *Cartographic Encounters: Perspectives on Native American Mapmaking and Map Use*. Chicago: University of Chicago Press, 1998.

Liberty, Margot. "I Will Play with the Soldiers." *Montana The Magazine of Western History* 14 (October 1964): 16–26.

Llewellyn, Karl N., and E. Adamson Hoebel. *The Cheyenne Way: Conflict and Case Law in Primitive Jurisprudence*. Norman: University of Oklahoma, 1941.

Lookingbill, Brad D. *War Dance at Fort Marion: Plains Indian War Prisoners*. Norman: University of Oklahoma Press, 2006.

Low, Denise. "Composite Indigenous Genres: Cheyenne Ledger Art as Literature." *Studies in American Indian Literatures* 18, no. 2 (Summer 2006): 83–104.

Lytle, Andrew Nelson. "The Hind Tit," In Twelve Southerners, *I'll Take My Stand: The South and the Agrarian Tradition*, 201–45. Baton Rouge: Louisiana State University Press, 1930.

McCoy, Ronald. *Kiowa Memories: Images from Indian Territory, 1880*. Sante Fe, N.Mex.: Morning Star Gallery, 1987.

———. "Miniature Shields: James Mooney's Fieldwork among the Kiowa and Kiowa-Apache." *American Indian Art Magazine* 20, no. 3 (1995): 65–71.

———. "Searching for Clues in Kiowa Ledger Drawings: Combining James Mooney's Fieldwork and the Barber Collection of the Cincinnati Art Museum." *American Indian Art Magazine* 21, no. 3 (1996): 54–61.

McGillycuddy, Julia B. *McGillycuddy, Agent: A Biography of Dr. Valentine T. McGillycuddy*. Palo Alto, Calif.: Stanford University Press, 1941.

Mama, Amina. "Enslaving the Soul of the Other." In *Beyond the Masks: Race, Gender and Subjectivity*. New York: Routledge, 1995.

Marzio, Peter. *The Art Crusade: An Analysis of American Drawing Manuals, 1820–1860*. Washington, D.C.: Smithsonian Institution Press, 1976.

Meadows, William C. "Black Goose's Map of the Kiowa-Comanche-Apache Reservation in Oklahoma Territory." *Great Plains Quarterly* 26 (Fall 2006): 265–82.

———. *Kiowa, Apache, and Comanche Military Societies: Enduring Veterans, 1800 to the Present.* Austin: University of Texas Press, 1999.

———. *Kiowa Military Societies: Ethnohistory and Ritual.* Norman: University of Oklahoma Press, 2010.

Merleau-Ponty, Maurice. *Phenomenology of Perception.* Translated by Colin Smith. London: Routledge, 1962.

Merrill, William L., Marian K. Hansson, Candace S. Greene, and Frederick Reuss. *Guide to the Kiowa Collections at the Smithsonian Institution.* Smithsonian Conributions to Anthropology Series, no. 40. Washington, D.C.: Smithsonian Institution Press, 1997.

Miles, Tiya. *The House on Diamond Hill: A Cherokee Plantation Story.* Chapel Hill: University of North Carolina Press, 2010.

———. *The Ties That Bind: The Story of an Afro-Cherokee Family in Slavery and Freedom.* Berkeley: University of California Press, 2006.

Miner, H. Craig. *The Corporation and the Indian.* Columbia: University of Missouri Press, 1976.

Mishkin, Bernard. *Rank and Warfare Among the Plains Indians.* Memoirs of the American Ethnological Society. New York: J. J. Augustin Publisher, 1940; reprint, Seattle: University of Washington, 1966; reprint, with introduction by Morris W. Foster Lincoln: University of Nebraska Press. 1992.

Mitchell, W. J. T. "Imperial Landscape." In *Landscape and Power,* edited by W. J. T. Mitchell, 5–34. Chicago: University of Chicago Press, 1994.

Montgomery, F. C. "United States Surveyors Massacred by Indians, Lone Tree, Meade County, 1874." *Kansas Historical Quarterly* 1, no. 3 (May 1932): 266–72.

Mooney, James. "The Cheyenne Indians." *Memoirs of the American Anthropological Association* 1, no. 6 (1907): 357–442.

———. *The Ghost Dance and the Sioux Outbreak of 1890.* North Dighton, Mass.: JG Press, 1996.

Moore, John H. *The Cheyenne.* Cambridge, Mass.: Blackwell, 1996.

———. "Cheyenne Political History, 1820-1894." *Ethnohistory* 21, no. 4 (1974): 329–59.

———. *The Cheyenne Nation: A Social and Demographic History.* Lincoln: University of Nebraska Press, 1987.

Nagy, Imre. "A Typology of Cheyenne Shield Designs." *Plains Anthropologist* 39, no. 147 (1994): 5–35.

Noë, Alva. "Life Is the Way the Animal Is in the World: A Talk with Alva Noë." Accessed March 3, 2009. http://www.edge.org/3rd_culture/noe08/noe08_index.html.

Nye, Wilbur Sturtevant, and William S. Soule. *Plains Indian Raiders: The Final Phases of Warfare from the Arkansas to the Red River.* Norman: University of Oklahoma Press, 1968.

Parsons, Mark L. "Plains Indian Portable Art as a Key to Two Texas Historic Rock Art Sites." *Plains Anthropologist* 32, no. 117 (1987): 257–74.

Pember, Mary Annette. "Graduating to Prison: Native Americans Sue School District" The Progressive (February 2007). Accessed November 3, 2010. http://www.progressive.org/mag_pember0207.

Petersen, Karen Daniels. *American Pictographic Images: Historical Works on Paper by the Plains Indians.* Sante Fe, N.Mex.: Morning Star Gallery, 1988.

———. "Cheyenne Soldier Societies." *Plains Anthropologist* 9, no. 25 (1964): 146–72.

———. *The Edwards Ledger Drawings: Folk Art by Arapaho Warriors.* New York: David A. Schorsch, 1990.

———. *Howling Wolf: A Cheyenne Warrior's Graphic Interpretation of His People.* Palo Alto, Calif.: American West, 1968.

———. *Plains Indian Art from Fort Marion.* Norman: University of Oklahoma Press, 1971.

Rand, Jacki Thompson, *Kiowa Humanity and the Invasion of the State.* Lincoln: University of Nebraska Press, 2008.

———. "Primary Sources: Indian Goods and the History of American Colonialism and the 19th Century Reservation." In *Clearing a Path: Theorizing the Past in Native American Studies*, edited Nancy Shoemaker, 137–57. New York: Routledge, 2002.

Richardson, Heather Cox. *West from Appomattox: The Reconstruction of America after the Civil War.* New Haven: Yale University Press, 2007.

Richardson, Jane. *Law and Status among the Kiowa Indians*, Monographs of the American Ethnological Society. New York: J. J. Augustin, 1940.

Rowe, Anne. *The Enchanted Country: Northern Writers in the South, 1865–1910.* Baton Rouge: Louisiana State University Press, 1978.

Rushing, W. Jackson. "The Legacy of Ledger Book Drawings in Twentieth-Century Native American Art." In *Plains Indian Drawings 1865–1935: Pages from a Visual History,* edited by Janet Catherine Berlo, 55–62.

Ross, Luana. *Inventing the Savage: The Social Construction of Native American Criminality.* Austin: University of Texas Press, 1998.

Schmittou, Douglas A., and Michael H. Logan, "Fluidity of Meaning: Flag Imagery in Plains Indian Art." *American Indian Quarterly* 26, no. 4 (Fall 2002): 559–604.

Shannon, Timothy J. "Queequeg's Tomahawk: A Cultural Biography, 1750–1900." *Ethnohistory* 52, no. 3 (Summer 2005): 589–633.

Smith, Caleb. *The Prison and the American Imagination.* New Haven: Yale University Press, 2009.

Smith, Marian. "The War Complex of the Plains Indians." *Proceedings of the American Philisophical Society* 78 (1938): 425–64.

Snyder, Christina. *Slavery in Indian Country: The Changing Face of Captivity in Early America.* Cambridge, Mass.: Harvard University Press, 2010.

Swan, Daniel C. *Peyote Religious Art: Symbols of Faith and Belief.* Jackson: University Press of Mississippi, 1999.

Szabo, Joyce M. *Art from Fort Marion: The Silberman Collection.* Norman: University of Oklahoma Press, 2007.

———. "Chief Killer and a New Reality: Narration and Description in Fort Marion Art." *American Indian Art* 19, no. 2 (1994): 50–57.

———. "Drawing Life's Changes: Late Nineteenth-Century Plains Drawings from Hampton Institute and Carlisle Indian School." *Native American Studies* 18, no. 1 (2004): 41–51.

———. "Howling Wolf: An Autobiography of a Plains Warrior-Artist." *Allen Memorial Art Museum Bulletin* 46, no. 1 (1992): 4–87.

———. *Howling Wolf and the History of Ledger Art.* Albuquerque: University of New Mexico Press, 1994.

———. "Medicine Lodge Treaty Remembered," *American Indian Art Magazine* 14 (August 1989): 52–59.

———. "Shields and Lodges, Warriors and Chiefs: Kiowa Drawings as Historical Records." *Ethnohistory* 41, no. 1 (1993): 1–24.

Taylor, Colin F. "The 'Tall Bear' Drawings in the William Blackmore Collection at the British Museum." *European Review of Native American Studies* 18, no. 2 (2004): 1–12.

Van de Logt, Mark. *War Party in Blue: Pawnee Scouts in the U.S. Army.* Norman: University of Oklahoma Press, 2010.

Vincent, Gilbert T., Sherry Brydon, and Ralph T. Coe, eds. *Arts of the North American Indians: The Thaw Collection.* Cooperstown, N.Y.: Fenimore Art Museum; Seattle: University of Washington Press, 2000.

Viola, Herman J. *Warrior Artists: Historic Cheyenne and Kiowa Indian Ledger Art Drawn by Making Medicine and Zotom.* Washington, D.C.: National Geographic Publishing, 1998.

Vizenor, Gerald. *Fugitive Poses: Native American Indian Scenes of Absence and Presence.* Lincoln: University of Nebraska Press, 1998.

———. *Manifest Manners: Postindian Warriors of Survivance.* Middletown, Conn.: Wesleyan University Press, 1994.

Wade, Edwin L., and Jacki Thompson Rand. "The Subtle Art of Resistance: Encounter and Accommodation in the Art of Fort Marion." In *Plains Indian Drawings 1865–1935: Pages from a Visual History,* edited by Janet Catherine Berlo, 45–49.

Warhus, Mark. *Another America: Native American Maps and the History of Our Land.* New York: St. Martin's Press, 1997.

West, Elliott. *The Contested Plains: Indians, Goldseekers, and the Rush to Colorado.* Lawrence: University of Kansas Press, 1998.

———. *The Last Indian War: The Nez Perce Story.* New York: Oxford University Press, 2009.

Wildhage, Wilhelm. "Material on Short Bull." *European Review of Native American Studies* 4, no. 1 (1990): 35–42.

Witmer, Linda. *The Indian Industrial School, Carlisle, Pennsylvania 1879–1918.* Carlisle, Penn.: Cumberland County Historical Society, 1993.

———. *Changing Images: The Art and Artists of the Carlisle Indian Industrial School.* Carlisle, Penn.: Cumberland County Historical Society, 2008.

Wong, Hertha Dawn, *Sending My Heart Back across the Years.* New York: Oxford University Press, 1992.

Woodward, David, and Brian Harley, eds. *The History of Cartography,* vol. 2, pt. 3. Chicago: University of Chicago Press, 1994.

Contributors

Melanie Benson Taylor is Associate Professor of Native American Studies at Dartmouth College and a member of the Herring Pond Wampanoag tribe. She is the author of *Disturbing Calculations: The Economics of Identity in Postcolonial Southern Literature, 1912–2002* (2008) and *Reconstructing the Native South: American Indian Literature and the Lost Cause* (2012).

Colin. G. Calloway is John Kimball Jr. 1943 Professor of History and Professor of Native American Studies at Dartmouth College. He has written many books on Indian history, including *One Vast Winter Count: The Native American West before Lewis and Clark* (2003) and *The Indian History of an American Institution: Native Americans and Dartmouth* (2010).

Deborah T. Haynes is Data Manager at the Hood Museum of Art, Dartmouth College.

Michael Paul Jordan is an assistant professor of Anthropology at Texas Tech University. His research focuses on the ethnohistory and expressive culture of the indigenous inhabitants of the Southern Plains.

Vera B. Palmer is a member of the Tuscarora Nation–Six Nations Grand River Band. She is Senior Lecturer in Native American Studies at Dartmouth College and teaches courses cross-listed in English, Environmental Studies, and in the Writing Program.

Joyce M. Szabo, Regents' Professor of Art History at the University of New Mexico, was the William H. Morton Distinguished Fellow at Dartmouth in the fall of 2010. A specialist in Native American Art and Museum Studies, Professor Szabo's area of particular focus is Plains drawing and painting from the late nineteenth and early twentieth centuries. Her publications include *Imprisoned Art, Complex Patronage: Plains Drawings by Howling Wolf and Zotom at the Autry National Center* (2011); *Art from Fort Marion: The Silberman Collection* (2007); *Howling Wolf and the History of Ledger Art* (1994); and *Howling Wolf: An Autobiography of a Plains Warrior-Artist* (1992).

Jenny Tone-Pah-Hote is an assistant professor of American Studies at the University of North Carolina–Chapel Hill and a member of the Kiowa tribe. She is currently completing a book manuscript on Kiowa expressive culture and nationhood in the late nineteenth and early twentieth century.

Mary Peterson Zundo did her graduate studies for the PhD in American art history from the University of Illinois, Urbana-Champaign, where she also received the MA and the MFA in Printmaking. Her dissertation, "Mapping Destiny: Cartography and Nineteenth-Century American Art of the Frontier," explores the intersecting roles of map-making, western expansionism, and nineteenth-century imagery of the Great Plains in constructing notions of nationhood, empire, and territorial sovereignty.

Index of Plates

Index

References to illustrations appear in italic type.

Copyedited by Jo Ann Reece
Indexed by Hazel Blumberg-Mckee

Book design by Julie Rushing
Jacket & cover design by Tony Roberts
Set in Warnock Pro
Image prepress by University of Oklahoma Printing Services

Printed by Oceanic Graphic International, Inc.
Printed on 157 gsm Gold East Matte